EXPERIENCES IN LANGUAGE

EXPERIENCES IN LANGUAGE

TOOLS AND TECHNIQUES FOR LANGUAGE ARTS METHODS

Fifth Edition

Walter T. Petty   **Dorothy C. Petty**

Richard T. Salzer *State University of New York at Buffalo*

Marjorie F. Becking   *contributed to previous editions*

91-1977

ALLYN AND BACON

Boston   London   Sydney   Toronto

Library of Congress Cataloging-in-Publication Data

Petty, Walter Thomas
  Experiences in language : tools and techniques for language arts methods / Walter T. Petty, Dorothy C. Petty, Richard T. Salzer. — 5th ed.
    p. cm.
  Includes index.
  ISBN 0-205-11932-8
  1. Language arts (Elementary) I. Petty, Dorothy C. II. Salzer, Richard T., 1934- . III. Title.
LB1576.P552 1989
372.6′044—dc19   88-39797
                                                      CIP

Series Editor: Sean W. Wakely
Cover Administrator: Linda Dickinson
Editorial-Production Service: Lifland et al., Bookmakers
Cover Designer: Lynda Fishbourne

Photos on pages 1, 15, 358, and 366 are by Talbot D. Lovering.
Photos on page 79 (top right and bottom) are also by Talbot D. Lovering.
Photos on pages 21, 44, 62, and 68 are by Christina J. Bogan.
Photo on pages 115 and 130 is by Christopher Morrow/Stock Boston, Inc. Used by permission.
Photo on page 355 courtesy of Lifland et al., Bookmakers.
Photos not otherwise credited are by Peter Walders, Richard T. Salzer, or Walter T. Petty.

Printed in the United States of America
10 9 8 7 6 5 4 3   94 93 92 91 90

To our children, grandchildren, and great-grandchild:
Anne, Claire, Ellen, Jonathan, Lee,
Matthew, Michael, Michelle,
Roy, Shelley, and Tom

Contents

Chapter 3   Language Learning and Young Children   53

Chapter 6   Listening and Learning   **151**

Chapter 11   Learning to Spell   291

Chapter 12   Children Learn to Read   321

Preface

*T*his edition of *Experiences in Language,* like previous editions, emphasizes a comprehensive treatment of all areas of the language arts. We attempt to base our descriptions of what should be taught and how it should be taught on defensible research evidence and established good practices. We believe in interrelating the teaching of the language arts and in integrating this teaching with the teaching of other areas of the curriculum. Integration, however, does not imply that the language arts—or any other subject area—should be taught incidentally. On the contrary, it requires thoughtful planning and recognition of the fact that the direct teaching of certain aspects of each language arts area is generally needed. Therefore, we have again included separate chapters on each of these areas—speaking, listening, spelling, writing, reading, etc.

Recognizing the vital role of the early years in language development, we include in this edition a chapter on preschool programs and activities and one on the language arts in kindergarten and the primary grades. In addition, we have expanded the two chapters on the important area of writing. The chapter on handwriting now covers writing by both hand and machine, thus reflecting the increasing use of computers in elementary schools. The use of computers as a resource is given attention in all chapters. Furthermore, we address the needs of elementary-school children to learn how to make effective use of the library and media center and to develop reading and study skills.

Our appreciation for help with this edition, as with earlier ones, is extended to teachers we know and have known and to the many students who have been in our classes. The courtesy shown us by the many teachers in whose classrooms we observed and photographed children is also appreciated. The teachers and staff of the Early Childhood Research Center of the State University of New York at Buffalo provided insights that have been incorporated into this edition, and we thank them. Finally, and especially, our appreciation is extended to Chris Langsam, children's librarian of the public library in Rogers, Arkansas, for her valuable suggestions and recommendations.

W.T.P.
D.C.P.
R.T.S.

EXPERIENCES
IN LANGUAGE

Chapter *1*

Language and the Language Arts

*T*he successful exchange of knowledge through language is crucial to every person's well-being. Those who lack facility in communication will find it increasingly difficult to participate fully in our complex society, whether as students, family members, employees, or simply individual citizens. The importance of raising the level of communicative competence in the general society must be recognized, and institutions must cooperate with one another to improve the literacy of the population. Nothing is more important than promoting children's language abilities. The home and family are instrumental in the early acquisition of language and in stimulation of its development, but the role of the school system is central.

Such books as *Ways With Words,* by Shirley Brice Heath, and *Family Literacy,* by Denny Taylor, describe many interesting language-learning episodes in children's homes.

LANGUAGE

Language may be defined in a number of ways, but human speech is usually thought of first. Communication occurs in many other ways, however. Animals communicate with one another or with humans in many ways, ranging from the tail wagging of dogs to the sounds made by dolphins. Computer language has become a well-established—and sometimes annoying—part of daily life. There are communicative sounds other than speech, such as drums, fog horns, and sirens. There are various types of graphic symbols, from marks on trees to the symbols commonly seen on highway signs or restroom doors. There are gestures, used with or without speech, the sign language of the hearing-impaired, and body language (well known to teachers, especially as exhibited by students who are restless or bored).

All of these are language in the broader sense because they are used to communicate—and both teachers and children should be aware of this. The principal focus in the classroom, however, is on language as defined in the narrower sense, that is, as the symbols, either vocal or graphic, that are produced in systematic patterns by one person in order to convey meaning to one or more others. The primary concern of this book is with teaching and learning the use of language defined in this way.

Language and Culture

Language grows out of people's need to communicate. The shared collection of understandings that accumulate from interactions in daily life is called culture. That is, culture is the beliefs and ways of doing things that characterize a group of people and differentiate it from other such groups, or societies. Language is a means of storing knowledge, but it is also the

2

means by which people see the world and process information. Language, culture, and thinking are interrelated in complex ways. For example, the English statement "The path runs around the lake" seems rather foolish when taken in a literal sense. In another language the same observation might be stated as "With respect to the path and the lake, circumscription," which appears to come closer to describing reality. In English one of the preferred sentence patterns implies that something does something to something else, even though that way of perceiving events does not always make literal sense. This is a cultural characteristic: English speakers expect events to have causes and therefore look for explanations. People from other cultures may be more likely to take things as they come, without insisting that there usually be causes and reasons. This is one way culture, thinking, and language are interrelated.

The Alaskan natives of the North Slope are said to know more than eighty different kinds of snow— and to have words for all of them.

Additional relationships exist between culture and language. Names for objects and events are created as communication needs arise. Seventeenth-century English did not include the word *electricity,* but this does not mean that the language was deficient or its users primitive; there was simply no need for such a word. Today, visitors unfamiliar with American English may express confusion about what menu to expect and how to dress when invited to attend a *lunch, brunch, supper, dinner,* or *cook-out.* And we are amazed when it is reported that some languages have no word for lying, or "saying that which is not." We might wonder what such a society would be like! Such language differences convey much about a culture, and this is why language experts and other scholars insist that a people cannot be fully understood unless their language is fully understood.

One of the most important ways in which language and culture are interrelated is that those with a way to communicate can share one another's experiences. Talking, singing, writing, and reading all combine to promote the development of common understandings. Through language we know about the lives of our ancestors, and we can speculate as to the fate of generations that are to come. We can know every detail of an imagined event that could never have taken place, and we can even become emotionally involved in a made-up character's adventures or problems.

Personal use of language is also related to culture. Conversations among individuals are always governed by certain rules that have been learned. For example, when meeting a prospective mother-in-law for the first time, the average person would not use the same vocabulary as he or she would when relaxing with friends. Every society has its own standards; there may be expectations about when eye contact is permitted or how close faces should be during conversation. Language permits us to think and communicate, but culture structures the methods and content of communication and thought.

Characteristics of Language

Language is symbolic.
Language symbols are arbitrary.
Language is systematic.
Language is a form of human behavior.
Language is a social instrument.
Language continually changes.

Characteristics of Language

The systematic arrangement of symbols is a key characteristic of language. The systematic nature of any language is shown by intertwined and interrelated principles that cause the language to operate in regular ways. Each language has its own system—a system peculiar in at least some respects to no other language—but every language is systematic and every language has vocal (and generally graphic) symbols that have been arbitrarily attached to the ideas and objects that are a part of the culture it serves.

Thus, arbitrariness is a part of language related to its systematic nature. The people of every culture have simply designated a sound or set of sounds to represent something they need to talk about. The French say *le chien,* the English say *dog;* both are arbitrarily designated symbols (both in sound and graphic forms) that represent the same object, and they do so regularly and systematically. Those who use a language also make it as complete as necessary for their culture. Modern English has the term *nuclear physics;* a Native American language of the year 1600 had no need for such a term. This difference makes neither language any less "advanced," complete, or systematic than the other. Each is a social instrument facilitating communication between people about the things they want to communicate about.

Still another characteristic of language is that it changes. Evidence of the change in English is apparent, for example, if one compares pages from the King James version of the Bible, a Shakespeare play, a Hemingway novel, and an issue of *Time.* These changes in language occur in many ways. We readily think of new meanings being attached to words and of new words or combinations of words being used for new or changed objects or ideas. Perhaps we can think of pronunciation changes or spelling changes, though the latter tend to take longer to occur, and we may not be aware of them unless we read something written a hundred or so years ago. And if we look back far enough we can even find changes in word order.

Language in Use

Most of the time we are not aware of the scientific aspects of language; we are simply using it in all aspects of life. Through face-to-face and telephone conversations, electronic media, newspapers, magazines, books, and advertising, we are constantly exposed to language in one form or another. The effectiveness of the communication that occurs in these encounters depends on the degree to which both the expressor and the receptor know the language and have, relatively speaking, the same abilities in using it. Knowing the language in this sense means having attained a level of development of those elements discussed above that make possible language use, including being aware (though perhaps not at a conscious level) of any social or cultural forces that may bear on the communication.

Language also often serves as a means of releasing tensions or reacting to a specific personal incident. Many of us talk to ourselves—sometimes using expletives—or sing or talk to a pet or even an inanimate object. We may mutter imprecations after a poor golf shot or while working on an income tax form, exclaim aloud at the sight of the Grand Canyon, or shout "Bravo!" in appreciation of an outstanding musical performance. Language used in such instances as these is personal; no communication to someone else is generally intended.

The role of language in thinking is possibly the most important use of

Compared to the 1966 edition of The Random House Dictionary of the English Language, *the 1987 edition has 50,000 more words and 75,000 new definitions for existing entries.*

New Words

greenmail
disinformation
palimony
byte
yuppies

The many ways language is used are thoroughly discussed in *Language Learning Through Communication,* by Allen, Brown, and Yatvin.

language. Although not all of the symbols used in the mental manipulation necessary for thinking are language symbols, the majority are. Primitive people could think in terms of mental images as they sought food and shelter, but as the need for communication developed and as rules, laws, customs, and social mores were established, representational symbols became necessary. Thus, language evolved, and now language symbols representing the many abstractions of our culture are crucial to thinking.

Language Variety

The language each of us uses is largely a reflection of early environment and education and the social situation of the moment. The variation in language that is most obvious is in **dialect.** Dialects, like the language of which they are a part, are systematic, adequate for communication among their users, and, to a large extent, predictable in structure and use. In general, dialects differ in matters of pronunciation and vocabulary more than they do in sentence arrangement. Some dialects are also characterized by rate of speech and variation in pitch. The slow drawl associated with the South and Southwest and the nasality of the southern hills are familiar examples. *Mary, marry,* and *merry* are pronounced identically by most natives of the northern Midwestern states, whereas native speakers in New England pronounce these words differently. Groceries are placed in a *bag* in some sections of the country but in a *sack* or perhaps a *poke* in others. There are

To get water, do you turn on the faucet, hydrant, spigot, or tap?

Some children speak one language at home and another at school.

How do you say these words?

creek
greasy
roof
wash
stomach
hog

many other instances of differences in pronunciation and vocabulary, but in the United States dialectal differences ordinarily do not extend to such basic features as the order of words in sentences.

Even though everyone (not just people in the South or Brooklyn or Boston) speaks a dialect, each person's language within a dialect is, to some extent at least, unique. This is an individual's **idiolect.** Also, each of us varies his or her language from one expressional situation to another, particularly after becoming an adult. Such variation is known as **register switching,** or, more commonly in written expression, changing styles. Each of us uses a colloquial or homely language in speaking with close friends and family. This language is certainly less formal than that used in giving a speech or writing an article. A person may also use particular words and expressions—localisms—in his or her own town or neighborhood that would probably be avoided in another geographical location. Thus, although we may say that a person speaks *a* dialect, that dialect has variations, just as there are variations among dialects.

Any dialect is an adequate means of communication for its users, but if it deviates too much from what the community at large considers to be standard or acceptable English (see Chapter 7), a problem is created for the speaker, one that the school must recognize and attempt to solve.

Language Change

English is a particularly adaptable and flexible language, partly because it is a polyglot one, rich in words taken from other languages, for example:

What others can you think of?

Dutch: *buoy, yacht, sleigh, waffle, skate*
French: *rouge, bayou, toboggan, vignette, coup*
Hebrew: *amen, cherub, sabbath, camel*
Italian: *violin, replica, ghetto, broccoli*
German: *bagel, delicatessen, kindergarten, schnozzle*
Spanish: *sombrero, guitar, mosquito, corral*
Kongo (African):   *gumbo, voodoo*
Persian: *caravan, bazaar, shawl*
Algonquin (Native American):   *caribou, hominy, squash*

And, of course, other languages have adopted English words; speakers of French or German use such Americanisms as *weekend* and *drugstore*.

Early settlers created these:

underbrush
bluff
gap
warpath

Besides adopting words from other languages, we create words to describe new commercial products, processes, or discoveries or new ways of thinking about things: *motorcade, jetliner, stereo, amplifier, missile, sneakers, Freon.* Other words actually are abbreviations, compounds, or acronyms: *OPEC, TV, pro, hype, motel, houseplant, scuba, offbeat, paperback, software.* Still others move into the language from slang, although much slang gives new meaning to words already in the language. However, very little slang gains permanent acceptance (one period's *square* is another's *nerd*), although such words as *crank, fad, pluck,* and *slump* were once considered slang.

Examining the Language

We use language as a complete experience of communication, but all communicative acts can be broken down into component parts and examined. Those who do this systematically are referred to as **linguists,** scientists who study language. Linguistics as a field of knowledge focuses on such areas as sounds of a language, combinations of sounds used as words or word parts, arrangements of words in sentences or parts of sentences, and the processes by which meanings are assigned to language experiences.

Sounds. The basic sounds of a language are called **phonemes.** A phoneme is the smallest unit of sound that produces a change in meaning. It is often not precisely a single sound; there are slight differences in the sounds indicated by *p* in *pin, spin,* and *lip.* Native speakers of English learn to hear these sounds as identical, however, and make no distinctions among them. On the other hand, the sound difference represented by *b* in *bit* and *p* in *pit,* although also slight, is one that native speakers know carries meaning and therefore acknowledge.

Phonemes are represented in written form by using virgules in order to distinguish between letters and the sounds they represent. For example, to show the sounds in mat, *the linguist writes /m/ /a/ /t/.*

Phonemes are not the same as letters of the alphabet in English. One sound may be represented by different letters or even combinations of letters. The phoneme /s/ is represented by *s* in *send, c* in *cent,* and *sc* in *scent.* Conversely, one letter of the alphabet may represent different phonemes. For instance, *g* is the graphic form of the initial sound in *gun* and *gene* and the medial sound in *regime.* These complexities are one of the important outcomes of the historical growth of the English language.

Phonemes identifiable in the flow of speech as a speaker uses voice, teeth, and mouth parts are called **segmental phonemes.** They can be segmented, or isolated, from other phonemes and are recognizable as meaningful units. Differences in analysis procedures and classification systems lead some authorities to state that there are only thirty-three phonemes in English and others to conclude that there are more than forty.

In addition to segmental phonemes, there are **suprasegmental features** that also describe speech. These include four degrees of **stress** in the flow of language, three levels of **pitch** in the voice, and four **junctures,** or interruptions in the stream of speech. Stress is most readily apparent when it shifts, as in the pronunciations of *expert* and *expertise.* Changing the pitch of the voice is done almost automatically when asking questions and even when the sentence is not in the form of a question (try saying "His name was Billy" giving the last word a higher pitch than the others). Juncture is exemplified by comparing "light housekeeping" with "lighthouse keeping."

Words. In ordinary speech we do not pay much attention to phonemes; words are thought of as the meaningful elements. Even quite young children learn that words have power to secure assistance and even to cause hurt. Linguists study morphemes rather than words. A **morpheme** is defined as the smallest unit of language that cannot be divided without eliminating meaning or changing it drastically. A morpheme is, in fact, often a word, such as *cat, walk,* or *laugh.* These are called **free,** or **lexical, morphemes** because they can stand alone in terms of meaning. A **bound,** or **grammatical, morpheme** is one that must be combined with another morpheme; examples are *-s, -ed,* and *anti-*. Thus, *cat* is one morpheme (three phonemes), and *cats* is two morphemes (four phonemes). The *s* in *cats* does have meaning ("more than one"); this is an example of why morphemes may be thought of as the building blocks of language.

Words may be classified into four large **form classes,** or parts of speech (nouns, verbs, adjectives, and adverbs). Placement in these classes in most contemporary descriptions of language is determined by four basic considerations, none of which gives particular emphasis to meaning or function in the traditional sense (for example, that a noun is the name of a person, place, or thing). The considerations that are used include affixes, word order, particular structures or function, and the sound stress given. Thus, a noun is a word that will take the inflectional endings *-s* or *-es, -'s,* and *-s';* that will take derivational suffixes such as *-er, -or, -ment, -ness,* and *-ism;* that may be signaled or marked by such words as *the, a, each, some, many,* and *my;* or that receives major stress on the beginning syllable (for example, *sus'pect* is a noun, whereas *suspect'* is a verb). A word can be classified as a noun if it meets one of these criteria, and there are a few instances in which all can be applied. For the other form classes—verbs, adjectives, and adverbs—word order, signal words, and affixes are used to determine the classification.

In addition to the form classes, English has **structure,** or **function, words.** These include the signal words already mentioned and qualifiers (*very, rather, quite,* and so on), prepositions (*on, in, after,* and so on), and conjunctions (*but, and,* and so on). The structure words relate words of the different form classes to one another and provide the framework that gives the language fluidity and cohesion.

Sentences. The arrangement or order of words in sentences or parts of sentences is **syntax,** which may also be defined as the grammar or description of a language. There are several approaches to describing word order in English sentences (see Chapter 7). Syntax is particularly important in English because it is the major way of showing relationships among words and is essential in making meaningful sentences. For example, each of the words in the string "selected book the quickly girl the" expresses grammatical meaning via structure signals and endings, but taken as a group their meaning is not clear until they are arranged into the syntactically correct "the girl quickly selected the book."

Meaning. Language conveys meaning, and making yourself understood and comprehending what others say and write are important areas of knowledge about language. Some linguists conduct studies of **semantics,** the meanings associated with words. They are concerned with the literal or objective meanings (a *plum* is a fruit) and also feelings and emotions that become attached to words (a *plum* is anything highly desired). The study of word meanings also involves examination of dialects and cultural influences

---

Function or Signal Words

Noun markers—*my, some, two, the, an*
Verb markers—*am, is, were, had, will*
Phrase markers—*into, above, down, up, out*
Clause markers—*because, that, if, why, how*
Question markers—*who, when, what, where, why*

British English

flat
lift
vest
biscuit
cooker
lorry
nappy

American English

apartment
elevator
undershirt
cookie
stove
truck
diaper

(*calling* in British English refers to a personal visit, not a telephone conversation).

Other areas of meaning touch on psychology and intellectual development, aspects of **psycholinguistics.** A person cannot understand language if the ideas expressed are totally unfamiliar or if they are complex beyond that individual's ability to comprehend. **Sociolinguistics** recognizes that social factors are also relevant in determining meaning. Class background, dialect, and sophistication with respect to context are all of significance. No teenager who has just demolished the family car would take the statement at face value when the parent says, "Well, we're certainly proud of you today."

LEARNING LANGUAGE

Nearly all children learn to talk without much difficulty. This learning begins at birth; the first sounds the child hears seem to trigger communication attempts. The fact that language is systematic facilitates this learning, as does the desire of persons around the child to communicate with her or him. As the child experiments and others respond, discovery and reinforcement proceed, and the language system begins to come under the child's control. Of course, not everything is grasped at the outset. For many years, including those spent in elementary school, children continue to learn about their language.

Children learn the language of the adults with whom they are in contact, but just how this learning occurs is not a matter of consensus. Several different theories to explain the learning of language have been advanced by linguists; these are discussed in the following section.

Theories of Language Acquisition

Theories of language acquisition and the work of Piaget are discussed in Chapter 1 of Pflaum's *The Development of Language and Literacy in Young Children.*

The theories concerning how language is acquired are complex and controversial. Advancing our understanding of the language acquisition process brings a better grasp of the nature of language. The theories are discussed here in terms of initial language learning, but the important points also relate to how older children learn in all of the language arts areas.

Behaviorist Theory. The behaviorist point of view is that each newborn infant has a potential for learning in general but no specific capacity for language learning. The development of language is a result of the environment: Japanese children learn Japanese, and American children learn English. More specifically, each child first learns a dialect, the language spoken in his or her immediate environment.

See Chapter 6 in *Inquiries into Child Language,* by Diane Nelson Bryen.

Under this theory, all learning, including language, results from positive reinforcement of desirable behavior and nonreinforcement of what is not wanted. Thus, the babbling infant is reinforced or rewarded for making certain sounds rather than others. Furthermore, according to behaviorists,

Children learn language best when in close contact with adults.

the environment controls a baby's language efforts in that those around the child respond positively when he or she produces an utterance close to something recognizable in the language. Sounds such as *buh-buh-buh* may be repeated by others, with accompanying laughter, smiling, and cuddling. Then, at some time near the first birthday, the child says "da-da" or "mama," and much excitement results. More words are learned in the same way, and the child gains the ability to try to say what others say. Repeating known words becomes enjoyable and reinforcing in itself, and the child goes on to say them over and over without urging.

Young children differ greatly in their tendency to imitate as well as their ability to do so.

The behaviorist theory, unlike other points of view, treats language learning (and all other learning) as essentially imitation and repetition guided by external events. In learning the language to which they are exposed, infants are not always able to repeat everything they hear, but, according to this theory, the stimuli and reinforcement provided encourage them to make the effort, to experiment, until they master the system to the extent necessary to function successfully in the environment where they find themselves.

Nativist Theory. The nativist point of view is not as well defined as behaviorism and differs principally from that theory in the assumption that humans are endowed with a specific capacity for learning language. According to the nativist theory, this innate ability or mechanism gives the learner a start in "knowing" the system of a language in its basic design. This inborn ability, called the **language acquisition device (LAD)**, needs only to be triggered by the language environment of the infant for the expression of language to occur rapidly.

Advocates of this theory hold that the imitation and reinforcement conditions of the behaviorists cannot account for the rapidity with which a child in any culture learns the essentials of language structure. Nativists also point out that a young child speaks sentences or parts of sentences that are not imitations of adult speech, which seems to indicate that exposure to adult models is needed only to give the learner examples from which to deduce the underlying rules that govern how the language system works. Although the LAD remains basic to the nativist theory, many nativists currently emphasize the interaction between the child and adults. The nature of this interaction, which is not entirely verbal since facial expressions and touching are included, is that adults use language differently when speaking with children than they do when talking to other adults. Adults do everything possible to help the learner see how the sounds relate to meanings and what the underlying language organization is.

In further support of their theory, nativists cite studies of language acquisition in different cultures; these have shown that children of differing intellectual abilities or even ones with physical or environmental handicaps will learn whatever language they have access to, and the acquisition sequence will always be substantially the same. On the other hand, experiments in teaching language to chimpanzees have seemed to challenge the nativist position that acquisition of language is restricted to humans. Some researchers have shown that chimps can be taught to utilize such language symbols as electronic sign boards and American Sign Language. The nativists counter this evidence by stressing the difference between acquiring a language from nothing more than exposure to it and being carefully taught to use it. They also point out that the chimpanzees do not go on to develop language use beyond the linking of a few symbols or signs.

Cognitivist Theory. A third point of view relates language to cognitive processes, or thinking. Although cognitivists accept the uniqueness of humans in language learning, they emphasize the development of basic thought structures prior to the development of corresponding linguistic structures, implying that thought is at least initially independent of language. Before being able to use language, the infant does solve some problems that appear to call for thought (for example, finding a toy by removing the cover placed over it). The LAD is not discounted in this theory but is considered to be related more to relationships of meanings than to the underlying organization of sentences and other word combinations. Semantic concepts are viewed as the generating force in the learning process, as the child constructs the meanings of the words he or she hears. Such construction is facilitated by language users in the child's environment, of course; thus, interaction with adults is considered important, as it is in the other theories.

Language Development

A child begins at birth to experiment with his or her vocal organs, to make sounds. This experimenting progresses through cries and cooing, sounds that are identified as expressing pain, fear, anger, or joy. These early vocalizations show little system or little relationship to the language spoken by those caring for the child. At about four months of age the infant shows signs of responding to human sounds—turning the head and eyes to look for the speaker. Shortly thereafter the cooing will change to babbling, which with increasing practice shows considerable mastery of the basic elements of the vocal mechanism. The child does more "practicing," gaining a great deal of control of volume, pitch, and articulation, as shown by the ability to repeat sounds that are heard. By the time the normal child has reached the first birthday, he or she is producing sounds to which adult listeners can genuinely attach meaning. Usually these first "words" are consonant-vowel in form—*ma-ma, da-da, bye-bye*—and the child may not be attaching the same meaning to them as the adoring father and mother do, although experimenting will soon enable the child to relate the sounds to the adult meanings. The majority of first words are usually nouns—*ball, man, bird,* and so on—but such action words as *want, give,* and *more* also appear before the child begins to put two or more words together.

Children's first words often seem to be attempts to express complex ideas, suggesting a words-as-sentences hypothesis. The term **holophrastic speech** is often used to convey this idea. Of course, there is no way for us to know if a child has the idea of the content of a sentence in mind. The child who says "milk" is likely to get more milk, but the adult who hears the word doesn't know whether the child had "I want more milk" in mind but was limited by memory, attention, or linguistic skill or simply recognized that the one word was sufficient to accomplish communication.

Most children acquire at least fifty words before beginning to put two or more of them together.

Children normally, however, begin to put words together at around eighteen to twenty months of age. The experimenting in doing this is similar to that done with words. The first combinations of words tend to follow the pattern of a few words in a particular utterance position joined with a variety of other words ("bye-bye, daddy," "bye-bye, mommy," "bye-bye, doggie"). The experimenting continues, with more of these singled-out words being tried out with other words and combinations of words. Gradually, then, the child perceives the notion of word order—that some words belong first and some words second. Sometimes this early perception is faulty with respect to the language system. More often, though, word order is satisfactory, but frequently some words are omitted. The child says "I see car" for "I can see the car." This is **telegraphic speech** (as in telegrams) and is simply further experimenting. All such experimenting is a normal stage in development, a stage in learning how the language works.

By the time most children are two years old they have a fund of words that represent objects and actions and are able to use them in ways that are understood. They test hypotheses about noun and verb endings, frequently overgeneralizing about the rules by saying "foots," "goed," or "mines." This "sorting out" continues for some time (for some aspects of syntax to about age nine and even beyond), but by the time the average child reaches kindergarten age he or she speaks in sentences, the complexity of which depends on mental maturity, language aptitude, and experiences.

From the very beginning the child's use of language is purposeful, not perfunctory. The child who has learned to talk enough to use language for satisfying immediate physical needs soon becomes absorbed in making the acquaintance of a great variety of things. Children ask "What's that?" over and over. Asking questions is the characteristic type of language activity at this stage of preschool language development. Two- to five-year-olds struggle to identify the many objects in the environment; they seek to bring order into a wide world of sight, sound, smell, and feeling. The responses to this exploring are very important to language development. Thus, narrow experiences and limited responses result in language development that is less advanced than that of the child who has had broad experiences and has secured responses to expressions of curiosity.

The family environment is the most important factor other than the child's maturity pattern in determining the language facility that develops and the speed with which it develops. For instance, an only child may have closer association with adults than does a child who has brothers and sisters. This closeness may result in the development of a larger vocabulary and more maturity in expression. Similarly, the child who is talked with a great deal develops language facility earlier than does one who grows up being ignored or told to be quiet. In addition to providing the child with language experiences, the family provides the language model—the kind of language to imitate.

In *The Meaning Makers: Children Learning Language and Using Language to Learn,* Wells describes how a group of British children developed language from early speech through the intermediate grades.

Children's mental development and progress in using language move along together, thoroughly interwoven with the experiences of life. Once children have a basic command of language the relationship between thinking and communication becomes significant. According to Piaget's theory of intellectual or cognitive development, the age of about six or seven is the beginning of the concrete-operational period and marks an important change in a child's thinking. One important consequence regarding language is that children past this age are much more likely to understand that a word may have more than one meaning. This is why kindergartners do not understand puns and riddles, whereas first and second graders love them. A child has to know that two meanings of a word can exist simultaneously in order to see the joke in the mayonnaise asking for the refrigerator door to be closed because "I'm dressing." Third graders are bored by all this because they are well aware of multiple meanings for words.

As children approach the age of ten or eleven, most are moving into what Piaget calls the stage of formal thinking. At this time they are ready

Language learning results from experiences and from talking about them.

for greater abstractions, so vocabulary involving amounts, comparisons, qualities, and characteristics takes a substantial leap. Their reasoning ability advances, and they have more need for connectives such as *since, because, whenever,* and *although.* They are able to suspend judgment and do propositional thinking, and this ability has some effect on their interest in such activities as reading science fiction and writing stories of their own.

Although there are different degrees of maturity in children of the same chronological age, the general relationships between levels of maturity and thought processes must be of concern to teachers. This concern must be reflected in the attention given to how and when it is best to teach concepts in various subject areas—mathematics, science, and social studies—as well as in the language arts. To the extent that teachers know how children think and how that thought is reflected in their language, they will be better able to organize the curriculum.

THE LANGUAGE ARTS

The language arts are the **receptive language activities** of reading and listening and the **expressive language activities** of speaking and writing. Involved in both reception and expression is thinking, which is sometimes called the fifth language art.

Although "language arts" is the most widely used term, there are other names given to the portion of the school program devoted to teaching language communication skills. "English," of course, is the historical term, but "the communicative arts," "the English language arts," and simply "language" are also used. It is also true that many teachers think of reading, spelling, composition, and the like rather than thinking more broadly of the language arts; thus, they use no inclusive term.

"The language arts" seems to be the designation that best describes the activities of speaking, writing, listening, and reading and recognizes their interrelatedness. It focuses on language, as opposed to the more narrow and traditional elements of writing, grammar, and literature associated with English or the broad aspects of communication involving sound, sight, feel, and smell without the use of language.

The Language Arts

RECEP-TIVE ↔	THINKING	↔ EXPRES-SIVE
listening		speaking
reading		writing

Elements of the Language Arts

The use of the term *language arts* aids in focusing on the interrelatedness of the four aspects of language communication. Using this all-inclusive term, however, requires that the various elements and how they are related to one another be specified.

Writing encompasses the skills of spelling, handwriting, punctuation, capitalization, and, most importantly, composition—putting together ideas and information in a coherent and appealing manner, recognizing the value of proofreading and editing what one has written, and using conventional forms where needed. The major element in speaking is also composition, but the skills of articulation, pronunciation, and voice projection, as well as those related to physical posture and manner, are also included.

Reading and listening have common characteristics. Both are concerned with perception of either graphic or oral symbols, with the identification of unknown words and terms, and with the use of these, along with one's experience, to gain meaning.

Thinking is very much a part of each of the language arts. Children think as they compose, spell, form letters and words, listen to a speaker, read a selection, and so on. Thinking is largely a language manipulation activity; therefore, any shortcomings in understanding how language works and how it may be used will adversely influence thinking. Conversely, limitations in thinking ability will limit the uses of language.

Cutting across the receptive and expressive aspects of the language arts as thinking does (and related to it) are elements of grammar, vocabulary, dialect, and usage. Equally important are the study skills involved in using a dictionary, locating information, and utilizing the library.

Furthermore, the language arts include attitudes toward language usage, communication activities, and the aesthetic components of these activities. For example, reading is more than merely gaining meaning, for literature is a part of this aspect of the language arts. In the same sense, listening is done both for useful purposes and for pleasure, and writing may be both practical and creative.

Interrelationships among the Elements

The interrelationships among the language arts are many and varied, as will become clear in the chapters that follow. At the heart of those interrelationships is the presence of language in each element of expression or reception and the fact that an experience affecting one facet will usually affect others. When one engages in a communicative act, many aspects of language, as well as of thought, are involved.

For example, in writing a letter to a family member or friend, you consider what is to be in it, using your thinking abilities to recall events that might be mentioned, to organize content so that it makes sense, and to devise especially effective or entertaining ways to express yourself. You also read as you write, going over what you've written, perhaps doing this aloud. You may even talk to yourself ("She'll get a blast out of this!") or to someone else or listen to that person ("Don't forget to tell about the cat"). Thinking is involved as you project events into the future, perhaps creating an image of what the recipient will look like or be doing while reading the letter or what the response to a particularly humorous part will be. You may write with a pen or type—in either case doing it with some care; you want to be courteous and want what you write to be legible. The words you write are ones you have learned through listening, speaking, and reading. Most are ones that appear in anyone's English, but a few might not be appropriate for "polite" conversation, and you may even use a word or expression that has meaning only for your family or circle of friends. The sentences you compose are likely to be varied: simple statements ("I have a vacation in June"), questions ("How's Harry?"), exclamations ("They were impossible!"), and statements with more complex constructions ("With the baby coming, a bigger house is something we have to think about"). Thus, even though producing a letter is basically a writing activity, there is significant involvement in the other principal language arts areas, all related to one another and to the thinking process.

You write a letter, however, without giving specific attention to each separate aspect of language. There is likely to be no overt concern with the placement of a particular comma or with the size of the loop on a letter, even though you subconsciously know that evidence of a possible lack of an ability or skill may detract from communication, the conveying of ideas to another person, which is your principal concern. Issues of spelling, word choice, and sentence patterns are also not likely to receive significant attention unless your thinking causes you to be concerned about detractions from the effectiveness of your message. Audience is important! When writing to a newspaper, for instance, or to an acquaintance, you would probably watch the organization of the letter, the sentence structures, and the spelling more closely than when writing to a close friend or relative. And, of course, when writing a letter of application for a job, you will be very concerned with good form and correctness.

Like writing, reading is a thinking act—one that requires knowledge of vocabulary and of how the language works (structures, relationships between graphic symbols and sounds, etc.). Organizational ability and even knowledge of spelling are necessary for successful reading. Listening is similar to reading in that many of the same skills are needed for determining messages. Ability in reading correlates significantly with development of vocabulary as well as with interest and proficiency in both speaking and writing. Speaking and writing are interrelated in a manner similar to the way listening and reading are.

At the elementary-school level the language arts program may sometimes be separated into particular facets—spelling, reading, handwriting, and so forth—for instructional purposes. The need for this partitioning must be acknowledged since some necessary skills and abilities may not be adequately learned without it. Rarely does any area of the language arts function independently, however, and this fact should be not only acknowledged but capitalized on in teaching. All language-related abilities, skills, processes, habits, and knowledge (or whatever terms are in current vogue) must be taken into consideration in instruction, and teachers must recognize that growth in one language area generally reinforces other areas and that language activities need to be rich and varied in order to assure optimum growth in each facet of the language arts.

Examine Newman's *Whole Language: Theory in Use* for examples of interrelated teaching of the language arts.

A FINAL WORD

In recent times the English language has become a virtually worldwide medium for commerce, science, technology, and transportation. Not surprisingly, then, English is widely studied, with people in many nations seeking to master it. All languages are worthy of study, of course, but, considering the international prominence of English, it is obviously necessary that children learn to use English well. In order to ensure this proficiency, teachers must have a thorough knowledge of the English language—the way it works, how it grows and changes, how children learn it, and the ways it affects the lives of all of us. In addition, teachers need to know what to teach, when to teach it, and the best procedures to use in teaching. The chapters that follow were developed to help you acquire such knowledge.

References

Allen, R. R.; Brown, Kenneth L.; and Yatvin, Joanne. *Learning Language Through Communication: A Functional Perspective.* Wadsworth, 1985.

Bryen, Diane Nelson. *Inquiries into Child Language.* Allyn and Bacon, 1982.

Chapman, Robert L., ed. *New Dictionary of American Slang.* Harper & Row, 1986.

Claiborne, Robert. *Our Marvelous Native Tongue: The Life and Times of the English Language.* Times Books, 1983.

Heath, Shirley Brice. *Ways with Words.* Cambridge University Press, 1983.

Henderson, Edmund. "History of English Spelling," in *Teaching Spelling.* Houghton Mifflin, 1985, pp. 5–36.

Holzman, Mathilda. *The Language of Children.* Prentice-Hall, 1983.

Linn, Michael D., and Zuber, Maarit-Hannele. *The Sound of English: A Bibliography of Language Recordings.* National Council of Teachers of English, 1984.

McCrum, Robert; Cran, William; and MacNeil, Robert. *The Story of English.* Viking, 1986 (companion to the Public Broadcasting System's series).

Myers, Doris T. *Understanding Language.* Boynton/Cook, 1984.

Newman, Judith M., ed. *Whole Language: Theory in Use.* Heinemann, 1985.

Pflaum, Susanna W. *The Development of Language and Literacy in Young Children.* Charles E. Merrill, 1986.

Seiler, William J.; Schuelke, L. David; and Lieb-Brilhart, Barbara. *Communication for the Con-*

temporary Classroom. Holt, Rinehart and Winston, 1984.

Taylor, Denny. *Family Literacy.* Heinemann, 1983.

Tompkins, Gail E., and Yaden, David B., Jr. *Answering Students' Questions about Words.* National Council of Teachers of English, 1986.

Wells, Gordon. *The Meaning Makers: Children Learning Language and Using Language to Learn.* Heinemann, 1986.

Teaching Resources

The materials listed below are only a limited sample of the available resources related to the content of this chapter.

Adelson, Leone. *Dandelions Don't Bite: The Story of Words.* Pantheon, 1972 (grades 3–5).

The Birth, Life—and Death?—of the Printed Word. Knowledge Unlimited (filmstrip).

A Common Tongue. Encyclopaedia Britannica (videotape).

Greene, Carol. *Language.* Children's Press, 1983 (grades 1–4).

Language—The Social Arbiter. Stuart Finley (film series).

Nevins, Ann. *From the Horse's Mouth.* Prentice-Hall, 1981 (grades 4–6).

News Words. Knowledge Unlimited (filmstrip).

Our Changing Language. National Council of Teachers of English (record).

Schwartz, Alvin, ed. *Tall Talk and Other Talk Collected from American Folklore.* Harper & Row, 1981 (grades 4–8).

Steckler, Arthur. *101 More Words and How They Began.* Doubleday, 1981 (grades 4–6).

The Story of English. Public Broadcasting System (videotapes).

Weiss, Ann E. *What's That You Said? How Words Change.* Harcourt Brace Jovanovich, 1980 (K–grade 3).

Activities for Preservice Teachers

1. Make a list of slang expressions currently used by high-school and college students. Ask people of various ages and backgrounds what these expressions mean. Report your findings to the class.

2. Analyze your own language history. What variety of English (or other language) is spoken by your relatives, friends, and neighbors? What influence has this had on you? What steps might you take to "improve" your English?

3. Watch several television situation comedies and quiz shows, paying particular attention to speech. What differences do you hear in sounds, vocabulary, and sentence structures?

4. Visit with some elderly people and ask what words they used in their youth to refer to games, candy, toys, and relations between boys and girls.

5. Videotape a two-year-old engaged in play or book reading with an adult. Note the child's range of vocabulary, speech patterns, and responses to what the adult says.

6. Look up the pronunciations of *aunt, berserk, data, heinous, orange,* and *route* in several dictionaries and then listen to how your classmates say them. What do you find?

7. Visit an elementary classroom for about two hours and closely observe one child. How much language does he or she use? What kinds of language? With whom does he or she talk? For what purposes? What proportion of class time is spent in listening, speaking, reading, or writing?

8. Begin a file of readings and language activities related to animal communication. Start with material

from encyclopedias about bees, dolphins, and primates.

9. Examine the treatment of the following in a number of other textbooks on teaching the language arts:
    a. Elements of the language arts
    b. Interrelationships among the language arts
    c. Language acquisition theories
    d. Language development in children

10. See if you can identify the region of the country associated with each of the words or phrases in these pairs: string beans and snap beans, pail and bucket, sweet corn and roasting ears, porch and stoop, cherry pit and cherry seed, pavement and sidewalk. Perhaps friends and family members can help.

11. Visit a classroom and talk with children who did not begin their schooling in the school they are now attending. Find out the reasons for their having moved. As the children talk, listen for variety in language patterns and usage. What might any or all of this mean to you as a language arts teacher?

Activities for Inservice Teachers

1. Watch two or three of the programs from the Public Broadcasting System's series *The Story of English*. Identify content that might be adapted for teaching to elementary students.

2. Videotape yourself as you make a presentation in your classroom or work with a reading group. What do you notice about your speech and general style of communication that might be improved?

3. Ask children to write about the meanings of well-known expressions such as those listed below. Tailor the selection to the maturity and sophistication of your group. Let them take these home for discussion with others—especially if you ask about the expressions' derivations.

neat as a pin	look a gift horse
picture of health	in the mouth
once in a blue	on cloud nine
moon	raining cats and dogs
barking up the	get up on the wrong
wrong tree	side of the bed

4. Identify a problem concerning language arts teaching in your school. Find out the names of state or federal resource people, and write to them for advice.

5. Discuss with pupils what constitutes appropriate talk for various settings: the dinner table at home, the living room when their parents have guests, the school bus, and so forth. Take note of the particulars they mention, the factors they consider important, and any language-related generalizations they make.

6. Talk with a highly experienced or retired teacher about how emphases in language arts teaching have changed over the years with regard to interrelatedness among the areas.

7. Investigate nonverbal, or body, language. Consult such sources as Edward Hall's *The Silent Language* (Doubleday, 1959) and Julius Fast's *Body Language* (Evans, 1970). Note the use of such language by children in your class.

8. Find some books about words for children (*The First Book of Words* by Epstein and Epstein or *More About Words* by Ernst, for example). Use these as a departure point for a unit on vocabulary, dictionary study, or spelling.

Chapter 2

Teaching the Language Arts

A hundred years ago, the list of language areas studied by students was long and included oral and silent reading, spelling, etymology, penmanship, elocution, composition, grammar, and literature. What do you remember about the language arts you studied when you were in elementary school? Possibly you engaged in many learning activities similar to those of a century earlier—participating in spelling contests, identifying parts of speech, diagramming sentences, filling in blanks, giving reports, drilling on handwriting forms, and reading aloud to the teacher.

Although the language arts are not as partitioned today as they were a hundred years ago, many of the same activities occur in some present-day classrooms. Increasingly, however, teachers are dropping or modifying these activities or adopting new ones in recognition of evidence from research. Also, newer activities such as videotaping or using a word processor have been introduced in many classrooms. Even though what to include in a program is determined to some extent by state and district requirements, the need to make fundamental decisions concerning the requirements and the organization of a class of children and the physical aspects of the classroom itself presents difficult problems a teacher must deal with every year and to some extent every day.

The purpose of this chapter is to give you an overview of effective language arts teaching and the planning and organizing that are so important in maximizing children's learning. The content of this chapter has application in each of the chapters that follow—and you may find yourself referring back to it as you study them.

PREPARATION FOR TEACHING

Who are the children?
How are they alike?
How are they different?
What are their needs?
How will you find answers
to these questions?

As a teacher, you need to know whom you are teaching, what it is that they should learn, and how you want to go about helping them learn. You may know quite a bit about children in general, but every class is somewhat different, and individual students can be extremely difficult to understand. You need to know what abilities, knowledge, skills, and attitudes your students have and what their interests, problems, and needs are. Determining all this for more than a few children is a huge task—one that has to be worked at all year long. Getting to know children is a rewarding experience, however, that will enrich your life as well as make you a more effective teacher. You can refer to test scores and other school records, of course, and consult previous teachers, but keep in mind that these records and opinions may be accurate or may be biased against a child because of personality conflicts, cultural differences, or judgments made hastily. Use records and others' judgments carefully, depending primarily on your own methods for learning about children (see the section titled "Recognizing Pupil Differences" later in this chapter).

Other important matters to consider when preparing to teach include the content of the program and the learning principles on which to base teaching activities as well as the decision-making process by which you integrate what you know about children, subject matter, and effective teaching strategies.

Content—What to Teach

What should be taught is important to organizing a language arts program, but how content is selected—on what premises and by what principles—is of utmost concern if teaching effort is to accomplish anything worthwhile. The findings of research, the contents of curriculum guides and textbooks, and the policies and standards of the school provide guides, but the responsibility for determining what is taught is primarily the teacher's. Some teachers say this is not true—that the principal tells them what to teach or that the textbooks and other materials structure the program for them— but this contention is too often an easy way to avoid planning and exercising personal initiative. The teacher presents whatever is presented in his or her classroom for the children to learn; the teacher is the major controlling force.

Examine textbooks for your class very carefully. Are these principles observed? Remember that a textbook is a resource, not a recipe.

Guiding principles for exercising this responsibility include the following:

- The content of the program should be selected after consideration of statements of objectives formulated by the school or district. If objectives have not been stated, are too general or not clear, or are simply thought to be understood, then the formulation of objectives is a necessary first step. For this formulation, reliance should basically be on research evidence rather than on custom, the opinion of some school authority, or the resources available.
- The emphasis in teaching should be on using the skills of communication rather than on learning subject matter. In other words, it is more important for a child to have the skills necessary for effective expression and reception of ideas and information than to know rules about language structure, punctuation, and so forth.
- The selection of content should take into account the communication needs of the children in the classroom—their experiences and development, the types of communication they can and cannot handle, the things they will need to have mastered before progressing further in school, and the ongoing activities that develop from day to day in the classroom.

To help you decide what skills, abilities, attitudes, and knowledge the children in your class need now and as they progress through their school years, you should ask yourself the questions below. Answering them may not be easy, but you should rely on your own honest, sensible judgment in seeking the answers rather than first turning to the teacher next door or to textbooks and their manuals. Both of these resources—and others—may help you to find answers, but essentially the answers must be yours.

- *How frequently is this needed and used in the life activities of children and adults?* For example, writers use colons much less frequently than they use commas, people do more storytelling than choral speaking, and seldom does one need to identify the adverbs in a sentence.

- *How important is this when the need for it arises? Will the need arise?* For instance, many people do not write business letters frequently, but when the need arises, it is usually important that the letter be well written.

- *How universally is this skill or ability encountered in the various life activities?* For example, giving a book report is a school activity for most people, but conversing is something everyone does.

- *What evidence is there that this will meet a permanent need?* For example, some of the first words a child should learn to spell are the same words adults use frequently in their writing.

- *Which children, if any, in my classroom are ready to learn this?* In other words, attention must be given to the needs of the children, the experiences they have had, and what they have already learned. Dictionary instruction will have little value for the child who has not learned alphabetical order.

Using Principles of Learning—How to Teach

For teaching to be effective, learning must occur in the individual who is being taught. In planning your teaching—how you will teach as well as what you will teach—you must recognize that learning is a complex act, and descriptions of the process are sometimes superficial or misleading. Research based on observations of learning, however, provides evidence as to how learning may be expedited. This evidence can be stated in several principles, which every teacher must heed.

Can you recall a college class in which these principles seemed to be successfully applied?

Learning is Individual. Children differ from one another in many ways, including the ability to learn. This difference is shown in learning capacities and rates and in the effectiveness of various instructional modes. Further, in addition to differences in inherited and intellectual and physical endowments, children differ from one another in terms of emotions, previous experiences, and motivation and may differ in age, sex, maturation, and physical condition. Thus, children's participation in a classroom activity will reflect these factors. A teacher can do something about some of the factors but not about others, yet all have to receive consideration in teaching.

Learning is an Active Process. Although much of what we know seems to have been learned subtly—possibly because the human mind is much like a constantly running computer ready to take in data—learning is a seeking process. An individual's environment almost constantly forces that individual to transact with it, to try to overcome any disequilibrium felt. The school environment must take into account children's backgrounds and needs in such a way as to facilitate many of their transactions even while presenting tasks that establish disequilibrium. That is, if the learning tasks are challenging rather than frustrating, the seeking process will be encouraged.

Learning is Developmental. Anything learned is built on and adds to previous learning. Learning will not occur without readiness; therefore, it is important to determine what children know, their maturation levels, and their learning rates and capacities, as well as to plan for the proper sequencing of their experiences.

Learning is Motivated. The disequilibrium that an individual's environment may cause him or her to feel is a motivation for reacting, for learning. As suggested, this may be a very subtle process. However, for much learning—particularly in the classroom—there is more than a simple reaction. There will be a conscious drive established if the challenge, the motivation, is strong enough.

Learning Requires Reinforcement. Anything learned but not used moves rather quickly out of the conscious mind. It may be forgotten. If it is used, on the other hand, it becomes established. Thus, those things that children are to learn in school need to be practiced. This practice, of course, needs to be meaningful and satisfying to the children. Reinforcement does not occur if what is learned is separated from its use.

Learning May Transfer. Ordinarily, transfer of learning takes place from one situation to another to the extent that identical elements are shared by both. Learning will transfer if proper attention is given to what is taught, when it is taught, and whether children are helped to see the similarity of the situations.

Thinking about Teaching—Making Decisions

Systematic instruction is planned instruction.

Every day a teacher makes dozens of decisions. Good teaching is largely a question of the ratio of better decisions to poorer ones.

Determining the content you plan to teach and acknowledging relevant principles of learning contribute significantly to your preparation for teaching, but other important decisions remain to be made. You must be sure that the content given priority receives adequate attention and is presented in an appropriate form and sequence to provide students with sufficient opportunities for learning. Very little should be left to chance. You have the responsibility to teach in the best way you know how and to ensure that children learn what you intend that they should.

This does not mean, however, that all unplanned learning opportunities ought to be ignored. In every classroom unexpected events occur that can become excellent vehicles for teaching. You should be ready to capitalize on such imbedded teaching opportunities whenever they will contribute to the achievement of instructional goals. The chances are very good that these unplanned activities will be memorable for the children and will lead to the

Plan for purposeful use of language.

planning of successful related experiences.

All decision making does not have to be done by the teacher alone. Teachers who plan cooperatively with their students find that this approach leads to improved performance and good attitudes toward learning and school. Effective sharing of decision-making responsibility does not just happen, though; it must be learned through gradual expansion of the chil-

Teachers should recognize and value children's planning.

dren's role. Children and teacher need to learn how to plan together. The following suggestions should help that process along.

- Keep your responsibility as a teacher in mind. Know what the children's abilities are at any given point, and share decision making appropriately.
- Make sure that genuine choices are available. This is the only way for students to see that they are really involved in planning.
- Attempt to implement the plans that have been made. It is worthwhile for even the results of poor planning to be experienced.
- Make certain that planning is not being done by only a few members of the class. True sharing means that everyone is included.

INSTRUCTIONAL PLANNING

An instructional plan is not something that can be made once and then shelved; a plan needs to be revised, dropped, or remade as circumstances change and as children learn. Although a long-term plan (what should be accomplished this year, this term, this month) is crucial, plans must be made also for intermediate periods of time and for daily lessons.

Daily, unit, quarterly, and yearly plans must mesh if goals are to be achieved.

This section describes the elements of an instructional plan—for any period of time—and suggests a model of a basic plan for teaching the skills needed in the various language arts areas as well as integrating this teaching with some aspect of a content subject that is a part of the classroom's total curriculum. Finally, there is an illustration of such a plan.

A Basic Instructional Approach

The Language Arts Instructional Plan shown here illustrates a framework for thinking about planning instruction. The diagram depicts the relation-

LANGUAGE ARTS INSTRUCTIONAL PLAN

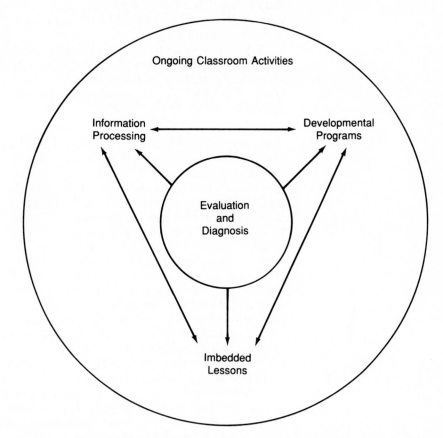

ships among the major factors to be taken into consideration as classroom planning is done and as instruction occurs. The larger circle represents the ongoing classroom program, instruction as it moves along from day to day, each day building on learning that has been gained and taking into consideration children's interests and their needs as determined by evaluation and diagnosis. The setting includes not only the curriculum requirements and the children but also external influences such as state-required and local testing, community preferences, and district policies. These and many other factors impinge on planning and, in turn, on instruction.

Inform parents of your instructional goals and plans. *Be specific.*

The smaller circle represents the evaluation and diagnosis—both formal and informal—that should be integral parts of all classroom activities. As a teacher, you evaluate the progress of students, the success of particular materials or activities, and the effect of your own planning and teaching. It is important to remember, though, that children have a responsibility for evaluating their own daily work and academic progress. Diagnosis seeks to determine each student's specific problems. Responsibility for diagnosis

Evaluation is an ongoing process, not something done only periodically.

Diagnosis also means finding out what is going well.

falls primarily on the teacher, but students can learn to identify their own weaknesses. They can also participate in discussions of problems and how they might be solved. With practice and guidance children can, as they become more mature, learn to honestly diagnose their own learning efforts.

The diagram focuses on three principal types of teaching activities: those based on instructional materials of a sequential, developmental nature; information processing activities involving realistic use of language, that is, language in communication; and imbedded lessons, which focus on practice and corrective or specific needs.

Developmental Programs.

Classroom teaching is strongly influenced by instructional materials of various types designed to teach skills in a developmental, sequential way. These materials primarily consist of textbooks but also include curriculum guides and, to some extent, kits, duplicated worksheets, computer programs, and simulations and games. The primary developmental materials used in language arts teaching are the basal readers, series of books that take children through a sequential set of experiences designed to lead to competency in reading. In addition, it is common for schools to have children study spelling and handwriting by completing programs that provide a definite sequence of learning activities. "English" or "language" books are also often used, but the developmental, sequential aspects in these have less basis in research evidence than do those in books dealing with reading, handwriting, and spelling.

If a teacher proceeds through such textbooks page by page, not much planning will be required, but this is not the best kind of teaching. At a minimum you need to adjust the use of any textbooks or other guides to the needs of your own students. And, as you plan other aspects of your classroom program, you will very likely see better ways to use textbooks than to simply progress through them page by page. After some experience you may even create your own developmental program, which will be different from that used by anyone else.

Information Processing.

Students process information as they clarify, identify, compare, inquire, survey, judge, create, solve, analyze, and evaluate.

Information-processing activities are ones in which students use writing, reading, listening, and speaking to express themselves and absorb knowledge. Information-processing activities involving all school subjects and various thinking and language abilities will have to be planned as you develop an effective classroom program.

Reading is often thought of as a subject to be taught for its own sake, but as a teacher you will want to plan reading experiences that are based in other areas of the curriculum. In science, for example, students will read about the process of photosynthesis and need to understand the description in terms of the stages involved. This type of reading is more difficult than the reading-for-sequence experiences presented in basal readers. Listening will be utilized as children are introduced to poetry and other types of literature. In social studies children will listen to recorded speeches and perhaps to reports made by their classmates. They must try to follow each presentation and grasp meaning at several different levels. When giving oral reports themselves, children will require assistance in learning how to prepare their material and make an effective delivery. Writing presents a great number of possibilities for thinking and expressive experiences.

These learning opportunities will have to be carefully planned if children are to derive maximum benefit from them. Some activities will be described in the teachers' manuals of textbook series in social studies and other subject fields, but the best ideas are likely to be your own because only you know the students and what activities will be most appropriate for them.

There are, of course, connections between developmental programs and information-processing activities. It seems logical that students should learn something in a developmental program and then be able to apply this directly to their information-processing experiences, but studies of human learning seem to indicate that this will occur with only a small proportion of learners. You will be more effective if you use relevant material from the language textbook at the time when the class is preparing for such an experience. Basal textbooks in spelling and handwriting may frequently be used as resources when other information-processing activities are proceeding.

Imbedded Lessons. Imbedded lessons also relate to information processing, but they are different in that they usually involve only a single student or small group for a brief time, during which the focus is on a specific skill or understanding. Imbedded lessons cannot be planned because of the impossibility of predicting when the situation will arise for teaching, re-

A brief time spent with a child can be an important imbedded lesson.

In her book *The Art of Teaching Writing,* Lucy Mc-Cormick Calkins gives examples of imbedded lessons taught to children as they write.

teaching, and practicing language skills that need attention. Experience will reveal what to expect in a general way, though, so you need only to be alert for good teaching opportunities. When children write stories, for instance, they may be vaguely aware of the need for quotation marks in dialogue but will have to be assisted in seeing exactly how they are used. This, then, is the best time to provide a few minutes of instruction—just when the child is ready.

Developmental program materials can be used with imbedded lessons as information-processing activities. For example, when learning about quotation marks in order to use them in a story, the child may be referred to relevant pages in the language textbook. Both language and spelling books are likely to include lists of commonly misspelled words, and children should be taught how and when to use these resources. Writers' guides covering many matters related to word choice, punctuation, and other questions are found in some language textbooks; this is a good type of aid to use in imbedded lessons. Also, when a child's handwriting seems to need attention, the teacher can refer him or her to a handwriting book for help and practice in correcting the problem.

Imbedded lessons are closely related to information-processing activities because such specific teaching is most likely to succeed when children are using language to learn content in the subject areas and to express themselves concerning what they have learned. Within the context of these comprehensive experiences there will be numerous opportunities to help children learn the specifics of spelling, handwriting, reading, using the dictionary, punctuation, vocabulary, listening, and speech. You can, however, plan for imbedded lessons only in a general way—by being alert for good teaching opportunities, knowing when a student is likely to be ready for a particular learning experience, and regularly refreshing your memory concerning the abilities and skills you want to emphasize.

Planning in Action

As indicated in the preceding section, daily language arts activities have many sources. Many come from textbook series and other materials that include detailed plans telling the teacher what to do. As a teacher, you should modify these materials as needed, making decisions about what to leave out and which aspects to emphasize and extend. Even if you tried to do it, you would not have enough class time to carry out all of the activities included in each set of published materials.

Decisions often involve choosing what to omit.

Another major consideration when developing lesson plans is to provide for language experiences in which knowledge and feelings are received or expressed within the framework of other classroom events. In science or social studies, for example, you will be planning lessons about magnets or pioneers that should involve children in writing, speaking, listening, and reading. Thus, language skills are integrated into other subject areas, where they may require specific attention at times—a few minutes on the use of capital letters for place names or how to find topics in an index, for instance. This kind of imbedded lesson advances the effectiveness of language skills and activities without diverting students from the subject matter being studied. In such situations learning opportunities for the language arts, just as those for mathematics or some other area of the curriculum, are included for purposes of reinforcement and transfer (discussed in the earlier section on principles of learning).

In addition to lessons already planned for you and lessons imbedded in expressional activities, there are the fully developed lesson plans that are truly your own. These you devise because of needs in the class, subject matter that is required to be taught, something that has come up in expressive activities, your desire to provide an experience that you believe important for the children to have, and so on. Planning is needed in all cases, and even the most experienced teachers will at least make a few notes about what is needed and what will be done. Those with less experience will usually want to be more thorough and complete a fully developed lesson plan.

Planning a Lesson

You probably have read about how to plan a lesson, or you may have done such planning yourself. A lesson plan may be for a single day or for several days (often the case for a social studies or science unit). Lesson plans also vary in amount of detail specified and in format; the extent of the detail included often depends on the teacher's level of experience. Every lesson (for either a unit or a day), however, involves tasks and learning opportunities that require planning, and careful thought must be given to what is to be taught, why it is being taught, how the teaching will be done, and how to measure the effectiveness of the teaching.

You may, of course, decide to deviate from the plan, making a "midcourse correction" in order to capitalize on an unforeseen learning opportunity. This flexibility is usually commendable and is one of the marks of a superior teacher. If you are a beginner, though, or someone who is more comfortable with established procedure, it is useful to identify specific objectives for a class session and to have a carefully thought-out plan and stay with it.

Suppose that the curriculum guide for your school requires you to teach a unit on colonial America. This is a **broad objective,** so delineation is required (if not specified in the guide). First, you and the children might discuss what they want and expect to learn from this unit. Perhaps the discussion would lead to these questions:

What famous people lived during that period? Why are they famous?

What events occurred during the period that are important to us today?

How did the people of that time live?

Since all of these questions cannot be answered in a single lesson—even if it lasted several days—one or two **specific objectives** should be identified for the lesson. Suppose, then, that you and the children decide to concentrate on the third question as the objective of the lesson being planned.

With this objective determined, the next step is to consider what you will need to do, what materials and other resources will be needed, and what learning activities the children will engage in. While keeping all of these thoughts in mind, attention should be given first to the resources. The children, knowing and understanding the objective, can provide some input. For example, they might suggest the class's textbook, the encyclopedia, and other books in the classroom and/or school library. Someone might also suggest that a nearby museum could be visited. You might propose a film, a local collector of antiques, or a speaker knowledgeable about the topic.

Certainly you need to list the long-range, or broad, objectives, the specific objective, and the resources, and it is also a good idea to list these on the board or a chart for the benefit of the children. Be realistic about resources, however. For example, if transportation to a museum is not likely to be available, a museum visit is not a viable resource for the lesson.

The next part of developing the lesson plan is deciding what procedures or activities will be used to help the children attain the specific objective. You may want to have the children work in small groups (permitting individual choices) or as individuals to gather information on such aspects of colonial life as food, clothing, housing, jobs, transportation, recreation, religion, and so on. Of course, a museum visit, a speaker, or a film would provide information to all and perhaps give an overall picture of colonial life; specific and more complete information about the various narrower aspects requires that the groups or individuals read and do research on their own. You, throughout all of this, should be guiding children with respect to finding resources, taking notes, and thinking about how they will report their information to the class (for example, oral reports, written summaries, demonstrations, displays, or dramatizations).

Beginners often find it helpful to include a time schedule in lesson plans. This provides a target for pacing.

You need to plan how much time will be given to gathering information and how much to reporting, thereby putting a time frame around the lesson. The broad objective of the planning example discussed here dictates that it will not be a one-day lesson (and few lessons are) but is likely to extend over a week or more.

A stage in any lesson—and one that should be recognized in any lesson plan—is an evaluation of the learning and of the effectiveness of the procedures followed. Perhaps having the children summarize orally is adequate; perhaps testing is appropriate. Certainly, evaluation must also include deciding what to do if the objective has not been accomplished. The children, of course, should be included in the latter aspect of evaluation and in looking ahead to the next lesson. Your evaluation often needs to be more than that done by or with the children, if such evaluation consists of only oral discussion and summarizing, important as these may be. You may need to consider what experiences were provided and note which particular skills or processes need more practice or attention. It is to be hoped, of course, that the children will eventually learn to evaluate themselves in terms of skills and behavior deficiencies.

Although the example discussed here is a social studies lesson, the same kind of planning is needed if the focus is science, health, language change, literature, or any other subject area. The significant point is that effective communication must be a second center of attention, no matter what the subject matter is. This is integration, and it is through such integration that language skills are most effectively taught. For a particular unit of study or a day's lesson to achieve its objective, children may use library skills, take notes, and organize material; they may introduce speakers, listen courteously, and discuss what they have heard; they may write reports, produce dramatizations, do videotaping, or perhaps even do some poetry writing. Some of the skills needed may already have been mastered; others will have to be introduced or reviewed.

Thus, planning a lesson involves certain necessary steps or stages. Also necessary is the children's participation in the planning and in execution of the plan. A plan for a single lesson, for example, might be recorded in a form like the following:

OBJECTIVES:

    Broad—Learning about life in colonial America
    Specific—Gaining information about how life necessities were acquired
            by colonists
            Improving skills in researching, studying, and reporting

MATERIALS:

    Chapter 2 of the social studies textbook
    Encyclopedias in the classroom and in the library
    Books on colonial America that have been set aside in the school library
    Large pictures of Plymouth Plantation

PROCEDURES:

1. Initiate discussion of camping (a topic familiar to many of the children), relating this to situations faced by colonists. Involve children in listing life necessities and discussing how these are met when camping.
2. Use pictures of Plymouth Plantation to show what a colony was like and to suggest how the colonists lived.
3. Encourage discussion about life necessities—which are truly basic and which are merely important? Have the class formulate a list.
4. Form groups consisting of four or five pupils, and have each group select a life necessity to investigate and report on.
5. Discuss available resources, at the same time providing lessons that review using a table of contents, skimming, and note taking.
6. Suggest that groups begin to plan how they will make their reports.
7. Conclude by reviewing what has been done and what will be done during the next class.

EVALUATION:

1. Do children have a clear idea of what the necessities of life are? Does each group understand what kind of information they are looking for?
2. Are pupils skimming resources to see whether they contain needed information? Is further practice in this skill needed by some or all of the children?
3. Are the notes that have been taken so far accurate and likely to be useful?

4. Are group members working well together, with each child making a contribution?

SUMMARY AND FOLLOW-UP:

1. Plan for a review of skimming and/or note taking for those who need it.
2. Decide, with the children, what other aspects of colonial life and times should be investigated.
3. Plan for variety in resources, grouping, and methods of reporting.
4. Determine what kinds of experiences can be included in the total unit, both those provided by you (trips, films, etc.) and those provided by the pupils (skits, demonstrations, oral and written reports, displays, etc.).

RECOGNIZING PUPIL DIFFERENCES

Refer to Chapter 16 regarding "special" or "exceptional" children and mainstreaming.

We know that each person is unique. Yet aside from observing obvious physical differences, a teacher may not really recognize the range of differences that exist among the children in his or her class. In terms of pupil achievement, only about one-third of a typical class achieve at or near the norm for that grade level on a standardized achievement test. The other two-thirds are usually about equally divided above and below the norm, with the range (distances from the norm) increasing as the grade level advances. For example, a classroom of sixth graders may show 40 percent at grade level, 20 percent at seventh grade level, 10 percent at eighth grade level or above, 20 percent at fifth grade level, and 10 percent at fourth grade level or below. And since the achievement test does not measure many of the language skills, the range among all pupils for all skills, abilities, and attitudes important to language communication is likely to be even more startling.

Teacher Identification of Differences

Make note of both strengths and weaknesses.

To identify the specific differences among pupils in order to determine their instructional needs, it is necessary to carry on a continuing program of evaluation. Relying on possibly casual observations and your memory about each child's strengths, weaknesses, and needs is likely to result in instruction that is less effective than it could be. More is needed, and below are specific evaluative devices and procedures you may use.

1. Observe and record on a note or checklist the speech performance of each child, including his or her speaking skills, mannerisms, and behavior as a member of an audience.
2. Make observational notes on individual pupils at regular intervals with re-

Neither does grouping need to be so lacking in flexibility that a child is always in the (so-called) "dumb" group.

Grouping is not easily done by many teachers, as observation of a number of classrooms soon forces one to conclude. However, a teacher who has confidence in the children and feels that he or she can rely on them seems to have much greater success with grouping than does another teacher who is more authoritarian or less inclined to involve children in the planning and conducting of activities. In addition, recognition of the limitations of evaluative instruments in pinpointing needs should not result in failure to use the instruments and to devise others to supplement them. Furthermore, grouping for instruction is easier when objectives are clearly defined.

In addition to the need for your objectives to be clear, you should think about the children's needs and interests and their personalities, the materials available to work with, how the groups will operate, and how you will handle time and space needs. Keep in mind that no grouping should be set in concrete. Sometimes plans just don't work out. Sometimes you have to revise your initial impression of individual children and their needs. Sometimes they take spurts in learning.

Individualizing Learning

There are many ways for providing instruction directed at meeting the individual needs of children. The plans and related activities suggested here are only a few that might be implemented. As you read other chapters and think further about the importance of individualizing learning opportunities, you will be able to add to the ideas presented in this section.

Many classrooms today have **learning centers,** areas that children are free to use during certain periods of the day. These centers may be simply tables or partly screened-off areas of the room or some kind of grouping of materials. The idea is to provide opportunities for independent study and work, usually involving something of particular interest to the children. How and how much the centers are used varies from teacher to teacher, based on the instructional goals of each. There are frequently centers for writing, listening, reading, science experimenting, and so on, with materials and equipment in each center related to its purpose.

The following paragraphs describe some ways in which assignments and special interests may be worked on individually or in small groups. Many suggestions for making this concept a reality are given in the chapters that follow, and at the end of each chapter are specific examples of independent learning activities. Like all other activities suggested in this book, these are only samples. If activities are to meet specific needs of individual children, they *must* be designed with those needs and those children in mind.

Regardless of the school or classroom organizational plan or plans, it is possible to provide individualized practice on specific skills for children who need such work. For example, some children can profit from exercise materials that require them to make decisions about which words should be capitalized. On the other hand, it is obvious that many language skills cannot be practiced with paper-and-pencil exercises. In fact, one of the big errors made by many teachers (and encouraged by some textbooks) is the use of written practice exercises as a means of changing the way children speak. However, discriminating use of practice materials, in ways such as those suggested below, may be helpful.

- Practice exercises can be secured from workbooks, old textbooks, and clippings from teachers' magazines. These materials should be cut up so that the exercises that apply to a particular skill can be filed together.

- It is often profitable to have two copies of workbooks that you intend to use in this manner so that the material on both sides of a page can be used. These exercises can be placed in clear plastic envelopes in order to keep them clean and to permit children to write on them with crayon that can be washed off. Answers to the exercises should be provided (perhaps on the back of the exercise page) so that pupils can check their own papers.

- Since many commercial materials (for example, the pages of a workbook or textbook or a card in a kit) may either provide unrealistic and useless practice or try to give practice on more than one skill, exercises that you make yourself may be the most helpful.

Be wary when using commercial and other types of individualized learning packages. They may provide a rigidity that you want to eliminate.

Many opportunities for individualizing instruction occur as language arts instruction is integrated with instruction in the subject matter areas of the curriculum, as the lesson described earlier shows. Individualizing instruction is as important in the subject matter areas as it is in language arts since children's abilities and knowledge vary in all areas. Integration with social studies is expedient because both receptive and expressive language are essential to most social studies activities. This is also true for other subject matter areas. For example, if a class of third graders is studying the use of water by plants, there would be a need for children to be given library research to do—and to report orally to the class. Individual children could be assigned to list and assemble materials needed for several experiments the activity would call for (plants watered and not watered, tracing the absorption of water by a plant, how water gets out of plants, etc.) while other children could keep records (of water levels, times needed for absorption, etc.). Children could write descriptions of the experiments, with the difficulty of these adjusted for individual pupil ability. Vocabulary words would have to be looked up in a dictionary and possibly written on a chart. All of the children would be involved in conversations and discussions about the activity.

Related to the above procedure is one in which children enter into contracts to do specific tasks. These contracts usually develop from pupil-teacher conferences in which previous work is evaluated in terms of objectives agreed on earlier. Since children vary in their capacities to plan and in their abilities to assess their own capabilities and interests, it is appropriate for the teacher to provide alternatives that may be contracted for. Suggestions may be made regarding pacing, although it is important for each child to discover his or her own working speed. Decisions must also be made regarding the way the product of a contract will be evaluated.

Children may need help in organizing for contract work.

Other suggestions for individualizing include the following:

- Children who finish assignments or activities before their classmates do may be encouraged to make copies for the bulletin board of something they feel they have written well.
- A child who does good work in a particular area may help others who are having difficulty.
- Each child may keep a notebook or journal for unassigned writing of a personal nature and should have the option of showing it to the teacher only if he or she wishes.
- Children who finish assignments early may be permitted to browse in the library, work on special reports, listen to recordings, and so forth.

MAXIMIZING CONDITIONS FOR LEARNING

From the moment children at any age level enter a classroom door, there are opportunities for developing their language abilities. Children are ready to learn, and your program should capitalize on their abilities, backgrounds, and interests. Specific and careful planning is needed, but this planning, this organizing, must take into account conditions not discussed earlier, including ones you need to create.

Experience and Learning

An effective language arts program recognizes in three ways the importance of experience in the development of children's ability to use language. First, the program is based on an awareness that every child entering school, whether he or she comes from a white middle-class neighborhood or from a highly diversified socioeconomic and ethnic one, has a background of many experiences. Although these experiences—including the language ones—may not have been used as learning tools and built on to the extent that is desirable, they are important. Second, an effective program provides experiences that build vocabulary and concepts, develop multiple meanings of words, and familiarize children with the kinds of sentence patterns and ways of expressing themselves that they will encounter in school. Third, an effective program provides these experiences in settings that focus on genuine, lifelike communication activities that have meaning for the children involved and provide motivation for learning.

Awareness that every child has a language background developed prior to entering school—one that continues to be developed outside of the classroom—means more than overcoming any bias with respect to a "disadvantaged" or "deprived" child's having had little language experience or being "nonverbal." Children's language backgrounds are simply different, and to assume a background of experience on the basis of family economic conditions, race, ethnicity, or anything else is a fallacy. It is important, though, to try to determine just what the experiential background of each child is and to find out which experiences important to the school curriculum are lacking. To take for granted a background of experience and an understanding of concepts is dangerous. For example, teachers frequently report that inner-city children do not have a concept associated with the word *pet,* yet reading readiness books and first primers usually have pets in their stories. One teacher recently told one of the authors that children (and these were not "deprived" children) in her class had difficulty choosing a picture of a writing pen as representing a word that rhymes with *hen.* They apparently knew *pen* as the name of an enclosure for the chickens, but they did not know another meaning for the word. Probably their parents write either with a pencil or with something called a "ball point." Another teacher found an entire class of sixth graders who could not verbalize a definition of *physician.* It is possible, of course, that they would have known *doctor* or *pediatrician.*

There is a need in language arts programs to build on children's experiences and for the focus of this building to be on developing language ability; experiences of children both inside and outside of the classroom are opportunities for this to happen. An experience is simply any occurrence, but more importantly it needs to be thought of as the reactions and feelings of the participants about the occurrence. Thus, the activities in a classroom provide differing experiences to different children, and some may provide little to any of them. The key is the quality of the activity—the experience— how it is planned, how it relates to the learning objectives, its realism, children's interest in it, and the guidance given by the teacher toward achieving the objectives.

Building on Experiences

Because of the differences discussed, there should be provision for diversity in children's school experiences. At the same time, a teacher should attempt to provide a common core of experiences because of the similarity of many children's needs. Children will be limited in their use of language by the experiences they have had. A child will not be able to express feelings about "early morning on the farm" if he or she has never been on a farm and arisen early. In the same way, a child will not react with feeling about the dazzling wonders of the snowflake if he or she has not seen snow—or if snow has only been something to contend with rather than to appreciate (though the opportunity may be present to help such a child discover the wonder and beauty that accompany the hardships of snow).

Prepare children for experiences. For example, before a field trip, encourage the children to help plan it, generate questions, and discuss vocabulary and possible follow-up activities.

Children must have an abundance of opportunities to gain new ideas, new impressions, and new feelings and to relate these to the experiences they have had. The number of ways to give children these experiences is almost infinite: reading aloud from a variety of materials; talking with them about news events and other things of interest; providing for interesting visitors to the classroom; making available television and radio programs, recordings, films, and still pictures; providing books in profusion and the opportunity to read them; and giving special attention to expressive words and apt phrases and how they may be used. Particularly important are excursions or field trips. These may be merely excursions into the schoolyard or another part of the building, they may be visits to various points of interest in the neighborhood, or they may entail more extended trips.

Talking about things that are real and important is beneficial.

A Few Awareness Books

Find Out by Touching by Paul Showers (Thomas Y. Crowell)
I See the Winds by Kazue Mizumura (Thomas Y. Crowell)
Rain Drop Splash by Alvin Tresselt (Lothrop, Lee and Shepard)
What Is Your Favorite Smell, My Dear? by Myra Gibson (Grosset and Dunlap)

Take time to observe:

the swooping of a swallow
the chugging and blinking of a helicopter
a bird's nest in a tree fork
the swaying of a tall pine
the ripple on the water caused by a fallen leaf
waves creeping up a sandy beach
the bouncing run of a rabbit

Helping children be more aware of their senses is particularly important and will result in input that builds language growth. Children, like most adults, are seldom good observers, although too often time for observing is simply not provided for in a crowded school day—and this is sometimes the case on a field trip or some other experience-building activity. Although various observation games are available or can be created—such as displaying a number of objects, removing one, and asking what is missing—the observation of natural phenomena is more helpful. Taking time to observe cloud formations, how the wind has drifted the snow, a flock of geese overhead, or the spread of the roots of a sprouting bean seed will interest children, cause them to use language, and facilitate their learning of new ideas and words.

Children themselves can provide much input. With very little encouragement they will bring butterflies, leaves, worms, rocks, and innumerable other objects to the classroom.

Activities such as the following are all useful in adding to children's knowledge and creating communication opportunities.

- Keeping an aquarium or terrarium
- Noting temperature differences in sunshine and shade
- Watching flying formations of birds
- Collecting leaves of different kinds or colors
- Collecting kinds and shapes of rocks

- Tasting particular substances, such as pickles, berries, fruits, spices, or nuts
- Feeling various materials, such as velvet, fur, aluminum foil, sand, wool, and silk
- Caring for a classroom pet
- Observing the growth of different kinds of seeds
- Keeping a weather chart
- Bringing in pictures of things of interest, such as a new baby at the zoo
- Feeding birds or squirrels in winter
- Observing soil erosion
- Listening to stories and recordings
- Participating in singing games

A Learning Climate

Children's learning is impeded if the atmosphere in the classroom is not positive, not warm and accepting.

Children's growth in language depends on many things, not the least of which is the atmosphere or climate in a classroom. The climate desired is one that fosters goodwill, respect, and friendliness on the part of all concerned. It is one in which an effort is made to ensure that each child will feel relaxed, at ease, and accepted as an important member of the group. Such a climate respects each child's personality, his or her heritage, and the social and emotional effects of his or her out-of-school environment. Creating the climate for developing each child's potential is largely the teacher's responsibility, and it will evolve chiefly from the children's feelings of acceptance, freedom, and shared responsibility.

Although there are differences among teachers (and who would want it otherwise?), every teacher ought to be a vital, interesting person, one who is sensitive and encouraging. These qualities are reflections of attitude, and attitude can be shown in many ways. These include the following:

- Show each child that he or she is an accepted and important member of the classroom group.
- Encourage an attitude of friendliness and mutual respect among the children—including respect for differences as well as likenesses.
- Talk with and listen to children individually and in groups, and encourage them to exchange ideas and experiences.
- Be receptive to ideas and interests expressed by the children.
- Show appreciation of each child's efforts at expression.
- Be enthusiastic—and allow the children to be—about the activities of the classroom.
- Show sensitivity to and awareness of the world about you—encourage children to notice the way things look, sound, smell, and feel.
- Let children see your own enjoyment of the stories you read, the way words sound, and the images they create.

Classroom climate is also affected by the general learning environment or climate of the school. The principal, office workers, lunchroom helpers, custodians, bus drivers, and teacher aides are all involved in setting the learning conditions in classrooms. The principal is a key person in this. He or she must understand children, know the curriculum and materials, and see the importance of a busy and interesting classroom, one in which the children are active participants. If a teacher has an aide, this person certainly should share the teacher's feelings about children and seek to develop the same attitudes that the teacher has or is developing. A custodian needs to be interested in what a class is doing and be willing to accept possible personal inconveniences such as a disarranged classroom. Other school personnel should also appreciate children's curiosity and enthusiasm. You cannot control the actions and reactions of these people, but you can do much to influence their attitudes by talking with them about what the children are doing and why they are doing it. Try inviting each of them to be a special guest of the class for a particular activity or program. Also, try involving them in a class activity—making something, telling about something, or giving their opinion on something, for instance.

Physical materials in the classroom are also important. Little stimulation of language growth or creativity will come from drabness. Wall and bulletin-board decorations, displays, pictures, and objects to handle and talk about are all important. And, of course, there must be language: signs, titles, and name plates to show the use of words; records, tapes, and tables and shelves of books as evidence of the delight and knowledge they can bring. Further, a classroom where language growth is taking place is one that shows evidence that the children themselves have taken part in planning, preparing, and arranging the decorations and displays and that many activities are in progress there. This does not necessarily mean neatness, though children must learn that materials left strewn around the room are not easily found when needed or may not be in condition to be used again. Nor does it mean that absolute peace and quiet must reign; children learn as they share their experiences, discuss their activities, and help one another with problems.

RESOURCES FOR TEACHING THE LANGUAGE ARTS

Parents should be told and shown how the textbooks and other resources will be used.

Anything in the children's world—in the classroom and outside of it—may be a teaching resource. In a more narrow sense, however, the principal resources are textbooks and materials intended to supplement them, such as workbooks, encyclopedias, videotapes, and audio cassettes. Computers are increasingly showing promise of becoming another significant instructional resource.

Textbooks

As discussed in the section on instructional planning, textbooks, particularly the sequential reading series, are the most readily available and important resource the language arts teacher has, but all textbooks (even those for reading instruction) are aids, not directors or regulators. To begin a year's teaching by starting an individual child or group of children on the first page of a textbook and to proceed through it page by page, day after day, fails to take into account the language abilities and needs of that particular child or group of children.

Furthermore, although they are very useful, textbook series cannot do everything; they are not assistant teachers. They do, however, provide a general view of the content the authors believe to be suitable for a particular grade level, thus serving as a reminder and a standard against which the instructional program may be measured.

Recognize weaknesses in textbooks as well as strengths.

The limitations of textbooks are many, particularly if they are relied on heavily. In the first place, a textbook-oriented program is likely to be too formal, with little involvement of the children in planning and too few hands-on learning experiences. In addition, the emphasis in many textbooks, particularly language textbooks, is on aspects of language study that children either know already or have no valid reason for learning. The practice exercises and activities suggested—even if they focus on what children need to know—are often inadequate in number and type because of limitations on the size of textbooks. Also, many language-learning activities must be oral in nature, and books simply cannot provide those.

Computers

Riedesel and Clements, in Coping with Computers in the Elementary and Middle Schools, *review the possibilities and problems associated with these important teaching aids.*

Computers have only recently become widely used as instructional resources in the elementary school. In many ways teachers are still learning how to

Use of the computer can begin at a very young age.

use them effectively. One of the difficulties is that computer-based learning and teaching tools proliferate at a faster rate than they can be incorporated into classroom organization and procedures. At the same time computers are increasingly affecting other aspects of the school program, such as information storage in the library.

Computers have made their most dramatic impact in the language arts as word processors for writing. (This development is discussed fully in Chapters 9 and 10.) Appropriate use of computers in several other areas of language learning is possible, too, and there are many good examples of such use that teachers should consider.

- *Spelling.* The computer can flash a word on the screen, accompanied by an illustration or the correct pronunciation. The word then disappears, and the student has a few seconds to type the word correctly.
- *Vocabulary building.* Simulation experiences involving such activities as operating a small business provide opportunities to use new terms—*asset, liability, inventory,* and *profit,* for example.
- *Beginning literacy.* A child types letters and the computer names them. After a group of letters has been typed (such as CAT or MNXEOFU), the child signals the computer to pronounce what has been written.
- *Reference skills.* Students can learn about information retrieval by supplying information to create a classroom data base. The computer will then answer questions about Sam's phone number or the names of all students having a dog as a pet.

Reviews of educational software may be found in specialized publications such as:

AEDS Monitor
Association for Educational Data Systems
1201 Sixteenth Street, N.W.
Washington, DC 20036

Classroom Computer News
Intentional Educations, Inc.
341 Mt. Auburn Street
Watertown, MA 02171

The Computing Teacher
Department of Computer and Information Science
University of Oregon
Eugene, OR 97403

Educational Computer Magazine
P.O. Box 535
Cupertino, CA 95015

Electronic Learning
Scholastic, Inc.
902 Sylvan Avenue
Englewood Cliffs, NJ 07632

School Courseware Journal
1341 Bulldog Lane, Suite C
Fresno, CA 93710

The use of computers requires careful selection of software, the programs that cause the machines to operate. Some programs are a waste of time; either they do not make much of a contribution to learning or what they provide is better done in some other way. Often programs are simply not appealing to children; material presented via a computer in a boring manner will not improve children's learning.

When selecting computer programs for classroom use, you should be guided by several general questions:

1. Does the program contribute to the achievement of appropriate long-term educational objectives?
2. Does the program make a contribution because it does something faster, better, or for more students than other approaches do?
3. Is the program attractive to students in terms of usability, color, movement, graphics, and sound?
4. Does the program teach rather than simply test?
5. Are there procedures for varying the difficulty level of the program through adjustments in speed and provision of more or less material?
6. Is it easy for the teacher to intervene at various points in the program in order to assist the student?
7. Is a record automatically kept of the student's successful and unsuccessful responses so that this information may be used for follow-up?
8. Is information on how well the student is doing in the program immediately available?

The Reading Teacher and *Language Arts* are professional journals that sometimes have sections devoted to reviews of software.

In addition to these general concerns, there are many specific points to consider when selecting and using software. When you need such information the best advice will probably come from an experienced teacher who uses computers extensively. There are also libraries and resource centers where programs may be tried and many periodicals that contain relevant information for teachers.

Other Resources

An effective language arts program uses virtually everything and anything as teaching resources. Children are interested in the world and want to communicate about it. They learn outside the classroom as well as inside; in fact, they may learn more outside. Thus, teachers lose touch with much of the child's world if they limit teaching resources to just those found within the school walls. Additional resources include trade and reference books, magazines, newspapers, displays, artwork, maps, puppets, bulletin boards, television and radio, film, audio and video cassettes, filmstrips, transparencies, photographs, and slides. Because such resources play an important role in attaining an effective language arts program, some of these resources are listed at the end of each chapter so you can bring them into your planning and instruction.

Audio and video recorders make a significant contribution to the language arts program.

These resources are often referred to as audiovisual aids, but they are more than aids. When used in a well-planned program, they will heighten motivation for learning, provide for better retention of what is learned (because of their concreteness and multisensory characteristics), give the program freshness and variety, provide reinforcement for other learning, encourage students' active participation, widen the range of experience in a manner that has special attraction, and appeal to varied abilities and interests.

Much of the above applies particularly to television. Too often television in the classroom is watched with little follow-up and less preparation. With the increased variety of content available on videotape, television can become an effective classroom resource in all subject areas. It is a way of communicating that deserves an important place in the language arts curriculum. Reading and writing activities readily grow out of television programs viewed both in the classroom and at home.

The greater availability of resources necessary for videotape recording, photography, and audio recording means that students can make greater use of such resources to produce their own work, which has important implications for language arts learning as well as learning in other subject areas. Children might write their own version of some historical event, for example, and then produce and videotape it with accompanying narration, recordings of music, and sound effects.

EVALUATION AND GRADING

Too often evaluation is equated with giving a grade, but it is much more than this. Evaluation is a process, an essential component of the larger process of instruction. It is directly related to instructional goals and to the attainment of those goals. Evaluation determines what has not been effectively taught—what else needs to be taught. Grading, on the other hand, is done for the purpose of reporting to pupils, to parents, and to school authorities. Grading should be based on evaluation; therefore, evaluation is necessary for grading. However, the converse is not true—grading is not required for evaluation.

The Role of Evaluation

Evaluation is a process that comprises all the procedures used by the teacher, the children, the principal, and other school personnel to appraise the outcomes of instruction. The general steps that must be followed in order to arrive at an appraisal include formulating instructional objectives that can be measured or assessed, securing evidence from representative situations and activities regarding the extent of the achievement of the objectives, summarizing and recording this evidence, interpreting or analyzing the evidence in terms of the objectives and the instructional procedures, and using the interpretation to extend and improve instruction.

Finding out what a child knows or can do is the first step in good teaching. Often, too much emphasis is given to what the child cannot do. Not many of us would want to spend hours trying to do something we found extremely difficult.

In relating these steps to a particular aspect of an instructional program (perhaps a writing activity, the giving of an oral report, or learning to use the dictionary), begin by giving an inventory test or by using some other appropriate means for appraising what the learner already knows or can do that is specifically related to what you plan to teach. Then teach the skills, knowledge, or attitudes needed by the learner as shown by this appraisal. Provide motivation for learning the things taught by designing situations in which they are actually needed and used; this will establish learnings firmly. Next, give a test or make an appraisal similar in content and form to that used during the inventory stage. Use the results of this appraisal to determine the extent of learning and discover specific deficiencies. And finally, reteach for these deficiencies, giving practice as needed; if necessary, continue the process by retesting, reteaching, and so forth.

Techniques and Instruments

As suggested earlier, instruments and procedures for evaluation vary widely in type, structure, and function. The procedures include the administration of tests, questionnaires, inventories, checklists, and observation forms, as well as conferences, examination of biographies and folders of pupils' work, and oral or written questioning. Tests vary, too—they may be oral or written, standardized or teacher-made, essay or short-answer. In addition, there are models, statements of standards, progress charts, logs and diaries, and scales.

Many of the instruments and procedures are discussed in later chapters where specific reference is made to their use. At this point the emphasis is on the importance of evaluation and the fact that there are many instruments and procedures available. It is also important to recognize the imprecision in commercial materials for evaluating oral and written language abilities—a fact reflected in the paucity of tests available for evaluating many important objectives. Thus, it is necessary to do much informal evaluation—to make use of checklists, records, charts, and inventories; to collect pupils' work in folders; to keep logs and diaries; to have conferences; and to help pupils develop models, scales, and statements of standards.

Reporting Progress

A teacher must observe the reporting policies of the school and district, of course, and in many cases this means putting letter or numerical grades on a report card. You can go further than this, though, by sending home samples of children's work, evaluative statements and explanations, and the results from using various instruments and procedures. Although some teachers think doing these things is too time-consuming and others simply don't know what to say in evaluative statements (often because of having done too little evaluating), the value of more adequate reporting cannot be denied. In addition to providing better and more detailed written reports, you should arrange to confer with parents about their children's progress and needs more often than once a year.

Try to have conferences with parents early in the year, before problems develop.

Children should also be reported to, but again this does not mean that every paper or activity has to be marked with a grade. Pupils will appreciate talking with you about their progress, seeing your marks on checklists and observation forms, and participating in interpreting data obtained via instruments such as tests and scales. This kind of active participation, along with helping to establish criteria before activities are begun, will help children to learn habits of self-evaluation and to understand what is expected of them.

Telephone or send a short note to parents about their child's accomplishments.

All reports—to parents, to pupils, and to school authorities—should be based on evidence that can be shown and understood; they should be made with consideration of the child and the effect of the report on the child and his or her learning; and they should be as accurate an assessment of achievement or progress as is possible and without subjective bias of any sort—or as nearly so as possible.

A FINAL WORD

Children acquire language facility in three principal ways: internally, through use, and through direct instruction. All three are of importance in the elementary school. The program and the teacher should support growth in each child's ability to use her or his language in writing, reading, speaking, and listening. Children learn in the subject areas of the curriculum through the use of language; they need to know everything from specialized vocabularies to the ways of thinking that characterize a field of knowledge. Language use is what enables children to expand their language abilities, and the language arts program must be organized and executed with this foremost in mind. This chapter has given a brief overview of the organizing and planning needed to teach language arts effectively; suggestions will be expanded on in the chapters that follow. Principles for selecting content and guidelines for planning become operational only when the teacher applies them in light of the particular children in a classroom—how well they speak and write, how well they listen and read, and what problems they seem to have. In the same way, the instructional plan and the means for implementing it can become truly meaningful only when considered in connection with specific content and procedures for teaching speaking, listening, reading, and writing.

References

Busching, Beverly A., and Schwartz, Judith I., eds. *Integrating the Language Arts in the Elementary School.* National Council of Teachers of English, 1983.

Calkins, Lucy McCormick. *The Art of Teaching Writing.* Heinemann, 1986.

Carkhuff, Robert R. *The Productive Teacher II: An Introduction to Instruction.* Human Resources Development Press, 1984.

Cushenbery, Donald C. *Directing an Effective Language Arts Program for Your Students.* Charles C Thomas, 1986.

Goodman, Kenneth S.; Smith, E. Brooks; Meredith, Robert; and Goodman, Yetta. *Language and Thinking in School*. Richard C. Owen, 1987.

Paley, Vivian Gussin. *Boys and Girls*. University of Chicago Press, 1984.

Pollard, Rita, ed. *Reading, Writing, Thinking, Learning*. National Council of Teachers of English, 1986.

Riedesel, C. Alan, and Clements, Douglas H. *Coping with Computers in the Elementary and Middle Schools*. Prentice-Hall, 1985.

Shepherd, Gene D., and Ragan, William B. *Modern Elementary Curriculum*. Holt, Rinehart and Winston, 1982.

Thaiss, Christopher. *Language Across the Curriculum in the Elementary Grades*. National Council of Teachers of English, 1987.

Teaching Resources

MAGAZINES FOR ELEMENTARY-SCHOOL TEACHERS

Childhood Education. The Association for Childhood Education International, 3615 Wisconsin Avenue, N.W., Washington, DC 20016.

Early Years. Allen Raymond, Inc., P.O. Box 1266, Darien, CT 06820.

The Horn Book. Park Square Building, 31 St. James Avenue, Boston, MA 02116.

Instructor. The Instructor Publications, Inc., 757 Third Avenue, New York, NY 10017.

Language Arts. National Council of Teachers of English, 1111 Kenyon Road, Urbana, IL 61801.

Pre-K Today. Scholastic, Inc., P.O. Box 644, Lyndhurst, NJ 07071-0644.

The Reading Teacher. International Reading Association, 800 Barksdale Road, P.O. Box 8139, Newark, DE 19711.

School Library Journal. P.O. Box 1978, Marion, OH 43305-1978.

Teacher. Macmillan Professional Magazines, Inc., 77 Bedford Street, Stamford, CT 06901.

OTHER RESOURCES

Computer Teaching Tips. Sunburst Communications.

Selfe, Cynthia. *Computer Assisted Instruction: Create Your Own*. National Council of Teachers of English, 1986.

Shillingburg, Patricia M.; Bareford, Kenneth C.; Pacita, Joyce A.; and Townsond, Janice Lubinsky. *The Teacher's Computer Activities Book*. Teachers College Press, 1986.

Tiedt, Sidney W., and Tiedt, Iris M. *Language Arts Activities for the Classroom*. Allyn and Bacon, 1987.

Watson, Dorothy, J., ed. *Ideas and Insights: Language Arts in the Elementary School*. National Council of Teachers of English, 1987.

Activities for Preservice Teachers

1. Develop a lesson plan that shows how you would try to teach average third graders social studies or science material in such a way as to give them experience in thinking and writing about a sequence of events.

2. Interview a college professor or school administrator who is particularly concerned with evaluation in the language arts. Find out what practices are common in evaluation and how problems are being addressed.

3. Discuss with an elementary teacher the children in her or his class. Ask about the ranges of their intellectual abilities and academic achievement and how he or she deals with these.

4. Describe the mandated language and reading proficiency tests for classroom teachers, college students preparing for teaching, and elementary and secondary pupils in your state. Compare these with the requirements of other states.

5. Make an appointment with a school administrator, and ask to be shown the different types of records kept in children's cumulative folders. Consider what relevance these might have for language arts teaching.

6. Go to your college's curriculum library or your school district's facility and examine a basal language series for elementary schools. Identify elements that

appear to be developmental or to relate to information processing as discussed in this chapter. Is there any mention of what might be thought of as imbedded lessons?

7. Interview several elementary school teachers from different school systems and ask how they group for instruction in various subjects. List as many different grouping designs as you can as well as what the teachers believe to be the strengths and weaknesses of each.

8. Obtain copies of your state and district syllabi for language arts. Study these to determine what children are expected to learn at each grade level.

9. List the advantages and disadvantages of subject-matter departmentalization in elementary schools. Indicate the sources you used for determining these.

Activities for Inservice Teachers

1. Interview other teachers at your grade level in your school system, asking them to identify language arts topics not receiving sufficient attention in the program. Can they (and you) agree on how time might be taken from other topics to make reallocation possible?

2. Find textbooks from language arts series that are at least eight years old. Note the similarities and differences between them and the materials currently in use.

3. Develop a plan (including techniques and/or devices) for evaluating your pupils in the language arts areas, one that will provide you with information helpful for instruction and for reporting to parents. Keep in mind both simplicity of use and adequate coverage.

4. Plan an interesting presentation for parents designed to explain your language arts program. Be sure that you cover your teaching goals, the program's importance, evaluation procedures used, and how parents might help at home or as volunteer aides in your classroom. Discuss what you've planned with your administrator before making the presentation.

5. Examine several pieces of language arts software with which you are unfamiliar. Use the criteria presented in this chapter to evaluate them.

6. Talk with those people who are on curriculum development committees in your building or school system and find out if there is any interest in making a concerted effort to teach language arts "across the curriculum"—perhaps in conjunction with increased attention to information processing, or children's thinking.

7. Over a period of two weeks note the number of imbedded lessons you teach to individuals and small groups. Can you increase the number by consciously looking for opportunities?

8. Examine some standardized achievement tests in language arts. Do the items match the content of your program? What do you think of the questions and format? Are the results reported in a way that makes them useful to you?

9. Review the electronic equipment and media available in your school. Draw up a list of needs, justifying each item on the grounds of its contribution to language arts teaching.

Chapter *3*

Language Learning and Young Children

Teachers rightly believe that the home has a powerful effect on a child's educational progress. In addition, most would agree that much of that influence is a result of the amount and kind of language experience provided by the parents. A high proportion of today's preschool children learn not only at home but also in group programs that they attend regularly. Parents and other adults who work with this age group need to be particularly concerned with language development.

In 1965, 500,000 children attended nursery schools; by 1985, the total was 2,500,000.

This chapter deals with the preschool years, although that may no longer be an entirely accurate term for the ages in question since prekindergarten classes are being introduced into the elementary schools of many communities. The teachers of four-year-olds in these classes usually have degrees in elementary education—you may be considering such a career yourself or one in nursery school education or day care. Those of you concerned with parent education will find in this chapter content that can be used to help you see what can be done at home to promote language development. And, of course, if you are a parent of a young child or likely to be one some time soon, you will find this chapter especially interesting. In many ways it is the foundation for what will be presented in the rest of the book.

EARLY CHILDHOOD EDUCATION

Parents may want to read *Choosing Child Care: A Guide for Parents,* by S. Auerback (available from Institute for Childhood Resources, 1169 Howard Street, San Francisco, CA 94103, or many bookstores).

A good general text on early childhood education is Morrison's *Early Childhood Education Today.*

Until children go to kindergarten, they may spend all their time at home or they may be enrolled in an organized group program. Whatever the setting, the learning principles operating are the same and are usually referred to as "early childhood education." Because of the age of the participants, so-called traditional teaching practices of scheduled lessons directed by teachers are not appropriate. When these practices are used, it is usually because the adults involved—whether parents or staff members of a group program—do not fully understand what is required for young children to learn effectively. A review of the basic principles of early childhood education is important.

1. *Young children require opportunities to move around and interact with others.* "Sit down and be quiet" is a nearly useless request when directed at young children. They cannot do this unless particularly fascinated by something they see and hear. They learn by engaging in physical activity and interaction with other children and adults.

2. *Interaction with concrete materials—blocks, puzzles, balls, paint brushes, and many other objects—is very important.* Young children manipulate these

and find out how they feel, what they can do, and how they respond when treated in certain ways. Important concepts grow out of these activities.

3. *Both large- and small-muscle activities are needed by young children.* Such small-muscle experiences as solving puzzles, cutting with scissors, and stringing beads should be provided. So should activities involving large muscles—running, climbing, sliding, and riding wheeled toys.

4. *Pretending and other expressive and creative experiences are necessary.* Young children need opportunities to draw, paint, sing, dance, dramatize stories, pretend to be someone else, and otherwise express themselves, their ideas, and their feelings.

5. *There should be balance and alteration in young children's activities.* The experiences of the young child should be balanced between active and quiet times, large- and small-muscle activities, and individual and group involvement.

6. *Adults should follow the lead of the child.* Parents and teachers should watch children for clues as to their reactions to experiences and should be prepared to switch to other activities if the reactions appear to be negative. Adults should not use bribes and threats to enforce their wishes.

7. *Young children must have opportunities to make choices.* Children should have the right, at least some of the time, to select activities and decide how long to remain with them. The choices available ought to include declining to participate.

8. *The way something is done is more important than the result.* The expression is "process, not product." How children feel about themselves and the experience is of significance—the tunefulness of their singing or the beauty of their pictures is not.

These principles apply to all types of experiences in the young child's life—playing at home, attending a group, going shopping, visiting a relative, and so on. This chapter is especially concerned with seeing what these principles mean for language learning, recognizing, of course, that this is only one area of growth and development.

YOUNG CHILDREN'S USE OF LANGUAGE

As discussed in Chapter 1, an infant may be observed listening to human voices, often moving the body in rhythm with the language heard. An infant will recognize some speech, especially the mother's, and will react to familiar voices by stopping crying or by waving and kicking in anticipation of being picked up or played with.

Babies do a great deal of vocalizing and, as the end of the first year approaches, may begin to produce sounds that are more and more like words. These utterances lack meaning in the beginning, but gradually some are associated with people and objects. The vocalizations lengthen, often lasting several seconds ("ooh-wa-duh-da-da-muh"), and babies will engage in a conversationlike game of taking turns making speech sounds. Hearing others talk and participating in the exchange of vocalizations stimulate very

Language growth requires interaction.

young children in their language development, and so does having adults recite nursery rhymes and sing to them, activities often accompanied by holding, rocking, and bouncing. Vocabulary items accumulate slowly at first but then increase to several dozen rather rapidly, particularly if others respond to the child's attempts, try to encourage language production, and show enjoyment of these activities.

Toddlers (children aged from about eighteen months to three years) have learned to walk and talk and so are able to engage in much interaction with family members and, very likely, other people as well. By age two or soon afterward children often know a hundred words or more, including the names of objects and of people and pets and some action words. They use this accumulated stock of words in many different ways: to make their needs known ("More milk"), to describe actions ("Throw ball"), and to relate to others ("Mommy kiss"). They can ask questions ("Daddy come?"), use modifiers ("red truck"), show possession ("Grandma car"), describe a situation ("Juice all gone"), and, of course, express characteristic negativism ("No! No bed!"). These two- and three-word "sentences" are gradually replaced by standard patterns of close approximations ("Me want that") as the child adds those words needed to hold the language together. At this age articulation is not perfect (for example *wif* may be used for *with* and *tar* for *car*), and improving it should not be considered an important goal.

By the time they are just over three years old, children have generally mastered the basics of speech. They have good vocabularies—over a thousand words in many cases. (It should be noted, though, that knowing a word does not mean that it can be used appropriately.) Some pronunciation difficulties persist, and there is likely to be some stammering as the desire to talk outstrips the physical ability to speak quickly.

Three-year-olds can usually use several different kinds of sentence patterns, including those starting with dependent clauses ("When it rains . . .") and prepositional phrases ("In the morning . . ."). Although they continue to use language in the same ways as toddlers, three-year-olds add such abilities as reporting on events ("And then we rode the ponies and then we . . .") and discussing consequences ("The smoke means it's hot"). They also ask many questions, often as a way of maintaining a conversation with an adult. Most importantly, however, threes generally begin to use language to talk about language: "What rhymes with 'funny'?" or "'Humungous' is bigger than 'gigantic.'"

Four-year-olds have language under rather good control. They may even hold fairly complex conversations with adults and moderately interesting ones among themselves. Vocabulary is increasing rapidly and is likely to reach two thousand words. Additional language uses for some four-year-olds include recalling events from the past ("Remember when we . . . ?"), discussing projected ones ("Next summer on our vacation . . ."), and describing imaginary situations ("The rocket ships will attack the dinosaurs"). Interest in language expands to include concern with making rhymes, spelling, and defining words.

LANGUAGE EXPERIENCES FOR INFANTS AND TODDLERS

See Cataldo's book on infants and toddlers (listed in the References) for descriptions of programs at this level.

Children younger than three may be in day-care situations, but most are found at home with their families. Home environments vary quite a bit, so it is not easy to generalize about the language experiences of infants and toddlers. In some cases English is not spoken by the family. Although in such a case the child may be learning to use another language rather well, he or she will need to develop English later. Some children grow up speaking a dialect that is significantly different from the English used at school. And in some families very little speaking is done, communication being restricted to a few commands and gestures.

See Chapter 16 for discussion of how to distinguish between normal speech characteristics and serious difficulties.

Most young children, though, have good opportunities to learn a usable form of English. They may not enunciate perfectly or always choose the right word, and they sometimes put words in an odd order, but they know what someone is saying to them and can make themselves understood. They learn through talking and participating in the many forms of communication used by those around them.

Talking with Infants and Toddlers

Nothing is more important for language development than speaking to a young child regularly and with loving attention. Babies smile and show delight when spoken to and move their arms and legs in rhythm to speech. As they grow a bit older, they join in singing, recitations, and conversation as best they can.

Parents and other adults who spend a lot of time with infants and toddlers need to find a correct balance between encouraging development and allowing natural processes to occur. The following guidelines are suggested for those who interact with very young children:

1. *Be a good listener.* Take the time to hear what the child wants to say and show interest in what he or she says.

2. *Be a good talker.* Speak with the child often about daily events and planned activities.

3. *Be a good speech model.* Without exaggerating, speak distinctly, simply, and at an appropriate speed.

4. *Be a model of courteous conversation.* Children who are given a good opportunity to talk without being interrupted will learn to treat others politely.

5. *Be careful in offering corrections.* Avoid criticism of the child's language and only occasionally discuss the pronunciation of a word or a better way to say something.

6. *Be sure the child has chances to express his or her needs through speech.* Create opportunities for the child to ask questions and make requests by deliberately not doing everything for her or him.

7. *Be sensitive to the child's need for assistance.* A child who wants to say something may require special attention such as touching, vocal encouragement, and/or extra time without interruption.

8. *Be a good provider of experiences.* Read to the child, go on walks together, look at picture books, tell stories, play games, sing, and enjoy language.

The Influence of Television

Some young children are exposed to TV for thirty hours a week—or even more.

Television sets are turned on for many hours each day in the average home, and infants and toddlers are exposed to what is being broadcast. For the most part they go about their usual activities without paying much attention to what is on the screen. Gradually, however, they begin to watch—commercials at first and then cartoons and other shows, mostly those directed at children. Color, motion, repeating images, and music are quite attractive to young children, and they readily learn to recognize musical selections and advertising announcements. Very often they stop what they are doing to watch favorite commercials and then resume the previous activity. They are also able to connect advertising with the products found in supermarkets and other stores.

By age two, or even younger, some children are watching certain programs regularly, everything from *Sesame Street* and other network and local television programs, for example, *Mr. Rogers' Neighborhood* and *Reading Rainbow,* to music videos. *Sesame Street* is popular for several reasons. The characters, including both real people and puppets (young children are not always sure which is which), appear regularly and are distinctive, so the children readily learn who they are and what they are likely to do. The same episodes appear frequently, and this familiarity also makes the program attractive to young children. Academic and intellectual activities on *Sesame Street* include classifying objects that go together and noting features such as shape and color. A large portion of the learning episodes are specifically related to academic skills: counting, for example, and learning the alphabet and how letters, sounds, and words are related. Most of this content is intended for preschool youngsters, but toddlers probably profit to some extent from being exposed to it.

Certainly children seem to learn a great deal from such television experiences, *especially when adults watch with them and discuss what is on the screen.* Follow-up activities are important, too, and parents can make use of the *Sesame Street* magazine and other books and learning aides related to that and similar shows. Again, most of this content is more appropriate for somewhat older children.

Reading to Infants and Toddlers

In many homes reading to the child begins quite early, often when he or she is no more than six months old. Infants and toddlers love to be read to, and there is every reason to believe that the activity is very important. Fortunately, there are many attractive books available that are made of materials that can withstand the kinds of treatment likely to be received from very young children. (Books for young children and reading to them are discussed more extensively in a later section of this chapter.)

Reading and Writing in the Home

In *Awakening to Literacy,* Anderson and Stokes report their finding that in homes identified as economically disadvantaged toddlers averaged eight literacy experiences a day—evidence that exposure to reading and writing is common to all households.

In every household there are writing and reading activities for which the young child is either an observer or a participant. Mail is received and read, letters are written and greeting cards sent, and papers are brought home from school by older children. In addition, there are newspapers, advertising circulars, and pamphlets from churches and community organizations to be read, grocery lists to be made, and telephone messages to be taken. Even if there are few books or magazines around, the family has the opportunity to offer the child important literacy-related experiences.

The International Reading Association has an excellent pamphlet for parents: *How Can I Prepare My Young Child for Reading?*

When a family is strongly oriented to reading and writing, the child will become familiar with printed materials of all kinds not only in the home but also in libraries and bookstores. In some cases children are exposed to typing and computerized word-processing as well as handwriting. Parents may make paper and markers available, purchase plastic letter sets for the refrigerator door, encourage the scribbling of "letters to grandma," take the child's dictation of stories, play word games and supply related electronic toys, and generally encourage understanding and exploration of the language.

Additional Literacy Experiences

Even the youngest children have many literacy-related experiences in their daily lives. They see advertising on signs as well as on television (not many fail to recognize the logos of their favorite fast-food restaurants). They may also be aware of words on street signs and building signs, such as STOP and EXIT. At the supermarket they recognize brand names of cereals, toothpastes, and soap products. Some words are seen so often that a few begin to realize what the letters m-i-l-k or j-u-i-c-e mean.

LANGUAGE EXPERIENCES FOR THREE- AND FOUR-YEAR-OLDS

In many homes children of ages three and four years benefit from the same sorts of language-related experiences as those described for infants and toddlers; they learn much from the everyday events in the household and from the special activities provided by their parents. In increasing numbers, however, children of this age group attend organized programs—nursery schools, Head Start classes, day-care centers, and prekindergarten classes—where they speak, listen, look at books, engage in dramatic play, scribble and draw, and participate in dozens of group and individual activities.

The areas of language growth are discussed separately in this section, but this should not be taken to mean that such experiences ought to be conducted in isolation from one another. Rather, as a teacher in an organized program for three- and four-year-olds, you should emphasize "holistic" activities—stories, poems, and finger plays—having possibilities for several different kinds and levels of learning. Also, threes and fours should be given wide latitude in selecting their own activities; there must be no "language lessons" at this level of education. Experiences in preschool programs should be planned in accordance with the principles of early childhood education presented earlier in this chapter.

Oral Language

Nearly everything that transpires in the early education environment promotes speaking and listening. You should have plans for encouraging children to acquire new words, use sentences of different kinds, and employ language in various ways as they explain their side of a dispute, ask questions when curiosity is aroused, and explore learning situations.

Of course, you can do much to stimulate the child's language. These guidelines are important:

1. Talk one to one and face to face as much as possible.
2. Talk about what is meaningful to children—pets, holidays, birthdays, home and classroom events, and so forth.
3. Talk about what children are doing as they do it, supplying needed words.
4. Ask them to tell what they are doing or planning to do.
5. With an unhappy child, show empathy by describing the emotions being experienced as well as you can.

6. Ask children to use language to express their feelings—to tell another child to stop taking toys rather than hitting or pushing that child, for example.

7. Show enjoyment of language by reciting funny poems, making up stories using the children's names, and using rhyming words in conversation.

8. Give children opportunities to memorize by using finger plays, poems, and stories over and over again and then providing extension opportunities that make use of the memorized materials.

9. Expand children's statements. When a child says "scissors," respond with "Betty wants scissors to do some cutting. What color, Betty?"

10. Relate language learning to classroom activities. Block building, picture painting, manipulating modeling clay, and many other experiences provide good opportunities.

11. Give specific sensory experiences in touching, smelling, tasting, listening, examining, and lifting. Use many different words to describe them.

12. Recognize that concepts develop slowly. Provide many opportunities to use such words as *green, tall,* and *triangle,* and do this over periods of several weeks or months.

13. Encourage good listening habits by asking children to listen for sounds in the environment, playing recordings of sounds for them, and having them listen to stories and repeat parts of what they hear.

The Alphabet

Young children see letters all around them, with the result that some become so interested in examining and naming the ABC's that they learn the complete alphabet by age three or even earlier. For those children, as well as others, you can provide appropriate experiences in the daily program. Singing the alphabet can be included in the group's repertoire of songs, and you can provide several ABC books. Reciting the alphabet will not mean much to some youngsters ("KLMNO" is often heard as one word), but others have learned it at home, perhaps from *Sesame Street,* and will associate names with specific letters.

In providing alphabet-related learning experiences, you should particularly adhere to two principles of early childhood education: the instructional materials must be of a size and type that can be easily handled by the children and the decision to explore them must be made by each child. Several kinds of alphabet sets are appropriate. Large wooden ones, about four inches in height, are popular, but somewhat smaller rubber or plastic ones are also satisfactory. The sets may be either loose letters or in forms showing the A-to-Z sequence. Traditional cube-shaped wooden blocks with letters, pictures, and numbers on them may also be used.

A visitor to one home with young children counted fourteen alphabet sets of various kinds distributed among all the rooms—including the bathroom.

Environmental Materials

Signs, advertising, and packaging materials easily attract children's attention, and you should be alert for opportunities to bring these into the classroom. Good possibilities are posters, fast-food packages, cereal boxes, milk

Alphabet letters should be available to young children in many forms.

and juice cartons, brand insignias from toy products, and advertising materials from local shops and markets. Such items may be included in the dramatic play of the group; playhouse corners and pretend stores are particularly good places for such use.

In addition to the use of commercial packages and signs, there are many other ways to introduce print materials into the early childhood classroom. In the playhouse corner, for instance, there can be telephone books, cookbooks, and magazines and newspapers, just as at home, as well as note pads for making lists and taking messages.

When you organize pizza restaurants or doctors' offices as settings for dramatic play there will be more opportunities to use signs, menus, order blanks, prescriptions, and charts. The same is true of outside play involving traffic signs for wheeled toys or refreshment stands for dispensing juice and crackers.

Classroom Centers

Permanent classroom centers may also be the focus of reading and writing experiences. Near the fish, gerbils, or plants, for instance, there might be signs that give their names and other information about them, pictures drawn by the children, and related library books. Writing materials may be placed nearby to accommodate children who want to draw or pretend to write something about the plants or animals. Even in the block corner a child may wish to make a street sign or a sign to identify a building.

Reading Books

Although reading to young children is discussed in a later section of this chapter, such reading is so important in early education that it is also examined here in relation to other language-learning experiences. The young child sitting beside you as you read is being given a very important opportunity to hear a particular kind of language—the vocabulary ("the ugly old troll"), the cadence ("and they lived happily ever after"), and the structure ("three pigs," "three daughters," "three wishes") of literature. Reading to a child provides both a listening experience and an introduction to the stories, novels, and poetry that comprise the storehouse of our cultural heritage. There will be an opportunity to practice oral language, too, as the child discusses characters and events and her or his own related experiences.

Learning about literature begins with nursery rhymes and traditional tales. Some adults wouldn't know what someone meant who called them "Chicken Little."

Group activities are also productive. When you read to an entire class, the experience will require some planning so that they will understand how to conduct themselves. You will need to talk with them about remaining seated, not interfering with others' opportunities to see and hear, and restraining their desire to interrupt with comments and questions. Even though you should be tolerant of such behavior—it indicates a desirable enthusiasm for book reading—the children should be guided to understand their role as members of an audience.

See Schickedanz's *More Than the ABCs: The Early Stages of Reading and Writing* for many good ideas about how to include literacy experiences in an early childhood program.

Reading, whether to individuals, small groups, or whole classes, supports the development of many literacy-related understandings. You should occasionally point to the print, showing that this is what is being read and that it goes from left to right and from the top to the bottom of the page. You may even indicate which printed words are the ones you are saying at a particular time. Some children will begin to recognize common words or even make a connection between the first letter of a word and how it is pronounced, and you should acknowledge these insights.

Children will want to have some books read repeatedly and this ought to be done, along with introducing new ones. And be sure to provide follow-up experiences after a book is introduced. There are audiotaped book sets that permit children to listen to the story while looking at the book as well as video cassettes of many popular stories. Favorites may be dramatized or recreated through the use of flannel boards and cut-out figures or puppets. All of these activities, plus others you can think of or find in various sources, should be provided.

Writing for Children

Children should sometimes be given the chance to see what they have to say written down in some form. Individual experiences are possible; for example, you can transcribe what a child wishes to tell about a recently completed painting. Of course, there should be no requirement to name a painting or tell something about it—initiation of such writing should come from the child.

Opportunities for group experiences will also occur. The children can describe what they saw on a trip to the zoo, and you can record their descriptions in the form of an experience chart. This gives the children the experience of seeing their own ideas in print—letters are made, there are spaces between words, there is punctuation, and the lines are placed under one another. Depending on the maturity of the group, you might mention some of these points.

Other kinds of personalized experiences can be made available, too. You may act as an interviewer and guide a child to make her or his own book. This can be done by talking with the youngster about preferred play activities, favorite foods or television programs, interest in animals, and other similar experiences. You then incorporate the child's responses into a booklet, with one sentence on each page, for example, ''Betty likes hot dogs,'' ''Betty has a new shirt,'' and so on. The child supplies drawings that illustrate the sentences, and a book results. Class books can also be made if each member provides a drawing with an accompanying dictated sentence.

Writing by Children

In early childhood children are likely to have seen adults writing at home (and if they have not, you will use the types of activities just described to provide them with this experience in the preschool program). Most have also scribbled with crayons, pencils, or markers from the time they were toddlers. Because of their limited coordination capacity, threes and fours cannot generally produce recognizable letters. A few can, though, and you should be sure to give them access to writing materials.

The Beginnings of Writing, by Temple et al., presents many examples of children's first attempts.

A classroom writing center is easily established; it can be called the writing table or office, and children should be encouraged to use it at will, like any area of the room. Such a center should have a variety of markers, pencils of different kinds, and crayons, as well as a good supply of old stationery, envelopes, and scrap paper. Add printing sets, stencils, and al-

Letterlike figures by a four-year-old.

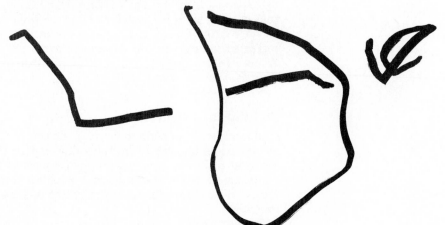

Many local libraries have a story hour for preschoolers, and there are librarians whose special interest is books for young children.

phabet letters for tracing and copying when the children seem ready. Other possible accessories are staplers, safe scissors, old magazines, and paste or glue.

Near the writing center there should be a chalkboard for the children to use. If fastened to the wall, it should be placed close to the floor; an easel chalkboard will usually have to be lowered, too. Both drawing and writing with chalk should be encouraged. Magnetic letters and numerals and other similar items should be placed on the board.

Children's Names

Children's names are very important to them. At home and in school they become aware that their names can be written, and they enjoy seeing this done. You should make sure that children's names appear on their lockers, paintings, and other projects as well as on charts, lists, and rosters. You might give the children the opportunity each day to find cards bearing their own names and place them in an "I am here" pocket of a calendar chart.

Knowledge of their names helps children learn other aspects of literacy. A child first recognizes the initial letter of his or her name, and will recognize the other letters a bit later. Being able to recognize the letters in their names encourages children to look for these familiar letters on signs and in other print. Of course, they will be anxious to try to write their own names. They may begin to notice sound/symbol relationships as they realize that their names sound like other words that begin with the same letter. When children first attempt to write texts to accompany their drawings, the rearranged letters of their own names are often used since these are the ones with which they are most familiar.

A three-year-old's responses to requests to write something (left) and draw something (right).

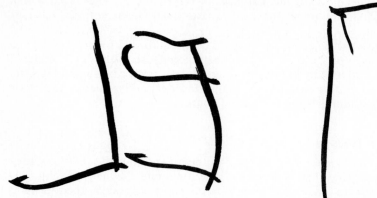

An early attempt by Jerry to write his name.

YOUNG CHILDREN AND BOOKS

Stories and books are very important for young children. Those who are read to regularly, have their own collections of books, go to libraries, and participate in family reading activities not only make good progress in school but also develop a lifelong love of reading. Nearly everyone can learn to read reasonably well, but those read to throughout their childhood years have the greatest likelihood of developing into "real" readers.

In a literacy-oriented home or school environment children are surrounded by books, even when quite young. By age two some have personal favorites that they carry around with them. At three they are likely to be familiar with a large number of titles and may even have bookshelves of their own. By the time they reach four most will have developed a preference for certain kinds of books or those about particular characters.

Four-year-old Phillip writes his name.

Families should give much attention to book reading with young children, and many do so. However, there are homes where not much reading is done. When you are responsible for teaching children from such backgrounds, it is imperative to make book reading an important activity. By giving regular attention to reading, you will be providing those children with a good start toward genuine literacy and a productive and enjoyable life.

Books and Babies

When reading to a baby, you should sit with the child on your lap and hold the book upright so that it can be seen. You should talk about the book, point to the pictures, and read any text. Gradually the child will begin to become involved in the activity, hitting the pages, vocalizing, and grabbing at the book. All of this should be encouraged.

As the baby becomes a few months older, he or she behaves differently. Taking turns at talking occurs, as the child vocalizes after you have said something. A baby may begin to point at illustrations and by his or her first birthday may enjoy turning pages and want to hold the book.

There are even "board-books" made of heavy cardboard or wood and plastic books especially for bath time.

A thorough discussion of the benefits of reading to young children is found in William Teale's chapter in *Awakening to Literacy*.

Infants ought to have their own books, but, as mentioned earlier, these must be durable—made of cloth, plastic, or stiff cardboard. It should be emphasized that the very young child will mostly play with these as with any object but will look at them occasionally as well. You may respond to a child's fascination with paper tearing by supplying old magazines and newspapers for that purpose, but naturally this activity must be supervised.

Infants derive several benefits from being read to:

- The association of reading and books with the pleasurable sensation of sitting on someone's lap and being held
- The hearing of sentence patterns and voice intonations that are different from those of ordinary speech
- Seeing how books are handled—how they are held and manipulated

Toddlers and Reading

Reading should be a regular event in the toddler's daily routine at home, involving both parents as well as other family members. In an organized program outside the home, as much time as possible should be devoted to reading to toddlers individually and in very small groups.

As children approach the second birthday, they become much more involved in the reading experience. They begin to pay close attention to illustrations, often pointing to small details as you ask them to find Big Bird or the pig with a hat. They can point and vocalize alternately with you, too. Animal books are popular at this time, and a certain routine often becomes part of reading them.

ADULT: Look! A cow. Where's the cow?

CHILD: (*pointing*) Dah!

With experience babies learn how to handle books.

ADULT: Yes, a brown cow. The cow says "moo."

CHILD: Muh!

A sort of game soon develops in which the child learns to say the names of animals and to give their characteristic sounds. This is important, because looking at books and talking about them is of significance and is one of the first kinds of conversation for the child.

In addition to animal books, toddlers enjoy Mother Goose books, alphabet books, and books with pictures of toys and common household objects. These books should have large, colorful illustrations that are relatively simple in design. Toddlers will learn how to handle books without damaging them and so should have some access to the family or classroom library. Whenever possible, you should store books with the front covers visible so that children can easily find their favorites.

Toddlers derive several benefits from being read to, in addition to those identified earlier:

- The ability to identify entire pictures and smaller components on the pages
- Increased vocabulary acquired from the story and from discussion of the illustrations
- The repetition of the story, which prepares the way for further discussion

Threes and Books

Enjoyment of simple story books begins at about age three. Rhymes and repetitious or patterned stories are popular, along with ABC, counting, and shape books. Three-year-olds will be interested in a variety of types of books, so this is an excellent time to begin making regular trips to the library.

Threes can begin to see that stories have parts: a beginning, a middle, and an end. You should introduce books with highly predictable texts, since threes very much enjoy knowing what is coming next and joining in. Children of this age are likely to start to say "the end" as you finish a book. Also, since an important kind of listening comprehension begins to occur at this age, you should be sure to read stories from beginning to end without interruptions, unless the child wants to comment or ask something. Discussion is important, but the youngster's lead ought to be followed; it may be that a book has to be really familiar before the child wants to talk about it. And threes will insist that the same book be read over and over again—something that you may not enjoy but should do cheerfully, recognizing it as an important contribution to their development of literacy.

Three-year-olds derive several benefits from being read to, in addition to those identified earlier:

- The memorization of stories and the enjoyment of turning pages and retelling what they have heard
- Familiarity with particular stories and characters and the pleasure of hearing about these over and over
- A rudimentary understanding of the characteristic features of stories

Reading and Fours

A high proportion of four-year-olds will spend time alone looking at books, and those who have been read to extensively will have solid knowledge of books and print. They will be able to discuss a title with you and will sometimes recognize an author's name. They are very likely to have some understanding that, although pictures are attractive and interesting, it is the print that you read to them.

Some fours will be able to listen to rather long stories, perhaps ones that continue over several days. They may very well develop preferences for certain kinds of books and stories—simple folk and fairy tales, perhaps, or books about trucks and machinery.

Four-year-olds derive several benefits from being read to, in addition to those identified earlier:

- Greater understanding of what makes a story: characters, a place, a sequence of events, and so forth
- Participation in more involved discussions of books and stories
- Greater familiarity with print and the realization that the words are read from left to right and top to bottom on the page

Suggestions for Reading with Young Children

1. Before reading, talk about the book.
2. Point to the words in the title as you read it.
3. Get children to turn the pages when possible.
4. Point to things in pictures and name them.
5. Point to words and move your finger from left to right across the text.
6. Read with expression in your voice.
7. Change voices for different characters.
8. Encourage children to participate by stopping and letting them supply a rhyming word, reading repetitious parts so that they can join in, and giving them lots of time to answer questions.
9. Read in a soft, pleasant voice.
10. Let the children see the pictures as you read.
11. After reading the book, talk about it together.
12. Ask story-related questions that have more than one answer.
13. Keep interruptions to a minimum while reading aloud.

A FINAL WORD

The good home and the well-organized early childhood education program have much in common. In both settings the child is treated with respect, and his or her special abilities are valued. This extends to language; the child is talked with and encouraged to use his or her capacity to discuss, recite, describe, pretend, imagine, and create. The best kinds of home and school environments stimulate interest in literacy. Children have frequent direct contact with books, are read to regularly, and see adults read. They also have access to writing materials and may explore writing just as they do reading. Your responsibility as teacher or parent is to act as a good model and supportive collaborator in these highly significant experiences.

References

Beaty, Janice J. *Skills for Preschool Teachers,* 2nd ed. Charles E. Merrill, 1984.

Bredekamp, Sue, ed. *Developmentally Appropriate Practice in Early Childhood Programs Serving Chil-*

dren From Birth Through Age 8. National Association for the Education of Young Children, 1987.

Butler, Dorothy, and Clay, Marie. *Reading Begins at Home.* Heinemann, 1981.

Cataldo, Christine Z. *Infant and Toddler Programs: A Guide for Very Early Childhood Education.* Addison-Wesley, 1983.

Clay, Marie. *Writing Begins at Home.* Heinemann, 1988.

Fallen, Nancy H., and Umansky, Warren. *Young Children with Special Needs,* 2nd ed. Charles E. Merrill, 1985.

Goelman, Hillel; Oberg, Antoinette; and Smith, Frank; eds. *Awakening to Literacy.* Heinemann, 1984.

Grinnell, Paula C. *How Can I Prepare My Young Child for Reading?* International Reading Association, 1984.

Harste, Jerome C.; Woodward, Virginia A.; and Burke, Carolyn L. *Language Stories and Literacy Lessons.* Heinemann, 1984.

Hough, Ruth A.; Nurss, Joanne R.; and Wood, Dolores. "Making Opportunities for Elaborated Language in Early Childhood Classrooms," *Young Children* 43 (November 1987), pp. 6–12.

Lamme, Linda Leonard, ed. *Learning to Love Litera-ture: Preschool Through Grade 3.* National Council of Teachers of English, 1981.

Lawton, Joseph T. *Introduction to Child Care and Early Childhood Education.* Scott, Foresman, 1988.

Machado, Jeanne M. *Early Childhood Experiences in Language Arts,* 2nd ed. Delmar Publishers, 1980.

Mahoney, Ellen, and Wilcox, Leah. *Ready, Set, Read: Best Books to Prepare Preschoolers.* Scarecrow Press, 1985.

Morrison, George M. *Early Childhood Education Today.* Charles E. Merrill, 1988.

Schickedanz, Judith A. *More Than the ABCs: The Early Stages of Reading and Writing.* National Association for the Education of Young Children, 1986.

Seefeldt, Carol, ed. *The Early Childhood Curriculum: A Review of Current Research.* Teachers College Press, 1986.

Spodek, Bernard; Saracho, Olivia; and Davis, Michael D. *Foundations of Early Childhood Education: Teaching Three, Four, and Five-Year-Old Children.* Prentice-Hall, 1987.

Temple, Charles; Nathan, Ruth; Burris, Nancy; and Temple, Frances. *The Beginnings of Writing,* 2nd ed. Allyn and Bacon, 1987.

Teaching Resources

Many appropriate video cassettes, filmstrips, computer programs, books, and kits of various types are available. Those listed here are a few good examples of teaching resources.

Beginner Books Filmstrips. Random House (various sets with six filmstrips and cassettes in each set).

Coletta, Anthony, and Coletta, Kathleen. *Year 'Round Activities for Four-Year-Old Children.* Center for Applied Research, 1986.

———. *Year 'Round Activities for Three-Year-Old Children.* Center for Applied Research, 1986.

Croft, Doreen J., and Hess, Robert D. *An Activities Handbook for Teachers of Young Children,* 4th ed. Houghton Mifflin, 1984.

Great Beginnings Activity Card Library. Thompson (box of cards with songs, games, finger plays, and language activities on them).

Hirsch, L., ed. *The Block Book.* National Association for the Education of Young Children, 1984.

Literacy Development in the Preschool. Heinemann, 1986 (filmstrip).

Mister Rogers' Plan and Play Book. Family Communications (records and audio cassettes).

Mother Goose Treasury. Greenleaf (videotape).

Taetzsch, Sandra Zeitlin, and Taetzsch, Lyn. *Preschool Games and Activities.* Fearon, n.d.

COMPUTER SOFTWARE

Easy as ABC. Springboard.
Rhymes and Riddles. Spinnaker (K–grade 3).
Stickybears ABC. Scholastic.

Suggested Stories and Books for Infants and Toddlers

TRADITIONAL STORIES FOR THE VERY YOUNG

The Three Bears
The Three Little Pigs
Red Riding Hood
Jack and the Beanstalk
The Three Billy Goats Gruff
The Gingerbread Man

FOR THOSE WHO ARE A LITTLE OLDER

The Elves and the Shoemaker
Rumplestiltskin
The Ugly Duckling
Peter Rabbit
Cinderella
Hansel and Gretel
Snow White

DURABLE BOOKS FOR INFANTS

Bonforte, Lisa. *Farm Animals*. Random House, 1981.
Bruna, Dick. *My Toys*. Methuen, 1980.
——. *Out and About*. Methuen, 1980.
Ford, George. *Baby's First Picture Book*. Random House, 1979.
Kunhardt, D. *Pat the Bunny*. Western, 1962.
Pfloog, Jan. *Kittens*. Random House, 1977.
Sesame Street. *Ernie and Bert Can . . . Can You?* Random House, 1982.
Smollin, Mike. *The Cow Says Moo*. Random House, 1979.
——. *Your Friends from Sesame Street*. Random House, 1979.

Wells, Rosemary. *Max's Ride*. Dial, 1979.
——. *Max's Toys*. Dial, 1979.

OTHER BOOKS FOR INFANTS

Ahlberg, J., and Ahlberg, A. *Peek-a-Boo!* Viking, 1978.
Broomfield, Robert. *The Baby Animal ABC*. Penguin, 1968.
Bruna, Dick. *B Is for Bear*. Methuen, 1967.
Charao, Kay. *Baby's Lap Book*. Dutton, 1977.
Curry, Nancy. *An Animal Is Red*. Bowmar, 1977.
Fujikawa, Gyo. *Gyo Fujikawa's A to Z Picture Book*. Grosset and Dunlap, 1974.
Rojankovsky, Feodor. *Animals in the Zoo*. Alfred A. Knopf, 1962.
Scarry, Richard. *Early Words*. Random House, 1976.
Tudor, Tasha. *Mother Goose*. Henry Z. Walck, 1976.
Weisgard, Leonard. *My First Picture Book*. Grosset and Dunlap, 1964.

BOOKS FOR TODDLERS

Brown, Margaret. *Goodnight Moon*. Harper & Row, 1947.
Carle, Eric. *Do You Want to Be My Friend?* Crowell, 1971.
——. *The Very Hungry Caterpillar*. Collins-World, 1969.
Conover, Chris. *Six Little Ducks*. Crowell, 1976.
Freeman, Don. *Corduroy*. Viking, 1976.
Krauss, Ruth. *The Carrot Seed*. Harper & Row, 1976.
Rojankovsky, Feodor. *The Tall Book of Mother Goose*. Harper & Row, 1942.
Slobodkina, Esphyr. *Caps for Sale*. Addison-Wesley, 1947.

Suggested Books for Threes and Fours

Ahlberg, A., and Ahlberg, J. *Each Peach, Pear, Plum*. Viking, 1978.
Anno, Mitsumasa. *Anno's Counting Book*. Crowell, 1977.
Barton, Bryon. *Wheels*. Crowell, 1977.
Carle, Eric. *Pancakes, Pancakes*. Pantheon, 1975.
Crews, Donald. *School Bus*. Greenwillow, 1984.

de Paola, Tomie. *Nana Upstairs & Nana Downstairs*. Putnam, 1973.
——. *Pancakes for Breakfast*. Harcourt Brace Jovanovich, 1978.
Dr. Suess. *Green Eggs and Ham*. Random House, 1960.
——. *Hop On Pop*. Random House, 1963.

Eastman, P. D. *Go, Dog, Go!* Random House, 1961.

Gag, Wanda. *Millions of Cats.* Coward-McCann and Geoghegan, 1977.

Gramatsky, Hardie. *Little Toot.* Putnam, 1978.

Gretz, Susanna. *Teddy Bear's ABC.* Follett, 1975.

Hoban, Tana. *Count and See.* Macmillan, 1972.

———. *Is It Red? Is It Yellow? Is It Blue?* Greenwillow, 1978.

———. *Round and Round and Round.* Greenwillow, 1983.

Hopkins, Lee Bennett. *Go to Bed! A Book of Bedtime Poems.* Alfred A. Knopf, 1979.

Keats, Ezra Jack. *The Snowy Day.* Viking, 1962.

Kellogg, Steven. *Pinkerton, Behave.* Dial, 1979.

Kraus, R. *Leo the Late Bloomer.* Dutton, 1973.

Lear, Edward. *An Edward Lear Alphabet.* Lothrop, 1983.

———. *The Owl and the Pussy Cat and Other Nonsense.* Viking, 1978.

Lionni, Leo. *Swimmy.* Pantheon, 1963.

Lowery, Janette. *The Poky Little Puppy.* Golden, 1942.

Maestro, Betsy. *Harriet Goes to the Circus.* Crown, 1977.

McCloskey, Robert. *Make Way for Ducklings.* Viking, 1941.

Piper, Watty. *The Little Engine that Could.* Scholastic, 1979.

Rey, Hans. *Curious George.* Houghton Mifflin, 1941.

Sendak, Maurice. *Where the Wild Things Are.* Harper, 1963.

Stevenson, Robert Louis. *A Child's Garden of Verses.* Franklin Watts, 1966.

Viorst, Judith. *Alexander and the Terrible, Horrible, No Good Very Bad Day.* Atheneum, 1972.

———. *The Tenth Good Thing About Barney.* Atheneum, 1971.

Zion, Gene. *Harry the Dirty Dog.* Harper & Row, 1976.

Zolotow, Charlotte. *William's Doll.* Harper & Row, 1972.

Activities for Preservice Teachers

1. Interview the parent of a two-year-old. Find out how much the child is read to, which are the child's favorite books, and how much access the child has to writing materials.

2. Visit a nursery school or a day-care center that enrolls preschoolers. Note the room arrangement, equipment and materials, child/teacher interaction, and scheduled activities. Pay particular attention to how language development is encouraged and how much contact there is with books.

3. Visit a preschool or kindergarten class. Make a note of differences among the children in size, physical coordination, willingness and ability to express themselves orally, and extent of vocabulary.

4. Try some software intended for young children. Evaluate the content and mode of presentation. What would be likely to appeal to young children? What are some problems that you see in the use of such software?

5. From friends who teach prekindergarten classes or parents of children aged three to five, collect samples of children's "writing." Can you read it? Are some letters conventional in shape? Is there evidence of linear motion in putting them on paper? Are some figures (possibly letters) repeated frequently?

6. Go to a library or bookstore and examine books for preschoolers. Which do you judge to be the best? What are your criteria?

7. Tell a story such as "The Three Little Pigs" to a three-year-old and then to a four-year-old. Have each child tell it back to you. What do you notice about the children's ability to tell the story in sequence?

8. Watch several *Sesame Street* programs and pick out some episodes that are designed to teach language. To what extent are the principles of early childhood education followed?

9. Begin a collection of poems and stories to be used with young children. Keep these on file cards in a box.

10. Examine several college textbooks on early childhood education. Note what they contain on such topics as language development and beginning writing and reading experiences.

11. Assemble numerous objects—blocks of various sizes and colors, puzzles, beads, cartons, toy vehicles, puppets, picture books, and so forth—and give them to a three-year-old. Observe what the child is interested in first, second, and so on, how long the interest lasts, and what the child does with the articles. Report your observations to the class.

Activities for Inservice Teachers

1. Interview some parents of preschoolers. Try to find out what they want the preschool to provide for their children. How informed are they about the intellectual development and learning abilities of their preschool children? Do they seem to favor an emphasis on academic learning or on social experiences?

2. Find out about your state's policy on providing early childhood education for all children. If a specific policy statement has been issued, obtain a copy and see whether it comments on the kind of program that ought to be provided for this age group.

3. Videotape a discussion with a three- or four-year-old. Analyze the child's speech in terms of the number of different words used and the average length of utterances. Be prepared to report your analysis to your class as well as possibly to show the videotape.

4. Examine some recently published versions of such old favorites as "Little Red Riding Hood" or "The Three Bears." How do they compare with the ones you remember from your childhood in terms of content and illustrations?

5. Observe young children (aged two to four) in a public place such as a restaurant, supermarket, park, or department store. What do the children seem to notice, and how do they investigate what they notice? Take notes on what they are interested in and what they do.

6. Interview some prekindergarten teachers. Find out about their expectations for the children's progress, the stated goals of the program, and their confidence that the results will be what is expected.

7. Prepare a checklist of language-related characteristics that could be used in discussions with the parents of young children to help them see how language development proceeds and how a good preschool program makes a contribution.

8. Make a list of dramatic play activities that would provide especially good opportunities for young children to use writing materials.

Activities for Children

In other chapters the section corresponding to this one is titled "Independent Activities for Children." Here the activities do not have an "independent" format, even though preschool youngsters will often behave independently during an activity.

1. Choose a topic (with input from the children), such as "Our Pets," "My House," or "What I Like to Eat," and write it on a chart or chalkboard. Then have each child draw a picture of a pet, house, kind of food, or whatever is appropriate. Try to have each child tell something about his or her picture and write it on the picture for them. Collect the drawings and bind them together, make a cover, and add a title. The children then can tell about, or "read," what is in their book.

2. Make a "Rhyming Box," a box containing objects such as a shell, a cork, a spoon, a rubber mouse, and so on. Ask the children to find in the box an object whose name rhymes with, for example, *house, bell,* or *fork.*

3. Provide a box of old clothing, shoes, and hats for children to use in creative play.

4. Discuss news items with the children—both ones that you suggest and those you hear them talking about. Follow up by providing them with paper to make individual drawings about the things that interest them.

5. Make a display of materials for children to handle and talk about. For example, a display of different cloth (silk, burlap, suede, velvet, nylon, wool, canvas, etc.) will lead to talk about differences, likenesses, feel, and so forth.

6. Give children sets of pictures from magazines and ask them to place them in sequence as stories. Mount the pictures on cardboard so that they will last, or even put flannel patches on the backs so that they may be placed on a flannel board.

7. Provide a box of odds and ends from which children may choose materials to create imaginary animals or other objects. Children may show these to the class, thus stimulating discussion, which, among other things, should lead to more use of the box.

8. Children may have innumerable learning experiences in a sandbox or with a tub of water. For example, they may build roads, houses, and lakes or check what will float and discuss what causes bubbles. Make sure these materials are provided.

Chapter 4

Beginning Language Arts Programs

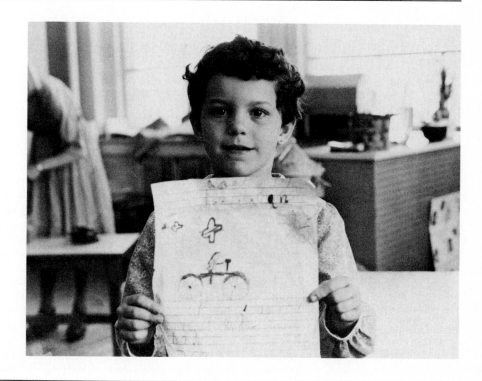

*I*n this chapter the discussion of the language development of children begun in Chapter 3 is extended with an overview of language arts programs for kindergarten and first and second grades. The language arts receive major attention at these levels because they are foundational for other learning and because young children are interested in learning to read and write and, in general, in gaining competence in using language. This chapter continues to emphasize continuity in children's language development and suggests learning experiences that will be meaningful to children and will not push them beyond their abilities and levels of maturity.

Many kindergarten programs are too structured for children of this age group. On the other hand, the activities offered should be sufficiently challenging to those students who are more mature and eager for the opportunity to engage in a wide variety of learning experiences, including beginning literacy instruction. It is important that differences in the development of children be recognized and dealt with appropriately by kindergarten teachers.

Many of the learning experiences and activities discussed in this chapter are introductory in nature or are only briefly described; if you are teaching at this primary level, you will want to supplement the suggestions with those made in later chapters.

LANGUAGE ARTS IN KINDERGARTEN

About 95 percent of eligible children currently attend kindergarten.

The Nebraska State Education Department and many professional organizations have taken a position opposed to making the kindergarten program heavily academic.

There are several types of kindergarten programs. What many people still mean by the term is a half-day session devoted mainly to free-choice activities in centers, along with music, stories, art activities, and outside play. In recent years, however, there has been some tendency for the kindergarten program to move toward the direct teaching of skills usually taught in first and second grades. The result is that in some kindergartens much less time is given to a playhouse corner, block building, easel painting, and other similar activities. Instead, teachers in these programs have total-class or even ability-group lessons on letters of the alphabet, writing, phonics, and numbers. The amount of time devoted to these lessons leaves little time in a half-day session for anything else. The response has been to change to an all-day schedule, meaning that five-year-olds attend for just as many (or almost as many) hours as older students. This arrangement has been justified on the basis that it satisfies all needs: there is time to conduct formal teaching, and there is time for free-choice and expressive activities. Concern has been expressed by many—particularly some authorities on early child-

Many types of experiences develop the language of young children.

hood education—that the full-day schedule may not be the best use of a young child's time, especially if play opportunities are less and less visible and the direct teaching ignores children's levels of readiness for learning what is presented.

Several rationales have been advanced for these changes in the kindergarten: that children know more today, that they have been attending group programs before kindergarten entrance, and that parents want the full-day schedule and more emphasis on academic study. These reasons do not seem sufficient to warrant the substantial changes in many kindergarten programs. Five-year-olds need a program that balances in-school and out-of-school experiences and provides for much self-selection of activities in an interesting and varied environment. There should be concern for the language development of children in kindergarten. Even in a structured program there should be opportunities for expressive and creative experiences—in fact, a sensitive teacher will see that there are. On the other hand, in a more child-oriented program a teacher should be sure that the children are gaining the skills and understandings they need for progress in important areas such as writing and reading.

Oral Expression in Kindergarten

Children's development in all areas of the language arts and, for that matter, their development and growth in all subject areas are so dependent on their opportunities for oral expression that such expression must be the foundation of all kindergarten activities. This means that there must be free-choice time for children to talk with one another about the bridge being built, a just-completed painting, the fish in the tank, or sprouting seeds. There must also be time in the playhouse area or on the climbing frame for children to engage in dramatic play and talking with one another in what they believe to be the language of parents or circus performers. And pairs of children or groups of three or four must be allowed time to quietly engage in highly personal conversations about pets, baby sisters, or plans to go skating.

If you make sure there are plentiful opportunities for oral expression, you will be able to note who seems to be making only limited use of language or who has specific difficulties. Observations may lead you to realize, for example, that James seems to stammer hardly at all when playing with Bobby but has serious difficulty when anyone else is involved. Dialect patterns can be easily noted in these informal moments, so pronunciations, common expressions, and usage variations can be recorded. Although some of this is only useful for you to know as background, other factors may be significant for program planning.

In addition to encouraging oral language during free times, you will want to provide structured opportunities and give guidance. Total-class and group sessions should include discussions, sharing, storytelling, dramatizing, and creative play. In group settings you can introduce matters based on observations made during informal periods. Of course, if there are formal academic requirements, you will need to teach particular lessons at such times.

Discussion. Discussion, or talking together, often occurs in the kindergarten as children gather around the teacher, who is preparing to play the piano or read a story or talk about plans while showing a calendar. The children should be seated on the floor and the atmosphere relaxed. At this age, considering how self-centered a five-year-old is, it is not reasonable to expect children to raise their hands and be recognized before speaking. With prac-

tice this may be learned, but rigid rules are not conducive to the spontaneous use of language.

Discussions, of course, don't always have to focus on something the
teacher is doing; extending the informal activities of the preschool is
appropriate. For example, a tub of water in the room, although sloppy,
stimulates children's talking. It reduces shyness and leads to discussions
about what will float, what won't, animals that live in water, and so forth.
Children will have a great deal of fun, and the possibilities for discussion
are innumerable.

A display of materials that children may handle will bring about new
understanding of words, as well as awareness of everyday things in our
world. Remember to encourage discussion of how things look, feel, and
smell, as well as of likenesses, differences, and uses of materials. The display might consist of burlap, cotton, suede, velvet, wool, and nylon. The
amounts needed are small and can be obtained easily and inexpensively
from a fabric shop.

Things that can be smelled provide a way to bring about a good deal of
talking. Children can be encouraged to describe the various smells and to
talk about smells they have encountered, which smells they like or dislike
and why. This may lead to a discussion of what smells tell us and the recognition that not all liquids that look like water are indeed water. In fact,
using water, rubbing alcohol, and white vinegar is a good way to begin a
discussion of the difference between looks and smells. Such a discussion
can lead to further vocabulary development and concept building.

Another simple way to start discussion is to ask every child in the room
to bring in the top from a jar or bottle. Each child may show his or her
top to the other children, who handle it and ask questions. For example, a
discussion may begin with "Is this from a catsup bottle?" "What do you
use catsup for?" "If I put mustard on my hamburger, why isn't the top of
the catsup like the top of the mustard? They are used for the same purpose." "Could we put a catsup cap on mustard?" Such a discussion might
lead to the discovery that differences may be very slight or not immediately
obvious. For example, though the consistency of both appears much the
same, catsup will pour, whereas mustard will not.

To expand this discussion you might bring in catsup, mustard, and a
variety of relishes and onions. The children may taste these and discuss the
differences in the tastes, which ones taste good or bad, and why. This lesson
is more enjoyable if hamburgers or hot dogs can be served, but that is not
always easy to arrange.

Other activities might include planting a terrarium, blowing soap bubbles, preparing fruit for eating, making and wearing paper masks, looking
at objects through a magnifying glass or a microscope, and examining by
feel and then describing objects in a sack.

Of course, there are many occasions for discussion when direct leadership by the teacher is needed. For instance, you will need to talk with the
children about the room and management—such things as where to keep
papers until taken home, who will care for the hamsters during vacation,
or what will be done about costumes for the Halloween party. The calendar

can be the focus for talking about the days of the week, what can be expected during a particular month, and whose birthday is near. Discussion of the weather brings up matters of clothing, outside play, and waiting for the bus.

A visitor to the room is an event that presents you with the chance to do some important direct teaching. Before a visit is the time to talk about such courtesies as raising hands for permission to speak, not interrupting others, and listening carefully to what is said. After a guest leaves is a good time to discuss what was said, who the visitor was, and what he or she does. The behavior of the class during the visit can also be talked about, giving you the opportunity to review the things discussed before the visit.

Reading to the class leads to many additional subjects for discussion; these are mentioned in a later section of this chapter.

Some good guests in kindergarten:

police officers
fire fighters
safety officers
musicians
dentists
doctors

Sharing. Sharing and the related activity "Show and Tell" are common language experiences in the kindergarten (and beyond). Children may bring toys, books, or other objects to show and talk about, or they may share personal experiences, for example, a visit with relatives or something seen on the way to school. For some children sharing is easy; many are eager to share. For others, holding an object while telling about it may relieve nervousness by taking attention away from self. Either type of sharing may be conducted in a total-class setting or in small groups, perhaps at tables. Sometimes shy youngsters will participate only if the group is small and composed mainly of friends.

Several suggestions are relevant to sharing:

Children can "Show and Tell" about:

a colorful rock
seashells
a bird's nest
a photograph
a self-drawn picture
foreign stamps
toys
books

1. Urge children to talk to the group rather than to you.
2. Encourage questions and comments.
3. Encourage attention and good listening.
4. Be a good listener yourself.
5. Be prepared to limit the number of children sharing each day, if necessary, to ensure that the others will be able to pay attention.
6. Do not overemphasize taking turns. Enthusiastic participants can stimulate others.
7. Invite and suggest, but do not require, participation.
8. Take special care to praise the efforts of shy children.
9. Do not fall into a pattern in which the children show while you do the telling.

Creative Dramatization. Activities based on creative dramatization were briefly described in Chapter 3, along with principles and guidelines to observe in fostering these activities. Kindergartners should have many opportunities for creative role playing since so much of children's emotional and social growth, cognitive development, knowledge about their environment, and, certainly, language development occurs through this form of creative experimentation and expression. Opportunities for creative play—child-inspired dramatizing—are present throughout the school day. Children in the kindergarten ought to continue to have the opportunity to pretend doing

Subjects for group pantomimes:

playing catch
a mouse is loose in the room
raising the flag
putting up a tent
gathering wood for a campfire

housekeeping, shopping at the market, driving a car, being a firefighter, and so on.

Another activity to continue is that of hearing and saying rhymes. More may be expected of kindergartners with respect to listening to and acting out in sequence the events in a rhyme. It is usually helpful, though, to select the most extroverted children for the first efforts at "acting out."

Children know much about rhyming and may pick up the wording of the rhyme, but memorization should not be required. Keep in mind that spontaneity of expression and ease with language are the goals. Some children, particularly those who are extremely self-conscious, may not readily respond to these activities, and to do some of them may take months, even with six-year-olds. Gently encouraging these children will help. Patience and knowledge of the particular children involved are the keys in planning such activities.

Some suggested Mother Goose rhymes to dramatize are these:

This Is the Way the Ladies Ride	Three Little Kittens
Rock-a-Bye-Baby	Baa, Baa, Black Sheep
Jack Be Nimble	Simple Simon
One, Two, Buckle My Shoe	Old King Cole
Jack and Jill	Polly, Put the Kettle On
Georgie Porgie	Old Mother Hubbard
Humpty Dumpty	Wee Willie Winkie
Little Miss Muffet	

Many others are as suitable as those listed. Always be on the lookout for poems well suited to dramatization or to pure enjoyment.

Other Teaching Considerations

Much that was said about programs for threes and fours in Chapter 3 also relates to kindergarten classes.

In every kindergarten class attention needs to be given to several factors. Some of these supplement the oral language activities just discussed; others are important to the writing and reading activities that follow. There are also potential problems of which kindergarten teachers must be aware and with which the program must be concerned.

The average kindergarten child has watched 5,000 hours of television.

Listening. Listening is not something new to kindergartners. They have been listening from early infancy. They have heard hundreds of people speaking, perhaps speaking different dialects or even other languages. They have listened to mechanical and natural sounds and to music of all kinds. They have listened to radio, records, and television. Most of what they know in the way of concepts and understandings has been gained through listening.

Listening is crucial to language learning, and this learning continues in kindergarten in very important ways. Therefore, among many other things, you should attempt to provide a good speech model so that children will have an opportunity to hear, for example, that it is not "liberry" but "library." You should also ask children of this age to make listening distinctions between words, because such distinctions are important in reading and spelling.

Many classroom activities provide listening experiences, and, with planning, all may be used to teach important skills. Children listen for their own names when you call them to get their coats in preparation for going home. They listen to find out about the sequence of the day's schedule and to follow directions for completing a classroom project. And the stories you read or tell furnish things to listen to—new words, interesting events, and character descriptions. (Chapter 6 discusses listening in detail and suggests various activities, many of which are appropriate for kindergarten.)

Speech. Speech is a major concern in kindergarten; as many as one-third of the youngsters are likely to use speech that may lead to problems. The speech of these children ranges from the common "baby talk" to serious problems that may prevent the child from being understood even by you. It is important, though, to distinguish between genuine problems and speech characteristics that are likely to disappear with maturity. To help with this, school districts often require kindergarten screening, a procedure that involves examination of the child's vision, hearing, motor coordination, and language ability. This kind of testing is often done during the months preceding enrollment in kindergarten or shortly after the beginning of the school year. Screening and follow-up examinations will generally identify kindergartners with speech problems requiring the attention of experts.

If a child has a serious speech difficulty, you should be aware of what the clinician is doing and be prepared to support that plan. Even children with minor difficulties may be seen by a therapist, possibly for only a few sessions, and the therapist will have suggestions as to what you can do to help in these cases. You should not, however, decide that every child who does not pronounce words in standard adult ways has a speech problem. In many cases maturity will eliminate potential problems. (Further discussions of speech are found in Chapters 5 and 16.)

Vocabulary. The development of vocabulary occurs rapidly in the kindergarten without any direct lessons about words and their meanings. Children of this age know as many as two thousand words and are constantly learning new ones. You can make an important contribution to this aspect of language growth by continuing the activities begun during the preschool years. That is, you should provide a good model, introduce words associated with the learning activities, play word games of all kinds, and, especially, read to the children and engage in discussions with them. Every kindergarten room should have objects that require naming. Some of these may be part of the furnishings, such as a balance beam or triangles for making music. Others might be a turtle, a microscope, or a scale. Especially valuable is anything that may provide an entirely new kind of experience, perhaps a work bench where children can hammer and saw.

Besides helping children learn new words, you have the responsibility for clarifying meanings for them. It is difficult for young children to grasp that a word may have more than one meaning, but once this occurs new areas of thinking and enjoyment (such as riddles) open up to them.

Studies based on vocabulary testing indicate that some children have particular strengths and weaknesses. For example, a number of youngsters from disadvantaged backgrounds seem not to know very many verbs. They are just as likely as other children to climb, peek, and pull, but they appear not to have these words in their vocabularies. You need to be aware of such possibilities and look for the chance to link activities and vocabulary. The backgrounds of these children have affected more than vocabulary development, however. Such things as self-image and freedom of expression are likely to have been affected, and a teacher must keep this in mind.

On the other hand, even if children speak reasonably well and seem to use words correctly, that does not mean teaching is unnecessary. Children may distort what they hear to make a word or statement fit their own ideas about language, as is exemplified by reports concerning the words children actually say in pledging allegiance to the flag (" . . . just dust for all"). The existence of such accounts points to the need for you to listen carefully and to attempt to clarify when it seems called for. One little girl, for instance, seemed to be confused about the words *neighbor* and *store,* but her teacher finally realized that what she had been hearing was "next store neighbor."

Young children learn best when they have meaningful experiences. Direct observations of people, things, and processes made possible by trips away from the classroom are particularly conducive to vocabulary development. These may be full-fledged field trips to such places as a museum, a farm, a factory, or city hall, or they may be short excursions to places close by, such as to the shrubbery at the edge of the school grounds to see the birds' nests or to the principal's office to learn what records are kept. Each trip should be a focus for discussions—on planning the trip; what will be, or was, seen and heard; and what to write on an experience chart. Each such experience can build vocabulary.

The Alphabet. Some children entering kindergarten may know the alphabet; that is, they may know the names of all or most of the letters and perhaps be able to recite or sing these in the correct order. Some of the children may be able to identify uppercase ("capital" or "big") and lowercase ("little") letters and write several of them, most likely ones in their names. Other children will know somewhat less, and a few will not be able to name or recognize more than a letter or two. Such a range of achievement levels makes it absolutely necessary to provide many different learning experiences, several alphabet sets to manipulate, and a writing table similar to the one described in Chapter 3.

Group and individual recitation of the alphabet should be part of the daily routine in a kindergarten class. Saying the alphabet will do no harm to those children who already know it and the practice is necessary to those who are still learning. In general, children need to know the alphabet and to recognize uppercase letter forms before they are taught to write either uppercase or lowercase letters.

Learning the names of the letters and being able to recognize them is

You will find it revealing to administer a standardized instrument (such as the Peabody Picture Vocabulary Test) to children from different socioeconomic backgrounds.

Studies indicate that the average child entering kindergarten recognizes fourteen letters of the alphabet.

The article by Salzer listed in the References at the end of this chapter contains a statement on kindergarten literacy programs adopted by the International Reading Association.

important, but the teacher needs to exercise judgment concerning what to introduce and how much to expect at any given time. Some school systems mandate the use of generally inflexible programs for teaching the alphabet. Often, though, the use of the inappropriate activities within such programs can be minimized. Although learning alphabetical order is important, it is really not necessary for kindergarten children to be drilled on it, since there is no real need for them to know it at this age.

Writing in Kindergarten

In Chapter 3 the writing interests and abilities of preschoolers were considered, and it was pointed out that many four-year-olds can make a few letters and some can print their own names. Some children entering kindergarten can print several letters other than those in their names, and a few can do more. Nearly all can make letterlike forms, although these may be upside-down or backwards. With the levels of writing ability they have, and because they know that pictures often accompany writing, kindergartners can begin to draw pictures and write texts to accompany them. Usually all that is required is for the teacher to say "Draw a picture and write about it. Use any letters you know." Some will say that they do not know how to write, but when the teacher's response is "Pretend you can," most will go ahead. When the climate is an accepting one, this is enough in nearly every case. Those who remain reluctant (sometimes these are very able children who

A proud beginning writer shows her work.

need to feel that they are always correct) may have to see the others partici-pating happily for a few days before they can risk joining in. Your accept-ance or, even better, encouragement of what they do, along with their pride in the work, will keep them writing, and the writing will keep maturing.

The text that kindergartners put on their drawings shows much experi-menting in making the letter forms as well as various interpretations of what children mean by "writing."

- *Writing the ABC's.* Writing to some kindergartners means making the alpha-bet letters; they will draw a picture and write all twenty-six letters or some of them. These are usually uppercase letters written in order from left to right, but less conventional arrangements are found, too. When asked to "read" this text, children are likely to supply a story or description related to the picture.

- *Using letters of their names.* Again using what is familiar, beginning writers may rearrange and repeat the letters of their own names when asked to write. For example, Michael's text is a string of letters, ALLHMEC, which, when "read" by him, tells a tale: "Me and my dad made a snowman."

- *Combining letters from several sources.* Some children begin to use letters other than those in their names, often scattering them around the page. When they string letters together, they sometimes appear to be observing "rules," such as "Letters next to each other have to be different; no doubles." To increase their supply of letters they will look around the room and copy from signs and books. Nevertheless, they are usually willing to "read" what they have written as something about the drawing or why they drew it.

- *Clustering of letters.* Groups of letters appear as kindergartners begin to make wordlike forms. Sometimes a cluster of letters will be placed near a compo-nent of the picture. There is a figure of a dog, for example, and the cluster KTMO nearby is identified as "dog." Many of these clusters will be written left to right.

- *Single letters as sounds.* As young writers become more familiar with the let-ters, they may try to represent words or parts of them with single letters. First, letter names may be used (U stands for "you") and then single letters that represent the initial sound of a word (H for "house"). This step signifies a very important discovery—that the letters are related to the sounds of speech.

- *Beginnings of invented spelling.* The alphabetic principle is soon extended to multisyllable words. RB is read as "rainbow," and AP as "airplane." Final sounds are then included; "house" is spelled HS, and "pond" is written PD. A few adventurous kindergartners will even try to spell long words such as *magnificent* and may come close to the correct spelling.

The active engagement of kindergartners in writing stories throughout the school year is accompanied by physical and intellectual maturing, so their handwriting should improve. Those who have not already learned to do so will begin to form letters correctly, orient them on the page in conven-tional ways, and reduce them in size. Unlined paper should be used and the exclusive use of uppercase letters allowed, since these are the ones the chil-dren know best.

Progress related to the conventions of writing is important, but the most significant element in anyone's writing—child's or adult's—is the content,

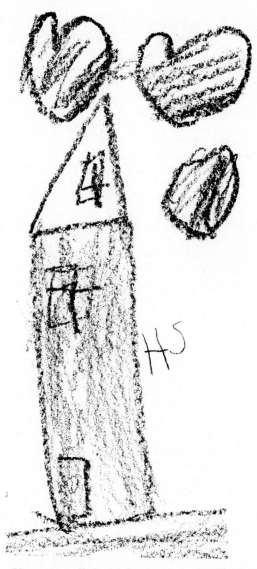

House *is spelled with beginning and ending sounds only.*

the message. Young children's first scribbles are done for the joy of movement and the satisfaction felt in making marks. Knowledge that the letters
signal meaning brings the desire to convey meaning, and this is the real gain
children make in kindergarten writing programs.

Reading in Kindergarten

If the language arts program is varied—much reading to children, saying
of nursery rhymes, writing by you for the children about their experiences,

and writing by the children themselves—many kindergartners will evolve into beginning readers without much direct instruction. This is because they are learning the language of books and what print does on the page. Also, as they write, they are learning how to associate speech sounds with the letters of the alphabet and, most importantly, that writing conveys meaning.

A varied language arts program enables you to respond to inquiries about what contribution the kindergarten is making to children's learning to read. This is important because many administrators and parents believe that only a formal reading program will accomplish that goal; they want kindergartners to be in highly structured prereading and reading programs, such as reading groups with regularly scheduled lessons. In pointing out possible problems with this formal approach, you will want to discuss the concepts associated with reading readiness and the various aspects of a reading program appropriate for all of the five-year-olds in a kindergarten classroom.

Reading Readiness. Long associated with first-grade reading programs but increasingly related to kindergarten programs, the term **reading readiness** has several meanings. One of these implies that a child may require time to mature before the next level of reading instruction is begun. For kindergartners the next level is the beginning of direct instruction; however, there are also several readiness levels for each child prior to entering school, and there are readiness levels for various aspects of a reading program beyond kindergarten and first grade. Another common meaning, quite different from the first, identifies reading readiness as an instructional program in which students are directly taught what they are thought to need in order to get ready to read. What is important to remember is that learning to read is a gradual process that begins in the first months of life when the infant is read to and continues throughout the early years, fostered by the kinds of experiences described in this chapter and the preceding one.

In a national report titled *Becoming a Nation of Readers,* "emerging reading" is used rather than "reading" readiness," reflecting the concept that reading is a learning process that begins during the first months of life.

Determining Readiness. An important aspect of kindergarten programs is determining reading readiness. The teacher needs to look at many factors in a child's development to determine which areas must receive attention prior to the initial instruction in actual reading skills. Once this determination has been made, attention can be given to building readiness in those factors needing it. There may be some children, of course, who do have the readiness for initial reading instruction when they come to school, but most will range from "nearly ready" to needing both time and considerable attention to most of the factors. It is important to remember that at any stage of development every human being is ready to learn something, but readiness is not static, nor does it proceed in regular cadence for all individuals. Two children might both be ready for the first steps in initial reading instruction, but both may not be ready for the next steps. You must continually seek to elevate a child's readiness and know what the readiness level is for instruction to be most successful.

Factors that generally must be assessed to determine the readiness strengths and weaknesses of the child before reading instruction begins are indicated by the following questions:

A. *Physical condition.* Is the child:
1. in general good health?
2. sufficiently rested and nourished?
3. able to see and hear adequately?
4. physically coordinated as well as others of the same age?
5. able to articulate sounds and pronounce words normally?
6. established as to eye, hand, and foot dominance?

B. *Intellectual and perceptual ability.* Does the child:
1. have the general intelligence and maturity of other children of the same age?
2. have the ability to discriminate visually among shapes, letters, and words?
3. identify words that rhyme or begin alike?

C. *Background experiences.* Has the child:
1. been on shopping trips to various kinds of stores?
2. visited places such as a zoo, farm, or office building?
3. gone on trips of some distance?
4. been to the library?
5. been read to and looked at many books?

D. *Language ability.* Does the child:
1. have the ability to describe experiences to others in a comprehensible way?
2. understand a variety of concepts and words, for example, that a peach is a fruit and a cow's baby is a calf?
3. know the meanings of common prepositions such as *over, under, between,* and *above?*
4. use and understand the language of the school, that is, what is meant by such expressions as "sit in a circle," "library corner," and "sharing time"?
5. have the ability to understand and restate oral directions?

E. *Social-emotional status.* Does the child:
1. adjust behavior when the situation changes?
2. work independently?
3. have the desire to learn and the ability to complete tasks?
4. relate well to other children?
5. listen to and react appropriately to others?
6. have a positive self-image?

F. *Letter knowledge.* Can the child:
1. identify uppercase letters?
2. identify lowercase letters?
3. identify some letters in his or her own name?
4. match some letters with speech sounds?

G. *Environmental reading.* Can the child:
1. identify common advertising signs?
2. recognize names on cereal boxes and other containers?
3. find common words such as *milk* on packages and containers?

H. *Book and print familiarity.* Does the child:
1. know how to find the front and back of a book and its title?
2. know that the print is read rather than the illustrations?

3. point from left to right with a finger to show how print is read?
4. recognize a few letters and words in printed material?

These are not all of the questions that might be asked, nor is a negative answer to one or even several of these evidence of possible failure in the beginning stage of learning to read. But such questions do get to the heart of the abilities, attitudes, and skills that are important to first instruction, and therefore many "yes" answers are needed. "No" answers indicate what needs to be stressed in the readiness program planned for the child.

The answers to such questions can be obtained by observing the children and talking with them, by interviewing their parents, and by administering commercial tests. Caution should be exercised in assessing readiness, however. Commercial tests are often not as diagnostic as is claimed, and there are differences among them as to what should be evaluated as evidence of readiness for initial reading instruction. Also, the things children and parents say may be misunderstood or may be inaccurate. The best procedure is to use a variety of means, formal and informal, but to remember that there is no absolute set of conditions that says a child is ready for the initial instruction.

It is also important to remember that the above questions are not only appropriate for kindergarten. For some children reading readiness will need to be assessed in first grade or, in some cases, even beyond.

Developing Readiness. Developing readiness is often thought of in terms of using commercial materials. These materials vary in quality, of course; although some may be helpful to teachers and to children, for the most part they include many more worksheets and dittoed exercises than are useful or should be used. Children's readiness, as noted before, is best developed in natural communicative activities.

The activities suggested earlier in this chapter—reading and telling stories, sharing, and vocabulary and listening activities—all develop reading readiness. Here are some other activities that build readiness:

- Have children arrange pictures to form a story sequence.
- Have children create new endings for stories read.
- Encourage dramatization of words such as *walked, ran, crept,* and *raced.*
- Write charts of children's experiences for them to "read."
- Have children show their understanding of relationships, for example, by putting objects of the same shape but different sizes together.
- Give children tasks, perhaps related to room "housekeeping," that require remembering a sequence of steps necessary to complete the task.

Neither these activities nor the ones suggested earlier should be thought of as things that must be done to build readiness. The point is that children's experiential backgrounds, language development, understanding of relationships, eye/hand coordination, attention spans, and/or adjustment to the school setting may need teaching attention, and there are many ways this may be given.

In her article "Testing in the Kindergarten," Durkin points out that readiness programs often involve too much stress on phonics.

Remember!

See that all readiness activities are planned and purposeful.

Make every lesson a diagnostic lesson.

Stop occasionally to think about how some of the things you do *routinely* can be made a part of the readiness program.

Don't overlook the fact that a readiness program must be individualized, since no two children need exactly the same program and very few children can move through a program at the same rate.

Utilize commercial readiness materials when they are suitable to your program and to the needs of individual children.

Finally, recognize that readiness never ends.

**Differences in Children That
Affect Learning**

1. Intellectual abilities
2. Mental maturity levels
3. Experiential backgrounds
4. Verbal facility
5. Emotional adjustment
6. Attitude toward learning
7. Exposure to print
8. Physical coordination
9. Visual and auditory
   abilities

Learning to Read. As stated earlier, learning to read is a gradual process; thus, it is entirely reasonable to expect a few children to come into the kindergarten with some reading ability, others to gain beginning reading ability by the end of the year, and still others to make progress toward learning to read. The kind of classroom program that best accommodates such a range of performance is informal in nature, providing the kinds of experiences described in this and earlier chapters.

A formal program—involving basal series, reading groups that meet at scheduled times, and workbooks—is inappropriate for most young children and has no place in a kindergarten. In such approaches to teaching the focus is not on whole experiences but on the teaching of specific skills in isolation: the sound represented by *h,* the blending of the sounds represented by *d* and *r,* or making a *k* in a particular way. In formal programs the child usually has few or no choices. Self-selected experiences must too often be postponed or abandoned because it is time for a lesson that is unrelated to what the child is interested in at the time.

In kindergarten you should stress informal and holistic experiences, both those that you plan and ones that occur naturally in a literacy-related environment. Such experiences are to be preferred because they are identical with the ways in which kindergartners have been learning all their lives.

Literature in Kindergarten

Teachers should read stories *daily,* not just to children who have not yet learned to read but to children at every elementary-school grade level. This important guideline cannot be stressed too much. In kindergarten, of course, reading to children is an extremely important component of the language arts program. Those who have been read to at home and in nursery school or other early childhood settings will continue to enjoy the activity. Others may not have been read to much before, so this introduction to books and stories will be especially significant for them.

The materials that you read should include several types. Old favorites are important because many children will have heard some of these, and children like what they know; familiarity with the text helps them to grasp the connection between print and associated speech. Hearing once again about Harry the Dirty Dog or Curious George encourages children to talk about events and characters—a very productive language experience. Introducing new stories is also important. These stories should be carefully selected to include some that are told in rhyme, others whose illustrations or vocabulary provide special interest, and still others that add to children's experiential backgrounds or describe personal relationships or feelings.

The primary purpose for reading stories—at any grade level—should always be to provide pleasure through language. But reading to children also provides opportunities for language growth. Children who are read to develop more varied language patterns, share ideas and feelings, and develop a "sense of story," which is important both to writing and reading.

An especially valuable introductory group experience is the shared reading of "big books." These are useful because both illustrations and text are easily seen by the whole class. Very often the text is highly predictable and

"Big books" are available from:

Holt, Rinehart and Winston
  of Canada
Rigby Education
Scholastic, Inc.
The Wright Group

can be memorized after only a few exposures. The children can then join in saying some of the words or sentences, thereby gaining valuable practice in following a printed text, a factor in learning to read. A next step, or a concurrent one, is to read a portion of a story on each of several consecutive days. This encourages children to recall what has occurred previously and to think about what might happen next. Such stories as those in the *Betsy* books by Beverly Cleary are especially good because they describe situations that are common in the life of a young child.

Kindergarten classes ought to go to the school library regularly just as older classes do. Here they may be introduced to many books and to the librarian, who will help them find books they particularly enjoy and tell them about new ones. If there is no school library, a trip to the public library may be possible. You should have a permanent classroom book collection, of course, one that includes some of the traditional favorites. In addition, when possible, there should be temporary inclusion of books borrowed from libraries.

Storytelling should be as important a part of the literature program as story reading is. Both activities require planning. Both also require using the voice skillfully to communicate plot, mood, setting, and so forth; gaining the attention and eye contact of the children; and anticipating interruptions and questions. But telling a story allows greater freedom in using gestures, permits better eye contact, and frees the hands for using aids such as flannel-board figures or puppets. Stories should not be memorized but should be known well and told without simplifying the language "because the children are young." You should learn how to tell stories, but you also can get help from librarians who tell stories to young children.

> Make every effort to see that each child has a library card for the nearest public library.

> Additional suggestions concerning literature and stories are in Chapter 15.

LANGUAGE ARTS IN FIRST AND SECOND GRADES

Children in the early primary grades are still quite young, so the principles of early childhood education apply to a large extent. Children of this age do best when classroom experiences have maximum meaning for them; much of what is done in the class should grow out of the interests and events close to their lives. They need opportunities to experience language and to use language skills in realistic situations.

Developmental and sequential learning activities need to be provided, of course, but in many classrooms this amounts to drills on skills, with the emphasis on drills. With this kind of teaching, children may spend most of their time answering questions to which there is presumably only one right answer and completing worksheets that result, at most, in limited learning. More than this, young children need experiences that utilize various forms of communication—movement, art, and music, as well as all of the language arts. Spelling, writing, reading, handwriting, and speech are certainly important, but concern with teaching skills must be balanced by activities that include attention to daily human experiences of a much more compre-

> Many activities described in Chapters 5 and 6 can be adapted for use with children in the primary grades.

hensive nature. If a class takes up the topic "Our Fire Department," for example, they should learn about local government, fire protection, water pressure, and many other things. They might interview firefighters or speak to other classes about fire hazards. They should certainly read several kinds of printed materials, learn new words, and do much writing. They might also paint pictures of fire trucks and try movement activities in which they pretend to be pulling hoses and climbing ladders.

The elements of the instructional planning guide presented in Chapter 2 have relevance to the following discussion of separate program areas. That is, developmental sequences should receive attention, but there should also be many opportunities for information processing as topics in social studies, science, and other areas are explored and as other activities proceed. And, of course, writing activities and those in other language arts areas need to be regarded as fertile ground for teaching various skills to individuals and small groups.

Language Development and Learning

Once children enter first grade there are nearly always more restrictions on their behavior than there were in kindergarten. One important difference is that there will be fewer and shorter periods during the day when they can move around the room and talk with classmates. In many classrooms they are expected to remain in their seats and to speak only under certain conditions. However, teachers of the primary grades tend to be tolerant of the problems children have with following rules exactly, so restrictions are often not imposed rigidly. Although spontaneous language does gradually become less frequent, oral expression should continue to be a prominent part of programs in the primary grades.

The average six-year-old knows nearly all of the words most used by adults.

Discussion Activities. In the first and second grades discussion activities to a large extent should be similar to those provided in kindergarten but should reflect the growth in the children's abilities. Sharing at the beginning of the day leads to discussing the weather, school activities, community events, and children's personal experiences. Other topics for discussion might include behavior on the bus, proper ways to treat one another, and management of the room. Discussions may also center around learning experiences—talking about what plants need in order to grow and how they are used by people, for example.

You and the children can plan both total-class and group discussion sessions. The group settings will work better if the children have had a fair amount of experience in total-class discussion and have received guidance in how to have good discussions. An agreement should be reached as to what the discussion is to accomplish, for example, deciding which of two television programs is better for children to watch. Specifying a goal will provide a focus to the discussion and thus make possible a decision. It's a good idea to work out with the children some guidelines or standards that should be observed, for example:

1. Speak loudly enough to be heard, but don't shout.
2. Give everyone a chance to talk.

3. Listen to what each person says.
4. Be polite when disagreeing.

Dramatizing. Dramatization activities continue to be important to language development in first and second grades—particularly as related to speech. The opportunities for such activities may be similar to those suggested for kindergarten, but additional ones may also be appropriate because of the broadened curriculum. Dramatizations may also be suggested by conversations or situations that occur on the playground or in the classroom. For example, suppose children playing a game get into an argument about the rules. Later, the situation could be dramatized, and the children themselves could work out a solution to the problem. Naturally, the focus should be on discovering a better way to resolve the disagreement, *not* on placing any child or children in an awkward or embarrassing position. This will not happen, of course, if the classroom is one in which every child feels that he or she is an accepted and important individual.

Formal dramatization at this level is seldom desirable. If you wish to plan a program for parents or another group of children, the informal dramatization discussed will suffice. It may be rehearsed, but only to a limited extent; and since spontaneity is a goal, the final version may vary from earlier ones. And by all means use only the simplest of props—half a yardstick can become an old man's cane or a soldier's sword, and an apron can transform a little girl into a mother, become a shawl for an old woman, or create headgear for a princess. Let the children's imaginations, not costumes, and props, create the desired effect.

Storytelling. Storytelling and many of the other oral activities discussed in Chapter 5 should, of course, receive attention in grades one and two. In fact, if storytelling, oral reporting, interviewing, and so forth are not introduced in the early primary grades, they probably will never become the significant bases for learning that they should.

Vocabulary development may occur from:

1. Making a mural.
2. Planning and giving a puppet show.
3. Looking at and discussing pictures.
4. Drawing pictures of objects, people, and places.
5. Writing stories.
6. Planning for and making an exhibit.
7. Viewing films and television programs.
8. Talking with classroom visitors.

Vocabulary Development. Vocabulary development continues as a major concern in first and second grades. Many teachers at these levels recognize that vocabulary building is best done through direct experiences. Therefore, they stress children's involvement with concrete materials—making things, solving problems, painting murals, and doing science demonstrations. Meaningful activities such as these provide the most advantageous settings for learning new words and new meanings and using and remembering them.

In class discussions there are opportunities to introduce such words as *missile, hurricane,* and *sympathy.* When giving special attention to words in discussion activities, the idea is not to teach the meanings of words directly but to make the discussions and related activities focus on the appeal of words and the many interesting facts that can be learned about them. One idea is to list on the board or on charts new words or new meanings encountered during the daily routine. These may be words from social studies, science, or other subject areas; words used by the children in the classroom or on the playground; or words they heard on TV, saw on a sign on

Picture Dictionaries

The American Heritage Picture Dictionary by Robert Hillerich (Houghton Mifflin, 1986)
The Cat in the Hat Dictionary by Dr. Seuss (Random House, 1964)
Charlie Brown Dictionary (Prentice-Hall, 1973)
The Macmillan Picture Dictionary (Macmillan, 1983)
My First Picture Dictionary by William A. Jenkins and Andrew Schiller (Scott, Foresman, 1982)
My Picture Dictionary (Ginn, 1977)
The New Color Picture Dictionary for Children by Archie Bennett (Children's Press, 1981)
The New Golden Dictionary by Bertha Morris Parker (Western Publishing Co., 1977)

the way to school, or heard used by a visitor to the classroom. Little learning will result, of course, unless these lists appeal to children.

Charts may be made of words in particular categories, such as "quiet" words, "sad" words, or "winter" words; these can be related to many activities. Charts may also be made of words to use instead of commonly overworked ones (*real, nice, pretty,* etc.) and of words for special occasions or special interests, such as football, camping trips, or art class. Charts of synonyms and antonyms can also help in building vocabulary. One class came up with thirty words that were better than *mad* to describe the incidence of *anger* in various contexts. Finding synonyms and antonyms for words is also an activity that could be on a task card in the language arts center of your classroom. Chart making can be an activity for the entire class, for individual pupils, or for small groups, and the charts can be made in final form or planned so that they may be added to.

Children can be encouraged to keep individual lists of words they have learned and want to use. For this project to succeed, the children must really be interested in the words; an assignment of so many words a day becomes drudgery. Each child keeps his or her own list; you should help each one find words that appeal, show interest in their words, and make learning new words an important part of classroom activities. Some provision should be made for having children tell about their words—perhaps in spare moments throughout the day different children can tell about words they have added to their lists.

Campaigning for the adoption of new words is fun, but it should continue for only a few weeks or interest will lag. Such a campaign may take the form of introducing one or more new words daily by showing pictures and drawings that give the meanings, by putting questions on the bulletin board asking "How is it pronounced?" "Can you find it in the dictionary?" "Have you heard anyone use it?" or "Can you use it in two sentences?" and by providing situations in which the new word can be used. Or possibly each day a different pupil might select a word and present it to the class. Some teachers like to supervise this selection; others prefer to let children exercise their ingenuity in finding words, even though some turn out to be less than useful.

Listening. Listening is an important skill in the primary grades because teachers ask children to pay attention while directions are given, materials are distributed, questions are asked, and discussions occur. Children must also listen to films, to audiotapes and videotapes, to visitors, and to each other. Because of all these demands, listening should receive particular attention in the classroom program.

Listening can be encouraged in many ways. For example, a story might be introduced by saying that it has funny parts or a surprise ending that should be listened for. Or reading a poem about rain can provide a time for children to listen carefully for words that make "water sounds." (Chapter 6 gives many suggestions for teaching listening skills, and some are appropriate to use in the early primary grades.)

Alphabetical Order. Children should know alphabetical order, and know it thoroughly, if they are to be able to use a telephone directory, card catalog, book index, encyclopedia, or dictionary both rapidly and efficiently. Although alphabetical order does not have to be totally mastered in grades one and two, it should be introduced and some specific teaching effort made.

In the early grades, the letters of the alphabet should be visible to the children throughout the school day. You might want to sing the ABC's as part of your opening exercises. Stress left-to-right order at the same time, using a pointer or yardstick to indicate each letter as it is sung.

First- or second-graders can also make their own ABC books, using pictures cut from magazines or catalogs. Assigning children to locate a picture of something that begins with B or some other letter can make them feel very important. Judgment should be exercised about using a picture of bread or a block to illustrate B; some teachers prefer not to use these "blend" pictures.

Large sheets of paper can be used to make a class ABC book, either before the children make individual books or at the same time. Use any available wall space to post the individual pages, being sure to keep the letters in alphabetical order and to show both uppercase and lowercase forms for each letter. As the children bring in pictures to paste on the pages, they will be practicing pronunciation, learning to work cooperatively, and gaining skill in finding the letters quickly. An activity such as this will add color to the room and will promote interest among parents when they visit during "Open House."

Many ABC books should be available in primary classrooms. These should be read to the children; the children can also "read" along with you, and they should be free to look at the books and read what they can. Some of the better books are listed below; your librarian can suggest others.

Anno, Mitsumasa. *Anno's Alphabet: An Adventure in Imagination.* Crowell, 1975.
Chess, Victoria. *Alfred's Alphabet.* Greenwillow, 1979.
Duke, Kate. *The Guinea Pig ABC.* Dutton, 1983.
Elting, Mary, and Folsom, Michael. *Q Is for Duck.* Clarion Books, 1980.
Feelings, Muriel. *Jambo Means Hello: Swahili Alphabet Book.* Dial, 1974.
Fujikawa, Gyo. *A to Z Picture Book.* Grosset and Dunlap, 1974.
Gardner, Beau. *Have you ever seen . . . ?* Dodd, Mead, 1986.
Grant, Sandy. *Hey, look at me!* Bradbury Press, 1973.
Hague, Kathleen. *Alphabears: An ABC Book.* Holt, Rinehart and Winston, 1984.
Lobel, Anita, and Lobel, Arnold. *On Market Street.* Greenwillow, 1981.
MacDonald, Suse. *Alphabatics.* Bradbury Press, 1986.
Rey, H. A. *Curious George Learns the Alphabet.* Houghton Mifflin, 1963.
Tobias, Hosea, and Baskin, Liza. *Hosie's Alphabet.* Viking, 1972.
Wall, Elizabeth. *Computer Alphabet Book.* Bayshore Books, 1979.
Wildsmith, Brian. *Brian Wildsmith's ABC.* Franklin Watts, 1963.

Select ABC books with more in mind than simply teaching letter names and their sounds in words. Certainly teaching these and the order of the letters is their primary purpose and should be uppermost in mind, but there are other purposes as well. *Brian Wildsmith's ABC* could be selected for its illustrations alone; *Q Is for Duck* introduces the letters through riddles (A is for zoo because animals live in the zoo; Q is for duck, of course, because they quack). The latter might prove useful in the second or third grade with children who need reinforcement or are still having trouble with letter names and sounds, as might *Jambo Means Hello*—its softly colored illustrations and words in the Swahili language add variety and introduce children to another culture. The city child will like *Hey, look at me!,* which uses actual photographs of city children performing actions that begin with the various letters, for example: digging, eating, splashing, and itching. There is an alphabet book suitable to virtually any child, but of course there should be a variety available so that children may broaden their experiences.

A number of activities can be devised to supplement books in the teaching of alphabetical order. For example, each letter can be written on a large index card, with one set of uppercase letters and one set of lowercase, and these cards can be used in various ways. A set could be shuffled and a child or a group of several children asked to put the letters in alphabetical order in the chalk tray. Or each child could be given a letter, and then several children asked to place themselves in alphabetical order at the front of the room. A variation might be for you to say, for instance, "Capital S, go to the front of the room." As soon as that child has done so, ask the children with the two letters that go before S to go to the front, and so on.

The teaching of alphabetical order can be combined with practice in handwriting. On the chalkboard or a chart, place rows of letters, with one letter missing at the beginning or end of each row. The children copy these, filling in the missing letters:

abcde___   ___bcdef

This can also be done with uppercase and lowercase letters:

A___B___C___D___   ___a___b___c___d

After the children become proficient at this, let them work with only one letter as a cue, for example, ___ g and g ___. Later they may move on to ___ k ___ and ___ ___ c or ___ ___ z. The "room alphabet" should remain visible during this activity so that children can check themselves if they are not sure of the correct order. Incorrect habits should not become established.

Handwriting in the Primary Grades

When very young children begin to make letters—some by age four or before—they will have their own ways of doing so. Letters may be turned one way or another and placed almost anywhere on a page. A child may want to begin at the bottom and curl an S up and around, or form the first part of A as an uninterrupted tent-shaped line. If children come to school already writing some letters, usually what they do will differ from the letter forms and the ways they are made that you are going to teach. Although it is advisable to work toward consistency among class members, with all writing the same way—preferably using movements that are economical of time and energy—this can be overdone. Too much attention to the "one right way'' at the outset can even cause a child who already writes some to lose confidence. (One girl, who had been writing her name in capitals for over a year and was trying other words, stopped writing entirely when her first-grade teacher said that she was not using lowercase letters as taught and was making some of the uppercase ones incorrectly.)

Beginning Instruction. Instruction in handwriting almost always begins in grade one. Most of the children are ready for this instruction, particularly if it is not done too formally. No instruction should be given, however, until a child possesses the necessary muscular coordination, the emotional and mental maturity required for learning the skills, and the desire to write. Many of the experiences described for kindergartners earlier in this chapter build the coordination, maturity, and desire needed. In addition, it may be helpful for children who are less mature and coordinated to have some practice in the basic movements needed for writing legibly: making clocks, stick figures, circles, various geometrical shapes, and so on.

Children are first taught printscript—probably more often called **manuscript.** The reasons for teaching manuscript rather than cursive form include the fact that it is considered easier to learn than cursive, since only simple curves and straight lines are required to form the letters, and that the formation of letters in manuscript is similar to that of letters encountered in reading. Manuscript is also typically more legible than cursive writing, and young pupils derive great satisfaction from their rapid progress in mastering it. The use of manuscript writing thus appears to contribute to achievement in reading and spelling, as well as helping children produce more and better written language products.

The teachers in a school and, perhaps, in a school system must make several decisions with respect to handwriting instruction. The most notable decisions concern which materials to use, since different materials may require different teaching approaches and involve differences in letter forms and how they are made. Commercial materials need not be used, of course, although even language and reading textbooks may include sections on handwriting. Commercial handwriting materials introduce manuscript forms in particular ways and indicate how letters should be made. Some teachers also have their own verbal directions, for example, "The *n* is one hill to slide down, and the *m* is two." Although individuality in giving directions may be appropriate and expected, it is best if a second-grade teacher (or a teacher of a higher grade) does not teach letter forms and ways of making them that differ from those first taught.

The most commonly taught manuscript form is the **vertical form,** which consists primarily of straight lines, circles, and parts of circles. Straight lines are usually made from top to bottom and circles from left to right. The pencil is lifted from the paper as a new line in a letter is made. There is also the **D'Nealian** or **slanted, form,** whose letters are oval rather than round and slanted rather than vertical. Most of the lowercase letters for this form are made in one continuous movement, without lifting the pencil. Advocates of this approach claim that it facilitates the transfer to cursive writing. On the other hand, continuous movement is more difficult, and the letter

---

Basic Objectives of Beginning Handwriting Instruction

1. To recognize and know the names of all the letters of the alphabet
2. To follow instructions about how to make letters
3. To sit, place the paper, and hold a pencil properly
4. To write his or her first and last name from memory
5. To write easily on lined paper a one- or two-sentence story
6. To observe a two-finger margin at the sides of papers and a one-finger space between words

Paper Position for Manuscript Writing

For manuscript writing the paper is usually perpendicular to the edge of the desk. Some authorities suggest an angle of about 10 degrees.

Don't try to force children to make letters of a size they cannot comfortably manage.

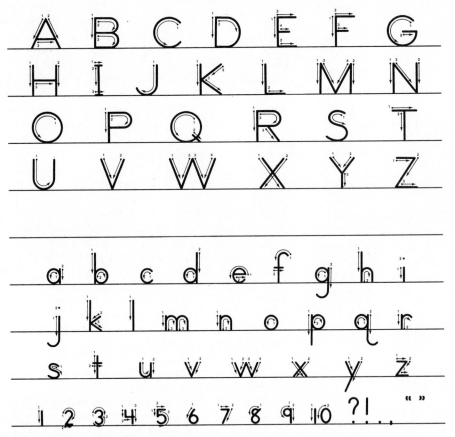

Zaner-Bloser Manuscript Alphabet

Used by permission of Zaner-Bloser, Inc., Columbus, Ohio. Copyright © 1984.

forms look less like print than do the vertical ones. Both of these types of manuscript alphabets are illustrated here.

The chalkboard is a good place to begin handwriting instruction, and some handwriting programs advocate it. There is space on the board to make large letters, which may be easier for some children (of course, children who have done a lot of writing on paper will not need to make such large letters), and corrections can be made easily. In addition, the board is a good place to show letter forms and movements, and children like to write on the board. Begin by choosing a word that is within the children's reading vocabulary and that has meaning for them. Demonstrate each letter of the word on the board. Call attention to how each letter is made. (You may want to call the vertical lines "bats" and the circles "balls.") Write the word, say what it is, and then write it again, asking the children to tell you how each letter is made.

$$a\ b\ c\ d\ e\ f\ g\ h\ i\ j$$

$$k\ l\ m\ n\ o\ p\ q\ r\ s\ t\ u$$

$$v\ w\ x\ y\ z$$

$$A\ B\ C\ D\ E\ F\ G\ H\ I\ J$$

$$K\ L\ M\ N\ O\ P\ Q\ R\ S\ T\ U$$

$$V\ W\ X\ Y\ Z\ ,\ '\ .\ ?$$

$$1\ 2\ 3\ 4\ 5\ 6\ 7\ 8\ 9\ 10$$

D'Nealian® Manuscript Alphabet

From *D'Nealian® Handwriting* by Donald Thurber. Copyright © 1987 by Scott, Foresman and Company. Reprinted by permission.

Demonstrate how to hold the chalk. Have each child stand directly in front of where he or she is to write, holding a half-piece of chalk with the index finger (the child may call it a "pointer") near the tip, the middle fingertip next to it, and the thumb underneath. For straight lines, children should start at the top and pull down; letters with round movements should be done according to the directions for the handwriting system being used.

Paper with lines is often used from the beginning in first grade, and this may be all right for those who have been writing in the kindergarten. Many beginners need to concentrate on making the letter forms rather than on keeping between lines, though, so writing on the chalkboard and on large pieces of unlined paper should precede writing on lined paper. As writing comes under the child's control, he or she will begin to align the letters and reduce their size; these are signals that paper with lines may be successfully introduced.

Pencils and markers of all kinds have generally been used by young children before they enter first grade. Therefore, large crayons or pencils may be needed by only a few first-graders. Be as flexible about the writing instruments children want to use as about the paper they choose to write on.

Continuing Development. Development of handwriting is needed beyond the learning of manuscript forms. You must provide for practicing manuscript in meaningful writing experiences. In addition, you must teach it to those children who still require instruction; even some second-graders may not yet have learned all of the manuscript forms. Objectives for handwriting development in second grade should include the following:

- Refining manuscript ability—keeping the letters well rounded; making firm, straight lines; spacing letters closely and evenly within words; leaving a space of one finger between words; and placing all letters properly on lines.
- Writing all the uppercase and lowercase letter forms correctly by the end of the year.
- Maintaining a consistently acceptable hand position—holding the pencil about an inch from the point, keeping the hand and elbow below the base line of writing, and keeping an air space under the wrist.

Of course, in some second grades there is instruction in cursive forms. Discussion of this transfer is in Chapter 8.

Reading in the First and Second Grades

Historically, reading instruction has begun in grade one. This instruction was typically preceded by activities and exercises that were purported to build readiness for the initial reading instruction. Now, for a number of reasons (discussed earlier in this chapter), many children entering the first grade will have a good start toward real reading ability. An even greater number will require less attention to readiness than did children of an earlier time. As suggested earlier, building readiness for the first instruction in how to read should not be ignored, but it ought to occur via meaningful activities, not worksheet exercises unrelated to the children's interests or backgrounds. This is, of course, still true for first-graders who are not yet ready for their first direct instruction.

The basics of reading instruction, including that for grades one and two, are covered fully in Chapter 12. However, some concerns, issues, and instructional suggestions particularly related to beginning instruction, are discussed in the following sections.

Invite parents to learn about your reading program. Be prepared to give them suggestions for helping their child become ready for your first instruction and for helping as the child is beginning to read.

Basal Series. Nearly all schools use basal series to provide a systematic approach to teaching reading. These series are attempts by publishing companies to provide materials that cover everything a child needs to know in order to read successfully. Basal readers generally represent for the reading program the developmental aspect of the instructional plan presented in Chapter 2. In first- and second-grade books, the reading selections are short, and the thought processes required for understanding the content are not at a high level. Vocabulary and sentence length are controlled, many colorful illustrations are included, and selections are often written as vehicles for the introduction of certain skills or practice on particular words. Teachers' manuals give detailed instructions for daily lessons on letter sounds, sight recognition of words, comprehension, and other aspects of reading. In addition to the reading books themselves, sets of basals include workbooks and several other kinds of teaching aids.

Examples of Seatwork Activities

1. Practicing handwriting
2. Studying spelling
3. Working in a reading workbook
4. Writing a story
5. Reading for fun
6. Working on a science experiment
7. Working on a social studies project
8. Doing learning games and puzzles
9. Practicing visual discrimination activities
10. Classifying objects
11. Listening to tapes and records
12. Following suggestions on task cards

Classroom Organization. In the early grades classroom organization for reading typically involves small groups of pupils who meet with the teacher daily, although individual attention should be given as often as possible. Frequently, there are three groups, although there may be two, four, or even five. These groups, whose membership is determined on the basis of ability, are taught either using the same basal series but proceeding at varying rates or using a different set of books with each group. Such grouping means that the teacher will meet with one group while pupils in the other groups are occupied with planned activities at their seats or with learning experiences located elsewhere in the room.

Shared Reading. The shared reading of "big books" with predictable texts is included in many basal programs. Usually "big books" are used in the first grade. The idea behind them is that all children in a group can see the text and follow it as one child reads. There are often small versions of the "big books" that pupils may take home in order to have the very satisfying experience of reading to family members.

A related kind of shared reading may occur if a class makes its own books from pages contributed by children. Although these books are similar to the experience charts used most often with younger children, they are books rather than charts, and the pages have been written by the children. These hand-produced books may be kept and used for months; children never seem to tire of reading something that means so much to them. Such

Writing can be an excellent seatwork activity.

very easy reading materials are important to building the skills and good attitudes needed by some youngsters who may not be succeeding very well with the regular reading program.

Phonics.   Reading programs give much attention to phonics. The object in teaching phonics is to enable children to identify words by relating speech sounds to letters. All basal reading programs provide extensive study of phonics, beginning in kindergarten and first grade. There are also various programs for teaching phonics alone or as the principal means for learning to read. These programs emphasize rules or generalizations about letter/sound relationships (for example, "When two vowels go walking, the first one does the talking"), which children are to learn so that they can "sound out" unknown words.

One of the problems with this emphasis is that the rules, many of them at least, do not apply often enough to allow children to rely on them as procedures covering all situations. The difficulty is magnified for beginners because they need to learn to recognize common words such as *give* and *said* that do not conform to the rules. (And, of course, the application of rules to specific situations is not a teaching procedure that fits the principles of early childhood education.) Another problem is that some children find it almost impossible to blend together isolated sounds to help them in recognizing the words. Certainly children need to learn letter/sound relationships, but, as was mentioned earlier in this chapter, this will occur as they try to find the letters they need to spell something being written. This is a much more child-oriented way to learn useful phonics.

Writing and Reading.   The skills of writing and reading are related in important ways. As the beginning writer reaches the stage of inventing the spelling of words he or she wants to use, attention is first given to the initial letters of words (P stands for *People*); then final letters are added (PPL); and, finally, the use of internal letters (PEPL) reveals that the child is grasping the significance of sounds in the middle of words. Obviously letter/sound relationships in English are not perfect, but there is enough correspondence for beginning writing of this kind. More importantly for reading, children who begin to represent sounds with carefully selected letters are indicating their readiness to make good attempts to pronounce unknown words encountered in reading.

As children write, they begin to understand more advanced aspects of literature and reading as well. They realize, for example, that books and stories are made up by authors attempting to communicate with audiences, just as they do when producing a story in the classroom. This makes it possible to have discussions with the children concerning what makes a good story and why they like books by a particular writer.

Literature.   Literature continues to be important to first- and second-graders, just as it is to younger children. Although it may sometimes be hard to find the necessary time, there is nothing more important than introducing readers to stories, books, authors, and illustrators. You should use all kinds of literature: fables, fairy tales, poetry, humor, adventure, nonfic-

Correct spelling is a concern of parents. Make sure that they understand your program.

Provide private places to read:

in an old bathtub full of pillows
in a papier-mâché cave (with a light inside)
in a large box
under a long table on a rug
in a carrell

A child invents a spelling for snake.

Common Invented Spellings

WEN
WR
GRIL
CLOS

Less Common Ones

FEEMAILS
STRUCKSHURE
OMOOSTE
VISTETER
SELAPERATE
PONIT
OWIS
FERSBYEE
UNICIL
DICIS
WOCHD
KCIINTS

Stimulate writing by providing *input:* reading, field trips, movies and videotapes, observations, new words, demonstrations, and so on.

tion books, and the classics. Children at this age level will enjoy having portions of *Heidi* or *Black Beauty* read to them each day, for example. (Chapter 15 gives many more literature selections for primary-age children along with suggestions for their use.)

Writing in the First and Second Grades

At the beginning of the school year many first-graders can print their own names and make a few other letters. Others can do even more. Teachers who emphasize writing in their first-grade classrooms begin in the first weeks to have children draw pictures and write about them. If this activity was introduced and repeated in kindergarten, first-graders will easily continue to produce such writing. Children who have not had the opportunity before will do what kindergartners do—produce a few alphabet letters or perhaps their names or copy words visible in the room ("CRAYOLA," for instance). Especially able pupils will invent the spelling of words right away and will carry out a suggestion that they put down sufficient letters to help them remember what they were writing. First-graders who are practicing letter forms for manuscript writing, reading books with you, and listening to stories will make steady progress in their ability to write. Second-graders who have had this background will produce very good results.

In first or second grade, writing matures if it has a focus in terms of the writer's purposes and the process being used. Three types of writing are especially appropriate for children of this age—journals, stories, and their own books—although, as is described later, these are not always separate types but merely different formats for the products. And with proper guidance, regardless of the type, the writing involves three stages, or aspects, of the writing process (discussed extensively in Chapter 9): prewriting, writing, and postwriting.

Journal Writing. In its simplest sense journal writing means keeping some kind of record in a "journal," a place for writing that is the writer's own. For young children a journal may simply be a few blank pages stapled together, although spiral notebooks or other forms of bound paper are desirable. The objective is to encourage the children to draw and write in the journal whenever they have the time and the desire to do so. Of course, children have to learn what a journal is for and how it should be used. Thus, you may need to set aside time to explain this kind of writing and to tell children that they may draw pictures and write about them in their journals.

Doing journal writing early in the morning—perhaps as the first activity on the schedule—works out well, since children usually come into school bursting to tell about the squirrel they saw, or their new sneakers, or a planned camping trip. You can respond by suggesting that such an event is something to be recorded in the journal, although the desire to talk about things should not be stifled; both sharing and writing can occur.

After a few weeks some children will want to show their drawings and read their journals to others. You can easily make such reading a part of sharing time. There is no need to be concerned with handwriting and spelling because the children will be doing the reading themselves and will need only a few clues from their drawing and writing to recall the content.

Journal writing may involve all three stages of the writing process. In the prewriting stage the child thinks about what to write. For young children this is accomplished almost immediately, since the usual topics are themselves and their own activities. Their natural self-centeredness enables them to write unselfconsciously about friends, new clothes, pets, and family events. In the beginning much time and effort will be invested in the drawings, but by late in the first grade some children may not want to draw before writing, and many second-graders will be ready for prewriting activities other than drawing.

During the writing stage the child produces letters, words, and sentences with a proficiency that reflects her or his maturity level. Those children having difficulty spelling a word may attempt to spell it as best they can, ask a friend for help, or look for it on a word list or in a book. Every first- and second-grade classroom ought to have beginning dictionaries. If you spell words for children, you will be spending much time that could be devoted to other more helpful activities. However, if you do help with spelling, the words should be written on slips of paper and given to the children rather than spelled orally.

Use folders of children's writing as a departure point for parent conferences. They furnish much to talk about—interests, creativity, use of language, improvement in handwriting, spelling, and so on.

Beginning dictionaries are listed in Chapter 13.

5/4/87

My family has 6 pep
ni ti Mom Dad Jack
and Me tegils
And My orei Cat.

You must all keep Mom very busy

A drawing and accompanying writing from a young girl's journal.

Children read what they have written in a small group.

Postwriting experiences for some children of this age may be similar to those described in Chapter 9. Most frequently, though, the postwriting stage for first- and second-graders consists of reading to a partner or to you or reading from their journals during sharing time.

Story Writing. A story often evolves out of the interests and experiences that children have written about in their journals. For example, Val's journal contains a great deal about her dog, Ollie, and she has also talked with the teacher frequently about him. Thus, it is natural for her teacher to suggest that she write a story about Ollie. The prewriting phase in this case has been fairly long and rich; Val has drawn pictures of Ollie and has written and talked about what he does. Additional prewriting activities may include bringing a photo of Ollie to school and talking with others about their dogs or other pets. Before Val begins to write, the teacher might also suggest to her that she make a **topic web** to help her remember the things she wants to tell about Ollie. Children need help in learning to use this type of schematic diagram. So the teacher draws a circle and writes "Ollie" in its center, then draws several other circles around the topic circle and connects them to it with lines, while explaining to Val that she can write words in the surrounding circles to show what she wants to say about Ollie: what he eats, the tricks he does, how friendly he is, and so on. Later, when Val has developed the habit of making webs for herself, she will find them very useful in writing stories (see Chapter 9). Keep in mind, however, that a web is not an end but only a means and should not receive so much attention that it inhibits the actual writing.

In producing a story the writing stage may require several days because there is so much to say. Again, the content is what is important; the teacher encourages Val to get ideas and words down on paper without much concern for appearance. False starts are simply crossed out, and arrows show

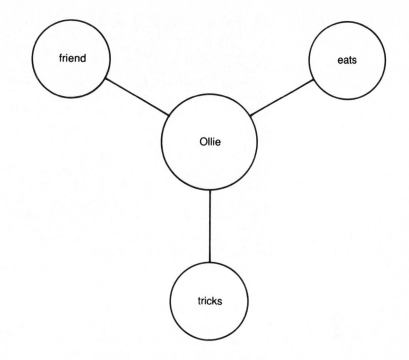

Children enjoy reading the books they have written to adults, such as the principal.

where something has been added to a sentence. Val is then invited to read over what she has written, sharing with classmates and the teacher. Reading and discussion will cause her to think of more that she wants to write about Ollie.

Since a good bit of revising will have been done before the story is finished, the postwriting stage will mostly involve reading, for instance, to the principal, to family members, or to Ollie. An additional postwriting possibility is to "publish" the story, to make a book that others may read for themselves.

Book Making. As an extension and refinement of story writing, making a book is a postwriting activity that can be very satisfying to children. The postwriting stage will probably involve completing a second draft of the story to improve organization and will certainly include editing, giving at-

A page from a child's book about her family's fishing activities.

tention to such matters as handwriting, spelling, and punctuation. Then, the child and the teacher will read over the text together to see what punctuation may be needed to help the reader. The class members have seen punctuation marks in books, have talked about them, and have used them in earlier writing, so attention to punctuation is not new. The same is true for correct spelling. In addition, neatness and overall appearance may need attention because, as the teacher might point out, books are neat, not messy.

Book writing, with the editing and rewriting suggested above, may be too much for some children, so expectations must not be unreasonable. On the other hand, if children are to become effective writers they need to be challenged to do their best.

After a child's book is completed it may be read to the class, placed in the classroom library for others to read, or taken home. If it becomes part of the library, a comment sheet may be placed in the back so that those who read it can write what they liked about it.

A FINAL WORD

This chapter attempts to show that the most effective language arts programs in the kindergarten and early primary grades are a continuation of the desirable home and preschool activities discussed in Chapter 3. Oral language growth and the related vocabulary and experience-building activities have been particularly emphasized as being fundamental to learning how to read and write.

In the kindergarten as well as in grades one and two classroom organization and programs are more structured than in preschool. Much is expected to be and needs to be learned in the early primary grades. Meeting all children's educational needs at this level requires a comprehensive, planned teaching effort that begins by providing what is needed by the least mature children and goes on to provide what is needed by all children, regardless of maturity and ability levels. The focus must be on the learners, not on textbooks, tests, curriculum guides, or publicized but false notions of what the program ought to be.

The chapters that follow extend the suggestions in this chapter and give more detail concerning the curriculum and teaching efforts needed in language arts programs.

References

Anderson, Richard C.; Hiebert, Elfrieda H.; Scott, Judith A.; and Wilkinson, Ian A. G. *Becoming a Nation of Readers*. National Institute of Education, 1985.

Biber, Barbara. *Early Education and Psychological Development*. Yale University Press, 1984.

Cochran-Smith, Marilyn. *The Making of a Reader*. Ablex, 1984.

Durkin, Dolores. "Testing in the Kindergarten." *The Reading Teacher* 40 (April, 1987), pp. 766–770.

Fields, Marjorie V., and Lee, Dorris. *Let's Begin Reading Right*. Charles E. Merrill, 1986.

Fromberg, Doris Pronin. *The Full-Day Kindergarten.* Teachers College Press, 1987.

Hill, Kathleen J. *The Writing Process: One Classroom Writing.* Thomas Nelson (Australia), 1984.

Jewell, Margaret Gree, and Zintz, Miles. *Learning to Read Naturally.* Kendall/Hunt, 1986.

Loughlin, Catherine E., and Martin, Mavis D. *Supporting Literacy: Developing Effective Learning Environments.* Teachers College Press, 1987.

Mayesky, Mary E. *Creative Activities for Children in the Early Primary Grades.* Delmar, 1986.

McVitty, Walter, ed. *Getting It Together: Organizing the Reading-Writing Classroom.* Heinemann, 1986.

Nebraska State Board of Education. *Position Statement on Kindergarten,* 1984.

Parker, Robert P., and Davis, Frances A., eds. *Developing Literacy: Young Children's Use of Language.* International Reading Association, 1983.

Rudolph, Marguerita, and Cohen, Dorothy H. *Kindergarten and Early Schooling,* 2nd ed. Prentice-Hall, 1984.

Salzer, Richard. "Why Not Assume They're All Gifted Rather Than Handicapped?" *Educational Leadership* 44 (November, 1986), pp. 74–77.

Spodek, Bernard, ed. *Today's Kindergarten.* Teachers College Press, 1986.

Teale, William H., and Sulzby, Elizabeth, eds. *Emergent Literacy: Reading and Writing.* Ablex, 1986.

Temple, Charles; Nathan, Ruth; Burris, Nancy; and Temple, Frances. *The Beginnings of Writing,* 2nd ed. Allyn and Bacon, 1987.

Teaching Resources

COMPUTER SOFTWARE

Easy as ABC. Springboard Software, 1984 (five games to teach alphabet).

Kids on Keys. Spinnaker.

Kindercomp. Listening Library. (K–grade 3)

Letters and First Words. C and C Software, 1984 (identifying letters, letter sounds, simple spelling; preschool–grade 2).

Listen and Learn/Sound Ideas Series. Houghton Mifflin, 1986 (series of word-attack and comprehension disks; K–grade 2).

Picture Dictionary. D.C. Heath.

Talking Text Writer. Scholastic.

Tiger Tales. Sunburst Communications, 1986 (disks and guide; reading practice for individuals and groups; K–grade 2).

Write On! Humanities.

KITS

Alphabet Fun. Random House (four filmstrips and four audio cassettes; K–grade 3).

Basic Reading Skills: Reading Readiness. Society for Visual Education (six filmstrips, six audio cassettes, skill sheets, and guide).

Books Talk Back. Library Filmstrip Center, 1986 (filmstrip, cassette, and guide; K–grade 3).

Fable Plays for Oral Reading. Curriculum Associates.

Fairy Tale Plays for Oral Reading. Curriculum Associates.

New Goals in Listening. Listening Library (nine cassettes and guide; grades 1–3).

Ready to Read. Richard C. Owen.

VIDEOTAPES

Aesop's Fables. Society for Visual Education (with guide; preprimary and primary).

Animals in Verse. Society for Visual Education.

Fairy Tale Masterpieces. Society for Visual Education.

Four by Dr. Seuss. Society for Visual Education.

Prewriting. National Council of Teachers of English, 1984 (literature and basal stories as stimuli for writing; strategies include brainstorming, story structure, and webbing).

Readers of the Lost Alphabet. Greenleaf.

Sesame Street: Learning about Letters. Greenleaf.

The Story Book Series. Society for Visual Education.

Writing the Alphabet. Greenleaf.

OTHER RESOURCES

Chappel, Bernice M. *Listening and Learning.* Fearon Teacher Aids (games and activities).

Geller, Linda Gibson. *Wordplay and Language Learning for Children.* National Council of Teachers of English, 1985.

Live Oak Media produces video cassettes, books, and sound film strips related to the content of this chapter.

Activities for Preservice Teachers

1. Collect samples of the writing of children aged four to six. Compare these samples with the samples reproduced in *The Beginnings of Writing,* by Temple et al.

2. Collect samples of the writing of children in grades two and three. Compare these with those you collected for the preceding activity and with examples in published handwriting books. Can you draw any conclusions from these comparisons?

3. Observe a reading group in a first- or second-grade classroom. What activities take place? What are the responses of the pupils? If a basal series if used, does the teacher follow the manual? What conclusions can you report to your class?

4. Visit a kindergarten or first- or second-grade class. Make notes on the differences you observe among the children in size, physical coordination, willingness and ability to express themselves orally, interest and ability in writing, and extent of vocabulary.

5. Try to do manuscript writing yourself on chart paper, an overhead projector, the chalkboard, and paper on which you might write a note. Where do you need to improve? How fast can you write?

6. Collect pictures of objects that children can use in a variety of ways: to identify beginning sounds, to find words that rhyme, to practice vocabulary by making up descriptions, and to match images and the appropriate words.

7. Interview a speech therapist. Find out what the common articulation problems of young children are. Ask which of these are serious and what teachers might do about them.

8. Investigate commercial materials intended for use in grades one or two. The listing under "Teaching Resources" represents only a small sample of materials available for reading, language, and so forth. Which materials do you believe to be useful? What criticisms of these materials do you have?

9. Investigate the use of computers in the elementary schools in your town or area. In particular, find out how often a child—any child in a class—can actually use a computer and for what purposes.

10. Observe a class doing the "morning news," where the teacher does chart writing. See how many opportunities there are for the inclusion of imbedded lessons in speaking, listening, skills related to reading, and punctuation and capitalization.

11. Develop lists of words that will interest children in early primary grades. For example, you might include words borrowed from Native American languages (*moose, squash,* and *pecan*), words that have become generalized (*kleenex, jello,* and *coke*), or new words (*cassette, paramedic,* and *fallout*).

12. Observe children on the playground or during a physical education period. Select several children to watch closely and compare their coordination with that of the other children. If any child seems to be notably lacking in coordination, ask the teacher how he or she compares with the others in articulation, handwriting, spelling, and reading.

13. Start a file of ideas for dramatizing traditional tales such as "The Three Billy Goats Gruff" or "The Tortoise and the Hare." Make flannel-board cut-outs of the characters and try these with a child.

Activities for Inservice Teachers

1. Examine two or three reading-readiness tests. What areas do they test? From the list included in this chapter what do they not test?

2. Find a second-grader who has not received much formal spelling instruction. Ask her or him to try some typical words from second-grade spelling lists and see what the results are.

3. Videotape a "show and tell" or "morning news" session. Use it as a basis for talking about oral expression, listening, and other language arts areas.

4. Examine *Writing with Computers in the Early Grades* (J. L. Hoot and S. B. Silvern, eds., Teachers College Press, 1988) for some ideas about using word processing with this age group.

5. Plan a unit on some familiar topic, such as the zoo. See how many relevant children's books you can find, and use these as bases for various activities.

6. Describe steps that might be taken to help a shy child participate more in classroom activities.

7. Use poetry to stimulate children to think of good words to use for specific descriptions. Try such authors as Shel Silverstein and Lee Bennett Hopkins.

8. Regardless of the grade level you are teaching, have the children compose a group story with yourself as the scribe. What evidence do you find of the children's story sequencing and organizing abilities? What else can you report about the experience?

9. Find out what is occurring in your school or a neighboring one with respect to writing and reading in the kindergarten.

10. Visit the instructional resources center for your school district. Look through catalogs for vocabulary development materials that are not presently available in your school but would be desirable and appropriate for the age and ability levels of the children you work with. Meet with your principal or immediate supervisor and explain why money should be allotted for these in the next budget.

11. Locate a basal reading series that uses selections from literature for most of its content. What has been used for the beginning levels? How well does it seem to work?

Independent Activities for Children

1. A materials center, including such things as fabrics, crayons, clay, clothespins, and whatever else you have available, can encourage both creativity and language use. Children can make various kinds of objects that they then name or tell about, either orally or in writing.

2. Collect and make a variety of puppets and, with the children's help, make a puppet stage. The children can use these to do puppet shows whenever they have time.

3. Make available to the children several children's magazines (see Chapter 15) and encourage individual children to engage in some of the activities suggested. Note the ones that most interest the children so that you may extend them.

4. Provide a writing center supplied with paper, pencils, crayons, and so forth, and encourage the children to use it whenever they have free time (that is, when they are not working directly with you). Each child should have his or her own place for storing whatever has been written or drawn. Visit the center frequently to assist children who want help.

5. Provide materials such as telephone books, encyclopedias, dictionaries, atlases, and other reference books for children to practice looking things up. Suggest things related to the ongoing activities of the classroom that the children can look for.

6. Individual children can look in magazines for words, phrases, and sentences to describe pictures that have been placed on a bulletin board. These can then be cut out and placed around the pictures.

7. Collect some of the alphabet books listed in this chapter—or others that you choose—and place them in a corner or on a table where they are readily available to the children. They will do their own exploring.

8. Individual children or small groups may make lists of words by categories. For example, a child might list all the food words he or she can think of. Or the category might be divided into lists of vegetables, fruits, and dairy products. Another child might list words identifying kinds of pets. Still another might list types of occupations. Lists can be exchanged, added to, talked about, and so on.

9. Find several versions of a well-known story such as "The Little Red Hen" or "The Gingerbread Man" (see the lists in Chapter 3 for suggestions), and make them available to the better readers. This should lead to group discussions about the different treatments.

10. Make it possible for children to create their own greeting cards to give to relatives and friends. This can be done by adding blank cards, half sheets, envelopes, fabrics, or whatever is available to the materials in the writing center.

11. Some children who have become familiar with such patterned pieces as "The House that Jack Built" may enjoy trying to create additional verses.

Chapter 5

Using Oral Language

Chapters 3 and 4 stressed the importance of oral language as the basis for the young child's learning of writing, reading, and other aspects of the language arts. Although early speech development is particularly significant, the need to increase competence in oral language performance does not diminish once children learn to talk reasonably well. As children progress through the middle and upper grades, systematic attention should be focused on fostering their inclination to converse with others and on furthering both this ability and the ability to speak effectively in various group situations. This chapter addresses matters related to the effective use of oral language in the classroom and in life activities outside the school setting.

THE IMPORTANCE OF SPEECH

Many teachers provide opportunities for children to talk, for they recognize that this is the way language power develops and that children have practical needs for speaking in various types of situations, both in and outside of the classroom. However, evidence of the cliché "the good classroom is a quiet classroom" still exists, and there are also classrooms in which children talk a good deal but where there is little evidence of guidance toward learning the skills and behaviors important to the speaking situations commonly met.

There are also many teachers, but not nearly enough, who recognize the importance of speech to children's success in attaining competence in listening, reading, and writing and consequently to their learning in many areas. Of course, levels of language maturity are not *always* reflected in a child's (or adult's) speech, but the preponderance of research evidence indicates that they usually are. For example, Loban, in reporting his thirteen-year study, stated that children "superior in oral language in kindergarten and grade one before they learned to read and write are the very ones who excel in reading and writing by the time they are in grade six."

The relationship between a child's proficiency in oral expression and his or her personal and social development is significant, bearing on the child's potential for learning and affecting the self-concept. Teachers have often noted that personality differences among children seem to be related to their speaking. An aggressive child frequently assumes a great deal of classroom leadership, possibly monopolizing speaking activities. Perhaps the child's assurance in speaking fosters this behavior, or possibly the aggressive personality provides speech confidence. On the other hand, a shy, retiring personality could be attributable to language immaturity, or it may be that the child's shyness has undermined his or her confidence in speaking. Cause-and-effect relationships are not clear, but the fact that there apparently is a relationship adds to the reasons for emphasizing oral language in language arts programs. Surveys have shown that many adults fear speaking before a group; surely it is reasonable to assume that giving little—or haphazard and sporadic—attention to speaking situations during children's school years may well result in their becoming such adults.

THE BASICS OF SPEECH

Skill in oral expression results from practice in the various situations in which an individual needs to speak. The instructional program, then, must provide many speaking situations, and it must utilize these situations to direct attention to speech skills, to behavioral attitudes and habits, and to content.

Naturally *what* is said, the content, is of primary importance in any speaking situation. Effectiveness in communicating this content is affected by its organization and development, by the vocabulary used, and by the skills discussed below: (1) control and use of the vocal mechanism, (2) use of facial and bodily expression, and (3) development of audience/speaker rapport.

Vocal Control

Effective speech is pleasing to the ear. It is produced with ease and confidence. It is rhythmic and free from hesitations, repetitions, and interruptions. The tempo and volume are suitable to the content and the audience, and all sounds are clearly articulated and distinctly enunciated. To aid children in developing this kind of fluency the teacher must do three things: help each child to feel confident and secure in speaking situations, help each child discover his or her own weaknesses and have the desire to improve them, and help each child learn to speak as clearly and distinctly as is physically possible.

A person's emotional state is often indicated by voice quality, tone, pitch, and tempo. This is especially true of children. A child who is upset, tense, or worried shows it in his or her voice. A self-reliant, alert child shows confidence by a pleasing voice. An eager, happy child is usually friendly and talkative. A diffident child who is emotionally and socially insecure is unable to achieve fluent, articulate speech. A child who is overly aggressive, perhaps also reflecting emotional insecurity, is apt to speak in a strident voice and insist on monopolizing speaking situations.

You cannot, of course, be expected to solve all of your children's personal and social problems, but you can create a classroom atmosphere in which children feel secure and free to speak. You can provide many activities and experiences that encourage talk and, by your personal and verbal interactions with each child, build his or her self-concept.

Choral speaking, which is discussed more fully in a later section of this

One fourth grade set these standards for oral expression:
1. Don't talk too fast.
2. Speak clearly and loudly enough that everyone can hear.
3. Be sure that you know how to pronounce all the words.
4. Don't use too many *and*'s.
5. Look at your audience.
6. Use good facial expressions and gestures.
7. Show your interest in what you are saying.
8. Try to look relaxed; don't fidget.

chapter, is an excellent activity for building the confidence of the shy child or for tempering the speech of the overly aggressive one. Choral speaking also has value in helping children develop an understanding of the importance of rate, pitch, rhythm, stress, and uses of pauses. Experimenting with different ways of reading lines helps them to see how these factors contribute to effective speech.

Few of us really listen to our own voices except through artificial means. Therefore, one of the best ways to help children discover their individual needs with respect to pitch, volume, and rate of speaking is to record their voices and have them listen to the recordings. This may be done individually, in small groups, or with the entire class participating. The clearly established purpose of the listening, of course, should be to seek ways to improve, not to find fault. Listening to recorded speech may also be helpful in formulating standards; these should not be unrealistic, but they are not likely to be if the children participate in setting them. They can be posted and referred to in evaluating each new effort—and refined as the children progress in speaking abilities.

Articulation

See Chapter 16 for suggestions for children with speech handicaps.

Children in the early grades sometimes do not articulate sounds clearly. This may be due to the retention of early speech habits, missing teeth, or eagerness in talking. Generally, such articulation difficulties are eliminated by the time children reach the middle grades, especially if teachers have been good speech models and the children have engaged in many speaking activities. There may be, though, some children who have real problems in making certain sounds correctly. The problems of these children may have been noted in a speech screening program, and the children may be receiving help from a speech therapist. However, if such is not the case, you may do the following:

1. Show the child how the sound is made as he or she listens and observes the movement of your lips and tongue.
2. Have the child imitate you and examine his or her attempts by watching in a mirror.
3. Have the child repeat the sound several times.
4. Have the child say syllables and words that include the sound.

In teaching the production of speech sounds, time should not be wasted in drilling on those that present only minor difficulties, since to be motivated to improve, a child must feel that proper production of the sound is important to communication and not just something to be done during a practice period. The child, of course, will readily recognize that minor speech faults do not interfere with communication.

Individual attention is usually more effective than teaching a given sound to the entire class. The instruction should be as close as possible to the time when the difficulty with the utterance occurs. Finally, throughout the instruction, make your own speech an example of good articulation, distinct enunciation, and correct pronunciation.

Gestures and Bodily Expression

Children need to be aware that oral communication often includes more than speech. It is virtually impossible for a person to express herself or himself orally without using some body movements, and these movements should be natural and in harmony with the speech activity and the content of the communication. Rhythmic activities, finger plays, and action verses used with younger children are both enjoyable and a means for developing harmony between speech and physical movements. Lack of such harmony may be shown by annoying mannerisms such as fidgeting, head jerking, hand twisting, exaggerated facial expressions, and other undue physical movements. The development of such mannerisms may be avoided if children engage regularly in the activities suggested above and if efforts are made to eliminate their self-consciousness. Children's self-consciousness can be reduced or eliminated by careful planning and participation in speaking situations that have real meaning.

Showing aids telling.

For a child in the primary grades the activity of showing an object while telling about it may relieve nervousness by taking the child's attention away from self. Similarly, the middle- or upper-grade child might use a map, chart, or some other object in giving a report; this will also encourage natural gestures and more purposeful body movements. Group and individual pantomimes, discussed below, as well as creative dramatics, can also teach the value and proper use of gestures and body movement. And, of course, you are a constant example; just as you try to set a model in speaking, so you should also be aware of your own use of facial expressions, gestures, and body movements throughout the school day.

Pantomime

Pantomime follows rather naturally and easily from the creative play and beginning dramatization described in Chapter 4. In addition to being fun, pantomiming is related to the oral expressn that will occur both before and after it is done; thus, it is an important part of language arts programs.

Pantomimes to try:

opening birthday presents
playing a video game
getting dressed in the morning
diving from the high board
practicing the violin
wrestling with an alligator
eating spaghetti
roller skating
walking an unruly dog

Pantomime is expression. It tells something. It is imitation. The familiar is easy for children to show by pantomime. Therefore, start with simple ideas. Encourage children to work their pantomimes from the inside out, to use their own thoughts and feelings, and to pantomime both in groups and individually. Children may imitate a parent driving a car, caring for a baby, shopping for groceries, or playing golf, or they may imitate the look on someone's face when that person is happy, surprised, angry, or sad. Other actions they may want to mimic are swimming, watching television, vacuuming a rug, playing with a dog or cat, or building a snowman.

The entire body is brought into use in pantomime when children pretend to be one of the following (add your own suggestions or have children add theirs): a rag doll, a tin soldier, a runaway horse, an angry dog, a dish of Jell-O, a monster, a tree on a windy day. Or perhaps they could be someone who just sat on a tack, a firefighter climbing a ladder, or even a coffee pot perking.

Pantomime activities can also be used to develop sense awareness. For example, a child might pretend to put a foot in a tub of ice water or might look at an apple, think how good it will taste, bite into it, chew it—and find half a worm. Another might act out putting a finger into a hot pie, eating a hamburger, smelling something burning on the stove, or hearing noises in the night. While one child does the imitation or pantomime, other children will enjoy guessing what role or activity is being portrayed. These pantomime activities, which appear to children to be a game, provide many opportunities for language development. Encourage questions and responses that go beyond one word. That is, when a child asks "Why?" it may be appropriate to ask "Why, what?" in order to get a good question. In the same manner, one-word answers may be changed to sentences.

A full-length mirror in the classroom will give children the opportunity to practice their pantomimes and try out variations before an audience of only one. (A mirror can also help children note mannerisms, physical movements, and general appearance.) Videotape recorders can be used as effectively in pantomime activities as they can in many other oral language situations.

Audience/Speaker Rapport

Aside from the explorative type of talking done by a young child—and the talking-to-ourselves that we adults often do—an individual speaks because he or she has something to say: an opinion to express, facts or information to present, a question to ask. The need is to say something to someone, to an *audience*. The audience may be one person or many, but the audience is very much a part of any oral expression.

It is important for a speaker to establish and maintain with this audience a relationship in which there is interplay, in which there is genuine communication. The people in the audience will show that this communication is taking place by their posture, their eyes, their facial expressions, their courtesy in listening, the incisiveness of their questions, and their voiced reactions. The skilled speaker shows a sensitivity to the audience in his or her response to their reactions. For the child this is often difficult; it is only learned through experience and careful planning.

OPPORTUNITIES FOR ORAL EXPRESSION

Natural situations—the class discussing a problem, a small group working on a project, two or three children conversing—should be the basis for much of the instruction in oral expression. In addition, the teacher must plan other opportunities in connection with the ongoing activities and studies of the class—reports, dramatizations, and so forth. Genuine and meaningful activities that are truly concerned with communication provide the best opportunities for giving attention to specific speech skills, to behavior related to speech activities, to the content of the speech, and to listening abilities.

Each school day will offer many such natural situations, since teaching and learning in every subject area require at least some oral expression. In virtually every chapter in this book some reference is made to using language orally, with suggestions or implications for its teaching. This section is devoted to the kinds of oral language situations and activities that are not adequately discussed elsewhere and for which particular skills, attitudes, and behaviors need to be taught.

Conversation

A wise teacher shows interest in his or her students by being available to talk with them when they first come to school in the morning and at other times during the day. Such "chatting time" should not be considered a waste, since some children have no one at home who will listen to or talk with them. To develop positive self-concepts, children need to know that others are interested in them and their experiences.

The desire to communicate thoughts and ideas to others is as pervasive for children as it is for any of us. Opportunities for conversing with one another persist throughout the school day: the rearranging of the classroom, an assembly program, a group social studies or science project, or a class discussion of current news events. In each of these opportunities certain habits and courtesies must be agreed on and practiced by those involved.

For a conversation to be effective the listener must be attentive so that he or she can react to what the speaker is saying; the topic must be of mutual interest; and both participants must be polite (even when angry) and tactful (especially when being forthright). A good conversationalist is friendly and remembers that a conversation is not a battle of wits in which one participant attempts to disarm another. A good conversationalist is also enthusiastic about what he or she has to say and about what others say. Being enthusiastic requires being informed and knowing about many things that become the subjects of conversations—books, movies, television, political and social events, and so on.

Many behaviors in conversational situations are suitable for dramatization by pupils or for discussion in large and small groups. The first week of school is a good time to discuss conversational abilities and courtesies, with a review whenever it seems appropriate.

Children will enjoy forming food, games, and decoration committees and meeting to plan a class party. Remind them of the guidelines for conversation.

It is important to remember that conversing is an activity of some intimacy and that the necessary intimacy is difficult to achieve in a formal physical setting with a classroom of children. A shy child who will not talk from his or her seat may find it easier to talk in a conversational group of four or five children where it is possible to talk in a low voice and to feel secure in the physical nearness of others. However, even in a small-group setting, it may be necessary to have one or more self-confident children included in order to keep the conversation rolling and to foster the participation of the other children. How you operate your classroom, especially the emphasis given to small-group work and teacher/child conferences, will

Planning sessions can be times for genuine conversations.

have a profound influence on the amount of genuine conversation that takes place.

Telephoning

Tips on Telephoning

1. For business calls, know what you are going to say.
2. For business and personal calls, identify yourself when making or receiving a call.
3. Speak as courteously as in a face-to-face conversation.
4. Be prepared to leave a message on an answering machine.
5. Ask permission before using another person's telephone.
6. Try to call people at times convenient for them.
7. Avoid monopolizing the telephone.

Some teachers say that since so many children begin using the telephone prior to their coming to school, instruction and guidance in telephoning skills and courtesies are not necessary. To some extent this may be true; however, it is still likely that some teaching and reviewing will be worthwhile. Certainly telephoning is an activity that provides its own motivation and opens the door for numerous language arts activities. If possible, actual situations involving the use of the telephone that arise either at school or at home should be used. Such situations might include telephoning the mother of a child who is ill to give information about assignments or class activities, phoning to make arrangements for an interview, using the telephone to ask someone to come and speak to the class, or calling to inquire about suitable dates for a trip to a museum or another place of interest.

Having a unit on using the telephone is sometimes a good idea since it will stimulate interest and provide the opportunity for direct attention to telephoning skills and courtesies. Telephone companies often have kits that may be borrowed for this teaching. Such kits may include materials about using telephones as well as telephone hookups for the classroom. Because it is increasingly possible to buy telephones relatively inexpensively and because a good many children in the upper grades have strong science interests, it is even possible that a school may have its own equipment for such a unit.

Discussion

Many of the problems that arise in the daily activities of the classroom lead to discussions among the pupils. With guidance these discussions can lead to the development of skill in critical thinking, reasoning, problem solving, and expressing ideas orally in a rational and organized manner. Through discussion children gain information, learn to stick to the point of the topic being discussed, and develop the ability to express themselves effectively.

Discussion differs from conversation in that it ordinarily has a topic that was at least somewhat agreed on and a more purposeful goal. It is similar to conversation in the need to take turns, to be courteous, to avoid repetition, and to speak so that all can hear. Discussion is not the same as arguing, although some arguments may occur as a discussion progresses. Arguments, however, arise from an attempt to defend a point of view, whereas a discussion seeks to arrive at an answer or a solution to a problem.

Discussions need not involve the entire class. Round-table and panel discussions are good activities and call for a limited number of participants, especially to prepare and to agree about rules for the discussion (order of speaking, amount of time each one has to speak, etc.). Audio and video recordings are useful to participants in round-table and panel discussions, since these give them the opportunity to judge their speaking skills and the content of what they have said as a basis for planning future similar activities. In addition to more or less formalized panel discussions, having a small group of children discuss a topic is often very useful and can be tied to having one or more of the group report to the entire class on the discussion and the conclusions reached.

In teaching skills for any discussion format, attention should be given to helping the children discover what needs discussing and to defining the subject accurately so that irrelevant talking can be avoided. However, the children also need to learn the importance of and reasons for various viewpoints. And they need to learn how to agree on rules or limitations to the discussion (such as the number of times an individual may speak and how a conclusion will be reached).

How We Discuss a Topic

1. Everyone thinks before speaking.
2. Only one person talks at a time.
3. Everyone listens carefully.
4. Everyone gets a chance to talk.
5. We keep to the subject.
6. We are polite.

Reports

The giving of oral reports is an extension of the "Show and Tell" activity of young children and should have many of the same characteristics. That is, the content of the reports should be organized, and reports be limited in scope rather than being rambling accounts, but many should be given because the children want to give them. Children beyond the primary grades will volunteer to show something or to tell about personal interests and events. This volunteering, if encouraged, can lead to effective reporting on social studies and other subject area topics, even if these report topics are assigned.

Good reports don't just happen—they need to be motivated and planned. A good report must communicate to an audience something that is important to them. Thus, children will need to develop the ability to select material appropriate to the topic and to the audience, the ability to collect

The use of charts improves oral reports.

and organize material (this will require skill in reading critically, taking notes, summarizing, and outlining), and the ability to face the group and give the oral report with accuracy, interest, and avoidance of "ah—hmm—well a—you know" and the like. They also need to recognize that a report can often be made more meaningful to the audience through the use of a map, diagram, chart, or flannel board with words or pictures relevant to the content of the report.

If topics are assigned to children, there should be some choice so that each child can select one that interests him or her. (Children should not have to give reports, however, if they need to develop more security in speaking through some other situation first.) Instruction is generally needed in location of information, preparation of notes, and the avoidance of plagiarism. Children will also need help in judging the amount of time available for the report, developing good beginnings and endings, and selecting visual aids.

A bulletin board display that gives steps for children to follow in preparing reports may be useful. Here is one example:

Steps in Preparing a Report

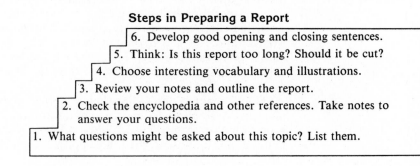

6. Develop good opening and closing sentences.
5. Think: Is this report too long? Should it be cut?
4. Choose interesting vocabulary and illustrations.
3. Review your notes and outline the report.
2. Check the encyclopedia and other references. Take notes to answer your questions.
1. What questions might be asked about this topic? List them.

There are many opportunities for genuine and useful reporting. Here are some suggestions:

- Topics related to social studies or science are suitable. See the end of each chapter in textbooks or in teachers' editions.
- Reports may be an extension of reading. Perhaps the class has read a story about a Scottish family and the children want to know more about Scotland. The more able readers could be asked to give reports on Scotland to the class after they have consulted additional resources.
- New plans or rules of the school can be examined and reported on.
- Extensions of current events topics may be the subjects of reports. For example, events as they are discussed in different newspapers would furnish excellent topics for reports during a study of propaganda techniques—detecting bias in a writer's viewpoint, the use of "loaded" words, and so on.
- Other opportunities for group or individual reports include interviews, trips to places of interest, and reviews of movies, books, or television programs.

When the children give their reports, you should be a model listener in the audience. But you should mentally note, and perhaps jot down, individual weaknesses in usage, organization of the material, eye contact with the group, voice control, and the like. The weaknesses you note, as well as strengths, can later be recorded on a checklist or put into a file of notes you are keeping on individual children or on various types of speaking situations.

Audio or video recordings may be useful to you and to the children in evaluating the success of report giving. Until children become accustomed to being recorded, however, you will want to use recorders sparingly. On the other hand, children's confidence is sometimes given a boost if viewing a videotape or listening to an audio recording causes them to believe they gave better reports than they thought they had.

Children should be encouraged to set up criteria and to evaluate their own reports. There is some danger that children will tend to set their standards too high, so you will want to participate in this process. Group evaluation should be carefully guided; children are sometimes thoughtless in their negative remarks. If your criticism is helpful and constructive, though, the children are likely to follow suit.

Announcements and Directions

Giving announcements has become a part of school life, and many schools broadcast regular opening announcements over a speaker system. Some schools encourage children to make announcements, and there are many opportunities in classrooms for children to do this. Outside of school, children may make announcements at scout meetings, club meetings, and parties.

Announcements should be given in a clear, brief, and friendly manner. They usually have a "who, what, when, and where" format. Standards for announcements should be developed by the class, taking into consideration the recommended format and the manner of presentation. These standards

Rules for Giving a Report

1. Pick an interesting topic and stick to it.
2. Have a good opening and closing.
3. Organize your information carefully.
4. Look at the audience.
5. Make your voice loud enough to be heard.
6. Use good sentences and interesting words.

Oral reporting can be fun.

can then be used as the basis for instruction and as a guide for the preparation and delivery of announcements by members of the class.

Children also have many opportunities to give and follow directions during a school day. They may give directions for playing a game, participating in a scavenger hunt, performing a science experiment, or getting to their homes. Standards for giving directions should also be established by the class as a group; these standards should stress accuracy and sequence, as well as delivery.

The skills and abilities necessary for making announcements and for giving directions are similar to those needed in most oral language situations. The language used must be organized and presented in terms that will be understood by the audience. Acceptable language should be used, but the most important aspects are the conciseness and clarity of the message and its appropriateness for the particular audience.

Interviews

An interview is a good method of securing information and provides the interviewer with the opportunity to use speaking skills, organize his or her thinking, and develop listening ability. And not to be overlooked is the fact that the results of an interview can be written and prepared for publication

Note taking and outlining can be taught with interviewing; see Chapter 13.

in the school or classroom newspaper. In fact, interviewing is an activity that makes possible the use of all of the language arts areas.

Many situations occur that give children the opportunity to conduct interviews. Intermediate-grade children studying a foreign country may wish to talk with someone who has lived in or visited that country. The children themselves may know of such a person, possibly a parent, a relative, a friend, or even a child in another class. If not and if you are new to the community, you may have difficulty in locating interviewees. Try one or all of the following:

- Talk with other teachers or the principal, who may know someone who has spent time in that country.
- Contact the local Chamber of Commerce office or a senior citizens' group to obtain a speakers' bureau list.
- Send letters to parents with a list of countries the class will be studying during the year, and invite any of them who have knowledge of a country to talk with the group.

Interviewing parents and other adults about their occupations or hobbies will also enrich the curriculum. In planning for such interviews, emphasize the importance of the job or avocation to the community, its uniqueness, or its relation to subjects being studied. It is amazing how unaware both children and adults are of services that are provided in communities. For instance, when children drop money into a juke box or soft-drink machine, do they think about how the machine got there or who keeps it running? Have they ever thought that someone earns a living this way?

What is necessary for an interview experience? First, preplan by listing questions that the class or individual would like answered. Develop enough knowledge of the topic that sensible questions can be asked. This often means that the children may need to do some library research. Above all, it is important that an interview have some purpose other than simply giving the child experience in interviewing.

Some people who cannot meet with the children in person may agree to a telephone interview.

Some people will be able to come to school for an interview, but others will not, and plans will have to include arrangements for these interviews. In addition, plans should include ways the information gained may best be utilized. Children may want to use a cassette recorder for an interview if one is available. They should know, however, that if an interview is to be recorded, permission should be obtained from the person being interviewed. Nonprofessional speakers are sometimes frightened by the thought of having their words recorded.

Standards that could be developed for interviewing include the following:

1. Introduce yourself and state the purpose of the interview.
2. Avoid sentences like "The teacher says we have to ask you about _____."
3. Remember that the interviewer should open and close the interview.
4. Have the questions to be asked firmly in mind or on paper so that you stick to the topic.

5. If it seems advisable, give the person to be interviewed a list of the questions to be asked. This can be done when the appointment is made, thus giving the person time to consider his or her answers.

6. Discover appropriate times for an interview appointment.

7. Give the person being interviewed some idea of the amount of time the interview is to last.

8. Take notes during the interview (see Chapter 13).

9. Find a way to end the interview other than "Well, our time is up, so we have to quit."

10. Always be courteous, listen carefully, and express appreciation for the information.

Debate

Debating is ordinarily considered a secondary-school or college speech activity. However, some children in the upper grades of the elementary school can be attracted to the idea of a "formalized" argument. If there are children in a class who are so attracted and if they are mature enough, then, for those children, doing the research that goes into preparing the arguments will be good practice for using reference skills and doing logical thinking.

Debating calls for two children to present one side of the debate topic and two children to present the other. Each speaker makes a presentation and a rebuttal, with a time limit set for each turn at speaking.

An entire class can become involved in a debate because they must listen to it in order to judge which team won. How to judge a debate usually should be a discussion topic for the class, with the discussion leading to the drawing up of standards for judging.

Meetings

Intermediate-grade children are of the "let's form a club" age. When this interest is expressed, it is time to teach parliamentary procedure. The name and type of a club should be chosen by the children. It is possible, for example, to have science, book, and class clubs all at the same time with different members and officers. A fair amount of guidance will be needed, though, since children sometimes become quite cliquish within clubs and may hurt others' feelings.

Interest in forming a club does not automatically mean interest in parliamentary procedure. Prior to starting one, you may need to initiate a discussion of the importance of learning how to operate a club effectively. The children need to be taught the purpose of rules for conducting a meeting as well as the rules to be followed. Although rules should not be too detailed or formalized for beginning groups, a chart of the rules agreed on could be posted and referred to during meetings.

As the children become more experienced with clubs and meetings, they will need to develop some understanding of parliamentary procedure and its vocabulary. What is a *motion*? How do you make a motion? What does

Basic Elements of Parliamentary Procedure

1. The chair calls the meeting to order.
2. The chair asks for minutes of the last meeting to be read; the secretary does so.
3. The chair asks for additions or corrections to the minutes.
4. The minutes are approved. Strictly speaking, this is done by vote, but in most cases the chair simply says, "If there are no objections, the minutes stand approved as read" (or corrected). Any objection, of course, requires a vote.
5. The treasurer's report is asked for, given, and acted on as above, except that the chair usually asks if there are questions concerning the report.
6. Committee reports are asked for, presented, and discussed as needed. No motions are made at this point.
7. The chair asks for old business. If there is any, proper motions are made, discussed, and voted on.
8. The chair asks for new business. New business is discussed; motions are made, discussed, and voted on; any necessary committees are appointed.
9. The chair asks if there is further business to come before the group.
10. If there is none, the chair asks for a motion to adjourn. This is voted on, and the meeting is adjourned.

it mean to *amend* a motion? What do we mean when we say that only one person may *have the floor* at a time? What are the possible omissions, additions, or corrections that may be asked about following a secretary's or treasurer's report?

The following guide to making motions and voting on them may be useful.

1. The individual who wishes to make a motion stands and says, "Mister (or Madam) Chair."
2. The chair replies, "The Chair recognizes Tommy Blank."
3. Tommy then says, "I move that we be permitted to have a morning and afternoon snack in our room." (Note that correct wording is "I move," *not* "I make a motion that . . . ")
4. Another child says, "I second that motion." (Remember that a motion must be seconded before it can be voted on.)
5. The chair then says, "It has been moved and seconded that we be permitted to have morning and afternoon snacks in our room. Is there any discussion?"
6. After discussion the chair may need to repeat the motion. The chair then calls for a vote by saying, "All in favor say 'Aye.' Those opposed say 'No.'" (If there is doubt about the outcome of a voice vote, a member may say, "I call for a show of hands.")
7. The chair announces, "The motion has been carried" (or defeated). Once a motion has been voted on, there need be no further discussion of it in the meeting.
8. Members of the club need to keep in mind that only one motion may be on the floor at a time and that a motion must be voted on before another motion may be made.

The above is a simplified list, but it should be quite adequate for the needs of most groups of either children or adults. If several children—or the entire class—become particularly interested in studying the fine points of parliamentary procedure, obtain a copy of *Robert's Rules of Order*.

Parliamentary procedure should *only* be taught when children have the desire and need for this procedure. If the children are not interested in clubs, or only in quite informal ones, it is not necessary to teach these procedures. However, some form of organization is important in even an informal group activity.

In addition to learning how to conduct and participate in club meetings, the children should also learn that meetings will be more orderly and fewer arguments will arise if a simple set of bylaws or standing rules is agreed on. These might include such items as the number of officers, the length of their terms of office, whether they can succeed themselves, the time and place of meetings, and the amount of dues (if any).

Storytelling

Storytelling by a teacher or librarian was discussed in Chapter 4 and receives further attention in Chapter 15, but children should not only listen to stories

Storytelling is natural for children if informality is maintained.

being told but should tell them, too. Storytelling is an activity they enjoy, both as tellers and as listeners, so it should be engaged in at all grade levels.

Children's first storytelling is usually the recounting of personal experiences, since storytelling is essentially an act of sharing. These first stories may be laced with both reality and fantasy, reflecting children's actual experiences as well as things they have heard about or seen on TV. But even very young storytellers do show a recognition that stories have a framework—although a teller's eagerness sometimes disguises this. Sketchy as such a framework may be, it does show that the element of organization has begun to enter into the child's thinking—an element vital to all communication, both oral and written.

These first experiences in sharing may be followed by encouraging the children to tell stories they've heard and liked and, later, ones they've read. In the telling of these, story beginnings and endings are used, characters and settings appear, and story lines are followed—again, aspects of composition. As important as this foundational element is, however, the major reason for encouraging children to tell stories should be the joy they will gain from both listening to a good story and being able to tell one—a joy that may be experienced throughout life. And, of course, telling stories leads directly to writing them.

Storytelling is more informal than most other forms of expression, but the speech skills needed are those required for all speaking activities. Listening to and watching an adult who is a good storyteller will help children to see the advantages of utilizing voice tone, gestures, and facial expressions. But experience is still the best teacher—children must practice the skills for oral interpretation and the techniques for holding an audience.

Jokes and Riddles

Books Children Will Enjoy

Beastly Riddles; Fishy, Flighty and Buggy by Joseph Low (Macmillan, 1983)

A Frog Sandwich: Riddles and Jokes by Marci Ridlon (Follett, 1973)

Monica Beisner's Book of Riddles (Farrar, Straus and Giroux, 1983)

Monster Jokes and Riddles by Norman Birdwell (Scholastic, 1973)

Nailheads and Potato Eyes by Cynthia Basil (Morrow, 1976)

Unriddling: All Sorts of Riddles to Puzzle Your Guessery by Alvin Schwartz (Lippincott, 1983)

What If . . . ? by Joseph Low (McElderry Book, Atheneum, 1976)

Witcrackers—Jokes and Jests from American Folklore by Alvin Schwartz (Lippincott, 1972)

When children are about seven years old, they develop a real interest in telling jokes and riddles. This interest can be utilized to help develop oral language skills. Begin by having joke and riddle books in the classroom library and occasionally reading a joke or riddle to the class.

Using jokes and riddles is often good at a time when you and the children are experiencing a letdown. One way to overcome such doldrums is to cover a bulletin board with black paper, cut out large white stars, and use a red marking pen to write a riddle on each star. Use another star as backing, since the marking usually goes through the paper. This second star, which has the answer printed on it, should be fastened to the one with the question. The bulletin board title might be "The Answer Is in the Stars" or "The Stars Know—Do You?"

After such a bulletin board display has been made and used, the children have listened as you read jokes and riddles, and they have looked at the joke and riddle books on the library table, they should be sufficiently motivated to want to tell jokes themselves.

A class discussion is called for to establish rules for telling jokes and the types of jokes to tell. The discussion may be used to bring out the point that jokes should never hurt another person's feelings or make fun of someone in any way. Children may want to tell jokes about nationalities, races, or religions because they have heard their parents or friends tell them and know that people have laughed. A child may say, "My dad tells jokes about _____ all the time." There is no good answer to this; certainly jokes about nationality, race, and religion are reappearing—and perhaps this is a sign that prejudices are beginning to disappear! Perhaps you might say that adults sometimes see things differently (children should certainly agree with that) and suggest that you might laugh at a joke about teachers when told by another teacher, but be very hurt if it was told by one of the children in the class. In short, avoid even implied criticism of a child's family or friends, but reemphasize that a joke should not hurt another's feelings. If interest is present and the class sufficiently mature, you might even go into the changes that have taken place in comedy—the disappearance of the blackface comedian, the lazy servant, and the Irish cop, for example.

From the class discussion, lead the children to set up rules for telling jokes. The following are good:

1. Tell the joke to the teacher first to be certain that it is a good joke for the class.
2. Look at the audience when telling a joke.

3. Know the order in which events happen in the joke so you don't have to say, "No, wait a minute; I forget; let's see—ah—then . . . "

4. Don't laugh at your own joke until it is over.

5. Remember the punch line. Use your voice to lead up to the punch line, and then deliver it quickly.

A good way to begin is to let the children take turns telling jokes or asking riddles as a part of the daily sharing time. Later, extend the class time for telling jokes and riddles to an assembly program. For such a program each child in the class might dress as a clown or wear another costume of his or her choice. The entire program could consist of jokes, riddles, funny songs, and funny dances. Many or all of the children in the class should know all of the jokes so that if one child is ill there is not a crisis—his or her spot can be filled.

Watching a comedian on television—although there are few who use content or appear at times appropriate for children—can help children learn about such things as expression, timing, and mannerisms for telling a joke. Children can report to the class what they have learned about telling jokes from watching a particular individual. Work on listening skills at the same time by asking each child to remember one joke the comedian told and to tell it to the class. Again, videotape recording can be used for rehearsal and for self-evaluation as well as for preserving a record of the final production.

The telling of jokes and riddles is a good way to develop many oral language skills. It is especially useful with children who have negative ideas toward school and learning, since it will develop interest and may cause them to decide that school can be fun. Reading is also taught, as children turn to books to find new jokes and riddles. For a child to remember a joke it is essential that he or she comprehend and remember what was read and understand the sequence of events. Even children with negative attitudes toward reading will generally read a book of riddles or jokes.

The telling of jokes and riddles can also be related to daily handwriting lessons in that children can work on their handwriting problems by copying riddles from the board or a book or writing their own. These handwriting papers can be collected and later made into a riddle book. Withholding the answers to the riddles until the end of the day will promote class conversation as children try to guess them.

Choral Speaking

Choral speaking is a most enjoyable way to interpret literature orally. Experience with choral speaking helps children learn to sense mood development, to understand the role of rhythm in speaking, and to realize the importance of volume, tone, and quality of voice. Fluency, clarity of enunciation, and speaking with expression are improved through choral speaking.

Choral speaking requires interpretation as well as thorough knowledge of the selection to be spoken. Sometimes a poem or verse may be memorized; other times it may be read. In either case, the children will need to read the selection several times and discuss the meanings of phrases as well as the entire piece. Speaking will need to be tried, varying the pace, rhythm, emphasis, and tone in order to decide how the piece may be most effectively spoken. However, this should not be overdone or children will tire of it. Trying out can be fun, though, and even disagreements about meanings and aspects of the reading can add zest to the activity.

Choral speaking also has value in helping children speak in other situations. Children who are too shy to speak tend to lose their shyness when they are just members of the group in choral speaking. Children who never seem to close their mouths learn to discipline themselves when they become a part of the group. Children who hate to read may develop more positive attitudes toward reading while engaged in this activity. As with everything else in the classroom, your enthusiasm will be the major factor in determining whether or not children enjoy choral speaking and profit from it.

Several types of choral speaking are described below. You will probably need to try different types with the children you are teaching before deciding what works best and what they like. You may also want to experiment and perhaps modify the suggestions given.

Refrain. A selection such as "Poor Old Woman" appeals to children, for it represents a form of choral speaking in which a soloist reads the narrative and the others join the refrain. When introducing this poem to the class, you can make it more appealing by showing pictures of each bug or animal as it is mentioned. These pictures can make a delightful bulletin board and certainly sharpen imagery and highlight meanings.

Give each class member a copy of the selection. Ask the class to follow with their eyes while listening to your reading of the selection, paying particular attention to the expression. Read it again with the children joining in on the refrains.

Sometimes holding up pictures of the animals encourages reluctant children to participate. Puppets or other objects suitable to the content may also be used. But don't overdo this.

POOR OLD WOMAN

(slowly and deliberately):

SOLO:	There was an old woman who swallowed a fly.
ALL *(dramatically):*	Oh, my! Swallowed a fly!
(slowly)	Poor old woman, I think she'll die.
SOLO:	There was an old woman who swallowed a spider.
(slowly)	Right down inside her, she swallowed a spider.
	She swallowed the spider to kill the fly.
ALL *(dramatically):*	Oh, my! Swallowed a fly!
(slowly)	Poor old woman, I think she'll die.
SOLO:	There was an old woman who swallowed a bird.
(said in an aside)	How absurd to swallow a bird!
(more quickly)	She swallowed the bird to kill the spider,
	She swallowed the spider to kill the fly.
ALL *(dramatically):*	Oh, my! Swallowed a fly!
(slowly)	Poor old woman, I think she'll die.

SOLO:	There was an old woman who swallowed a cat.
(slowly and deliberately)	Fancy that! Swallowed a cat!
ALL:	She swallowed the cat to kill the bird,
	She swallowed the bird to kill the spider,
	She swallowed the spider to kill the fly.
	Oh, my! Swallowed a fly!
	Poor old woman, I think she'll die.
SOLO:	There was an old woman who swallowed a dog.
(as if telling a secret)	She went the whole hog! She swallowed a dog!
ALL:	She swallowed the dog to kill the cat,
	She swallowed the cat to kill the bird,
	She swallowed the bird to kill the spider,
	She swallowed the spider to kill the fly.
	Oh, my! Swallowed a fly!
	Poor old woman, I think she'll die.
SOLO:	There was an old woman who swallowed a cow.
(slowly and carefully)	I don't know how, but she swallowed a cow.
ALL:	She swallowed the cow to kill the dog,
(with increasing momentum)	She swallowed the dog to kill the cat,
	She swallowed the cat to kill the bird,
	She swallowed the bird to kill the spider,
	She swallowed the spider to kill the fly.
(slowly and deliberately)	Oh, my! Swallowed a fly!
	Poor old woman, I think she'll die.
SOLO:	There was an old woman who swallowed a horse.
ALL:	She died, of course.

Antiphonal. Antiphonal choral speaking contrasts light voices with heavier ones. For example, some children may read questions and others the answers, or poems containing dialogue may be used. Poems of contrast are also excellent, with heavier voices taking parts that contain long vowels. Middle- and upper-grade children do well with this type of choral reading.

Give the children copies of the selection and have them follow as you read aloud to give the pattern for the children to imitate. Have several children try parts of the selection until class agreement is reached on voice quality, inflection, and timing. One good selection is Christina Rossetti's "Who Has Seen the Wind?":

HEAVY VOICES:	Who has seen the wind?
LIGHT VOICES:	Neither I nor you:
HEAVY VOICES:	But when the leaves hang trembling
	The wind is passing thro'.
LIGHT VOICES:	Who has seen the wind?
HEAVY VOICES:	Neither you nor I:

Use audio or video recorders so that children may hear themselves.

LIGHT VOICES: But when the trees bow down their heads
The wind is passing by.

Of course, this poem could also be done with one group asking the question in each stanza and the other responding, but the above division is a bit more unusual and gives each group an opportunity for creativity in reading the lines.

Other poems that can be used in this way include "Baa, Baa, Black Sheep" (Mother Goose), "Little Boy Blue" (Mother Goose), "Night" (Sara Teasdale), "It Is Raining" (Lucy Sprague Mitchell), "The Little Elf" (John Kendrick Bangs), "Father William" (Lewis Carroll), and "What Is Pink?" (Christina Rossetti).

Line-A-Child. In the line-a-child choric form, a single child or small groups of two to four children speak a line or couplet. The selection is continued by another child or group, then another, and so on until the end. It is necessary that the selection have lines or couplets that are naturally separated from one another—possibly marked off by semicolons or periods.

A bulletin board display or individual pictures may serve as an introduction to the selection. Each child should have a copy of the poem, and you should point out where each line or couplet ends. (You can combine this oral language activity with a written language lesson on thought units and punctuation.) Read the selection with the children listening to get the feeling of the poem and to determine which words or expressions need emphasis. Discuss these and then place the individuals or groups according to the order in which they speak so that they can remember their turns. Speaking on cue is essential for the continuity of the poem.

Good poems to try include "Jump or Jiggle" (Evelyn Beyer), "The Little Turtle" (Vachel Lindsay), "The Barnyard" (Maude Burham), "My Zipper Suit" (Mary Louise Allen), "The End" (A. A. Milne), "Only One Mother" (George Cooper), "Merry-Go-Round" (Dorothy W. Baruch), "Mice" (Rose Fyleman), "Someone" (Walter de la Mare), "The Wind" (Robert Louis Stevenson), "Spring Rain" (Marchette Chute), and "Very Lovely" (Rose Fyleman).

Unison. Teachers are often surprised to discover that unison speaking is the most difficult of all choral work. Children in the primary grades have great difficulty in coordinating their voices, and this precision is essential for quality unison speaking. This form also requires the greatest skill by the director. If you wish to see whether young children can do unison speaking, try Mother Goose rhymes, as they are easily interpreted and can serve as a beginning for pantomime and dramatics.

Many poems are suitable for unison speaking in the intermediate and upper grades. One example is "The Purple Cow" by Gelett Burgess:

I never saw a purple cow,
I never hope to see one;
But I can tell you anyhow,
I'd rather see than be one!

Try these:

"There Was a Crooked Man" (Mother Goose)
"Galoshes" (Rhoda W. Bacmeister)
"Silver" (Walter de la Mare)
"Snow" (Dorothy Aldis)
"The Sun" (John Drinkwater)
"Someone" (Walter de la Mare)
"The Monkeys and the Crocodile" (Laura E. Richards)
"Witch Ways" (Ethel Jacobson)

Choral reading or speaking has advantages as an assembly presentation. First, all the children in the class become involved and are on stage. Second, all children will learn the selection; if the child selected as soloist comes down with measles on the day of the production, others know the part. Those who have been involved with the trauma of having a sick child on the day of a program will appreciate this advantage of choral speaking.

Creative Dramatics

Some of the suggestions in Chapter 10 for stimulating writing are adaptable to creative dramatics.

Creative dramatics in the elementary school as discussed here is essentially a continuation of the activities and suggestions made in Chapter 4 about creative play and dramatization of stories and rhymes. The emphasis should still be on informality and creativity, with no more attention to scenery, props, costumes, or memorization of lines than is natural for the children to be concerned about. Dramatics in the elementary school should seldom, if ever, reach the production level of high-school presentations. Formal productions of plays are time-consuming, may be traumatizing to children, and hinder rather than foster creativity.

The essence of creative dramatics is improvisation; children are inspired to use imagination in choosing words and actions that will convey the desired impression. They can experiment with tone, rate of speaking, use of gestures, and even bodily stance as they try to create a believable mood or character. All of these require creative thinking.

In addition, the use of creative dramatics promotes both personal and social growth. Children release energy and express emotions as they respond to music or some other stimulus and as they create characters and scenes. A shy child can gain confidence through pretending to be someone else, as well as through working in a group. The aggressive child learns to work as a part of a group, and all children learn how important cooperation and planning are to achieving a desired outcome. And, finally, children gain a better understanding of themselves and others as they "become" other people and discover the commonality of human emotions.

Dramatize moods and reactions, such as surprise, excitement, happiness, sorrow, pain, and so on.

Children can also react to personal problems they are experiencing or have heard or read about or plan how they will behave in particular situations (for example, conducting an interview or going on a field trip) through **role playing,** a form of creative dramatics. This has the value of possibly clarifying issues, solving problems, and indirectly teaching skills and behavior.

If the children have not had a background of experience in dramatic play and other oral activities, it would probably be best to start at the beginning of the year with activities such as rhythmic response to music, pantomime, and re-creation of incidents from literature. Dramatizing an incident such as Charlie's visit to the chocolate factory or Tom Sawyer conning his friends into whitewashing the fence is not difficult, yet it presents an opportunity for creativity. And such an activity might be extended by using a different ending to a story or creating another incident involving the same characters (for instance, "What do you think might have happened if Tom's friends had decided to turn the tables on him?").

Creative dramatics can add understanding and depth to almost any area of the curriculum. A child who has helped to create a rhythmic dance based on a mathematical concept (a square, subtraction, etc.) will not find arithmetic dull. Similarly, dramatizing a day spent traveling across Kansas in a covered wagon will give students a deeper understanding of the hardships of the westward expansion.

All the skills required for any oral activity can be developed through creative dramatics. Like any other activity, it should not be overdone, but it should be an integral part of the language arts program.

Puppetry

Puppets and marionettes can be useful tools for teaching oral expression. Besides, they are fun! Puppets are less difficult to use than marionettes and therefore generally more useful. A marionette is usually operated from above by strings, which often isn't easy for children to do, whereas a puppet is operated by hand from below. Interest in puppets may first be developed when a child brings a hand puppet for "Show and Tell." Children may wish to use this puppet to recite a favorite Mother Goose rhyme. Talking for a puppet instead of one's self tends to bring out a shy child. Once interest has been generated, you will want to encourage each child to make his or her own puppet. Making puppets and putting on a play is an excellent way to teach children to follow directions and to strengthen language skills. And the children will have a delightful time while they are learning.

When making puppets, start with simple ones such as cut-out stick puppets, empty-bag puppets, or vegetable and fruit puppets.

Puppet Books

Easy-to-Make Puppets by Joyce Luckin (Plays, 1975)

Magic of Puppetry: A Guide for Those Working with Young Children by Peggy Davidson Jenkins (Prentice-Hall, 1980)

Mitt Magic; Finger Plays for Finger Puppets by Lynda Roberts (Gryphon House, 1985)

Potpourri of Puppetry: A Handbook for Schools by Enid Bates and Ruth Lowes (Fearon, 1976)

Wooden Spoon Puppets by Audrey Dean (Plays, 1976)

Using puppets is fun and helps develop speaking skills.

Styroform Stick Puppet

Paper Bag Puppet

Sock Hand Puppet

Box Puppet

Cut-out Stick Puppets. For cut-out stick puppets, figures or faces may be drawn, colored, and cut from cardboard, or paper dolls may be used. Coloring books often have outlines of figures or faces that can be pasted on cardboard. Tongue depressors or popsicle sticks can be glued to the bottoms for the children to hold. If a puppet needs support up the back, a longer stick will be needed, one long enough so that the hand holding it will not show if the puppet is used in a puppet stage. Stick puppets can be clothed with either cloth or paper. Old wallpaper, leftover gift wrap from Christmas, or even colorful shelf paper can be useful for making attractive paper clothes, and remnants or scraps of cloth can provide materials for cloth garments.

Empty-Bag Puppets. Children can make and use empty-bag puppets if the bags are not too large for them to handle. Place the bag flat, with the folded bottom part up. Draw or paint the upper part of a face on the bottom of the bag, and the lower part of the face on the side. If you want the puppet to have a moving mouth, the upper part of the mouth should be on the bag bottom, and the lower lip on the side. If the eyes are to move, the lashes should be on the bottom, with the lower part of the eyes on the side. Yarn, crepe paper, or cotton can be glued on for hair. The puppet is operated by placing fingers in the bag so that the folded-down bottom can be moved up and down to move the mouth (or eyes, eyelashes, or eyebrows).

Vegetable and Fruit Puppets. Potatoes, carrots, beets, radishes, apples, and oranges are a few of the vegetables and fruits that can be mounted on sticks and used as other stick puppets are used. Faces can be made in a variety of ways: they can be cut out with a vegetable peeler, drawn on with paint or a felt-tip pen, or made from paper or felt and pasted on. Or thumb tacks or paper stars may be used for eyes, with other features added in one of the above ways.

More Advanced Puppets. At a little more advanced level are sock puppets. These are simply socks with buttons sewed on for eyes and with crayons or paint used to make other features. The stuffed-bag puppet is a modification of the empty-bag puppet. The bag is filled about halfway with crumpled paper. (This simply fills out the bag, which is used in about the same way as described above.) If the bag is large, it can be partly drawn together with a string to represent a neck and shoulders below the face. Stuffed-bag puppets usually are decorated or dressed more than the simpler puppets.

The Puppet Stage. You will need some kind of stage in order to use puppets for dramatization. Of course, hand puppets are good for storytelling, getting children's attention, and just talking, but to get full value from the puppets children make, dramatization is needed.

The puppet stage should be inexpensive and easy to make. Tip a card table on its side; the children can sit behind it and raise puppets above the table edge. A large box or carton—the kind refrigerators or stoves are shipped in—also works well. Part of a side is cut out and the part visible to the audience is painted. The children sit inside and raise their hand puppets to the "stage floor" level.

The Story. Almost any situation can be dramatized with puppets. Here are some ideas:

- Accepting responsibility for tasks at home and at school, such as cleanliness of a room or completion of a task. Let the children plan their own dialogue for this.
- Good sportsmanship on or off the playground.
- Correct behavior in social situations.
- Stories from literature. Try these:
  Amiable Giant (Louis Slobodkin)
  The Three Bears
  Andy and the Lion (James Daugherty)
  Hansel and Gretel
  Snipp, Snapp, Snurr (Maj Lindman)
  Pet Show (Ezra Jack Keats)

ADDITIONAL TEACHING CONSIDERATIONS

Improving children's oral expression through the speaking opportunities described above involves some important practices and concerns. These are discussed in the sections that follow.

Video Activities

Many elementary students are quite familiar with video recorders from home experiences, and video equipment is available to some extent in nearly every school system. As mentioned earlier, videotaping is a way to provide feedback to speakers to let them know how their presentations look and sound as well as a means of preserving a record of a panel discussion or an interview. Puppetry and creative dramatics are also obvious opportunities for such recording.

Video equipment has been used in other ways as well. Some schools have a cable system throughout the building that permits "morning announcements" to be presented via television, with students giving the news and carrying out other activities, just as the announcers on a television news show might do. Of course, there are many opportunities to use video equipment in science and social studies classes. A science demonstration may be seen better by the whole class if it is shown "live," while at the same time

Doing the news "on TV" is an excellent oral language activity.

being taped and commented on by a student. In social studies the camera and recorder may be taken on a field trip, and the videotape can be used later back in the classroom. Very often such productions require scripts, and, of course, these have to be written—so the experience actually involves all of the language arts areas.

Videotaping by elementary-school children has proved to be highly satisfactory. Making "home movies" was attempted by classes in the past, but with generally unsatisfactory results. A video recording, however, has sound, requires no developing, is immediately available for viewing, and can even be copied if the school has at least two recorders. Also, some inexpensive video recorders may be used without much preparation by children in the primary grades.

As they do videotaping, children are learning about an important form of communication as well as a possible vocational field.

Oral Language and Social Amenities

It is not enough to be able to speak at a functional level; to communicate effectively requires the ability to express oneself in particular forms in particular settings. Some of these have been discussed. There are, however, situations in which particular social behaviors—social amenities—are important, and children should learn about these.

Social amenities are best taught as rehearsals for occasions when they will be needed. Many teachers would like to think that these forms of behavior are taught at home, but most know that often they are not. It is the responsibility of the school to acquaint children with at least the minimum requirements of courteous behavior.

The atmosphere in the classroom and your attitude toward teaching and toward each child are of utmost importance in teaching proper social behavior. Many influences in society tend to promote or excuse rudeness, including much of what children see in daily life and on television. You must stress the dignity of every person and mutual respect among the members of the class if you are to begin to overcome these effects.

Social amenities that children particularly need to learn are those concerning making introductions and extending and responding to greetings. Children need to learn the conventions that are followed in such circumstances, and this is best accomplished during the genuine occasions that arise in every classroom. For example, visitors who come into the classroom may be greeted by a room host or hostess, who introduces them to the teacher and the other children. Good practice for older children can also occur during an open house, parents' night, or similar occasion. In addition, these amenities can be introduced and practiced through dramatizations.

Situations That May Be Dramatized

introducing a parent to a school friend

introducing one friend to another

a parent introducing his or her child to a friend or guest

introducing oneself to a stranger

introducing a visitor to the class

In making introductions children should learn to say "Mrs. Smith, this is Sue" or "Mary, I'd like you to meet Jimmy." The first name mentioned should be the person honored—an older person or a special guest. Children should also learn how to respond: "I'm very glad to meet you, Sue" or "How do you do." Encourage them to shake hands firmly (but not too firmly) and to look at the person they are being introduced to.

Rules that are helpful include these:

1. Speak each person's name clearly (if a name is not understood, ask that it be repeated).
2. Use an introduction to start a conversation, with the person making the introduction beginning the conversation.
3. When introducing yourself to another, be certain to give your name clearly and add some identifying remark.
4. Speak the name of a person to whom you are introduced and use it when speaking to him or her to help remember it.

Discuss with children the awkwardness of a situation in which two people are talking and are joined by a third person, known to one of the first two but not to the other. The person who knows the one who has joined them does not introduce her because of having forgotten her name. This should be no excuse; the person should simply apologize, ask her name, and then introduce her. Children will be relieved to know that many people feel shy and embarrassed in this kind of situation—that this is natural but needs to be overcome.

Other situations to discuss with children might include the following:

• What can be said to make a new child feel welcome?
• What words should be used in such situations as thanking an aunt who has given a boy a shirt that he thinks is ugly? What can he say about the shirt without lying or hurting the aunt's feelings?
• What might be said and done if a group of children are playing ball and notice some strange children watching?
• Suppose you are having dinner at a friend's house. What do you do and say after dinner?
• What do you say if you want a person to sit in a particular place?
• A friend invites you to a movie. What do you say?
• What are some situations in which you should offer assistance? For example, in removing a coat, what do you say?
• Suppose the teacher asks, "Who discovered America?" and a child replies, "George Washington." Is it polite to laugh?
• How do you respond to courtesies shown you?
• Someone knocks at the door. How do you greet this person?

Classroom Courtesy

Manners and courtesy are essential if people are to get along in a pleasant atmosphere. It might help to begin the year with a discussion of what everyone in the class needs to do to make the room a pleasant place in which to live and work. This may also be the time to discuss the ways in which courtesy and safety work together. The discussion of classroom behavior might well lead to a unit on courtesy and the necessity for obeying the rules on school buses, in the lunchroom, and on the playground.

You can get help with such units from several sources. For example, most police departments will send someone who will talk with children about safety. Some bus drivers and cafeteria workers may be pleased to help. Inquiry should also be made to state education departments, AAA offices, and organizations such as the Boy Scouts and 4H. Materials related to safety and courtesy may often be obtained from insurance agents, since many insurance companies provide a wealth of materials on these subjects. For example, write to Public Relations, Kemper Insurance Company, 4750 Sheriden Road, Chicago, IL 60640, for free material on several aspects of school safety.

The library is an important resource when teaching courtesy; there are numerous books, films, and filmstrips available on this topic. You might want to read to your class *What Do You Say, Dear?* by Sesyle Joslin. Magazine pictures may also be used to promote discussions of good manners; use these on a bulletin board or show them to a group using an opaque projector.

Also by the same author are *What Do You Do, Dear?* and *Dear Dragon* (Harcourt Brace Jovanovich).

After discussing courtesy in the room and the importance of courtesy and safety when coming to or going from school and on the playground, discuss courtesy and safety in the school building—the corridor, cafeteria, auditorium, and office. Perhaps the principal will be able to come to the room to discuss the importance of courtesy and how the children can help by being polite and following school rules (or a child may interview the principal). Teachers are often hesitant about asking school administrators to talk with their classes, but many are flattered to be invited. Other people who work in the school building may be willing to discuss their jobs with the children and tell how good manners make their work easier. Or a safety patrol member or crossing guard may discuss why good manners and following directions are essential for safety.

Children may also discuss behavior and courtesy in public places such as stores, museums, libraries, zoos, parks, restaurants, pools, movies, and ball games. Courtesy and safe behavior on escalators, elevators, streets, and public buses should also be discussed. It is essential that children learn appropriate physical and verbal behavior, since there really is no excuse for rudeness by people of any age.

Through dramatization—actually playing roles—children can learn many social amenities that will be useful to them. In fact, teaching amenities provides an opportunity to use a variety of oral language experiences. Discussion, role playing, telephoning, interviewing, committee work, puppet plays, making announcements, and giving directions can all be used to further children's understanding of behavior that shows concern for others. Here again, video equipment may be helpful, especially for recording dramatizations of "good" and "bad" ways to act in particular situations.

The Role of Parents

It is the sharing of experiences that broadens children's knowledge of the world about them, increases their vocabularies, and develops their ability to express themselves. Most teachers agree that it is from a child's experiences and his or her discussion of them that concepts necessary for future learning are developed. Yet schools are not able to provide all the experiences that a child needs—a great deal must be left up to the parents. Consider planning a program for parents with the purpose of informing them of the role of experiences in learning. Include in such a program an explanation of the importance of talking with and to children at every age level. If a program is not possible, perhaps you might speak to the principal about possibly getting an article published in the local newspaper. Sending a letter home with children informing parents of your teaching objectives is always a good idea. Caution is needed in wording any such message, however, as most parents do not want to be told how to raise their children. At the same time, parents generally do want their children to do well in school, so pointing out the importance of encouraging language development may be taken as a reminder.

EVALUATING ORAL EXPRESSION

There are tests of articulation ability, auditory discrimination, and verbal development. They do not measure abilities in social speaking situations.

There are no standardized tests for measuring children's abilities in the types of oral communication activities described in this chapter, but the skills and abilities of children in speaking situations should be evaluated. Evaluation can and should be a part of virtually every speaking situation. This does not mean formal evaluation or the testing that may first come to mind, but it does mean appraisal, or determining what children can and cannot do adequately for their maturity levels. Such evaluation must be a basic element of teaching if children's speaking skills and abilities are to improve from one speech activity to another.

The evaluation or appraisal should be based on the objectives of the total program and the objectives for specific speaking activities: conversation, discussion, interviewing, and so forth. To some extent these objectives may be set by curriculum guides developed for your school and/or formulated by yourself. Even in consideration of these, however, the objectives determined by pupils must not be overlooked.

Standards

Guidelines, rules, or standards for performance can be developed for all oral language situations. These standards should be developed by you and the pupils. They should reflect the children's way of looking at things, but if children's original suggestions are too restrictive or are beyond the performance levels possible, some modification may be necessary. Standards should always be thought of as evolving.

Evaluation should always be made in terms of the standards developed by you and the children and, most importantly, in terms of each individual child and the amount of progress he or she has made toward achieving these goals. In addition, you should evaluate the extent of each child's capabilities in the speech skills discussed earlier in this chapter, as well as his or her efforts to make any needed improvement. The evaluation of oral expression is bound to be somewhat subjective, but the effects of subjectivity will be minimized if goals are clearly understood, if progress in achieving these goals is discussed regularly by you *and* the children, and if each child is evaluated according to individual abilities, needs, and achievements.

Checklists

Checklists are similar to lists of standards in that they also suggest appropriate behaviors. The items on a checklist are usually questions that can be answered with "Yes," "No," or a check mark. Checklists may be used by individual pupils for self-evaluation or by the teacher.

A checklist may be extended to include questions about specific usage items of concern, physical mannerisms exhibited by pupils, and more details regarding the content and organization of the material.

Checklists should be used at regular intervals, and comparisons made of the responses from one time to another. And checklists, like standards, may need to be revised as children's abilities progress.

Checking Up on My Speech

	YES	NO
1. Is my voice pleasant to hear?	_____	_____
2. Do I speak so everyone can understand me?	_____	_____
3. Do I adjust the volume of my voice for different situations?	_____	_____
4. Am I prepared for speaking activities?	_____	_____
5. Do I think before speaking?	_____	_____
6. Do I use good words and sentences?	_____	_____

Other Records

Checklists are relatively easy to use, but they may not be constructed so that enough details about individual children's strengths and weaknesses can be recorded. Some teachers prefer to keep notebooks with pages for individual students. Still others like to keep individual files, putting notes in them from time to time. Whatever the record system used, there should be provision for determining growth. The system should also deal with specifics so that instruction can be focused on needs.

A FINAL WORD

There are many ways in which effectiveness in using oral language enhances a child's life. As children speak, they use new words they have learned and make them their own; they also experiment with sentence patterns and may even try one that they have never heard before. Talking also improves thought processes; elementary-school children often work out what they understand and believe as they talk about a topic. Using oral language well is crucial to academic development and to social and emotional growth. People who are confident when speaking have a definite advantage over those who are tentative or halting. In discussing the goals of instruction in reading, writing, and the other language arts, later chapters will point out the extent to which their full realization depends on students' oral language abilities.

References

Considine, David M. "Visual Literacy and the Curriculum," *Language Arts* 64 (October, 1987), pp. 634–640.

Cottrell, June. *Creative Drama in the Classroom, Grades K–3.* National Textbook Company, 1987.

———. *Creative Drama in the Classroom, Grades 4–6.* National Textbook Company, 1987.

Geller, Linda Gibson. *Wordplay and Language Learning for Children.* National Council of Teachers of English, 1985.

Kimeldorf, Martin. *Teaching Is Dramatic.* Endick Communications, 1985.

Language Arts 65 (January, 1988) (issue on drama), pp. 14–55.

Mayher, John S., and Brause, Rita S. "Learning Through Teaching: Teaching and Learning Vocabulary," *Language Arts* 60 (November/December, 1983), pp. 1008–1016.

McCaslin, Nellie. *Creative Drama in the Intermediate Grades.* Longman, 1987.

McTear, Michael. *Children's Conversation.* Basil Blackwell, 1985.

Moffett, James, and Wagner, Betty Jane. Chapter 5 in *Student-Centered Language Arts and Reading,* *K–13: A Handbook for Teachers,* 3rd ed. Houghton Mifflin, 1983.

Nilson, Allen Pace. "Children's Multiple Uses of Oral Language Play," *Language Arts* 60 (February, 1983), pp. 194–201.

Nugent, Susan Monroe. *Integrating Speaking Skills into the Curriculum.* National Council of Teachers of English, 1986.

Ontario Ministry of Education. *Drama in the Formative Years.* Ontario Ministry of Education, 1984.

Seiler, William J.; Schuelke, L. David; and Lieb-Brilhart, Barbara. *Communication for the Contemporary Classroom.* CBS College Publishing, 1984.

Sloyer, Shirlee. *Readers Theatre: Story Dramatization in the Classroom.* National Council of Teachers of English, 1982.

Stewig, John Warren. *Informal Drama in the Elementary Language Arts Program.* Teachers College Press, 1983.

Stewig, John Warren, and Young, Linda. "An Exploration of the Relations Between Creative Drama and Language Growth," *Children's Theatre Review* 27 (1978), pp. 10–12.

Teaching Resources

BOOKS

Brown, Marc. *Finger Rhymes.* Dutton, 1980.

Burns, Marilyn. *The Hink Pink Book.* Little, Brown, 1981.

Carlson, Dale, and Fitzgibbon, R. *Manners That Matter.* Dutton, 1983.

Glazer, Tom. *Eye Winker, Tom Tinker, Chin Chopper: Fifty Musical Finger Plays.* Doubleday, 1973.

Hand Rhymes. Dutton, 1985.

Livo, Norma J., and Rietz, Sandra A. *Storytelling Activities.* Libraries Unlimited, 1987.

———. *Storytelling: Process and Practice.* Libraries Unlimited, 1986.

Playmakers. Cambridge University Press (grades 2–6).

Renfro, Nancy. *Puppetry in Education Series.* Renfro Studios, 1985–1987.

Ring A Ring O'Roses. Flint Public Library, 1026 E. Kearsley, Flint, MI 48502 (finger plays).

Rosenbloom, Joseph. *World's Toughest Tongue Twisters.* Sterling, 1987 (grades 2–8).

Walker Plays for Oral Reading. Curriculum Associates (grades 3–6).

Williams, Mary Young. *Let 'Em Talk: Oral Language Activities for the Classroom.* Dale Seymour (K–grade 8).

Young, Karen Romano. *Please Come to My Party.* Children's Press, 1986.

VIDEOTAPES

Communication Fundamentals—Five Basic Skills. Phoenix/BFA (primary–intermediate).

How to Make a Speech. Greenleaf.

Persuasive Speaking. Greenleaf.

Your Communication Skills—Speaking. Coronet Instructional Films (grades 1–6).

OTHER RESOURCES

Challenge Boxes. Dale Seymour (fifty projects in creative thinking; grades 4–8).

The Storyteller. Educational Activities, 1986 (computer software; grades 4–6).

Talking Time Series. McGraw-Hill (Two sets of eight filmstrips each; grades 2–6).

Activities for Preservice Teachers

1. With a group of classmates, do a video production—a commercial, sports commentary, travelogue, or skit. Focus on what you can learn that will help you use video equipment with children.

2. Plan some creative dramatics activities for a specific grade level. Collect simple props (such as hats, dolls, badges, telephones, luggage) that are likely to stimulate children to come up with creative ideas.

3. Learn several stories well enough to tell to children. Try your storytelling skill with neighborhood children or those at a nearby school. You may want to practice with peers first.

4. Make a list of the ways in which audio and video recorders might be effectively used in elementary classrooms. Discuss your list with classmates; ask for their reactions.

5. Start a collection of poems that are appropriate for choral speaking. Determine the type of choral activity each poem is best suited for.

6. While observing in a classroom, try to identify a child whose shyness or lack of confidence seems to be inhibiting her or his full participation in oral activities.

Devise particular activities and experiences that could be used to give that youngster a gradually increasing sense of confidence in such situations. If the activities and experiences can actually be used, identify those that seem to help most.

7. Develop a plan for moving from pantomime to dramatization with children. Show how, over a period of a few weeks, it might be possible to do group pantomimes, rehearsed individual pantomimes, and, finally, dramatizations. Some subjects might be "The Cafeteria Line," "Riding on the Bus," and "Cheering for the Team."

8. Interview a speech therapist who works for a school district to find out what kinds of speech problems he or she encounters and what kinds of remedial procedures are used.

9. Observe a class during some oral activity, and use a checklist to assess the group and individuals. Decide which skills, attitudes, or abilities should have instructional priority.

10. As you prepare a report for one of your own classes, apply the suggestions presented in this chapter.

Activities for Inservice Teachers

1. Videotape a particularly vigorous and expressive speaker (in person or from a television broadcast). With your class, analyze what this person does and how well the techniques seem to work.

2. Assist the children in your class in forming a club based on some interest shared by many (a fan club for

a local sports team, perhaps). Along with the many possible language-related club activities, see that they learn about and use some parliamentary procedures.

3. Plan a choral speaking activity that your class might present to another group. Videotape a re-

hearsal, and use the tape as a basis for group evaluation.

4. Plan to make puppets with your class. Get the students involved in the planning—deciding what purpose the puppets will have, what kind to produce, the materials needed, the procedures to be followed, and so on.

5. Prepare a card file of books of jokes, riddles, and word games that children may use.

6. Develop a lesson that uses creative dramatics in science, social studies, or math. Did it seem to promote understanding of the content? Would you try something similar again?

7. Arrange for your students to interview various people within the school (custodians, cafeteria staff, etc.) after reviewing with the children the suggestions made in this chapter.

8. Start a drama book shelf that holds books containing good stories to dramatize. Criteria for selection of stories should include simple sequences, clear-cut climax, significance of content, and varied characterizations.

9. Organize a field trip to a local TV station. Then ask one of the announcers (the weather reporter, for instance) to visit your classroom—and perhaps be videotaped by the children.

10. Have children plan a program in which they announce various things: what they have to sell or buy (or, perhaps better, borrow or lend), events of interest, or plans for a class activity, for example. Make sure that standards are developed and observed.

Independent Activities for Children

1. Two children may work together to plan a play to demonstrate good manners. For example, one might be a guest visiting the classroom and the other could greet and introduce her or him, or they might illustrate ways to disagree in a conversation without being discourteous.

2. Have individual children plan skits for special days (Citizenship Day, the anniversary of the Boston Tea Party, United Nations Day, Flag Day, etc.). The planning may include writing a script, getting props, researching, and selecting participants. A child may get help from other children with the planning.

3. A child can relate to a small group an incident in a story he or she has read, telling it as though he or she had been one of the characters. (The child may wish to rehearse this before a mirror or record it on tape before presenting it to the group.)

4. Allow children to select a "visitors' committee" who will greet guests to the classroom, explain activities of the class to them, and otherwise act as hosts. Ask school personnel and parents to visit regularly to provide practice for the hosts. New members should be appointed at regular intervals.

5. Children can make puppets independently if they are provided with a place and materials—paper bags, paint, scissors, socks, sticks, stapler, and so on. Have a few puppet models, but encourage children to do more than merely copying these.

6. Stories can be made up to tell using puppets. Children may make up these stories independently and practice them in front of a mirror before telling them to the class or to a small group.

7. Paper dolls and their clothing can be cut out and used for dramatic play. Children should do the cutting, of course, and may create plays for the figures.

8. Children may write the material for "commercials" to "sell" the reading of library books to their classmates. The presentations can be made directly or might be videotaped for later showing.

9. Keep a card file of topics or situations calling for oral activities. These might be filed under types (conversation, discussion, interviews, storytelling, explanations and directions, etc.), or they might be labeled simply "individual" and "group." When children have free time during the day, they can draw a card at random and develop the activity suggested. Group activities can be enjoyed and, perhaps, evaluated by those participating; individual activities can be videotaped or presented to the class at odd moments—before lunch, for example. Topics should not be too specific or directive. A conversation card, for example, might read "A new neighbor has moved into the house next door. Decide just how you might meet and carry on conversation. Be yourself, not some imaginary person." The children should be encouraged to add top-

ics; they may also help to rotate cards so topics do not become stale.

10. Give a child a list of words that are sometimes not pronounced correctly or that are not clearly enunciated so that they are confused with other words. Have the child record these and listen to herself or himself. You may also check the recording or have two children do this together so that they check one another. Some words to use are *quote, quota; compile, compel;* and *partial, parcel.*

11. A child can prepare a talk to give to the class on a topic such as:

How to make a kite
How to build a snowman
How to build and care for an aquarium
How to begin a stamp collection

12. Give a child a collection of pictures from magazines and have him or her record on tape a story based on these pictures.

13. Children may also record original stories on tape. At a special time, such as once each week, tapes may be played to the class for practice in listening and discussion.

14. Let children keep a file of pantomime ideas. Provide a mirror in a corner of the room where individual children can experiment with pantomimes and prepare to present them to the class or to small groups.

15. Individual children may prepare and present announcements at school assemblies or over the school public address system.

Chapter 6

Listening and Learning

*E*vidence indicates that most adults spend about half their communication time listening to the speech of others. For students the proportion is often higher—60 or even 80 percent in some classrooms. An activity that is so prominent a part of people's lives certainly deserves more attention than it usually receives in schools.

Most of us are concerned about effective listening. We want to receive the newscaster's words accurately as well as those of associates and family members. Children should learn how to listen effectively, and teachers can help children attain this ability.

LISTENING IN THE SCHOOL PROGRAM

By the time children come to school for the first time they have had five or six years' experience in listening. From listening they learned the language of their homes, of their neighborhoods, and possibly of much of the world (through travel and television). No one has taught them to listen, although they have likely been told many times to "pay attention." They have probably acquired some listening habits and skills, but they have probably not developed the concern and many of the practices for learning by listening that teachers desire.

It is accepted by most authorities that we listen at an efficiency level of about 25 percent.

Although we sometimes say we "half listen" and although we often listen intermittently or in a somewhat passive manner to music or to someone talking, real listening requires participation. Like the reader, the listener must actively engage in the perception and recognition of words and phrases, in the comprehension of ideas and facts, and in conscious or emotional reaction to these in relation to his or her background of experience. Listening is not an activity that should be separated from expression. Listening to speech requires a speaker. Listening to music requires a performer. Someone or something is always producing the sounds heard; this is further evidence of the active nature of listening.

Hearing and Listening

Listening is affected by the acuity with which a person receives sound waves of various frequencies (tones) at various intensities (levels of loudness). An inability to respond to normal frequencies and intensities represents a hearing loss, which may range from minor to serious. Although a hearing loss affects an individual's ability to perceive sounds and discriminate among them, it is possible for a person to have normal hearing and yet have difficulty with sound perception and discrimination. This is particularly the case with people who have speech problems and with those unfamiliar with a language or a particular dialect. There should be, at most, only minimal problems with children who speak the language or dialect and who do not have speech or hearing problems. Many children who seem to have difficulty with perception and discrimination are probably exhibiting a lack of understanding of what they are asked to do, unfamiliarity with aspects of the language (for instance, the words used), little motivation to retain (remember) what they heard, or inattention.

Hearing is also affected by fatigue and masking. **Masking** is simply a failure to hear because of the superimposition of sounds that interfere—the many voices at a cocktail party, for example. Related to this, but with a physical base, is inadequate binaural hearing. **Binaural hearing** may be thought of as similar to depth perception in vision; that is, without adequate binaural hearing the individual cannot locate a particular speaker among several talking at once.

There are a number of factors related to hearing and listening that may interfere with reception.

Speech that is too rapid for reception (usually because the content is unfamiliar)
Slow speech, which leads to "mind wandering"
Lack of interest in the topic or speaker
Waiting for the opportunity to take issue with the speaker
Inadequate knowledge of the topic
Distractions caused by sounds, movement, or the physical surroundings
An "overacceptance" of the speaker and/or the topic
Inadequate development of the skills needed for listening
Poor organization of the material to be listened to
Preoccupation with personal interests and problems
A hearing loss

Listening and Reading

Since listening and reading are receptive acts, there are many similarities between them. Both require as a first step readiness for reception. This means that interest in what is to be heard or read must have been aroused; there must be appeal or curiosity—a motivating force. Both reading and listening also require accurate perception of sounds. If *build* sounds to the listener like *filled,* it may not be possible to get the message. Similarly, the child who sees *black* instead of *blank* will have trouble understanding the sentence "Fill in the blank spaces." Reading and listening also both require that the words or other lexical units (for example, *rocking chair, push broom, town house*) heard or read are ones whose meanings are either known or can be determined from the context or other clues.

Comprehension in both reading and listening results from understanding phrases, sentences, and statements of greater length—the paragraph, for example—rather than a single word. Therefore, both require relating what is received to past experiences, so that the content of what is heard or read can be thought about and examined creatively and critically. Further-

Children should learn to note signal words and expressions, for example, *next, at the same time, after, my next point*, and *thus*.

more, both processes require active attention to signals—punctuation marks, pauses, intonations, key words (for example, *next, for instance, perhaps, on the other hand*).

Reading and listening can take place in many situations and can be done for many purposes. The closeness of their tie has been shown over and over again by the similarity of activities and exercises designed to teach their skills. In fact, since listening has begun to receive instructional attention, many reading series provide listening activities and suggest that teaching listening skills is one way to improve reading skills.

Ability to listen and ability to read do not necessarily go hand in hand, but a planned program that builds on the relationships between them should improve children's skills in both areas. For example, children may follow a story with their eyes and listen to it being read (using earphones to listen to an audio cassette). Other examples of activities to develop listening are giving oral directions (they may be taped) for reading assignments, presenting material in social studies and other curriculum areas through both listening and reading, and motivating reading by having pupils listen to stories with related themes or subjects.

Types of Listening

We all listen in different ways at different times and in different situations, and this fact needs to be taken into account in an instructional program. Although listening is an active, interacting process, the level of activity on the part of the listener varies. Interest in what is being heard affects this level, as do emotional and intellectual factors. Sometimes we only listen marginally, as when a radio is on, but we are basically thinking about whatever we are working on. We often listen to music for sheer enjoyment, perhaps being involved to some extent emotionally but to a lesser extent cognitively. At times, we listen for particular information but are not otherwise actively involved. At other times, we are very attentive, listening totally for understanding and perhaps critically analyzing what we are hearing. There is response to any listening, of course, or it is not listening, but the response is rather passive in marginal listening situations. However, in situations in which the listener seeks information or understanding, desires satisfaction of an emotion, or wishes to make a judgment, the listening act is an active one.

Types or levels of listening are not as discrete as perhaps is suggested above. Certainly, listening instruction should not have the objective of "moving" children from a "lower" (marginal or passive) level to a "higher" one. Rather, the objective is to teach children how they may listen more effectively in the situations and settings where they have the need to listen.

THE LISTENING SKILLS

Listening skills have been listed by many researchers, but with the increase in the number of these lists there has arisen more and more skepticism about their validity. Obviously, though, there are factors that make the reception of sounds meaningful. Possibly listening is something of a state of mind. The young child who has received no instruction in listening can listen well when he or she wishes to do so—no child who is hungry has to be called twice for lunch. Every child has shown considerable effectiveness in listening in order to have learned the language he or she speaks and the ideas and concepts that he or she can express.

Yet young children have generally not had occasion to listen for the kinds of purposes that exist in classrooms. Even older children often lack many of the skills that would aid their listening, or perhaps they do not know what they should be listening for in various situations.

Listening to speech, like the related receptive act of reading, is an information-processing experience. In both reading and listening, it is not a single sound, letter, or even word that is the basic unit of comprehension, although the reader or listener may use the clues any of those provide in the processing. Essentially, the process of listening first requires perception of something that is meaningful to the receiver—language structure that is known and used, a "chunk" of language whose content is related to something the listener already knows, or perhaps only a word, a tone, or a gesture that gives a clue to the meaning. A listener (unlike a reader) cannot stop listening in order to analyze a sequence of sounds, and usually it is not possible to "go back" and relisten. Yet a listener can learn to gain meaning from (1) the context of what is heard, (2) the clues in a speaker's facial expressions or gestures, (3) the organization of the content, (4) the redundancies that occur in most speech, (5) the voice inflections—tone, rhythm, and volume—a speaker uses, and (6) the clues provided by such signals as *on the other hand, first,* and *however.*

Some Purposes for Listening

1. To get the main idea
2. To select details
3. To establish a mood
4. To answer questions
5. To summarize information
6. To separate fact from opinion
7. To gain a visual image
8. To appreciate and enjoy
9. To recognize propaganda, bias, or prejudice
10. To determine the speaker's purpose
11. To adapt information presented to a particular need
12. To evaluate in terms of some criteria
13. To perceive relationships
14. To interpret unusual or especially appealing language
15. To show courtesy

The perception of all or some of the language heard, by the listener's knowledge of elements of it or by any of the ways suggested above for gaining the necessary understanding, is only part of the listening process. Responding to the information perceived completes the process. For such responding to occur, the listener must be skilled in such information-processing abilities as (1) determining the main idea of what was heard; (2) accurately noting relevant details; (3) following directions; (4) understanding denotative and connotative meanings; (5) following the sequence of a plot, explanation, or argument; (6) recognizing relationships of cause and effect, time, space, and place; (7) understanding figurative and idiomatic language; and (8) distinguishing among fact, fiction, and fantasy.

These skills are closely related to the purposes for listening—purposes that arise throughout each day for almost everyone. For example, in the classroom children and teacher must listen to one another as they discuss topics of interest, plan activities, and stimulate each other's thinking. Each child needs to listen so that he or she can answer questions about social studies events, a story the class has read, or an arithmetic problem. The child must listen in order to separate fact from opinion (in a newscast, a political speech, a TV advertisement, or a talk given to the class); he or she must listen in order to summarize material (such as that given in a science report), follow directions for a game or a project, or get the main idea from a story, a TV program, or a class report. Children also listen to gain appreciation of music, a story, or a poem. They listen to establish a mood for thinking and reacting. They listen to music and other nonspeech sounds to start ideas flowing for a creative writing activity. And sometimes they listen to show courtesy to a classmate or a guest.

Guidelines

A number of guidelines or principles are helpful in planning a program to improve children's listening. To begin with, a classroom climate that is conducive to listening avoids distracting physical and emotional conditions. This climate includes a relaxed, unhurried, nonthreatening teacher's voice, along with facial expressions that are expressive and varied and are directed at promoting accurate listening.

Second, purposes *for* listening should be suggested or developed with the children; the teacher should not simply demand that children listen *to* something. Listening should be done *for* information that can be gained, *for* appreciation of the language in a poem, *for* propaganda words, *for* directions, and so forth. Establishing standards, providing for class reactions, and discussing listening behavior will all help children discover the need for and the importance of listening.

This discovery will be further expedited if listening activities are related to the ongoing activities of the class—this is the third guideline. These activities should be within the interest and comprehension levels of the pupils so that they become personally involved, thus preventing "tuning out." Interest is also more likely to be maintained if the listening periods are not too long and if a change of activity is provided—questions, discussion, drawing, or writing something as a result of the listening.

As much variety as possible should be provided in the experiences used for teaching the listening skills. For example, films, debates, individual and group reports, dramatic activities, demonstrations, music, descriptions, explanations, discussion, and conversations may all be used. Some variations in the seating arrangement will also help. That is, when you are reading a story and showing illustrations from a book, the children might be grouped closely about you, whereas for a film they might sit in rows (with care taken to see that children at the perimeters can see well).

An effective listening program also provides for individual differences. This will include seating those children who have hearing losses as advantageously as possible, as well as providing activities of varying levels of difficulty and with varying purposes for different individuals and groups.

Of course, and most importantly, provision must be made for activities and lessons for learning and practicing the listening skills or abilities identified earlier. Directions for these activities should be well organized, and they should be presented once, with children being encouraged to think before asking to have them repeated. Attention should also be given to helping children practice ignoring distractions.

Listening can be improved by:

1. Setting specific purposes for listening.
2. Giving directions only once.
3. Listening courteously to children.
4. Setting an example by clear enunciation and accurate pronunciation.
5. Organizing material presented orally to children so that it is systematic, explicit, and brief.

The teaching of listening provides opportunities for planned integration.

Teachers' Listening

In planning instruction for children, teachers should first give attention to their own listening. They should genuinely "pay attention," "be courteous to speakers," and manifest all the other behaviors that they try to instill in children. Doing so will avoid such catastrophes as that of the teacher who responded, "Isn't that nice, dear. Now go play and have fun" after a child announced that his grandfather had died last night!

You may find yourself at a loss for words when given some valuable piece of information by a pupil. If a child says, "We got new gravel in our driveway," you may find yourself wondering, "Who cares?" But the child does care; this is something to talk about. Perhaps you might begin a discussion of stone size or the difficulty one encounters in riding a bicycle on new gravel. Give the child a sense of pride by truly listening and giving a positive response.

Teachers also need to remind themselves of factors that foster their own listening effectiveness, as well as those that block their listening. Doing so should cause them to recognize that the same factors bear on children's listening. Even the most positive conditions for listening will not ensure that a child who is hungry, sleepy, or emotionally upset will listen effectively. None of us listen very well if we are anxious or sad, thinking of other things, or simply not interested in what is being said.

> Listening is important to information processing, and its importance should be stressed in all areas of the instructional program.

LISTENING EXPERIENCES

Ideally, the improvement of listening skills should be a general goal for the entire classroom program, with children receiving frequent reminders, clues, and instruction about how to listen more effectively. It is true that listening gets little attention in some classrooms—possibly because there are no textbook series on the subject. However, both language and reading textbooks do usually contain some lessons devoted to listening skills, and these may serve as an indication that the area is worthy of inclusion in the school program. Listening is not likely to be improved much by a few book-oriented lessons, though; what is required are many experiences based on real information-processing tasks. Children need to listen for a reason. In one-to-one contacts with individual pupils you can gain a good impression of how well they listen and what might be done to help them listen better.

> **Listening for Sounds Around Us**
>
> *Street sounds*—horns tooting, gears grinding, dogs barking, people talking
> *Sounds on a trip*—getting on the bus, the bus going over a bridge, entering a pet store
> *Classroom sounds*—footsteps, blocks falling, singing, whispering

Listening Experiences for Younger Children

As discussed in Chapter 4, children in the early grades are expected to listen for many purposes: to pick out rhyming words, to discriminate among speech sounds and relate them to letters, and to identify nonspeech sounds. They listen to music and rhythms and experience listening as a stimulus for imaginative thinking and for basic communication purposes.

Young children should also be encouraged to listen for meaning. They

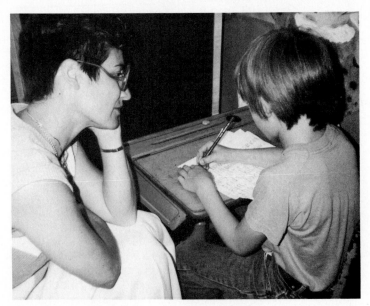

A teacher should model good listening behavior.

can listen to stories, responding with their ideas about characters, a story's ending, or what it reminded them of. And, as suggested in earlier chapters, attention to meaning can be emphasized as pupils listen to one another at sharing times, when directions are given, and as they engage in creative dramatics.

Word play is important for young children since they are constantly refining their pronunciation, increasing their vocabularies, and becoming aware of how words relate to one another and are put together. Experiences may include asking children to think of pairs of words that rhyme (*cold* and *told, fast* and *last,* etc.), to identify the rhyming words in nursery rhymes or even think of replacements ("What if the line were 'Little-Bo-Peep has lost her *dog*'?''), and to come up with answers to rhyming riddles ("I rhyme with sled and you sleep in me''). Particularly able children may enjoy such challenging activities as providing a sentence whose last word rhymes with the final word of a previous line, for example:

TEACHER: I baked a cake.

PUPIL 1:   You baked a snake?

PUPIL 2:   No, she backed into a lake.

PUPIL 3:   She baked a snake and stepped on a rake.

PUPIL 4:   My goodness sake!

A related activity is for the teacher to provide a common word ending and have the children supply a consonant or blend that will make it a word (for example, *end* becomes *send* or *ink* becomes *blink*) and then go to the board and write and pronounce the word. Or children may suggest words that begin with a different consonant or blend but end with the same letters. Once the list is fairly lengthy the children may dictate silly rhymes such as:

> I had a hen
> Who talked with men
> As she sat in the den
> And wrote with a pen.

These may be collected and put into class books for children to illustrate and read.

A simple completion activity that helps develop attentiveness is to give the beginnings of sentences that children are to complete: "Our class is going to . . ." or "Jimmy is . . ." At first a one- or two-word completion is sufficient; later, depending on the maturity of the children, they can be asked to expand on an original completion by adding words and phrases: "Jimmy is a boy," "Jimmy is a tall boy," "Jimmy is a tall boy with a red sweater," and so on.

Children of this age love to be given the responsibility of going on errands around the school building, and you can capitalize on this to help them form good listening habits. Let them carry oral messages: "Darryl, go to the office and ask Mrs. Brown for a box of chalk" or "Jennifer, please tell Mr. Johnson that the sink is leaking." More mature children can be given instructions that are complex: "Tony, collect the pictures that are finished and put them on the round table. Then put the ones not finished yet on the shelf near the door." To avoid confusion and attract the attention of the child being addressed, always say the child's name before giving directions.

Since giving instructions is so much an integral part of the school day, there is little need to construct opportunities. It is helpful, however, to be guided by three principles:

1. Use some signal to gain attention (this might be a name, a question, possibly even a note struck on the piano).
2. Speak clearly so that those involved can hear accurately.
3. Form the habit of giving directions only once.

Primary-grade children are not too young to begin to select what is relevant to a particular listening purpose. Try giving a list of objects—for example, *cookie, muffin, fork, cake, bowl*—and asking them to name those that belong in the same category. Or pronounce a series of words—such as *red, bed, loud, bread, like*—and ask which ones do not rhyme, which ones end with the same sound, or which ones begin with the same sound.

Activities for helping children learn to listen more effectively should of course be genuinely interesting and appealing. Carefully selected stories, read or told, have this appeal and are an essential part of the language arts program. For example, the book *Harry the Dirty Dog* has great appeal, and when you read it you might ask the children to listen to find out why Harry ran away (main idea) or what happened after Harry ran away (sequence). Listening to a story for the purpose of retelling it is also excellent for learning sequence—as well as for providing valuable oral language practice.

You may need to help children ferret out the main idea, determine what the sequence really is, or identify important details. Sometimes ideas that seem obvious to adults are missed by children. Try asking what is important about a story or report that could be told in one sentence (main idea). Listing details on the board will help children learn to discover those that are important and to determine sequence or organization. Telling part of a story can aid in developing many skills. Children will need to listen for the main idea, for the sequence of events, and for particular information to adapt. In addition, such an activity will help them learn to draw inferences from what they hear, since the end of the story must fit the characters' personalities, the scene, and the events that have gone before. With young children, begin by using a single sentence and having the children add another: "As I was walking through the woods one dark and stormy night, I suddenly saw a flash of light. . . . " If this is too difficult at first, you might make several suggestions and write them on the chalkboard; the children can then decide which ones fit best with the original sentence.

Listening Experiences for Older Children

In the middle and upper grades there are increasing opportunities and needs for giving oral reports and engaging in various forms of discussion; thus the possibilities for a more direct focus on listening as an information-processing activity widen. Again, success is more likely if the discussions and reports are on subjects of concern to the pupils. The construction of a new playground, for example, is a good occasion for a discussion about features especially desired by the children, such as swinging bridges and climbing ropes. Some ideas offered are likely to be pertinent; others are not. Listeners should have paper on which they can make notes—separating fact from opinion, recording details, listing questions, and so forth. After a talk by a guest speaker, the group should discuss its content and the manner of presentation.

Another listening experience valuable for this age group is to have children listen to newscasts and to comments made by political figures, especially during a campaign. Such an activity is particularly good practice in determining what is fact and what is opinion.

Children can tell stories or give descriptions, to which their listeners are to respond by making drawings illustrating what they have heard. For example, at Halloween the ugliest monster imaginable could be described. This will surely result in drawings appropriate for the season.

Activities derived from listening to your reading are also valuable. Read a particularly descriptive passage to the class and have them do drawings of the scene. Read descriptions of well-known people—popular television or rock stars as well as historical figures being studied—and have children guess who they are. Read a folk tale aloud but stop before the ending, and allow the children to guess what happens.

A Listening Tip

Before reading to the children, write on the board words which may be unfamiliar to them. Have the children pay particular attention to gaining meanings of these words.

Children of all ages enjoy poetry. They can listen to poems in order to determine the mood, or feeling. Edgar Allan Poe's "The Raven" is especially good for this type of listening (and there are many others). In addition to mood, children may also listen for pitch, stress, pauses, rhythm, and tone. Poetry and stories unknown to the children may be read for several purposes (other than enjoyment and related literary ones). Two such purposes are to determine an appropriate title and to give practice in the use of context clues to figure out word meanings.

Sentences with one or more words omitted may be read, and the children asked to supply the missing words. For example, "Last year the _____ nearly killed a man, even though the park rangers affectionately called him 'Old Grizzle.'"

As children listen to many types of stories by a variety of authors (and write stories themselves), they can be asked to note how a writer creates an atmosphere by using certain words. They can also note how sentences may be used in particular ways; for instance, a series of short, choppy ones gives a sense of movement or excitement.

Videotaping of commercial television broadcasts can provide many possibilities for listening activities. Tapes of popular situation comedies can be played so that children can study the dialogue to see how much of the story is told via speech and how much through visual content. The language of sports commentators, cartoons, and commercials can be examined to identify examples of "incorrect" language usage and pronunciation. Commercials can also be examined for techniques used to convince viewers to make purchases. And, of course, newscasts and other worthwhile programs can be used to focus on listening skills.

The use of audiovisual aids can add much to listening activities. For instance, before giving an oral report, a child can list on the board or use an overhead projector to show questions pertaining to the report. Afterward, these questions can serve as a guide for a discussion of the main ideas, details, and sequence of what was said. At first, the children will need help in selecting and wording the questions.

Repeat-and-add games keep children interested and help to develop interesting sentences as well as to foster good listening habits.

A Bulletin Board Idea

A GOOD LISTENER

1. Has a purpose for listening.
2. Thinks while listening.
3. Is not distracted from listening.
4. Controls his or her emotions.
5. Recognizes his or her responsibility to the speaker.
6. Prepares to react to what is heard.

PUPIL 1: Thunder.

PUPIL 2: The thunder roared.

PUPIL 3: The thunder roared and the lightning flashed.

Another activity that is fun for the children is to listen to classmates reading orally and try to determine the punctuation. They may also evaluate the reader in terms of his or her ability to read with feeling, to "capture" the audience, and to convey the author's message. Encourage questions related to specific listening skills. For example: "What did Jim talk about?" (main idea) or "What did he say first, next, and last?" (details and sequence). Giving tests orally also provides useful practice in listening. That is, instead of writing questions on the board or passing out written forms, read test questions to the class (this works best with questions requiring short answers). Also try assigning various children the task of listening to and recording assignments so that they can be telephoned to a child who is absent.

An activity that is valuable in helping children understand usage problems, appreciate differences in speech, and understand various speakers is listening to different dialects. The New Englander's speech is not the same as that of the Southerner or the Midwesterner. Likewise, the male adult's speech and female adult's speech often present different listening tasks. Try recording the speech of friends and acquaintances who speak different dialects, have high or low voices, speak rapidly or slowly, and so on. Keep in mind, too, that music, such as the songs of Stephen Foster or modern country-western songs, offers excellent opportunities for listening to dialects.

LISTENING LESSONS

Plan for:

children to listen to each other
your listening to children
a balanced and not over-powering amount of listening
readiness for a listening activity

The following are examples of the types of direct instructional activities that may be used in a classroom to teach listening skills. Content for these activities may be taken from textbooks for the subject areas or may even be adapted from reading exercises in teachers' manuals or workbooks, since the purposes for reading and listening are so closely related. As was stated earlier, though, daily attention to listening in meaningful classroom activities should preclude the need for the direct instruction represented by these

Talking and listening occur naturally as pupils work in cooperation with one another.

examples. On the other hand, such lessons can confirm how effectively the children are learning the listening skills as well as provide the practice that some may need.

Selecting Details

Ask the children to listen for details about Virginia City and how it became a ghost town as you read the following:

> The miners living in Virginia City in 1860 lived in frame shanties and tents made of canvas, potato sacks, old shirts, and blankets. Two years later, however, the shacks and tents had been replaced by hotels, rooming houses, and homes—all of substantial construction. Three years after that the silver mines were closed because the silver ore began to give out. It seemed that Virginia City would become a ghost town, but new veins of silver were discovered and the life of the city revived. In 1875 a fire devoured the city, and that event, combined with a decline in mining, brought on the ghost town appearance of Virginia City as it is today.

Follow the reading by asking questions such as these:

> What were the tents of the early miners made of?
> When was the fire in Virginia City?
> What was mined in Virginia City?
> Why did Virginia City become a ghost town?

Finding the Main Idea

Write these sentences on the board and cover them:

> The burro is a very gentle animal.
> Children ride on their burros.
> The burro is a favorite pet in Mexico.
> The children give names to their burros.

Ask the children to listen carefully to what they are about to hear and to think of the one idea it tells about. Read the following paragraph:

> Many children in Mexico have burros for pets. The burro is so gentle that a small child can take care of him. The children enjoy riding on their burros. Sometimes the children ride them in parades. They call their pet burros by name, and talk to them just as they talk to one another. Often a boy will carry sugar in his pocket. His burro will follow him, sniffing in his pocket to get the sugar.

Uncover the sentences and read them aloud. Ask the children to write the sentence that is the main idea of the paragraph.

Following Directions

Try several activities involving one child telling another how to draw a figure or do something similar while their backs are turned to one another. This will cause them to think carefully about what they are saying and hearing.

Give a sheet of lined paper to each pupil and say something like "Today we are going to make a terrarium. But first we need to go over the directions. I'll read them to you, step by step. Listen carefully, and write down just a few words to remind you of each step. When we know exactly what we must do to build the terrarium, we will begin." The directions might be as follows:

1. Lay out the pieces of glass (except the piece for the top) on the table. Put the largest piece in the center and the smaller pieces around it, matching the smaller pieces with the sides of the large piece.
2. Fasten the largest piece of glass (the bottom) to each of the side pieces using wide adhesive tape.
3. Make sure that all exposed edges of the glass are taped.
4. Use tape to hinge the glass for the top to the rear of the terrarium.
5. Remember that the top is taped to the rest of the terrarium only on the rear side.
6. Tape the edges of the hinged top so that no glass edges are exposed.
7. Place the terrarium on a solid surface, and cover the bottom with about an inch of fine, clean sand.
8. Place the plants in the sand, leaving them in the pots.
9. Add pieces of driftwood, rocks, and other objects to make the terrarium attractive.

Getting Word Meanings

Write the words *exalt* and *ravine* on the board. Ask the pupils if they know the meanings of them. Write the meanings they give on the board and then ask them to listen to this paragraph to find out if they were right:

A little way off, to the left, stood a small house; and to the right was another, before which stood the wagons belonging to his father. Directly in front was a wide expanse of rolling prairie, cut by a deep ravine. To the north, beyond the small farm, which was fenced, a still wider region rolled away into unexplored and marvelous distance. Altogether it was a land to exalt a boy who had lived all his life in thickly settled Wisconsin.

Following the reading, the meanings of the words should again be discussed and looked up in a dictionary if necessary.

Distinguishing Between the Relevant and the Irrelevant

Ask the pupils to listen to the following selection and to be ready to tell which sentences are needed to gain the meaning and which do not really relate to the remainder of the selection.

There were six boys beside the campfire. The dry sticks blazed and the heavy logs glowed with the heat. It was almost time to put the fish in the frying pan. The boys had poked the potatoes in their foil wrappings and already they were softening. Jim's older brother had stayed at home. He was going to college this fall. All the boys were hungry and were anxious to eat. Bill put on more wood and Bob got the frying pan.

Ask the pupils to tell why the sentences that do not relate to the remainder of the paragraph are not needed to gain the meaning.

Drawing Inferences

Tell the pupils to listen to the following paragraph in order to answer some questions that can only be answered by listening "between the lines."

The air was crisp and clear, but a wet snow had pelted the windows last night. I breathed deeply, glanced toward the snow-covered cars parked along the curb, and thought, "What a beautiful day." Suddenly I came down with a bump on the sidewalk.

Ask these questions and discuss the meaning of making inferences:

Why did the speaker fall?
Does the speaker live in town or in the country?
Had it stopped snowing?

AIDS FOR DEVELOPING LISTENING SKILLS

Many resources are available to aid teachers in the development of more effective listening. Activities as diverse as adapting reading comprehension exercises and using videotape recordings are possible. With some creative thinking and careful preparation you can have a stimulating and successful program.

Audio Tape Recorders

For information on obtaining tapes of educational radio programs, write to National Public Radio, 2025 M Street, N.W., Washington, DC 20036.

Inexpensive audio cassette recorders allow teachers many opportunities to extend their teaching. You can record directions, test questions, stories, and various types of information, leaving you free to observe the children as they work, give individual help, and devise further activities. Many teachers record their spelling tests, for example, as described in Chapter 11. Directions for practice exercises can also be put on tape: "In the first row make a mark on the object whose name begins with the same sound as ball." Or you might tape study questions to be used with reading assigned in social studies or some other subject area. You can even allow space on the tape for recording children's answers so that the cassette can be used later for studying.

A "Listening Center" consisting of cassette players on a table allows individual and small-group listening.

Children can be encouraged to use a cassette recorder to extend understanding in science, social studies, and literature. They might tape a famous

A listening center may be used in many ways.

passage from a book, for instance, and then play it for classmates to see who can identify it (they might also take it around to other classes or even to adults in the building). An individual child can select a character he or she has learned about in social studies and prepare a tape of this person supposedly talking about herself or himself. The tape can be made available for anyone to listen to, and it might even be the basis for a "Guess the Mystery Guest" contest. A variation of this activity might involve taping several statements about a particular person; the other children then discuss these and decide which are fact and which opinon.

Children can also be encouraged to use the cassette recorder to evaluate their own performances and discover their own errors. The child who has enunciation or pronunciation problems may enjoy "playing teacher"—recording his or her own reading of a story and then listening to the tape to discover and correct errors. You will need to work with most children to help them learn this technique, but if you think children cannot hear their own mistakes, try listening to your own recorded voice and see how many speech mannerisms and habits you discover that you were unaware of. Taping is also very effective when children are preparing for a play, a choral reading presentation, an oral report, or any other activity to be presented before an audience—even if that audience is only the class itself.

You will find recording helpful for activities suggested in other chapters as well. For example, in connection with a unit on interviewing, the children will enjoy taping and then listening to an opinion survey program on a topic such as the following: "Should the frog replace the bird as a decorative symbol?'' There could be a discussion of frog wallpaper, frog placemats, frog lampposts, frog's nest soup, frog watchers, and who knows what else to stimulate listening and stir creative thinking.

Taping chapters or portions of chapters may help children who do not read well with difficult reading in the content areas. To establish listening purposes, preface the reading with taped questions, perhaps selected from those given at the end of the chapter. As reinforcement, provide written copies of the questions to be answered or begin the tape with an instruction something like this: ''Before you listen to the tape, turn to page 46 in your textbook and read questions 1, 2, and 3. Read carefully; then reread to be sure you remember what to listen for. Keep your book open as you listen so you can check yourself. Now turn off the tape recorder until you have read the questions and are ready to begin listening.''

Video Recorders

Chapter 5 described many possible uses of the video recorder in developing oral language, and this aid has equal relevance to listening. Many of the activities suggested for the audio cassette recorder will be even more effective if video equipment is available. Of particular value are recordings made of talks by guest speakers. (A television weather commentator, for example, may be willing to come to a class and discuss both weather forecasting and

Inexpensive video equipment makes it possible for children to make tapes and then look at and listen to them.

television broadcasting.) Students can watch such a tape several times to see how the "pro" is trying to help them listen better.

Recorded Music

Using music activities to develop listening skills is both helpful and enjoyable. For example, children can be given pictures of musical instruments along with information about the sounds produced by each instrument. Then, as they listen to "Peter and the Wolf," for example, the children hold up the picture of each instrument as it is played. This may be varied by giving each child only one or two pictures; the children will need to listen carefully so that they will not miss their instruments.

A good motion activity is to play music and have the children move in time to the rhythm. They love to march to something like Sousa's "Semper Fidelis." (Older students might be stimulated to learn more about Sousa and his life as bandmaster of the United States Marine Corps band.) More creative interpretations of rhythm and mood may result from "The Dancing Doll" (Edward Poldini) or "Claire de Lune" (Claude Debussy).

Such pieces as "Claire de Lune," "Parade of the Wooden Soldiers," and "Danse Macabre" are good for drawing out what the music makes a child think of. (The children should not be told the titles.) Sometimes their interpretations might be in the form of pictures that can be displayed and discussed. The composer's purpose can also be discussed, with this discussion leading to a comparison of the composer's inspiration with their reactions.

This procedure may be reversed, of course, by telling the children the story behind a particular composition, such as "The Sorcerer's Apprentice" (Paul Dukas), and then having them listen to see how the music and the instruments reflect the theme and mood of the story.

Poetry, normally thought of as being most effective when listened to as it is read, is also enjoyable when set to music. A good example of this is Maurice Sendak's "Really Rosie." Others include Shel Silverstein's "Where the Sidewalk Ends" and "A Light in the Attic." Although not totally set to music, "The Chinese Red Riding Hoods" and "Poems and Songs of the Middle Earth" might also be used.

Music is a natural corollary to social studies. Martial music of different wars, folk songs of many types and lands, spirituals—these and many other types of music will help children to truly understand the people who lived in other times and in other lands. Ask your school music director for help in selecting music of these types.

Books

There are many books that build interest in listening, suggesting things to listen to and for. Many others have stories that are appealing to listen to and are helpful in making children aware of listening and in teaching listening skills. Here are some:

Baylor, Byrd. *Plink Plink Plink*. Houghton Mifflin, 1971.
Borten, Helen. *Do You Hear What I Hear?* Abelard-Schuman, 1960.

Branley, Franklyn M. *High Sounds, Low Sounds.* Crowell, 1967.
Brown, Margaret Wise. *The Indoor Noisy Book.* Harper & Row, 1942.
Elkin, Benjamin. *The Loudest Noise in the World.* Viking, 1954.
Emberley, Ed. *Klippity Klop.* Little, Brown, 1974.
Erdoes, Richard, ed. *The Sound of Flutes and Other Indian Legends.* Pantheon, 1976.
Erwin, Betty K. *Behind the Magic Line.* Little, Brown, 1969.
Hamilton, Virginia. *Zeely.* Macmillan (Aladdin Books), 1986.
Hanson, Joan. *More Homonyms: Steak and Stake and Other Words That Sound the Same but Look as Different as Chili and Chilly.* Lerner, 1973.
Johnston, Tony. *Night Noises and Other Mole and Troll Stories.* Putnam's 1977.
Mayer, Mercer. *What Do You Do with a Kangaroo?* Four Winds, 1973.
O'Neill, Mary L. *What Is That Sound?* Atheneum, 1966.
Rand, Ann and Paul. *Sparkle and Spin.* Harcourt, 1957.
Showers, Paul. *The Listening Walk.* Crowell, 1961.
Spier, Peter. *Crash! Bang! Boom!* Doubleday, 1972.
Tresselt, Alvin. *Wake Up, City!* Lothrop, Lee and Shepard, 1957.
Wahl, Jan. *Crabapple Night.* Holt, Rinehart and Winston, 1971.

Of special interest in the area of listening are "predictable" books of the kind mentioned in Chapter 4. These books are written in such a way that patterns occur or there are other good clues as to how sentences are likely to end. If the children listen, they can anticipate what is coming next, which enhances their enjoyment of the book and also promotes careful listening. Here are some examples of this kind of book:

Brown, Margaret Wise. *Goodnight Moon.* Harper & Row, 1977.
Carle, Eric. *The Very Hungry Caterpillar.* Putnam's, 1986.
Duff, Maggie. *Rum Pum Pum: A Folk Tale from India.* Macmillan, 1978.
Hutchins, Pat. *Rosie's Walk,* Aladdin, 1971.
Martin, Bill. *Brown Bear, Brown Bear, What Do You See?* Holt, Rinehart and Winston, 1973.
———. *Fire! Fire! Said Mrs. McGuire.* Holt, Rinehart and Winston, 1970.
Parkes, Brenda. *Who's in the Shed?* Rigby Education, 1986.
Zemach, Harve. *The Judge: An Untrue Tale.* Farrar, Straus and Giroux, 1969.

EVALUATION OF LISTENING

Am I a Good Listener?

1. Do I pay careful attention and not do anything distracting?
2. Do I show appreciation without calling attention to myself by commenting or laughing too loudly?
3. Do I jot down questions or notes for later discussion with the speaker?

Without some form of measurement or testing, a teacher does not know whether listening lessons and activities are achieving the desired objectives. Equally important is the fact that each child needs feedback to guide his or her learning. Of course, well-designed lessons provide considerable evidence to both the teacher and the children of how effective the listening was for the particular lessons. However, some evidence beyond that attained in such a way is needed to determine growth.

Standards

Developing standards or guidelines for specific types of listening activities or lessons—for instance, oral reports or panel discussions, watching a film, listening to a story—is very useful. Not only do such standards provide a measure of guidance to speakers, but they give individual children a means for making judgments about their listening. They also provide guidance for a class or group evaluation.

The following is an example of a set of second-grade standards:

> *A Good Listener*
>
> Looks at the person talking.
> Doesn't talk.
> Thinks about what is said.
> Remembers what he or she is listening for.

Standards should become more specific than this example as the children mature and as they focus on different types of listening situations and purposes. Standards should always, however, be developed with the children rather than being imposed on them. Intermediate-grade children can develop standards based on such questions as these:

Do I keep in mind the main idea of what I'm listening to?
Am I courteous in my listening?
Do I reserve judgment until the end of a presentation?
Am I aware of transitional phrases and what they mean?
Do I recognize bias on the part of the speaker?
Do I remember what I am listening for?

Checklists

Statements of standards can be translated into checklists such as the one below, and these can be used by pupils to keep a written record of their listening skills.

My Listening Checklist

	YES	NO
1. Could I hear and see the speaker?	——	——
2. Was I ready to think about what the speaker said?	——	——
3. Was I ready to learn?	——	——
4. Was I able to discover the direction the speaker was taking?	——	——
5. Did I determine the main idea?	——	——
6. Did I use clues the speaker provided?	——	——
7. Was I able to pick out information supporting the main idea?	——	——
8. Was I able to summarize what the speaker said?	——	——

Tests

There are published tests that purport to measure listening ability or skills. These may be examined to see whether they are suitable for your program. You may, however, construct your own tests for detecting particular types of weaknesses in listening ability and for giving focus to the specific attention you need to give to listening. For example, to test pupils' abilities to listen for details, present material that contains details to listen for either orally or via a recording. In the same manner, you can direct test content and questions at evaluating skill in separating fact from opinion, in answering specific questions, in getting the main idea, in recognizing propaganda, or in using contextual clues to get word meanings. The listening lessons suggested earlier in this chapter provide examples of the way such tests can be constructed.

A FINAL WORD

An effective elementary-school language arts program exposes children to a broad range of listening experiences and relates these to speaking, reading, and writing. In school or out, much information processing occurs from listening, and this processing needs to be done as rapidly and effectively as possible. Thus systematic attention to children's listening attitudes and skills is necessary, including instruction in the skills as needed.

References

Basic Listening Skills. Illinois State Board of Education, 1982.

Devine, Thomas G. *Listening Skills Schoolwide*. National Council of Teachers of English, 1982.

Lundsteen, Sara W. *Listening: Its Impact on Reading and the Other Language Arts*. National Council of Teachers of English, 1979.

Oregon Listening Curriculum, Primary and Intermediate Units. Oregon Teaching Center (239 North 4th Street, Redmond, OR 97756), 1976.

Seiler, William.; Schuelke, David; and Lieb-Brilhart, Barbara. *Communication for the Contemporary Classroom*. Holt, Rinehart and Winston, 1984.

Teaching Resources

Most films and videos of an educational nature made for children can provide worthwhile listening experiences. Many companies, several of which are identified in various chapters of this book, produce worthwhile films, sound filmstrips, and videotapes.

Listening Between the Lines. Alfred Higgins Productions (video; intermediate).

Listening Comprehension Skills Kit. Curriculum Associates (two levels; cassettes, etc.).

Listening Corner. Houghton Mifflin (manual, worksheets, cassettes; K–grade 3).

Listening Skills Unit. Aquarius People Materials, 1983 (grades 1–6).

Listening with a Purpose. Random House (twelve audio cassettes, response books, manual, and guide; grades 3–7).

Scholastic Listening Skills. Scholastic (kit).

Your Communication Skills—Listening. Coronet (video; grades 1–6).

Activities for Preservice Teachers

1. Obtain the instructor's permission to read a news article aloud to one of your classes and then give a comprehension test. How much variation in listening ability is there in the group? Do you believe that the best listeners are also the best students? (Repeat the test a week later and see what happens.)

2. Examine basal series in reading and language and identify "lessons in listening." Do you find any? What do they consist of? Report your results to the class.

3. Try to improve your own listening. Anticipate what speakers are going to say by looking for clues as to how the material being presented is organized and paying particular attention to summaries and conclusions. Do you notice any improvement in your comprehension?

4. Plan an activity for which specific directions must be given. Go over what you have prepared very carefully, noting where you have been incomplete or vague. Then try out the directions to see if someone can follow them exactly.

5. Add to the list of "listening books" given in this chapter.

6. With the permission of the speaker, record a lecture using both audio and video cassettes. Play both tapes several times, noting differences between the two formats.

7. Talk with several teachers about what they do to teach listening. Do they relate teaching of listening skills to teaching in the content areas of the curriculum? Do they use audio recordings they make or ones marketed commercially? What do they do about listening that is related to their teaching of reading? Report to the class on your findings.

8. Examine publishers' and distributors' catalogs for materials useful in teaching listening. Also check sources that review such materials (for example, *Language Arts, The Reading Teacher,* and *The School Library Journal*). Give particular attention to materials that relate listening to other aspects of the curriculum.

Activities for Inservice Teachers

1. Find out how many of the children in your class have their own cassette recorders. If several do, begin to plan some ways in which they could use the recorders to contribute to their class work.

2. Review the requirements for listening in your daily program. What changes might be made with respect to the amount of listening expected of the children and the amount of guidance in how to improve their listening? Discuss this with the children.

3. Consider establishing a "listening center" in your classroom. What materials will you need? What space can be used? What sorts of activities will be emphasized?

4. Talk with a curriculum consultant or supervisor about some activities you might try that combine listening, thinking, note taking, and other study skills. (See Chapter 13 for further information.)

5. Try out different physical arrangements in your classroom and see if any seem to have a positive effect on listening behavior.

6. Visit the instructional media center of your school or district to determine what materials are available (such as video and audio recorders and players, prepared tapes, and activity kits) that might be used in teaching listening.

7. Tape discussions of small groups and then permit children to listen to them to see how much of what was said was actually listened to.

8. Tape directions for games. While the children are listening and following the directions, you can observe how well they listen.

9. Examine state or district curriculum guides in language arts to see what they recommend concerning listening. Discuss the need for attention to listening with members of a curriculum committee or an appropriate supervisor.

10. Prepare sets of listening lessons of the types discussed in this chapter for use with your children. Try these lessons, and report the results and your observations to the class.

Independent Activities for Children

1. Tape-record various sounds—street traffic, children playing, sports crowds, and animal noises, for example—and ask children to listen to these and write as many associated words as they think of. The children can then write stories and poems based on these words.

2. Have pairs of children use "walkie-talkies" to practice taking messages and making notes (they can pretend to be secret agents or police on a stakeout).

3. Tape recordings of stories can be useful in many ways. For example, one child could listen to the story and select the best title from a list of possibilities provided on a card. Another could listen for the main idea or the sequence of events. A third could listen to discover the feeling or mood or to find words that bring to mind particular pictures—tall house, round face, worn shoe, and so on.

4. Have a child perform an experiment or construct an object after listening to directions only once. Directions may be taped, or they may be read by another child. Taped directions should be spaced to allow time to perform each step; the tasks might be simple ones such as folding paper to make a hat. Oral directions for three to five simple tasks could be given all at once, for example: "Go to the window and raise the shade about two inches. Then come back, sit down in your chair, and fold your arms." Children will enjoy thinking up unusual directions and attempting to perform tasks accurately.

5. Record tests such as those in *My Weekly Reader* for children to take individually.

6. Have a child listen to a recorded story or description and then draw a picture of the scene described or an episode in the story.

7. A child can listen to a recorded story and then prepare cut-outs to use with a flannel board while telling the story to other children. Listening individually permits the child to relisten to parts of the story in order to develop the sequence and to decide what illustrations she or he needs.

8. Have a child make a list of all the sounds heard in a particular place—for example, in the lunch line, on the playground, or at a certain street corner on the way to school. As an added bonus, the child might use the list to write a "sound picture" of the spot or try to find the best words to describe each sound.

9. As a variation of the preceding activity, a child can sit quietly in a corner of the room listening for sounds such as a clock ticking, a car going by, a whistle, a buzzer, a dog barking, or walking in the hall. He or she should write down a word or two for each sound heard. Or two children can listen for the same period of time and compare the number of sounds they have heard.

10. Children can work in pairs, with one child reading a sentence and the other listening for words that sound alike. Sentences such as the following might be used:

> Jane knew that her mother would bring a new dress.
> The whole class saw the hole in the fence.

11. A child can listen to the weather report on radio or television and be prepared to present a forecast to the class, including expected temperature range, probability of precipitation, and so forth.

12. Newscasts can be listened to for the major topic reported, the name of the newscaster, the name of a public figure mentioned in the newscast, and so on.

13. Have a child take notes on an assembly program or a program presented to the class for the purpose of preparing a written summary for the class diary.

14. Oral presentations may be improved if a child tapes a poem or story she or he is going to read to the class and then listens to it several times to discover ways to improve the reading.

Chapter 7

Grammar and Language Usage

*T*he teaching of grammar has been a longstanding tradition in elementary schools, and in an earlier day these were called "grammar schools"—an appropriate name then, since a major portion of the curriculum was devoted to learning grammatical terminology, memorizing rules, and doing exercises. It was presumed that these activities would teach children to speak and write acceptably, certainly an admirable goal, not only then but now. The presumption was not and is not valid. However, despite evidence provided by both research and experience, the tradition unfortunately continues in too many schools today. The grammar taught today may be "new" rather than "traditional" (that is, a noun may be identified by the presence of a "noun marker" rather than being defined as "the name of a person, place, or thing") but the teaching is often just as formal and unproductive. Some schools and some teachers, however, are discovering that there are better ways to teach children to speak and write effectively and correctly. This chapter discusses these better ways. In addition, it describes the difference between grammar and usage as well as that between both of these and mechanics or conventions, examines the terms *standard English* and *dialect,* and shows how all of these areas relate to the development of an effective language arts program in the elementary school.

LEARNING AND TEACHING GRAMMAR

To many people the word *grammar* means "the rules" of sentence construction for speaking and writing correctly, including those rules concerning punctuation, spelling, and handwriting. Less concern is shown—particularly outside of schools—to the term *usage,* which refers to the form of expression, the choice of words a person makes when writing or talking. Saying "It is me" instead of "It is I" or "We was going" instead of "We were going" is a usage choice. Grammar, on the other hand, refers to the system of word structures and word arrangements in expression. All four of the examples just used are grammatical; however, expressions such as "Were going we" and "All the boy and girl are going" are ungrammatical.

Development of Grammar

Native speakers of English have the ability to judge whether or not a string of words is arranged in an acceptable manner, "acceptable," that is, in the sense of conveying meaning without regard to appropriateness for use in all social and business situations. Native speakers know the grammar of the language, at least in a general sense; they learn it at the *intuitive* level by communicating thoughts and acquiring meanings as they grow up. They would possess such knowledge even if they never went to school.

This learning of grammar begins to be apparent at the age of eighteen to twenty months when babies put together two-word combinations. Most of these early expressions (called "telegraphic speech") involve a few words used in a particular position with a variety of other words. This type of experimentation lasts only a short time, but it is an important step. The child who says "Chair mama," "Chair dada," and "See chair" is trying out word order. Very young children gradually become aware that some types of words come first and others second. As compared with that of an adult, the child's understanding is sometimes faulty but, even so, it provides evidence of the development of a language system, or grammar, characteristic of the child's level of maturity.

Children learn the classes of words early (although not, of course, the grammatical terminology), as they demonstrate by using many of their first words in different contexts. The repeated words are likely to be nouns and verbs or, less often, adjectives. At this stage the meanings expressed are largely dependent on the context. The child who says "Mommy sock" may mean "Mommy, put on the sock" or, perhaps, "This is Mommy's sock." Toddlers continue to talk predominantly about the here and now but begin to use longer utterances, such as "Me push truck" or "Go outside swing now." Various sentence types appear: "He no hit you" and "Where Daddy go?" Pronouns begin to be used: "I go bed" and, of course, "Mine! Give me!"

This early development shows that children attach meanings to the words they use, that they know that the functions of these words may differ, and that they realize conveying meaning depends on the order in which the words are spoken. Their utterances provide clear evidence that young children develop an early understanding of the language system. Although this grammar is not the same as that of a mature speaker, it is a definite step toward it. Young children have not yet learned how such elements as auxiliary verbs, prepositions, and inflectional endings work, but as their experimenting continues, they do learn to use them. In fact, they begin to try out noun and verb endings with such constructions as *foots, goed, mines,* and so forth. Using these overgeneralizations, they gradually learn from the responses of others that some ways of saying things are approved and others are not. As they mature, children learn how to make many generalizations about language use, but some of this learning takes a while.

Children entering a nursery school or even kindergarten or first grade are not yet literate in the generally accepted sense of the word, but they understand rather complex sentences when they hear them and know if a part of a sentence has been omitted or is in the wrong place. They speak in phrases and sentences that reflect their knowledge of language patterns. They know many words, and they know the language system well enough to realize that structural changes can be made in some words to achieve particular purposes and meanings (for example, adding endings such as *-s, -es, -er,* and *-ing*). Some children of this age occasionally confuse word order, add the wrong ending or fail to add an ending at all, or have prob-

A four-year-old knows, without being taught, that we say "two red balls" but not "red two balls."

The examples of utterances are from Chapter 4 of Bryen's *Inquiries into Child Language.*

lems with tense or person, but the basic understanding of the system is present and developing. If it were not, the children would not have been able to communicate during their preschool years.

The important fact to recognize is that children have reached quite an advanced level of language development by the time they enter school. However, since not all children are at the same level at this or any other point during their school years, language development must be a concern of the school. This concern should be focused on the individual child as much as possible, since further development is likely to be sporadic—some children will only be able to grasp the basics, others will soon be ready to learn about placement of modifiers, using the passive voice, and developing complex sentences.

The Place of Grammar Teaching

Hillocks (see References) has reviewed the evidence accumulated from research over many years that studying grammar has no effect on ability to write well.

As was stated earlier, the teaching of grammar—of any type or description—is supposed to help people write and speak more effectively. Actually, there is no evidence that learning classification systems, memorizing rules about word relationships, or diagramming sentences has any such outcome. In fact, there is evidence to the contrary, evidence that has been accumulating for more than eighty years. Elementary-school children (and secondary-school students as well) do not improve in expressive abilities by learning abstractions and applying rules. They gain communicative competence from direct experiences and attention to such specifics as variation of sentence patterns, vocabulary development, and the use of the most effective language. Children learn to write by writing and to speak by speaking, while receiving ongoing guidance from teachers who are sufficiently sensitive and knowledgeable to see where progress can be made.

Weaver (see References) gives an overview of grammar and grammar teaching.

For years elementary-school teachers have been prodded into teaching grammar by complaints, both real and imagined, from secondary-school teachers that pupils come to them unable to identify the parts of speech or tell a subject from a predicate. Of course, such inability has no direct bearing on developing effectiveness in speech or writing, and there is no evidence that the teaching of grammar in the secondary school has any more bearing on writing and speech than it does in the elementary school. Pressure has also come from secondary-school foreign language teachers. Complaints from these teachers about students not "knowing" grammar reveal an apparent unawareness that there is no "universal grammar" and that nearly fifty years of research evidence shows that the teaching of English grammar—of whatever type—has no bearing on the learning of a foreign language.

Many teachers, even some who know better, feel pressured to teach grammar by the language textbooks they are assigned to use.

However, if the kinds of informal teaching procedures suggested in this book are followed, pupils entering junior or senior high school will very likely be able to identify subjects, predicates, and parts of speech. Certainly, if a teacher says to a student "Can you think of a better adjective to use?" it is legitimate to expect the student to know which word is the adjective. And the same may be said for the other major grammar items. But such knowledge can and should be taught as a corollary to actual speech and writing, not in isolation or as something of value in and of itself.

Examining Grammars

Grammars—defined as descriptions of the structure of a language—have developed and continue to develop in different forms and at different times. This process has been documented as linguists seek better explanations for the workings of the complex phenomenon that is language. The following discussions of the grammars most commonly identified are necessarily brief and not intended to provide a thorough understanding of any one. Nor are they intended as something to be taught to elementary-school childen. But as a teacher of language arts, you should have a solid understanding of your language and its workings. If you do not, you should obtain that knowledge through further study, so that you may be better prepared to teach children "about language."

Traditional Grammar. **Traditional grammar** is a description of English that is based on the system of the Latin language. Historically, it was called simply *grammar;* the modifier *traditional* was added only recently when other grammars began to appear. This description first arose about four centuries ago as an effort to explain why particular words were used or certain sentences constructed, and, since Latin was at that time the language of scholars, it was natural to choose Latin as the basis for the description. Words were classified into eight categories—nouns, verbs, pronouns, adjectives, adverbs, prepositions, conjunctions, and interjections—and there were subclasses for most of these (for example, common and proper nouns, transitive and intransitive verbs). Rules and definitions were formulated to show how these categories are related to one another and how they can be combined into "correct" sentences.

The problem with this description was the assumption that all languages have the same system—all do, of course, have some system. But English is a polyglot language. It is descended to some extent from Latin, but it also has origins in the Germanic languages. Thus, it was—and still is—difficult to formulate rules that accommodate the many irregularities of English. Consider, for example, the formation of plurals: a majority of nouns form their plurals by the addition of *s* or *es,* but that "rule" does not cover the question of whether a final *s* should be doubled before the *es* is added or the multiplicity of exceptions, such as *knife* and *knives, foot* and *feet,* and *child* and *children.* Furthermore, there is great irregularity in the conjugation of some commonly used verbs; even people who think they know English grammar fairly well may sometimes have to consult a dictionary to make sure of the correct past tense or participle.

Despite these problems, traditional grammar was for years (and too often still is) taught formally, in the belief that learning its rules and definitions would teach children to write and speak "correctly." Perhaps because of being taught so formally, traditional grammar has become prescriptive rather than descriptive and has not reflected the facts that there are different levels of usage and that so-called correct usages that are awkward or difficult to learn are likely to change or become obsolete. Children have spent many hours learning to say "It is I" or "The stranger was he," but this type of structure is seldom used in writing and is today considered

Textbook exercises are generally useless for teaching more effective speaking and writing.

stilted in speech. Similarly, much time has been wasted in doing exercises that involve selecting *who* or *whom* (often in badly constructed sentences), even though an examination of current writing (at all levels) would demonstrate that *whom* has virtually disappeared from our language.

It should be noted, however, that those who attempted the first description of English were pioneers. There may have been some flaws in their description, but their classification of words is still valid. Words such as *the* and *my* are now often called noun markers rather than articles or possessive pronouns; conjunctions and prepositions may be called connectors, clause markers, or phrase markers; but the four major classifications—noun, verb, adjective, and adverb—are still recognized. The important thing to remember is that English is a hybrid, complex, growing language, yet children have learned to use it well enough to satisfy their needs even before coming to school. They will learn to use it more effectively not by studying grammar, either traditional or modern, but by having many and varied experiences involving reading, writing, speaking, and listening.

Structural Grammar.   A product of the scientific study by linguists of the way English is spoken and written, **structural grammar** does not prescribe what is "correct" but simply reports the language as it exists. The ways words are put together have been categorized, producing certain principles and patterns. These include basic sentence patterns, a rather small number in English, as shown here:

1. Birds fly.	Only two words—one the subject and the other the verb
2. Birds eat seeds.	Subject, action verb, and the recipient of the action
3. Birds are animals.	Subject, linking verb, and a noun which completes the meaning
4. Birds are beautiful.	Subject, linking verb, and an adjective which completes the meaning
5. Birds give me pleasure.	Subject, verb, indirect object, and direct object
6. Birds make people happy.	Subject, verb, direct object, and an adjective which completes the meaning
7. They called birds vampires.	Subject, verb, direct object, and a noun which completes the meaning

In traditional grammar a word is described in terms of its meaning: "A noun is the name of a person, place, or thing" or "A verb expresses action, being, or state of being." In structural grammar, on the other hand, words are described in terms of form and function. As mentioned previously, the four major classes of words are called by their traditional names, but words such as *the, my,* and *some* are called determiners or noun markers; they signal that the word that follows is a noun. There are also verb markers (such as *can, could, might*), clause markers (*because, if, how*), phrase

Children may enjoy creating nonsense words and making sentences with them. This activity is fun, but there is no evidence that it leads to better use of the language.

markers (*in, down, toward*), intensifiers or qualifiers (*very, just, less*), and connectors or conjunctions (*and, but, for*).

This system also has its problems, however. One way to illustrate some of them is to examine a nonsense statement: *Ra jerfuls buked ra vaky marm pugly. Ra* is almost certainly an article, or noun marker, since it appears twice in a position where these are ususally found. *Jerfuls,* then, is probably a noun (it also ends in *s,* an indication that it may be a plural form of a noun), and it occurs in the place where the subject is found much of the time; so tentatively *jerfuls* can be identified as the subject. *Buked* appears to be the verb, since it is in a typical position for a verb (this also confirms *jerfuls* as the subject, since the verb usually follows) and ends with *ed*, indicating past tense. At first glance, *vaky* might be the direct object but *marm* is more likely to be, since *vaky*—because of its position and *y* ending—is probably an adjective describing *marm*. And *pugly* must be an adverb because of its position in the sentence and *ly* ending.

Although this is a logical way to go about examining and explaining the way the language works, again the hybrid nature of English creates problems. Consider how many times the word *probably* or its equivalent was used in the preceding description. There is a very good reason for this; suppose, for example, that the translation of the nonsense sentence is "The girls called the expensive dress ugly" or "Our enemies found our ally most unfriendly." Then, neither its ending nor its position makes *pugly* an adverb or *vaky* an adjective, and we must fall back on meaning to make a determination. Other possibilities exist, of course, but these are sufficient to illustrate the difficulties faced by the linguist.

Another difficulty lies in the fact that not everyone speaks the same way; that is, there are social and regional differences in usage and pronunciation. Furthermore, English is spoken and written at different levels. All of these problems make the scientific examination of the language difficult. Of course, these difficulties also affect other grammars, but since the basis of structural grammar is its scientific determination, they introduce some limitations to generalizing about the completeness of its patterns as a description of the language system.

Transformational Grammar. **Transformational grammar** (sometimes called **generative** or **transformational-generative**) came into being after the development of structural grammar, as a result of the recognition by some grammarians of the impossibility of securing factual information on all possible sentences the speakers of a language may use. Transformational grammar has a theoretical base rather than an empirical (observable or factual) base like structural grammar. To avoid the problems associated with examining actual utterances, transformational grammar assumes the existence of a **deep structure** system that leads to a **surface structure** (the sentences actually said and written). There are two basic types of sentences: kernel and transformed. **Kernel sentences,** of which there are a relatively small number, are the core of the system. They are sentences that cannot be derived by analysis from other sentences. The basic patterns for kernel sentences were illustrated in the preceding section, but these may be changed by speakers and writers to provide a great diversity of sentences, or **transformed sentences.** If the kernel sentence is "Birds eat seed," for example, several kinds of transformed sentences are possible. Three of the most common transformations are these:

Birds do not eat seeds.	Changing to the opposite meaning
Do birds eat seeds?	Changing to a question
Seeds are eaten by birds.	Changing so that the direct object becomes the subject

Other kinds of transformations are possible. In writing, sentence combining and sentence expansion (both discussed in Chapter 9) are especially significant. In sentence combining, two or more sentences are restated as one. For example, "Birds eat seeds" and "Birds eat worms" become "Birds eat seeds and worms." Through sentence expansion, kernel sentences are made more informative and interesting by adding words (such as "many" and "yellow"), phrases ("from my garden"), and clauses ("when I am not at home"): "Many yellow birds eat seeds from my garden when I am not at home."

Transformational grammar makes use of terminology similar to that used in structural grammar. Like structural grammar, it is not prescriptive, except in the sense of indicating whether or not a sentence is grammatical. There is no prescription as to correctness of the words used. However, transformational grammar can be taught as formally as was traditional grammar, and this often is the case. Teaching it (or structural or any other grammar) can have the same emphasis on rules, relationships of words and phrases to one another (usually by a new kind of diagramming), isolation of the study from the expression of children, and activities that have little interest for or little meaning to children.

A Functional Approach

There is no place in elementary schools for formal, direct instruction in grammar. Children have learned to understand and use the language spoken in their homes and neighborhoods, and they do this effectively for their own purposes. (If the language spoken at home is not English, there is even less reason to teach English grammar in any kind of formal way.) But teachers certainly have the responsibility for providing good language models and should take advantage of opportunities to use grammar-related terms such as *sentence* and *verb,* (as well as *period, comma,* etc.) to build readiness for more sophisticated understandings. Teachers also need to know the research evidence concerning grammar teaching, to understand and be able to explain the difference between grammar and usage, and to know the kinds of things that can be done to improve youngsters' speaking and writing. They must also know a good deal about the kind of language study that will appeal to children.

Children are not likely to feel much enthusiasm if the program is centered around a textbook that insists that it is wrong to say "Don't go *in* the house" and that it is normal and proper to say "The team is *we,* the athletes." Nor will they have much interest in exercises calling for identifying the nouns, verbs, and adjectives in sentences, for underlining the "complete" predicates, for categorizing common and proper nouns, and so on. Children like to talk and they like to write; they want to tell what they have discovered and what they think about something. Thus, the program should focus on *using* language—speaking, writing, reading, and listening. A textbook may suggest ideas for using language. It also may be a source of examples and explanations (as suggested in Chapter 2). The grammatical terminology need not be taught or the exercises used.

As suggested above, grammar can be taught in a formal manner or dealt with in a functional way. In functional teaching of grammar the focus is on expression and its purpose rather than on the elements of the grammar. To the extent that grammar enters into it, however, there is the implication that the grammar taught is of value—is functional—in making expression more effective. Although there is little evidence in favor of bringing grammar into teaching with this focus, if grammar is taught (for any of the reasons suggested), it seems to make sense that an effort should be made to relate it to expression rather than to teach it as something entirely separate from the natural expression that occurs as children communicate.

Teaching about language functionally means that teaching about nouns cannot be allocated to the fourth grade, nor can it be done in a series of isolated lessons. Functional teaching requires that understanding be developed from the very first contacts teachers have with children. The kindergarten or first-grade teacher who says "Who can give me another sentence telling about one thing we saw at the bakery?" is teaching grammar. So is the fifth-grade teacher who says "Let's see how we can make this sentence more exact. Have we used the best adjectives to describe the carts the natives use for hauling grain?"

If children construct sentences well and thus convey the messages they intend, there is no need to teach grammatical items. On the other hand, if a child says "The boys is going," the opportunity *may* be present to teach about agreement of subject and verb. Certainly the child may be taught that *is* is a verb, not just something referred to as "this word." In a similar way, if a child describes the black bear in a film the class has viewed as simply a "black bear," there is a functional situation for teaching about using other adjectives (*big, lumbering, awkward,* etc.) to give a better word picture of what the child has seen.

There is no need to avoid using grammatical terminology when it is natural to use it. A verb is more properly called by that term than by "action word," and *verb* is no more difficult to learn than many other words that children readily use. We don't call a television a "box that shows pictures" or a wheel "something that goes around," and children have no trouble with these words or the basic concepts they represent.

In the middle and upper grades, as students learn to combine their ideas into longer and more complex sentences, it is perfectly natural for a teacher to begin to use terms such as *phrase, clause,* and perhaps even *antecedent of the pronoun,* but these should *always* be introduced in relation to actual expression. The language arts instructional plan suggested in Chapter 2

Don't burden children with meaningless exercises. Let them write, talk with one another, read, and so forth.

can provide the framework for such teaching. In this way the teaching of language skills will not be left to unplanned or incidental occasions; rather, careful planning will give rise to opportunities that require the use of particular language skills and therefore provide situations for functional teaching.

Activities

As you think about ways in which grammar-related content may be taught within the context of normal classroom learning activities, consider what you might do by starting with a basic sentence such as "Birds sing," for example. At the beginning level children may think of adjectives to describe the birds—"yellow," "angry," and so on. Then they can go on to work with sentence structure, making the sentence more complex and varied by turning the adjectives into phrases, clauses, verbs, or adverbs. For example, "the angry screeching yellow birds" might become "the angry yellow birds with the screeching cries" or "the yellow birds that screeched at us with angry cries" or "the yellow birds screeched angrily at us." This kind of learning activity can also involve discussions of how words change form and position when used differently and, if done often, should lead to much greater variety in students' sentences.

> Chapter 10 has many suggestions about sentence construction and sentence combining.

To teach word order, present simple sentences in jumbled arrangements, for example, "had many about airplanes Joe books read." Children will have little trouble putting this sentence in order, but if phrases or clauses are added ("in the fourth grade" or "which were used in wars") they will soon discover that word order is important to sentence sense. This kind of activity should be helpful to children who misplace sentence parts: "Having just eaten a rat, John saw that the snake was going to sleep." By using some of the children's own sentences noted during writing conferences (see Chapter 9), you will be able to help them see how the way a sentence is put together can contribute to meaning and effectiveness.

> "Clotheslines," magnetic boards, and word charts with slots are all good devices for allowing the rearranging of word order.

A similar activity that encourages understanding of sentences involves using strips of tag board on which are printed parts of sentences (subjects and predicates or noun and verb phrases, depending on the terminology used). Distribute the strips to the children; then ask each one to find all possible combinations that make meaningful sentences. As the children advance in their mastery of sentence construction, add strips containing coordinating conjunctions (*and, but,* etc.) and subordinating conjunctions (*if, because, when,* etc.). One child might be chosen to begin a sentence, with others volunteering to continue and complete it. The class judges whether the resulting sentence is a good one and possibly experiments with revisions. This activity can also be done in several groups, and results compared.

Another useful way to help children discover the importance of word order and sentence structure is to use the overhead projector to show a paragraph in which all sentences are simple ones with the same structure (for instance, subject–verb–direct object). To demonstrate the need for variety, have them rewrite each sentence in the paragraph in the same way, and do this several times for the entire paragraph. Depending on the maturity of the children, they might first invert word order and make every active verb passive ("Birds eat seeds" becomes "Seeds were eaten by birds"), add an adjective before each noun in the subject position, begin each sentence with a prepositional phrase, or make all sentences compound by connecting pairs with the word *and*. After redoing the sentences in several ways, have the children select one sentence from each rewrite to make a new paragraph, perhaps experimenting with several different combinations. Evaluate the results by reading several paragraphs aloud and comparing them with the original.

In the upper grades the value of variety in sentence structure can be illustrated by rewriting a famous speech such as the Gettysburg Address or Patrick Henry's "Give me liberty, or give me death" oration, keeping vocabulary the same, insofar as possible, but structuring all sentences in the same way.

As children write more in the middle and upper grades they often have difficulty with tense sequence, agreement, and staying in the same person. Activities such as those suggested in the preceding paragraphs can be structured to develop a better understanding of the way language works in these areas as well. For example, if you are using the tagboard strips, include various tenses of the same verb, both singular and plural forms of nouns, or a selection of pronouns (definite and indefinite, singular and plural, all persons). Or play a game in which no one is allowed to use plurals, past tense, or a particular pronoun for a certain period of time. This could be done in several ways; one is similar to "Ghost," with a child becoming one-third of a ghost the first time he or she uses the forbidden construction, two-thirds the second time, and so on. Obviously, some badly constructed sentences will result, but the children will become more aware of the grammatical need for different kinds of constructions.

These are only a few suggestions; obviously, the activities selected for a particular class must be chosen according to the needs and maturity of the children. The important point to remember in planning activities is that they should be directed at helping children see how the structure of language works in a positive way to make expression more effective and more meaningful.

USAGE AND DIALECTS

This and earlier chapters have emphasized that the language any of us use is largely a matter of early environment—although by the time a person is an adult he or she has learned a great deal about choosing language appropriate to the communication situation. Such choosing does not mean that a person invariably changes the pronunciation of words or modifies the expressions learned in childhood, but most people do pick up the jargon of their profession and social group and, in some situations, will avoid language that might be labeled "nonstandard."

The above suggests that there are levels of language, and a few years ago differences in usage were seen as being on different levels. These levels were often termed *formal, informal,* and *colloquial,* and sometimes—in an attempt at finer distinctions—*illiterate, homely, informal standard, formal standard, literary,* and *technical.* There was also the idea that an individual used the language of one of these levels—apparently all or most of the time. We now know that each person's language usage varies. However, usage is still largely termed as standard and nonstandard, even though these terms are difficult to define.

Acceptable Usage

Deciding what the school should do about usage teaching is a major problem. In the first place, determining what items of usage are unacceptable is difficult at best. A textbook is only a partially satisfactory guide, as it is directed at a hypothetical classroom rather than an actual one, and the focus is often on grammar rather than on usage. Also, the usage items that textbook authors list as unacceptable are often not realistic. For some years language scholars have been recommending that only a very few usage items should receive instructional attention in elementary schools. In support of this position, one authority stated:

Examine Pooley's The Teaching of English Usage (see the References).

(1) the constant repetition of a relatively small number of deviations constitutes over 90 percent of the nonstandard usage problems in the elementary grades [and] (2) a large number of ''errors'' listed in textbooks and language workbooks are not errors at all but standard colloquial English appropriate to the speech and writing of children and adults alike.

The reluctance of many teachers to accept certain usages is the major reason why the number of usage items identified here and in most textbooks is not more limited. A study done more than thirty years ago showed that teachers were only about half as accepting of ''*Can* I have another helping of dessert, please?'' ''Everyone put on *their* coats and went home,'' ''Go *slow*,'' and ''It is *me*'' as were a group of editors and writers. A later study by Johnson (see References) showed that five items of usage identified as acceptable by linguists were regarded by teachers as incorrect (particularly in writing, but also in most cases in speech). Observations by the authors of this book suggest that the extent of nonacceptance by many teachers has not changed much. The Johnson study dealt with the following examples of ''incorrect'' usage:

1. Everyone put *their* name in the upper left corner of the paper.
2. I *will* go to the store tomorrow.
3. The *reason* the page is missing *is because* Johnny tore it out.
4. They invited my friends and *myself*.
5. *Who* did you see?

Even more startling, this research also showed that ninety-nine out of the hundred teachers participating in the study actually used at least one of the ''incorrect'' usages in either their own writing or speech, or both!

The list below is intended to be a guide to the kinds of usages that should receive attention in the elementary school. It is not likely that the children in any one class will use all of them—and of course they should only be focused on if the need is present. In no case, however, should all of them receive direct teaching effort in a single year. If a large number of them are used by the children, it is best to select those that occur most frequently and concentrate on them so that teaching effort is not dissipated.

ain't or *hain't*	*hadn't ought*	where *it* at?
yourn, hern, ourn	he *give,* he *walk*	where is she *at?*
hisen, theys	*me and* Mary went	he *run*
youse	she *taken*	have *saw*
onct	I *likes* him	I *says*
hisself, theirselves	I *drunk, drunks*	he *seen*
hair *are*	*can't hardly*	*them* books
a orange	*does* we have	*this here*
have *ate*	my brother, *he*	*that there*
they *eats*	*her* and *me* went	*us* boys went
was *broke*	there *is* four	we, you, they *was*
he *brung*	there *was* four	with *we* girls
he *come*	they *knowed*	have *went*
clumb	I, they *growed*	have *wrote*
had, have *did*	haven't *no,* isn't *no*	the *mens*
she, he *don't*	*leave* (for let)	*learn* me a song
it *don't*	haven't *nothing*	
didn't ought	that's *mines*	

Since language does change and since the studies cited earlier suggest that teachers and textbooks are often slow to recognize this change, a teacher may need help in deciding what to teach. Two ways to obtain this aid are to listen to the speech of educated people and to read current newspapers and magazines; doing these with particular usages in mind can be very revealing. Since so many young people, particularly but not exclusively, use *goes* for *said* and *you know* at every pause in their speech, keeping current about language that is acceptable (and those two examples are not) in many social and business settings is important. Of course, appropriateness of words and expressions can be checked in reference books about usage, but sometimes these are not really current and may largely reflect the point of view of their authors.

Dialect Differences

It is certainly true that the pronunciations, vocabulary, and language structures of some children are such wide departures from the standard language or prestige dialect of the community that they cannot be ignored in classrooms. On the other hand, the dialects of other children may differ from the prestige dialect, yet not depart widely from the language that one hears and reads in the community. Thus, the attention given to these usages may be minimal, since many of the differences will cause no real communication difficulties and will add color and individualism to expression.

Dealing with dialect differences becomes very important, however, if other children laugh at the way a child speaks or say "He talks funny," if the dialect is of such low prestige and differs so markedly from "school" language that a genuine problem exists, or if understanding the child is difficult. If a youngster pronounces words such as *pin* and *pen* or *cheer* and *chair* the same way, there is a possibility that he or she will have difficulty with phonic analysis in reading—that is, a lack of sensitivity to a child's language may create a reading problem. Similar kinds of problems may affect spelling instruction, but in neither of these language arts areas, or in any others, should it be assumed that the youngster's pronunciation *must* be changed or that the child should be told he or she is speaking incorrectly. All that is needed is to know the child's dialect and be able to reinforce learning when necessary.

Grammatical differences from the standard or prestige dialect of a community are often characteristic of the dialects of the disadvantaged. The following are the principal types of grammatical differences that may be found:

1. Absence of inflectional endings (*s, es, 's, s', en, ed, ing*) for noun plurals, noun genitives, third-singular present indicative, past tense, present participles, and past participles.

2. Analogical forms such as *hisself* or *theirselves* and the absolute genitives *ourn, yourn, hisn, hern,* and *theirn.*

3. Double comparatives and superlatives, such as *more prettier* and *most lovingest.*

4. Omission of the copula *be* (usually *is,* for example, "He a cop") with predicate nouns, predicate adjectives, and present and past participles.

5. *Be* as a finite verb ("He *be* fast" for "He runs fast").

6. Differences in the principal parts of verbs, such as *growed, drawed, taken* as past tense, *rid* as the past participle of *ride,* and *clum* or *clim* as the past tense or past participle of *climb.*

These differences in grammatical features result in such expressions as the following:

He be absent yesterday.
She come to school every day.
He ax me can I go.
She had three sister.
Daisy is more taller than Eileen.
I drawed the picture.

It is important to recognize that a child using such expressions is not being careless. Careful listening will reveal that there is a system to the sentence construction as well as to the pronunciation and the vocabulary used. The child is using language that is familiar and that has worked well in meeting his or her communication needs.

In addition, no teacher should overlook the fact that his or her speech may not be fully understood by a child. Not only may the teacher use words unfamiliar to the child, but the pronunciations or the names given to objects or actions may be new as well.

Standard English

Parents and others in our society expect schools to teach "good English," meaning that they want children to learn the English that "important" people in the community use. This is the **standard English** referred to earlier that is so difficult to define. In fact, it simply cannot be defined in terms of specific words or pronunciation. However, it can be thought of as expression that is appropriate to the purpose of the speech or writing, that is consistent with the system of the language, and that is comfortable to both the expressor and the audience. It is language that is natural and uncramped by rule, reflecting custom that is widely accepted by society because it serves the needs of society. It is never static but changes with the communication needs and other changes in society.

This definition is based on criteria that the National Council of Teachers of English has long urged teachers to observe: acceptable usage (1) is determined by the living language of today, (2) recognizes dialectal, geographical, and vocational variations, (3) is judged by its appropriateness for the purpose intended, (4) recognizes that there are situational levels of speech, and (5) takes into account the historical development of the language.

TEACHING USAGE

Judgments about people are frequently made on the basis of the language they use. Fair or not, this is a fact. Thus, even though the way a child uses language at home and in his or her neighborhood may be useful for immediate communication needs, it may not serve lifetime needs, and the child may later feel cheated if the school has not attempted to teach a more widely acceptable dialect. It is important, therefore, to help each child to see the advantage of learning and using standard English, but it is equally important to do this without condemning his or her original dialect.

Procedures for teaching language usage are not as well defined by either research or established practice as would be ideal. However, the following sections suggest instructional principles and practices that appear to have the best foundation in research evidence and learning theory and to have received the greatest acceptance by teachers. These should help teachers who are frustrated by the failure of efforts they have made to bring about changes in the language children use. Many teachers do not modify their procedures in spite of being aware that what they have been doing is often fruitless—possibly because they do not know how these procedures might be changed. It is also possible that they do not really appreciate the fact that language habits are really that—habits—and habits are not easily changed.

As students give reports, usage problems can be observed.

To expect children to change their language habits because a teacher or a textbook says they should be changed is unrealistic. What is realistic is to recognize that the daily program in every classroom presents numerous opportunities for children to use a more generally acceptable language for genuine communication purposes. What is also realistic is to realize that pupils learn by doing. If children are to speak and write a standard dialect, they must have practice in speaking and writing it. Rules and exercises are too far removed from genuine communication to have much value.

Determining Usage Problems

It is not possible to indicate the specific items of usage that an elementary teacher may need to teach, since the language backgrounds of children vary widely. The usage items suggested earlier in this chapter are a guide, but the specific needs of the children in a class must be determined by a survey of the oral and written usage of the children in that class.

At the top of the next page is an example of a survey form you can make and use to record usage items that need instructional attention. Listening to the children in the classroom and on the playground and observing their writing will provide the usage items. Note language patterns (grammatical structures) as well as individual words.

The form at the bottom of the next page may also be useful. This one

	Usage survey for _____			
	verb forms	pronouns	redundancy	illiteracies
Michael	he growed			yourn
Amanda			John he	
Scott			this here	
Toni	be tall			yourn
Debra	axt			
Brian				
Jeffrey		it's		
Julie	has took			

	Chris	Kelly	Jill	Todd	Kurt	Miguel	Danielle	Rosalita	Linda	Barbara
I goes	✔		✔	✔				✔		
brung	✔	✔		✔						✔
he don't				✔		✔	✔			
hisself	✔	✔								
me and _____			✔		✔		✔			
drawed	✔	✔				✔				
he be late	✔		✔	✔						
he a tall boy	✔									
rid for rode		✔								

focuses on items previously selected; if filled in at regular intervals, it provides a simple means for noting particular improvements by the children.

Instructional Procedures

The most vital factor in teaching acceptable usage is motivation. Therefore, every possible device must be utilized to relate the activities of the classroom to the basic goals of each pupil. Children must be made to feel that standard English is actually in widespread use (thus, as suggested earlier, the items taught must be realistic ones) and that learning it will benefit them personally. They must be shown that their communication is, at least in many situations, more effective when they use standard English.

Elimination of a particular item (for example, "Me and him went") begins only when the child recognizes it in his or her own speech.

Acceptance of children and the language they use is most important in teaching usage. Finding fault doesn't work; this is a fact that all adults recognize in their own experiences. And acceptance means more than simply recognizing that children can and should use their own dialect when it is appropriate—on the playground, for example. It means also accepting each child's cultural heritage—family, neighborhood, style of living, and so on. It means encouraging children to talk and write about their experiences and the things that are important to them.

Begin by surveying your class early in the year and at intervals throughout the following months. From these surveys choose only a few usage items for concentrated teaching effort. A few items will probably apply to the entire class, and these may receive total class instruction. Items needed by only a few may be worked on individually or in small groups. Only the most frequently used and grossest departures from acceptable usage should be selected for teaching—perhaps by comparing the children's speech with lists of divergent dialect features or misused words such as those presented earlier in this chapter. After these have been selected, identify them for the children, along with the reasons for their selection, without making any child feel inadequate because he or she employs a particular usage.

These items may be attacked in two ways. First, and most important, opportunities must be provided for the children to use accepted alternatives to the particular items being emphasized in natural communication. The focus should always be on the communication rather than on the usage, but teaching directed toward attacking the particular items need not be minimized by this focus. Simply see to it that the children use the accepted forms of the items selected, and do so without fault-finding or placing undue stress on them. Second, continue to work toward building interest in words and expressions—and in language generally. This is done principally through providing many experiences with language of many kinds. Read to children often from prose and poetry, imaginative and factual materials; call attention often to the pictures created by words, as well as to the emotional reactions they call forth. Particular attention should be given to variations in language used for different purposes—for example, a science lesson and a story containing conversation.

If you have a particularly good relationship with a class, you may be able to get them to use a signal (buzzing like a bee, perhaps) whenever anyone hears a particular form the group is trying to avoid.

This kind of activity can be combined with discussions about dialect, colloquialisms, and differences in situational usages. Children might collect sentences heard on the playground and revise them into language appropriate for an assembly announcement and for a social studies report. Activities such as those suggested earlier in this chapter for teaching grammatical concepts can also be adapted for usage practice. For example, tagboard strips containing noun and verb phrases can be combined, with children saying sentences aloud as they are formed. Both seeing and hearing the accepted forms will help to provide reinforcement.

As much as possible, the children themselves should assume the responsibility for making changes. Encourage them to work independently, both individually and in groups, keeping their own lists of individual problems and charting progress they make in learning new forms. This will help to focus their attention on their own particular problems and provide motivation by concentrating on improvement.

In short, then, providing for much use of language (both oral and written) in meaningful situations, presenting many opportunities for children to see and hear language that is well used (through books, records, films and filmstrips, and your own language), and including frequent, *brief* drill on a limited number of items that have been selected for your particular pupils should result in some measure of success in teaching children to use language effectively.

A FINAL WORD

Grammar and usage are two aspects of the language arts for which instructional decisions must clearly be made by the teacher rather than taken from textbook materials. For this reason *you* need to understand the English language as thoroughly as possible, including the usages that are acceptable or unacceptable in particular situations, and to appreciate and have some knowledge of various dialects. You also need to understand and be able to use the techniques suggested here for teaching your students about our language, its structure and usage, and how it may best be employed in communicative situations. The extent to which a class needs help with standard English or is interested in or ready for examination of sentence structure can only be fully understood by a knowledgeable teacher who interacts with them daily. Much time and effort will be wasted if, instead, teaching of grammar and usage is based on textbooks or duplicated worksheets.

References

Baron, Dennis E. *Grammar and Good Taste.* Yale University Press, 1982.

Bryen, Diane Nelson. *Inquiries into Child Language.* Allyn and Bacon, 1982.

Daniell, Beth. "Rodney and the Teaching of Standard English." *Language Arts* 61 (September 1984), pp. 498–504.

Hillocks, George, Jr. "Grammar and the Manipulation of Syntax," in *Research in Written Composition,* pp. 133–151. National Conference on Research in English/ERIC Clearinghouse on Reading and Communication Skills, National Institute of Education, 1986.

———. "Syntheses of Research on Teaching Writing." *Educational Leadership* 44 (May 1987), pp. 71–82.

Holbrook, Hilary Taylor. "ERIC/RCS Report:

Whither (Wither) Grammar?'' *Language Arts* 60 (February 1983), pp. 259–263.

Johnson, Robert S. "A Comparison of English Teachers' Own Usage with Their Attitudes Toward Usage." Doctoral dissertation. Teachers College, Columbia University, 1968.

Lindfors, Judith Wells. *Children's Language and Learning.* Prentice-Hall, 1980.

Non-native and Nonstandard Dialect Students. National Council of Teachers of English, 1982.

Pooley, Robert C. *The Teaching of English Usage.* National Council of Teachers of English, 1974.

Temple, Charles, and Gillet, Jean Wallace. *Language Arts: Learning Processes and Teaching Practices.* Little, Brown, 1984.

Weaver, Constance. *Grammar for Teachers: Perspectives and Definitions.* National Council of Teachers of English, 1979.

Teaching Resources

Many companies are developing and distributing software related to grammar. Much of the material is drill-like, and even if the content is learned, it is likely to be of little value in helping children write, speak, or read better. Examine all materials carefully—including those listed here.

COMPUTER SOFTWARE

Dragon Games. Educational Activities (disk and guide; grades 3–6).

Grammar Gremlins. Scholastic.

Kid Bits Words Fair. Potomac MicroResources, 1982 (K–grade 4).

Microcourse Language Arts. Houghton Mifflin, Software Division (diskette; grades 3–8).

Noun Bound. Scholastic.

Usage. JMH Software of Minnesota (tape and diskette; grades 3–8).

VERBatim. Scholastic.

Wally's Word Works. Sunburst, 1985 (guide, three disks, and record sheet; grades 4–6).

VIDEOTAPES

Basic Grammar Series. Society for Visual Education.

Grammar As Easy As ABC. Greenleaf.

The Search for the Stolen Sentence. Society for Visual Education.

OTHER RESOURCES

Goffstein, Marilyn B. *School of Names.* Harper & Row, 1986.

Morley, Diane. *Marms in the Marmalade.* Carolrhoda Books, 1984.

Terben, Marvin. *Your Foot's on My Feet! And Other Tricky Nouns.* Houghton Mifflin, 1986.

Activities for Preservice Teachers

1. Ask others in your classes to define such terms as *adjective, reflexive pronoun, weak verb,* and *subordinate clause.* What do they say? Do they recall studying definitions for these in school? If they recall the school definitions, ask them how frequently they've needed to know them. For what purposes?

2. Videotape television programs that make extensive use of characters with strong dialects (don't forget British and Australian programs on the Public Broadcasting System's stations). Pick out particular characters and play their scenes several times. How do their dialects differ from yours? Try to speak as they do. Ask others to tell you how you do.

3. Compose a paragraph using only simple sentences (as suggested on page 184), and plan the kinds of revisions you might ask a particular class to make.

4. Observe a particular class over several days, and listen to their use of language. Make a record of nonstandard items that require attention. Based on your observations and record, to which items would you give teaching priority? Why?

5. Work out some techniques that you might use for the items you identified in the preceding activity.

6. Note differences in usage that you hear on television and radio and among your associates. Divide

those you find into examples of dialect differences and examples of nonstandard usage.

7. Examine several elementary-school language textbooks to see how much attention they give to grammar definitions and rules. Does the content of these books appear to be seeking to teach *about language* or *about grammar*? Is there enough content about *using language?* Which, if any, of the textbooks would you want to use?

8. The work by Robert Pooley listed in the References may seem "old" to you, but the evidence he reports and the suggestions he makes are worthy of your study. Plan to engage in a discussion concerning "standard" and "nonstandard" language use.

Activities for Inservice Teachers

1. Ask the teachers in your school to estimate the proportion of pupils who speak standard English. What do they think? Is there agreement? What kinds of definitions do they seem to be using? Ask some secondary-school English teachers the same question.

2. Find out from supervisors or members of a curriculum committee in your school district how much concern there is with the teaching of grammar and usage. To what extent is the concern about "correct" grammar as opposed to language use?

3. Carefully examine the writing of one of your favorite authors (Vonnegut or Oates, for example). Do you find any sentences that do not meet the definition of a sentence as given in many elementary-school language textbooks? Do you find any other constructions that seem to break traditional grammatical rules?

4. Videotape some programs that have characters who do not speak standard English. Being careful to avoid racial stereotypes, discuss some examples with your class, and use this discussion as a departure point for sensitizing them to the issue of there being appropriate language for given situations.

5. Prepare a survey form similar to one shown in this chapter, and evaluate your class. Then contract with children to eliminate a few common problems.

6. Ask a publisher's representative why there is still so much traditional grammar in elementary-school language textbooks when research has indicated that it is inappropriate.

7. Review the language-teaching activities in this chapter, and select several to use with your class. Keep a record of the use, including the planning.

8. Evaluate your own ability to identify parts of speech. Assess this knowledge in terms of the degree to which you use this knowledge in writing and speaking. In light of this assessment, evaluate some of the exercises and practice materials commonly given to children.

Independent Activities for Children

1. Have pupils make individual checklists of expressions to try to avoid in their writing. For example, someone might list these in two columns:

Words I Use with Friends	Words I Use in Writing
I ain't gonna do it.	I am not going to do it.

Only a few expressions should be worked on at a time. When these have been mastered, the child can add others.

2. Record children using nonstandard and standard forms, and then let them listen to themselves. The contrast will help them identify the differences. Expressions to start with might include these:

have at	have went	was broke
she give	he brang	them books

3. Write on cards sentences in which the child is to substitute phrases. For example, a sentence such as "He wanted to go to the store" might be used with directions to the child to substitute other phrases after the first *to* (for example, "ride around the block," "play ball," "go to the circus").

4. Prepare a set of cards with a two-word sentence on each ("Boy walked." "Dog barked." "Snow fell."). Adding one or a few words at a time, the child is to expand each into a series of sentences, for example:

Snow fell.
Snow fell steadily.
Snow fell steadily all day.
Snow fell steadily all day long.

5. To help individual children with word order, make cards with simple instructions, such as the following:

Write a simple sentence. Then add an adverb to make your sentence more specific. Tell how, when, or where. For example:

The horse jumped.
The horse jumped *suddenly.*

Rewrite the sentence with the adverb in another position. Keep your adverb list to use in free writing time.

6. Prepare cards or ditto sheets from which the child can select sentence exercises such as the following:

Put in missing words.
The ____ man ____ scolded the ____ boy.
There was a ____ storm ____ night.

Directions may include listing as many words as possible that would "make sense" for each blank.

7. Give the child tagboard strips containing noun and verb phrases. Have her or him see how many can be matched so that they make meaningful sentences. An extension is to provide coordinating conjunctions

(*and, but,* etc.) and subordinating conjunctions (*if, because, when,* etc.) on other strips for forming compound and complex sentences.

8. Using cards of various colors, make stacks of different classes of words and phrases: determiners, nouns, verbs and verb phrases, adjectives, adverbs, prepositional phrases, and conjunctions or clause markers. Pupils may experiment with word order and structure by making sentences from these. At the upper levels, gerunds and participles may be added. Children can try to make the funniest sentences, longest sentences, most descriptive sentences, and so on.

9. Using the letters in their own names, children can list adjectives that they believe describe themselves:

JOAN   *j*oyful, *o*bedient, *a*ctive, *n*ice
TOM   *t*errific, *o*rganized, *m*ighty

Or they can do the same with verbs that tell what they do:

DIANE   *d*rives, *i*nvestigates, *a*nnounces, *n*ails, *e*njoys
SAM   *s*kates, *a*rgues, *m*oves

10. Individual children can make lists of incomplete sentences to share with the class at a later time. Other children then try to think of words and/or phrases that fill the blanks and make interesting sentences.

I looked out the window and saw ____.
Sitting on the front doorstep was ____.
He ____ the cake ____.

Chapter 8

Writing by Hand and Machine

*F*or several understandable reasons handwriting has declined in importance. For years the typewriter has been the principal means for written communication in business and is used increasingly in personal communication. Certainly, too, the telephone is now used to conduct much business that was formerly done by mail and has in many cases replaced the letter to friends or relatives. Another important development that has affected both personal and business communication is the growing availability of electronic devices of various kinds. For example, some families now regularly exchange audio or video tape recordings and find these much more satisfying than letters. Photocopying machines have reduced the need to take notes from print materials or otherwise use handwriting. Typing by means of computerized word processors has also become increasingly popular.

But writing by hand continues to be done, too. A typewriter or word processor is not always available, of course, and is inappropriate for some tasks anyway. People often need to take messages, make lists, leave notes, and send greeting cards, and such writing is generally done by hand. Students are able to make photocopies of one another's class notes, but first someone has to take them in readable form. Even for material that is typed the preliminary work is usually handwritten and often has to be good enough to be read by others. And many people simply feel that a handwritten letter or note is more personal than a typewritten one and that more thought can be given to a handwritten letter than is possible during the give and take of a telephone call.

The elementary-school program must give attention to both handwriting and writing by machine. Much of this attention can be incorporated into work in the subject areas, but writing itself also deserves specific instructional attention. Beginning writing was discussed in Chapter 4. It was emphasized that manuscript writing meets the criteria of legibility, ease of execution, and similarity to the print that children of that age are learning to read. This chapter describes instruction in hand and machine writing and suggests activities that should be a part of an effective elementary-school language arts program.

HANDWRITING IN TODAY'S SCHOOLS

The major rationale supporting handwriting instruction is that handwriting is still important. It must be legible, and it must be done with reasonable speed. Therefore, instruction—in letter formation, instrument position, and movement—and practice are needed. Handwriting is a complex skill that involves both mind and muscles and the coordination of the two.

Children's handwriting improves when they are motivated to diagnose their own handwriting needs, to evaluate their own progress, and to receive direct help with their problems. This motivation is largely based on their doing purposeful writing. Thus, handwriting should be taught throughout the day rather than being relegated only to instructional periods, although specific times should be reserved for working on problems or for teaching forms and movements.

Handwriting must be legible. Letters should be well formed and of the proper relative size, with adequate and uniform spacing between them. There should be uniformity of forward slant to the letters (or a lack of slant in the case of manuscript letters) and adequate and uniform spacing between words.

Good handwriting is done with ease. To write easily, the writer must have a comfortable posture (body, arms, and hands), writing instruments and paper correctly positioned, free movement of the arm and hand, and a rhythm to the writing movements.

Finally, your own handwriting, your understanding of the developmental nature of handwriting skill, the knowledge you have of effective teaching procedures, and your skill in using these procedures are important factors in creating a successful program.

Manuscript Writing

Some commercial handwriting materials provide for practicing manuscript forms at every elementary-school grade level.

Although manuscript writing is usually taught only in the first years of school (as discussed in Chapter 4), it is becoming accepted as a valid form of writing for personal use. There are clearly several valid reasons why children should continue to practice and use manuscript writing throughout the elementary-school years and beyond. When the need arises to label drawings, make signs, or fill in forms, those who can write manuscript have a distinct advantage. Also, if the legibility of the writing done by many adults is any indication, children's manuscript is much easier to read than their adult cursive is likely to be.

In *Handwriting: Basic Skills for Effective Communication*, Barbe, Lucas, and Wasylyk report on studies demonstrating that manuscript writing is easier for children to do, just as fast as cursive and more legible.

It is particularly unfortunate that, just as children begin to master manuscript after two years or so of instruction and to use it effectively for writing stories and other texts, instruction stops, and in some cases the school even begins to require that all the children's work be done in cursive. A better practice is to provide for the maintenance of acquired manuscript skills. This can be done with little instructional time; as suggested above, manuscript use can be encouraged when children are labeling posters, filling in forms, and so on.

Transition to Cursive Handwriting

Learning to do cursive, or "real" writing as children often refer to it, usually occurs in the third grade, although some schools teach it earlier and a few do not teach it at all. Cursive can be difficult for children to execute since there are many upward movements, some awkward connections of

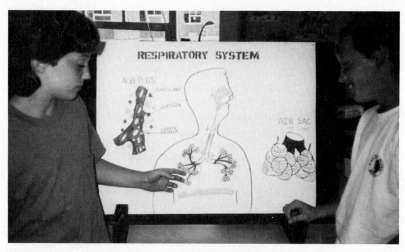

Manuscript writing is needed for labeling charts.

letters, and the need to keep a legible and consistent slant to the letters. There seems to be an advantage in beginning instruction by showing the children that the new way of writing is similar to the old. This is done by connecting manuscript letters and tracing cursive forms over manuscript equivalents where possible. Letters such as lowercase *f* and uppercase *G* can then be taught as exceptions.

The teacher should show how to connect the letters in cursive writing.

Commercial handwriting systems include instructions for teaching cursive forms, and it is generally a good idea to consider following the suggestions provided with the materials you are supposed to use. However, the following suggestions may also be useful.

- Show the relationships of cursive forms to manuscript forms by illustrations such as the following:

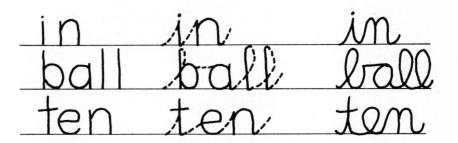

- Move from the simple to the complex. Introduce lowercase letters first, starting with the ones that are easiest to make: *l*, *e*, *i*, *t* (undercurve and slant strokes).
- In introducing letters, use parallel guidelines on the board to show how each straight line slants the same way as the others. The parallel lines will also help in showing spacing between letters, the width of humps in *m*'s and *n*'s, the width of the loop in an *l*, and so on.
- Introduce letters in words on the chalkboard, calling attention to the strokes, to the way the word begins, to the way the letters join, to the size of the letters, and to the ending stroke of the word.
- Introduce new letters in several words, so that a new letter will appear in various positions—at the beginning, in the middle, and at the end of a word.

Handwriting in Intermediate and Upper Grades

After cursive handwriting has been introduced and adequately learned, practice continues to be important if children are to maintain their skill. As more and more handwriting becomes necessary in school work, students need to increase their competence so that handwriting will be a tool to serve them rather than something that takes up a great deal of time and attention. Further, as speed increases, legibility often declines, so teachers in the intermediate and upper grades must be prepared to assist students in evaluating their handwriting and taking steps to improve it. You should focus attention on helping students achieve these specific objectives:

- To write all letters legibly in both manuscript and cursive forms and in upper and lower case
- To understand how the terms *shape, size, spacing, line quality,* and *alignment* apply to evaluating their own handwriting

- To be aware of posture, hand position, and movement when writing
- To evaluate their own handwriting in terms of class standards, commercial models, and diagnostic materials

EMPHASES FOR HANDWRITING INSTRUCTION

The preceding section discussed the transition to cursive writing, showed the need for maintenance of manuscript after the transition, and presented an overview of handwriting in the intermediate and upper grades. This section discusses specific aspects of instruction that require attention.

Emphasis on Practice

In addition to teaching handwriting directly and maintaining skills through the use of teachers' and pupils' guides and textbook materials, you should capitalize on opportunities to give attention to handwriting in all of the pupils' writing. Handwriting skill will diminish unless it is practiced, and this practice must include corrective work on factors that cause the writing to be illegible or cause it to be done awkwardly or in a tiring fashion.

Discuss expected difficulties (as shown in the chart on pages 208 and 209) and determine the extent to which any appear in the children's writing.

Keep a checklist for recording individual problems that need correction. Search for the causes of handwriting faults as well as for the faults or errors themselves—check for poor posture, improper paper position, poor lighting, a too tightly held pencil, or a writing instrument that is too large, too small, or too short. In addition to the checklist, it is a good idea to keep samples of the children's writing collected at intervals throughout the year. Supplement your analysis of the handwriting on these samples by asking the principal, or perhaps the next-door teacher, to rate them.

Children should also evaluate their own writing. They should make comparisons with levels of achievement shown on commercial scales as well as with their own previous writing efforts. Their efforts toward improvement may be encouraged by displaying samples on the bulletin board, holding a writing clinic with several of the best writers acting as "doctors" for specific problems, having children report on their handwriting (each child indicating his or her best letter, the most difficult letter to make, why his or her handwriting is improving, etc.), and giving emphasis to handwriting in all areas of the curriculum.

Opaque and overhead projectors are useful for looking at children's writing. In showing children's writing, emphasize improvement rather than finding fault. Do not stress details too much: dwelling on "the tail of the q is too long" or "the o is not round enough" will make handwriting improvement more difficult to achieve. Instead, have the children refer to handwriting charts to form their own judgments. Some discussion of handwriting will help focus on particular problems. For instance, one day talk about the effect of the slant of letters on speed and legibility. On other days attention can be given to uniformity of letter size, spacing, formation of letters, and so on.

Using the overhead projector involves a specific writing skill.

Handwriting practice should grow out of the needs that arise as the children write stories, poetry, reports, summaries, diaries, minutes, letters, notes, announcements, signs, and so forth. Genuine communication will foster an appreciation of the importance of good handwriting to attaining that communication. It is usually helpful to set up one main objective for the class each week, with each pupil paying particular attention to any personal handwriting faults that relate to that objective. The objective might be maintaining parallel slant, gaining uniformity of letter size, closing letters properly, maintaining good margins, or having good posture when writing.

Instruction Time

Research evidence indicates that ten to fifteen minutes of concentrated work each day should be sufficient for teaching and maintaining handwriting skills. Most primary-grade teachers will find occasion and need for daily handwriting periods, whereas perhaps no more than a five-minute lesson on alternate days will be adequate at higher grade levels. The use of less frequent and shorter periods presupposes, of course, that attention is being given to individual diagnosis and practice.

Handwriting maintenance in the intermediate and upper grades requires only a few minutes (three to five) several times per week if attention is given to legibility and adequate speed.

In addition to having specific handwriting periods, devote attention during the day to handwriting skills in all areas of work in which writing is involved. Pupils must feel responsible for legibility in all their writing.

The way to eliminate poor handwriting is not to spend more time in handwriting periods but to better utilize the time that is devoted to its teaching and practice.

Paper Position for Cursive

The relaxed angle of the forearm across the desk and the maximum convenience of the forearm and fingers to the paper decide the position of the paper. Usually the angle of the bottom of the paper with the edge of the writing surface should be 30 degrees. For the left-handed writer, the paper should be angled in the opposite direction.

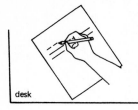

desk

Position and Movement

A child's handwriting is affected by the fit of the desk and the child's position in relation to it. Handwriting is also affected by the position of the paper, the way the writing instrument is held, and the movements of the arm and hand during handwriting strokes. If attention is given to each of these factors at the proper times, much time and energy on the part of both the child and the teacher will be saved.

A child should sit comfortably, with both feet touching the floor and both arms resting in a relaxed position on the writing surface. The writing instrument should be held lightly, and the index finger should be placed nearer to the point than the thumb, with both at least one inch above the writing point. The writing movement should involve smooth coordination of the whole arm, the wrist, and the fingers.

Speed of Writing

Attention to speed is not only useless but harmful if it begins before letter formation is spontaneously good. No end is served by making letters, words, and sentences rapidly and illegibly. Speed is important once letter formation has been properly established, since we all need to write rapidly at times. However, pupils usually make their own adjustments according to the nature of the work—pressure work, personal writing, or work that needs to be particularly neat and pleasing in appearance. Speed norms (see scale samples later in this chapter) are only rough averages and should not be used as arbitrary standards for all children or for every product of a child's writing.

Differences in Letter Forms

A common instructional problem, particularly in the intermediate grades, is that different children in a class will write a number of different forms of the same symbol. These differences are particularly apparent for many capital letters, and they usually simply reflect the fact that the teachers the various pupils have been instructed by in earlier grades have used different commercial materials. Since there seems to be no conclusive evidence to demonstrate the superiority of a given letter form over other forms of the same letter, it is reasonable to permit pupils who have learned different forms to continue to use these so long as they are legible and can be made with sufficient ease and speed. However, it is a good idea for a school to adopt a single system, so that teachers will not confuse pupils by advocating their individual ideas. Before adopting a system, a school may want to simplify some letter forms (removing loops and swings).

Handwriting Materials

Materials for handwriting include chalk, chalkboard, paper, crayons, pencils, pens, and usually commercial handwriting books. There is great variation in the use of these materials in different programs. Most programs call for the use of chalk and crayons in the primary grades, and many call for large beginners' pencils. As to the latter, there is less emphasis today on a larger than normal pencil diameter, but the lead should be thicker, since the essential requirement is that the beginning writer be able to make a line that is easily seen.

There is also variation in what paper is advocated for the various grade levels. You should insist that several types of paper be available to the children in your classroom—not all paper in grade two should have lines that are a half-inch apart, for example. In addition, there should be stationery available for letter writing. The following is a guide to appropriate paper for practice and instruction:*

Don't force children to make letters of a size they can't comfortably make.

Grade 3	9 x 12, lined the long way with lines 1 inch apart
	9 x 12, with lines ½ inch apart alternating light and heavy
	9 x 12, with lines ½ inch apart
	8½ x 11 inch, with lines ⅝ inch apart
Grade 4	8½ x 11 inch, with lines ½ inch apart
	8½ x 11 inch, with lines ⅜ inch apart
Grade 5	8½ x 11 inch, with lines ⅜ inch apart

A left-handed child does manuscript writing.

*Paper varies in size. Some beginning lined paper, for example, is 8½ x 11 inches (with the lines running the long way).

The Left-Handed Child

Five to ten percent of the pupils in a classroom are likely to be left-handed. These pupils are in a right-handed world and are probably taught by a right-handed teacher. If the pupil cannot imitate the teacher as the right-handed pupils do, he or she starts off with a problem. It is important, therefore, that you be aware of the left-handed pupils in your classroom, since their need for instruction is equal to that of right-handed pupils. First of all, it is necessary to recognize that left-handed children can be taught to write as well and as quickly as the right-handed ones. On the other hand, the time needed for development of particular skills is not necessarily the same for the left-handed pupils as for right-handed ones. In any case, it is important to avoid the implication that a child needs special attention because he or she is left-handed—simply pay attention to this child's individual needs as you do to those of other children.

Attention does need to be given to special instructional problems. For example, there should be much writing at the board in the early years, since when a child is writing at the board it is practically impossible to use the upside-down style some improperly taught left-handed writers use. The best way to prevent the acquisition of this habit is to make sure that the paper is angled in the opposite direction from that suggested for the right-handed child. In addition, encouraging the left-hander to hold the writing instrument slightly farther from the point helps, as does making sure that the top of the pen or pencil is pointed toward his or her left shoulder.

It is possible that some left-handed pupils will have developed the upside-down writing habit before they come into your classroom. Whether or not a teacher should attempt to change this habit after about the fourth grade depends on a number of factors. The pupil may not be psychologically or emotionally responsive to a change. In such cases, if the handwriting is reasonably legible and can be done with adequate speed, no attempt to change it is advised.

Left-handed writers should not be expected to write with the same slant as the right-handed ones, although some may do so. However, if the paper is placed properly and the writing instrument held correctly, it is logical for the left-handed child's writing to slant in the direction of the writing movement—that is, to the right.

Maintaining Interest

Young children are eager to learn to write. Later, they are also highly motivated to learn cursive form. However, interest in practicing handwriting may lag. For a program to be successful special attention must be directed toward creating interest in handwriting and providing a freshness to instruction. Try using some of the following activities to supplement the preceding suggestions and furnish motivation:

- Combine spelling review with handwriting practice by having the children compose sentences using the spelling words.

- Children can use bags or envelopes to make individual mailboxes. These mailboxes are then placed beside the pupils' desks, and the pupils may use them to send daily notes to one another. Legible notes may be read; illegible ones are sent to the dead-letter office where a committee of students studies them and reports on their weaknesses.

- Pupils may do research on the history of handwriting, kinds of paper and how paper is made, the handwriting of famous people, kinds of handwriting tools, italic writing, graphology, or the handwriting of pupils in other grades.

- Children may report on writing they do at home, for example, letters, thank-you notes, shopping lists, and telephone messages. To help show the importance of writing, they may also report on writing their parents do.

Novelty can be added to practice through the use of such sentences as the following:

Zillions of zebras zipped by.
Well, Willie works willingly.
Buzzy, a busy bee, buzzed by.
A snapping turtle snapped at the stick.

To provide further variety in practice, tape a paragraph or two, speaking slowly but evenly and paying strict attention to the number of words per minute. If you have several tape recorders with listening stations, different children can practice writing different paragraphs (different content, different speeds, etc.).

Planning a handwriting project with another teacher of the same grade level can also provide motivation for practice. Pupils can write selections (without names on papers) to be exchanged between classes for other children's evaluation. A variation of this is to exchange letters with pupils in a more advanced grade or some other part of the country.

If a child's handwriting remains poor, consider the possibility that he or she may have an emotional problem. If so, it would probably be wise to forget about any intensive effort to help the child improve. Instead, try to give emotional support and look for ways to help with the problem. Persistently poor handwriting may also be caused by poor visual-motor control. Vision should be checked, of course, but sometimes readiness activities merely need to be continued.

EVALUATING HANDWRITING

Handwriting can be evaluated either formally through the use of published scales or less formally by the teacher and the pupils. Since evaluation should lead to corrective practice and remedial teaching, the latter procedure is recommended. This evaluation should be pupil-focused and systematic and should be used as the basis for further teaching.

Diagnosis and Remediation

Most publishers of commercial handwriting materials can supply instruments helpful in locating handwriting faults. Some extracts from one handwriting chart, "Handwriting Faults and How to Correct Them," are given below.*

[This chart] is designed to reveal whether or not the pupil's handwriting violates one or more of the following essential qualities: (1) uniformity of slant, (2) uniformity of alignment, (3) quality of line, (4) letter formation, and (5) spacing. Three levels of quality—excellent, mediocre, and poor—are shown for each trait. In addition to illustrating these qualities, the chart contains excellent suggestions on ways to test a pupil's handwriting for each quality. The chart is particularly helpful because it enables both the teacher and the pupil to discover specific handwriting weaknesses that are in need of remedial treatment and makes helpful suggestions for correcting the defects.

How to test legibility: Make a letter finder by cutting a hole a little larger than the letter in a piece of cardboard. Place the hole of this finder over each letter in turn and mark the letters which are illegible. Have the pupils practice these letters separately, then write the word again and test as before.

How to test slant: Draw slanting lines through the letters and mark all letters which are off slant. If the slant is too great, the paper is tilted too much. If the writing is too vertical, the paper is too upright, and if the slant is backward, the paper is tilted the wrong direction.

How to test for spacing: Draw parallel lines between letters (see diagram). Place the paper in front of you and mark all letters and words which are unevenly spaced.

*Chart published by Zaner-Bloser Company in 1937 and periodically revised. Used by permission.

correct   incorrect

spacing   *spacing*

How to test alignment: Alignment and size are closely integrated and should be studied together. Use a ruler (a diagnostic ruler is best) and draw a base line touching as many of the letters as possible. Also draw a line along the tops of the small letters. Mark the letters above or below these lines.

correct   incorrect

alignment   *alignment*

How to test size of letters: Draw lines along the tops of the letters. Remember the minimum letters, i, u, v, etc., are ¼ space high; t and p are ½ space; capitals and l, h, k, b, d, are ¾ space high. All the lower loop letters extend ½ space below the line.

Comparative size of letters.

How to test for quality of line: Make a letter finder by cutting a hole a little larger than the letter in a piece of cardboard. Place the hole of this finder over each letter in turn and mark the letters which are illegible due to the quality of line.

Have pupils practice these letters from their writing books separately until the letters are perfectly legible. Then have them write the whole word again and test as before.

Handwriting Scales

Handwriting scales are often not used because of the feeling that children will attempt to copy the handwriting on the scale and thus lose the individuality of their writing. However, scales do not have to be used for *grading* pupils' handwriting; they can simply be bases for the pupils to use in making their own judgments about the legibility of their handwriting.

One commercial instrument, *Guiding Growth in Handwriting Evaluation Scales*, provides five specimens of handwriting for each grade level and suggests that samples comparable to these specimens be rated as good, medium, or poor.* There is also a numerical score for each of the five specimens. Two of these specimens are reproduced below.

Specimen 3—Medium for Grade 5. Similar cursive handwriting may be marked 75. The standard speed for this grade is about 60 letters per minute.

> I live in America. It is good to live where you have freedom to work and play. As an American, I support my country and what it stands for.

Specimen 5—Poor for Grade 5. Similar cursive handwriting may be marked 65, and writing poorer than this may be evaluated accordingly.

> My name stands for me. I want to write it well.

Checklists

Procedures for evaluating handwriting were suggested in the section on handwriting practice, since practice should grow from diagnosis and evaluation. You can make a legibility checksheet such as the one shown on the next page, but be sure to list only the letters causing difficulty for your class. The checksheet can be added to if new problems are noted.

*Scales published by Zaner-Bloser Company in 1966. Used by permission.

	NOT THIS	BUT THIS
Straight back stroke for e, l	*e, l*	*e, l*
Avoidance of loop in a, i, n, t, u	*a, i, n, t, u*	*a, i, n, t, u*
Points on r and s	*r, s*	*r, s*
Well-rounded curves on m, n, u	*m, n, u*	*m, n, u*
Carefully crossed t	*t, t, t*	*t, tt*
Open loops on b, f, h, k	*b, f, h, k*	*b, f, h, k*
Avoidance of lazy ending on h, m, n	*h, m, n*	*h, m, n*
Open loop on g, p, y, q	*g, p, y, q*	*g, p, y, q*
Dot over i, j in line with letter	*i, j*	*i, j*
Closing of f on the line	*f, f*	*f*
Careful closing of a, d, g, q	*a, d, g, q*	*a, d, g, q*

WRITING BY MACHINE

Handwriting has advantages, not the least of which is that the equipment needed to do it is simple and completely portable, so it can be done nearly anywhere. Handwriting is highly personal, too. You can probably recognize that of several people you know, and some people even claim to be able to deduce much about the personalities of writers from samples of their penmanship. Also, the use of handwriting conveys feelings; lovers do not ordinarily type intimate messages, and an angry note executed with emphatic graphic flourishes has a certain impact.

However, notwithstanding all these uses, machines are taking over most writing functions. Typewriters and computers have advantages of speed, accuracy, legibility, and storage capability, which are highly important in commerce and communications. A practical consideration for schools is that computers are found in more and more homes, and large numbers of children are learning to use them to write. It seems clear that the elementary-school program must include writing with machines as a part of the language arts curriculum.

Typing

Keep in mind that typists—whether children or adults—need to be able to write by hand legibly and with adequate speed for various tasks.

The advantages of being able to type are obvious. Students may benefit from possessing this skill at any level, but at the secondary level and above, they may be required to submit typewritten assignments. Those who cannot type for themselves must either pay for the service or make arrangements to have it done at times that are not necessarily convenient. Even if an instructor accepts handwritten assignments, there is always the likelihood, supported by some evidence, that typed materials receive a higher evaluation.

In the article listed in the References at the end of this chapter, Hoot mentions some of the studies which show that typing seems to improve the academic performance of elementary-school children.

Typing has not been widely used in elementary classrooms but the results that are available indicate that those students who type produce longer texts, spell and use punctuation more accurately, and write better in other ways. Routine typing may be difficult for children, however. The customary "hunt-and-peck," or two-finger, method is slow, and there is no conclusive evidence as to how old children need to be to learn touch typing, although some have learned as early as the fourth or fifth grade. In addition, the noise level in the elementary classroom will be unacceptably high if a group of children are hammering away on typewriters while they practice touch typing. And errors mean lots of messy erasing or starting over—just as with handwriting. Electric typewriters are easier for children to use, and many have automatic erasing mechanisms, but having enough machines and using them without disrupting the class remain problems. Some of the benefits of typing can be enjoyed, however, before children learn the touch method or when there are only a few typewriters available to them in or near the classroom.

It is usually only when business machine companies or other agencies have supplied the necessary funds or equipment for typing classes that there has been the opportunity for young children to make much progress in typing. And, very often, such classes are held in a room devoted to that activity, an arrangement that does not lend itself to making typing an integral part of the instructional program. Thus making typing a part of the elementary-school program has looked promising, but expectations have not been met.

Computers and Word Processing

Computers have been a major aid to handicapped students.

Personal computers are used in many ways, and one of the most common is for typing or word processing. The computer is much more than a typewriter, of course. One principal difference is that what is typed is displayed on a television screen rather than being directly printed on a piece of paper. While the text is on the screen, erasing, changing, and adding of material may be accomplished very easily and this is why writers find using computers to be a very advantageous method of composing. Also, at any time, the writer may activate a printer, which types the current text onto paper. What is typed may be the text in final form or a draft that the writer can change further at a later time. The computer is also able to remember what has been typed. Its own memory can hold relatively short texts, and longer ones can be stored on magnetic disks. Disks are also used to hold the **program**, the electronically coded set of directions that tell the computer how to process what is being typed by the person at the keyboard. Many different word-processing programs are currently marketed; among those available, several are appropriate for use in elementary classrooms.

Whether adult or child, a writer using a word-processing program has to know how to activate and employ its operations. The writer must be able to type a text, examine it to see what changes need to be made, make those alterations, and then either print the material or store it for later additional revision. In carrying out such operations, he or she will use equipment— several pieces of **hardware** such as the keyboard and the screen, as well as **software**, the programs that are stored on disks and tell the machinery what to do. Thus, to do word processing a writer needs to know something about the equipment and a great deal about the procedures involved in using it.

The Equipment. Most people have some familiarity with computers; you may be quite proficient in using them yourself. However, some people have done little more than type in a few words or numbers at a library or teller machine. Personal computers have the potential to be used for word processing but several components are required to make a word processor: the computer itself, a keyboard, a screen, disks and disk drives, and a printer.

The computer is taken for granted; common usage is to refer, inaccurately, to the entire system as "the computer." This generally creates no problem in daily life, but students should understand that the computer is only part of the system; it is most likely contained under the platform the screen sits on and is composed of silicon chips and complex circuitry. This **central processing unit** is what permits such complicated procedures as those described for word processing. The typist hits keys representing the letters of the alphabet and punctuation marks, and the computer very rapidly translates each strike of a key into electronic signals, which are further manipulated. The computer then puts the signals back into letter form so that the writer can read them on the screen and proceed to develop the text.

The keyboard used with the computer is quite similar to that on an ordinary typewriter. There are some additional keys and other controls, and the locations of keys for some characters or functions may not be the same as on a typewriter. Although there has been some experimenting with different keyboard patterns, unless alphabetical sequencing is used, none of the variations seems to be better than the others for elementary-school children. Even rather young children, however, seem to learn the locations of letters fairly quickly.

The screen, or monitor, for the computer resembles that for a television set and is quite like it. The screen is designed to accommodate a certain number of lines and columns, which is important to keep in mind when doing word processing because when the text is actually printed, it may not look just as it did on a screen that is narrower than a piece of typing paper. Color monitors permit the use of programs that produce differently colored letters and/or backgrounds; some people prefer such a color option, but the letters are sometimes difficult to read on the screen. The screen has a small lighted area the size of a letter space called a **cursor**. The cursor is a place holder; it tells the writer where the next character to be typed will appear or which character will be erased if that is the signal being sent.

The disk drive for programs is a boxlike unit that usually sits alongside the keyboard and screen. It has a slot in it and the writer inserts into that slot a magnetic disk that contains the program to be used. As mentioned earlier, it is this word-processing program that governs how the various keys will type or make changes in the text. The program must be transferred into the computer's memory before typing can begin. When the word-processing session is over, the program disk is removed; until the disk is reinserted, the computer "forgets" how to do word processing.

The disk drive for files is another unit like the disk drive for programs but the disk that is inserted is a blank one initially that will furnish a record of what has been typed. When the writer wants a text to be preserved in electronic form, the computer can be signaled to put it on the writer's disk. Texts stored on disks are called **files.** A file can be put back into the computer at any time the writer wishes to continue working on it.

The printer is usually separate from the other pieces of hardware and is not present in some computer systems. At any time the writer can have the printer put part or all of the text on paper. These typed pages are called **hard copy** and may be taken from the screen, the memory in the computer, or the disk files. The hard copy may be written on just like any paper, so writers may make notes on the pages of changes they plan to make when they again have that text on the screen.

Children's disk files are most conveniently kept in a covered box near the computer (although those with machines at home will also want to use them there).

Procedures for Using Word Processors. Each word-processing program is somewhat different from the others, but there are some general procedures common to nearly all of them. Going through a simple writing activity step by step demonstrates what happens when children begin to use a word processor.

1. Select a program disk and place it in the disk drive. In a minute or so the program is "booted up," or transferred to the memory of the computer. The system is then ready to be used for writing.
2. Type the text, correcting errors that occur along the way, if desired.
3. Read the text and make any necessary changes, in anything from the spelling of a word or the placement of a comma to the location of a word, sentence, or several paragraphs.
4. When the writing is finished, activate the printer to obtain the hard copy.

Many other procedures are possible, too. Making a file for later revision or printing has already been mentioned. In addition, there are program features that permit the writer to decide how lines will be spaced when the printing is done, whether or not there will be an even margin on the right-hand side of the page, which words should be changed each time they appear in the text, and more.

WORD PROCESSING IN THE CLASSROOM

Significant numbers of elementary-school teachers are using word processing in their classrooms, and the ones with the most experience have identified and at least partially solved the problems encountered in implementation. They are convinced that the major difficulties can be overcome and that the contribution made by word processing is so valuable as to be worth the effort. Several factors that seem to be particularly important to the effective use of word processing in the classroom are discussed in the sections that follow. (This discussion emphasizes the use of word processing as an alternative to handwriting. The actual process of composing with the computer is a separate concern discussed in Chapters 9 and 10.)

Proficiency of the Teacher

If the school has a special instructor who teaches about computers, she or he can supervise the children as they become familiar with word processing, and their classroom teacher can very probably learn along with them. Otherwise, word processing should not be undertaken in a classroom until the teacher has become proficient at it. Some adults are able to learn the procedures on their own using only the instruction books. However, most cannot succeed in this way; they need a teacher of their own.

Availability of Computers

In order for computers to be available to pupils on a reasonable basis there should be one or more in each classroom. Several are needed to make word processing an effective tool for children's writing efforts.

In elementary schools computers may be located in separate "computer rooms," in library resource centers, or in regular classrooms. When a computer room serves an entire school population, its use usually involves taking a whole class there on a regular basis to acquire "computer literacy," or general knowledge about computers, and to get some experience in operating them. In such circumstances it is not likely that students will be able to use the machines to learn word processing; there simply will not be enough time for them to do so unless the school is quite small. When computers are located in a library or resource center, it is sometimes possible for individuals or small groups to use them for a variety of purposes, including writing activities. Generally, the students who do this will have to be those who are able to work without much supervision, however.

When computers are in classrooms permanently, or at least for large blocks of time, doing word processing is quite feasible. Much can be learned even if there is only a single unit in a classroom, but the availability of three or four makes a big difference. The reason why even a single unit is advantageous is that word processing is not necessarily a solitary activity. Because the text is on the screen and easily seen by anyone in the vicinity, others can observe the writer, and comments about everything from spelling to content may be expected. Some teachers have children work in small groups; one child may be making notes and another reviewing hard copy, while others are composing on the screen and still others are reading the story or other composition to themselves or aloud as it is being written. In such a situation the sense of writing for an audience is immediate.

Learning Keyboarding

When children are introduced to word processing, they should simultaneously be taught to do touch typing, typing with all fingers and without looking at the keys. Otherwise, they will learn to use less efficient methods, habits that will have to be broken later if they are to become efficient typists. Fortunately, if physically capable of doing so, children learn keyboarding quickly. There are some very good teaching devices, including several computer programs that have been developed to teach keyboarding skills. Several principles guide such instruction for elementary-level students:

Keyboarding is a skill, and the skill-related learning generalizations apply. For instance, there should be frequent, brief periods of meaningful practice.

- There should be a typing teacher or other keyboarding expert who oversees the teaching.
- Classroom teachers should have at least general knowledge of the methodology of keyboarding instruction.
- Emphasis should be on accuracy rather than speed.
- Keyboards should be readily available for individual practice.

Selecting Appropriate Programs

Word-processing programs vary in their possibilities, capacities, and complexity of operation, so choosing which one to use is a difficult decision. An elementary-school student should usually concentrate on learning only one, which means that a school ought to plan to designate a particular program for use by everyone. This choice should be made with several criteria in mind, including ease of use by beginners as well as potential for providing assistance to advanced writers. If you, as teacher, must select a program for a class, you should consult with several experienced people who know computers and have worked with students of the same age group as the class.

Teaching Word Processing

By fourth grade some children are very competent typists—producing 40 words per minute or more.

When elementary-school children are being taught to do word processing, several important considerations apply. Until the students learn to type reasonably well, they should concentrate on their keyboarding skills. Before they are proficient typists, their attempts to compose on the word processor will not be especially successful because the procedure will be too time-consuming and frustrating for many. In order to provide a better experience for these students, teachers may have them do their initial writing by hand and then enter this draft into the word processor. Typing a familiar text in this way can be good practice. Alternatively, an older student or adult may do the typing for a beginner. Once the text is in the computer, the writer should take over, however, and give attention to revision.

A FINAL WORD

Years ago the principal tools for writing were pencils or pens to be dipped in ink. School children worked on their "penmanship" for hours each week, and some went on to work in occupations requiring that they be able

Children can teach one another how to use a word processor.

to "write a good hand." Now there are many means for written communication, and people who do the most writing use machines much of the time. Actually, all individuals should learn how to type and use a word processor; ideally, these skills can begin to be taught in the elementary school. However, handwriting must also be taught in the elementary school, and the emphasis of this instruction should be on reasonable legibility and speed. All children need to be able to write legibly and quickly, but writing forms do not have to be identical for every member of the class, nor does the writing need to be a work of art. And, finally, since there are innumerable forms to be filled out in this modern world and machines are not always available, children should be encouraged to maintain and use manuscript writing even after they have learned cursive.

References

Barbe, Walter B.; Lucas, Virginia H.; and Wasylyk, Thomas M.; eds. *Handwriting: Basic Skills for Effective Communication*. Zaner-Bloser, 1984.

Chandler, Daniel. *Young Learners and the Microcomputer*. Open University Press, 1984.

Handwriting Resource Book, Grades 1–7. Ministry of Education, British Columbia, Canada, 1981.

Hoot, James L. "Keyboarding Instruction in the Early Grades: Must or Mistake?" *Childhood Education* 63 (December 1986), pp. 95–101.

Hoot, J. L., and Silvern, S. B. *Writing with Computers in the Early Grades*. Teachers College Press, 1988.

Kaake, Dianne M. "Teaching Elementary Age Children Touch Typing as an Aid to Language Arts Instruction." *The Reading Teacher* (March 1983), pp. 640–643.

Teaching Resources

Elements of Legible Handwriting. Zaner-Bloser, 1974 (pamphlet).

Evaluating Handwriting. Zaner-Bloser, 1977 (pamphlet).

Fry, Edward. *Computer Keyboarding for Children.* Teachers College Press, 1984.

Handwriting Evaluation Scales. Zaner-Bloser (kit).

Keyboard Cadet. Mindscope (software).

Learning the Keyboard for Children. Random House (six cassettes, keyboard fingercharts with colored key stickers, and lesson sheets; K–grade 6).

New Links to Cursive: *A Power Approach to Handwriting.* Curriculum Associates (kit).

The Print Shop. Scholastic (software).

Rainbow Keyboarding. Scholastic (software).

SRA Lunchbox Handwriting Kits. (separate kits for manuscript and cursive; K–grade 4).

Success with Typing. Scholastic (software).

Touch N' Write: *Palmer Manuscript Penmanship.* Sunburst Communications, 1986 (grades 1 and 2).

Activities for Preservice Teachers

1. Practice your handwriting—manuscript and cursive—on many surfaces and with all kinds of writing instruments. Evaluate what you write in the ways suggested in this chapter. Keep in mind that some people judge a teacher by the quality of her or his handwriting. (And, of course, the children have to be able to read it!)

2. Obtain handwriting samples from college students (preferably class notes, not something for display). How is the legibility? Are letters similarly made? Do those from the same schools write similarly? Can you tell who is left-handed?

3. If you do not type, take steps to learn. Typing classes are offered by adult education departments of public school systems, by community colleges, and by commercial schools, and many individuals have learned touch typing on their own using a high school typing textbook. As you learn typing, examine computer programs developed to teach children keyboarding.

4. Observe handwriting lessons at several grade levels. Note differences in posture, hand and arm movements, quality of handwriting produced, degree of insistence on uniformity throughout the class, and so forth.

5. Examine samples of commercial handwriting materials for a grade level or levels of interest to you. Decide which you would choose if the decision were up to you.

6. Obtain several samples of children's handwriting and evaluate them using a handwriting scale.

7. Visit a classroom, computer room, or resource center where elementary-school children are learning keyboarding and word processing. Do they seem interested? What difficulties do there seem to be? What software is being used? Is the teacher an expert in typing and/or computers?

Activities for Inservice Teachers

1. Ask a colleague to do a critique of your handwriting—on the board, on the overhead, and on children's papers. Are there areas in which you could improve? What specific plan can you devise for improving?

2. Have children at one grade level write the same paragraph and then identify three or four levels of quality among the samples. Offer these to your colleagues as the beginning of a handwriting scale for the building. What reaction do you get?

3. Start a file of examples of good and poor handwriting by adults. Try to get examples that are not signatures. With the children, examine the poor examples to determine why they are illegible—bad letter formation, spacing, slant, and so on.

4. Ask college professors, administrators, and parents what they think about eliminating cursive writing from the school program and concentrating on manuscript, typing, and word processing. What do they say? What reasons do they offer in support of their positions?

5. Find out what your school or district's policy is on teaching word processing. What provision is there for helping teachers to learn how to do word processing?

6. Try several computer programs that teach keyboarding to elementary-school students. Which one seems best to you? What recommendations would you make to those responsible for purchasing such items?

7. Prepare activities for the children in your class to do individually to improve their handwriting.

8. Make an informal survey of the handwriting in your school. Collect papers and analyze them for specific handwriting faults. Note the amount of writing done, types of assignments, and so on, and see if you can relate such factors to handwriting ability.

9. Make a survey of local school systems to see how computers are being used by students at various grade levels for their written work. What do you conclude? What are the opinions of the most experienced teachers regarding computer use by students?

10. Acquire some books on graphology. Use the study of graphology to stimulate interest in handwriting among upper-grade students.

Independent Activities for Children

1. Each child can keep a personal handwriting improvement record by filing dated samples of writing and reviewing these periodically, using some of the diagnostic and evaluative suggestions in this chapter to see where improvement has been made and what needs to receive attention.

2. Encourage pupils to use a diagnostic chart such as the one presented in this chapter to examine their handwriting for common problems.

3. Make available a device for determining the legibility of a single letter in a word. An easy device to make is a piece of tagboard about 1 inch wide and 3 inches long; near one end punch a hole with a hole punch. The child places the hole over individual letters and practices making those that are illegible.

4. For individual practice, prepare a folder with a pocket on one side and a sheet of acetate on the other (fasten it to the folder on one long side and on the bottom). In the pocket, place cards containing directions for the formation of letters and lists of words using those letters. A child selects a letter to work on and places it under the acetate. Using a marking pencil and with the card as a guide, the child first traces the letter, then writes it without tracing, and finally writes the words, comparing them with the model.

5. Some attention to speed is necessary in the middle grades, although legibility must remain paramount. To practice speed, individual children can write short paragraphs and time themselves. Prepare paragraphs that should take about a minute to copy (about forty to sixty letters) at first. Paragraphs and sentences may be taken from handwriting scales, textbooks, or familiar books or stories.

6. As an incentive to improve, suggest that a child prepare a sample of his or her handwriting (enough so that most letters—upper- and lowercase—and numerals are included) and write a letter to a pupil in another part of the country to send with the sample suggesting an exchange several times during the year.

7. To encourage the learning of touch typing, provide keyboard shields or color-coded keys (with corresponding stick-on finger dots) for children whose hands are large enough and who have adequate eye/hand coordination.

8. Children who have learned to use a computer program such as *Print Shop* by Scholastic can make attractive book covers, posters, and banners for special events in the class or school.

9. Arrange for children who are doing very well in touch typing to see a local speed typing champion in action. Such a visit should be a real treat for them, since they have some realization of the skill involved.

10. Children can collect samples of writing by adults and older children and practice identifying illegibilities

in this writing. In some instances, if it can be done without offending, they might point out to the writers (perhaps their parents) the illegibilities.

11. Have a child find examples of early picture writing and/or other alphabets—hieroglyphics, Native American picture writing, the Greek alphabet—and prepare a demonstration for the class. As a part of the demonstration, several children might develop symbols depicting an activity the class is involved with and have the other children try to "read" what they have written.

Chapter 9

The Writing Process in the Classroom

*W*riting "compositions" has been a part of school programs for many years. Results have seldom been encouraging, though, possibly because instruction so often emphasized everything but writing itself. Activities receiving the most attention were identifying parts of speech, diagramming sentences, filling in blanks with the "right" word, and providing punctuation for sample sentences. When students actually wrote compositions, teachers or textbooks supplied such stereotyped topics as "What I Did on My Summer Vacation" or "A Funny Mistake." Teachers' expectations usually focused on neat handwriting, accurate spelling, and "complete" sentences, each beginning with a capital letter and ending with the appropriate punctuation mark. Very often, the products fell short of the expectations, and the teacher had to "correct" them for rewriting in approved form. Quite understandably, under this sort of regime not many children enjoyed writing. Getting their compositions back all marked up with red pencil and receiving instructions to do them over again caused most children to dread the entire procedure.

Now, many teachers work in a different way. They teach writing as a process, as was briefly described in Chapter 4. The first section of this chapter further describes that process and focuses on the writing done in the middle and upper grades. The value of the process is that it encourages children to write, develops writing confidence and ability, and has applicability to all types of writing. Furthermore, children like it and can easily do it if they are properly taught and the teacher encourages its use.

Books by Elbow and Murray (see References) have good discussions of the writing process.

COMPOSITION AS A PROCESS

There are several advantages to emphasizing the process of writing in your teaching. One of the more important benefits is that attention is directed away from the finished product and to the act of writing. A piece of writing is not simply done and then given to someone to read; much has to be accomplished before there is any reason to be concerned about preparing the text to be read by others. Another advantage is that the student who develops a real understanding of the writing process learns a procedure that can be applied to many tasks. Techniques and terminology associated with the process become familiar, and, as a result, students and teachers may talk with one another about "drafting," "having conferences," and "editing." The process becomes an internalized one that writers can use on their own for the rest of their lives.

The process stages are prewriting, writing, and postwriting. For young children, depending on their maturity and writing experience as discussed in Chapter 4, these stages are rather brief and simple. For example, the child may draw a picture, write a related text, and then read that to the teacher or a friend. As children gain more experience and maturity, each stage becomes more complex. Before writing, the child usually decides on a topic, generates ideas, and generally builds enthusiasm for writing. In beginning the writing, the first step is getting ideas down on paper, recognizing that what is being done is a draft, an attempt that can be discarded entirely or extensively modified. The draft may be reread, discussed with others, and revised during the postwriting stage. A final step is publication, if that seems appropriate; this involves editing and making the piece available to others to read.

The Prewriting Stage

When you have a major writing task, it is most likely related to academic work, a term paper perhaps. If the end result is to be successful, much preparation is required; you read, talk with others, use resources, take notes, and make an outline. This is all a rehearsal for writing, and elementary-school students need to go through a similar process, deciding what to write about and collecting their thoughts. They must talk with the teacher and the other children, because as they hear responses to the ideas they express, their thinking will be stimulated. Reflection on these interchanges will put them in a much better position to begin writing. Time spent on prewriting activities is time well spent.

Selecting Topics. Subjects to write about come from several sources. The best ones are those that are important to the writer. If children keep journals as described in Chapter 4, they will have been writing about trips, play activities, experiences with their friends, and other events important to them. Journal writing is a means of exploring experiences and thoughts about important subjects, some of which may be interesting enough to be treated more fully. To help children select topics for further development, ask them to look in their journals.

Topics may be supplied by the teacher occasionally, especially if children have trouble deciding on things to write about among their own concerns. However, it is usually better for them to make such decisions themselves. Specific activities may be planned for the purpose of helping children to think of topics and clarify them.

Discussions among children can promote the generation of ideas about subjects for writing. Younger children will need some guidance; otherwise, they are likely to be heavily influenced by classmates' choices. Opportunities to discuss such broad topics as animals—including those on farms, in zoos, in the classroom, and at home—will usually generate sufficient exchange of ideas to permit everyone to identify a promising topic for writing. Older children, particularly those with several years of experience with the writing process, can discuss a variety of topics among themselves and give and receive advice as to the ones that will be most interesting to try.

Conferences between the teacher and an individual child concerning

Children will write about things they know about, things they have experienced, and things that have meaning for them. Make sure that children in your class keep adding to—and broadening—their experiences.

Professional writers often say that writing is "a process of discovery," meaning that they sometimes don't know what they are actually going to write until they write it. Some even say that they are occasionally surprised or shocked at what appears.

A teacher and student have a conference about writing.

topic selection may be very brief when the child has a definite idea and the teacher sees good possibilities in it. Such conferences may also be rather brief if the teacher has some doubts about a choice but believes it is advisable to encourage the child to go ahead and try. In such cases, though, the teacher should be sure to watch for the development of any difficulties as the child proceeds. Other conferences may involve some discussion to help the writer clarify his or her thinking about possible topics. In such cases, the teacher can ask general sorts of questions concerning out-of-school activities, hobbies, sports interests, holiday plans, and other areas that might offer possibilities. Many times teachers find that such conferences are not only productive for the writing program but also worthwhile in establishing relationships with children, since they provide excellent opportunities for talking with individuals about what interests them.

   Lists of possible topics can be kept by children for use as needed. A classroom list may be used, too, but only when it seems obvious that it is needed to move a child along. Items on the classroom list should be general: sports teams and players, popular outdoor activities, seasonal events, social occasions, classroom activities, trips, local events, scouts and clubs, and any others that seem likely to capture the children's interest. The list should reflect local concerns and events so that writing remains close to the children's experiences. Of course, as children's knowledge in various subject areas expands, the list may also include topics related to these.

Children get input from:

reading and being read to
observing things in nature
listening to sounds, music, and language
finding, listing, and discussing new words
attending dramatizations
and much more

Exploring a Topic. Once children have decided on their topics, it is usually helpful to teach them ways of generating related ideas. Too often, when a topic is assigned by the teacher or taken from a textbook and there is little or no exploration of what it means to them, children will write a few perfunctory sentences and announce that the assignment is completed, or they will ask how much writing is required. Whatever the source of the topic, writing about it can be made easier and better if writers learn how to use pictures, diagrams, and topic webs (introduced in Chapter 4), how to do brainstorming or free writing, how to consult books and other resources, how to conduct interviews and conferences, and how to take notes.

Pictures and drawings can be used by younger writers as described in Chapter 4, and the same idea may be appropriate for older children. Although they may not be interested in drawing a picture, some types of writing may be aided by making sketches or diagrams. When writing about figure skating, for example, a child may wish to draw stick figures in various body positions before trying to write descriptions of particular leaps and movements. A student interested in aircraft or rockets will often make elaborate drawings of individual pieces or scenes before writing about them. Of course, to make such sketches usually requires some research by the pupil.

Brainstorming is the process of coming up with many ideas that might be related to a topic. This should be done as a group experience at first—involving either the whole class or a subgroup. Once the process has been introduced, individuals may use it, although group results are usually more satisfactory. In brainstorming the goal is simply to generate ideas, whether they are good, not so good, or useless. During the procedure, participants may not evaluate suggested ideas, but may only produce new ones or expand on someone else's. Ideas can be represented by isolated words, short

Older children can produce high-quality illustrations for their writing.

phrases, or sentences. After a dozen or so have been produced, related ones may be grouped together. From a list of brainstormed ideas a writer will likely be able to see what can be used to get the writing started. Ideas that do not appear to be helpful can be ignored.

Free writing is similar to brainstorming in that the writer permits ideas to flow without exercising much control. Usually only older children can do this with any success, since it requires writing as fast as possible in an attempt to keep up with thinking. The child simply writes about a topic for a few minutes without stopping and without really thinking about what is being put down on the paper. There should be no going back to read or any attention to corrections, changes, or punctuation. (However, the writing does have to be legible enough to be read later). Through using this technique the writer explores ideas and feelings and, hopefully, discovers something worth keeping and developing.

Teacher conferences for the purpose of getting started provide an opportunity for the teacher to ask questions that may help a writer focus on the chosen topic and explore it, looking for aspects that have the most personal significance. The child should also be led to examine his or her reasons for writing and to consider what audience might be interested and what that individual or group will already know or might want to know. During these conferences, intrude as little as possible. Resist any temptation to tell a child how the writing might begin or even to offer hints and suggestions. Instead, follow the lead of the child, bearing in mind whose piece it is and the importance it might have to the author. This kind of conference is an opportunity to point out the value of making notes as a means for reminding the writer of the need for information from another person, a book, or some other source.

Peer conferences put children in the role of a teacher as they help classmates think about their topics and what they might mean to others. Children will learn to employ the same techniques they have observed the teacher using—asking how interest in the topic came about and other appropriate "when," "where," and "why" questions. You may want to listen in on some peer conferences (but only infrequently) to encourage the most beneficial lines of discussion. Another benefit of having such conferences regularly is that children will begin to ask themselves questions as they write, anticipating what their classmates are likely to want to know about in the conferences.

Webs, or semantic maps, are tools a writer may use for jotting down ideas or information related to a central topic. Writing the items in a schematic form such as a web gives a focus to the central idea and is helpful for remembering related or supporting items and how they are related. The first webs used are usually relatively simple, but they should become more complex. For example, a simple web used by a student named Val to write about her dog Ollie was shown in Chapter 4 (see page 109). If Val were more experienced, she would number the related circles within a web to help her decide what to write about first, second, and third. And, in the middle grades and beyond, she would put in a third set of circles to support or describe the second, as shown in the example on the following page.

In *The Art of Teaching Writing,* Calkins presents very thorough descriptions of what can be accomplished in conferences.

Webs can be thought of as clusters of ideas and information that are related to a central thought. They can be useful in any learning activity for relating ideas to one another.

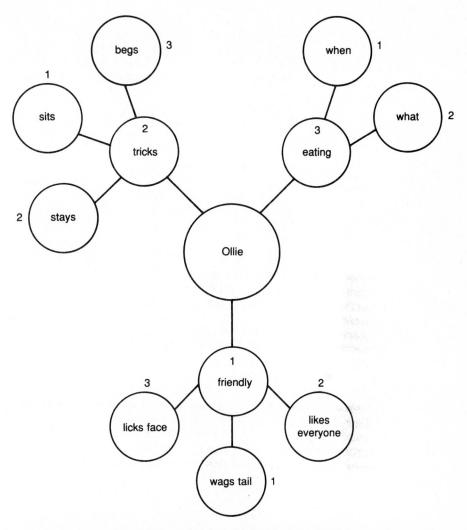

As webs become more complex, they are very useful as a first step in outlining. Effective writers will jot down ideas—perhaps in a schematic form such as a web—as a means for collecting these ideas (or information) so that they will not be forgotten and can be culled, added to, ordered, and so on. Some writers will go on to put the elements of the web into an outline form. This doesn't have to be a formal outline—even though it may later (in some cases) be turned into one—but it should show some order and reflect the relationships among the ideas.

Writing

The writing stage involves getting an organized text on paper so that the writer (at least) can read what has been written. For some types of writing there will be only one draft, especially for writing done by younger children and particularly for journal writing in the upper grades. More experienced writers, however, should come to see their initial efforts as first drafts that will be changed, extended, and improved at a later time. Such an attitude permits them to take risks in trying particular topics, in exploring their thinking about a subject, or in simply dealing with the subject as accurately and completely as possible.

When sitting down to actually write, the writer should call on all that she or he has done in preparation, including notes from brainstorming, free writing, conferences, reference sources, and a web or outline. The sources and the organizational aids provide the basis for "getting something down" on paper. As thoughts begin to come to mind, the writing must be done fairly rapidly so that ideas are not lost. Giving too much time to selecting just the right word or worrying about spelling is not advisable at this point. Building momentum and seeing what there is to be said about the topic should occupy the writer's attention.

The following guidelines may help to clarify for children what should be emphasized during initial writing:

Even professional writers sometimes find it necessary to write "just anything" in order to get started.

- *Use scrap paper for first drafts.* Writing on something other than good paper reinforces the transitory nature of these initial attempts. Backs of printed materials and worksheets and paper that might otherwise be discarded, such as computer print-outs, serve very well for drafts.

- *Try different "leads," or beginnings.* Getting started may require that several approaches to a topic be tried until the writer finds one that is effective in keeping the ideas coming.

- *Cross out rather than erase.* Drawing a line through what is being changed or discarded is faster and easier than erasing it. Also, text that has been crossed out can still be read; it might turn out to be the better alternative after all or useful in some other place.

- *Use arrows and other marks to show how sections of the text relate to one another.* During the writing of a first draft some additions and transpositions may be necessary. These can be done with notes and other markings that indicate what comes next. It doesn't matter how messy the text is as long as the writer can read it to someone else.

- *Do not be concerned about handwriting, typing, spelling, or punctuation.* During initial writing, concentration should be focused on ideas, not on mechanics. Children need to be cautioned that the handwriting should not be so bad that they cannot read it themselves, of course. Other matters will receive attention later.

Speaking and Writing K–12, edited by Thaiss and Suhor, gives attention to how thinking, talking, and writing are related.

- *While writing, also read, think, and talk.* Writers must shift among reading over what has been written, writing some more, thinking about the ideas to be expressed, and talking with others. One activity leads to another, and this interaction will keep the writing flowing.

A ten-year-old may have a "writer's block" just as an older and more experienced writer may.

- *Recognize that sticking points will sometimes occur.* Even when they are familiar with many techniques for maintaining the momentum of writing, children will occasionally be unable to make progress. At these times the best solution is often to put the piece away and come back to it later. A fresh look may then bring new ideas.

Writing first drafts will become easier as children get more experience with the writing process. As they gain that experience, concern about mechanics or even word choice or the awkwardness of sentences will lessen. They will know that all of these aspects can be dealt with after the first draft is made. In addition, they probably will have learned how to anticipate the questions that you and their classmates are likely to ask (What does that mean? Can you tell more about this part?), and such knowledge will enable them to think about these points as they write. All of this will gradually lead them to produce more successful first drafts.

Postwriting Activities

After the first draft of a piece of writing has been completed and, perhaps, read to others, the writer needs to decide whether or not anything further should be done with it. Acknowledgment of the ownership of the material and respect for children mean that a decision by a child to discard material has to be accepted. On the other hand, you should encourage children to keep all of their written work in folders. Something that does not seem satisfactory may be used later with a different result.

What seems an unsatisfactory story might evolve into a really good poem.

Children should be encouraged to select first drafts that are good enough for revision. It is through criticism of their own work and deciding what changes will improve it that they will learn to write. Beginning in the first grade, nearly every child will be able to revise something he or she has written and make it better. As children grow older and gain experience, an increasingly higher proportion of their writing will be taken through the postwriting steps of revision, editing, and publication.

Learning about Revision. Once students have been through the writing process a few times, they will understand the difference between writing a

Revision is an important step in the writing process.

first draft and making a revision. In the early grades, however, or when the process is being introduced to older children for the first time, you will need to take specific steps to familiarize them with revision procedures.

Most importantly, writers will need guidance in learning how to see the differences between what they wanted to express and the actual products that resulted. Of course, total satisfaction with a product cannot always be achieved, but it is extremely important that children learn to identify problems in their own writing. With experience they will begin to find ways to express themselves more effectively. Beginners generally think of revision as mainly adding more to the text or correcting spelling and punctuation. More experienced students realize that major changes in organization or even switching to an entirely different form of writing are sometimes necessary.

Reading a first draft and revising it as a group activity is helpful for demonstrating what revision involves. You may present a sample piece of imperfect writing (not the writing of a class member) on a chart or overhead projector, read it with the children, and discuss how it might be changed for the better. Changes should actually be made, based as much as possible on the children's suggestions. Cross things out, make insertions, and use whatever revision strategies seem to be appropriate, while encouraging the class members to discuss these and their effectiveness. After children have participated in several such group activities, some will be able to apply the revision techniques to their own work; others will need to be helped further. You can give them help by going over their texts with them privately but in a way similar to that used with the group.

Revising a First Draft.   After children have participated in group revision activities, they should be encouraged to examine their own drafts and identify at least some things that require attention. As a first step, they should read what they've written aloud to themselves (softly, of course) and apply questions such as were suggested in the group sessions: "Is this what I wanted to say? Does it make sense? Could I say it better?" Since children should have begun to recognize that they are writing for audiences, other points should also be kept in mind during their reading: "Will anyone want to read this? What more will they want to know? How can I make it more interesting?" Attempts to answer such questions will produce helpful ideas for revision.

Some written guidelines for revision should be provided. Posting a chart that summarizes the writing process will help children to remember the distinctions between first-draft writing, revision, and editing. Also, a checklist of basic, specific writing features to be examined when revising may be duplicated and handed out to the class, or perhaps the textbook may contain one that is applicable. Such a list should not be overly long and ought to be updated from time to time as writers gain in proficiency. Once a particular writing feature has been discussed by you and the children, it may be added to the list. The emphasis should be on meaning and ideas, although checklists certainly need to cover punctuation and spelling, particularly if the meaning of the children's writing is not clear because of problems with these aspects.

Reading aloud or listening to a recording of that reading will usually help a writer think of changes that need to be made.

How the
President almost got killed because of the friendship
~Ronald Reagan~ Festival

The president gets got on board a plane to Russia.
It was a ~so he~ festrade Of Friendship. After 18 hrs. hours of Being in
a airplane ~they~ got there. The president was Ronald Reagan
iDelighted to see the festival people dancing and
singing. the sight was amazing. The president
Ronald Reagan
was inttorducedst to the people in Russia. Some people ~where~ were booing. Th-
dressed in
en the presidents gurd sees ~some one~ a person pull a black
heavily armed top secret gun out, ~before his~ the guards heart was pounding
shot
gun echoed.
hard. Before ~you~ he could turn around the president
Ronald
was on the ground breathing hard and ~dying~ loud. — They
rushed him to the hospital but they didn't let
because the us
them operate. So they fixed it up enough so he could ~dying~ didn't trust ~them~ the Russian doctors.
get to the us without dying

They ~we~ went to the airport and ~went home~
on the way home the engine blow. The flight pilot
panicked
paneked. ~They~ They were expecting a storm—

A fifth-grader's first draft with revisions.

A checklist of writing features should direct the children to read their drafts and then respond to the questions on the list. A beginning checklist might have these questions:

Does the piece begin in an interesting way?
Does it tell enough?
Does each sentence make sense?
Could better words be used?

For suggestions on how to help upper-grade children with their writing, see Atwell's book, listed in the References.

For more advanced writers other questions can be added:

Is the topic developed in an interesting way?
Does each sentence fit in with what comes before and after?
Are there gaps that need to be filled in?
Are synonyms or more expressive words or phrases needed anywhere?
Could some sentences be combined?
Does any sentence need to be divided into two or more?
Is each sentence really a sentence?

Conferences with the Teacher. You should be available to confer with children about their first drafts. As what they write becomes longer, more time will be required for them to read the drafts to you. Once peer conferences begin, however, this demand on your time will be at least partially alleviated because they will read to one another. A conference may require only a few seconds for a discussion of word choice or several minutes for consideration of text organization.

During such a conference you should be giving direct assistance—but not specific directions—as well as demonstrating a procedure that the children will be able to use with one another and by themselves when working alone. Try to keep the following considerations in mind:

- *Ask questions that encourage children to talk.* You will learn a lot by listening, and the students will explore their ideas more fully.
- *Respond honestly but with discretion.* Finding something good in the piece and mentioning that should be the goal.
- *Ask the writer to identify something that needs attention.* Work on what the writer identifies, holding your own questions until later.
- *Deal with only a small number of concerns at any one time.* Too much attention to problems creates the wrong kind of atmosphere.
- *Encourage children to react to what they have written.* Remember that the child's opinion of something she or he has created is more important than the opinion of anyone else.

Pose questions that direct the writer's attention to the text:

How is this piece going?
What do you like about it?
What part are you going to work on first?
Who will read this?
What else would they like to know?
How do the parts fit together?
Does the beginning do what you want it to?
Are there problem places?

If children ask questions or otherwise indicate readiness for a particular learning experience, conference time can be used for direct teaching. This is an effective means for promoting growth in writing.

Conferences with Peers. After you have modeled the conference procedure in individual sessions, children should begin to meet in pairs or small groups to read and discuss their drafts. Emphasize to the children that their remarks ought to concern positive aspects of what a peer has written and they should concentrate on productive questions and suggestions rather than on negative criticism. When a positive atmosphere prevails, writers feel more free to express in writing what they really believe is important to them.

Reading one's work to peers also creates a genuine audience situation. Children should realize that they do not write only for themselves or the teacher; this will help them develop writing that will hold the attention of their classmates. The audience needs to be recognized in the revision of almost every type of writing.

Keep in mind the importance of an audience.

Writing Additional Drafts. In the elementary school a second draft is usually sufficient to make a piece satisfactory to the writer, although occasionally, a child will be so caught up in a topic that she or he will want to do a third or even fourth version. Such enthusiasm is not common, but it certainly deserves encouragement. All writers must know that perfection is seldom achieved, however; those who write must come to accept that they will often have to stop working on something they don't feel is "finished" yet.

A student refers to an edited earlier draft to write a final draft.

As children prepare to do second drafts, they should begin by working directly on the first—replacing words, making insertions, and even cutting up pages to move sections around. In general, the more mature the writer, the greater the extent of revision. More experienced and interested students will occasionally revise a piece of writing so that it is quite different from the original text. All drafts, even ones that have been changed a good deal, should be kept in each child's writing folder; then, during conferences, you and the child can review and discuss what occurred at each step in the revision. This should help the child to understand her or his development as a writer as well as giving you some hints as to what teaching is needed.

Editing. If children read their own writing to classmates, teachers, and parents, there is little reason to be greatly concerned about handwriting, spelling, punctuation, and usage. (But do make sure that parents understand what your teaching procedure is.) However, if a piece is being prepared for others to read, other standards prevail; common sense and courtesy require that writers adhere to accepted conventions.

It is important for young writers, particularly, to feel that they "own" what they have written.

Every teacher has had the experience of attempting to read something that was difficult if not impossible to decipher because of improper punctuation (or lack of punctuation) and incorrect spelling. Even though a reader may be able to see value in content that is poorly presented, a writer who wants a piece to receive the attention it deserves must edit for readability. This includes, even for elementary-school children, at least basic punctuation, the correct spelling of common words, and evidence that thought has been given to organization.

It is not necessary to insist on perfection during the editing stage; even the best newspapers and magazines sometimes contain misspellings or inappropriately used commas. Ownership should be kept in mind, too; it is the child's piece that is being put into good order, not the teacher's. If you take over during the editing process, much of what has been accomplished in the teaching of writing may be undermined. The child has selected the topic, explored it, done the writing, and made revisions; the work is his or hers in a very personal way. No one, not even the teacher, should step in at this point and make "corrections." Spelling, punctuation, sentence improvement, and so on do need to be taught, as is discussed later in this chapter and in other chapters. In the revising and editing stages of the writing process, however, what is most important is establishing classroom procedures that encourage children to check their own texts carefully in preparation for being read by others or for publication. These procedures should include evaluating the legibility, spelling, usage, vocabulary, and punctuation of the piece of writing. Several steps may be taken in each area of concern.

Developing a handbook of writing forms and conventions for a classroom (or even better for a whole school) will help both children and teachers.

Handwriting or typing requires attention from the writer before a piece is ready for publication. The writer needs to be sure that the best handwriting possible has been done or that the typing has been well executed. If a piece is to be published in handwritten form, this is the time to give attention to individual handwriting problems as described in Chapter 8. With respect to typing, others may type for the children, but it is preferable for them to have access to typewriters or word processors (classroom procedures for these are also discussed in Chapter 8).

Spelling errors are usually the first thing noticed by a reader who is examining a written product. Therefore, a writer needs to check for correct spelling before publishing. There are a number of things that can be done to help young writers with spelling. First, spelling should be properly taught, as described in Chapter 11. Second, dictionaries of varying degrees of inclusiveness should be available, as well as lists of common words and common spelling errors (also found in Chapter 11). In addition, children ought to maintain individual lists of words they have trouble with. And, finally, the most expert spellers in the class can be used as resources—but only during the editing stage.

Usage and vocabulary problems must also be considered in the editing stage. The choice of words can be particularly important for more experienced writers. With respect to usage, whatever specific items have been identified for attention in the classroom (see Chapter 7) should be checked for in editing. This will support usage learning in a significant way. Vocabulary may receive attention through the use of lists of synonyms for overworked words and lists of imprecise words to be avoided. Older children or the most proficient younger ones can be encouraged to use a thesaurus when editing.

Punctuation items are discussed in a later section of this chapter. From the chart on page 249 you can formulate a checklist that will be appropriate for your class. Initially, such a list should be fairly brief; add to it gradually as the children can be expected to be aware of and properly use more items.

As one part of the editing and proofreading procedures, a system of symbols should be introduced and used by everyone in the class. This saves time, promotes communication, and gives students a sense of being involved in adultlike activities. Lists such as the one shown below are often found in language textbooks.

A Bulletin Board Idea

THINGS WE AVOID IN OUR WRITING
1. Overworked words
2. Inactive verbs
3. Vague references
4. Misplaced modifiers
5. Stale, worn-out phrases
6. Inaccurate expression
7. Sweeping generalizations

Marks Used by Proofreaders		
≡ Make a letter a capital.		ℒ Take out a word or phrase.
/ Make a letter lowercase.		∧ Insert a word or phrase.
⊙ Put in a period.		(sp) Fix the spelling.
↑ Put in a comma.		¶ Indent to begin a paragraph.

Publication

Publication, the final stage in the writing process, involves sharing a finished product with classmates, other students, teachers, family members,

Market Guide for Young Writers (available from Child Write, Inc., 26409 Timberland Drive, Kent, WA 98042) tells where to send children's writing.

Publishers of Children's Writing

Chart Your Course!
G/C/T Publishing Company
Box 6448
Mobile, AL 36660-0448

Chickadee
59 Front Street East
Toronto, Ontario M5E 1B3
Canada

Ebony, Jr!
820 Michigan Avenue
Chicago, IL 60605

Jack and Jill
1100 Waterway Boulevard
P.O. Box 567B
Indianapolis, IN 46202

Odyssey
Astro Media
Kalmback Publishing Company
625 E. St. Paul Avenue
P.O. Box 92788
Milwaukee, WI 53202

Pathways
Inky Trails Publications
P.O. Box 345
Middleton, ID 83644

Stone Soup
Box 83
Santa Cruz, CA 95063

Each year Raintree Publishers (310 W. Wisconsin Avenue, Milwaukee, WI 53203) selects a book written by a child and publishes it.

or even people in the community. (Of course, the final product can be a play, a videotaped reading, or some other type of performance, but publication generally means producing a text for someone to read.) For younger children such sharing often consists of taking a single page written in careful handwriting and placing it on a special shelf, displaying it in the corridor, or carrying it home in a transparent folder. For older writers a fairly lengthy book may be the product of the writing process, with typed copy and illustrations. Such books may be placed in the classroom, school, or even public library. A few children may write well enough that their work can be submitted to a magazine that publishes children's writing.

In addition to those just mentioned, there are many other good ways for children to share their finished writing. Some are listed below, but you can probably think of others.

- Read a piece to younger children or place it in their classroom for them to read.
- Set up displays of writing in stores, banks, libraries, or shopping centers.
- Read the writing products to community groups such as senior citizens.
- Have a schoolwide "Young Authors' Day" when children read and display their work to other students and guests.
- Encourage the children to submit their writing to the school newspaper or magazine.
- Invite an author to come to school to discuss writing and to look at what the students have written.

Publication fulfills several important functions with respect to the writing process. Most significantly, it demonstrates to the children the validity of questions about audience and purpose. When you ask a child "What will they want to know about this?" or "How can you explain what your feelings were at that time?" the idea of writing for an audience will have more meaning to the writer. When you inquire about the reasons for selecting a particular topic or treating it in a particular way, a child who has been through the full writing process a number of times will be better able to discuss the type of writing he or she is attempting to produce.

THE CLASSROOM WRITING PROGRAM

The writing process just described provides an overall structure for children's writing experiences, one that takes the writer from first idea to a finished piece of work. Use of this process will encourage students to write and to improve their abilities. Just as importantly, following the process will provide opportunities for you to teach specific skills at the right moment—precisely when a child has a real need for them. In addition, writing experiences offer many opportunities for children to learn and grow in such areas as self-concept, exploration of their own thoughts and experiences, and communicating with others. There are also opportunities for teaching that written expression is most effective when its content is organized so as to clearly convey the thoughts of the writer, that sentences need to be well constructed and interesting, and that the words used should both reflect precisely the meaning intended and show variety. Use of the three-stage writing process can allow you to accomplish these important goals. Some helpful suggestions and activities are described in the sections that follow.

As emphasized in Chapter 2, effective instruction is largely dependent on an organized and systematic program, one that recognizes children's abilities and needs as well as curriculum goals. The following guidelines are basic to effective writing programs:

In *The Art of Teaching Writing,* Calkins calls for an hour of writing each day—and she doesn't mean writing words in blanks on ditto sheets!

The book by Hansen listed in References gives many good examples of activities involving reading and writing.

1. Organize the day so that large blocks of time are available, rather than segmenting related areas. Since writing includes spelling, handwriting, vocabulary, and other aspects of language usage, the teaching of these ought to focus on how they relate to more effective writing.

2. Use the writing process in science, social studies, and literature. Writing is a good way for children to learn about many kinds of subject matter since it requires them to explore and extend their thinking.

3. Provide for a wide variety of oral expression: sharing, discussing, role playing, and other activities described in this book. Listen to the children, encouraging them to clarify and extend their thinking and language.

4. Guide children toward being observant of the world around them, from spellings used in some advertisements to how geese fly in formation or how an author ''draws a picture'' of a character.

5. Stimulate children with stories, poetry, field trips, and visitors to class; bring in curious objects and other unusual materials; discuss movies and television programs.

6. Encourage children's curiosity and creative thinking. Explore possibilities for having them engage in creative problem solving or ''Olympics of the Mind'' activities.

For information on the ''Olympics of the Mind,'' write to OM Association, P.O. Box 27, Glassboro, NJ 08028.

7. Have a comprehensive writing program, one that includes the various forms of written expression described in Chapter 10 along with any others that you and the children may think of.

8. Respect the children's privacy by not giving their work to other children without permission. Do not read everything children write yourself; remember that adults do not want to share everything they write.

9. Set up a writing center that includes all kinds of paper and writing tools, dictionaries, word lists, charts of the writing process, editing checklists, a typewriter, and regularly changed lists of suggested topics and questions related to writing.

10. Have each child maintain a folder in which all writing is kept. This is a practical way to avoid lost pages and also serves as a means for reviewing the child's progress.

11. Show that you value ideas, originality of expression, and precision and vividness of language by calling attention to examples in the children's writing and in literature.

12. Teach as much as possible via imbedded lessons. When children have a specific need to use something, such as quotation marks, make a brief presentation to an individual or a small group. If this is done effectively and attention

is given to maintenance of the skill, proficiency will gradually spread throughout the class.

13. Accept that growth in writing ability occurs in spurts. Performance will vary among members of the same class and even for the same child. Writing is affected by many things that influence the child and is itself complex, so progress is not steadily upward.

14. Use textbooks primarily as resources for writing. Have the children use only what will help from what the textbooks offer. For example, many have thesauruses, writing manuals, and lists of words often spelled incorrectly.

15. Write yourself—perhaps occasionally at the same time as the children, if the children are working well independently. Writing will help you think of ways to help the young writers in your class and will, very likely, give you some satisfactions that come only from writing.

Organizing Content

The best way to present a thought effectively is to organize the expression of that thought so that it sticks to the point and presents the information interestingly and in a suitable sequence. Attention to organization is reflected in the construction of sentences, paragraphs, and the whole piece. No expression—one sentence or more—is effective unless it is well organized and thoughtfully composed.

When a child begins to recognize relationships, he or she is beginning to organize. Activities such as the following utilize organizing skills and are closely related to learning to organize thoughts in written form:

- Putting pictures related to a story into proper sequence
- Telling in sequence the things seen on a trip
- Deciding what classroom tasks should be done
- Telling how to play a game
- Thinking of words that are associated with special days or events

Guidance in helping children organize their expression should begin as they tell about experiences and continue as they dictate more than a single phrase or sentence and write independently. Organization is a thinking skill that develops through guided practice; therefore, early guidance in oral expression is particularly important to organized writing. This guidance should be subtle, so that free expression is not stifled, but it does need to be offered. Dictation to the teacher provides especially good opportunities for such guidance, and this is the major reason that dictating to teachers by individuals and groups should not stop just because children have begun writing.

As children engage in the writing process, it is important to help them focus on organization of content. Activities such as the following may be helpful:

1. Write a short paragraph on the chalkboard or duplicate it. Have the children tell the main idea of the paragraph in one sentence. The paragraph may be taken from a social studies or science book.

2. Have children look at and discuss the content of a picture and then state in one sentence the main idea of the picture. A variation of this activity is to choose a title for the picture (without regard to whether it is a sentence).

3. Write several sentences on the chalkboard, and have the children select the ones that could be put together into a paragraph.

4. Provide the children with paragraphs in which there are one or two sentences unrelated to the main idea. Have the children cross out the unrelated sentences.

5. Provide the children with a paragraph in which the sentences have been scrambled, and have them rearrange the sentences in the most effective order.

6. Give children paragraphs in which the beginning or ending sentences are missing. Have them compose appropriate sentences to make the paragraphs complete.

7. Provide opportunities for pupils to discuss ideas and information and make lists of these before they begin writing. This should be done regularly at all grade levels; it is one of the most valuable ways in which you can help children learn to organize their thinking.

8. Encourage the children to watch for ways in which professional writers move skillfully from topic to topic and use paragraphs in their writing.

Developing Sentence Sense

Much written expression is not as effective as it might be because of faulty sentences. Although there are no shortcuts to developing skill in constructing effective sentences, there are some things teachers can do to help students, as well as some that are often done but probably do not help. In the latter category are teaching a grammatical definition of a sentence, identifying parts of speech in sentences, and having children do sentence construction, punctuation, and capitalization exercises totally unrelated to their interests and their own writing. Basically, children need to learn that a sentence is a means of expressing an idea. The focus is on the idea and on expressing it in a way that is clear and exact, a way that makes sense. The expression of the idea must be lucid and complete; it must avoid trying to tell so much that the meaning becomes confused or lost.

Don't overlook opportunities presented by conferences and other feedback situations for encouraging children to focus on creating sentences that *make sense*.

As has been mentioned frequently, children should have many opportunities to express themselves orally, and when they do, encourage them to express ideas clearly. This does not mean that every response has to be a "complete" sentence in the sense that most of us have had drilled *at* us in grammar study. However, questions may be asked or issues and problems advanced that require more than a "yes" or "no" answer.

The development of sentence sense is greatly helped if children frequently hear good sentences. A major way to accomplish this is to read well-written material to children in a voice that carries "sentence feeling." Sometimes it is helpful to have children listen to recordings of their own speech, noting how the voice tends to drop at the end of a group of words—that is, at the end of a sentence. Another way to illustrate good sentence structure is to write two stories in contrasting forms—one in which good sentence sense is evident and one in which the sentences are poorly or improperly constructed. Then have the stories compared and evaluated and the poorly written one reconstructed.

Activities such as those suggested in the preceding paragraph can be used at all grade levels by simply varying the length and difficulty of the material used, as can dictation exercises on punctuation and capitalization (particularly helpful after a new item has been introduced), exercises in which children match subjects in one column with predicates in another, or those requiring pupils to organize sentence elements into their proper relationships to make good sentences. At every grade level, expose children to good sentences that are read well.

You may also want to try activities such as those suggested below. They are listed in an order that reflects increasing difficulty, but many can be varied to suit different ability levels.

1. Display a large picture to the class and ask "Who can give us a sentence about this picture?" A picture of a firefighter, for instance, might elicit responses such as these:

   The firefighter has a big hat.
   She is holding a big hose.
   We had a fire on our street.

   Write the sentences the children give you on the board. Do not write a child's response unless it is a sentence. Don't be too negative about this, though; simply suggest that the child rephrase the thought.

2. Write sentences on the board from a story the children are reading or have read, scrambling the order of words. Have individual children or small groups rearrange these so that sentences are formed.

3. Give each child an envelope containing words printed on small pieces of durable paper. These may be words taken from their reading and other class activities. Each envelope should contain nouns, verbs, adjectives, adverbs, connectives, determiners, pronouns, and so forth, so that sentences can be made. Have the children see how many sentences they can compose, making sure that each sentence makes sense.

4. Write a sentence on the chalkboard. Ask the children to add phrases to make the idea clearer. A variation is to add adverbs and adjectives rather than phrases.

5. Write on the board several phrases that elicit mental pictures, for example: a pile of clothes on the floor, wet leaves on the window pane, the smell of bananas. Have pupils combine and/or add to the phrases to make sentences.

6. Have the children revise sentences found in their reading in which time relationships are expressed, for example:

   When Edith's father came to the door of the kitchen, all of the children were exclaiming about the dessert.

   This might be revised in one of these ways:

   The children were exclaiming about the dessert as Edith's father came to the door of the kitchen.

   Edith's father came to the door of the kitchen just in time to hear the children exclaiming about the dessert.

7. Write a sentence such as "She will play" on the board. Have the children add details that provide more information; they can do this by asking them-

selves such questions as "Who?" "What?" "How?" "When?" and "What kind?"

She will play with Bill.
She will play baseball with Bill.
She will play baseball with Bill on the school diamond.

Remedying Sentence Faults

Children's thinking sometimes runs ahead of both their speaking and their writing, resulting in the omission of some sentence elements. Children also tend to run sentences together by overusing *and* or, in writing, by simply running them together without a conjunction or punctuation and capitalization. Other common faults include using launchers (such as "you know" or "well"), which do not function as transition words or contribute to meaning, and making unnecessary repetitive and/or irrelevant statements.

Activities such as those suggested for developing sentence sense will help to remedy these faults. The idea of "making sense" causes children to realize that these faults interfere with clarity, that they make communication less effective or even impossible. Exercises that provide practice in distinguishing between fragments and sentences, in correcting run-on sentences, in adding or deleting words to make sentence meaning clear, and in making sentences out of nonsentence groups of words may also be helpful. Here are some examples of exercises that you might try:

1. Write on the chalkboard a story composed of a series of run-on sentences. Have several children take turns reading the story, stressing the idea that they are to attempt to read it paying attention only to the punctuation they see. Following such attempts have the story read again, this time emphasizing how natural reading shows where sentences begin and end. Then have the children rewrite the story, breaking it into sentences and omitting *and* when they think it preferable.

2. Write sentence fragments (perhaps from children's own work), such as:

   Because she did not go
   After the story ended
   While the class finished the game

   Have the children decide whether these are sentences and then how each might be made into a sentence.

3. Write sentences on the board, such as:

   Linda said that it was a good story.

   The children can then try various changes to make the sentence more interesting, for example:

   Linda declared that the story was very appealing.
   "What a good story!" said Linda.

4. Have children write sentences in different ways, experimenting with the placement of parts, for instance:

   During recess she will play with her friends in the gym.
   She will play with her friends in the gym during recess.
   She will play in the gym during recess with her friends.

5. Write sentences on the board for the children to rewrite and clarify, such as these:

> He saw four live ducks on the way to the market.
> There was much action in the movie that I didn't understand.

Sentence-Combining Activities

One difference between writing done by younger children and that done by older children and adults is that the more experienced writers use sentences that contain more and longer clauses. Since readers tend to prefer a style that has fewer and somewhat longer sentences rather than numerous short ones, a useful revision strategy is for writers to look for places to do sentence combining, to make two or more sentences into one. Skill in sentence combining may be improved to some extent by having children do exercises that require several sentences to be replaced by a single one through compounding, subordination, or substitution. Such exercises appear in most language textbooks. Usually these books have models demonstrating such combining, followed by a number of groups of sentences to be combined as those in the model are. Although this kind of practice may have some value, it often has the disadvantage common to many drill materials—that of being unrelated to the work and interests of the children in a specific classroom. It is better to write sentences related to things the children are studying, talking, or writing about, and then let them experiment with combining to achieve greater clarity, emphasis, focus on the image the writer desires the reader to have, ease of reading, or variation in style.

These are *example* sentences. Use ones related to your children and their activities.

You might simply write two sentences such as the following on the board and ask the children *if* they can be combined into one sentence:

> The fifth-grade classes are having a party.
> The party will be in our room.

The children will easily find several ways to combine such sentences, and then you can move on to asking them to combine several sentences into one. Emphasize that the ideas from sentences can be combined in different ways. For example, one might take the following sentences:

> The children got off the bus.
> John got off the bus first.
> As soon as the bus emptied the driver closed the door.

These might be combined in two ways, at least:

> John was first as the children got off the bus, just ahead of the closing door.
> John got off the bus first, and after the other children followed him, the driver closed the door.

You may want to emphasize combining in particular ways to show how style may be changed. For example, sentences such as

> The girl played hard.
> The girl won the game.

can be combined in several ways.

1. Using a connector:

   The girl played hard, and she won the game.

2. Not using a connector:

   The girl won the game by playing hard.
   By playing hard, the girl won the game.

Still another activity is to write words such as *when, after, until, there, where, if, because, then,* and *since* on the chalkboard. Then write pairs of sentences such as these:

Everyone sat down to dinner.
The children came in from playing.

We will go to the airport early.
My grandmother is coming from Syracuse.

Have pupils combine the sentences in each pair using one of the words from the board, for example:

After the children came in from playing, everyone sat down to dinner.

There are many variations in these sentence combining activities that may be used for showing children ways that sentences may be constructed. Children are usually intrigued by the possibilities in manipulating language, and these activities have appeal if they are not used to the extent that they become boring or interfere with writing for the many purposes suggested in Chapter 10.

Improving Word Choices

The quality of the words in a piece of writing is as important as the quality of the sentence structures. Care in choosing words can add brightness, vitality, and appeal to the writing, as well as communicating the content more effectively. Thus, children need to be guided in making the best choices possible to convey the information, ideas, and feelings they seek to express.

Precision and *vividness* of language are aspects of writing products to be especially valued. Precision means exactness, so children should be encouraged to replace such words as *thing, something,* and *a man* with the name of the object or person. Replacing such expressions as *made a face* with *scowled* or *frowned, slowly walked* with *sauntered,* or *got away* with *escaped* will improve exactness as well as be more appealing to readers. Thus, vocabulary building is vital, since choosing better words is possible only if the writer has a storehouse of words to choose from. Choosing can be aided, though, by the use of a thesaurus or sometimes a dictionary.

Children usually know many more words than they use in their writing, however. This may be because they can't spell some of them, but it is more likely because they have not been encouraged to substitute better words for those they have been accustomed to writing. Only slight encouragement is necessary to get children to list substitutes for "overworked" words. And they may be intrigued enough to search for others to add to the list. Making lists may not mean that the words will be used by the children in their writing, but calling attention to such words will remind the children that they can and should be used, and consequently at least some of them probably will be.

Since a word is a symbol that stands for or refers to an object, action, idea, or possibly a relationship, one might assume that its referents will be known if the word is known. This isn't true, though. Many words have multiple meanings, and others mean different things to different people. Writers need to be aware that if they use words for which they and their readers may have different referents, the intent of their writing may be lost. To avoid this, children should use words whose referents are as specific as possible. For example, *T-shirt* is more specific than *shirt, pizza* is more specific than *food, oak* than *tree,* and *spaniel* than *dog.* Such attention to word choices may appear to be too advanced for elementary-school children, but it need not be. Questions that probe what a writer really means to say and whether meaning could be misunderstood or lost because of some words, if used frequently and in a supportive manner, will accomplish a great deal.

Writing is also improved by vivid verbs that carry the weight of several adverbs with them, for example: *amble, trudge, march, slink,* or *pace* rather than *walk.* Similarly, adjectives should be carefully chosen; such words as *bulky, enormous, huge, vast,* and *burly* convey meaning much more accurately than *big.* As stated above, children will know better, more vivid verbs and descriptive adjectives, and they will be interested in learning even more and using them more often as they realize that the words add clarity and appeal to their writing.

Charts may be made of words in particular categories, such as "quiet" words, "sad" words, or "winter" words; these can be related to many activities. Charts may also be made of words to use instead of commonly overworked ones (*real, nice, pretty,* etc.) and of words for special occasions or special interests, such as football, camping trips, or art class. Charts of synonyms and antonyms can also help in building vocabulary. One class found thirty words that were better in various contexts than *mad* to describe the incidence of anger. Finding synonyms and antonyms for such words is an activity that could be on a task card in the language arts center of your classroom. Chart making can be an activity for the entire class, for individual pupils, or for small groups, and the charts can be made in permanent form or planned so that they may be added to.

Figures of speech, including personification, simile, metaphor, and certainly onomatopoeia, should be used in children's writing. Personification—the granting of human characteristics to nonhuman objects—is no stranger to children who know the Gingerbread Man, Br'er Rabbit, the Care Bears, Kermit the Frog, Little Toot, and so on. Perhaps they are less familiar with the simile, an expression that makes a direct comparison, such as "as slow as molasses in winter" or "fought like a tiger," although many will surely have heard a cake described as being "light as a feather" or of something happening "as quick as a flash." Children also may have heard metaphors such as "She has a finger in every pie" or "He blew his stack"; in these a comparison is implied, not directly stated. Children also know about onomatopoeia, the use of words whose pronunciation imitates or

Changing "the Picture" by Changing the Sentence

The bear came down the road.
The bear ambled down the path.
A brown bear shuffled along under the trees.
A small brown bear loped down the path.

Some Noise Words

thump
thud
sigh
slurp
murmur

suggests specific sounds; from their earliest years they've been delighted by such words as *tinkle, boom, pop, purr,* and *zoom.* These forms ought not be taught formally, with definitions and distinctions, but children should be encouraged to try them.

On the other hand, too much emphasis on figures of speech, highly descriptive adjectives, and other word choice features can lead to distraction from the meaning to be conveyed. Often children will overuse similes or become preoccupied with adjectives, particularly as they first experiment. Helping them focus on exactness of meaning but with enough variety to add appeal will soon remedy this.

Form and Convention in Writing

Most teachers seem to agree that the vital element in written expression is the content. Unfortunately, though, some appear to believe that the conventions of writing—the mechanics, the matters of form and appearance, the agreed-on customs of putting language symbols on paper—are of little importance. Such teachers are probably doing their pupils a distinct disservice.

Certainly conventions must be kept in proper perspective in writing. They are aids to communication, not ends in themselves. Children do need to learn that communication may not take place if attention is not given to the conventions. But, as suggested earlier, during the rough draft stage of writing, the primary concern should be getting ideas on paper. Yet even at this stage, if absolutely no attention is given to conventions, the meaning could be lost to even the original writer of the draft. In addition, since habits, good or bad, tend to "stick," all stages of the writing process should be followed frequently to encourage the learning of good habits with respect to the conventions.

Keep the focus on content. Teach form and appearance in the context of the children's writing.

A Bulletin Board Idea

> **THIS IS THE WAY WE HEAD OUR PAPERS**
>
> name
> school
> grade
> date
> title

Form and Appearance. A neat and attractive-looking paper, whether a letter, a report, an announcement, or a story, constitutes a courtesy to the reader and helps make the writing more effective. Although there are few strict rules about matters of form, there are some generally accepted guidelines about such matters as leaving margins at the top, bottom, and sides of the paper, indenting the first line of a paragraph, placing a title, avoiding crowded writing at the end of a line, and eliminating untidy erasures and messy blots. Children should learn about these and know what is expected of them. It is a good idea to work with the children early in the year to establish standards of form and appearance for written work once it reaches the publication stage. These standards should be simple and should include only items needed for identification, neatness, and correctness. Items to cover might be position of name and date on papers to be handed in, the extent of margins, regulations about writing on one or both sides of the paper, types of paper to be used for written work, and so on. By all means let the children themselves participate in setting these standards. Discuss the reasons for having such standards, and then post them until habits become established. Also, make sure that the standards are adhered to consistently in order to avoid confusing the children.

Punctuation. Punctuation can be overemphasized, but it does have an important place in writing: it helps to transmit meaning. Simply stated, punctuation is a means of showing, by the use of a number of specially designated marks, meaning that cannot be shown—or is only partially shown—by words and the arrangements given to them. In speech these meanings are usually transmitted by the rising and falling tones of the voice, by emphasis or stress on certain sounds, and by pauses in or the breaking off of the stream of speech.

There are, of course, punctuation marks that are unique to written discourse—marks used in writing that are not meant to symbolize speech features. These include such things as a period after an abbreviation, a hyphen to show the division of a word, the underlining (or italicizing) of a book title, and quotation marks around the title of a story.

There are also features of stress, pitch, and juncture in speech that are not reflected by punctuation in written expression. Stress is usually shown by meaning, for example:

> She signed the *contract* without hesitating.
> As the pavement began to *contract,* a crack appeared.

Pitch can sometimes be shown by punctuation, as in the sentences ''He will go with us'' and ''He will go with us?'' Although end punctuation is the most common clue to an intonation pattern, other punctuation marks sometimes indicate the need for a change in pitch. For example, ''The boys without coats were very cold'' will not be read orally the same way as ''The boys, without coats, were very cold.''

The breaks in the stream of speech, the junctures, can sometimes be signaled by punctuation marks; for example, the pronounced juncture at the end of a sentence is signaled by a period. However, since any sentence (The man/next to me/was laughing) has breaks in the flow of its utterance (as indicated by the /), it is a fallacy to assume that every pause requires a punctuation mark. This is particularly true given the current deemphasis on close punctuation. We see ''My friend Jim Smith will go with us'' just as often as ''My friend, Jim Smith, will go with us,'' and no one fails to get the meaning. Also, when one wants to indicate a pronounced interruption (a double-bar juncture or //, for example), there is no particular punctuation form that must be used. The sentence ''My brother (actually my half-brother) will meet me in Boston'' can be written ''My brother—actually my half-brother—will meet me in Boston.'' Nothing about the way the two sentences are said indicates the difference in punctuation.

Punctuation practices vary. For example, a comma may or may not precede and *in sentences containing words in a series.*

Teaching about punctuation may be aided by relating the items taught to intonation patterns in speech when this is appropriate. When children read orally, opportunities for calling attention to punctuation marks and what they signal often arise. Major attention, however, should be given to functional and direct teaching. That is, punctuation should be taught as it is needed by pupils in their writing, and attention given to only those items that are important to that writing. This type of instruction should begin early in the primary grades. The first sentences put on the board, seen in a book, or written on a chart or under a child's drawing provide opportunities for teaching punctuation. Although this teaching should be informal and secondary to expression, it can be specific and direct. Children should be allowed to take what they can from these experiences.

It is through reading and writing that older students will most readily learn about punctuation, as well as other conventions, but this learning should not be left to chance. As has been stated, you have the responsibility of determining what an individual is ready to learn as you observe and confer with him or her, and this applies to learning proper punctuation. The best type of learning experience is always one that grows out of a child's questions, interests, or thoughts. The teacher, however, must follow through on the interest to ensure learning.

The following sections discuss the most common punctuation marks, the ones that are first taught, and how they should be taught.

The Period. The first writing children encounter calls for a period *at the end of a sentence,* for example:

We went to the park.

Call attention to the period. Point out that the little dot is a traffic signal called a period. It means that a stopping point has been reached and there must be a pause before going on to the next set of words. Later a more formal explanation may be given, such as "A period tells us this is the end of a statement."

As children begin their own writing, remind them of the need to signal the end of each statement they write. To help them, provide charts with properly punctuated sentences as models.

Early in children's experience they will also encounter three other uses of the period. They will see it in *abbreviations of titles of persons and of place names,* for example:

Mill St.
Dr. Hill

They will also find it after *initials in proper names,* for example:

H. O. Downs

Finally, they will encounter it after *numerals in lists:*

1.
2.

Each of the above four uses of the period should be introduced to pupils in kindergarten and first grade and directly taught in the first, second, or third grade as pupils begin writing and encounter situations that require such uses.

The Question Mark. First-grade children should be introduced to the question mark. Since children are always asking questions, it is natural for you to place a question mark *at the end of a direct question* in a story they dictate. It is also natural for them to write questions in their first stories,

Such exercises as having pupils memorize "the eighteen ways to use a comma" are a waste of time. A child learns how to use punctuation by writing a great deal over several years.

and they will readily place the correct mark if it has been introduced. In fact, children probably have less trouble with question marks than with any other type of punctuation.

A second use of the question mark is *after a direct question in the context of a larger sentence,* as in

"Are you going to the store?" Billy asked.

This is more difficult for children to understand and should not be introduced until the late third or early fourth grade.

The Comma. There are many uses for the comma, but children should be taught only those they actually need in their writing. In the primary grades, as you write experience stories children dictate and notes that the children may copy to take home, and as they begin writing themselves, some uses of the comma will, of course, be introduced. These may include the comma between the date and the year, between city and state, after the salutation in a friendly letter, and after the complimentary close of a letter. The need to teach these is dependent on the emphasis that is being given to letter writing. In much of the writing that children do independently, they become aware of the comma used to separate words in a series; direct teaching of this is usually done in the third grade.

Quotation Marks. Children in the primary grades will encounter quotation marks in their readers and storybooks and will naturally have questions about them. That is the right time to introduce their use. A good way to do this is to have children take the parts of characters in stories in which the speech is set off by quotation marks. They will learn that these marks signal speech. The use of quotation marks may also be shown in group stories you write on the board as the children dictate. Have the children create these group stories often, even after they begin to write compositions of more than two or three sentences by themselves, for such stories are useful in many ways—for example, for developing vocabulary and organizational skills. As you write, point out punctuation marks and paragraphing, making special mention of the placement of commas and question marks in relation to quotation marks. Put some of the stories on charts, and the children can use them as models. And, above all, work with the children in individual conferences; if good habits are established from the beginning, many problems may be avoided.

The punctuation marks and their uses discussed in this section are not all of the marks and not all of the uses that should receive attention in the elementary school. The chart on the next page suggests grade levels for the introduction, direct teaching, and maintenance teaching of the various punctuation marks usually taught in the elementary school. Keep in mind, however, that these are approximations only; each class progresses at its own rate, and so does each child. If punctuation is taught in connection with situations where there is a need to communicate and if children are shown that it contributes to the success of communication, there should be sufficient learning.

Capitalization. Capitalization is another convention of written expression about which a great deal is known in relation to children's needs for instruc-

ITEM	USE	K	1	2	3	4	5	6	7	8
Period	At the end of a statement	*	*	†	′	′	′	′	′	′
	After initials	*	*	†	′	′	′	′	′	′
	After abbreviations	*	*	*	†	′	′	′	′	′
	After numerals in a list	*	*	†	′	′	′	′	′	′
	After letters or numerals in an outline				*	*	†	′	′	′
	In footnotes and bibliographies						*	*	†	′
Question mark	After an interrogative sentence		*	†	′	′	′	′	′	′
	After a question within a larger sentence				*	†	′	′	′	′
Comma	Between the day of the month and the year	*	*	†	′	′	′	′	′	′
	Between city and state	*	*	†	′	′	′	′	′	′
	After a salutation in a friendly letter		*	†	′	′	′	′	′	′
	After a complimentary close		*	†	′	′	′	′	′	′
	To separate parts of a series			*	†	′	′	′	′	′
	To set off words of direct address				*	*	†	′	′	′
	To separate a direct quotation					*	†	′	′	′
	Before and after appositives					*	*	†	′	′
	After introductory clauses					*	*	†	′	′
	After introductory words: yes, no, interjections					*	†	′	′	′
	Before the conjunction in a compound sentence						*	†	′	′
	Before and after a nonrestrictive clause						*	*	†	′
	Before and after parenthetical expressions						*	*	†	′
	In footnotes and bibliographies							*	†	′
Apostrophe	In contractions		*	*	†	′	′	′	′	′
	To show possession		*	*	*	*	†	′	′	′
	To show plurals of figures and letters				*	*	*	†	′	′
Quotation marks	Before and after a direct quotation		*	*	†	′	′	′	′	′
	Before and after titles (other than titles of books)			*	*	*	†	′	′	′
Exclamation mark	At the end of an exclamatory word or sentence		*	*	*	†	′	′	′	′
Colon	After the salutation of a business letter				*	*	†	′	′	′
	To separate the hour from minutes			*	*	*	†	′	′	′
	Before a long series or list					*	*	*	†	′
	To denote examples						*	*	*	†
Hyphen	At the end of a line to show a divided word		*	*	*	†	′	′	′	′

*Introduction   †Suggested teaching   ′Maintenance

Capitalization Chart

WORDS TO CAPITALIZE	GRADE								
	K	1	2	3	4	5	6	7	8
First word of a sentence	*	*	†	'	'	'	'	'	'
First and last names of a person	*	†	'	'	'	'	'	'	'
Name of street or road	*	*	†	'	'	'	'	'	'
The word I		*	†	'	'	'	'	'	'
Name of a city or town		*	†	'	'	'	'	'	'
Name of a school or special place	*	*	†	'	'	'	'	'	'
Names of months and days	*	*	†	'	'	'	'	'	'
First and important words in titles	*	*	*	†	'	'	'	'	'
Abbreviations: Mr., Mrs., St., Ave.	*	*	†	'	'	'	'	'	'
Each line of a poem^a			*	†	'	'	'	'	'
First word of a salutation of a letter		*	†	'	'	'	'	'	'
First word of a complimentary close		*	†	'	'	'	'	'	'
Initials		*	*	†	'	'	'	'	'
Titles used with names of persons			*	*	†	'	'	'	'
First word in an outline topic				*	*	†	'	'	'
First word of a quoted sentence			*	†	'	'	'	'	'
Names of organizations			*	*	†	'	'	'	'
Sacred names			*	*	*	†	'	'	'
Proper names generally: countries, oceans, etc.			*	*	*	†	'	'	'
Proper adjectives					*	*	†	'	'
Titles of respect and rank and their abbreviations			*	*	†	'	'	'	'

*Introduction   †Suggested teaching   'Maintenance

^aBe sure to point out that there are exceptions to this, particularly in modern poetry.

tion. For a specific class these needs can be determined by examining the children's writing. Textbooks and course guides often give recommended grade levels for introducing and teaching capitalization uses (see the capitalization chart on page 250), but, as always, such lists are merely guides, not firm requirements. The best guide is the writing the children actually do.

Capitalization is introduced to children at a fairly young age. When children first begin to learn about letters, they discover that each letter has two sizes (actually the forms usually differ as well as the sizes). Later, when they see words and sentences written on charts or on the board or printed in their storybooks and textbooks, they encounter many words that are capitalized. The experience stories children dictate to you provide opportunities to point out capital letters as they are written: "Notice that I am beginning the sentence with a capital letter" or "Bruce begins with a capital letter because it is a name."

Direct teaching usually begins when children first start to copy words from charts or the chalkboard; words that are capitalized should be pointed out (and the reasons given) so that children begin with an awareness of the need for both capital and small letters.

When children begin to write independently, it is important to look over their written work, noting their needs (without red-marking the papers) and planning lessons to address problems and to introduce new uses as they become appropriate. At this point children are fascinated with writing anything, so group and individual dictation can be used to give practice in capitalization uses to which particular attention is being given or which pupils find difficult. Pupils can also compare their writing to models that illustrate capitalization and make their own corrections. Group correction of papers, with special attention to capitalization, is possible if an overhead or opaque projector is used. Remember that forming good habits at the very beginning is far more effective than any amount of corrective work.

Good habits in the conventions of writing are like good driving habits—they become established through regular use.

If good habits are formed, unnecessary capitalization will probably not be a problem. However, with some children you may have to reteach certain usages or provide practice activities to eliminate unnecessary capitals. In particular, children who capitalize words for the purpose of emphasis should be helped to overcome this habit.

Above all, however, teaching children to revise and edit their writing will generally accomplish more than any amount of direct teaching.

Punctuation and Capitalization Activities. In the lower and middle grades, the teaching of punctuation may be enlivened by making cardboard stick puppets representing various punctuation marks. These can be given names such as Rollo Period, "Slim" Exclamation Mark, and Paula Apostrophe—or let the children choose names they like. Each character can tell what he or she does and from time to time can come out and remind pupils of what they have forgotten.

Children can also play matching games, matching punctuation symbols with their uses. Make tagboard cards, printing a symbol or a use on each one. For example, make a period on each of four cards; then on four additional cards print the words "at the end of a sentence," "after an abbreviation," "after initials," and "after a numeral in a list." (A symbol card is needed for each use.) If desired, an additional set of cards can show illustrations of the uses.

The importance of punctuation and capitalization can be shown in many ways. One is to have pupils find examples of specific punctuation and capitalization uses in books, newspapers, and magazines. For instance, they might look for sentences in which commas set off words in a series, a period is used after an abbreviation, a word is divided by a hyphen, or parentheses are used to enclose material that is not part of the main thought. These examples can be used to make charts or a bulletin board display.

Another way to emphasize the value of punctuation and capitalization is to present the children with a paragraph that has none. Choose this paragraph carefully, selecting one in which meaning is actually obscured by the lack of signals. Or let the children try reading some of Don Marquis's *Archy and Mehitabel*—this will quickly convince them.

It is fun occasionally to present ''trick'' sentences for pupils to punctuate. Sentences such as these can be used:

> Sixty, three, and eleven are the numbers.
> Sixty-three and eleven are the numbers.

> No water is coming through the pipe.
> No, water is coming through the pipe.

> Bill, said Joe, is very noisy.
> Bill said Joe is very noisy.

An important aspect of teaching any skill is helping children to become aware of their own errors. A good way not only to help them become aware of their errors but also to lead them to assume responsibility for overcoming them is to have pupils keep individual folders for papers that have punctuation and capitalization errors marked. From these they can compile lists of items that need to be studied and select practice exercises or activities to help them overcome their problems. Papers should be dated so that children can examine them regularly (perhaps once a month) to determine their own progress.

Avoid workbook types of practice activities in which there are several or even many different items on a single page. Individual children or groups may be helped by using practice activities, but the practice should be focused on a specific need. For example, these exercises focus on (1) capitalization of proper names and (2) commas to set off words of direct address:

1. Write each sentence, using capital letters wherever they are needed:
   it was uncle jim who took me.
   we went to the zoo in glenwood park.
   will mrs. jones be at the picnic?
   last christmas we visited sarasota, florida.

2. Write the following sentences, using commas where they are needed:
   Where did you get the bike Jim?
   I think Mom that I may be late.
   John come over after school and play.
   Alice aren't you going to school today?

Exercises can be made up from the children's own sentences if this can be done without embarrassing anyone. You can gather sentences by listening and making notes as they talk or possibly from their writing. Exercises can also be made by copying material from textbooks in reading, science, or other subject areas without capital letters or punctuation marks (perhaps just the particular marks being studied). The children can capitalize and punctuate where they think necessary and then compare the results with the textbook.

Dictation exercises can furnish variety, and they can be used in several ways. Children can dictate to each other, or dictation can be recorded and used by individuals who need practice on particular items. Spelling words that need review can even be included in dictation drills. Dictation can also be done by the teacher when a large group or the entire class needs practice on a specific skill or as a general review. When dictating, read the selection three times: once so pupils will know the length and get the gist of what is said; a second time, very slowly, so they can write it; a third time, more rapidly, so the writing can be checked.

A duplicated paragraph is good for a general review of punctuation and capitalization, again with specific directions as to the number of items to be supplied.

Directions: Rewrite the following paragraph, using eight capital letters, three periods, and four commas.

no one was allowed to leave boston and this could have been disastrous for paul revere had he not known the city so well in the darkness he was able to reach the charles river where he had hidden a rowboat a few days before and two friends were waiting to row him across it would be a very dangerous mission for their boat would have to pass near the enemy

It is a good idea to have a generous supply of practice materials of all types for individual children or small groups to use when they need drill and to keep these materials filed in such a way that the particular type can be found quickly. These can vary in difficulty according to the grade level and the needs of the particular children in the class. Answer sheets should be included in each folder so children can check their own work.

Writing with the Word Processor

Solomon, in her book *Teaching Writing with Computers*, presents a very thorough overview of this subject.

Chapter 8 pointed out that increasingly some writing, even by elementary-school children, is being done by machine rather than by hand. Few elementary schools are likely to have enough typewriters or word processors to enable children to use them to do the quantity of writing that is necessary for learning to write effectively. However, most schools now provide at least some experiences with word processors. This is desirable since word processing is like the revision and editing aspects of the writing process in that what has been written can be brought back and changes made in it. The changes may involve removing or inserting individual letters, words, sentences, paragraphs, or even more. In addition, blocks of the text (of any size) can be relocated by the machine. The writer, then, can adjust the text

For children word processing is usually a cooperative activity.

by making deletions, insertions, and relocations so that it is as he or she wishes. All of this is revising and editing done by means of a machine that "takes orders" from a writer who knows what needs to be done.

Some word-processing programs offer options concerning the size and style of print. Others make possible the production of newspaperlike hard copy—pages with columns, headlines, and illustrations. Still other programs will identify typing and spelling errors or even possible grammatical mistakes and overused words. Some programs actually prevent errors; for example, if *seperate* is typed the computer will print *separate*.

Children obviously need to be taught to use a word processor by someone who knows how to use it and is familiar with the various programs available. It is not likely that elementary-school children will be able to make revisions of their writing on the screen without going through the intermediate step of marking up the print-out of a first draft. However, the capability of the machine to do revising will motivate children in this revising and editing.

A FINAL WORD

The introduction to this chapter pointed out that the teaching of writing was for a long time dominated by an overemphasis on handwriting, mechanics, and grammatical rules. A high level of awareness of the significance of the writing process has now largely redressed this imbalance. Many elementary teachers are giving the necessary attention to how children express what they want to say and are carefully guiding the children so that this expression is successful. Of course, this approach does not mean that matters such as organization of content, sentence construction, spelling, and punctuation are unimportant; these elements should be focused on at the appropriate points in each child's learning. This is the challenge you face as a teacher—asking the right questions and making useful suggestions at the moment when these will be of the greatest benefit. When such a goal is achieved, children will be stimulated and encouraged, and well-written, attractively presented texts will be the result.

References

Atwell, Nancie. *In the Middle: Writing, Reading and Learning with Adolescents.* Boynton/Cook, 1987.

Calkins, Lucy McCormick. *The Art of Teaching Writing.* Heinemann, 1986.

Collins, James L., and Sommers, Elizabeth A. *Writing On-Line: Using Computers in the Teaching of Writing.* Boynton/Cook, 1985.

Elbow, Peter. *Writing with Power: Techniques for Mastering the Writing Process.* Oxford University Press, 1981.

Graves, Donald H. *Writing: Teachers and Children at Work.* Heinemann, 1983.

Hansen, Jane. *When Writers Read.* Heinemann, 1987.

Hansen, Jane; Newkirk, Thomas; and Graves, Donald. *Breaking Ground: Teachers Relate Reading and Writing in the Elementary School.* Heinemann, 1985.

Hillocks, George, Jr. *Research on Written Composition.* National Council of Teachers of English, 1986.

Huff, Roland, and Kline, Charles R., Jr. *The Contemporary Writing Curriculum.* Teachers College Press, 1987.

Langer, Judith. *Children Reading and Writing.* Ablex Publishing, 1986.

Murray, Donald. *A Writer Teaches Writing.* Houghton Mifflin, 1985.

Olson, Carol Booth, ed. *Practical Ideas for Teaching Writing as a Process,* rev. ed. California State Department of Education, 1987.

Proett, Jackie, and Gill, Kent. *The Writing Process in Action.* National Council of Teachers of English, 1986.

Solomon, Gwen. *Teaching Writing with Computers: the POWER Process.* Prentice-Hall, 1986.

Stewig, John W. *Read to Write.* Richard C. Owen, 1986.

Thaiss, Christopher, and Suhor, Charles, eds. *Speaking and Writing K–12.* National Council of Teachers of English, 1984.

Tiedt, Sidney W., and Tiedt, Iris M. *Language Arts Activities for the Classroom.* Allyn and Bacon, 1978.

Wresch, William. *A Practical Guide to Computer Uses in the English/Language Arts Classroom.* Prentice-Hall, 1987.

Teaching Resources

COMPUTER SOFTWARE

Bank Street Writer. Scholastic.

SRA Writing Skills: Punctuation. Science Research Associates (diskettes, guide book, and back-up disks).

Writer Rabbit. The Learning Co.

The Writer's Assistant. InterLearn, Inc.

The Writing Adventure. Developmental Learning Materials.

The Writing Workshop. Milliken.

VIDEOTAPES

The Authoring Cycle: Read Better, Write Better, Reason Better. Heinemann.

Celebrating Children's Writing. National Council of Teachers of English, 1985 (includes mini-lessons on grammar, punctuation, and spelling).

Prewriting. National Council of Teachers of English, 1984 (grades 4–6).

Teachers Teaching Writing. Association for Supervision and Curriculum Development (six videos and discussion guides; grades 3–12).

Teaching Writing: A Process Approach. Maryland Department of Education (nine half-hour videos; elementary through secondary level).

The Writing and Reading Process. Heinemann.

The Writing Conference. National Council of Teachers of English, 1984 (middle grades).

Writing as Discovery. National Council of Teachers of English.

OTHER RESOURCES

Basic Writing Skills. Society for Visual Education (two groups of six filmstrips and six audio cassettes each; intermediate and upper grades).

Lessons in Proofreading. Curriculum Associates (kit).

Suid, Murray; Lincoln, Wanda; and Gatheral, Maryann. *For the Love of Editing.* Scholastic (grades 2–6).

Activities for Preservice Teachers

1. When doing the next assigned paper for some course, make a conscious attempt to use the writing process described in this chapter. Does using it seem to help? If so, in what way? How different is the process from what you would have done anyway? What modifications to the process, if any, would you suggest?

2. Select one of the references listed in this chapter, and report on it to the class. Make sure that your report conveys the substance of the book and include your personal reactions to what the book says.

3. Report to the class on what one language textbook series does with respect to teaching sentence sense, organizational skills, and making word choices so as to improve children's writing. (Several students could each analyze a different textbook series.)

4. Make a checklist to use in assessing children's writing. Include such factors as vividness of language (intensity, freshness, vigor), picturesqueness of speech, involvement of feelings, element of surprise, and so on. Decide on the range of points you will assign each item. Check out your list and the points awarded for each item with someone who is now teaching.

5. Prepare a set of transparencies to be used for group practice in proofreading at a particular grade level.

6. Plan a bulletin board display of "fun" sentences in which the meaning is changed by changing the punctuation.

7. Act as a teacher and have a conference with a friend who is writing a paper for a course. Can you help just by listening? Try to ask helpful questions. Resist the temptation to step in and "take over."

8. Observe some writing activities in elementary-school classrooms. Are the teachers using elements of the writing process as described in this chapter? What kinds of problems do the children have, and what does the teacher do about them? What happens to the children's writing when they are "finished"?

9. Find out if there are any writing competency tests for prospective teachers in your state. When are these taken? What are they like? Are you preparing for them?

10. Report to the class your assessment of what the average person, the public media, and the professional literature in education believe to be "basic" to teaching children to write effectively.

Activities for Inservice Teachers

1. Select a child in your class who does little writing. Observe this child closely for a week or two. Note his or her activities, interests, and abilities. What does the child do when he or she could be writing? Analyze your observations and plan what you might do to create more interest in writing and to develop confidence in doing it.

2. With the children in your class, prepare a bulletin board display on editing. The editing signs (sp = spelling error, lc = small or lowercase letter, etc.) will interest children.

3. If you do not already hold regular conferences with the children in your class about their writing efforts, try it for a few weeks. Does it seem worth the effort and time? Do you find that you understand individual children better?

4. Visit a newspaper office with your class or have a newspaper staff member come to school to talk about how stories get edited. Get copies of edited material if available (more and more newspapers do everything on word processors). Put up a bulletin board display that summarizes the newspaper production process, including proofreaders' marks and their use.

5. Inventory the types of writing the children do in your class: making class books, keeping journals, trying fiction, preparing reports, contributing to the school newspaper, and so on. Develop a plan for adding two or three additional types over the next several months.

6. Start a newsletter for parents. Children can write stories about what is going on in the classroom. If you have access to a photocopier, they can include drawings, pictures, and cartoons. One of the early issues should be about the writing program so that parents can see what is being done about sentence construction, spelling, punctuation, and so forth.

7. Review the writing of the children in your class, making notes on common punctuation and capitalization problems. Share the list with the children, and ask for their assistance in planning activities or procedures that might help reduce the number of problems.

8. Call attention to the relationship between oral reading and some forms of punctuation. Have children read their own writing and decide where periods, question and exclamation marks, and commas are needed. Follow up—depending on the maturity level of the children—by examining punctuation marks that usually are not determinable from oral reading.

9. When the children are writing, join them by writing yourself. You will need to be brave enough to share what you've written if you ask the children to share theirs. Most children will especially appreciate stories about the times you got into trouble when you were their age.

10. Report to the class your reactions, based on your teaching experiences, to the content of this chapter, especially the description of the writing process and the suggestions made relative to it.

11. Investigate different ways for children to manufacture their own books and then try them in your class. (Tiedt and Tiedt, in *Language Arts Activities for the Classroom,* offer several suggestions.)

Independent Activities for Children

1. Provide bulletin board space for an "Announcement Center." Children may post sign-up sheets for use of classroom facilities such as the computer or materials such as the unabridged dictionary, notices of scout or club meetings, advertisements of articles for sale, and so on. Announcements should be carefully prepared and well displayed, and someone should be in charge of removing out-of-date materials periodically.

2. Provide time for journal writing, preferably at the beginning of each day. In general, the older children are, the less they will want to read aloud what they have written, a feeling that should be respected. But you can circulate to see that they are writing *something* and express your interest in reading whatever they want you to see.

3. Encourage children to write about classroom activities: how the plants are growing, what the gerbil did, the best things that happened this year, the play the fifth-graders did, the trip to the zoo, and so on. Plan activities that are likely to produce good writing opportunities.

4. Videotape short sequences from TV programs, and play them back with the sound turned down. Ask pupils to write a script that could be associated with the action on the screen.

5. Children who have pets can write about them, or they might want to write a daily journal as though the family dog or cat were keeping it.

6. Have a child adapt a story for dramatization and videotaping, writing a script with dialogue and staging

and camera directions, perhaps including recommendations for musical background, too.

7. Editing checklists, punctuation charts, and lists of usage forms to be avoided in writing can be made by children working in groups. This can be followed up by the groups deciding how the lists and charts will be used.

8. Invent an imaginary character called, for example, "Ralph the Rotten Reporter," who keeps publishing a newspaper with all kinds of mistakes in it: punctuation and spelling errors, gross usage problems, jumbled paragraphs, and so on. Anyone who wants to can act as Ralph's editor. Those who are really interested may want to be Ralph and write something with many deliberate mistakes. Make sure the editor does his or her job so that the ones acting as Ralph aren't establishing bad habits.

9. "Pattern" books of fill-in sentences are sometimes useful in getting a pupil started in writing. These can be only a few pages long. Possibilities for sentences include:

I like _____ but I don't like _____.
The good news is _____; the bad news
  is _____.

10. Encourage children to share good ideas. In the writing corner, place a suggestion box in which pupils can place notes about what they think would make a good story. Children can then go to the box for ideas when they are "stuck" and don't know what to write about.

11. Have the children make a chart showing commonly used abbreviations. The chart can be illustrated with pictures of a street, an army officer, a medical doctor, and so forth.

12. One child can prepare a set of sentences with different punctuation marks at the ends. He or she can then read them to a friend, giving the necessary (but natural) inflection. The second child guesses what the punctuation mark is. This activity can gradually be extended to punctuation marks other than those that go at the ends of sentences.

Chapter **10**

Children's Writing Experiences

*T*he writing process described in Chapter 9 should be the basis for all instruction in writing. The process is one that focuses on composition, on getting writers to put on paper what they want there. This chapter describes the many forms, or types, of writing important to children and how these can best be learned. The writing process is crucial to each type; once writers have learned—or at least begun to learn—how to think in terms of drafts, revisions, and audiences, this process can be applied to letters, reports, poetry, and many other forms of written expression. This chapter also includes discussions of writing with word-processing software and the evaluation of writing and the writing program.

WRITING ACTIVITIES

Many opportunities for children to write for purposes that are meaningful to them occur in classrooms every day. An opportunity may stem from a science lesson, a field trip in social studies, the information brought to health class by a resource person, the development of a story, or any of numerous other activities that are integral parts of the curriculum. This section identifies many possible writing situations and suggests the kinds of activities that can and should be planned for in a classroom where children are encouraged and helped to communicate their ideas and feelings.

Cooperative Writing

Gradually expand the length and complexity of the writing when you are acting as the scribe. This provides opportunities for using various types of sentences and forms of punctuation.

Much writing done by younger children occurs in group situations, and the teacher does the actual writing as a text takes shape on the chalkboard or a chart. The purpose of the writing may be to report or summarize something learned or to be learned, to create a story, or to record the class's response to a visitor, for example. Other types of writing described in the sections that follow can also be done cooperatively. Cooperative writing, however, should not be thought of as something to be done only in the primary grades; it also has a place in higher grades as a way of helping to give focus to particular information, bring unity to a class, or illustrate a particular form of writing. In the middle and upper grades, of course, the scribe may be one of the students.

Cooperative writing permits children to focus first on the composition of the message or text—its organization and whether what gets written is what was intended. Mechanical skills, vocabulary, use of effective sentences, and other aspects of revision can also be attended to in a group setting, since revision is an important element of writing (as was described in Chapter 9). Working on compositions in small groups allows all of the children to be involved and to observe such techniques as sentence combining being used. Such participation and observation will provide them with a basis for doing similar sorts of work when writing on their own.

Depending on the maturity of the children and their experience with the writing process, you may need to get the group started by asking questions: "How shall we start? Who has an opening sentence? Can someone think of another way?" Sometimes questioning may also be needed to help the children develop the piece and then to end it. Revising may also call for questions, more of which will be focused on skills. However, it is not wise to introduce a great number of skills at one time or dwell on any for too long, particularly when doing cooperative writing with young children.

Personal Writing

An important form of writing for elementary-school children is the regular recording of day-to-day events in a journal. Children who keep journals gain some important understandings. They discover that they can reflect on their own experiences and then write pieces that they themselves enjoy reading. They can also read some of what they have written to classmates and the teacher and find that others seem interested in what they think and do. In addition, journals can furnish material that serves as a departure point for further writing—material that can be expanded on, revised, and even published in some way.

Journals must be private; no one should read another's journal without permission, because such writing is sometimes quite personal. Writing about a problem or a painful experience can be helpful in relieving stress and achieving understanding of what has happened—many of us have felt better after composing an angry letter, even if it was never sent. Older children should not be routinely asked to read aloud from their journals. Rather, these children may designate parts to be read or read sections they choose to you or to classmates.

A unique kind of personal writing occurs when the teacher and a child initiate a written dialogue. A child may write a note about a forthcoming birthday, for example, and the teacher responds, sharing in the excitement. The child may then write again, giving information about gifts received and the like. The exchange continues as long as there is a reason to do so. This type of writing helps to establish good teacher/pupil relations, and the teacher's participation in it clearly demonstrates the value she or he places on written communication.

Story Writing

Story writing really begins when children first participate in oral sharing and experience writing activities, for which, in many cases, the teacher is the scribe. Story writing is also similar, or often even identical, to writing

Send stories to *Shoe Tree:
The Literary Magazine by
and for Children* (National
Association for Young
Writers, Inc., P.O. Box 452,
Belvidere, NJ 07823).

For information on creativity, see articles in the *Journal of Creative Behavior.*

about a topic. To children, particularly young ones, a story is something they want to tell, and they will do this both orally and in writing when they are encouraged to do so and have the necessary skills.

Children's first stories are usually about something that happened to them or that they have learned about. These first stories (described in Chapter 9) are factual in the sense that they reflect children's beliefs and knowledge. But given their inborn imaginative and creative abilities, their stories soon become ones that they "make up" or at least embellish considerably. Teachers generally encourage children to use their imaginations, "to be creative," and, of course, the encouragement of children's creativity—in all of their endeavors—is desirable. But creativity is more than imagination; it draws on imagination, but it also draws on an individual's emotional resources and propensity to be curious and to think independently. It requires divergent thinking, but the expression of this thinking—the product—results only if there is some degree, at least, of convergent thinking.

This is not meant to imply that there should be any diminishing of teachers' efforts to foster children's creativity. In fact, teachers should generally exert more effort. This effort, however, must be more than simply telling children to "write something creative." Too often this direction results in wildly imaginative pieces that have few characteristics of stories and/or creative expression—even though such a piece may contain ideas or ways of phrasing them that are indeed genuinely creative. Too often, too, there is no encouragement or guidance in revising this writing. Stamping a smiling face or writing "good" on the paper does nothing to teach writing. It isn't even satisfying to the child.

An informal writing conference.

Children can be awakened early in their experiences to features of stories. Dictating to the teacher—with questions by him or her that help children think about catching a reader's interest with the story's beginning, the order in which they want to tell the story, and so on—will help. The same sort of thing can be done in time spent with children as they consider writing they have done themselves. As a teacher reads or tells stories or relates personal experiences, children will begin to learn the importance of sequence in relating events and details. And, of course, pointing out these characteristics of stories is an integral part of teaching reading and listening comprehension. Yet when children begin to write, many of their "stories" may have an appealing beginning, but then the sequence of events becomes confused, a climax is absent, and finally the "story" just stops (often with the child writing "THE END").

Trying too hard to be imaginative is one cause for a story's being poorly developed, but attempting too broad a scope is possibly even more often a cause. Limiting a topic—for a story or for other forms of writing—is a problem for all writers, whether children or adults. Help children to discover that if the scope is limited to a particular event or time span, the story can be developed more interestingly. For example, the title "Sam Got Out of the House Last Night" lends itself more readily to sequencing events and using specific details than does "My Pet Cat." Or "The First Indian I Ever Saw" is more easily handled than "Crossing the Prairie in a Wagon Train."

Deciding how to limit the topic, as well as what needs to be included and in what sequence, is a part of exploration, the prewriting phase of the writing process. Using the prewriting techniques discussed in Chapter 9 will prove helpful to making such decisions. Particularly, your listening to and talking with children as they formulate ideas will help them to clarify their thinking. For children in the middle grades, it might be useful to formulate standards that can be posted and called to their attention each time they write. These might include such points as the following:

Things to Think about Before I Write

1. What is the story about?
2. Where did it happen?
3. Who are the characters and what are they like?
4. Who is telling the story?
5. How will it begin?
6. What is the high point, or climax, of the story?
7. What events or actions lead up to this climax?
8. How will I end the story?

This may seem like a good deal for a child to think about, but children are often capable of more than teachers expect of them—especially when they have some idea of what to do. And if the standards are posted, children can refer to them as they plan and as they write.

Children should learn, of course, that such preplanning is not iron-clad. Sometimes plans need to be modified—possibly even abandoned. But preplanning does help in getting started and in organizing content. The child who has some idea of where he or she is going is more likely to produce an interesting story than one who simply begins.

Even with planning and modifying of the plan during the writing, stories usually need revising once the writer contemplates them or they are read to peers or the teacher. Thus, reference will need to be made to standards or "story guides" and to what listeners or readers say.

If attention is given to all that is said and implied above, dashing off a "story" in a Friday afternoon "creative" writing period is not possible. Time is needed to produce stories satisfactory to their authors and readers. This is true for authors of any age—as teachers who have tried to write stories themselves have found out.

Letter Writing

Letter writing is one of the most frequently used writing forms and therefore should receive instructional emphasis in the elementary school. Like other writing forms, it is best taught in situations where the need is genuine rather than manufactured. Such situations are plentiful in the average classroom; some example are listed on the next page. Probably you can think of other occasions or of other people for children to write letters to. You might try asking parents to send in names and addresses of grandparents and other relatives to whom children could write. In fact, arranging for children to start their own address books is a good idea.

The point is that letter writing can be done for genuine purposes. Practice will be real. Children will learn when it is appropriate to write notes of sympathy or congratulations, that one should write a thank-you note to someone who has sent a gift or done a favor, that it is courteous to express respect when writing to someone older than they are, how to acknowledge invitations, and to give reasons when regrets are necessary. They should also develop the ability to select appropriate writing materials (paper, pen, typewriter) and the realization that letters should be answered and mailed promptly. Like any other piece of writing, a letter should be read by the writer before publication, that is, before it is mailed, and attention should be given to spelling and neatness. And, finally, a letter is personal; one should not read a letter addressed to someone else unless asked to. Courtesy in this regard may be emphasized by asking children's permission before using their letters in some way, such as posting them, and by respecting a child's wish *not* to have his or her letter read by others.

Although younger children will have some occasion to write business letters, principal instruction should begin in the middle grades, with emphasis on the need for more formal language, appropriate salutations and closings, and the kinds of information that should be included in the body of the letter (whether money is enclosed, how to write out dollars and cents, the importance of stating exactly where merchandise or information is to be sent, etc.). Whenever children first write to an individual (rather than a firm) and request a reply, they should learn that a stamped, self-addressed envelope should be enclosed. And they should know that any letter written

---

Names of pen pals are available from:

Junior Pen Pal Network Directory
Postal Department
Washington, D.C.
20260-3100

Student Letter Exchange
308 Second Street NW,
Austin, MN 55912

Two books about letter writing, *P.S. Write Soon!* (elementary) and *All About Letters* (upper elementary and high school), produced by the United States Postal Service and the National Council of Teachers of English, are available from the latter for $2.50 each. Both have many ideas about places and people to write to, as well as addresses.

Use charts and models to show acceptable formats for letters. Label these parts: heading, greeting, message, closing, and signature.

Occasions Calling for Letter Writing

Invitations	To friends to visit the classroom To parents to come to an activity To another class or school to come to a program To the principal or supervisor to observe an activity To a guest to show slides or give a talk To the custodian or nurse to tell about his or her work
Replies	Of acceptance of an invitation from another class Of regret at not being able to come to a program
Sympathy	To a sick classmate, teacher, or relative To a teacher or family of a classmate after a death or accident
Greetings	To others at school on a holiday To parents on birthdays, Mothers' or Fathers' Day, and other special occasions To the principal and other teachers on birthdays To various friends on special occasions
Friendly letters and postcards	To another classroom or school To a former classmate To last year's teacher To a student in a foreign land To authors of favorite books To grandparents To a sports star
Thank-you notes	To someone for talking to the class To friends and relatives for presents To another class for the use of books or other materials To a parent for the loan of materials To the principal for some special favor
Requests	To a company or individual for information To a shopkeeper for materials To someone for permission to visit his or her business or home To the principal for permission to take a trip To organizations for free materials
Orders	To a business for class supplies To a publisher for a magazine subscription
Applications	For a position on the school paper For a job in the school office For summer work For after-school jobs
Complaints	About an article in the newspaper About a practice on the playground About a product to a consumer agency

Learning about the parts of a letter.

to a stranger—even if it is a letter of complaint—should always be courteous; rude or angry letters seldom get the desired results.

In the upper grades many, perhaps most, of the students will know how to type or use a word processor; therefore, it is important to introduce or reinforce any of the conventions of letter writing with which the children do not seem to be familiar. The teacher should also bring in, discuss, and post business letters having various formats, such as the block and indented styles. At this level, the students should know that it is good form to both write *and* type the signature on a business letter.

Most of us do not write business letters often, but when we do it is sometimes important that they convey a particularly good impression (letters of application, for instance). Impress children with the importance of neatness, the placement of the letter on the page, and the inclusion of needed information in the body of the letter. Again, no letter should be sealed and mailed until it has been proofread. One or two inked-in corrections are better than mistakes left uncorrected; if there are many errors, the letter should be rewritten or retyped.

There are many matters of form that are particularly important in letter writing: the placement of the parts of a letter, capitalization of particular items, abbreviations of titles such as Mr. or Dr., wording of the salutation or complimentary closing, and so on. Children will master these only by having real letter-writing experiences. Certainly letters should not be emphasized to the exclusion of other forms of writing, but letters are often crucial, and therefore the writing of letters should not be neglected in the school program.

Middle-grade children will enjoy *Dear Dragon* by Sesyle Joslin.

More Ideas for Teaching Letter Writing

1. Post model letters, including those written by children.
2. Show letter make-up by outlining the form with a felt pen.
3. Use dittoed worksheets, lined in such a way that the child is forced to write in correct form.
4. Keep collections of letters showing various forms.
5. Use construction paper cut-outs to show form and shape.
6. Have pupils exchange letters for correction of matters of form.

Reporting

There are always many opportunities for children to write reports. In fact, the classroom activities that pursue children's interests and recognize that the teaching of writing should not be separated from the teaching of other subjects—social studies, science, health, and so on—demand the writing of reports. Among the kinds of reports are the following: summaries of books, speeches, articles, movies, and television and radio programs; summaries of student council, class, or club meetings or of assembly programs; research accounts based on interviews, reading on specific topics, or science experiments; accounts of personal and class experiences.

Reporting begins in the primary grades, both in many "stories" written by children themselves and in those dictated to teachers, when the emphasis is on conveying information. This early reporting is a good foundation for later reporting on many topics and of all types. The following should suggest the almost unlimited possibilities for reports:

When Writers Read, a book by Hansen, discusses many relationships between reading and writing.

Sending reports home informs parents about their children's learning.

Writing one-paragraph reports on famous people
Visiting a museum and reporting on an object observed
Writing a report on a hobby or special interest
Keeping records of baseball and football games and reporting on them
Explaining the organization and work of a club
Describing an incident from a particular point of view
Reporting on controversial issues in committee meetings
Writing an account of a holiday celebration
Reporting briefly on the history and derivation of a word
Giving personal reactions to characters and situations in books
Reporting on the steps through which a character in a story changes

Writing is a part of the learning process in social studies and other subjects.

Reporting on the history of a custom, superstition, or place name

Reporting on an interview with the principal

Summarizing newspaper articles on a topic of current interest

Reporting on background information relative to a current news story

Chapters 13 and 14 discuss teaching children to locate information, take notes, outline, and correlate information—skills needed for making reports as effective as possible. Since reporting, either orally or in writing, is important to many classroom activities, it is a good idea to initiate a class discussion aimed at formulating a set of procedures. For children in the upper grades, these should probably include the following steps:

Don't overlook the possibility of putting cover pages on reports so they can become part of the classroom library.

1. Decide what facts or information should be included.
2. Determine the most likely sources for this information—observation, interviews, reading, and so on.
3. Use these sources to find the information needed.
4. Recheck step 1 to see whether all needed information has been found and whether new items should be included.
5. Decide on the order in which facts should be presented and the best way to present each one—illustrations, details, or reasons.

Books on Writing for Children

How to Read and Write Poetry by Anna Cosman (Watts, 1979) (grades 4–7)

In Your Own Words: A Beginner's Guide to Writing by Sylvia Cassedy (Doubleday, 1979) (grades 6–9)

Where Do You Get Your Ideas? Helping Young Writers Begin by Sandy Asher (Walker, 1987) (grades 3–7).

Write Your Own Story by Vivian Dubrovin (Watts, 1984) (grades 5–8)

Writing Your Own Plays by Carol Korty (Scribner's, 1986).

The Young Writer's Handbook by Susan and Steven Tchudi (Scribner's, 1984) (grades 6–9)

Reviews

A review is a specialized type of report. Reviews may be written about books, television programs, movies, and cultural events. A review should be a teaser, a reaction by the writer, not a dull account of "what happened." Before children write reviews, particularly of books they have read, they should be made familiar with reviews such as those found in *Language Arts* and *The Horn Book*. Most newspapers have reviews (of varying quality) of television, movies, books, and local plays or concerts. Various reviews should be discussed with children so that they learn how a review differs from other kinds of reports.

Essays

The word *essay* has fallen into disuse, except in literature classes, yet it is an apt term for a type of writing that offers endless opportunities for expression. In simple terms, an essay is the written presentation of one's beliefs or feelings about a person, a place, an event, or an idea. Thus, much of the writing and speaking that we do, both as children and as adults, has some of the qualities of an essay—even a personal letter is a loosely organized essay, since it expresses the writer's personality. Similarly, many of the experience stories that children write or dictate to the teacher are essays.

The essay has several advantages as a vehicle for written expression. First, it is a form with which children have had experience; therefore, they can focus most of their attention on choosing the best way to express their thoughts and feelings. Second, by its very nature the essay is creative, since it is a personal expression. Third, children want to express their likes and dislikes, their fears and desires, so this form should appeal to them. Writing essays may even help to improve the self-image of a child who believes that his or her feelings are unimportant to others. And finally, the essay is some-what similiar in form to the kinds of writing most commonly used by children and adults—more so, at least, than are stories and poems. Thus, children can learn organization and methods of developing ideas while they are also developing their creative talents.

News Articles

A classroom newspaper can be extremely effective for motivating writing. Children will become intrigued with discovering and reporting events around the school, in the neighborhood, and in their homes. The newspaper can be handwritten by the children (in manuscript form), typed (parents and older siblings might help), or composed on a word processor. (As mentioned in Chapter 9, there are word-processing programs that will produce newspaperlike output.) However a classroom newspaper is produced, it can have the organizational features of a regular newspaper, such as a staff, editorials, and various sections. It can be published weekly, monthly, or only occasionally for special holidays and events. Frequency should be determined principally, of course, by the amount of learning and enjoyment the children gain from this activity, but other factors must be considered too. Will this frequency of publication fit into the schedule without replacing other activities that may be as or more valuable? Can the paper be planned to call forth the kinds of writing practice and skills needed by the children? Is time available for typing and duplicating, or can parents and/ or students be depended on to do at least a part of this work?

The writing in a newspaper may be of many types, since newspapers ordinarily include many things: news stories, special features, letters to the editor, jokes, advertisements, poems, and comics. Organizational skills are also called into play in making decisions about what things should be included and how they should be placed.

Many upper-grade reading programs include material on how to read a newspaper. This may provide a starting point for a class or school newspaper. Children might read newspapers in class and analyze them, cutting out clippings of various sorts to illustrate what they have learned. Various sections of a paper (sports, world news, society news, etc.) should be noted, and special attention should be given to the sources of material for these sections—syndicated columns, wire services, publicity handouts, and local reporting. Journalism has its own vocabulary, and children can learn the special meanings of words such as *copy, deadline, proofreading, layout*, and *editor*. The school newspaper should receive high priority in a program of written expression because it is a live (not drill or textbook) activity, it builds class and school spirit, and it appeals to all children, regardless of creative abilities. Every child in the classroom may participate in some way, because such a wide variety of forms of writing is needed. And almost every area of the curriculum may be utilized in the newspaper—social studies, science, art, health, and so forth.

Records

Children's interest in nature and in everything going on around them provides motivation for writing records of things that happen. Since most record keeping requires straightforward, factual writing, and not a taxing amount, many children who have difficulty with other forms of writing can keep records. Here are some kinds of records that can be kept:

> The time the sun sets, recorded at weekly intervals
> Weather calendars
> Growth of plants in the classroom windows
> Steps followed in making pudding
> Spelling words missed by the class
> Classroom duties assigned to pupils
> Class diary of daily events
> Books read by each child (avoid making this too competitive)
> Daily temperatures, wind direction, etc.
> Dates of appearance of first robin, geese flying south, etc.
> Height and weight records
> Foods eaten for breakfast, hours slept, etc.
> The changing appearance of polliwogs, cocoons, etc.
> Visitors to the classroom
> New words learned in various subjects
> Science experiments
> Points to remember about a film
> Daily attendance and daily schedule
> Standards or rules for class activities
> Events to be reported on in the yearbook

Forms

Everyone has occasion to fill out forms. Neither children nor adults can avoid doing so; therefore children need to learn and to practice this kind of writing. There are many day-to-day activities in which children must fill out forms. These situations should be utilized to teach careful reading, the importance of legible writing (or printing), and the need for accuracy. Some school situations for filling out forms are these:

> Enrollment cards
> Questionnaires regarding personal history
> Questionnaires concerning health facts
> Library loan cards
> Call slips for books at the library
> Information called for on a standardized test
> A money order for materials for the class
> An application card for an account in the school savings bank
> A deposit slip for a school savings account
> A withdrawal slip
> A subscription blank for a magazine
> Coupons for samples advertised in magazines
> An order to a publisher for a reference book
> An application blank for membership in a magazine club
> A book plate for use in a textbook

Announcements, Labels, and Notices

Many school activities call for written notices, labels, titles, and announcements. This type of writing requires specificity and brevity. Moreover, such writing may not be read unless it is interesting and clear. Teaching emphasis should be on these factors. Activities such as the following may be helpful:

> Making oral announcements that hold to standards of brevity, accuracy, etc.
> Giving oral directions for a game or other activity
> Examining the weaknesses of notices and announcements in newspapers
> Reporting on notices, signs, and labels seen around the school
> Scoring announcements and notices as to appeal, clarity, neatness, etc.

The factors to be considered can be listed on a score sheet and points assigned to each as an announcement or notice is examined.

Poetry and Rhymes

Books for Children to Read

City Talk by Lee Bennett Hopkins (Alfred A. Knopf, 1970)
For Me to Say by David Mc-Cord (Little, Brown, 1970)
It Doesn't Always Have to Rhyme by Eve Merriam (Atheneum, 1966)
Miracles by Richard Lewis (Simon and Schuster, 1966)

Things to listen for:

the first raindrops tapping tentatively at the window
a lonely puppy wailing in the night
the howling wind demanding to be let in
the crunch of rubber boots on new snow
the light laughter of young children at play

Every child should have some experience with poetry—hearing it, reading it, speaking it individually or as part of a group, and writing it. Certainly no one class will produce many—if any—poets of great stature, but the number of children who can create a truly charming, humorous, or actually poetic bit of verse is often surprising.

Children should not be expected to write poetry unless they have heard a great deal of it. Poetry in its various forms must have been read to them, and they should have experienced saying it in choral speaking activities. Opening activities in a classroom provide a natural time every day for reading poetry to children, but many other times will come up if you have appropriate poetry ready to read (see Chapter 15). There are equally many natural and fun times for children to experience speaking poetry. Important, too, as background for children's writing of poetry are experiences that have extended their language powers: finding and talking about words and phrases that create visual and sound images, words with a musical lilt, new ways of saying things, and words related to their emotions.

A class poem is a good beginning. Decide on a type of poem with which the children are familiar and which they have enjoyed, read aloud several examples, and then suggest that they might compose a poem like this. If they have the background suggested, children should be able to think of topics, words and phrases, rhyming words (if needed), and even entire lines. Possibly you may need to encourage such suggestions by stimulating one or more of their senses. Even a weed picked on your way to school may prompt thoughts about its structure, color, or smell and bring forth words and phrases about how ugly or beautiful it is, its uniqueness, and so on. The children can then discuss which words and phrases sound best or fit the subject or rhythm best. In this way they will learn how to go about the process of creating a poem.

It is not important to teach poetic techniques as such, but call attention to them when it is appropriate. For example, kindergarten children cannot be expected either to pronounce or to remember *onomatopoeia*, but they can readily grasp that *buzz* is something like the sound that a bee makes.

Upper-grade pupils, on the other hand, might be extremely proud of the fact that they have used a technique called **alliteration** in creating a phrase such as "the sad, silken syllables of the breeze." Emphasis should always be on expression rather than on techniques, however.

After several class poems have been composed, it may be appropriate to encourage group poems (by three or four children) in order to give children more confidence, since the responsibility for success or failure does not then rest on a single child and the exchange of ideas often leads to better language choices. With little encouragement some children will want to write poetry themselves, once they have heard a good many poems and if they are not forced into attempting a form that doesn't appeal. Others will do little poetry or verse writing by themselves regardless of the amount of poetry they hear or read and the encouragement they receive. They should not be pressured to write poems, but the door should be kept open for them to try when and if they want to. Sometimes a simple observation or sensory experience will elicit feelings—words and phrases—from even the most reticent child and may lead to an almost spontaneous writing of verse.

Writing poems based on a specified pattern or formula will assist some children. Although such writing to pattern can be overdone, there are several short and rather structured forms that children particularly enjoy using. The form itself creates a challenge and furnishes rather definite guidelines, thus helping them to achieve greater success with their first efforts.

Magazines That Publish Poetry by Children

Child LIfe
P.O. Box 10681
Des Moines, IA 50336

Children's Digest
P.O. Box 10681
Des Moines, IA 50336

Cricket
Open Court Publishing Company
1058 Eighth Street
LaSalle, IL 61301

Highlights for Children
Cobblestone Publishing Company
20 Grove Street
Petersborough, NH 03458

A Couplet:

For all the long day
We searched for a way.

A Triplet:

A large pig
Went to dig
For a fig.

Couplets and Triplets. Preschool activities that call attention to rhyming words may stimulate children's first attempts at composing verses. Early attempts at rhyming should not be hampered by a concern with rhythm, although children love rhythm and may well try to produce it. Simply encouraging them to make a second sentence that rhymes with and is related to the first is sufficient.

Helping children to find words or phrases that sound better or improve the rhythm will help them develop aural discrimination, but working on rhyming and rhythm does more than this and more than helping them learn about sentences, capitalization, and end punctuation. Writing couplets, triplets, and other simple forms of poetry is a first step toward developing creativity and—even more important—is fun to do.

Cinquain. Cinquain is not difficult to write, and it is excellent for helping children to become aware of the special quality of poetry—its appeal to the emotions and the senses. It has a very specific formula:

First line:	One word, giving title
Second line:	two words, describing title
Third line:	three words, expressing an action
Fourth line:	four words, expressing a feeling
Fifth line:	one word, a synonym for the title

This is too restrictive a form to stay with for very long, but it does allow some freedom in the choice of words and phrases, and almost any child can achieve some degree of success with cinquain. To show how the formula works, here are two examples:

SAM

Warm, friendly,
Licks my face
To show his love.
Puppy.

DARKNESS

Thick, eerie;
I whistle loudly;
I fear the night;
Black.

Free Verse. Free verse places no restrictions on total length and number of syllables or words to a line and prescribes no rhythmic pattern. The writer decides where to break lines or begin new stanzas and when the poem is complete. In a sense, free verse may be thought of as *free thought*. The length of the thought might be one sentence by a third grader or several stanzas by a creative sixth grader.

If children experience activities in which they talk about and use words and phrases that express their feelings about commonplace but important things to them—family, friends, fear, happiness, pain, and so forth—then writing down these feelings will follow.

Limericks. Middle-grade children can have a great deal of fun with limericks, and certainly children should know that poetry can be humorous as well as serious. That, in fact, is the essence of poetry—it expresses all our emotions at one time or another. Limericks have a set form with which most of us are familiar: the first, second, and fifth lines rhyme; the third and fourth lines rhyme and are shorter. Show children that the "trick" is to find a number of words that rhyme and then see if several of them suggest an idea; they will need at least three rhyming words for lines one, two, and five. Then show them how they can experiment with word order or find synonyms in order to make the meter work out correctly. The beginning couplet should be developed first; then the same kind of experimentation can produce lines three and four. The final line should come rather easily after this much has been done.

There was an old woman named Snow.
Who couldn't get flowers to grow.
She planted some seeds
But grew only weeds.
What happened I really don't know!

Other Forms. Obviously there are many more verse forms than have been discussed here, and children may be encouraged to try any that they are interested in. **Haiku** is a lovely Japanese verse form that many teachers have children try. Haiku has a total of seventeen syllables in three lines: the first line has five syllables, the second seven, and the third five. There is no rhyme or meter. The central image is usually from nature, with the final line making an observation about life.

The beauty of haiku lies in the right choice of words to create the image and express the idea of the poem. However, in the opinion of most authorities on poetry, elementary-school children are not likely to have the vocabulary and life experiences to write haiku since it involves much more than syllable counting. The same may be said for other Japanese poetry forms: *tanka*, which starts with the same structure as haiku but adds two lines of seven syllables each; and *senryu*, which has three lines but may add two or three syllables in each line.

Some teachers, working with their students, have invented their own forms, such as *triante* and *diamente*. These can be structured according to the age and abilities of the children. Triante is appealing because it calls for "sense" words, as follows:

First line:	one word, giving the title
Second line:	two words, telling how it smells
Third line:	three words, telling how it feels
Fourth line:	four words, telling how it looks
Fifth line:	five words, telling how it sounds

Poems can also be made in shapes; that is, a poem about a cloud might be shaped like a drifting cloud, or one about Halloween might be in the shape of a pumpkin. The important fact to remember is that poetry is yet another way in which ideas and feelings may be expressed. In the kind of world we live in today, it is important for children to learn to express their emotions verbally and to exercise care in selecting the words they choose to express those emotions. In addition, reading and hearing poetry can add dimension to their lives, and creating poetry will undoubtedly extend this dimension.

Other Writing Activities

Many other activities can serve to stimulate children's writing. In particular much of what children read will serve this function, and the writing done will also be a useful reinforcement and supplement to reading lessons as well as to reading in other curriculum areas. The following are forms of writing that may be based on reading experiences.

See Chapter 15 for writing suggestions related to literature.

Character Sketches. Sketches based on the characters in a story may be written by children. They should think about the character selected, search for details about that character and the things he or she does, and speculate about his or her behavior. A character sketch can take any of several forms; it can be thought of as a "verbal snapshot" or an impression gained by a "first glance," a description that tells what kind of human being a person is, a combination of these, or a sketch that concentrates on an example or examples of one trait.

Biographies. Children can research and write biographies of people in the news or people they have learned about in social studies. They can also write "made up" biographies or autobiographies of characters in stories. These provide not only fun but also good motivations for reading. Techniques such as personification can be used if the writing lends itself to such treatment. An old car, a horse, or a towering tree can write its early life through the imagination of the child.

Stimulate writing by reading all types of literature:

fables
tall tales
autobiographies
fairy tales
historical fiction
science fiction
folk tales

Descriptions. Literary selections often demonstrate how a professional writer uses composition skills. For example, at the beginning of "Rip Van Winkle," Washington Irving describes the Catskill Mountains:

> . . . swelling up to a noble height, and lording it over the surrounding country . . . when the weather is fair and settled, they are clothed in blue and purple, and print their bold outlines on the clear evening sky; but sometimes, when the rest of the landscape is cloudless, they will gather a hood of grey vapors about their summits, which, in the last rays of the setting sun, will glow and light up like a crown of glory.

In discussion, help the children to discover how the use of devices such as personification and simile adds vigor to a description, how the use of verbs as well as adjectives and adverbs gives strength, and how a few well-chosen details, instead of a wealth of them, can set scene and mood. This can be followed by asking the children to think about a familiar setting and give details about it. These details can then be woven into a description.

Book-Related Letters. Corresponding with an author is a way for a child to share with others some of his or her reading experiences. The possibilities for such correspondence may be limited, but trying it might bring surprising results.

Children can also write letters to the librarian, to another teacher, or to children in another grade about the books they have read. These are effective whether the writer is recommending or criticizing the book.

In the middle grades, book characters may exchange letters. Have pupils write to one another as the characters might have done. For example, Henry Reed might ask Homer Price all about the doughnut machine, and Amos might be very interested in discussing French customs with Anatole.

Commentaries. Another variation of the book report is the commentary, which involves encouraging children to relate the most humorous incident in a book, the most exciting happening, the part they liked the best, or the saddest part. This will help children learn to seek certain types of materials from books and stories.

Riddles. Children can prepare a series of clues concerning a character, a setting, an event, or an object in a story. The reader must guess who or what is being described. Sometimes it is possible to create interest by deliberately choosing ambiguous terms.

Captions and Headlines. For children who have difficulty expressing ideas in writing, short forms of composition should be tried. Writing labels for pictures related to stories is one example. These labels should be more than simply one or a few words. Instead of writing "The Snowstorm," a child might be encouraged to write a sentence, such as "When I woke up, everything was white and clean."

In addition to writing labels for pictures, less able children may be encouraged to write headlines—to give in short sentences the "big idea" of a story they have read.

Diaries. When studying colonial times or other periods in history, students may pretend to be living during the period and keep diaries. They can also write letters to friends telling about some of the experiences or first-person stories in which they describe events as though they had participated in the action. It is particularly important to limit the scope in this kind of writing. For example, a diary entry might cover only one day, or even a part of a day; a first-person account could be limited to a single aspect of an important historical event—for instance, what the foot soldier felt like at Valley Forge.

MORE ON MOTIVATION AND WRITING

Once children have used the writing process for some time, the chances are good that they will have a very positive attitude toward writing. When this is the case, there are no significant problems with motivation; indeed, some children will write in their free time in school as well as during out-of-school time. But, if the bulk of the teaching they have experienced has stressed isolated skills rather than purposeful writing, motivating them to write may be a real problem. Of course, beginning with the writing process and emphasizing personal reasons for writing will help, no matter what the age of the class members. For some children, though, more specific stimulation for writing will be needed.

A "Writers' Corner," partially screened if possible and furnished with necessary materials, will encourage children to write.

Even children who have had numerous and productive writing experiences will also occasionally benefit from a suggestion by the teacher or an initiating activity. This is particularly true for writing that does not have the directly communicative purpose of a letter, a report, or an announcement. If some children are asked to write stories, essays, or poetry, a bit of a push or some immediate form of motivation may be needed. Most will require only a glimmer of an idea—a word or two, a picture, or an object—to get them on the way to thinking and writing.

Specific Topics

If a teacher simply writes a topic or topics on the board and asks children to begin writing—even if he or she provides time for them to think before actual writing begins—the expected writing may not result. In fact, some children may write little or nothing.

Students are very proud of the books they have produced.

There are several ways to avoid this. First, it is probably better to provide a choice of topics; a single topic is not likely to suit the interests and abilities of all the children. If the general topic is one that has come from a particular study unit, suggest different ways of treating the topic or different aspects that might be dealt with. Second, it is wise to take a few minutes to discuss the topics, suggesting—or having the children suggest—ways in which they might be treated; this may spur pupils to think of others themselves. Another possibility is to select a particular topic and list on the board, again with the children's help, some words that might be suitable to use in connection with this topic. The list need not include every word that can be dredged up—only enough to get the children's thinking started. It should, however, include nouns, verbs, and adverbs as well as adjectives; children should discover early that adjectives are not the only words that describe. Topics should be chosen with an eye toward children's interests and experience—either actual or vicarious. No one can be expected to write well about something that is uninteresting and unfamiliar. Finally, topics determined by children themselves are almost always more appropriate than those a teacher suggests.

Writing done to fulfill an assignment is usually far less expressive than that done out of personal interest.

It is true, of course, that a person often knows more about something than he or she may be aware of. Sometimes children can be stimulated by writing on the chalkboard questions such as these:

What do I know a lot about?
What do I want to learn something about?
What would my friends like most to read or hear about?
Do I know how to do something that I could tell about?

Some children may not think they have answers to such questions, but perhaps if they are interviewed by other children they will have.

Pictures

Other ways to provide stimulation:

listening to music
attending plays
observing dancers
visiting an art gallery

Using pictures as bases for ideas is another technique for getting children to write. Collect pictures of various sizes and on various subjects, mount them on heavy paper if necessary, and file them for ready reference. The filing is usually by topic (for example, dogs, winter, children, farm animals, colors, etc.). Mounting pictures adds to the amount of filing space needed, but it also keeps them from becoming dog-eared; probably temporary mountings are best, since they may need to be changed for different purposes.

Pictures can be used in several ways: a large picture can be displayed to the entire class; smaller pictures can be distributed to individual pupils; or individual pupils or small groups can choose from a display in the chalk tray, pictures in story books, or those in readers or other textbooks. Showing a large picture to the entire class is usually good for beginning writing activities because the ensuing discussion often stimulates many ideas.

The following suggest the kinds of "thinking about" and "talking about" questions that are helpful:

What is happening in the picture? (Encourage various possibilities.)

What kind of people are these? Do they belong to the same family, are they friends, or what? Do you think you would like them?

What might have happened just before the time the picture shows? What might happen next?

Think of words and phrases that describe the action in the picture. What words might describe the people or the way they feel?

What are some words that describe the scenery in the picture?

If you were going to tell a story about this picture, how would you begin?

It is important that such questions be exploratory, not directive; creative writing does not result in every child's turning out the same story. On the other hand, children should discuss whether or not suggestions fit the picture; a wrinkled, ragged crone might find a long-lost child, but she is not likely to marry Prince Charming or find a lucrative job unless she is in disguise or a fairy godmother goes to work!

A Story Framework

If a topic or a picture does not give a child enough of a setting to start his or her thinking and writing, an elaboration or extension of the topic may be helpful. Such an extension usually provides a framework around which a story can be created. Sometimes, too, the framework stimulates thinking that leads to a story that is not directly attributable to the framework. A file of such "frames" can be useful; listed below are some that have proved successful.

1. You are a young boy who plays the drum for an army company that is part of Washington's Revolutionary Army. Tell what happens one day while you are waiting in camp for the general to arrive.

2. You are traveling on a wagon train from St. Louis to California. Many of the wagons are lost crossing the Red River. What happens the next morning?

3. Pretend you are an inanimate object such as a parking meter, a "No Parking" sign, or an object on display in the drugstore window. Describe your feelings about one of the people who passes daily.

4. You are a famous explorer who has just returned from a trip. Tell about one of your discoveries and why it is important.

5. You wake up suddenly in the middle of the night. Everything is quiet, and it is pitch dark. Suddenly you hear a clanking sound that reminds you of a TV program. Tell what happens next.

6. The chair is rocking, but no one is in it. As you watch, the rocking increases in speed and a faint glow of light travels across the room. What happens next?

7. You are lying on the bank of a lake watching your fishing line. Suddenly you hear a rustle in the bushes behind you, followed by some loud sniffing. Tell how you feel and what happens when you discover what caused the noise.

8. Describe some common happening as though you were an invisible observer from another planet visiting the earth for the first time.

9. Pretend you are a statue in the park. Tell about some of the things you have seen and the changes that have occurred over the years.

10. Think of some of the things you have done on Halloween, some of the ways you have dressed, some of the things you have seen and heard. Think, too, of smells and tastes and how they were related to what you did. Can you make up a story about an ideal Halloween?

A Story Beginning

Sometimes a child who cannot think of a beginning for a story will be able to finish one or even add more than simply the ending if the beginning is appealing. Furthermore, most children enjoy writing a story from a given beginning. One way to write stories is for the class as a group to make up an opening and then each child finishes the story individually. Magazines for teachers and for children often have story beginnings that can be used as they are or with modifications for local circumstances. Many kinds of beginnings may be used. Some actually indicate how the story should end, and only minor variations are possible. Others simply start the "wheels" turning, so that the various stories the children write reflect their creativity and individuality.

It is a good idea to have some story beginnings on hand, just as you have files of topics, pictures, and story structures. Here are some beginnings that teachers have used:

1. There was a strange silence along the main street of the town, even though it was only 9 p.m.

2. On the table was a stack of books; the top one was open.

3. Bulldozers began climbing the hill as the sun appeared.

4. The rain beat against the window pane as the sky darkened and lightning flashed.

5. There was a fluttering of wings, and the quail rose from the bushes.

6. She looked over the edge of the building and gasped at what she saw many floors below.

7. The door banged. Then it opened quickly and a tall, grizzled cowboy came through.

8. All the way home I kept looking at my clothes and thinking about what I might say to my mother.

9. The old house looked interesting. The rocking chair on the porch had a red cushion in it, and the screen door was hanging by one hinge.

10. As I passed the house, I caught a whiff of . . .

11. Susan stood on the dock; her legs felt stiff and refused to move. Then she felt dizzy.

12. He was very tall. I mean really tall. I wondered why he would take a job like that.

Story beginnings that go beyond a sentence or two are also helpful. All that is needed is something to start children thinking about what they could and would be interested in writing about. The following are more examples of beginnings that you might try:

1. John and his younger brother were playing on the beach when they found the strange footprints. They seemed to come from the water and to go along the shore toward the trees in the distance. John started to follow his brother, who was racing after the footprints.

2. The last weak rays of the sun streaked coldly across the graying sky. Linda shivered and touched her heels gently to the horse's flanks, remembering that the field would soon be swallowed by the fog and clammy darkness. The she heard the scream—a piercing, wailing cry.

3. George manages the family, but not always very well. He forgets that he is a dog and that there are some things a dog can't do. I remember when he tried to . . .

4. I could see the fire in the distance. The blaze danced above the tree tops and the smoke billowed away in a darkening cloud. Just then three deer burst through the undergrowth and dashed past me. What should I do?

5. It's fun to watch ants. They are so busy and seem to know what they are doing. Sometimes I have fun pretending I am an ant.

6. The roar of the waterfall could be heard above the patter of the rain on the trees. I listened carefully for another sound. No, I could not hear it. I wondered why. I surely was close enough. Maybe I was on the wrong side of the river.

7. The strange sound got louder and louder until it was almost deafening. We had stopped walking when it started, and now we stared at one another. Fright began to show on John's face, and Bill's eyes were blinking. Then

the sound stopped and an eerie silence ensued. We wondered what might happen next, but we still didn't talk.

8. I pounded and pounded, but the door wouldn't open. Looking around for something to use as a hammer, I spotted a large rock lying in the driveway. I ran to get it and was hit by . . .

9. The light got brighter and brighter as the spaceship settled toward the earth. Then there was a slight flutter and it came to rest. I held my breath, wondering what would happen next. Suddenly a hole opened up in the bottom of the ship and a ladder came swiftly down. The figure that followed was round, spindle-legged, and silver colored—just as an "outer space" creature was supposed to look. What should I do? Should I speak? Should I run? I decided . . .

10. It was a very good movie, especially the music. It reminded me of the time we went camping, although we didn't have the trouble with bears that the girl in the movie had. But wait, let me tell you about it.

Words and Phrases

Words about Weather

sunny	blustery
bright	hot
foggy	stifling
sultry	warm
snowy	humid
stormy	changeable
cloudy	windy
dry	smoggy
wet	drizzling
cold	tepid
clear	misty

Seeing and discussing words and phrases that remind them of experiences or stir their imaginations may stimulate children to write. Often such words and phrases can be collected by the class, and perhaps those may work particularly well. Sometimes, however, pupils may need help in getting thinking started. Phrases such as these may help them to think of others:

pelting rain on the window
a prancing horse
silver-gray smoke rising
a seagull floating noiselessly above
sunlight dancing upon the blue water
the swaying, bending trees
a dewy spider web in the bush
snow blowing in waves across the field

Nothing creative is likely to result from such phrases, however, unless children have come to enjoy words and the way they are used. As you read aloud to children, comment on an unusual word or show your appreciation of an apt phrase. Talk about words; help children to enjoy the way they sound and the way they conjure up pictures. Encourage them to discover new words and learn new meanings for words they already know. Only a true appreciation of language will bring about expression that shows sparkle and imagination.

EVALUATING WRITTEN EXPRESSION

Evaluation is one of the major elements in the total teaching/learning process. From evaluation both you and your pupils should discover what has been learned and what has not. From evaluation you should plan future teaching. But because evaluation is often difficult and because there is a reluctance to criticize a child's creative efforts, some teachers do little evaluation of children's writing or of their own teaching of writing.

However, evaluation need not be as difficult as it is often thought to be if its focus is realistic and instruction-centered rather than directed at giving grades, making red marks, and finding fault.

Evaluating Your Teaching

Writing Teacher, a magazine for teachers of kindergarten through eighth grade, is available from ECS Learning Systems, P.O. Box 791437, San Antonio, TX 78279.

The first concern in evaluation should be the program itself—its objectives and the teaching procedures and materials used. Such questions as these should be considered:

1. What is the atmosphere in the classroom? Is it one in which each child feels free to express ideas and make contributions to projects and discussions? Is there anything that might tend to repress individual expression?

2. Does the physical appearance of the classroom reflect creativity (on the part of both teacher and children), or is it less attractive than it could be?

3. Is there sufficient input of many kinds throughout the year and in all areas of the curriculum?

4. Do children have many opportunities to read and hear well-written stories, poems, and so forth? Is there a real interest in words and the ways they are put together?

5. Do children have enough skill in the mechanics of writing to be able to express their ideas? Is the emphasis on mechanics so great that they are afraid to try new ways of expressing themselves?

6. Are motivation and preparation for writing adequate, or are children expected to write without really having a purpose or knowing what is expected of them?

7. Is writing a genuine part of the total curriculum? Is advantage taken of the many opportunities that occur for children to do purposeful writing?

8. Do the children write in many forms and for a variety of purposes and audiences? Do they have adequate knowledge of the many forms of and purposes for writing?

9. Does each child receive constructive responses—from you and others—at various stages in the writing process? Does each child feel free to ask questions, try out ideas, and seek help?

These are questions to be asked and answered by you, the teacher. In part, though, your answers must come from a consideration of the children's writing. Is the writing generally vapid, superficial, and trite? Does it neither interest nor communicate? Surely children are not like this. They are eager and sad, exhilarated and frustrated, interested and bored, possessive and giving. If their writing fails to express these feelings, if it is unimaginative and nonindividualistic, then something has happened. Something has come between the children's natural expressiveness and the papers they turn in.

Possible causes for children's failure to achieve the results desired (both by them and by the teacher) include the following:

- Lack of direction and guidance
- Fear of teacher disapproval
- Stifled oral expression
- A meager vocabulary
- Ignorance of the forms of writing
- A deficiency of input
- Failure to recognize the importance of the audience
- No working knowledge of composition skills
- Putting paper before the children too soon
- Overemphasis on teaching mechanical skills

Evaluating Specific Products

Evaluation of any piece of writing is largely an appraisal of its quality in terms of its purpose. Not everything children write should be evaluated, of course. But, as was stated earlier, when children have matured to a level in their writing where they are preparing finished products, evaluation is necessary. It is a major stage in the writing process. This evaluation includes examining the thought, idea, or topic, the organization, the clarity and appeal of the final product, and the courtesy shown to readers in the form of legibility, correct spelling, acceptable language usage, and meaningful punctuation.

As a child writes to communicate and to express, as all children will unless their desire for expressing themselves by writing is shut off by the classroom program, he or she should appraise what was written. Children's self-evaluation can be aided by providing them with models, when possible and appropriate (formats and styles for letter writing, for example), to use

Artwork adds to the meaning of written material.

Checklist for Written Reports	Linda	Ian	Kim	Carlos	Marie
Information					
Organization					
Vocabulary					
Sentence structure					
Appearance					
Usage					
Punctuation					
Capitalization					
Spelling					

for guidance and comparison. Proofreading and editing checklists and lists of standards to be observed will also be helpful. The checklists and other aids to evaluation ought to be developed with the children's participation. An example of a checklist for evaluating reports is shown above. Such a form should be useful to you, of course, but it may also be modified and duplicated for children's use. That is, the spaces where the children's names appear could instead be used for a child to write in information identifying specific pieces of writing. Thus, the child could determine which areas he or she needs to work on most, where improvement is occurring, and so on, particularly if points (for example, in a range from 1 to 5) are assigned to each item rather than "yes" or "no."

A checklist can be expanded, but only if there is time available and background has been laid down for using the expanded version. For example, organization can be broken down into introduction, body, and conclusion; appearance can be divided into title, margins, and handwriting. Items included, of course, should vary according to grade level and standards previously established.

Individual pieces of writing may also be evaluated for content, organization, mechanics, style, and so forth, by a scale that provides for the assigning of points for each of the aspects of writing in the scale. Scales will have either short examples of different levels of quality for the characteristics being assessed or statements on which to base judgments, as in this example of a portion of a scale:

Sequence

High	The order of events is clear even if the writer at times tells about the past or the future.
Middle	A few times it is not clear which event happened first.
Low	It is impossible to determine which event comes first or follows any other event.

Any teacher can make a scale to aid in judging writing products. With guidance, children can do this too. A scale has particular value in guiding consistency in judgments about pieces of writing from the same individual and in aiding an evaluator to form judgments about examples of writing from a whole class.

Writing products are increasingly being evaluated by a *holistic method.* That is, rather than evaluating aspects of composition and assigning points, which are then totaled for a score for the piece, the evaluator makes a judgment as to the quality of the piece as a whole. Holistic scoring is usually done on a schoolwide (or even broader) basis to get an assessment that can be compared with earlier ones or ones in other settings. Judgments of the quality of each piece of writing (preferably more than one piece per writer) are made by two or more teachers who have come to some agreement about the bases for their judgments. Holistic scoring has some advantages but does not have the diagnostic features that scales and checklists have for determining what aspects of writing need teaching attention.

The New York State Education Department recommends a five-point "holistic scale" for rating the writing of elementary-school students. Factors considered are organization, sentence variety, word choice, and mechanics.

Informal Records

Making valid judgments about the quality of an individual's writing as a whole or about aspects of it is not easy. Certainly, since writing ability grows in spurts and every writer has "off days," judgments should not be based on evaluating one or even several pieces of writing. In order to determine a child's strong points and weaknesses, various techniques should be used. One is using a checklist or scale at intervals during the year. Others include keeping folders of children's writing; anecdotal records for each child—derived primarily from individual conferences; observational records of prewriting, writing, and postwriting behaviors; and tests of knowledge and application of punctuation and capitalization skills, paragraphing, and showing variety in sentence structure.

Parents are interested in such records, which are a good means for giving them evidence of their child's ability and growth.

Standardized Tests

There are standardized tests that purport to measure ability in written expression or some aspect of it. However, these measures do not actually do what is often claimed for them. For example, a test may determine a pupil's knowledge of grammatical terminology or rules, but this kind of knowledge has nothing to do with writing ability. Identifying good and poor sentences (or fragments), choosing acceptable words and expressions (standard usage), arranging sentences in order, identifying misspelled words, and indicating where punctuation items should be placed are other activities that appear on standardized tests (although not all of these appear in all tests that purport to measure writing ability). These items, of course, are all related to writing, but they simply sample the test-taker's ability to distinguish between standard and nonstandard forms and to proofread for some types of errors. Standardized tests do not reveal much about performance in the individual's own expression.

Assigning Grades

Assigning a letter or number grade to a child's paper should be avoided unless there is a school policy requiring it. If there is such a policy, the grade assigned should be supplemented by noting commendable aspects of the writing, such as a good choice of words, an apt expression, a neat margin, or good organization of thought. Every written product from every child has something about it that can be commended. Perhaps it may only be a better formed letter, fewer erasures, or greater promptness in turning the paper in, but, whatever can be praised should be made the focus rather than the grade.

Grading in some form is necessary, since grading is reporting—reporting first to the child and later to the school system and the parents. However, whenever possible, such reporting should be done by a statement or series of statements rather than by the traditional letter grade.

A FINAL WORD

Teaching children to express themselves effectively by writing is one of the most complex tasks of the elementary-school teacher. Ideas, organization, knowledge of forms, sentence structure, vocabulary, usage, and spelling—all these and more are inextricably bound up with written expression. When we speak, gestures, facial expressions, personal appearance, and intonation can supplement the actual words; further explanation or argument can even be added if the thought is not understood or accepted. On the other hand, written expression must often stand alone. This does not mean that the teaching of oral expression should be minimized in language arts programs, but a letter of application, a friendly note, the minutes of a meeting are often matters on which one is judged. It is important, then, that children know how to write in these and other special forms and have the skills to do so effectively. The ability to write effectively is also an aid in thinking and a means for self-expression, both important aspects of life.

References

Benjamin, Carol Lea. *Writing for Kids.* Harper & Row, 1985.

Diamond, I. M., ed. *A Guide to Helping the Reluctant Writer.* University of Wisconsin, 1980.

Evans, Christine Sobray. "Writing to Learn in Math." *Language Arts* 61 (December 1984), pp. 828–835.

Hall, Nigel, and Duffy, Rose. "Every Child Has a Story to Tell." *Language Arts* 64 (September 1987), pp. 523–529.

Hillocks, George, Jr. "Synthesis of Research on Teaching Writing." *Educational Leadership* 44 (May 1987), pp. 71–82.

Hollingsworth, Helen, and Eastman, Susan. *Teaching Writing in Every Class*: *A Guide for Grades 6–12.* Allyn and Bacon, 1988.

Kintisch, Lenore S. "Journal Writing: Stages of Development." *The Reading Teacher* (November 1986), pp. 168–173.

Mayher, John S.; Lester, Nancy; and Pradl, Gordon M. *Learning to Write/Writing to Learn.* Boynton/Cook, 1983.

New York State Education Department. *Composition in the English Language Arts Curriculum.* New York State Education Department, 1986.

Petty, Walter T., and Finn, Patrick, eds. *The Writing Process of Students.* Department of Learning and Instruction, State University of New York at Buffalo, 1975.

Phillips, Kathleen C., and Steiner, Barbara. *Creative Writing, A Handbook for Teaching Young People.* Libraries Unlimited, 1985.

Sealy, Leonard; Sealy, Nancy; and Millmore, Marcia. *Children's Writing.* International Reading Association, 1979.

Smith, Carl B., and Dahl, Karin L. *Teaching Reading and Writing Together.* Teachers College Press, 1984.

Taberski, Sharon. "From Fake to Fiction: Young Children Learn About Writing Fiction." *Language Arts* 64 (October 1987), pp. 586–596.

Tiedt, Iris M. *Teaching Writing in K–8 Classrooms: The Time Has Come.* Prentice-Hall, 1983.

Teaching Resources

COMPUTER SOFTWARE

Build a Book. Mindscope.

Explore-a-Story. D.C. Heath

Kidwriter. Spinnaker Software, 1984 (diskette and guide; grades 1–5).

Letter Writer. InterLearn (diskette; grades 3–8).

Magic Slate. Sunburst Communications.

Story Book Starters. Mindscope.

Story Builder. Random House (tape, diskette, and guide; grades 3–6).

Story Maker. Scholastic (four diskettes and guide; grades 2–6).

Story Starter. Random House (tape and diskette; grades 2–4).

That's My Story. Learning Well, 1983 (two diskettes and guide; grades 3–8).

The Writing Adventure. DLM Educational Software (grade 4 and up).

Writing Skills. Milliken.

Writing to Read. IBM, 1984 (diskette; K–grade 3).

VIDEOTAPES

Think 'N Write. Society for Visual Education.

Write a Letter. Barr Films (grades 1–6; also available as a film).

Writing in the Content Areas. National Council of Teachers of English.

OTHER RESOURCES

Hall, Mary Bowen, and Mansfield, Sue. *Why Are There Wars?* Scott, Foresman, 1986.

James, Elizabeth, and Barkin, Carol. *How to Write a Great School Report.* Lothrop, Lee and Shepard, 1983.

Report Writing Skills. Random House (eight audio cassettes, worksheets, and guide; grade 4 and up).

Urdang, Lawrence, and La Roche, Nancy. *Picturesque Expressions*: *A Thematic Dictionary.* Gale, 1983.

The Write Source. Knowledge Unlimited (handbook).

Writer's Workshop. Scholastic (kit).

Writing Is Reading. National Council of Teachers of English, 1985 (booklet).

The Young Writer's Handbook. Scribner's (handbook).

Activities for Preservice Teachers

1. Keep a diary for two or three weeks. What do you find yourself writing about? Is it easy to write every day? Do you think daily writing may be beneficial?

2. Write a letter you "owe" to a relative or friend. Do you include anything you would not say in a telephone conversation? Do you express something differently than you might in speaking?

3. Plan writing activities for a fifth-grade class working on a unit in social studies or science. See how long and varied a list you can compile; ask others for their ideas. Consider also how similar subject area activities might be planned for.

4. Collect some magazine pictures and other materials that would be especially useful in teaching writing. Plan activities related to them, for example, generating word lists, formulating questions, creating original phrases, writing dialogue, and writing descriptions.

5. If you feel sufficiently confident of your writing skills and your college has a center where students may go for help with their writing assignments, volunteer to be a tutor. See what the directors of the center suggest to students to help them improve their writing. How does whatever is recommended compare with the content of this chapter and the preceding one?

6. For a specific grade level, plan an activity to encourage highly imaginative writing. For instance, have children write a TV commercial, conversations in "balloons" over the heads of cartoon characters, or a newspaper advertisement for a new kind of toy.

7. Write about a personal problem or an important decision you have to make. Does such writing help? Do you experience any sense of discovery?

8. Prepare several paragraphs to use in teaching organization, incorporating the suggestions in this chapter or devising ideas of your own.

9. Investigate the free materials that can be secured by writing letters. Give special attention to those that could be written for by the children.

Activities for Inservice Teachers

1. Identify two or three pupils in your class who write very little. Begin to confer with them frequently concerning what they might write about and how they might go about it. After several conferences, make an assessment as to the improvement shown in the children's writing.

2. Conduct an interest survey in your class—or, better yet, have the children do it. Find out what sports, hobbies, reading materials, TV programs, music, and board games the children are interested in. Could any of these be used as departure points for writing?

3. Collect samples of children's writing at one grade level. Apply ratings to these (use the New York State scale mentioned in the marginal note on page 285 if it can be obtained; if not, get one from another source or make one up). See if other teachers agree with your assessments.

4. Collect sports articles from newspapers and magazines, and have pupils look through them for colorful language and such specific items as metaphors or similes ("The Lions were toothless tabby cats last night" or "Rogers covered Smith like a steel sleeping bag").

5. Parents often state that they have no idea what their children do in school. Plan a biweekly newsletter for reporting class activities to parents. Precede this activity by a study of newspapers and a visit to a local paper.

6. Survey your classroom as objectively as possible to determine the degree of creativity fostered by the environment. Are children's ideas evident or have they been suppressed? Is the classroom yours or does it "belong" to the entire group?

7. Investigate the possibility of establishing a "post office" in your classroom or in the entire school. Children can write letters to one another and to you (and to siblings and friends in other rooms if the whole building is involved). Letters can be picked up each day, sorted, and delivered. The importance of clear handwriting and correct spelling can be stressed.

8. With other teachers in your school, plan for publishing a schoolwide writing anthology. Decide what kinds of writing will be published—poetry, stories (consider limiting the length), jokes, riddles, and so on. Also decide on due dates, the form in which the writing should be submitted, who will decide which writing is accepted (children should be involved in this), and so on.

Independent Activities for Children

1. Children may collect letters from a variety of businesses and offices (including the school office). They can make displays of these, noting the various ways in which parts are arranged, the efforts to make the letters attractive, and the variety in content.

2. Contact a local nursing home or convalescent center and ask for names of people who might enjoy corresponding with children. Children can write letters telling about class activities, what they are interested in, plans for the future, and so forth. Possibly poetry or stories could also be sent from time to time.

3. If a child seems interested in an important public issue, encourage him or her to write a letter to the editor of the local newspaper. This should be well planned and done carefully. You may want to include a note to the editor, explaining the circumstances.

4. Ask businesses for out-of-date forms of any kind; many children will be interested in attempting to complete them. This is good practice in using legible manuscript writing.

5. For the child who can't think of a story to write or who doesn't believe his or her experiences are worth relating (or doesn't know how to relate them), keeping records about a window garden may be the answer. Have the child bring the soil and container (paper cup, egg carton, etc.), and you furnish the seeds.

6. Prepare collections of materials to spark children's writing. The collections (usually a box is needed for each) might include the following:

> Comic cartoons from newspapers
> Photographs of interesting places and events
> Cloth and other objects of different textures
> Newspaper stories
> Pictures from magazines

7. Children can write letters to their favorite TV personalities (and usually get some kind of response).

(Name of Star)
ABC-TV Public Relations
1330 Avenue of the Americas
New York, NY 10019

(Name of Star)
NBC-TV Information Services
30 Rockefeller Plaza
New York, NY 10020

(Name of Star)
CBS-TV Entertainment
51 W. 52nd Street
New York, NY 10019

8. Cut up workbooks to obtain pictures that tell a story in sequence. Fasten each group together with a paperclip or rubber band, and keep them in a shoe box covered with gift wrap or contact paper. A child selects a group, places the pictures in sequence, and then writes a sentence about each, thereby making a paragraph.

9. Children can write poems according to particular restrictions. For example, the first letter of each line spells a word:

> Fair skies, but
> Across the
> Lake comes a
> Long blast of cold air.

Or, there are only two words per line:

> **CLIMBING**
>
> Up faster;
> Out farther;
> And farther;
> Down quickly.

10. When children need to learn about the use of hyphens to divide words at the ends of lines, turn to the newspaper. Because newspaper columns are short, they contain many hyphenated words. Have the children look for these, cut out the columns, and circle the hyphens with red crayon. Put the articles on a chart or bulletin board. Using the display, help the children formulate generalizations about the use of hyphens to divide words.

11. A child or several children working together might do any of the following:

> Make lists of colorful phrases
> List adjectives describing objects in the classroom
> Find good beginning sentences for stories
> Collect objects that provide sensory feelings

12. Have children collect particularly good similes, metaphors, and images. They might then work in groups to compile booklets of those they like best.

13. Two children can play a game with cards bearing various types of punctuation—periods, quotation marks, exclamation marks, and so forth. One child draws a card; he or she must compose a sentence that uses the mark on the card, giving the proper inflection. The other child guesses which mark was on the card. Individual children can play this game by drawing

cards and then writing sentences using the marks correctly.

14. Two children can work together: one writes a question, using the correct capitalization, spelling, and punctuation, and the other writes a statement in reply to the question. The children can check each other. (This is also excellent practice in spelling, changing person and forms of verbs, etc.)

15. Suggest that children exchange stories or other writing with children in other schools. These may be children whose names were obtained from one of the sources for pen pals, or they may be children in a nearby school. Each child should write to another child, inviting him or her to exchange writing and reactions to that writing.

Chapter 11

Learning to Spell

*T*he ability to spell words correctly is often viewed as being less significant than other language skills. Indeed, some otherwise well-educated people make no secret of their inadequacies in this area and do not appear to be concerned about them. The oral spelling of isolated words is not a common activity, being restricted mostly to spelling contests, television quiz programs, and responses to children's requests by teachers and parents. But spelling is important as a component of writing, and knowledge of how words are spelled and why contributes to a fuller understanding of our language. Spelling is a subject worthy of study in the elementary school.

GOALS OF SPELLING INSTRUCTION

A 1972 study by Thomas showed that 1,000 words account for 83 percent of all words used in children's writing; 2,000 words account for 89 percent.

The basic goal of spelling instruction is to teach children to spell the words they use in their writing. This means the writing they do in school *and* the writing they will do after their school years. Of course, it is impossible to determine all of the words any person may need to spell in a lifetime, but everyone should learn to spell the words that are most frequently written. It is also important to encourage children's increasing awareness of the structure of their language and how aspects of this structure relate to spelling specific words. Finally, a positive attitude toward spelling correctly and habits that support this attitude need to be developed.

Another study found these words account for over 36 percent of all words written:

the	of	on
I	is	they
and	was	that
to	have	had
a	my	she
you	are	very
we	he	will
in	for	when
it		

Since spelling requires putting into written form words that are familiar from speaking, reading, and listening, two important abilities are needed. One of these is the ability to recall how words look—the words that the child has studied and those that have frequently appeared in materials he or she has read. The other basic ability is that of associating letters and patterns of letters with specific sounds. These two abilities become closely allied in the spelling efforts of most children, and both are influenced by the children's understanding of the language.

Of course, a child should possess many spelling-related abilities treated in other chapters of this book. For example, good handwriting will reduce the likelihood of confusion about how a word has been spelled. The child should also know how to alphabetize words and how to use this knowledge to find the spelling of words in dictionaries and glossaries. He or she should be able to pronounce words clearly and accurately and to use the diacritical markings and key words in a dictionary, as well as phonetic and structural aids, to help with pronunciations.

A person who spells well shows a concern for doing so by proofreading his or her own writing, by looking up the spellings of unknown words, and

See Chapter 13 for a discussion of dictionary skills and activities.

by establishing a specific study procedure for learning to spell new words. Thus, teaching the child habits of proofreading, studying, and using the dictionary properly is very important.

These basic objectives should be kept in mind as you read the remainder of this chapter, as you plan your program, and as you select and use materials in the program.

THE SPELLING PROGRAM

It has been reported that children who start with "invented spelling" in kindergarten or first grade are making normal progress with "standard" spelling by the third grade.

For many children—in fact, most—learning to spell begins with their first writing efforts, even though this writing may be described by most people as "scribbling." This first learning arises from the children's seeing letters and words as they are read to and as they handle books. These experiences lead to "invented spelling" (see Chapter 4) and later to learning to spell from reading and writing. This continues for most people throughout the school years and into adulthood, but the rate and amount of such learning varies greatly from individual to individual. Unfortunately, the spelling skills mentioned above are not achieved by most children if the program consists only of informal learning—important as it is, and as much as it needs to be encouraged. Each teacher should have a specific spelling instructional program. When this instruction should begin *should* vary from child to child, but, given the constrictions of school programs (generally a spelling workbook for each grade level), it often is not. Spelling ability varies greatly among children at any age. A good teacher, though, recognizes the developmental nature of spelling ability (and of other abilities) and seeks ways to provide appropriate experiences and instruction. In this chapter ways to provide effective instruction for all children are suggested.

Learning to spell is a series of:

> *impression*
> ↓
> *recall*
> ↓
> *impression*
> ↓
> *recall*

As has been pointed out, the ability to spell is largely contingent on the effectiveness of two processes: impression and recall. Impression comes from *recognizing* letters, noting their sequence, and associating with them sounds and knowledge of word structures, individually or in patterns. Recall requires *remembering* the sequence of letters and/or remembering associations that aid in achieving the correct sequence. Essentially, then, these processes are what children engage in as they invent spellings and seek to improve their inventions. A specific spelling program gives them practice, and the practice concentrates on words that research has shown are written with great frequency.

Are you a good speller?

Do you believe that correct spelling is important?

Do you proofread for spelling errors?

Do you know several ways to find out the correct spelling of a word?

Do you know a good way to learn to spell a new word?

Fostering Positive Attitudes

A truly good speller is one who endeavors to spell all words correctly. A good speller possesses an attitude of concern and knows how to learn to spell a new word, how to get help in spelling unknown words, and how to make the best use of the knowledge of words that he or she has. Good attitudes toward spelling may be encouraged through continuous attention to correct spelling in your own writing. Show the children that correct spelling really matters by proofreading your own writing and by using a dictionary when necessary.

Showing the children that the words they are required to learn to spell are ones they consistently use in their writing and have need to spell is also useful. A simple tabulation of the words they write or of the words written by their parents and friends will show this—and will produce a list very similar to the one on pages 295 and 296.

Requiring the children to learn only those words that spelling tests and actual writing situations have shown they are unable to spell makes sense to the children and prevents the development of the negative attitudes that often result from studying words that are already known. It is also important to make certain each child knows and uses a specific and efficient method of learning to spell new words.

Some adults have a poor attitude about spelling—they "don't care" or say they "never could spell." Children can develop such an attitude.

Encouraging in the class a spirit of mutual pride and cooperation in spelling achievement builds good attitudes. Children enjoy helping one another study, giving proofreading help, and providing encouragement to one another. Also emphasize individual and class progress in spelling, making each pupil aware of the progress he or she has made. Records of progress should be kept by the pupils themselves, although you may want to keep supplemental ones.

Encouraging high standards of neatness and accuracy for final drafts of writing is very helpful. Standards can be developed for the children to apply, and these should be referred to as often as is necessary to be sure that they are maintained. It also helps to use the time set aside for spelling instruction efficiently—avoid dragging tests out too long or developing procedures that encourage dawdling and other poor habits. Negative attitudes toward spelling should be dealt with immediately, although fault-finding should be avoided in favor of determining the causes of spelling failures and encouraging and stimulating the efforts children make.

Developing Desirable Habits

Even though a favorable attitude toward spelling is basic to a successful program, the mere desire to do well will accomplish little unless appropriate habits are established in the class. The following are particularly important:

Correct spelling is a concern of parents. Make sure that they understand your program—especially if you encourage "invented spellings" in first drafts of written work.

- *Being concerned about the spelling of words used in written expression.* First-draft writing does not require perfect spelling, but when a piece is to be read by someone else, the writer should realize that misspelled words will interfere with communication. The habit of being concerned about correct spelling is established by the development and maintenance of standards and by the concern you show about correct spelling in writing products.

Be alert to children's establishing incorrect spellings as a habit.

- *Proofreading systematically.* Writers must accept responsibility for examining their drafts carefully, word by word and letter by letter. Anyone can spell a word incorrectly through carelessness or temporary confusion, and imperfect skills in handwriting or typing may also be the cause of difficulty in some situations. In proofreading for spelling errors, each word must be looked at letter by letter.

- *Checking the spelling of all words about which there is any doubt.* Writers should be conscientious about checking words if there is any question in their minds about them. Children ought to know how to use a variety of sources—human and print—and should be willing to continue the search until verification is made.
- *Using a specific procedure for learning the spelling of new words.* Although the specifics of study procedure will vary somewhat from child to child, there are steps in studying that are important, and each child should understand these and use what works best for her or him.
- *Working efficiently during the spelling period.* Following a specific study procedure is an important aspect of working efficiently during the spelling period, but listening attentively to the pronunciation of words during testing times and completing spelling exercises with attention to correctness and detail are also necessary to establishing this habit.

Teaching Specific Words

A great deal of evidence has been accumulated about the words people write most often. Many commercial spelling materials provide for the teaching of these words, although some materials tend to emphasize the teaching of words that illustrate "spelling patterns" (for example: *cap, cat, catch, pack, cab, cad, badge, bag, jam, pan*) even though some of these words are not likely to be written—at least not frequently—after the completion of the lesson.

The commercial spelling books that seek to teach a core of important words usually present 3,000 to 4,000 for children in first through eighth grades to learn. Materials emphasizing spelling patterns may include a greater number of words (including many of the "most commonly written" ones) in order to illustrate the patterns and to show exceptions to them.

The following words are of particular importance. Elementary-school children should be able to spell these words without hesitation by the time they reach the fifth grade (or sooner).

a	as	big	cat	didn't
about	asked	black	children	do
after	at	book	close	does
again	away	boy	coat	dog
ago		boys	cold	doing
all	baby	bring	come	doll
along	back	brother	coming	don't
also	bad	but	could	door
always	ball	buy	country	down
am	be	by	cut	
an	because			
and	bed	call	daddy	each
another	been	called	day	eat
any	before	came	days	end
are	best	can	dear	even
around	better	car	did	every

fall	hold	much	sat	too
far	home	must	saw	took
fast	hope	my	say	top
fat	hot		school	town
father	house	name	see	tree
feet	how	never	seen	two
few		new	send	
find	I	next	she	until
fire	if	nice	should	up
first	I'm	night	show	use
five	in	no	side	
for	into	not	sister	very
found	is	now	sleep	
four	it		snow	walk
friend	its	of	so	want
from		off	some	wanted
fun	just	old	something	was
		on	soon	water
game	know	once	started	way
gave		one	stay	we
get	land	only	stop	week
getting	large	open	such	well
girl	last	or	summer	went
girls	let	order	sun	were
give	letter	other	sure	what
glad	like	our		when
go	line	out	take	where
going	little	over	teacher	which
good	live		tell	while
got	long	part	than	white
grade	look	people	that	who
great	looked	place	the	will
grow	lost	play	their	wish
	lot	played	them	with
had	lots	please	then	work
hand	love	pretty	there	would
happy		put	these	write
hard	made		they	
has	make	rain	thing	year
hat	man	ran	things	years
have	many	read	think	yes
he	may	red	this	yet
hear	me	rest	thought	you
heard	men	ride	three	your
help	milk	right	through	yours
her	more	room	time	
here	morning	run	to	
him	most		today	
his	mother	said	told	
		same		

A Spelling Program Plan

The spelling program in a classroom is often determined by the textbook
or other materials available. Most commercial spelling textbooks make use

Many schools use a commercial spelling series in their program. The weekly lesson described here should be the basis for using any commercial program.

of one of two basic plans. These are usually called the *test-study* and *study-test plans.* Evidence favors the test-study plan as the most efficient and satisfactory approach because it focuses on individual differences among pupils and fosters positive attitudes by requiring pupils to study only those words they do not know how to spell. The test-study plan consists of these features:

1. A test is given at the beginning of the term or month to determine the general level of spelling achievement of the class and of individuals in the class. It can be constructed by randomly selecting words from the lessons to be covered during the term or month. Select as many words as the pupils can attempt without becoming overtired or losing interest (usually twenty to twenty-five words are enough).

2. Pupils may be grouped for instruction on the basis of the preliminary test, or individualized teaching may be planned. For example, high achievers may be released from spelling instruction for other activities and low achievers may be assigned special materials, given fewer words, or provided with planned, individualized study help.

3. The weekly assignment begins with a test. This permits you and each child to determine the specific words that require study. You may want to precede this test (perhaps only occasionally) by pronouncing the words and having the pupils pronounce them. If you think there are words whose meanings are not known, these may be discussed. However, this is usually not necessary if the words have been selected properly.

4. The words that each pupil misspells on the pretest are identified by the child and become his or her study list for the weekly spelling lesson (see the following section).

5. In studying each word, the children use the steps that have been worked out by the class, or by you and individual children if modifications in the class steps seem to be necessary.

6. A final weekly or lesson test is used to determine the degree of mastery each child has achieved (a midweek test is also usually advisable, since attempting to spell—trying to recall—for a test is a good learning procedure).

7. Each child keeps a personal record of spelling achievement on a chart or similar device.

8. To prepare for reviewing, each child records in a notebook all words misspelled on the final test. Review words are studied using the steps followed in studying new words.

9. Each child is tested on the words in his or her review list at regular intervals until these words have truly been mastered.

10. A final term or monthly test is given to measure the progress made since the administration of the first test. This test may be a sampling of the words or it may include all of the words taught during the period of time (perhaps in more than one sitting).

A good instructional plan in spelling also provides for allowing children to correct their own tests and for giving most tests in list form. Having pupils correct their own tests makes the testing a learning experience, for pupils see exactly what mistakes they have made. Having the test corrected by another pupil or by you practically eliminates the possibility of any learning occurring from the procedure.

Some variation in testing is useful. For example, you may dictate sentences, each containing a spelling word, or perhaps a paragraph containing several or all of the words in a lesson. However, the difficulty with this form of testing is that other words used may not be known by the children. Thus, the list test should be used most often because it saves time and focuses on the objective of learning to spell the words in the lesson.

The Weekly Lesson

The spelling of a word used often in writing should be taught whenever the opportunity to do so occurs. However, as suggested, it is necessary to have a developmental program. The following are the principal features of a five-day lesson plan. The weekly lesson may be done in three days by including the second day's activities with those given for the first day and the fourth day's activities with those for the third day. Also, some children may not need all of the visual and auditory impression activities; and, as suggested in the preceding section, especially good spellers may need little or none of the weekly program.

First Day. Administration of a pretest of the words in the lesson (pronouncing the word, using it in a sentence, and pronouncing again); checking the test (each pupil checking his or her own); making individual study lists of words misspelled; discussing the words as necessary—their meanings and use, any unusual spellings, the application of any rules, or etymological matters that are appropriate and of interest.

Second Day. Visual and auditory study of structural and phonemic elements in the words; direct study of the words on individual spelling lists.

Third Day. Administration of a test (usually including all words in the lesson as a means of ensuring that guessing did not account for some correct spelling on the pretest); checking the test again with each pupil checking his or her own; studying the words misspelled.

Fourth Day. Continued practice in visual and aural analysis of the words; learning new meanings for the words; extending word knowledge through practice in using linguistic principles; studying words misspelled on the third-day test.

Fifth Day. Administration of the final test; checking the tests, with each pupil again checking his or her own; writing words in a review list; marking achievement on a progress chart.

In addition, time may be given as it is available to practice in using the dictionary, to use of vocabulary building exercises, and to participation in games and enrichment activities. Some study of language, particularly of word origins, is also appropriate for inclusion in the lesson as time permits.

Research shows that no more than 75 minutes per week should be devoted to direct spelling instruction.

Children learn to spell many words from their reading; therefore, they may know how to spell many of the lesson words.

Words misspelled on the final lesson test should become words to study in future lessons.

Grouping for Instruction

The weekly lesson plan calls for much of the learning and teaching effort to be individualized; for example, each pupil makes his or her own study list, each pupil individually studies the words he or she misspells, each pupil writes his or her own review words, and each pupil marks his or her own progress chart. However, the plan does not indicate how to go about grouping for instruction.

Actually, grouping is not difficult. It may be done in a manner similar to that used for reading or mathematics instruction. The first step should be administering a quarterly, semester, or yearly pretest of twenty-five to seventy-five words (depending on the ability of the pupils to handle the mechanics of writing). The words on this test should be randomly selected from the words for the particular quarter, semester, or year. Children who misspell none or very few of these may be considered high achievers; those who misspell 10 to 50 percent should be considered the average group; and those who misspell more than half of the words should be considered the slow group. Some teachers make the average group larger than suggested and limit the slow group to only a few pupils.

The high and average groups should be given all of the words in a lesson. Some enrichment words may be added to the list for the high group if such words are carefully selected because they are needed in writing.

Pupils' Study Procedures

There is general agreement among spelling authorities that the spelling of a word is learned by a series of steps involving impression and recall. The impression, or image, steps generally include visual, auditory, and kinesthetic impressions. The recall steps usually involve "seeing" the word in the mind and then writing from memory. Children who are very good in spelling can often learn a new word after seeing it only once; for them, the other steps may not be necessary. The poorer spellers need help and encouragement in learning the steps and putting them into practice. They may also need to have the steps individualized by the addition of extra ones to help them say the words properly or to gain better visual, auditory, or kinesthetic impressions.

The following method of study is suggested as suitable for most children. You may wish to modify it in some manner for your class, but keep in mind that alternating impression and recall procedures are needed.

1. Look at the word carefully and pronounce it correctly. Say it slowly, naturally, and clearly, looking at it as you say it.
2. Cover the word with your hand or close your eyes. Say the word and think how it looks. Try to visualize exactly the way the word is written as you say each letter in sequence to yourself.
3. Look at the word again to be sure that you said it and spelled it correctly. If you did not, start again at step 1.
4. Cover the word and then write it, thinking carefully about how it looks.

5. Check your spelling. If you misspelled the word, begin again at step 1. If you spelled the word correctly, go on to the next word.

Electronic Aids

Audiovisual equipment and computers offer many possibilities for spelling practice. Word lists may be put on audio cassettes, and children can listen to pronunciations and test themselves by writing the words they hear. This is particularly effective for an individualized program since several lists at different levels of difficulty can be produced by the teacher and used repeatedly by the students. Students should keep track of their progress and the words they need to study; this will promote acceptance of responsibility for their own learning.

Overhead projectors are sometimes helpful in the gamelike activities described later in this chapter. Writing on the platform of a projector more closely approximates the usual spelling environment than does writing on a chalkboard. Some projectors have the very useful capacity of projecting on a screen what is typed on a typewriter or computer keyboard.

As mentioned in earlier chapters, typing and word processing are likely to have a positive effect on students' spelling—interest is heightened, what is produced looks like real print and so is more easily recognized, and

A word processor may motivate children to practice spelling.

changing the spelling of a word may be relatively simple on an electric typewriter or word processor. At a basic level, a computer can flash a word on its screen and then remove it, giving the student a few seconds to type the correct spelling before signaling "right" or "wrong." Other spelling experiences are offered through a variety of software programs. Knowledgeable teachers are able to program the computer to test children and then direct them to particular spelling lists and activities. The computer can also keep a record of each child's success rate, achievement level, and problem words.

Practices to Avoid

Several of the techniques sometimes employed for teaching spelling are inappropriate. Often these are used because the teacher is confronted with a difficult program or simply does not know that they are of no value or even potentially harmful. For instance, calling attention to possible "hard spots" in words might implant spelling difficulties that could be avoided through a positive approach to learning. The practice of "writing" words in the air is also used, presumably to give children a kinesthetic-tactile impression. This is not a valid technique, since gaining a true "feel" for a word requires that the shape of letters be felt (in sand or on a writing surface) and that the muscle movements approximate those used when the word is actually written.

Some teachers have children write problem words ten or even more times without intervening attempts at recall. Simply copying a word is not likely to create a permanent impression. Such a practice is related to the even more objectionable one of assigning the studying or writing of spelling words as a punishment for misbehavior. Neither technique does anything to promote a positive attitude toward spelling.

It should be emphasized that spelling is a writing activity. We may admire people who win "spelling bees" by orally producing strings of letters, but this skill is not one needed in school or in later life.

Some words used in the finals of a national spelling contest:

heirolatry
micaceous
propylaeum
taknonymy

OTHER TEACHING CONSIDERATIONS

Other matters related to spelling instruction are discussed in this section. There are differences of opinion concerning some of these, and these differences are frequently reflected in the content of commercial spelling materials. Even with the less controversial matters there is disagreement regarding the amount of instructional attention each should receive.

Language Structure and Spelling

There is a long history of attempts to relate in some way the twenty-six letters of the English alphabet and the approximately forty (depending on the dialect) sounds, or phonemes, the letters must represent, so that learning to spell can be simplified. Various rules for representing or spelling some sounds have been promulgated in commercial spelling books for many years. Most research regarding this effort has focused on discovering how the various phonemes are represented. For example, Ernest Horn reported about thirty years ago that an examination of 10,000 words showed that "the *k* sound is spelled with *c* 64.36 percent and the *s* sound with *s* 71.19 percent of the time." A few years later researchers at Stanford University reported on a study of 17,000 words in which they took into account phoneme position in syllables and the stress given a syllable, as well as letter representations of the phonemes. Some of their findings regarding representations were similar to Horn's, and others were different, but these researchers used the word "regular" to identify the most common letter representation of each phoneme and suggested the teaching of generalizations concerning them. This study influenced the content of many commercial spelling materials and school programs despite the fact that these researchers had also shown that programming a computer with an algorithm of several hundred complex rules resulted in only 50 percent of the words being spelled correctly.

Other researchers have extended the Stanford study by pointing out that the representation of a sound may be influenced by the sounds adjacent to it, concluding that the percentage of "regularity" would be higher if this were done. For example, one points out "that the final /j/ sound of *fudge* is spelled *dge* because it follows a short vowel sound but is spelled *ge* in words such as *huge* and *large* because they contain other kinds of vowel sounds" (from Hodges, p. 6; see References).

The importance of this information to a spelling program, valid as it is, seems debatable. Will a child seeking to spell *pajamas* be helped by knowing this? The /j/ sound does follow a short vowel, as it does in *pageant* and *digit*. And the child may need to spell *gem, jug, general, joy, agent, tragedy, urge, major reject,* or *hinge,* for example.

Children do need to learn likely representations of sounds in order to avoid completely irrational spelling attempts. And it is true that some sounds are represented by a single letter or a cluster of letters with considerable frequency (the /b/ sound, for example), but others, particularly vowels, are variously represented in many commonly used words. Further, if the dialect variations in speech are taken into account, the "regularity" of representations decreases. So it seems that efforts to teach generalizations about "regular" sound representations are likely to be unprofitable, if for no other reason than that, as stated in the report of one study (see entry for Johnson, Langford, and Quorn in References), "A comparison of words that children have difficulty spelling with words that can be constructed from common spelling patterns will show very little overlap. Words that confuse children include *said, friend, their, too, beautiful, people, holiday, finally, scared, experience,* and *silver.* These words cannot be constructed from common spelling patterns and yet they are words that children commonly use in writing and which they frequently misspell." Certainly time used in attempting to teach generalizations about sound/symbol correspondences and word patterns could be better spent.

Researchers are currently giving less attention to phoneme/grapheme correspondences and more attention to verification of theories concerning

Attention to "correct" pronunciation must take into account dialect differences that occur in pronunciations—for example, some people give the vowels in naughty *and* knotty *the same sound.*

the nature of English orthography. They are discovering that the nature of this orthography closely parallels what mature, efficient spellers know about the language system and its graphic representation. The thrust of researchers' advice regarding spelling programs is that children should be provided with many opportunities to explore the ways in which their knowledge of spoken language relates to spelling. Many of them also admit that learning to spell is complex enough to warrant regular spelling programs.

Many teachers and researchers have long recognized that the issue, variously identified over the years as "phonics and spelling, " "linguistics and spelling," or "pattern spelling," is really one of *teaching versus learning*. The average mature speller has *learned* the most likely representations of individual sounds and patterns of sounds and exceptions to them. The mature speller has also learned that in deciding how to spell a word consideration must be given to the placement of its sounds in syllables and to their sequence, to the stress given to these syllables, and to the relationship of the word to other words in terms of meaning and structure. How this learning has occurred, though, is less well-known. Many recognize that mature, efficient spellers have done much writing and reading. However, the role in this learning of what some writers like to label "traditional" spelling programs cannot be discounted.

Spelling Rules and Generalizations

Use rules cautiously. Will rules help you spell these?

birch	curse	beard
church	hearse	weird
perch	terse	feared
search	worse	leered

Despite the evidence cited in the preceding section, the spelling program should give attention to generalizations that are helpful to spelling. A helpful generalization should not be taught in such a way that children simply learn to verbalize it but then show no ability to apply it in spelling as they write. Rather, generalizations should be presented during lessons on words to which they apply or at times when children encounter a spelling problem that a generalization will help to eliminate. No more than one generalization should be dealt with at a time, exceptions to it should be noted, and opportunities for reviewing it and other generalizations should be provided. Any instruction should also take into account dialect differences; the fact that pronunciations given to some words vary with the context of speech, the situation, and their grammatical use; and the fact that generalizations which may be useful in reading may not be useful in spelling. An example of the latter is a commonly used reading generalization: "When there are two vowels, one of which is final *e,* the first vowel is usually long and the *e* is silent" (*bake, tone, fine*). This is helpful to a reader seeking to pronounce the word and thus determine what it is, but the reader is *looking* at the word. A child hearing or thinking of such a word gains no clue from this generalization about how to spell it.

Particularly important generalizations that have few exceptions are the following:

1. Words ending in a silent *e* usually drop this *e* before a suffix beginning with a vowel (*make-making*) but keep the *e* before a suffix beginning with a consonant (*time-timely*).

2. For words ending in a consonant and *y,* change the *y* to *i* before adding a suffix, unless the suffix begins with *i* (*candy-candies, baby-babying*).

3. For words ending in a vowel and *y,* do not change the *y* to *i* when adding a suffix (*play-played, enjoy-enjoying*).

4. For those words of one syllable or accented on the last syllable that end in a single consonant preceded by a single vowel, double the final consonant when adding a suffix beginning with a vowel (*run-running, begin-beginning, need-needed*).

5. The letter *q* is always followed by *u* in common English words (*quite, quart*).

6. English words do not end with *v* (*believe, give*).

7. Proper nouns and most adjectives formed with proper nouns begin with capital letters (*France, French*).

Rules concerning the use of the apostrophe are also useful, since improper use of the apostrophe is the cause of many spelling errors. The following are helpful:

It is also correct to simply add an apostrophe to singular nouns ending in s (for example, Ms. Jones' house). However, it is simpler for children to learn one rule than two.

1. The possessive of a singular noun (including those ending in *s, z, ss,* or *x*) is formed by adding an apostrophe and *s.*

John's idea	Congress's action
father's hat	box's top
Ms. Jones's house	Buzz's pitch

2. The possessive of a plural noun ending in *s* is formed by adding an apostrophe.

girls' coats	Matthewses' relatives
Smiths' house	states' rights

3. The possessive of a plural noun not ending in *s* is formed by adding an apostrophe and *s.*

women's hats	data's use
teeth's whiteness	children's books

4. Personal pronouns do not take the apostrophe to show possession.

his	theirs
hers	whose
its	

5. Pronouns that are not ordinarily possessive show possession by adding an apostrophe and *s.*

someone's coat	each other's dog
everyone's house	another's name

6. An apostrophe is used to indicate missing letters in contractions, letters omitted to show speech, and numbers left off the beginning of the year.

don't (do not)	we'll (we will)
it's (it is)	you're (you are)
'ere's to you	your 'ome
the winter of '92	the class of '72

There are some rules regarding the formation of plural forms that are also useful:

1. Plurals of most nouns are formed by adding *s* to the singular.

   boy–boys   book–books

2. When a noun ends in *s, x, sh,* or *ch,* the plural is generally formed by adding *es.*

   buses   foxes   bushes   churches

3. A noun ending in *y* preceded by a consonant forms its plural by changing the *y* to *i* and adding *es.* Words ending in *y* preceded by a vowel do not change *y* to *i.*

   body–bodies   boy–boys

4. Plurals of a few nouns are made by changing their forms.

   woman–women   mouse–mice   scarf–scarves

Relationships Between Spelling and Writing

Earlier chapters indicated that spelling is an important part of the writing process but by no means the most important part. In doing initial writing, the chief concern is to get ideas on paper; during revision and editing, attention is given to sentence structure, word choice, punctuation, and spelling in order to produce a piece of writing that fulfills the writer's purpose and is meaningful to the reader. If too much emphasis is put on spelling in early drafts, children are often inhibited from using expressive language since the words they think of may be difficult for them to spell. This may result in writing products that are error-free but they are not likely to be compelling to read.

Properly treated, however, spelling instruction makes a significant con-

Teacher and students discuss the spelling of a word during an editing session.

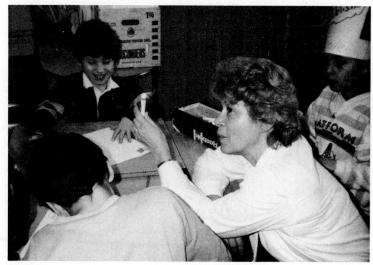

tribution to a child's writing ability. Similarly, writing may make a significant contribution to an individual's ability to spell. When a child refers to word lists, spelling books, and dictionaries for spelling assistance while editing, she or he is learning both how to spell certain words and how to use appropriate sources. Even when another child or the teacher provides a correct spelling, the writer is getting practice in seeing a sequence of letters, writing them, and seeing the word as it should be written. This practice will make a difference the next time the word is used, particularly if a personal list of such words is kept in a notebook.

There are, of course, situations in which writing is done only once by the child and not revised, such as when workbook exercises are done, tests taken, and notes or letters written for personal reasons. These are examples of materials that may be read by others, so accuracy in spelling is needed. Thus, the teaching procedures are crucial, and the resources for help with spelling should be utilized; particularly, the procedures and skills learned for the editing phase of the writing process should be applied. Those children who have serious difficulties in spelling correctly must receive additional attention concerning what to do in editing, their attitudes concerning the importance of spelling correctly, and how they study spelling. However, depending on the purpose of the writing, the writer may be given help with the spelling in order to stress to her or him that writing intended for someone else to read—personal letters, for example—should be free of spelling errors.

Special Spelling Problems

Some words are frequently misspelled (these are the "demons" that most teachers know about) and will require persistent effort from you. There are reasons for their difficulty, however, as discussed below.

Many words are misspelled because the children do not know or do not apply the rules that are workable, do not understand the use of the apostrophe, fail to capitalize properly, or do not have the linguistic knowledge they should have (for example, how compounds are formed). Here are some that are frequently misspelled:

coming	I'll	it's	studying	tried
didn't	I'm	getting	Sunday	truly
don't	its	sometimes	that's	writing

Homonyms also often cause difficulty. For pupils to learn these requires that meanings be thoroughly taught and that visual images be gained. Spelling authorities disagree about whether homonyms should be taught together. For the first instruction it seems better to present them separately. However, since much review of them is necessary, they should be presented together in the review to emphasize the differences:

there	hear	your	know	some
their	here	you're	no	sum
they're				

two	four	write	buy	piece
to	for	right	by	peace
too				

Improper pronunciation is a frequent cause of errors. Such words as *and, going, third, ask, today, Saturday, pretty, hundred, kept, been, library, children,* and *desk* are pronunciation and spelling problems for some children.

Phoneme/grapheme irregularity that results in misspelling because of the misapplication of a generalization is also a problem. Commonly written words that fall into this category include:

ache	believe	enough	thirty
across	birthday	friend	though
afraid	build	guess	thought
again	color	heard	tonight
among	could	one	very
answer	cousin	sure	were
beautiful	decide	the	when
because	does	they	women

The following list of spelling "demons" has been developed from studies of misspellings of elementary-school children. These words are important and should be learned by every pupil.

about	before	doing	good
address	birthday	don't	good-bye (good-by)
afraid	bought	down	grade
afternoon	boy		guess
again	boys	Easter	guest
all right	brother	enough	
along	brought	every	had
already		everybody	Halloween
always	can		handkerchiefs
am	cannot	father	has
an	can't	February	have
and	children	fine	haven't
answer	Christmas	first	having
anything	close	football	he
anyway	clothes	for	hear
April	come	fourth	hello
are	coming	Friday	her
arithmetic	couldn't	friend	here
aunt	cousin	friends	his
awhile		from	home
	daddy	front	hope
baby	day	fun	hospital
balloon	December		house
basketball	didn't	getting	how
because	different	goes	how's
been	dog	going	hundred

I'll	now	snowman	tonight
I'm	nowadays	some	too
in		something	toys
isn't	o'clock	sometime	train
it	October	sometimes	truly
it's	off	soon	two
its	on	stationery	
I've	once	store	until
	one	studying	
January	our	summer	
just	out	Sunday	vacation
	outside	suppose	very
knew		sure	
know	party	surely	want
	people	swimming	was
lessons	play		weather
letter	played	teacher	well
like	plays	teacher's	went
likes	please	Thanksgiving	we're
little	pretty	that's	were
lots		the	when
loving	quit	their	whether
	quite	them	white
made		then	will
make	receive	there	with
maybe	received	there's	won't
me	remember	they	would
Miss	right	they're	write
morning		think	writing
mother	said	thought	
Mr.	Santa Claus	through	you
Mrs.	Saturday	time	young
much	saw	to	your
my	school	today	yours
	send	together	
name	sent	tomorrow	
nice	sincerely		
November	snow		

ENRICHMENT ACTIVITIES

The spelling program can be enlivened through the use of games and other activities directed at learning the words in the spelling lessons and at building vocabulary. Activities and games are useful for motivating pupils, allowing for individual differences, and providing variety in the program.

Vocabulary

Vocabulary and spelling are closely related, so carefully selected word-study materials may make a contribution to your program. The activities in them, of course, should be adapted to the needs of your children rather than carried out exactly as suggested. Other experiences may come directly from classroom work, for example, having children find substitutes for such overworked words as *awful, funny, scared, pretty, good, nice, real,* and *sure;* synonyms for such words as *small, cold, sad, big, work, see, happy, strong,* and *tired;* and homonyms for *blue, do, fair, great, hail, made, pain, rain, read, sew, sight, tail, whose, wait,* and *pause.* These can be found and put on charts by individual pupils or groups, or the project can involve the entire class.

Similarly, antonyms may be collected (try finding them for *rise, new, bottom, full, empty, colder, front, never, short,* etc.); lists can be made of words that have the same root (*report, portable, import, portage,* and *portly,* for example); and words that have more than one acceptable spelling can be found (*judgment* and *judgement; gayly* and *gaily; driest* and *dryest*).

Exercises can be made that ask pupils to build compound words from other words. Words to start with might include *day, news, hall, base, stand, light, band, paper, ball,* and *way.* Or you might have the children form plurals for irregular words such as *wife, foot, mouse, leaf, woman, man,* and *calf.*

Children can become quite interested in words because of their origins, their forms, or changes that have occurred in them. For example, they might be asked to find the origins of such words as *braille, boycott, vandal, cologne, maverick,* and *nicotine.* They might also enjoy tracing the origins of words from other languages (*cipher, kimono, oasis, parka,* and *pretzel*) or compound words (*warehouse, chairman, downtown* and *statehouse*). Listing words builds spelling strength; in particular, you can emphasize that the spellings of the parts of a compound word do not change in the compounding.

There is also value in teaching the meanings and spellings of important roots, prefixes, and suffixes. The teaching may develop the meaning of a root (for example, *port*) and then add as many prefixes and suffixes as possible (*report, import, deport, portage, portable, porter, reporter, export,* etc.). Learning the spellings and meanings of roots and affixes can obviously help in reading, speaking, and writing as well as spelling.

Other interesting activities include seeing how many uses can be found for such common words as *run, head,* or *board;* finding words with different sounds represented by the same letter or letters, or vice versa (*enough* and *though, graph* and *rough, taught* and *taut*); discovering different ways in which the same meaning is expressed in various parts of the world where English is spoken (*lift* for *elevator, petrol* for *gasoline, lorry* for *truck,* and *sweet* for *dessert* in England; *tap* for *faucet* in Canada; etc.); and finding new words that have been added to the language and determining why they were created.

Games and Exercises

As in other curriculum areas, spelling activities that resemble games, puzzles, and quiz shows interest children and build class spirit. It is important, though, that such activities in spelling call for writing the words or seeing them in written form (reinforcement of visual impression) rather than spell-

Dictionary Challenges

How many can you find?
1. Synonyms for smart
2. Meanings for dark
3. Adjectives that describe food

ing them orally (a nonrealistic experience). Writing may be done on the chalkboard, the overhead projector, chart paper, or individual "slates" made by painting hardboard black or green (these, written on with chalk, are also useful in handwriting, mathematics, and other subjects and so are worth making or purchasing).

Races or other forms of competition may add to the frustration of poor spellers, so they should be used with discretion. Many of the activities described here (and at the end of the chapter) are noncompetitive or can be adapted to eliminate the competitive element.

Jumbled Words. Individuals or groups are given a specific selection of plastic letters or letter cards and instructed to make a word. Clues such as "name of an animal" or "something related to music" may be given. All the letters have to be used, and the word must be spelled correctly.

Word Mysteries. The teacher or a student gives a clue: "I'm thinking of a word that rhymes with *blue* and is something you eat." Others write answers. Answers may vary, but words have to be correctly spelled.

Plurals. The singular form is pronounced, and students write the plural (or the reverse). Use common (*mouse*) or uncommon (*sister-in-law*) words, depending on the maturity of the group.

Team Spelling. Each of four children is given a large card on which one of the letters S, T, O, or P is written. The children are told to arrange and rearrange their cards in a line to spell as many words as they can, using all four letters (many variations on this are possible: three children and R, A, and T or E, A, and T; five children with E, A, S, T, and L; etc.).

Concentration. Weekly spelling words or other well-chosen lists of words are written on cards. The cards are all turned face down. A child writes a word from memory and then tries to turn over the corresponding card for a match. To win a point, the child's spelling must be correct.

Contractions. The teacher or a student pronounces two words for which a contraction exists. The rest of the class or group try to write the contraction (this activity may be reversed, with the contractions being pronounced).

Add-a-Letter. Teams are given the same word to spell. Each team member goes to the board to write a single letter and then gives the chalk to a teammate (who has until then remained seated) to write the next letter. A judge—either child or adult—rules on the accuracy of the spelling. Coaching of teammates may or may not be permitted.

Drawings. Children may make drawings with the idea of causing others to think of and write words. These may be limited to words in the spelling lesson or words written may be limited by requiring the use of only some letters—as on TV quiz programs.

Pyramids. Children can make pyramids by starting with any letter, adding another to make a word, and continuing to add one letter at a time, always making a correctly spelled word with each addition. The objective is to make the longest list of correctly spelled words.

t	o	m
at	on	am
ate	one	ham
late	tone	sham
plate	tones	shame
plated	stones	shamed
		ashamed

Roots and Affixes. The children start with a root word such as *happy* and make other words by adding prefixes and suffixes: *unhappy, happier, happiness,* and so on. The object is to see how long a list of correctly spelled words can be made.

Baseball. Movable markers on a chart or chairs can be used as bases; children get a hit if they write the correct spelling for a word that is pronounced or make an out if they misspell it. A variation involves using lists of increasing difficulty for singles, doubles, triples, and home runs, with players selecting the level they want to try. Better spellers may then make "outs" more frequently.

Filling Grids. A two-dimensional grid is created that has columns headed by alphabet letters (E, H, T, and S, for example) and rows labeled by categories (Foods, Games, Clothing, and TV shows, for example). Teams or individuals compete by filling in the grid row by row. All words must be spelled correctly.

	E	H	T	S
Foods	*egg*	*ham*	*tomato*	*soup*
Games				
Clothing				
TV shows				

Changing Words. Individuals or teams try to transform one word into another by changing one letter at a time, always obtaining a correctly spelled word. Good word pairs to use are *wet-dry* (one solution: *wet, set, sat, say, day, dry*), *rich–poor, slow–fast, easy–hard,* and *rain–snow.*

Finding Little Words. Hold up a large card with a long word on it (for example, *together*) for a few seconds, during which children may not write. After the card is removed, they try to write any little words they recall seeing in the long word.

Identifying Correct Spellings. A large card with incorrect and correct spellings of a particular word (a "demon" perhaps) is held up for a few seconds for students to study. Then they try to write the correct spelling of the word.

Other Activities

Try having the better spellers make crossword puzzles using words from the spelling lesson or other words they might have occasion to write. Some commercial materials provide puzzles to use as models.

- Playing word games such as Scrabble and anagrams
- Providing riddles that can be answered with words from a list
- Providing crossword puzzles and having children make puzzles for classmates to work
- Finding the histories of words such as *desperado, digit, festival* and *vocation*
- Rewriting trite sentences using more interesting and specific words
- Reporting on new words added to the language because of the space program, computer technology, environmental problems, etc.
- Making charts of synonyms, antonyms, contractions, abbreviations, or some other category
- Having groups or individual children find words for various categories such as food words, TV words, words about our city, or holiday words.
- Using words in some form of creative writing—for example, children might write a story using *bronco, radar, calico, lizard* and *desert*
- Making individual graphs of spelling progress; making lists of words that are difficult; making lists of new words to learn to spell
- Finding modifications of spelling in newspapers, TV advertisements, and signs
- Making a word-picture dictionary
- Searching for the origins of surnames (they are often related to places or occupations)
- Writing descriptions of objects, using as many new descriptive words as possible and using them accurately

ASSESSMENT IN SPELLING

Assessment should begin with an examination of how to determine the extent of attainment of the spelling instructional goals. As was pointed out earlier, the goals of a complete spelling program are to develop a number of attitudes, habits, abilities, and skills and to teach the spelling of a basic core of words. Each child's ability to spell the assigned words on the basic list can be tested by you during the year, but a realistic assessment of the effect of the program with respect to attitude and, to some extent, general spelling ability cannot be made until some later time—perhaps even several years after the child has left elementary school. As you observe what the children do when studying spelling words and how they spell in all their writing, you will gain some impression of their attitudes, habits, and the approaches they take in finding out how to spell a word.

One type of assessment regarding an individual pupil's achievement in spelling is done by making a comparison with standards of national per-

A bulletin board can display reminders about how to study for and take spelling tests.

formance ("What is her percentile rank on the achievement test?" or "What proportion of other fourth graders in the country can spell that word?"). Comparisons can also be made with other children in the class ("He is not one of the best spellers but it's an able group") and with the child's own previous performance ("She is getting fewer words wrong on each weekly list"). In addition, a child's writing can be examined for clues as to types of misspelling, groups or types of words giving the most difficulty, and so forth.

Spelling Development

A group of researchers (see the book by Henderson listed in References) has presented descriptions of children's growth in spelling ability as evidenced by their representations of sounds. These researchers' descriptions may provide some guidance in interpreting pupils' misspellings as ones either to be expected or entirely out of place, considering their age, grade, and ability levels.

If, for example, a first-grader writes "WN" for *when,* this is considered an expected "spelling." If a third-grader is still spelling in that way, ignoring the need for a vowel, the child has a problem. However, if a child in the third grade writes "palushun" for *pollution,* this is considered "normal" because the vowels are all represented and the double *l* is not evident from the sound. Using *-shun* for *-tion* is not a normal expectation for a sixth-grader, however, since common affixes ought to be under better control by then (-*sion* would be a more mature attempt than -*shun*). These types of understandings should be helpful to teachers in their planning of spelling assessment because they bear a close relationship to how children are thinking about words and ways to represent them. Thus, assessment should focus on what is being done well and what is not being done in the spelling instructional program.

Tests

Since there are words that are used regularly in the writing of every person—child or adult—it is important to determine whether the spellings of these words have been learned. Several testing procedures, described below, can provide this information and thus give the teacher and each pupil a specific focus on words to be studied and habits and attitudes to improve.

- The regular teaching program should include several weekly tests, perhaps monthly tests, and a test at the end of each term. Each of these tests should include only the words the children should have learned (or a sampling of them) during the particular time period. Provision should also be made to test words learned earlier (including previous grade levels). The form of these tests should be that suggested earlier for the weekly lesson.

- A standard spelling scale can be used to compare the spelling of your class with that of children of the same grade level as reported in the scale. The only usable spelling scale today is *The New Iowa Spelling Scale* (Bureau of Educational Research, University of Iowa, Iowa City, Iowa), which lists the percentage of children in grades two through eight who spelled each of 5,500 words correctly.

- Testing through the spelling section of standardized achievement tests provides limited measures of spelling ability. The form of most tests is one of recognition rather than recall, and there are so few words tested that the results are useful only as guides.

Checklists

A checklist such as the one shown at the top of the next page or some similar device can help to systematize evaluation of children's attitudes, habits, and abilities.

Pupil Self-Evaluation

Children like to know that they are progressing in learning the spellings of words they need.

Children should participate in evaluation whenever possible, including evaluation of the program and materials. They should especially learn to evaluate their own spelling, whether this is done in the spelling class or in their writing. Some ways in which they can engage in the evaluation process are the following:

- Keep individual progress charts of scores made on spelling tests.
- Keep progress charts on written activities that contain misspellings. For example, such charts may record the number of words misspelled for every fifty or hundred words written and whether some words are repeatedly misspelled.

November Name	Proof-reads spelling pages	Proof-reads other work	Uses diction-ary	Uses study proce-dure	Uses gener-aliza-tions
Bill	*no*	*no*	*no*	*no*	*sometimes*
Roy	✓	?	✓	*no*	✓
Mary	✓	✓	✓	✓	*no*
Julie	✓	✓	*some-times*	✓	✓

- Keep records of the proofreading of written work.
- Correct their own spelling tests and analyze the errors made.
- Participate in class discussions of spelling achievement, study habits, and attitudes toward correct spelling.

Children may enjoy keeping progress charts that have the form of a graph, for example. The one shown below charts the results of final tests for weekly lessons, and the one on the following page depicts progress within each lesson.

My Progress Chart

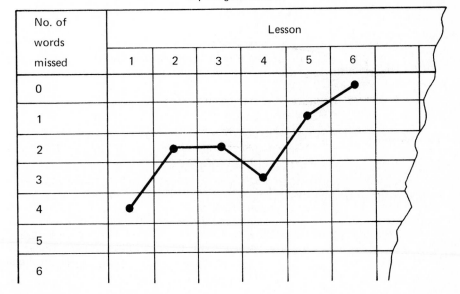

No. of words missed	Lesson							
	1	2	3	4	5	6		
0								
1								
2								
3								
4								
5								
6								

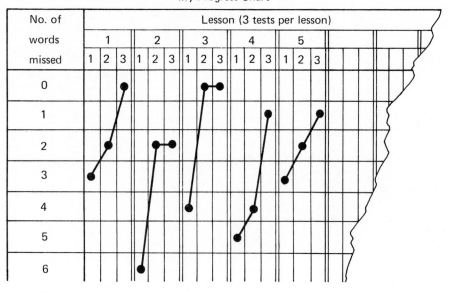

My Progress Chart

A FINAL WORD

Spelling is most productively studied in a classroom environment in which language is highly valued—where vocabularies are being developed through deliberate word-study activities, where play with words is encouraged, and where writing is frequently done for a variety of purposes. Both direct teaching of spelling and instructional attention to how words are spelled throughout the day are necessary. A carefully constructed program based on these principles will lead to effective teaching of spelling.

References

Anderson, Kristine F. "The Development of Spelling Ability and Linguistic Strategies." *The Reading Teacher* 39 (November 1985), pp. 140–147.

Betza, Ruth E. "Online: Computerized Spelling Checkers: Freinds or Foes?" *Language Arts* 64 (November 1987), pp. 438–442.

DiStefano, Philip P., and Hagerty, Patricia J. "Teaching Spelling at the Elementary Level: A Realistic Perspective." *The Reading Teacher* 38 (January 1985), pp. 373–377.

Downing, John; DeStefano, Johanna; Rich, Gene; and Bell, Aula. "Children's Views of Spelling." *The Elementary School Journal* 85 (November 1984), pp. 185–198.

Fitzsimmons, Robert J., and Loomer, Bradley M. *Spelling Research and Practice.* Iowa State Department of Public Instruction and the University of Iowa, 1977.

Gentry, J. Richard. "Learning to Spell Developmentally." *The Reading Teacher* 34 (January 1981), pp. 378–381.

Hall, Susan, and Hall, Chris. "It Takes a Lot of Letters to Spell 'Erz'." *Language Arts* 61 (December 1984), pp. 822–827.

Henderson, Edmund. *Teaching Spelling.* Houghton Mifflin, 1985.

Hodges, Richard E. *Learning to Spell.* Clearinghouse on Reading and Communication Skills and the National Council of Teachers of English, 1981.

Holbrook, Hilary Taylor. "ERIC/RCS Report: Invented Spelling." *Language Arts* 60 (September 1983), pp. 800–804.

Horn, Ernest. "Phonetics and Spelling." *The Elementary School Journal* (May 1957), pp. 431–435.

Johnson, Terry E.; Langford, Kenneth G.; and

Quorn, Kerry C. "Characteristics of an Effective Spelling Program." *Language Arts* 58 (May 1981), pp. 581–588.

Kamii, Constance, and Randazzo, Marie. "Social Interaction and Invented Spelling." *Language Arts* 62 (February 1985), pp. 124–133.

Middleton, Mildred L. *Improving Spelling Performance.* Kendall/Hunt, 1981.

Petty, Walter T. "The Teaching of Spelling." *Bulletin of the School of Education* (Indiana University) 45 (November 1969), pp. 79–98.

Sears, Nedra, and Johnson, Dale. "The Effects of Visual Imagery on Spelling Performance and Retention Among Elementary Students." *Journal of Educational Research* (March/April 1986), pp. 230–233.

Thomas, Ves. *Teaching Spelling, Canadian Word Lists and Instructional Techniques.* Gage Educational Publishing, 1974.

Teaching Resources

COMPUTER SOFTWARE

Computer Scrabble. The Writing Company.

Customized Flash Spelling. Random House (grades 2–6).

Fundamental Spelling Words in Context. Random House, 1982 (grades 1–8).

Magic Spells. Scholastic.

Maze-O. D.C. Heath (grades 2–6).

See It, Hear it, Spell It! MultiMedia Software (all grades).

Spellagraph and Spellakazam. Silver-Burdett (grades 2–8).

Speller Bee (Talking Notebook Series). First Byte (preschool and up).

Spell It. Davidson.

Spelling Wiz. Developmental Learning Materials, 1983 (guide and record sheets; grades 1–6).

Webster: The Word Game. Spoken Arts (grades 1–5).

Wizard of Words. Computer Advanced Ideas, 1983 (grades 2–7).

OTHER RESOURCES

Ellyson, Louise. *Dictionary of Homonyms: New Word Patterns.* Amereon, 1979.

Espy, Willard. *A Children's Almanac of Words at Play.* Dale Seymour Publications (grades 4–6).

Grant, Niels, Jr. *Vocabulary and Spelling Activities.* Fearon Teaching Aids.

Manchester, Richard B. *The Mammoth Book of Word Games.* Hart Publishing, 1976.

Spelling Wordfinder. Curriculum Associates (book).

Tompkins, Gail E., and Yaden, David B. *Language, Answering Students' Questions about Words.* National Council of Teachers of English, 1986.

Vocabulary Building. Zaner-Bloser (kit).

Activities for Preservice Teachers

1. Try some of the spelling-related computer programs listed in the Teaching Resources section above (or other programs to which you have access). What are the advantages and disadvantages of the ones you examined? Be prepared to discuss in class whether or not you would use one of these programs and why.

2. Attempt to spell the "demons" listed in this chapter. Be sure that you have mastered all of them. Then begin to compile a list of your personal "demons"— words you know give you trouble.

3. Study teachers' manuals and advertising materials

for several sets of spelling books to find answers to the following questions: How were the spelling words selected? What is the total number of words for each grade? Does the series use the test-study or study-test method? Are provisions made for both good spellers and poor ones? What activities are provided other than tests and direct study of words? Are study steps suggested?

4. Select a spelling book for a particular grade level, and plan a spelling program for a week, basing it on one of the weekly lessons in the book. Show how you would provide for upper, average, and slow groups; in what ways you would use individualized instruction; how you would use activities in the book; what enrichment activities you would add; and how the lesson might be integrated with other subject areas or other areas of the language arts. Be sure to stay within suggested time limits, except possibly when integrating spelling with other areas.

5. If you were a fifth-grade teacher and had several requests from parents that their children be given spelling homework, what would be your response?

Plan in some detail what you would do and report to the class.

6. There is no doubt that children invent spellings of words they need to write if they don't know the accepted spellings. However, there are differences of opinion among teachers and other professionals about how much such inventing should be encouraged, how long and under what circumstances it should be accepted, its relationship to direct teaching of spelling, and so on. Examine the professional literature concerning this, and be prepared to discuss in class what you have determined.

7. Discuss children's spelling with several elementary-school teachers to determine (a) what they consider to be children's chief problems, (b) the range of abilities in their classes, and (c) if they are using practices advocated in this chapter.

8. Do you know the spelling generalizations and rules for using the apostrophe given in this chapter? If not, learn them.

Activities for Inservice Teachers

1. Assume that a decision has been made to emphasize homework in your building, and your grade level is to concentrate on spelling. What activities could you justifiably use? What problems would you expect to encounter?

2. Be prepared to discuss in class several aspects of teaching spelling in your school or district. For example, is there a requirement that a certain amount of time be devoted to teaching spelling? Are spelling materials specified for each grade level? Is there a policy against displaying writing that contains misspelled words?

3. Bring to class samples of invented spelling from the children in your room or from younger children to whom you have access. Analyze these attempts to determine the extent to which what the children have done "makes sense" and/or conforms to correct spelling. If possible, include in these samples examples that show progress toward and arrival at standard spellings.

4. Start a file of spelling games and puzzles, including the ones described in this chapter. Get ideas from other teachers, professional magazines, and textbooks.

5. Try out some spelling-related computer programs that may help you solve a particular problem you have in teaching (record keeping, providing individual practice, providing enrichment activities, etc.).

6. Develop a schoolwide list of words on which children at every grade level above second are tested each year. Plan a way to determine if there is steady progress in learning these words from one grade level to the next. Are there words that need particular teaching attention? How might you determine if the yearly testing of basic words has a positive effect on spelling performance?

7. Review the reading levels of children in your class. Consider general performance, strengths and weaknesses in vocabulary and word attack, and the results of any informal inventory you have given. Then review each child's spelling performance. Are there any relationships between reading and spelling that might help you plan spelling activities for individual children?

8. Examine some standardized achievement tests in spelling (or the spelling sections of more inclusive standardized tests). How were the words selected? What is the task—identifying correct or incorrect words, ac-

tual writing of the words, or something else? Administer one or more of the tests to a few children. Compare the results of this testing with your assessment of their spelling abilities.

Independent Activities for Children

1. Children, particularly ones who are good spellers, will enjoy looking for misspelled words on supermarket windows, on hand-lettered notices on bulletin boards, in newspapers (perhaps those from local colleges), and in advertisements. Have an award ("Spelling Spy") for those who find errors made by adults.

2. Have a child prepare a chart for the bulletin board listing the most commonly used contractions: *don't, aren't, can't, I'll,* and so on. Another child might make a chart giving the use of the apostrophe (other than in contractions).

3. Two children can take turns drawing small letter tiles that have been turned over so they do not know what the letters are. The first player to make a predetermined number of correctly spelled words is the winner.

4. Each child should keep his or her own list of spelling "demons"—words missed in writing activities or consistently misspelled in review lessons. He or she may study these during free time and practice using them in sentences.

5. Sheets can be prepared with questions, directions, and spaces for the child's responses. Such entries as the following might be on the exercise sheets:
    a. Change the first two letters of *fright* and write the new words (*bright, slight, flight*).
    b. Put prefixes before the words so that antonyms are formed:

    _____ clear   _____ true
    _____ spell   _____ correct
    _____ patient   _____ sense

    c. Write synonyms for these words:

    throw   (hurl, cast, pitch, toss)
    shut   (close, bar)

    d. How many compound words can you make by adding words to these words?

    fire   (fireworks, fireplace, fireside)
    ball   (baseball, football, basketball)
    man   (fireman, chairman, mailman)

6. Put a series of compound words on cards—one word on each card. The child may add as many other compounds as possible that include one of the words

in the given compound word. Some compound words to use are *playground, bathroom,* and *mailbox.*

7. Prepare cards, each with an interesting activity, from which children may select an assignment. Cards might have the following activities:
    a. Write the plurals of these words:

    wolf   woman   fish
    leaf   sheep   church
    shoe

    b. Rearrange the letters in each group and write the words:

    lrig   pllse   drow   eerd

    c. Combine these words into compound words:

    ball   way   net
    fish   door   foot

    d. How many words can you write that begin with these letters?

    cl   st   gr   tr   bl

8. A child can categorize words according to spelling patterns. Various patterns can be used, for example:
    a. Words with a certain sequence of vowels and consonants (vcv—*begin, major, music;* vccv—*summer, dollar, filled*)
    b. Words ending in *-ing* or *-ake* (*sing, bring, thing; cake, lake, take*); two-syllable words (*later, truly, pilot*)
    c. Words that begin with a two-symbol consonant cluster (*br—brother, bring, bright; sl—slip, sleep, sly*)

9. A slow learner may be helped by the use of crossword puzzles made up of words from the spelling list for the week or a list of words that have caused special difficulty. If desired, the puzzle may even be used in conjunction with a list of words to be used, so the child may practice the correct spellings as he or she copies the words from the list.

10. In a shoe or boot box, place letters cut from tagboard and backed with flannel, making sure to provide duplicates of vowels and the frequently used consonants (a Scrabble board provides a good guide to the number needed). Line the top of the box with flannel. Two or more children may take turns drawing let-

ters; as soon as a child can form a word with his or her letters, the child places them on the flannel lid, each child keeping his or her words in a separate column. The first child to form a predetermined number of words is the winner.

11. Make a list of words commonly misspelled in children's writing, and have children make crossword puzzles from it. Children's puzzles then can be exchanged.

12. Have the children look in dictionaries (adult ones) for variant spellings of words. These can be put on a chart, which can then be used in a group discussion of why differences arise.

13. Children can find and list pairs of homophones. A variation of this would be to make a list of words which the children then match by sound with other words, for example: *plain, weigh, write, cent, feet,* and *mist.*

14. Prepare cards, each with a word that has several fairly common meanings. A child should find as many meanings as possible for each word and write sentences illustrating them. Words to use might be common ones such as *left, right, train, dress,* and *ship* or less well-known ones such as *bond, idle, type,* and *trim.*

Chapter 12

Children Learn to Read

Chapters 3 and 4 pointed out that learning to read is a process that begins in the early years and continues as the child has many experiences with books and print. Effective beginning programs offer many opportunities in literacy—in both writing and reading. Like writing, reading should not be an isolated activity for young children nor should it be taught as a sequential series of skills that are presented and practiced apart from actual use. Instead, reading instruction should be based in the children's oral language, and reading should be taught in such a manner as to use all that each child has learned from listening and speaking as well as from seeing letters, words, books, and other written materials.

The same principles apply to programs for older students. Learning to read must be viewed as a lifelong process: most adults regularly encounter some puzzling new reading task, such as trying to follow computer directions or struggling to understand a new tax form; and it seems that students in the upper elementary grades and beyond have more and more to learn each year. Schools cannot meet such demands simply by adding minutes to the reading class; even if that were a good idea, there would not be enough room in the school's daily schedule. With better teaching as well as a more efficient use of time, much of what needs to be learned about reading can be integrated with the other language arts and with the content areas. In this way children will find many avenues for growth in reading ability. This chapter examines reading as it relates to the total classroom program and to the lives of individual children.

READING: AN OVERVIEW

Two concerns must prevail in the teaching of reading: children should understand what they read, and they should have the desire to read. What reading means in the school program and how it relates to the students' life experiences are directly related to these two objectives. Comprehension best results when readers have a purpose for reading that grows out of some personal need or strongly held goal. The need to cultivate a good attitude toward reading is indicated by the large number of individuals who *can* read but do not *do* much of it.

The term aliterate *is sometimes applied to those who can read but don't.*

What Is Reading?
Reading is a complex process that involves a series of equally complex sensory and mental processes. But this complexity does not mean that learning

to read is difficult. Speaking is similar in complexity, yet children learn to speak, apparently without great difficulty.

Defining reading is not easy. Try to think of a one-sentence definition. What do you include? Is it attaching a sound to each squiggle that we call a letter so that putting the sounds together forms a word that the reader knows? Is it getting a clue to what several squiggles represent by any means possible—from pictures, from the shape of the pattern of squiggles, or by guess and inference? Is it saying each word either audibly or silently? Is it recognizing the meaning of a word, a phrase, or a sentence? Is it relating one's experiences to those of the writer? Is it a process of thinking that is stimulated by a special kind of object?

Over the years people identified as reading experts have defined, redefined, charted and modeled, and mulled over what it means to read. Definitions have ranged from "reading means getting meaning from certain combinations of letters," to "reading is a complex mental process that involves the doing of several things simultaneously," to "reading is a psycholinguistic guessing game," to "reading is proceeding from cognitive confusion to cognitive clarity." The educational literature is full of such definitions and more, ranging from the glib to more thoughtful ones. You should formulate your own definition after further study, but this definition is worth considering as your starting point:

See *Teaching Elementary Reading* by Tinker and McCullough.

> Reading involves the identification and recognition of printed or written symbols which serve as stimuli for the recall of meanings built up through past experience and further the construction of new meanings through the reader's manipulation of relevant concepts already in his or her possession. The resulting meanings are organized into thought processes according to the purposes that are operating in the reader.

No definition of reading, glib or extensive, will tell you how to teach reading. On the other hand, almost any definition reflects an interpretation of the reading process that suggests, at least, a method for teaching. But no one really knows *a* best way to teach reading, and it is true that some children learn to read regardless of the method and some do not.

Factors Affecting Reading

The extent to which any reading act is successful is affected both by the reader and by the material he or she is seeking to read. The reader must be ready for the specific reading effort. That is, he or she must have the mental capacity, experiential background, language maturity, and skill development required, as well as an interest in doing the reading. These factors are not unique to reading, however; none of us is successful in anything we attempt to do without readiness for doing it. If we do not have a background of some related experiences, an understanding of what is involved and what we need to do, and the physical and/or mental ability required, our effort will not be successful. And, of course, we would not even try any task if we weren't interested in doing it.

The content of the material and the vocabulary used in it also affect

Differences in Children That Affect Learning

1. Intellectual abilities
2. Mental maturity levels
3. Experiential backgrounds
4. Verbal facility
5. Emotional adjustment
6. Attitude toward learning
7. Exposure to print
8. Physical coordination
9. Visual and auditory abilities

reading, but these factors are directly related to a reader's experience and ability. Because of this, they are especially important in reading instruction. Children can attain a high degree of success in reading material whose content is generally familiar to them, especially if it does not contain too many words or language structures that they have heard infrequently or do not use.

Other factors that affect reading include the ability to visually perceive adequately, the emotional state of the reader, and, particularly for the child just learning to read, the empathy and encouragement shown by the teacher.

Objectives of Reading Instruction

The overall objective in teaching children to read is to develop in them the attitudes, abilities, and skills needed for securing information, fostering and reacting to ideas, developing interests and tastes, and deriving pleasure by reading. This fundamental objective may be met by a program which pursues these objectives for each child:

1. The ability or skill to
   a. recognize many words at sight
   b. gain meaning quickly upon meeting unknown words and expressions by using one or a combination of the following:
      analysis of structure
      phonics
      configuration of the graphic symbol
      contextual analysis
      the dictionary
   c. comprehend and interpret the meanings of words, phrases, and sentences
   d. read silently at speeds appropriate to the content of the material and the purpose of the reader
   e. read orally with fluency, suitable speed, expression, correct pronunciation, and attention to enunciation
   f. evaluate the content of what is read
   g. use books efficiently—locate information, use the library, etc.

2. The provision of many opportunities for rich and varied experiences through reading

3. The development of a lasting interest in reading

Integrating Reading Instruction

Reading, like the other language arts, is an all-day, all-life activity; wise teachers are aware of this and use it to their advantage in reading instruction, in building children's understanding that reading and the other language arts are our means for communicating, and in meaningfully integrating the curriculum.

The more the various areas of the language arts and other subjects are meaningfully related in instruction, the greater the possibility that learning will be enhanced and interest developed. Chapters 13, 14, and 15 cover

Children have not learned to read until they can comprehend the content of their textbooks and other nonfiction materials, including understanding concepts, directions, and questions.

studying, library skills, and children's literature and add to the instructional suggestions offered in this chapter. The interrelatedness of all the language arts and the need to use language skills and abilities in all areas of study make it easy to relate the teaching of reading to vocabulary study, spelling, and handwriting, as well as to science, mathematics, and social studies. Because the sharing of personal experiences, either orally or through writing, is highly motivational, such sharing can also be related to reading instruction. In many ways the interrelating of the various instructional areas is easy, but careful planning is required if the objectives are to be achieved. Numerous aids to such planning have been suggested in earlier chapters, and others will be discussed in the chapters that follow. However, an alert teacher will find many more ways throughout each day to relate his or her instruction in reading and the other language arts to all the other areas of the curriculum. These natural occurrences are usually better than the suggestions made in any book, because they relate activities to real people in a genuine situation.

THE CLASSROOM PROGRAM IN READING

As you consider how reading might be integrated into your total classroom program, you need to think as well of specific approaches to reading instruction. This instruction will probably involve at least some use of one or another of the many published basal reading series. (Such series were briefly discussed in Chapter 4 and are further examined in a later section of this chapter.)

However, a basal series should not constitute the totality of your program, even if the particular series used presents a balanced developmental approach to learning the skills, attitudes, and abilities needed to read. Basals can only go so far—partly, at least, because they are directed at a hypothetical "typical" class. In addition, important areas of a comprehensive program are limited by the content and format of basal series. For example, both children's books and teachers' manuals generally contain less than is needed in such areas as literature, reading for instructional purposes, and personal reading. Furthermore, basals fail to reach the instructional goals of providing many opportunities for rich and varied reading experiences and fostering the development of a lasting interest in reading.

Developmental Reading

Even if a skill or strategy has been "covered," you cannot expect it to be ready for use.

Basals contain a great deal of material designed to teach basic reading skills and to increase children's reading abilities. Sometimes, though, teachers or school systems come to feel that more and different materials are needed. The reasons underlying such a feeling vary, but they include differences in the abilities and personalities of teachers, recognition of the uniqueness of the individual children in each class, failure of children to do well on standardized tests, and simply dissatisfaction with the basal program. Unfortu-

The beginning of a lasting interest in reading.

nately, too, some teachers simply use many of the materials in the basal program as a means for keeping children busy.

Workbooks. Reading series generally include practice books, which provide exercises related to the stories in the readers as well as other activities. Other workbooks that are independent of any series—or form a sort of series of their own—are also available, and school systems or individual teachers often adopt them. Chief among these are phonics series that are sequenced by grade levels and provide practice in letter/sound relationships, the application of phonics "rules," and the analysis of words. Other types of workbooks focus on comprehension practice, with exercises that involve answering different kinds of questions after reading brief selections. Word-study workbooks are sometimes used as well; these provide specific attention to vocabulary development.

In general, workbooks seek to teach skills in isolation from reading; this makes remembering and applying what has been learned rather difficult, especially for those students who need help the most. Occasional use of workbooks may be good for an individual child or a small group, but they should generally not be used as a regular activity; they simply are not a good use of the limited time available in the classroom.

Comprehension should only be given attention after an entire selection has been read—an article, story, or book. There is no such thing as "comprehending" a sentence apart from its context.

Kits of Reading Materials. Boxes of study cards related to school subjects are often referred to as "kits." Most of those related to reading focus on comprehension; they have short reading selections and accompanying questions printed on a collection of cards. Other kits deal with phonics or vocabulary study. The cards are often organized in successive levels of difficulty, and students work their way through the box.

Such materials may be used by children working independently, and therefore do not require large blocks of class time. Kits may also serve as enrichment or remedial activities for a few pupils. In particular, some youngsters seem to get satisfaction and encouragement from seeing their progress recorded in a concrete way as they go through the successive exercises. For the most part, however, you will probably find that teaching goals can be accomplished more readily in other ways.

Duplicated Worksheets. Worksheets are often included with basal series, but independent sets may also be acquired. These may be in the form of masters to be copied or packages ready for direct distribution to children. Most worksheets have been designed to reinforce specific reading skills and provide extra practice for those having difficulties. However, it must be said that in some classrooms worksheets mostly serve as a way of keeping some students busy while the teacher meets with another reading group or does something else. Not much can be expected from the use of worksheets, however; the need is for activities that are much more stimulating than anything provided in this way and are more specifically directed at the needs of the individual pupils.

Giving the same seatwork to all children is an injustice to them. Make sure that all seatwork has a purpose and is not just something to keep a child "busy"!

Programmed Materials. Programmed materials used in reading instruction may be either books or collections of worksheets. Teaching using this type of material is based on the idea that whatever is to be learned should be broken down into small pieces and presented to the child bit by bit. This point of view considers learning to read to be a highly organized process that occurs in such a way that exactly what should be taught and how it ought to be done are known. In such a program all the pupils go through the same exercises, only at different rates; no other recognition of individual differences is provided for.

A programmed set of materials is often combined with testing to create a diagnostic-prescriptive system in which pupils are examined for their level of success in manifesting certain skills and then assigned exercises intended to teach them what they do not know, according to the results of the test. These programs often identify dozens, or even hundreds, of isolated skills to be tested for, taught, and then tested for again. This kind of teaching presents several difficulties. First, there is the question of transfer of learning; assuming that what has been taught can be appropriately used in an actual reading situation may be invalid for many pupils. Second, many children find the test-teach-test format boring and consequently develop poor attitudes toward reading. Finally, and most importantly, activities of this kind are not really reading, and time given to them must be taken away from what should be the major thrust of the reading program—dealing with meaningful content.

Computer Programs. Developmental reading exercises of various types—from phonics and word recognition to comprehension questions for

New computer programs are discussed regularly in such journals as *Language Arts* and *The Reading Teacher*.

difficult texts—are available in the form of computer programs. In many cases the activities presented to students on the screen differ little from what is offered on worksheets; the only advantage is that some children enjoy using the computer. This is not true for all software, however; some programs are superior to paper-and-pencil exercises.

General advantages of computer-presented material include the facts that the computer provides instant feedback concerning accuracy of an answer, can keep records of the progress of each student in the class, enables children to study in relative privacy with some control over the difficulty of the work being attempted, and has infinite patience in presenting similar exercises for as long as the pupil wishes to keep trying them. There are specific advantages, too, depending on the area of reading involved.

Many programs are available in the areas of phonics and word identification. Computers and programs with the capability of producing vocalizations are especially effective since it is a great advantage to hear the pronunciation of whatever is on the screen. If an exercise deals with "word families" (for instance, *hat, fat, cat, sat*), letter substitution is often involved. The computer presents the word *man* and a matching picture along with a picture of a pan, and the student attempts to change *man* to *pan*. The computer pronounces whatever the pupil types and produces a special signal when the target word is typed. Engaging in such an activity is superior to doing a similar one in a workbook, which cannot speak or respond.

Other software focuses on comprehension activities. For example, texts with missing words (called the "cloze procedure") may be presented to the child, who types in what seems a suitable word. The program informs the child whether or not the selection is appropriate. If it is not, the software package may have the capability of bracketing the text that should be reread before another attempt is made. Usually the student is in control of the difficulty level of the material presented and can try easier or more complex passages.

Reading Literature

Some teachers (and even entire schools or school systems) have children read only literature selections in the reading program. They do not use basal series.

Throughout this textbook it has been stressed that literature should be a central part of the classroom program, and this recommendation obviously applies to reading. Literature is significant to the reading program in several ways. Reading classic stories to the class is important because it is the way most of them will be introduced to the best authors. After you have read a good book on horses, for example, several children will want to read other similar titles. As children develop interests and read extensively on their own, they will build up speed in their reading, extend their vocabularies, and acquire such mature abilities as appreciating how writers use descriptive phrases.

Writing in response to literature can be a significant part of the reading program, and the relationships between this type of writing and reading are discussed in a later section of this chapter. Also, Chapter 15 is devoted to children's literature, and in it you will find many suggestions concerning materials and activities to be used in elementary classrooms.

Reading for Information

Reading is vitally important as an avenue for learning, of course, and this aspect should receive maximum attention in your teaching. Children need instruction in how to read their textbooks in science and the other school subjects. Each subject area has characteristic ways of presenting content and developing understandings. When reading textbooks, students will find themselves exposed to various challenges. Thinking about the accuracy of descriptions, keeping a sequence of events in mind, and reading for significant details are quite naturally of concern when reading textbooks and similar materials, and that is when to teach about them, not using reading workbooks with their brief, unrelated texts. Chapter 13, on reading and studying, discusses how the reading process relates to the systematic organization of subject matter.

Finding and using content in encyclopedias and other reference works are also frequently necessary in the classroom. Discussion of this aspect of reading ability is found in Chapter 14, on library skills, as well as in Chapter 15, on children's literature. It is absolutely essential for these types of reading to be incorporated into the daily work of children if they are to benefit completely by learning how to make effective use of their growing ability to read.

Personal Reading

As children grow older and their interests emerge, reading takes on personal significance for many of them. Use of reading in daily life is an indicator of the success of the school program. Those children for whom reading becomes important will not only learn to read and study and become acquainted with literature but will also find it possible to use their ability to accomplish significant personal goals.

Children will do most of their personal reading outside of school hours, but some materials for "recreational" reading should also find a place in the classroom. Children read for amusement, just as adults do, so they should have access to popular children's and sports magazines, books of jokes and riddles, and stories that appeal to their age group. Of course, some discretion may need to be exercised with respect to comics and popular magazines that the community might not accept as being appropriate for school.

Elementary-school children will sometimes want to read realistic fiction and other material with serious content. There are stories and nonfiction books that deal with divorce and other serious subjects, even at the primary level. Increasingly, such topics as drug and alcohol use and AIDS are treated in materials directed at elementary-school children. For personal reasons and from a desire to better understand the world around them, children will want to read these materials, and in many cases they should. Children should be encouraged to read anything they are interested in and are capable of reading, although the views of parents and the community need to be considered.

Some pupils who have "reading problems" in school can follow printed directions in order to operate complex electronic devices.

There is extensive evidence that poorer readers spend more time doing workbook exercises than they do reading. The way to learn to read is to read *something that is interesting.*

Choosing Good Books for Your Children, Reading Aloud to Children, and *Upbeat and Offbeat Activities to Encourage Reading* can be ordered from Reading Is Fundamental (600 Maryland Avenue, S.W., Suite 500, Washington, DC 20560).

More Children's Magazines

Boy's Life.
1325 Walnut Hill Lane
Irving, TX 75038-3096

Children's Playmate
P.O. Box 10681
Des Moines, IA 50381

Faces
20 Grove Street
Peterborough, NH 03458

Owl
The Young Naturalist
  Foundation
51 Front Street East
Toronto, Ontario M5E 1B3
Canada

Scienceland
501 Fifth Avenue
New York, NY 10017-6165

Your Big Backyard
The National Wildlife
  Federation
1412 Sixteenth Street, N.W.
Washington, DC 20036

The school should treat young people as citizens who require reliable sources of information. These can be provided in part by making newspapers and news magazines available in the classroom. Weekly newspapers prepared especially for elementary schools are quite good, but the content of a community newspaper will be closer to the daily experiences of the children. Children do not necessarily know how to use newspapers and similar reading materials; they must receive some instruction concerning the organization and functions of the different features as well as how news is presented.

Other kinds of personal reading will be related to preferred leisure activities. Some children will read about their hobbies—collecting something or following the careers of favorite television personalities. Others may be intrigued by outdoor activities or family pursuits such as raising show dogs and will read magazines and books related to these interests. You should invite children to bring their personal reading materials to school. Such a skill as reading for detail may be much better learned by reading a cookbook than by doing a workbook page. There are important affective benefits, too, when a child sees that you and other students find her or his special interest worthy of attention and even admiration.

ORGANIZING FOR READING

In addition to choosing the materials to use in your reading program, you need to decide how to organize your class. Any group of children manifests significant differences in intelligence, reading ability, interests, and work habits, and all of these have to be taken into consideration in the organizing you do as well as the materials you use. Because of this variation in needs and capabilities, some learning activities will have to be carried out with the entire class, some with small groups and some with individual students.

Whole-Class Activities

Some years ago, in a large number of elementary classrooms, all children read the same story in their books at the same time. This meant that some children easily read the material; others had a bit of difficulty; and some struggled constantly or even failed to read anything. This sort of procedure might still be found in a science or social studies class but is not likely to occur as a part of the reading program. There are reading experiences that are appropriate for whole-class participation, though.

When you read aloud to the children, valuable and varied learning will take place, with every class member participating. For example, you might read the book *The Secret Garden;* all the children will be able to listen, understand the story, and join in discussions. Those with the interest and the ability may get their own copies and read along with you, or they may even hurry through the book on their own and then ask for suggestions of similar stories to read. A few children who are very involved in writing may decide to compose a story about the same characters. Most of the class will simply enjoy hearing the book read but perhaps may need some help in understanding about dialects or life in nineteenth-century England. Thus, a story can be enjoyed by an entire class and followed up in several ways. Everyone can participate at his or her own level by dramatizing scenes, reading favorite parts aloud to someone else, drawing pictures, or writing about the events, setting, or characters.

Thematic reading is also a good whole-class activity. Books on a single topic—dogs, perhaps—can be read by everyone; each child can select something at the appropriate level of difficulty. All of the children can contribute to follow-up discussions and related activities, and even less able readers are likely to have found information their classmates will find interesting.

A popular whole-class, or even whole-school, activity is Sustained Silent Reading (SSR). In SSR a certain amount of time (at least 30 minutes in the upper grades) is set aside regularly for reading, with everyone joining in (including, in many schools, the principal and the clerical and maintenance staff). During SSR time, everyone reads a personally selected library book. Doing other school work, talking, or any other kind of interruption is not permitted. SSR promotes the habit of reading and communicates to the children a sense of the great value placed on reading by the adults around them.

Reading Groups

The most widely used form of classroom organization for reading involves assigning children to ability groups—usually three or four in a class—and

Periods of Sustained Silent Reading (SSR) are a regular feature in some school programs.

Use of groups does not mean there should be less individualized reading instruction.

then meeting with them each day to provide instruction by means of different levels of basal readers. The idea of ability grouping is to narrow the range of achievement differences so that the same book and a single set of objectives are appropriate for all the students in a group. Thus, in a class in which pupils read on all levels from first through sixth grade (the range to be expected in the average third grade), four groups might be formed, each with its own instructional program. The children in one group would all be reading at the third-grade level, using the same book and receiving instruction in many of the same skills. Another group would be working in a similar way at the second-grade level. A third group would include those students still dealing with beginning-reading tasks; activities for them should be individualized as much as possible. The most capable readers, the ones who generally read independently, would make up the fourth group because they also require and deserve some instruction.

Utilizing ability groups in the teaching of reading calls for an organizational plan that permits the teacher to give undivided attention to one group while the others are productively occupied. The following is an example of a way to schedule time for three groups. A similar arrangement could be drawn up for four or any other number of groups; however, the management of more than four groups is difficult.

AMOUNT OF TIME	GROUP		
	A	B	C
10 minutes	Teacher reading aloud, sharing newspaper reports, choral reading, and so on		
30 minutes	Teacher-directed activity	Reading library books	Independent work
30 minutes	Independent work	Teacher-directed activity	Reading library books
30 minutes	Reading library books	Independent work	Teacher-directed activity

Some Seatwork Activities

1. Practicing handwriting
2. Studying spelling
3. Doing personal reading
4. Writing and revising
5. Using a science kit
6. Working on a social studies project
7. Using learning games and puzzles
8. Listening to or watching tapes
9. Using the computer
10. Following suggestions on task cards
11. Drawing illustrations for a book

More or less time than that indicated on the chart may be needed for some groups. Particularly slow-learning children may need more teacher direction, while a group of high-achieving children may work independently, with only occasional teacher checking. All grouping, however, requires that children work independently at times while the teacher is teaching the others. For this to work, there must be meaningful independent or group activities that do not require much direct teacher attention. Listening to children read is not teaching, especially if the teacher is giving a substantial amount of attention to the other children in the room.

Ability grouping is sometimes done by grade level or even schoolwide. Children identified as reading at the same level attend reading class together in a specific room with a given teacher. This form of organization for reading instruction requires that all teachers schedule the reading period at the same time, with one taking the group of the very best readers from all classes, another taking the poorest group, and so on. Each teacher, then, sends most of her or his pupils to other rooms, keeping only those reading at the level being taught in his or her room. A disadvantage of this plan is that teachers may know the reading levels but not the interests and problems of the children from other classes. Also, the scheduling of "a reading period" by each teacher suggests that reading is taught only in that period rather than throughout the day, as should be the case.

Grouping for reading may also be done on some basis other than achievement. Interest groups might be created in which, for example, mystery-story or horse enthusiasts come together to read in their chosen field. Ability differences are not so important if the topic is a popular one. Work groups in science or some other subject area may read materials of varying difficulty and then be responsible for a report, a display, or a demonstration that shows what the group has learned. Or, when several children have enjoyed the same book, they can come together to plan an activity based on the story.

Individual Reading Experiences

Whether as one of a class or as a member of a small group, it is always the individual student who does the reading, of course, and reading is one of the most personal of experiences. Thus, the school program should support this type of activity. In some situations "individualized reading" describes this aspect of a program. It is somewhat similar to Sustained Silent Reading in that children select library books and read from these on their own for much of the time. They also meet regularly with the teacher to confer about what they are reading. These conferences are times for the teacher to talk with each youngster, to encourage progress, and to assess how well he or she is doing. Teacher and student keep records of what has been read and which reading abilities the child is still developing. Like the writing conferences described in Chapter 9, such sessions have many instructional as well as social and emotional advantages.

Individualized teaching provides an excellent opportunity to assist students who are at the two ends of the achievement range—the ones doing quite poorly or very well. Usually those with severe difficulties have been identified for some type of remedial teaching and go to a specialist regularly for assistance. You must do what you can to support the efforts of that specialist, however, since only if all those involved cooperate will the child have a good chance of making progress. Besides, you will have the child in your classroom most of the day, and teaching reading is an all-day activity. If there is no remedial service, you are responsible for observing the child closely, discovering what is needed, and doing the necessary individualized teaching. Utilizing individual reading inventories, as described elsewhere in this chapter, ought to be one of your techniques. It is also possible that computer-based activities might be helpful to such children.

Superior readers will probably find the typical reading-group activities

Those who have used individualized reading suggest that at least a hundred different books be available to children at the primary level and as many as five hundred to those in intermediate grades.

In her book *When Writers Read,* Hansen describes how to organize and conduct "reading conferences."

uninteresting, since they are likely to already possess the skills being emphasized. Individualized reading will probably benefit these readers because it involves self-chosen books and opportunities for discussions with the teacher, in which the teacher can identify and help with the skills they've not learned. Computer activities are also a possibility for high-ability students—for teaching study skills and for general enrichment. Superior readers may qualify as gifted students in your school system and therefore have sessions with a specialist teacher. Again, even if that is the case, your responsibility to provide support and experiences is not lessened.

Putting It Together

The successful teacher of reading must have a very thorough knowledge of children's literature.

A successful classroom program will have reading activities for the whole class, for groups, and for individuals. The emphasis you place on these components will be a function of your preferences and capabilities, the demands of building or district policies, and the needs and abilities of the children. In general, children should, as much as possible, move toward individual reading of the best literature. The routes by which such a goal is attained will be different, and you must not be impatient.

THE READING LESSON

Many types of learning activities make up an effective reading program. As described in the discussion of instructional planning in Chapter 2, a comprehensive approach includes developmental teaching, information processing, and lessons imbedded in other teaching activities. Developmental teaching in reading usually consists of the lessons presented in a basal series, although other materials are also used for that purpose. Information-processing activities arise in all areas of the curriculum where reading is required; the children should gain proficiency in reading from these activities, but their principal goal is the understanding and use of the information being gained. Improvement of reading ability is a by-product of any such learning activity, as is the students' realization that reading is important. Imbedded lessons are found in all subject areas and in personal reading matter, too, as the teacher finds opportunities to call the child's attention to such specifics as how a text presents a sequence of events or the new way in which an author has used a word.

The term "reading lesson" or "directed reading activity" usually refers to the developmental, planned activities of the kind to be found in basal series. Only you can decide how much of the basal lessons to use as presented and how often to develop your own lessons. To do this, you should have a good grasp of the essential features of a lesson as described in the section that follows.

Essentials of a Lesson

Naturally, a teacher must be flexible enough to vary the techniques used from day to day and from one particular teaching situation to another. Not every lesson should follow the same format; variety is good, and only you, the teacher, can plan really effectively for and with a group of children. Thus, the plan suggested here should be regarded as an outline of what is essential.

   I. Developing readiness for the reading activity
      A. Through a discussion of experiences that are related to the material to be read
      B. Through the introduction of new words and new concepts and the relating of these to known words and concepts
      C. Through relating children's interests to what is to be read and establishing purposes for the reading

  II. Guiding the first or survey reading of the selection
      A. By asking questions and responding to children's questions so that the child is motivated to read for the purpose or purposes of the lesson
      B. Through noting the organization of the selection

 III. Rereading for specific purposes, such as
      A. Answering specific questions
      B. Doing interpretive oral reading
      C. Finding specific words or explanations of particular concepts

 IV. Developing important habits and skills
      A. Through direct instruction and practice in using word recognition techniques, comprehension skills, and so forth
      B. Through the use of computer, workbook, and teacher-prepared materials
      C. Through evaluation of progress and the establishment of further instructional goals

  V. Providing for enrichment
      A. By following up on activities during rereading
      B. By relating what has been read to interests and needs in other curriculum areas
      C. By suggesting supplemental readings and other activities

Planning a Lesson

Even an experienced teacher makes plans; these include writing out reminders of things to do during a lesson, planning the probable sequence of activities, and gathering together needed materials prior to the lesson. An inexperienced teacher should make rather detailed plans—even if the teacher's edition of the children's reader has extensive suggestions. The following indicates the general outline of a reading lesson plan, along with some suggestions regarding each point.

Objectives. Write out the objectives in terms of what you want the children to know or be able to do as a result of the lesson. Think about how you will be able to observe what each child has learned. An objective is of value only to the extent that its achievement can be determined. For example, if an objective is to teach the children the meanings of certain words, whether or not they have learned them can easily be determined.

Materials. List everything you will need for the lesson: books, word cards, sentence strips, objects illustrating new words and concepts, pictures, and so forth.

Time. How much time must be spent on this lesson? Is it a lesson that should extend over more than one day?

Readiness. What will you do to get the children ready to do the reading and to learn the new words and skills? If you are going to have a discussion of a preceding story in the unit, what will you do to relate the discussion to this particular story? Readiness for the skills to be introduced or practiced must also be considered. Perhaps you will want to write sentences using the new words in a context more familiar to the children. You might need to list words that can help provide configuration (shape) clues, illustrate a phonic or structural principle, or teach a skill that can be used to determine meaning.

Reading the Story. How much of the story do you plan to have read at a time before discussing it—a paragraph, a page, or some other unit? Or do you want the children to read the story in its entirety before it is discussed or otherwise reacted to? (Beginning readers should read no more than one page before discussing and responding to questions.) How are you going to use the pictures? Will you have the class discuss them to help build readiness? Reading should usually be done silently first and then orally, but not every line needs to be read aloud. You will need to think about the purposes for specific reading acts. For example, you may list purposes such as the following: Read to find out why everyone in the picture is laughing. Now find out what happened next. See what the story tells about this picture.

Skill Development. The portion of your class devoted to skill development should include structural analysis and phonics activities, vocabulary-building exercises and activities, and work on comprehension skills. Some of this can be done before the story itself is read. However, you may want to see if the children can independently identify or determine the meanings of words that are new to their reading experiences. If they cannot, this may mean that a phonics principle (for example) needs to be discussed, examples given, and the relation to known words and other principles shown after the actual reading is completed. Activities in a workbook or a computer program are usually closely tied to this part of the lesson and should be used as long as you have ascertained their suitability to your purposes and their relationship to the teaching procedures you have planned.

Evaluation. Don't wind up your lesson by asking, "Did you like the story?" Instead, discuss the mood or plot of the story, how the story relates to real life, and so on. Plan evaluation in terms of the objectives. Are you going to give the children a worksheet in which they match words and definitions? Are you going to ask questions requiring answers that show understanding of the story read? What are those questions?

Enrichment. There are usually enrichment suggestions in the teacher's editions of reading textbooks at the end of either a story or a unit. Typically these suggestions include books that are related to the story or unit, films or filmstrips that extend understanding and build further interest, and dramatic activities that relate to the reading. These enrichment suggestions should always be considered. Although it may not be feasible to use all of them, those that can be utilized should be. Sometimes, too, the suggestions will cause you to think of other things to do.

TEACHING READING

Once children are beyond the stage of beginning reading, demands on their abilities, in terms of variety of tasks and complexity of materials, increase rapidly. The abilities and techniques needed are not taught and learned in a few months, however. Development occurs over several years, and there are very large differences in achievement among children of the same age and grade level. Some students seem to require little direct teaching; they read extensively and show that they understand reading processes. Others need more than experience; teachers must be prepared to conduct instructional activities that cover necessary areas of performance.

This section discusses procedures and activities for helping children learn how to read and for encouraging them to want to read. You will probably wish to examine other descriptions of teaching approaches found in textbooks on reading methods, professional journals, and commercial materials intended for use with children.

Sources of Further Activities Helpful in Teaching Reading

Reading Activities for Child Involvement, 3rd ed., by Evelyn Spache (Allyn and Bacon, 1982)
Reading: Teaching for Learning, by Vera Southgate (Macmillan, 1984)
Teaching Reading: A Practical Guide of Strategies and Activities, by Roger L. Rouch (Teachers College Press, 1984).
Teaching Reading Using Microcomputers, by Robert Rude (Prentice-Hall, 1986)

Word Recognition

The ability to recognize, recall, or otherwise identify or determine a word is basic to reading. There are several intertwined skills involved in word recognition. No one of these always works, nor do all children need an equal amount of instruction in all or any one of them. Some activities related to gaining these skills are discussed in the following sections.

Sight Recall. Adults generally recognize at sight most of the words they encounter in their reading. We simply know the words and do not have to stop to figure out what they are. We have gained this ability by our experiences. We have heard many words, seen them often in written form, and possibly have written most of them ourselves. In other words, how they appear in graphic form has been memorized. Of course, we sometimes look up a word in a dictionary, ask someone what it is, or possibly stop long enough to see a clue in it that we relate to a word we do know.

One of the principal goals of teaching in the early grades is the development of a beginning "sight vocabulary" (the importance of recognizing words in print was discussed in Chapter 4). These known words are used for the reading tasks in which they are learned and as a basis for learning unknown words and the development of strategies for dealing with new words.

In the middle and upper elementary grades children should have a very large sight vocabulary—of at least several hundred words. Like adults, these older readers will have seen the most common words countless times. Less frequently occurring words will be in their listening and speaking vocabularies and will be quickly recognized because of the context in which they are found. Children in the middle and upper grades whose sight vocabularies are not very extensive should be presented chiefly with low-reading-level, high-interest material so that they will get meaningful practice in sight recall.

Context Clues. The most important skill for determining the meanings of unknown words is that of using context clues. These clues are available to a reader because of some degree of shared experiences with the author of the materials and because of the reader's knowledge of how the language works. Although most of the clues are verbal, pictures also provide clues to meaning, since they generally relate to the content. Thus, a reader using context clues to determine the meaning of a word that he or she does not recognize at sight draws information from the remainder of the sentence, other sentences in the context, pictures that appear to be related, and experiences that he or she has had with related ideas. In a sense this is a guess (as, actually, are all word-recognition techniques other than using a dictionary), but it is an informed guess.

Children's skill in using context clues is closely related to the breadth and depth of their vocabularies. Knowledge of the multiple meanings of many words is necessary, as is knowing that many words have synonyms, that figures of speech and idioms have special meanings, that modifying phrases and clauses serve specific purposes, and that particular words suggest the author's pattern of thinking (for example, *first, also,* and *on the other hand*). Activities such as the following can help develop this skill:

1. Write sentences in which one word has been omitted and have pupils supply as many words for the blank as possible. Vary this procedure by writing different first letters in the blank:

   John _____ to the store.
   John w_____ to the store.
   John r_____ to the store.

2. Write homographs (*bear, stick, fleet, flat, fair,* etc.) and illustrate their meanings with sentences:

   I cannot *bear* to see you suffer.
   The *bear* ran down the road.

3. Think of all the possible descriptive words that could be related to a particular object or action.

4. Write as many sentences as you can showing different meanings of common words. Try words such as *run, walk, back,* and *step.*

5. Write synonyms for words in a story. Will all synonyms for a word always fit the context?

6. Circle the clues to the meanings of the underlined words in these sentences:

   The <u>submarine</u> is a reliable underwater craft.

After Bob bought the groceries for his mother, he <u>purchased</u> candy with the change.

Structural Analysis. Structural analysis involves looking for known parts within unknown words. Determining whether a part of a word is known by the reader—that is, that it has meaning that is understood—often leads to identifying the unknown word. Many words are compounds, and a reader may know the meaning of one of the words forming the compound. This may be enough of a clue (especially if other word-recognition skills are used) for the reader to get the meaning of the compound. Further clues may be provided by other word elements: inflectional endings (*s, ed, ing, ly,* etc.), prefixes, suffixes, and roots. Knowledge of how contractions work, plurals are formed, and words may be divided into syllables is also helpful in structural analysis.

Various teaching procedures or approaches—in which varying emphasis is given to each of the elements—are used for teaching structural analysis. Often the ideal time to teach structural analysis is when unknown words that lend themselves to such analysis are encountered by a reader. However, timely as such teaching might be, a reader who is excitedly fulfilling his or her purpose for doing the reading should not be stopped. In such a situation the wise teacher will simply supply the unknown word, but will note it for later teaching. Activities useful in such teaching include these:

1. Write inflected and derived forms of words (for example, *happier, making, shorter, carries, flies,* etc.) and have pupils identify the root word of each.
2. Have pupils find the root common to all (or a certain number) of a group of words (for example, *reporter, portable, portage,* etc.).
3. Make lists of words that have the same suffix (for example, *helpful, tearful, hopeful, fearful*) and have the pupils see if they can determine the meaning of the suffix.
4. Have pupils make lists of compound words or put words together to make compounds.
5. Provide lists of words to be divided into syllables.
6. Write prefixes on cards and place them in a box. Then have each pupil draw a card and give a word that has the prefix as a part of it.
7. Have children classify words in a list into those with common suffixes, prefixes, syllabication rule, or root.
8. Provide lists of contractions (*shouldn't, can't, I'll, won't,* etc.) for pupils to change to the contracted words.

Phonics. Chapter 4 discussed phonics as a method of teaching beginning reading, one in which children are expected to study the "sounds of letters" and be able to blend these together in such a way as to pronounce words that are in their listening and speaking vocabularies. As you may recall, this method of introducing children to reading is considered controversial. What hardly anyone disputes is that phonics makes an important contribution to reading performance. When used in conjunction with analysis of word structure, phonics is helpful to the reader who has a good grasp of the content—that is, has the experiential background—and can profit by having some good clues as to what a given word might be. The key is not to "overdose" children on phonics but to provide them with what is most useful at specific times.

There are many activities for developing phonics skills. Here are some:

1. Change the beginnings and endings of words to make new words (*man–can, meat–meal, walk–talk*).

2. Underline the common elements in a series of words (the *cl* in *clouds, climb, clap, clang*).

3. Make charts of pictures illustrating words that begin with the same blend (or letter, prefix, etc.).

4. Have children come to the board and point to the letter (or blend or digraph) that begins the word you say.

5. Substitute vowels to form new words (*cap–cup–cop, big–bag–beg–bug*).

6. List "families" of words (*cake, take, lake, make, sake, rake, bake*).

7. Have pupils sort cards with words on them into groups with the same vowel sound (or same beginning sound, ending sound, beginning blend, etc.).

8. Match words with specific sounds at the beginning to words with the same sounds at the end.

9. Add letters to beginning blends to make words (*cr* becomes *crash, creek, crazy, creep*, etc.).

10. Make lists of new words that contain a part from a familiar word (*shoe* gives rise to *shop, ship, show, shine*, etc.).

11. Pronounce pairs of words (*pay–pat, head–said, cap–hat*) and have the pupils tell in which pairs they hear the same vowel sound.

12. Match cards to make words. Initial consonants may be matched with phonograms (*an, ink, eat*, etc.); suffixes may be matched with bases; or two words may make a compound.

13. Match pictures whose names rhyme (or begin with the same sound).

14. Write words with medial vowels omitted (*r___d, t___n, p___n*) and have children insert as many different letters as possible.

15. Have the children write the first letter or first two letters of the words you say.

Chapter 13 describes techniques for teaching dictionary skills.

The Dictionary. Children should begin to have experiences with a dictionary as soon as they begin to make letters and know the names of letters. Not only will they learn many words as they investigate beginning dictionaries (see Chapter 13), but they will also learn that a dictionary is a reliable source of meanings of unknown words they encounter in reading. Although words in the listening and speaking vocabularies of readers can be recognized and their meanings determined by the other means suggested, some words readers meet cannot. At those times a dictionary is needed.

A Focus on Comprehension

The ability to read is more than identifying the words that the graphic symbols represent. The purpose of reading is to gain meaning, to comprehend;

and comprehension is an active mental process. The printed page itself contains no meaning. It is just ink on paper. Meaning comes from the mind of the reader. Comprehension requires the reader to relate his or her background of experience and knowledge of how language works to the words that have been recognized or decoded. Comprehension, then, occurs when the reader has a significant background of experience to relate to the content of the reading material and thinks about what he or she both knows and wants to know regarding this content. Thus, the problem in teaching comprehension is one of using and building on children's experiences, developing vocabulary related to those experiences, selecting reading materials that relate to experiences the reader has had, and utilizing the skills that facilitate comparing the language on the printed page to this experience.

The building of children's experiences has been emphasized in many sections of this book. The broadening and strengthening of children's backgrounds must be a continuing process if children are to comprehend the contents of their textbooks, library books, and reference sources. No stage in this process is ever complete, though; vocabularies must be continuously enlarged. New words—and new meanings of known words—should be explored and discussed in relation to new experiences as well as the children's earlier ones and their interests.

In addition to extending their experiences and providing opportunities for them to gain in language ability, a teacher must make sure that children acquire a number of specific skills that will aid them in comprehension; children must know how to read for the main idea, for details, and for the organization of the content; and they need to be able to skim, to read critically, to outline, to use the dictionary, and to vary their reading rate (these skills are discussed in Chapter 13). Children must also be taught to go beyond a literal interpretation of what they read. They must learn to do cause-and-effect reasoning, to draw inferences, to arrive at conclusions, and to make generalizations.

Comprehension is practiced even before the first reading instruction. In fact, listening to stories and accounts requires many of the skills and abilities of comprehension possessed by the mature and highly effective reader. Comprehension is a thinking activity and should not be thought of as something to teach after word-recognition skills have been learned and a storehouse of sight words accumulated. Children seek to comprehend from the beginning what they attempt to read. Thus, instructional attention should always be on reading purposefully, comprehending what is read, and assimilating or reacting to it.

All classroom activities that aid the development of children's thinking powers help to improve their reading comprehension. To encourage thinking, of course, the activities must be purposeful, must relate to the children's experiences and interests, and must require some degree of reasoning or the testing of ideas. Here are a variety of activities to use or adapt to your class:

1. Encourage children to raise questions regarding a selection before they read it. Also encourage questioning during and after reading; the focus should be on meaning rather than on words or manner of reading.

2. Ask questions that require more than recalling facts and oral reading in response. Ask questions that call for judgment and reasoning.

3. Question children about cause-and-effect relationships in things they talk about as well as read.

4. Aid children in constructing their own questions they want answered from their reading.

5. Have individual conferences with children to help determine how effectively they are comprehending what they have been reading and to aid comprehension by the exchange that will occur in the conferences.

6. Help children to recognize and interpret punctuation marks in material they read.

7. Ask children to paraphrase or tell in their own words what they have read.

8. Make specific efforts to teach sentence sense, variations in sentence and paragraph order, and organization of sentences, paragraphs, and larger units.

9. Encourage wide reading about topics of interest rather than intensive "digging" in only one source.

10. Have children illustrate favorite events in a story by drawing a picture or by dramatizing.

11. Encourage children to volunteer for oral reports on definite topics of special interest to them.

12. Have many projects going on around the classroom (science experiments, games, seatwork exercises, etc.).

13. Take time to point out and discuss figurative, idiomatic, and picturesque language. Encourage children to find other examples of these forms.

14. Have children describe a place or activity in one word and tell why the word is an appropriate description.

15. Use seatwork activities such as matching questions with answers in lists, paragraphs with titles, words with their synonyms (or antonyms), and pictures with sentences (or words or paragraphs). Other seatwork activities include using selections in which the main idea is to be found, details related to the main idea listed, directions followed, an inference that is justified stated, or a conclusion written.

16. Have children prepare short oral or written summaries of science experiments or social studies units.

17. Have children fill in from words in a list missing words (usually every fifth word) in paragraphs whose content is not too unfamiliar to them.

Reading Rates

Not all reading should be done as rapidly as possible. The type of thinking the content requires should determine the rate of reading. Thus, much of the problem in developing effective reading rates centers on helping the child to recognize the type of reading required—appreciative, critical, or informative. Talk with the children about how different materials, such as newspaper articles, cartoons, science experiments, arithmetic problems, and social studies books, should be read. This kind of discussion gives focus to reading purposes.

Give attention to reading rates in the middle grades (combine with teaching the use of a stopwatch and the computation of averages).

In addition, direct attention should be given to increasing reading rates. Try timed reading activities. Pick selections with words the pupils are likely to know and have them read for one or two minutes (gradually increasing the amount of time). Then have the pupils count the number of words read and divide by the number of minutes to get their reading rate per minute. Some testing of comprehension should accompany these exercises.

Oral Reading

An Oral Reading Guide

1. Make sure there is a purpose.
2. Prepare in advance and practice.
3. Read carefully and clearly.
4. Speak loudly enough to be heard.
5. Read with appropriate expression.

Oral reading, in contrast to silent reading, is slow, requires the pronouncing of each word, and is inefficient for many purposes. Its indiscriminate use in a classroom can do much to develop bad reading and listening habits. It is most indefensible in reading activities of the "round robin" or "barber shop" type in which children in a group "follow along" while they wait for their turn to read aloud. Oral reading, nevertheless, is a form of communication and has a place in the classroom.

There are two types of oral reading: (1) sight reading, in which the reader has not prepared for the oral presentation; and (2) prepared oral reading for communication to and/or enjoyment of an audience. The first type can legitimately be used to determine a child's ability in (1) recognizing and pronouncing words and enunciating their sounds and (2) phrasing and observing of punctuation marks in the content. This type of oral reading should be done individually, with only the teacher for an audience. It is for

Reading orally into a tape recorder and then listening to the tape can be a useful activity.

assessment and guidance as to what teaching needs to be done. The second type of oral reading calls for preparation so that what is read effectively relates a story, proves a point in a discussion, answers specific questions, announces something, or seeks to give enjoyment or create feelings, such as in dramatic and choral situations. It is communicating to an audience.

Oral reading of the second type requires that the reader not only recognize the words and understand the content but convey this understanding to the audience. Because of the need to convey understanding, silent reading (except as noted above) should always precede oral reading so that vocabulary and meaning problems are resolved before the reader faces the audience.

Attitudes Toward Reading

Reading ability is of little significance if people do not use it to read. A reading program that does not result in a great deal of reading of all kinds of materials cannot be judged successful. Large numbers of educated adults do no more reading than is absolutely necessary. This is unacceptable in a democracy and detrimental to the quality of everyday life.

There are many possible ways to stimulate children to read. Some specific ones such as Sustained Silent Reading and the provision of a wide variety of reading materials in the classroom have already been discussed. Other possibilities include the following:

1. Show interest yourself. When an interesting question comes up, seek out relevant reading material.
2. Talk with children casually about something you have read or are reading.
3. Find out what your students need to do to obtain a card at the public library and help them to do so.
4. Work with school and public librarians on programs to encourage reading.
5. Bring in a rug, an easy chair, or some pillows for a classroom reading area (see also suggestions about a reading corner in Chapter 15).
6. Make a special effort to identify books in the school library that might be of interest to your pupils.
7. Dramatize portions of popular books, do art activities depicting favorite characters or scenes, and select music to be played in the background as particular texts are read aloud.

INFLUENCES ON READING INSTRUCTION

Reading programs have had common elements over the years, but at different times some influences have been more significant than others. Basal series have been extremely important, and it is likely that they will continue to be central to reading instruction. These materials do undergo some changes from time to time, however. Developments in teaching methods and curriculum planning are also influential and merit attention.

Reading in an informal setting is enjoyable.

Basal Reading Series

Discussed in Chapter 4 and earlier in this chapter, basal reading series provide a sequential presentation of skills, abilities, and understandings and a plan for teaching them. This approach to the teaching of reading has been so widely adopted in elementary schools that estimates of the extent of its use are around the 90-percent level. Reading series became popular more than fifty years ago when "developmental reading" was defined as the process of growth youngsters go through in moving from reading readiness to initial instruction based on whole words and very simple texts, to independence and identification of unfamiliar words, to wide reading of many types of materials, and, finally, to mature reading and the knowledge of how to study. The teaching of all of this, or at least a significant proportion, was included in early basal reading series.

The first reading series were sets of books that gradually increased in difficulty, one for each grade level. Then practice materials or workbooks were added, and now basal series (often called "systems") include students' texts (sometimes more than one per grade level), teachers' manuals or guides to instruction, workbooks, materials for duplicating practice sheets, filmstrips, audio and video tapes, tests, charts, and computer programs. Not surprisingly, their complexity and wide use have made basal series in

Millions of children have learned to read from instruction based on basal series, but some have not.

reading thought of as one of the major enterprises in our educational system.

Over the years basals have been criticized for a variety of reasons. For example, male and female characters were often portrayed quite differently, males being depicted as active and adventurous and females as passive and timid. Also, the family situations on which most beginning reading selections were based consisted of an employed father and a mother at home with two or three children in a nice house where a dog and cat also resided. In most cases there were no characters who seemed to be from minority-group backgrounds or even lived in cities. But these things have changed, so much so that a different group of critics has complained that girls and women are not being represented as sufficiently "feminine" and that minority-group members are unrealistically overrepresented.

In general, basal series take a moderate position in terms of teaching methods, but criticism has also led to changes in this area. Some time ago, basals were faulted for giving too little attention to phonics, so phonics were added—to an extent that seemed to some observers to be excessive, especially at the beginning instructional level. More recently, the content of basals was criticized as being mostly composed of unappealing stories manufactured for the purpose of presenting certain words and particular skills. Such materials were unfavorably compared with "real" literature, stories whose language was more expressive and whose plots and characters were more interesting and memorable. The publishers of several series then began to select content written by widely known authors.

Another concern about basals is that their teachers' guides must, of necessity, be quite prescriptive in describing what the teacher is to do in a detailed way. This may be helpful to a beginning teacher or to someone teaching at a particular grade level for the first time. When a teacher has taught the same program for several years, however, the chances are good that she or he will have excellent ideas for learning activities that would be an improvement on those of the basal series. Such initiative is not always encouraged, and it can be quite frustrating when school policies requiring strict adherence to the series limit the more imaginative teachers. Such regulations exist because of a mistaken belief that only total implementation of the published materials will guarantee maximum achievement by the children. Attempting to do everything recommended in a basal series is likely to be an impossible goal, however. The amount of material contained in the children's books, teachers' manuals, and ancillary teaching aids is so large that all the activities could be conducted only if very nearly the entire school day were devoted to reading lessons.

Increasingly, though, as teachers demonstrate thorough knowledge of reading methods and have opportunities to exercise their professional judgment, basal series are viewed more as anchors and general outlines than as recipes to be strictly followed in daily teaching. You may well consult your basal series for a description of major points to be concerned with at your grade level and use these to establish the essential features of the classroom program. It will be obvious that much of this content can be taught through Sustained Silent Reading, individualization, interest groups, and reading lessons imbedded in all subject areas of the curriculum.

Literature and the Reading Program

As was just noted, basal series increasingly include many literature selections. Such content is important because it introduces children to aspects of our cultural heritage and encourages them to read more widely. These benefits are not nearly as likely to be realized if most materials are written specifically for a basal series, but some series do contain a very high proportion of literature-based content—stories, plays, essays, and poems.

In some situations teachers have largely done away with basal series and developed in their place classroom reading programs based entirely on literature. School systems that take such an approach usually have a plan that specifies certain stories and books for particular grade levels and supplies teachers with instructions as to how to guide the reading. This means that multiple copies of the chosen books must be made available—a dozen or so for small groups and class-sized sets where appropriate.

Whatever the organization, an emphasis on literature in the reading program seems to have several advantages:

Books by Moss and by Somers and Worthington (listed in the References) present many examples of how reading abilities can be improved through the use of literature.

1. Works of literature are more fully developed than basal materials and therefore more likely to capture children's interest.
2. Literature is written because authors are trying to communicate ideas important to them; reading is then a genuine writer/audience interaction.
3. The child's imagination is much more likely to be stimulated by a time-honored work of literature than by a basal selection.
4. The wider vocabulary and more expressive language of literature make a significant contribution to a child's cultural education.
5. Students are introduced to stories, characters, and authors that they will remember all their lives.
6. They are also learning about literature as a field of study, becoming familiar with forms of writing, story plots, character development, and dialogue.
7. Literature touches children's lives in significant ways—their hopes, fears, sense of humor, and personal experiences.

Relationships Between Reading and Writing

As was discussed in Chapters 9 and 10, there are advantages to exploring relationships between writing and reading. As children write, they reread their own texts, and when doing this, they want to know whether or not what they have written makes sense and does what they had hoped. If they have had many experiences in judging printed texts—noting, for example, the presence of a main idea, the use of supporting data in an argument, and the logical ordering of paragraphs—they will be more likely to use such features in their own writing.

When children read, they have many experiences related to writing; in turn composition skills relate to reading abilities. Consider the following:

- In the early stages of writing children spell some words the way they sound; this provides experience in thinking about letter/sound relationships.
- Since children will think about using just the right word to convey meaning

as they write, they will be more likely to notice when an author has made a good choice.

- Young writers who try to construct good sentences, paragraphs, and texts should notice when another writer has been particularly effective or ineffective.
- Readers who write see more readily how other writers use quotations, dialogue, and other features to make their texts interesting and lively.
- Doing sentence combining in their own writing may help students more readily comprehend complex sentences in what they read.

EVALUATION OF READING PERFORMANCE

Because children's reading achievement is considered so important in our society, there is a great deal of attention to evaluation of their progress. In many states and districts, assessment of reading ability is mandatory at several times during the elementary years. In addition, tests are included in the published reading programs, and informal evaluations are done by teachers. Most testing is intended to furnish information to interested groups: parents, school boards, state officials, national agencies or groups, administrators, and district supervisors. Different evaluation procedures other than testing are more likely to be useful to the classroom teacher in making daily decisions about the class and individual children. Also important is the fact that the children themselves ought to know whether they are gaining in ability. The various types of assessment for these several purposes and groups may be classified as either formal or informal in nature.

Informal Procedures

Informal assessment refers to those types of procedures that examine the reading behavior of children in activities that closely resemble the actual reading situation.

Observation. Observation of each child during reading should be continual, of course, with the teacher noting behavior during lessons. There should, though, be some system to this assessment by observation so that the results will be recalled accurately in planning instruction. This system can be very simple. A stack of notecards or a notebook with a page for each child is all that is needed to make notes on word identification problems, failure to observe punctuation marks (and which ones), phrasing difficulties in oral reading, and so on. The notations made should be as specific as possible since future instruction should be based on them. The alert teacher will observe children's reading at all times during the school day, noting such things as the use or nonuse of a dictionary or reference sources, library books chosen (and whether they are actually read), and problems a child appears to have in doing seatwork.

Individual reading lessons and interviews make possible detailed notations. Frequent interviews with children in which they talk about what they have been reading and problems they have had are especially useful both for noting something that has not been observed earlier and for providing clues about things to watch for in future observations.

Observation results may also be recorded in checklists and charts. Using these may simplify the noting of things observed. For example, children's names may be listed on a checklist that provides spaces for checking how each one is achieving in using various decoding skills or in reading for details, main ideas, and so forth. Teachers often have two or three types of checklists in order to note items related to all of the program objectives. Examples of types of checklists are given in other chapters.

Informal Reading Inventories (rev. ed.) by Johnson, Kress, and Pikulski (International Reading Association, 1987) contains many useful suggestions.

Inventories. Informal reading inventories, or "running records," of a child's reading ability may be used to determine levels of performance and to identify specific difficulties. These procedures involve taking careful note of how a child reads a particular selection orally. The notations are usually done in a systematic way and require some practice on the part of the observer, who writes on a duplicate copy of the passage read by the child. Texts at several levels of difficulty should be used, since one of the objectives of this assessment is to determine what the reader does as the material becomes more complex. How the child actually reads the selection—substitutions, omissions, inversions of word order, repetition, miscallings, and refusals—must be recorded and carefully studied for evidence as to the strategies the child uses well or poorly. (You may wish to use audio or even video recordings occasionally, especially if a child's reading problems are particularly puzzling and will require the help of a specialist.) Selections may also be read silently and followed by questions and discussion; this enables you to further assess the child's capacity to comprehend what has been read.

Formal Procedures

For a comprehensive discussion of reading tests, see *How to Increase Reading Ability* by Harris and Sipay (listed in the References).

Formal assessment generally involves testing a number of students at the same time, although such tests can be used with a single individual. The tests are usually administered to classroom groups, and the same procedures are followed in every administration so that the results will be comparable. The tasks presented are generally reading isolated words or answering question about a short passage—activities that may not resemble actual reading very closely.

Basal Reading Tests. Tests are included with basal series as part of the set of materials. These tests are usually "criterion referenced," which means that they are designed to reveal whether or not students have gained particular understandings or can perform specific tasks that have been included in the teaching program. If you use this approach, you administer the test after finishing a particular section of the reading textbook; the results should tell you the extent to which individual students, as well as the class or group, learned what was presented and point out specific needs for additional study in areas identified as deficient.

Standardized Reading Tests. Standardized tests are usually administered in order to obtain information concerning how results from an individual, class, or larger group compare with those from a large sample of similar students. Such tests are described as "norm referenced," since norms have been developed from the scores of many children from the same grade level. A student's score may be the same as the average for others at his or her grade level, somewhat above or below, or substantially above or below.

A widely used but misleading way to report results from such tests is by means of grade-level equivalents. For instance, a child in the fourth grade (4.0) might do very well on a standardized test and be reported as reading at the eighth-grade level (8.0). This does not mean that the child should be given eighth-grade books to read, nor does it mean that the pupil scored as well on the test as the average eighth-grader. All that such a result should legitimately be interpreted as meaning is that the child is a very good reader—something her or his teacher ought to know without giving the test. Grade-level equivalents are used in reporting the results of achievement testing because school systems and state agencies find them convenient.

See also *Reading: What Can Be Measured?* by Roger Farr and Robert F. Carey (International Reading Association, 1986).

Of greater significance than grade-level equivalents are percentiles, numbers that tell that a child scoring at, for example, the thirty-eighth percentile did as well as or better than about 38 percent of the group on which results were systematically collected and less well than about 62 percent of that group.

There are many reading achievement tests on the market and selecting one is a complex task. How the test was formulated, the nature of the group on which norms have been based, the ease with which it can be administered and scored, and the extent to which it is consistent with program objectives should all be considered important factors. A significant problem regarding the use of such tests is that teachers and others who receive the results of testing must be careful when interpreting what they mean and how they might legitimately be used.

A FINAL WORD

Sometimes, because of society's concern about children learning to read, teachers become too anxious about the very important task of teaching reading, and they use materials and spend time and effort that may not actually help. Reading is a complex process, but it is one that every child of reasonably normal intelligence can and should learn. The language arts are inextricably interrelated, and therefore suggestions are included in almost every chapter in this book that in reality bear on the teaching of reading.

This chapter has emphasized two major concerns for the elementary-school reading program: children ought to read with enjoyment, and what they read should mean something to them. The use of a teaching plan that lists hundreds of supposedly essential skills or specific behaviors every child must master before reading is possible will make it all too easy to lose sight of the truly important goals. Worse yet, some educators argue that children cannot possibly read without having learned skill *x* and that skill *y* certainly must precede *x*. This is fallacious. Many successful adult readers apparently lack some of these specific skills, and some four-year-olds read moderately well but cannot pass skills tests. There are, you should bear in mind, few hard-and-fast rules about teaching reading; if you strive to help children love to read, you will have made a significant contribution to society.

References

Alvermann, Donna E.; Dillon, Deborah R.; and O'Brien, David G. *Using Discussion to Promote Reading Comprehension.* International Reading Association, 1987.

Anderson, Richard C.; Hiebert, Elfrieda H.; Scott, Judith A.; and Wilkinson, Ian A. G. *Becoming a Nation of Readers.* U.S. Department of Education, 1984.

Choate, J. S., and Rakes, T. A. *Detecting and Correcting Special Needs in Reading.* Allyn and Bacon, 1988.

Cooper, J. David. *Improving Reading Comprehension.* Houghton Mifflin, 1986.

Cullinan, Bernice E., ed. *Children's Literature in the Reading Program.* International Reading Association, 1987.

Ekwall, Eldon E., and Shanker, James L. *Teaching Reading in the Elementary School.* Charles E. Merrill, 1985.

Finn, Patrick J. *Helping Children Learn to Read.* Random House, 1985.

Hansen, Jane. *When Writers Read.* Heinemann, 1987.

Harris, Albert J., and Sipay, Edward R. *How to Increase Reading Ability: A Guide to Developmental and Remedial Methods,* 8th ed. Longman, 1985.

Jewell, Margaret Greer, and Zintz, Miles V. *Learning to Read Naturally.* Kendall/Hunt, 1986.

Karlin, Robert, and Karlin, Andrea. *Teaching Elementary Reading,* 4th ed. Harcourt Brace Jovanovich, 1987.

Laughlin, Mildred Knight, and Watt, Letty S. *Developing Learning Skills Through Children's Literature.* Oryx Press, 1986.

Moss, Joy F. *Focus Units in Literature: A Handbook for Elementary School Teachers.* National Council of Teachers of English, 1984.

Reinking, David, ed. *Reading and Computers.* Teachers College Press, 1987.

Searfoss, Lyndon W., and Readence, John E. *Helping Children Learn to Read.* Prentice-Hall, 1985.

Somers, Albert B., and Worthington, Janet Evans. *Response Guides for Teaching Children's Books.* National Council of Teachers of English, 1979.

Strickland, Dorothy S.; Feeley, Joan; and Wepner, Shelly. *Using Computers in the Teaching of Reading.* Teachers College Press, 1987.

Tinker, Miles A., and McCullough, Constance M. *Teaching Elementary Reading,* 4th ed. Prentice-Hall, 1975.

Tway, Eileen, *Writing Is Reading: 26 Ways to Connect.* National Council of Teachers of English, 1985.

Vacca, J. L.; Vacca, R. T.; and Gove, M. K. *Reading and Learning to Read.* Little, Brown, 1987.

Teaching Resources

KITS

Clues for Better Reading. Curriculum Associates (grades 1–5).

Developing Reading Power. Zaner-Bloser (grades 3–6).

Fantastic Reading. Dale Seymour (grades 5–6).

Reading Laboratory. Science Research Associates (several kits, with cassettes, teacher's handbook, and booklets; various grade levels).

Society for Visual Education produces kits for primary and upper grades that focus on comprehension (each has filmstrips, audio cassettes, skill sheets, and a guide).

LITERATURE SETS

Bridges. Scholastic (K–grade 6).

I Can Read Book and Cassette Library. Harper & Row (twenty-four storybooks and audio cassettes).

Language Works. Modern Curriculum Press (all grade levels).

MCP Literature. Modern Curriculum Press (grades 3–6).

Odyssey. Harcourt Brace Jovanovich (K–grade 6).

Quest Extenders. Scholastic (study guides; grades 4–6).

COMPUTER SOFTWARE

Cloze Plus. Milliken, 1983 (grades 1–6).

The Comprehension Connection. Milliken (grades 4–6).

Comprehension Power. Milliken (grades 4–6).

Context Clues. The Learning Well, 1984 (grades 1–4).

Customized Alphabet Drill. Random House (grades 1–6).

Explore-a-Story. D.C. Heath (K–grade 5).

Kittens, Kids, and a Frog. Hartley (primary grades).

Microcourse Reading. Houghton Mifflin (grades 3–6).

Mystery Mazes. Educational Activities (intermediate grades).

Reading to Learn. Society for Visual Education, 1986 (grades 3–6).

Return to Reading Series. Media Basics, 1984 (grades 4 up).

Snoopy's Reading Machine. Random House (primary grades).

Sound Ideas. Houghton Mifflin, 1986 (grades 1–4).

Speed Reader II. Davidson (intermediate grades).

Stickybear Reading Comprehension. Weekly Reader (grades 1–6).

Success with Reading. Scholastic, 1985 (grades 3–6).

Word Detective. Sunburst (grades 1–6).

Writing to Read. IBM, 1984 (intermediate grades).

FILMSTRIPS AND VIDEOTAPES

Encyclopedia Britannica has several collections of stories on sound filmstrips, including the following:

America's Legendary Heroes (intermediate grades), *Famous American Stories* (intermediate grades), and *Four for Fun!* (kindergarten and primary grades).

Fantastic Series. Thomas S. Klise (series of five filmstrips; intermediate grades).

Mythology. Thomas S. Klise (series of four filmstrips; intermediate grades).

Teaching Reading Comprehension. WETN (3319 West Beltline Highway, Madison, WI 53613-2899. Fourteen 30-minute videos; grades 1–4).

The Writing Company distributes videotapes of such children's favorites as *Charlotte's Web, Heidi, The Hobbit, The Jungle Book, Old Yeller, The Red Pony, Where the Red Fern Grows,* and *The Yearling.*

BOOKS

McCracken, Robert A., and McCracken, Marlene J. *Stories, Songs, and Poetry for Teaching Reading and Writing.* American Library Association, 1986.

Moore, David W.; Readence, John E.; and Rickelman, Robert J. *Prereading Activities for Content Area Reading and Learning.* International Reading Association, 1982.

Rowell, Elizabeth, and Goodkind, Thomas B. *Teaching the Pleasures of Reading.* Prentice-Hall, 1982.

OTHER RESOURCES

Guinness Toucan Books for children eight and older include *Bullet Trains and Underwater Tricyles . . . and Other Amazing Mechanical Records* and *Bomber Bats and Flying Frogs . . . and Other Amazing Animal Records.* Sterling Publishing, 1986.

Little Books for children five to twelve include such titles as *The Great Wild Egg Hunt* and *The Bee That Could Never Be Killed.* Children's Art Foundation.

Spotlight on Vocabulary. Random House (books for grades 3 to 8).

TV and Movie Tie-Ins. Creative Education, 1983 (set of seven books that deal with movies and/or TV shows).

Activities for Preservice Teachers

1. Examine the teacher's manuals of several basal reading series for a particular grade level. How are word-attack skills taught? How much emphasis is there on phonics? What recommendations are made

concerning the methods of teaching phonics? What do the manuals include on diagnosis and evaluation?

2. Select two standardized tests that have reading sections (*Stanford Achievement Test, Metropolitan Achievement Test,* or *Iowa Test of Basic Skills,* for example) for examination. What aspects of reading are covered by these tests? What kinds of tasks are pupils asked to do? How are the results compiled and reported?

3. Compare two or three basal reading series, focusing on how much literature is included. Are there fables, poems, legends, and so on? What authors are represented? Does it appear that the selections have been extensively rewritten for use in the basals?

4. Examine several computer programs designed to teach reading or to supplement reading instruction. Do you think that children would enjoy using them? How effective do you believe they would be for teaching reading skills, compared to other possible activities?

5. Interview teachers with twenty or more years of experience in teaching reading. Ask them to describe some of the changes they have seen in reading pro-

grams during this time. Also ask them what teaching problems still persist.

6. Find out if there is a chapter of Literacy Volunteers or other comparable agency in your community and explore the possibility of participating in helping adults learn to read.

7. Observe a reading group in a particular classroom for a week or more. What are the principal activities? What variations in the lesson does the teacher use? Do the pupils appear to be paying attention and learning? How much actual reading do they do? How are they prepared for doing seatwork?

8. With some other college students, check your own reading rate, comprehension level, quality of oral reading, and other skills. Identify some areas you need to work on and see how much you can improve in a month or two.

9. Choose a grade level for which you can design exercises for finding the main idea, selecting important details, and understanding the organization of a selection. Compare what you have developed with commercial workbooks and worksheets.

Activities for Inservice Teachers

1. Examine your classroom program for opportunities to include realistic oral reading activities. For example, pupils might read directions to one another, a child could read selections from a favorite book in an attempt to get classmates interested in it, or two pupils might read actors' parts from a scene in a play.

2. Try having a Sustained Silent Reading period in your class daily for two weeks. If it seems to be successful, invite the principal or reading teacher to participate occasionally.

3. Visit a curriculum materials center, district reading office, or library to find out what reading-related computer programs are available for examination. Select some to try out yourself for possible inclusion in your program.

4. Conduct a survey of reading interests in your class, and then work with a school or public librarian to see how many relevant titles can be made available to your pupils over the course of several months.

5. See what can be done in your school district to divert funds from the purchase of practice materials to

library books. If changes in the law are necessary, find out how that might be accomplished.

6. Attend meetings of a local group of teachers affiliated with the International Reading Association. Find out what the benefits are of being a member at local, state, and national levels.

7. Consider having your two or three top readers and the same number of those with serious problems meet with you individually rather than as members of their regular groups. Plan some activities for these students but mostly emphasize the reading of books they have selected. If this seems successful, add others to this program of individualized reading.

8. Organize a "book fair" if your school does not already have one. Pupils can be involved by making posters about their favorite books. An author of children's books might be available to make an appearance. Bookstores and public libraries may be willing to participate.

9. Develop a plan for keeping parents informed about your reading program and about how they can help.

10. Work with the school librarian to assemble a list of books related to stories in the basal series you use or topics in other subject areas. Send these lists home with the children with a note encouraging parents to extend the school's reading program using some of these books.

Independent Activities for Children

1. Provide paragraphs in which a few words that may be unfamiliar to children are represented by blank spaces. (Make sure the content of each paragraph is of interest to the children.) A child reading such a paragraph attempts to understand what it says. Provide some way (perhaps by writing them on the back sides of the paragraph sheets or cards) for the child to find out what the omitted words are. The purpose is to show the significance of context in reading.

2. During Sustained Silent Reading children can identify particularly exciting, funny, or affecting parts of books that they can later read aloud to a partner or small group.

3. Children can work in pairs reading stories and re-writing them:
   a. From a different point of view
   b. In another setting
   c. With a different ending

4. Better readers can be introduced to genre reading in which they read nothing but Greek and Roman myths for a while, then science fiction, and then something else. This works best if children work as partners or in a small group.

5. Partners may read orally to one another. The listener should ask questions and attempt to predict what will come next in the story being read.

6. Activities such as the following can be done by individual children or small groups for practice in structural analysis:
   a. Match cards that have root words written on them with other cards containing prefixes or suffixes.
   b. Write the missing inflectional suffixes in sentences, for example:

   We are go____ to town.
   This is the small____ of the three balls.

   Put such sentences on cards and place them in a file.
   c. Prepare cards containing various words with common base forms. Have the child separate the cards into base-word categories. Words might be *green, greener, greenest; report, portal, portage, import;* and so on.

   d. Word cards can be sorted into those with particular endings (*-ed, -ing, -ness,* etc.), particular combinations of letters (*ake, ime,* etc.), or particular beginnings (*b, gr, str,* etc.).

7. Supply children with maps, graphs and charts suited to their level and ask them to interpret the information provided.

8. Activities can be constructed to provide practice in auditory discrimination and letter/sound association.
   a. Prepare sets of unlabeled pictures. A child can then group them according to the initial or final sound of their names.
   b. A child can sort words on cards according to the number of syllables in the words, words containing syllables that begin with a particular letter, those that rhyme, and so forth.

9. Prepare a bulletin board (one the children can reach) on which each section shows a letter or combination of letters. On each section thumbtack a box. Children can find pictures of objects whose names begin with the letters and place them in the correct boxes. This activity can be varied. For example, instead of showing letters, the bulletin board sections can contain pictures. Another variation is to find pictures of things whose names have ending sounds that match the letters on the board.

10. Children who like a particular character in a story may enjoy making a puppet of that character and dramatizing some scenes from the story.

11. To give individual children reading practice, prepare cards that children can read and then respond to by:
   a. Writing answers to questions about the selection
   b. Following directions
   c. Listing particular details given in the selection

12. Place small pictures from magazines or ones that you draw on three-by-five cards. Print the name of what is pictured on each card. With enough of these cards children can make up their own games, for example, matching pairs of homonyms, homophones, antonyms, or synonyms. After you get them started, children can make or find pictures to add to the set.

Chapter *13*

Reading and Studying

Study skills are not the exclusive domain of the language arts program. They are an integral part of teaching—and learning—in every curriculum area and at every grade level. When a kindergarten teacher asks "When we go out to peek at the nest in the big mulberry bush, what are we going to look for? How will we have to behave?" he or she is laying the foundation for good study procedure by helping the children to set both purpose and method. In the fourth grade a teacher may say "Before you start to write, *think* about your subject; draw a topic web or just make a list of the things you want to include. Then decide what should come first, second, and so on." This teacher is helping children to organize. Both are guiding children to familiarity with techniques that will aid them in learning effectively and independently. Providing this guidance is one of a teacher's most important tasks.

LEARNING TO STUDY

Parents are too frequently told by a teacher, "Your daughter would do better if she worked harder." But the meaning of "working harder" may not be clear to the student or her parents. They may assume that it means she needs to spend *more time* studying—and possibly it does. However, it may also mean that what she really needs is to learn *how to study*.

Study skills are an integral part of the instructional approach described in Chapter 2—especially as related to information processing.

Results of a great deal of investigation and testing demonstrate that elementary-school children do rather well in the basics of reading, that is, word recognition and the other abilities described in Chapter 12. Too often, however, children do not know how to read for information or what to do with information they have. Yet these skills, as well as others associated with them, are vital to success in school—and beyond. Thus it is the responsibility of the school to teach children how to study—how to read for different purposes, locate information they need, take notes, and organize information into meaningful reports, demonstrations, or discussions. Closely allied to these skills are the abilities to read, listen, and observe critically and to relate new information to what is already known.

Helping children acquire the skills and abilities they need to approach their tasks efficiently and successfully will almost surely have two-fold results: not only will their academic work improve, but, since we all enjoy what we do well, they should become more interested and participate more in class activities. This chapter discusses the particular skills needed and suggests ways in which they may be taught.

Assignments

Well-made assignments are essential if effective instruction is to occur.

Studying usually grows out of assignments, which, when properly made, lead naturally into activities—usually reading—that have a good chance of being successful. The assignment should be something more than a chalkboard notice that reads "Social Studies—read pages 140–145." It ought to be part of a comprehensive teaching plan designed to integrate purposeful reading with other modes of learning. And, of course, there should be several reading sources so that children of different ability levels can be accommodated.

To be truly meaningful, an assignment must guide study so that the desired learnings will occur. It should tell the child *what* he or she is supposed to do, *why* it is to be done, and *how* it is to be done. This requires more than simply assigning page numbers; it includes providing motivation, filling in necessary background, and giving specific purposes for the lesson. Suppose, for example, that pages 140–145 in the social studies text concern the colonial Southeast. The assignment might involve the following three steps:

I. *Motivation*: This could take the form of discussion centered around questions such as the following:
   A. When we talked about the colonization of the New World, we discussed how the different colonies were founded. Do you remember how Virginia and the Carolinas began? What about Georgia and Florida?
   B. Do you suppose life in the southern colonies was the same as that in New England or different? In what ways might it have been different?
   C. What is the climate like in the South? Might this have anything to do with the crops they raised and the way they made their living?
   D. We know that slavery developed in the South rather than in the North. Can you guess why?

II. *Background*: This might include briefly reviewing pertinent facts that the children may have forgotten, possibly listing the names of the southern colonies, and introducing new terms and vocabulary.

III. *Specific Purposes*: No assignment is complete until the children have specific things to look for as they read. You might duplicate or write on the board several questions to guide their reading, you might use some or all of the questions that are found at the end of a section or chapter in the text, or you might suggest the following procedure:
   A. As you read, notice the headings in dark print. Turn each of these into a question and see if you can answer it in one or two sentences. For instance, on page 141 you see the heading "Important Money Crops in the Southeast." Turn this into a question: What were the important money crops in the Southeast? Read the paragraph and see if you can answer the question in one sentence.
   B. As you read, try to discover one particular topic that you would like to find out more about and report on to the rest of the class. A list of suggestions is on the board, but you may be able to think of another topic that would make a good report.

The above example not only illustrates one way of making an assignment meaningful but also demonstrates how the language arts can be related to one another and to all curriculum areas. Since pupils need to use study skills in many different classroom activities, they need to be *taught* those skills. The particular assignment described above, for example, gives rise to the need to use the library (Chapter 14) and to use such reading skills as locating information, skimming a text, finding the main idea and related details, and answering specific questions. Writing may also be involved as pupils attempt to present what they have learned. The writing may consist of answers to the questions, notes taken concerning the answers to the questions, or a report on some aspect of the reading. And the studying will present opportunities to use other aspects of the language arts—speaking, listening, spelling, and so on. As with any skill, actual use of study skills makes their learning more meaningful.

The three steps in the example assignment—providing motivation, furnishing needed background, and outlining specific purposes—are vital to every type of assignment at all grade levels. These general steps can be adapted to suit almost any kind of learning activity—solving an arithmetic problem, planning a field trip, or setting up a science experiment. Obviously, variety can and should be introduced; nothing could be duller than to have nearly every lesson presented in exactly the same manner. Providing

Studying together is often helpful to children.

motivation as well as background, for example, might involve reading a story or poem, bringing in some stimulating pictures, looking at a videotape, or simply saying to the class something like "We decided to write for materials for our work on electricity. What do we need to do?" Provide variety in specific purposes as well; converting topic headings into questions is a valuable study technique, but children would soon lose interest if they were required to do that with every heading in a textbook.

Study Steps

SQ3R stands for *Survey, Question, Read, Recite,* and *Review.* The other acronyms denote similar study plans.

In addition to the guidance provided in assignments, a child in the middle grades needs help in learning certain study steps to use either in reading a textbook or in doing independent reading. A number of systems for reading and retaining written material have been advanced, and in keeping with current fashion, most are known by acronyms, for example, PQRST, POINT, EVOKER, and SQ3R. The number of steps in these varies, but for most purposes good study procedure boils down to four basic points:

1. *Preview*: Read the introduction if there is one. Look at section headings, pictures, maps, graphs, and so on. This will help you get an idea of what the chapter (selection, unit, story) is about.
2. *Purpose*: Read the questions at the end of the chapter (and/or questions prepared by the teacher as a part of the assignment) *before* reading the chapter itself. This will help you to know what kind of information you are looking for—it establishes a purpose for reading.
3. *Read*: Read the chapter carefully, keeping in mind the questions to be answered.
4. *Review*: Read the questions again, and see if you can answer them. If not, review necessary sections. Or, look at section headings again, turn each into a question, and try to answer it in one or two sentences. For some assignments or for particularly difficult material, you may wish to use both of these methods.

When these steps are first introduced, children often think they are time-consuming and therefore not worth using. But if you can persuade them to try this method, they will discover that they read faster because they know what information they are looking for, and that they are better prepared to take part in discussions or to report on their reading.

Children should also be shown that these steps can be adapted to many kinds of assignments and activities and can help them in many ways. The preview technique can be adapted for selecting a book for pleasure reading—a child might read the first few paragraphs, look at chapter headings and illustrations, and perhaps skim a page or two here and there to get a fairly reliable impression of whether he or she would enjoy reading the book. Or the child might use this technique to discover whether a particular article or book contains the information needed for a report. In this way, children may learn how to avoid wasting time reading something that is not suited to their particular purposes.

In a similar way, children may learn that establishing purposes for read-

Discourage reading merely to find answers to specific questions through thought-provoking questions that call for more than factual information and discussions centering around *why, how, what was the result*, etc.

ing—that is, beginning with specific questions in mind—is also time-saving. The child who knows what he or she is looking for and who uses the preview method will be able to prepare a better report because the time spent will be devoted to fruitful efforts.

Further, the review step furnishes an excellent way to study for tests. Far too many students, even in high school and college, spend the night before an exam trying frantically to reread all the material covered; using the suggested review procedure will not only refresh one's memory but will reveal those sections that do need to be read more closely.

Learning Logs

By the time they reach the middle grades, students may be encouraged to keep "learning logs" to aid them in their studies. In his or her log a child keeps a record of assignments, sources of information, study questions and notes, suggested topics for writing reports, lists of vocabulary words and personal spelling "demons," and—especially if children do their own evaluations—records of achievement in various subject areas.

Encourage pupils to use their logs to record questions that come to mind as they study. These may be points requiring clarification or topics for discussion or further reading.

The log should not be confused with the journal, which should contain a variety of writings, both finished and unfinished, including some that are private. The log, on the other hand, should be highly organized, perhaps by subject or interest area. Materials in it should be arranged in an orderly fashion so that it will be useful for study or review and needed information can be found quickly. The log, then, should be separate from the journal, although both may be kept in the same notebook, especially if it is a loose-leaf one allowing the use of dividers and the insertion or removal of pages.

Learning logs can also provide a focus for regular teacher/pupil conferences. They can give both you and the child additional insight into problems and progress, as well as reveal the skills or abilities that need to be taught or reinforced.

LOCATING INFORMATION

In addition to learning how to study texts, children need to know how they can locate information they need and record what they find in a form that will be useful. Library-related skills are thoroughly discussed in Chapter 14. The areas given attention in this section are using alphabetical order, becoming familiar with dictionaries, and taking notes.

Alphabetical Order

Children must know the alphabet thoroughly in order to use a telephone directory, a card catalog, a book index, an encyclopedia, or a dictionary efficiently. As younger children learn the alphabet, they may not immediately understand the importance of alphabetical order and why it is needed. They almost certainly cannot alphabetize when it requires referring to the second or third letter of each word; some adults fail at that. Older children

A major step in locating information is checking the card catalog.

often do not have the skill necessary to find items in an alphabetized listing or to arrange words in that way themselves.

Practice exercises for the initial learning of alphabetical order were given in Chapter 4. However, some children may need reinforcement of this learning. For these, keep a file of exercises such as those mentioned there, along with some that are more difficult—for example, ones involving clusters of letters with some missing (a b c _ e f or _ m n o p) or single letters that cue those that come before or after (_ x _ _ or _ _ _ j).

Most or all children in the late primary or middle grades will probably have to practice using alphabetical order in order to learn to do so quickly and efficiently, particularly when the use involves inspecting more than the initial letters of words. Activities such as the following should prove helpful:

Keep several alphabet sets on display during all alphabetizing activities.

1. Combine practice in using alphabetical order with handwriting practice in activities related to other curriculum areas. For example, pupils might list the names of green vegetables as a part of health study and then copy these in their notebooks in alphabetical order.

2. Have each reading group keep a dictionary to which individual children add their new words daily, placing each word neatly under the correct letter. These words will serve as a reading review and as a beginning dictionary for

a child to refer to for the spelling of a word needed in writing. Or, if you prefer, each child may keep a personal dictionary.

3. When teaching about the telephone, make a class directory in connection with a handwriting lesson. Children can copy the names and numbers from the board in alphabetical order, probably doing only a few each day until the directory is completed. Addresses may or may not be included, depending on the age of the children.

4. From the picture file, select pictures showing things whose names begin with a variety of letters. Hold up a picture, and let children tell you the name of the picture, the letter the name begins with, and whether that letter is found at the beginning, the middle, or the end of the alphabet. A card with this information on it can be stapled to the back of each picture so that children can play the game when they have free time. Or these cards can be separate, and children can match them with the pictures. Another alternative is to print vocabulary or spelling words on cards and use these to play the game described.

5. In small groups (possibly reading groups), have children play a game in which they try to open the dictionary to a given letter. The child who finds the letter first may call the next letter, or points might be given for opening closest to the right letter, finding it first, and so on.

6. After children know letter names and sequence, they can try to alphabetize words by second letters, and later by third letters. Using reading, vocabulary, or spelling words for this exercise will make it more meaningful and help to fix these words in the children's minds.

Dictionary Skills

Test yourself:

Can *you* turn quickly to the portion of a dictionary where a specific letter is located?

Although dictionary skills are usually emphasized in the middle grades, children should begin in the first grade to learn the uses of this valuable tool. Every primary classroom should have at least one picture dictionary, and children should have specific instruction in its use. Begin by making certain that they understand the relationship between the illustration and the printed word, as well as the arrangement of the words in the book. As they begin to write, help them to discover how the arrangement helps them to find words quickly and how the dictionary can help them to find the correct spelling of words they want to write.

As children progress through school, their knowledge and use of the dictionary will increase. In other words, dictionary usage is a developmental activity in which skills are taught, reinforced, and added to as children move through the elementary grades. These skills and understandings fall into four general categories.

The first category is that discussed in the preceding section—alphabetical order. Children should recognize early that not only dictionaries but nearly all other references they will use are arranged in alphabetical order not only by initial letters but by however many letters there are in the words. Thus, efficient use of a dictionary requires a virtually automatic familiarity with letter sequence, as well as with the relative positions of letters (the *d's* come in the first third of the dictionary, the *y's* in the final third, and so on).

The second category involves understanding the particular characteristics of the dictionary that aid one in using it efficiently. Children should learn to use guide words to locate the page on which a word may be found and that words are listed by their base forms (*have* is listed, but *having* is not).

The third category consists of pronunciation aids provided by the dictionary: accent marks, phonetic respellings, diacritical markings, and key words. In this connection, children also need to understand how syllabication is shown and how it is useful to pronunciation and to division of words in writing.

Finally, there is the wide variety of information other than definitions and pronunciations that the dictionary can provide. It may give abbreviations, synonyms, antonyms, and variant meanings of words; it may show related forms, irregular plurals, principal parts of irregular verbs, and meanings of prefixes; and it may contain many special features, such as tables of weights and measures, a gazetteer, a list of foreign words and phrases, and so forth.

Dictionary Activities. The activities suggested here are intended for several levels of dictionary users. There is a progression from the general and simple skills to the more specific, although many of the activities can be used in varying ways and at varying levels. Select those that appear suitable for the children in your class, and supplement them with others of your own devising as they are needed.

Some Elementary-Level Dictionaries

Houghton Mifflin Intermediate Dictionary, grades 3–6 (Houghton Mifflin, 1986)
Houghton Mifflin Primary Dictionary, grades 1–2 (Houghton Mifflin, 1986)
Macmillan Beginning Dictionary, grades 3–5 (Macmillan, 1987)
Macmillan School Dictionary, grades 5–8 (Macmillan, 1987)
My Second Picture Dictionary, grade 2 (Scott, Foresman, 1987)
School Dictionary, grades 5–6 (Macmillan, 1987)
Webster's Beginning Dictionary, grades 1–2 (American Book, 1980)

1. Point out the glossaries in books the children are using. Help children to develop the habit of looking up the word meanings needed for comprehension in reading.

2. As children progress in their dictionary skills, they may begin using a dictionary such as those listed on this page. Such dictionaries usually have sections explaining their use, and some have teacher's guides and/or exercises to give children practice in using dictionary skills.

3. Teach new vocabulary words associated with the dictionary itself. Show and explain *entry words, guide words*, and *definitions*. It might be helpful to make a bulletin board display or chart showing a sample page from the dictionary, with the guide words, entry words, and definitions labeled.

4. Have the children write on note cards questions that can be answered by using a dictionary and then exchange questions. Each child finds the answer, writes it on the back of the card along with the number of the page where the answer was found, and then reads it to the class. (Encourage good sentence formation, handwriting, capitalization, and punctuation on the cards.) Make a tree of knowledge on the bulletin board with these cards. The following are a few sample questions:

   Does a badger wear a badge?
   Does a foothill wear a shoe?
   Could a person play an oboe?

5. Select a list of words found in the children's readers. Have the children divide the words into syllables and place accent marks where they feel they should go. Then have them check their answers in the dictionary.

6. Randomly select a guide word from the dictionary and say the word. The first child to find that word gets to say a guide word for the others to locate.

7. Write phonetic spellings of several words on the board. Children are to determine what each word is and then write a sentence using it. Allow them to use the dictionary to check their answers.

8. Children can make their own glossaries of library, social studies, health, or science words.

9. Have the children learn a word a day, with each child getting a turn to select the word. The others locate it in the dictionary, discuss it, record the meaning(s) and part (or parts) of speech it may be, and write a sentence or two using it.

10. To develop speed in locating letters in the dictionary, give a letter name such as *I*. The child who opens to the letter *I* or closest to it gets to say the next letter.

11. Children in the upper intermediate grades should be taken to see the different dictionaries in the library. Allow them sufficient time to look through these and discover their special features.

12. Have children compare a dictionary with a thesaurus and list differences and similarities in both format and use.

Commercially published worksheets designed to reinforce dictionary skills can be time-savers, but make sure they fit the needs of your class.

Other Exercises. It will prove helpful to keep a file of dictionary exercises that may be used with one, several, or possibly all of the children in a class when specific skills need to be learned or reinforced. The suggestions below can be adapted to fit the needs of a particular class.

1. *Guide Words:*
   a. You might run into the words below when studying about airplanes. Find each of the words in the dictionary and write the two guide words that are on that page.

Word	*First guide word*	*Second guide word*
autopilot	_____	_____
runway	_____	_____
pressurized	_____	_____
jet propulsion	_____	_____
air drop	_____	_____
beacon	_____	_____
radar	_____	_____
ceiling	_____	_____

   b. *Nest* and *new* are the guide words on page 268 in a certain dictionary. Underline the words in the following list that will be found on that page.

lake	nerve
net	neither
neutral	nail
neglect	nettle
nestling	next

2. *Syllabication and Accent:*
   a. Divide the following words into syllables and place accent marks where they belong. Use your dictionary if you are not sure. When you are finished, use the dictionary to check each word, even if you are sure you are right.

galaxy	lunar	geography	continent
atmosphere	astronaut	mountainous	ocean

b. Sometimes two-syllable words are accented on the first syllable when they are nouns and on the second when they are verbs. Look up the following words and write three sentences for each, using a different meaning in each sentence. In each underline the syllable that should be accented.

conduct	compress	project	contrast

3. *Diacritical Markings and Key Words:* After each of the following words, write the phonetic spelling you find for it in the dictionary. Be sure to show the accent and the diacritical marks above the vowels. In the third column write the key words that will help you to pronounce each word. Be prepared to pronounce each word correctly.

Word	*Phonetic Spelling*	*Keys word(s)*
menace	_____	_____
vegetation	_____	_____
mammal	_____	_____
locust	_____	_____
debris	_____	_____
swarm	_____	_____
rubbish	_____	_____
larva	_____	_____
mesquite	_____	_____
retrieve	_____	_____

4. *Selecting Appropriate Meanings:* In front of each sentence put the number of the meaning that fits that sentence. Use the word in four other sentences, one for each of the four meanings.

support (sup-port'), v. 1) To hold up; to keep from sinking or falling; as, pillars support the porch. 2) to bear; to endure; as, he could not support the pain any longer. 3) to take sides with; to back up; as, to support a candidate. 4) to provide with food, clothing, shelter, etc.; as, he supports his mother.

____ She could not support the suspense any longer.
____ Many people must support a man to get him into office.
____ She helped to support her family by working after school.
____ The shelf was supported by braces.

5. *Finding Correct Spellings:* Below you will find the phonetic spellings of a number of words. Using your knowledge of the way various sounds may be spelled, find these words in the dictionary and write their correct spellings. [For this exercise be sure to use the phonetic spellings that are found in the particular dictionary that your children use. Select words that have appeared in reading they have done or that might appeal to them. Begin with simple words that the children know and work up to those which might be spelled in a number of ways—pneumonia, physical, pylon, heather, etc.]

These exercises are intended, of course, as examples only. Wherever possible, practice in using the dictionary—or any other reference tool—should be done in connection with actual needs. For example, new words in a science unit might be used for finding diacritical markings and phonetic spellings—and meanings, too, of course.

Note Taking

The abilities required for taking effective notes are essentially the same as those required for reading comprehension: getting the main idea, selecting supporting facts or important details, and putting ideas into sequence. The foundation for these skills is laid down even before children begin to write for themselves, when the teacher makes charts showing what to do during a fire drill, who is responsible for various housekeeping chores, what was seen on a trip, plans for a Halloween party, or how to care for the plants in the terrarium. If this kind of activity is presented on a regular basis, children will begin to understand the value of writing down important facts and organizing information.

The writing young children do in their journals may also be thought of as being foundational to their recognizing the need for note taking. Although the "notes" in a journal are essentially reminders of personal experiences and are not based on reading or study or necessarily used to recall something, the fact that they are written and often used as the basis for other writing teaches children the importance of learning note-taking skills.

As children advance in reading and writing ability, they should begin to use the study techniques discussed earlier. At this time they may wish to take notes in their learning logs to remind them of important facts or answers to study questions. Setting specific purposes for assignments will, of course, serve to guide them, but it is wise to give specific instruction in note taking as well. Group activities are a good way to start. Before introducing such

Note-taking skills facilitate independent learning.

activities, however, help the children to develop standards for note taking. At first these may be quite simple:

> ### *Tips for Note Taking*
>
> 1. Decide exactly what you want to find out.
> 2. Write down only important facts on the particular information you are looking for.
> 3. Use your own words. *Do not copy.*

With the standards firmly in mind, try these activities:

1. From one of the class texts choose several paragraphs that are particularly easy to take notes on. (This is an opportunity to integrate; don't simply select at random, but choose material that you had planned to assign anyway and that the children will be expected to understand.) Have all the children read the material and take notes, reminding them of the standards that have been established. After all have finished, select several to go to the board and write what they have written. Compare these and compile a composite, letting the children decide which facts to include and add any important information they think has been omitted.

2. Use an opaque or overhead projector to show a brief article from a magazine or book. Again, this should be something that pertains to the curriculum. Follow the procedure suggested above, or use the projector to show individual children's notes. (Papers should be handed in without names, so no child will be embarrassed.)

3. Have children take notes as a film or videotape is shown. Before the showing, write on the board a list of questions for which the children should seek answers. After the showing, have each child use his or her notes to write answers to the questions. The questions should include some that call for specific information and some that require drawing inferences.

4. Use audio or video recordings frequently to give children practice in noting only important details or finding answers to specific questions. This will help them to avoid the usual tendency of beginning note-takers to write down everything they read or hear, since the time will be controlled. Do this regularly throughout the year in connection with units of study in content areas, making sure always to provide guidance by giving children specific information to look for.

5. Have children watch specific television shows or particular kinds of shows at home and take notes on advertising techniques, use of dialects, or new vocabulary words, for example. Let children who have seen the same show compare information and prepare a group report for presentation to the class.

6. Let individual children who need practice work with tapes or cassettes in the listening center, making sure that they have questions to guide their listening. Allow them to stop the tape or replay portions in order to find the information they need, just as one would reread a portion of a book or article.

In the middle and upper grades, children will be preparing reports to give to the class, and for these they will need to use reference materials obtained from the library. Since each child will be using several sources and will be investigating different sources to discover material, standards will need to be more refined and inclusive:

1. Skim; that is, glance through the article to see whether it contains information that is important to the report.
2. Write down the name of the book, author's name, and page numbers on which the information is found. For encyclopedias, write the name of the encyclopedia, volume number, subject heading, and page numbers.
3. Write down only the important facts or the particular information you are looking for. Use you own words; *do not copy*.
4. If you do wish to use the author's words for some particular reason, use quotation marks, and *write down the exact page number*.
5. Check names, dates, and figures for accuracy.
6. Skim once more to see if you have missed anything important.

Checking information is important.

When children first start making individual reports based on notes they have taken from several sources, guidance from the teacher is particularly important so they will learn to locate materials quickly and to select the important information, as well as to avoid the pitfalls of unintentional plagiarism and forgetting to write down sources.

ORGANIZING AND REPORTING INFORMATION

The skills required to write the component sentences and paragraphs of a report are essentially those required for any writing; they are discussed in Chapter 9. Of particular concern for the report as a form of writing are organization of material, intended audience, and giving credit to sources of information.

Organizing for Writing

You are an important model for pupils. When planning and organizing activities, you should explain what you are doing and demonstrate how to do it.

All the activities of a classroom at any grade level require organization. Children should learn at an early age that they cannot even have a successful class picnic without planning what they will need and who will provide it. When they begin to write stories, it is necessary to plan the sequence of events and provide for the inclusion of details that will be of importance to plot development and will stimulate reader interest. A child who is going to write a business letter should jot down ideas about what items to include and the order in which they will be placed. And even for oral activities, children should be shown that a written outline can help keep a speaker from omitting important points.

Actually, planning should begin even before a child starts to collect information for a report, whether oral or written, to serve as a guide in deciding what information to look for. For a short report, perhaps a simple list of questions to be answered will be sufficient. For a longer one or one using several information sources, an informal outline might be used. Such an outline should simply list main ideas and subtopics; no particular attention should be given to sentence structure or formal outline form. Some children prefer to use a topic web (such as was discussed in Chapters 4 and 9), with the main topic at the center and related ideas branching off from it, which may be subdivided into additional components, all becoming parts of the web. Children often find these diagrams both fun to make and helpful in organizing their thinking, since, as the work progresses, new branches can be added easily.

Whatever method is used, however, children should learn that preplanning not only saves time but results in better organization and therefore more effective writing. They also need to understand that this preplanning is neither complete nor static. Revisions may be needed in the light of information found, some ideas that seemed fruitful may be dropped and others added, or what seemed to be a minor aspect may evolve into a major one. The list, outline, or web therefore grows and changes as work progresses.

Outlining

Perhaps the most difficult aspect of preparing a report occurs after a child has collected the information needed and is ready to begin writing. Faced with what seems to be a jumble of disorganized facts, the child must somehow put them in order. The solution is to use an outline. At this point the preplanning list, outline, or web, which has been growing and changing during the process of gathering information, should become the basis for organization. The outline form will probably work best for this purpose, since it clearly shows the order in which items should be discussed and which are major points or supporting and explanatory ones.

The outline used for organization, like the one used in preplanning, may be subject to change as writing progresses, but changes should be minimal if sufficient thought has gone into preparing it. Also, like its predecessor, this outline may be an informal one, unless it is to become a part of the final report.

Children should, however, become familiar with correct outline form, since they will find it both useful and necessary as they progress in school. Outlining is a developmental skill, with forms increasing in complexity as children mature and gain practice; therefore, activities are described here at three levels of sophistication.

Beginning Level. Children can become familiar with outline form in the early grades. The example below, which might be entitled "Our Trip," illustrates the kind of outline that can be put on the board or a chart for children to see. They should participate in preparing it, although they may need help in putting the statements into the correct form.

    I. On the bus
        A. Stay in seats.
            1. Talk quietly to neighbors.
            2. Keep hands inside.
        B. Do not eat.
            1. Keep food in a bag.
            2. Don't trade food or bags.

   II. At the zoo
        A. Find the animals that live in a warm climate.
        B. Find the animals that live in a cold climate.

  III. Back at school
        A. Write a report about the zoo.
        B. Draw pictures.

Opportunities for using outlines in planning and reporting class activities are numerous. For instance, directions or plans for a class picnic or party can be outlined on the board. Or, when children have finished reading or listening to a story, ask them to dictate the first main idea, details, and sequence, then the second main idea, and so on. Write these on the board or on chart paper; then reread the story to check the outline form. This kind of activity will help demonstrate to children how their own stories can be improved if they jot down their ideas and organize them into a meaning-ful sequence. As a follow-up, have them suggest several story ideas; then, with you as scribe, they can decide on a series of events and select the sup-porting details for each. At first, simply list the suggestions, then work with them to organize these into an outline for the story. Several of these might be written on charts to serve as models. The final step is to use one of them as the basis for a class story. You might divide the class into groups, having each group either develop one of the outlines or make their own outline and write a story from it.

Intermediate Level. Outlining must have a useful purpose if it is to have value for children. Many children will outline simply because they are told to, but it is important to convince them that outlining has value whenever they sit down to write or to prepare for an oral report.

The outline form can best be taught by using a chalkboard, chart, or overhead projector. Although the purpose and need for using outlining are the most important points for children to learn, some attention needs to be given to the outline form and why such a form is followed. The following should be taught:

I. Use Roman numerals for main topics—the most important points.
    A. Indent and capitalize letters for subtopics.
        1. Use Arabic numerals for the details.
        2. Because you have one, you need at least one more detail about sub-topic A.
    B. This is another subtopic of Roman numeral I.
        1. Give one detail about B.
        2. One B detail needs a second.

An object, chart, or drawing rather than a report can be made after doing research.

II. List another main topic.
   A. Subtopic.   Details may or may not be needed here.
   B. Subtopic.   Again, if there are two or more parts or details, there will
       need to be a division of the subtopic.

A movie or videotape may provide an excellent experience for teaching outline form. The choice of what to show should be carefully made, with a view toward its suitability for outlining, and preparation should be thorough so the children will not be frustrated in trying to identify important points. Before viewing, the class should be instructed to take notes that will be used to outline the content when the movie is over. Afterward, ask the children to tell what they saw or learned, and write everything they say on the board. The next step is to organize this information—to select the first main idea and then the related details, the next main idea and details, and so on, until everything has been covered. As the children select the main idea and details, help them to put them in an outline, using the overhead projector or chart paper. When the lesson is completed, the children can copy the outline and file it in a folder of "Movies I Have Learned From" or with pictures, reading notes, and so forth that pertain to the same unit of work. Naturally, the movie or the videotape, and therefore the outline, should be an integral part of a particular unit of study—there is no point in showing something or making an outline that does not apply to anything the class is doing.

The discussion of content area subjects in class also provides a good opportunity for teaching the value of outlining. As discussion takes place, write in outline form any information that you want the class to remember. The children can copy it in their notebooks and use it as a basis for study.

Advanced Level. Once children have become fairly proficient at outlining, have them use this skill regularly to promote its having some effect on their thinking and study habits. Both oral and written activities can be improved on by the use of outlining techniques. Also, show that you rely on this skill by outlining important facts on the board as they are discussed and by distributing study guides and other materials prepared in outline form.

At this level children may need help in correlating information from several sources for an oral or written report. When they do, the following procedure should prove helpful:

1. Using an overhead projector, show three different articles about the same subject. All should contain some common information, but each should include facts not found in the others.
2. Have the children take notes on each selection. This may be a group effort, with notes being taken on the chalkboard.
3. With the children's help, outline the notes from each selection.
4. Make a composite outline, including important points from all three. You may wish to have the children place numbers (1, 2, 3) in parentheses after each point, both to illustrate how the material is correlated and to help them locate information quickly if they need to refer to the articles in writing their summaries (step 5).

5. Have each child use the outline to write an individual summary of the information obtained from all three selections.

Preparing Footnotes and Bibliographies

The first-grader is often heard to say "My teacher says . . . " or "My father told me . . . ." This is the foundation for learning that we all depend on sources outside ourselves for much of what we know. As the child learns to read and write, he or she will refer to a dictionary for the meaning or spelling of a word and later will consult various references for needed information, especially if this sort of searching is encouraged. Help children to recognize that no one—not even you—knows everything, that what we know today, and what we will discover tomorrow, is built on knowledge that has been accumulated by others. As children begin to use reference materials in preparing reports, help them to understand that appending a bibliography strengthens a report in two ways: first, if a writer has authorities to back up what is said, the reader will know that the subject has been studied and that the writer knows what he or she is talking about; and second, the bibliography gives readers the opportunity to find out for themselves if they doubt the information or wish to learn more about the subject.

Children love big words, and there is no reason why they should not use the word *bibliography* to show their sources. In the beginning, the form should be simple. A chart may be used to help with the punctuation and with the spelling of *bibliography*.

> ### *Bibliography*
>
> Adams, Richard. *The Story of Canada*, pages 21–26.
> *The World Book*, Vol. C, pp. 1166–1195.

By the time children reach the sixth or seventh grade, they should be ready to include slightly more information in bibliographies. For example, the items given below should probably be included. Again, charts should be used to help with punctuation and the order of items; children should not be expected to remember these, especially since various authorities suggest different punctuation. The punctuation items and order given in the language text the class uses should be the guide.

TRADE BOOKS	ENCYCLOPEDIAS	PERIODICALS
author	title	author (if named)
title	most recent copyright date	title of article
publisher	volume number or letter	title of magazine
copyright date	pages	date
page numbers		pages

In the upper grades, some children may learn how to use footnotes. Generally there is little need in the elementary grades to require the use of footnotes, particularly for anything other than direct quotations. In a short paper, the source of a particular item of information can be found, if needed, by checking the bibliography or the pupil's notes. They will later learn that in longer papers it is sometimes desirable to footnote certain types of information that is not directly quoted; however, elementary-school children should *never* be assigned to write long "term papers." The important learning involved is the ability to correlate information from several sources and to organize it into a well-written report; if subjects are sufficiently limited in scope, children can concentrate on organization and good form in writing rather than sloppily throwing together a great volume of information.

As mentioned earlier, standards for note taking should be established as soon as children begin to take notes from reference materials, and one of these should always be a prohibition against copying. Point out to children that borrowing words is like borrowing books: people do not write their own names in books borrowed from friends or from the library; nor should they pretend that someone else's words are their own. As they begin to write longer reports and take notes from several sources, some children may find it less time-consuming to copy some information than to rephrase every item. This is the time to point out that notes can become extremely voluminous (and therefore more difficult to organize later) if too much copying is done. It is also the time to emphasize that they should *never* copy directly from a source without putting quotation marks around the words that were copied so that they will not borrow another's words without meaning to. Introduce the word *plagiarism*, explain its meaning, and invoke severe penalties if it should occur, even unintentionally—children will thank you for it later. Take the time to check sources if you are suspicious; the formation of bad habits will negate the positive aspects of note taking and reporting.

Help children to learn that a paper should be more than simply a series of quotations strung together, however well organized, and that it is "dirty pool" merely to transpose a few words or phrases and consider the writing original. The ideas and information in a report are gathered from other sources, but the organization and wording should be original. Quoting is done when it will strengthen the report in one of two ways. First, the writer may wish to use an author's own words to illustrate a point. For example, in discussing a poet, one might well quote from one or more poems; or a paper about a famous person might be enriched by the use of that person's own words. Second, it is sometimes desirable to use a quotation to show a particular person's opinion, especially if he or she is a well-known authority.

Footnotes may be in simple form. Author, title, and page number are sufficient; anyone who wishes more complete information can check the bibliography. There is no need to add the extra burden of learning about specialized forms, such as *ibid.* and *op. cit.* The important facts for children to learn are that they may not copy someone else's words without giving credit and how this credit may be given. Footnote form, like bibliography form, can be illustrated on charts to help children with punctuation and order of items. There is no need for them to memorize these, since, as mentioned earlier, forms vary. Point this out and explain that they should use whatever form is required by a particular teacher or school.

USING READING SKILLS

Many skills are needed for effective reading. The foundational ones were discussed in Chapter 12; those discussed here are the ones particularly associated with the study skills—skimming and critical reading.

Skimming

Children should be taught how to skim in the intermediate grades, since this important skill will help them to study and to locate information more efficiently. Skimming is not a skill that is simply acquired as children grow in reading abilities; it must be specifically taught. Habits to be developed are discussed in the following sections.

Reading the First and Last Sentences of a Paragraph. Both you and the children should be aware that the topic sentence of a paragraph is not always first or last, but it is frequently in one of those positions. Even when it is not, these sentences should give clues to the general content. In longer selections, the first and last paragraphs might be read quickly.

Looking for Cue Words. Cue words are of two types. First, if a child is looking for a specific piece of information, he or she should watch for words related to that information. For example, if a child only wants to find out where a particular tribe of Indians lived, then place names—California, northern plains, or Mississippi River Valley, for instance—should be looked for. Second, there are general cue words. The way they are used is illustrated in this paragraph. The heading has given the main idea. The first sentence uses the words *two types*; the words *First* and *Second* lead immediately to these two types. Number words (or the numbers themselves) are perhaps the most helpful of all cue words. If these had been omitted, however, *For example* in sentence three should send the reader's eyes back to the preceding sentence to discover one of the two types. Other cue words that can help children to locate ideas are words like *causes, reason, however, principal*, and *furthermore* and phrases such as *in addition, on the other hand*, and *in conclusion*.

Using Format Clues. As was suggested in the section concerning study steps, one of the quickest ways to discover the general content of a long selection is to glance through it and read the various types of section headings, as well as the captions for pictures, graphs, maps, and so forth. A child who is preparing a report can be led immediately to the information needed by using this technique, particularly if it is used in conjunction with the card catalog, table of contents, and/or index (see Chapter 14).

Materials used for teaching skimming should be selected carefully if these habits are to be established. This does not mean that the materials should not be related to the subject matter of content areas—only that you must select them with an eye to their suitability in developing a particular habit or skill.

Begin with short selections that clearly illustrate the habit you are developing. The first few times you may wish to underline the parts that are important—beginning and ending sentences, cue words, or topic headings. Give the children specific questions to answer and discuss what procedures might be used to find the answers. At first, simply ask them to decide what the selection is about. Later, proceed to more detailed questions, such as "What kind of homes did the Indians live in?" or "Find three reasons why the colonists came to America."

Divide the class into teams for "skimming contests." Award points for finding the correct answers to questions and for finding them in the least time.

Using an overhead projector to show practice exercises makes it possible to control the time more easily. Another method is to write the selection on the chalkboard in a spot where it can be covered by a pulldown map or screen. The time allowed can be cut as the children become more skilled in using clues. Regular, brief practice will improve speed. For example, say to the class "Turn to page 142 in your text and find the name of the Indian who guided the Smith family through the forest. As soon as you have found it, close your book and hold up your hand. Remember, find the name of the Smiths' Indian guide."

To help children who have difficulty with skimming, some teachers have tried drawing a vertical red line through the middle of a paragraph. As they look for clues, the children are to look only at the words that touch this line instead of letting their eyes go across the type line horizontally. Or you might try two vertical lines, dividing the page approximately into thirds. The idea is to help children learn to move their eyes quickly *down* the page, looking for clues, rather than looking *across* each line horizontally.

Observe children as they study and work on reports based on supplementary reading. Guide individual children by reminding them of clues to look for, and provide reinforcement exercises when the need is indicated.

Critical Reading and Thinking

Children show a tendency to believe everything they read. Most people eventually learn that not everything in print is true, but often they do not learn this well enough or soon enough. Thus, thinking critically about issues, listening critically to what is heard on radio or television, and reading information critically are skills that need to be taught. Many of the ways words are used to give a false impression are well-known. For example, a newspaper reports that a large number of young people attending a music festival were treated at the medical center for overdoses of drugs, upset stomachs, and cut feet. This is a fairly unadorned statement of fact, yet some readers might conclude from it that the use of drugs at the festival was widespread and that the principal cause of treatment at the center was drug overdose. This conclusion could be due (perhaps largely) to the reader's own preconceptions, but it is encouraged by the use of the words *large number*, the placement of the drug item in first position in the list, and the lack of specific numbers or percentages. Even numbers can be misleading, or course. Suppose the newspaper reports that 10 percent of those who came to the center were treated for drug overdose; this percentage is still not meaningful unless the reader knows the total number treated and how this number relates to the total number attending the festival.

It is important not only to teach children to read but to teach them to read critically. To develop into critical readers, children must learn to approach the printed words with inquiring minds, to evaluate what is read in the light of known facts or objective evidence, to examine the logic of the presentation, and to distinguish between fact and opinion. All learning, of course, is related to previous knowledge and experience, but the critical reader learns to suspend judgment and personal opinion until the total selection has been evaluated and assimilated, to seek out other knowledge and opinions, and to draw inferences from what has been read.

Reading materials designed for classroom use commonly provide children with the opportunity to make inferences, or "read between the lines." This kind of reading can be encouraged by asking questions: "Why do you think _____? Could this be true? What do you think really happened?" It is important to stress that answers must be based on information given or knowledge gained from other sources, not simply on opinion or personal preference. One way to help children develop this kind of thinking is to begin with sentences from which inferences can be drawn, such as the following:

> It is a beautiful day for a walk, but there is a sharp wind blowing. (Perhaps we will need jackets when we go out.)
> Bruce Smith has been practicing running and passing all summer. (He wants to go out for football this fall.)
> Mrs. Jones puts on her glasses the minute she gets up in the morning. (She can't see well without them.)
> Ordinarily, we have frequent showers in the summer, but this year the grass is brown and the trees look thirsty. (This has been an unusually dry summer.)

Another way to help children learn to draw inferences and base their thinking on known facts is to read or have them read part of a story and then ask them to write or tell a possible ending. This need not be the same as the ending used by the writer of the story, but it should be logical in terms of what is known about the characters and the events that have gone before. Begin with something short and fairly obvious, such as "The Boy Who Cried Wolf," and advance to stories in which character might decide the outcome.

As in developing other language abilities, it is wise to begin teaching critical thinking with group activities so that the children may learn from each other. This can be done even at the kindergarten level with activities such as the one suggested in the preceding paragraph. Be sure to ask not just "What do you think happened next?" but also "Why do you think so?" Try to get a number of responses, examine them critically (in a constructive way), and decide together which ones fit best with the known facts.

Besides supplementary reading materials, there are also filmstrips and cassettes designed to further critical thinking. These are useful because they are more readily associated with television, which influences so much of our thinking these days. They also provide variety, and they can be used with the entire class, with groups, or by individual children who need additional experience.

Closely allied to drawing inferences is distinguishing fact from opinion. Activities such as these can help children to develop this ability:

1. Have the children select famous personalities and write opinions about them: "I think Laura Ingalls Wilder must have lived in South Dakota because she wrote about life there so realistically" or "I think Jack Clark hit more home runs last year than any other player in the National League." Then have them use their library skills to determine whether these are only opinions or really facts.

2. Cut from magazines several full-page color advertisements, clipping off all printed material pertaining to the product. Show only the pictures to the children and ask them to write statements of fact and opinion about them, for example:

   Facts
   A woman is sitting on a patio with a collie.
   The woman is smiling.
   There are flowers and trees surrounding the patio.

   Opinions

   The woman is smiling because her new toothpaste got her teeth so white.
   She is smiling because the flower seeds she bought made her yard beautiful.
   She is smiling because a particular fertilizer made her garden grow especially well.
   She is smiling because her dog likes that new dog food.

   Check to make sure the facts are really facts, and lead the children into a discussion of whether such statements as "The woman is beautiful" and "The collie is a thoroughbred" are facts or opinions. Then show the printed material that was cut from the picture so children can find out which of their opinions were correct (at least according to the advertisement!).

3. Help children evaluate newspaper accounts by looking for key words that indicate opinion rather than fact. Here are some statements of the type to look for:

   There is *probably* more snow here than any other place in the country.
   The remains just discovered *may* be the missing link.
   This *appears* to be the driest spot in the nation.
   The students *think* that this is the best school in the city.

4. A variation of the preceding activity is to have children separate fact from opinion.

   Yesterday's rain, which lasted for five hours, was probably the worst downpour in our history.
   Fact: It rained yesterday. The rain lasted five hours.
   Opinion: It was the worst downpour in our history.

   Jim Simmons, who is exactly six feet tall, must be the tallest boy in school.

   Fact: Jim Simmons is six feet tall.
   Opinion: He is the tallest boy in school.

Mrs. Gotrocks, often said to be the wealthiest woman in the country, was shopping yesterday in Zayre's.

Fact: Mrs. Gotrocks was in Zayre's yesterday.

Opinion: Mrs. Gotrocks is the wealthiest woman in the country.

5. Have the children listen to television newscasts for several days and make a collection of phrases that are used to introduce statements that are not definitely known to be true, such as "It has been reported that," "Reliable sources inform us," "One witness said that," "Rumor has it," and so on.

6. Children should also be shown how the choice of words can sway opinion. Let them try showing opposing views of the same event:

Congressman Wilkins smirked sardonically, then snapped, "I have nothing to say at this time."

The weary Congressman attempted a smile, then said simply, "I have nothing to say at this time."

7. As a follow-up to the above, have the class compare newspaper accounts of the same event written by different writers. A football game between teams from two cities, for example, would be written up quite differently by sports writers from each of those cities. Follow by having them attempt to sort out facts and opinions.

Coordinate the teaching of listening strategies with activities such as these.

We are bombarded daily by propaganda of various sorts; those who have learned the skills of critical thinking are better prepared to make decisions based on reason rather than emotion. By the time children reach the middle grades, they should begin to draw conclusions from what they read or hear, distinguish between fact and opinion, and recognize that words have connotations as well as denotations. At this point they are ready for a more direct study of the ways in which people attempt to influence our thinking. Perhaps a good place to begin is with advertising techniques, since advertising is the most obvious type of propaganda. Begin with the most common categories:

- *Plain folks:* The president of the company started as a janitor. He still enjoys pitching horseshoes with the boys during the noon-hour break. (He understands ordinary people and wouldn't try to cheat them.)

- *Bandwagon:* More doctors recommend this pill than any other. (Notice that it doesn't say any other *what*.)

- *Repetition:* Sticky Goo holds your false teeth so you can munch, munch, munch for your lunch, lunch, lunch. (A more common type of repetition currently used involves frequently repeated slogans or jingles, which appear so often on television that even small children can repeat or sing them.)

- *Testimonial:* The star pitcher for the Oakland A's eats Ironies for breakfast. (If you eat Ironies, you can be a big leaguer too.)

- *Snob appeal:* Come out and see this executive house in an exclusive neighborhood. (Buy here and you can be part of an exclusive group.)

- *Emotional words:* Good mothers buy Junkie sneakers for their children. (If you don't buy your child Junkie sneakers, you aren't a good mother.)

- *Rewards:* Buy at Smith Brothers' Store and get double coupon value. (Also common today is the cash rebate, offered on everything from grocery items to automobiles.)

A bulletin board display might be a starting point. Ask children to bring in examples of the various advertising techniques, and let them judge which ones are the most representative and therefore the best to post. They may also enjoy collecting phrases commonly found in advertising. These might include the following:

huge savings	for better mileage
this week only	discount prices
buy with confidence	money-back guarantee
service with a smile	for preferred customers

An extension of this study that will appeal to children is to have them watch television commercials and decide which groups they are directed at—small children, women, teenagers, etc.—and which techniques are used for each group. They will be fascinated to discover that variations of the same technique are used for every age level: the four-year-old demands a certain cereal because there is a toy in the box, and the child's father buys a particular car because the company pays him a cash bonus.

As the children become expert in detecting the techniques, have them watch for overlapping ones. For example, "All responsible parents buy Dryer raincoats for their children. Your children deserve the best" includes the bandwagon, emotional, and snob appeal approaches.

As a concluding activity for the unit, divide the class into small groups and let each group select an item to "shop for." Each group should collect all the advertisements they can locate about their item. Then they should evaluate each one, write reactions to it, and report their findings to the class, including the reasons they decided to buy a particular brand or shop at a particular store. Items might include a swimming pool, a pool table, a jar of peanut butter, a snowmobile, a video game, or a pair of jeans.

If it is valuable to recognize the advertising ploys used by those who are trying to sell their products, it is even more important to recognize that virtually the same techniques are used by those who want to sell *ideas*. During every political campaign, for example, we are bombarded by the same spot announcements on TV and radio to keep candidates' names before us; film stars and other entertainers endorse their favorites, and so on. In fact, we are surrounded daily by propaganda of many types.

Children should learn to recognize propaganda, but they should also learn that it is not necessarily bad. Rather, it is a part of our way of life. TV stations, for instance, commonly telecast what they often call "public service announcements," warning young people against the use of drugs, advertising public clinics that give immunizations against various diseases, and so on; prominent athletes plug not only shaving cream but also fund-raising drives against multiple sclerosis or heart disease. No one is completely without bias; therefore, what a person writes or says is colored by his or her own beliefs. This "slanting" may be intentional, or the writer may make every effort to present an objective view. The important thing is that children should learn to search for bias or motive, to distinguish fact from opinion, to examine opposing views, and to draw their own conclusions. The following are some of the types of activities that can help them to recognize and evaluate propaganda:

1. Use reading exercises that call for making inferences and for distinguishing fact from opinion, as suggested earlier.

2. Begin even in the early grades to help children find themes in stories they read, for these are a type of propaganda—they represent the writers' beliefs. Begin with simple questions: "Do you think the person who wrote this story likes dogs? What makes you think so?" As children mature, they can grasp more subtle and complicated themes.

3. To help children think about the purposes and qualifications of writers when evaluating what they have to say, show a variety of articles from newspapers and magazines by means of an opaque or overhead projector. Then discuss such questions as the following:

   Did the writer simply want to sell more newspapers or magazines? (New Clues Uncovered!)

   Is the writer encouraging you to vote for a candidate or an issue. (Mr. Christopher is an all-around family man who lives in a neat, modest suburban home.)

   Is the writer qualified and competent to write on this subject? (Has the writer studied the subject sufficiently or had enough personal experience with it to know what he or she is talking about?)

   Does the writer present both sides of an issue or only one? (Those who oppose this issue base their objections on emotion alone; there can be no valid objection.)

4. Have children bring in two accounts of a political speech appearing in newspapers with opposing political views, or have them listen to reports of a speech on different television channels—or both. Then compare these and note the ways in which each supports its point of view.

5. An extension of the preceding activity is to videotape the speech itself and compare the various reports concerning it as to both accuracy and bias.

6. Have the children write papers either supporting or opposing a particular school or community issue on which opinions are strongly divided. Then have the class research the subject through whatever means are available— guest speakers, reading, and so on—and write new opinions based on what they have learned, telling why they have or have not changed their minds.

A Bulletin Board Idea

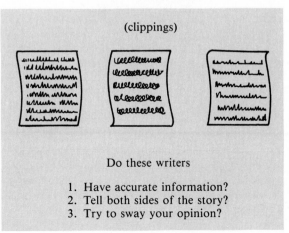

(clippings)

Do these writers

1. Have accurate information?
2. Tell both sides of the story?
3. Try to sway your opinion?

7. Bring in several articles concerning a current problem or issue. Show these on the opaque or overhead projector and have the children evaluate them in terms of propaganda techniques used, presentation of facts rather than opinions, use of "loaded" or emotional words, and use of logical reasoning.

Developing critical thinking takes time and effort. Broaden the children's horizons by providing many experiences and materials of various kinds. Make your classroom one in which a spirit of inquiry exists, where questions are freely asked and answers diligently sought. Help children to question what they read and hear and to acquire the desire and the skills to find answers.

A FINAL WORD

This chapter has focused on studying—on the skills students should know and use if they are to be genuinely successful in school. Basically, how effectively study skills are used depends on abilities in reading, abilities that go beyond mere word recognition and literal comprehension. But these skills also involve knowing how to use dictionaries and other reference sources effectively, how to take notes and organize information for written and oral presentation, and how to read for various purposes. Such skills are vital to success not only in the elementary school, but even more in later school years and in various activities of adult life after schooling is complete. The elementary school, then, is where these skills should be taught—and they must be directly taught, not just "picked up" incidentally. This teaching, of course, should and can be in the context of meaningful study activities.

References

Askov, Eunice N., and Kamm, Karlyn. *Study Skills in the Content Areas.* Allyn and Bacon, 1985.

Beyer, Barry K. *Practical Strategies for the Teaching of Thinking.* Allyn and Bacon, 1987.

Bragstad, Bernice Jensen, and Stumpf, Sharyn Mueller. *A Guidebook for Teaching Study Skills and Motivation,* 2nd ed. Allyn and Bacon, 1987.

Cunningham, Patricia M., and Cunningham, James W. "Content Area Reading-Writing Lessons." *The Reading Teacher* 40 (February 1987), pp. 506–512.

Devine, Thomas G. *Teaching Study Skills*, 2nd ed. Allyn and Bacon, 1987.

Duffy, Gerald G., and Roehler, Laura R. "Teaching Reading Skills as Strategies." *The Reading Teacher* 40 (January 1987), pp 414–418.

Eggen, Paul D., and Kauchak, Donald P. *Strategies for Teachers: Teaching Content and Thinking Skills,* 2nd ed. Prentice-Hall, 1988.

Fry, Edward B. *Skimming and Scanning*, 2nd ed. Jamestown Publishers, 1982.

Heimlich, Joan E., and Pittelman, Susan D. *Semantic Mapping: Classroom Applications.* International Reading Association, 1986.

Hill, Walter, R. *Secondary School Reading: Process, Program, Procedure.* Allyn and Bacon, 1979.

Jay, M. Ellen, and Jay, Hilda L. *Building Reference Skills in the Elementary School.* Shoe String Press, 1986.

Robinson, H. Alan. *Teaching Reading and Study Strategies: The Content Areas*, 3rd ed. Allyn and Bacon, 1983.

Winograd, Peter, and Smith, Lynne A. "Improving the Climate for Reading Comprehension Instruction." *The Reading Teacher* 41 (December 1987), pp. 304–310.

Wray, David. "Teaching Information Skills in the U.K. Elementary School." *The Reading Teacher* 41 (February 1988), pp. 520–524.

Teaching Resources_____

WORKBOOKS AND KITS

The Brigance Prescriptive Study Skills: Strategies and Practice. Curriculum Associates (kit of reproducible pages; grades 3–7).

Dictionary Skills. Curriculum Associates (workbook; grades 3–6).

Exploring Language with the Dictionary. Schoolhouse Press (workbooks; intermediate grades).

Flowcharting. Houghton Mifflin (workbook; upper grades).

HM Study Skills Program. NAESP Educational Products Center (guide, kit, and student text; grades 3–4).

Learning to Study. Jamestown Publishers (six workbooks and teacher editions; various grade levels).

More Lessons in Outlining. Curriculum Associates (skillbook; grades 5–8).

Reading and Thinking Strategies. D.C. Heath (kits; grades 3–6).

Sprint Reading Skills Program. Scholastic (kits; grades 1–5).

COMPUTER SOFTWARE

Alphabet, Sequences, and Alphabetizing. Random House, School Division (grades 2–4).

Building Comprehension. A. W. Peller and Associates (three sets; details, sequence, predicting outcome, etc.; K–grade 4).

The Cloze Technique for Developing Comprehension. A. W. Peller and Associates (two disks; grades 3–6).

How to Read in the Content Areas. Educational Activities (intermediate grades).

Let's Alphabetize. Unicorn Software (K–grade 3).

Library Adventure/Reference and Study Skills. Listening Library (grades 2–6).

Random House Dictionary. Sensible Software (intermediate grades).

Reading Comprehension: Main Ideas and Details. Milton Bradley (intermediate grades).

Report Writer. Society for Visual Education (teacher's guide; intermediate grades).

Storytree. Scholastic (intermediate grades).

Supermind: Advertising and Propaganda. Educational Activities (intermediate grades).

Tutorial Comprehension—Critical Reading. Random House (intermediate grades).

Who What When Where Why. Hartley (intermediate grades).

FILMSTRIPS AND VIDEOTAPES

Basic Thinking Skills. Society for Visual Education (videotape; intermediate grades).

Curious George Learns the Alphabet. Random House (filmstrips, cassettes, duplicating masters, and chart; primary grades).

Developing Effective Study Skills. Listening Library (six filmstrips with cassettes).

The Dictionary. Society for Visual Education (four filmstrips, four cassettes, worksheets, and guides; grades 3–6).

The Dictionary. Society for Visual Education (videotape, skill sheets, and guide; primary and intermediate grades).

The Dictionary. Thomas S. Klise (filmstrip and guide; upper grades).

Encyclopedia Brown Introduces Report-Writing Skills. Society for Visual Education (filmstrips, skill sheets, and teacher's guide; intermediate grades).

Go Find Out! Thomas S. Klise (intermediate grades).

How to Read the Newspaper Intelligently. Knowledge Unlimited (filmstrip; grades 5–6).

The Research Paper. Society for Visual Education (four filmstrips, four cassettes, worksheets, and guide; upper grades) (also available in video).

Using the Encyclopedia. Thomas S. Klise (intermediate grades).

BOOKS

Don't Believe Everything You Read. PEM Press (intermediate grades).

Fact Finders. Dale Seymour (grades 4–6).

For the Love of Research. Dale Seymour (grades 4–6).

Independent Research Student Handbook. Dale Seymour (grades 4–6).

Margrabe, Mary. *Media Magic: Games and Activities for Total Curriculum Involvement*. Acropolis, 1979.

Meinbach, Anita Meyer, and Rothlein, Liz Christman. *Unlocking the Secrets of Research*. Scott, Foresman, 1985 (grades 5–8).

Pirie, Jennifer, and Pirie, Alex. *Thirty Lessons in Note Taking*. Curriculum Associates (worksheets; grades 5–8).

Reading a Newspaper. Janus (intermediate grades).

Research Skills. Coronado (grades 4–6).

Tassia, Margaret R. *Games for Information Skills*. Libraries Unlimited, 1983.

Activities for Preservice Teachers

1. Analyze your reading and study habits. Do you use any particular plan? Try some of the procedures described in this chapter that you don't ordinarily use. Are any applicable to your situation?

2. Try skimming through magazine and newspaper articles about celebrities or political figures to find information concerning their childhood experiences or early education. What is your approach to skimming? Do you look at the first few words of each paragraph? Do you look for key sentences? Do you look for particular words?

3. Spend an hour taking a close look at a college-level or unabridged dictionary. What parts does it contain that you were not aware of? What information about the English language is presented? What lists are presented? Do you understand how to use the pronunciation guide?

4. Talk with instructors who are subject-matter specialists in chemistry, economics, or other technical fields. Ask them to describe some of the reading and study problems in their fields.

5. Think up a lesson concerning one of the seasons, and plan some related dictionary activities for the children at a particular grade level.

6. Plan the assignment for a social studies or science lesson at a particular grade level. Show exactly how you prepare the children for this assignment, assuming certain things about the children. Include motivation, background, and specific purposes.

7. Plan a lesson in drawing inferences for any specific grade level.

8. Collect materials for a bulletin board display relating to a lesson on advertising techniques or propaganda.

9. Observe some classrooms where teachers are likely to make assignments. Analyze the assignments made in terms of the points raised in this chapter. Note any attempts the teachers make to reinforce reading skills as they prepare children for carrying out assignments. Also note the extent to which they integrate the language arts with the teaching of content areas.

10. Examine some workbooks or worksheets that focus on specific reading skills, such as finding facts or following a sequence. Then find passages in science or social studies textbooks for the same grade level that would be better vehicles for emphasizing the same skills.

Activities for Inservice Teachers

1. Evaluate the way you assign homework. Experiment with the techniques suggested in this chapter for helping children learn how to study. Note any improvements in children's attitudes about homework and the quality of learning that might be attributed to better assignments.

2. Coordinate dictionary activities with activities in various subject areas. For example, make a list of new words in a science lesson and after introducing these, have the children use a dictionary and/or thesaurus to find synonyms, related words, and variant meanings. This will not only help them to better understand the new words and build vocabularies but will also give them practice in using these resources in their studying.

3. Collect a number of pictures from magazines. Have children write sentences, identifying facts and opinions. Have them look at headlines and captions for further instances of facts and opinions. This kind of

activity can also be done using videotapes of television programs.

4. Show a film or videotape whose content lends itself to outlining and the use of a web (or semantic map or flowchart). Have children do a web first, showing what the main topic is and how the subtopics relate to it. Then help them convert the web into an outline.

5. Attend a meeting or conference where a variety of teaching materials are displayed. Examine these to see the extent to which they might make a worthwhile contribution to your program. Decide on the wisest way to spend any funds that might be available to support your reading program.

6. Choose a local public issue that is not too emotional (there aren't many) and have your class analyze pamphlets and news stories to see what advertising and other persuasive techniques are being used by the different sides.

7. With your class, select several topics for reports, perhaps from a social studies unit or a current event of local concern. Have each topic reported on by a group. Depending on the children's maturity and abilities, have the groups locate materials in the library, take notes, and collate information from several sources. Groups in the middle grades should be able to make outlines, write drafts, prepare bibliographies, and write (perhaps type) final reports.

8. After completing a story or a lesson in a subject area, ask the children to develop two or three good newspaper headlines based on the lesson or story. Then see if they can restate their headlines to alter the meaning. Discuss how the changes affected the meaning. An alternative to this is to give the children two slanted headlines for the same story; then have them listen to or read the story to select the headline that fits best.

Independent Activities for Children

1. Have newspapers available so that children may use them to examine advertising copy, noting how words and sentences are used for certain purposes. Encourage the children to study how newspapers are organized into various sections (such study may lead to developing a class newspaper).

2. Children can prepare note cards to use when giving oral book reports by putting on each card a main idea followed by a list of important details they want to include.

3. Children can use a thesaurus to find synonyms and antonyms for words in spelling lessons and other words of interest to them.

4. A child can gain practice in finding the main idea by reading articles in the school newspaper, a local daily newspaper, or a children's newspaper such as *Weekly Reader* and then putting the main idea of each article into a single sentence.

5. Put lists of words on cards—on the front list the words in any order and on the back in alphabetical order. Vary the difficulty to allow for differences in the children's abilities. An individual child can select a card, put the words in alphabetical order on paper, and check the result by looking at the back of the card.

6. An individual child or a group of children might prepare a bulletin board display showing the elements in a dictionary: guide words, entry words, pronunciation key, syllabication, and so on.

7. A child who needs more experience in putting events into sequence can draw a picture sequence of everything he or she did between getting up and arriving at school. The pictures might then be put into a strip like a comic, and dialogue added in "balloons" over the heads of the people.

8. Prepare a number of outlines by listing main topics in order on the left side of the page and subtopics in

jumbled order on the right side. Children may select appropriate subtopics for each main idea and place them in appropriate sequences. On the back of each page, show how the subtopics should be placed.

9. Copies of current news articles related to children's interests (sports, local festivals, etc.) can be made available for study. Encourage the children to note how bias might be entering the articles, to determine fact and opinion, and to consider how certain expressions have been used. These aspects can be discussed in a group situation after enough of the children have read one or more of the articles.

10. Dictionary exercises for individual children may include ones like the following:
    a. Circle the words that come between *club* and *enough* in the dictionary.

clown	easy	draw	country
family	dust	cover	evening
oval	cloth	egg	explore
desk	close	ever	could

    b. Write the entry words for each of these dictionary respellings.

    bütz _____   kül _____
    mün _____   tüth _____

11. Prepare specific questions related to the content being studied in social studies, science, or other subject area. Children will utilize the study skills in locating answers to these questions.

12. Be sure that your listening center is well supplied with tapes designed to provide practice in finding main ideas, detecting the use of emotionally loaded words, putting information in sequence, and so on. Children need to learn how to do these things with content they both hear and read.

Chapter 14

Children and the Library

*T*oday's library is a storehouse for both pleasure and information, containing not only the books, magazines, and newspapers traditionally found in libraries, but also records, tapes, cassettes, filmstrips, videotapes, picture files, and displays of many kinds. Besides all this, there probably are special rooms or areas (and equipment) for viewing or listening, computers and the software to accompany them, microfilmed materials and readers, copying machines, and even areas and equipment for making videotapes, filmstrips, and other visual aids. Even small libraries, including those found in schools, may have many of these things, although on a lesser scale than in university or large city libraries. Because of the addition of such materials and equipment, school libraries may now bear such names as "Instructional Materials Center." This too, however, could be considered a misnomer, since it seems to emphasize the teaching/learning aspects only, ignoring the delight, inspiration, and simple contentment children should find there as well.

Whatever its name, though, one of the most important—and pleasant—tasks a teacher has is to help children develop the habit of turning to the library for both pleasure and information. To do this, they must have the ability to locate the information needed or the particular item that will provide pleasure. This chapter discusses ways of developing the needed library skills: helping children to get familiar with the library as a whole, use the card catalog, locate books and other materials, learn to use equipment such as computers and video recorders, and become acquainted with special references of many kinds.

GUIDING PRINCIPLES

Provide time—and a place—for individual reading in every school day and at every level.

Despite the library's wealth of other materials, its main focus is still books, and these should also be the main focus of your teaching about the library. There are two reasons for this. First, as suggested above, children should get to know and love books. The child who forms the habit of visiting the library regularly will seldom be bored or have "nothing to do." Reading will supply relaxation after a hard-fought basketball game, while away a rainy afternoon, or provide a quiet activity before going to bed. Think of how many hours most of us spend during our lives simply waiting—in the dentist's office, airport, beauty salon, and so on. The habit of carrying a book on these occasions can make them times for enjoyment rather than annoyance. The second reason for placing emphasis on books is that they are the chief source of specific and detailed information. Computers have provided both speed and convenience in storing information as well as in regurgitating it, and most of us get much of our news and entertainment from television. But when we want to know more about a news event or study something in depth, we turn to newspapers, magazines, and books. Similarly, in the classroom you use films, cassettes, pictures, and other aids to provide motivation or add interest and variety to your lessons in all subject areas; yet texts and supplementary books are the basis for most of your teaching. And when the middle- or upper-grade student prepares an oral or written report, he needs more than is provided by a filmstrip, or she needs facts that require the use of an encyclopedia, an atlas, and an almanac. Thus helping children learn to turn to books for both pleasure and information and to be at home in the library should have high priority in your program.

The most valuable ally to enlist in teaching the library skills is the librarian, since most librarians have chosen their profession because they like books and want to share them, just as most teachers like children and want to help them grow. Naturally not all of the teaching can or should be turned over to the librarian. To a great extent, motivation for using library skills must come from classroom activities, and children will need a great deal of individual help and reinforcement both in the library and in the classroom. But an enthusiastic librarian who believes that books and other materials should be off the shelves and in children's hands will do much toward providing a stimulating and interesting environment in which children may learn.

Library skills must be taught directly and completely if they are really to be learned and used. Like any other skills, they are best learned in a situation where they are being used for a meaningful purpose. Therefore, they are best introduced when children want to locate information, find a book about something they are interested in, listen to a cassette as they read a particular story, or perhaps simply explore what this fascinating place is all about.

A spirit of discovery must exist in a classroom for library skills to be needed. As children explore, seeking to satisfy their curiosity, motivation for learning the library skills will be created. The major task, then, is introducing children to ideas, to information that appeals to them, and to new thoughts. Reading frequently to children—and this should be a habit exercised daily—is a good way to introduce them to the world beyond their experience and at the same time show the importance of books. A multimedia and multitext approach to teaching in all areas will also help children to learn to look beyond a single source for information. This does not mean that every child must have several texts for each subject, but rather that additional resources of many kinds should be available to children and should be a part of their daily activities.

A classroom such as this will of course have an attractive and well-supplied room library, which children are allowed and encouraged to use. The room library can supply the initial focus for teaching beginning library skills as you help children look up information, find books for pleasure reading, or locate a filmstrip for viewing.

Your own attitude is a vital factor. Even a simple act such as looking up the correct spelling of a word in the dictionary or turning to the atlas for a

Children's Magazine Guide (7 North Pinckney Street, Madison, WI 53703) indexes thirty-seven magazines most read by elementary- and middle-school children.

Room libraries are more fully discussed both in the following section and in Chapter 15.

specific fact will demonstrate to children the usefulness of library tools. Bringing in additional resources, showing your own interest in books, and encouraging (and helping) children to look up information will provide motivation for acquiring library skills.

A final *must* is knowing the children, their interests and abilities, and what they do outside school. A child who doesn't know how to use the card file or take notes is ill-prepared to go to the library alone to find information for a report. Nor can a reluctant reader whose only interest in life is football be expected to become enthusiastic about learning library skills in order to find out about the history of ballet—but he or she might do surprisingly well at finding out about the career of John Elway or Dan Marino or how and when football was first played. Thus, knowing when individual children are ready to take the next step and building on the knowledge they already have are as vital to teaching library skills as they are to any other learning activity.

INTRODUCTORY ACTIVITIES

At the primary level, as children are first beginning to look at and read books, they can also learn how to use and handle them, how to talk about them, how to locate the ones they want, and how to check out and return them. The same applies, of course, to materials and equipment in the media center.

These learnings can begin in the room library. Some teachers like to make this a materials center (especially if the school library is set up in this fashion), housing filmstrips, cassettes, picture files, and so on, as well as books. Certainly such an arrangement fosters the understanding that libraries contain more than books, but it has the disadvantage of increased noise and traffic. If you prefer this arrangement—or if space requires it—be sure to have a "quiet spot" nearby where children can read comfortably and without distraction.

However, most libraries—including those in many schools—have separate areas, even separate rooms, for different kinds of materials or activities. Therefore, the best arrangement seems to be to have the media center adjoin the library, possibly with a central "check-out" for both (if your school permits books and/or materials to be taken home).

The Media Center

Almost all children have watched a great deal of television; many have played video games or watched others play them; and many have had experience with cassettes or other software. Therefore, they are at least partially prepared for using the media center. Not all will be equally well prepared, however, and all will need guidance in using and caring for materials. Even very young children can learn to use filmstrip and slide projectors, to insert a cassette, or to operate a computer, but they should also learn from the beginning that any such equipment is not a toy and must be used and cared for properly. Work with them as they learn, and help them to set up their own list of standards for using media. This might be something like the following:

When You Use Media
1. Work quietly and don't disturb others.
2. Don't get fingerprints on filmstrips, slides, tapes, or lenses.
3. Don't tear or bend filmstrips. Handle all materials carefully.
4. Be sure you know how to work machines before using them.
5. Put materials away when you are finished.

Selecting materials for the media center should receive as much attention as is given to selecting books for the library—there is great variation in quality. Well-chosen materials can be used to enrich the curriculum as well as to guide children to books. For example, a beginning reader is likely to enjoy listening to a cassette recording as he or she "reads" Ezra Jack Keats's *Whistle for Willie*, and children will rush to find Pat Hutchins's *Rosie's Walk* after viewing the film (distributed by Weston Woods).

The amount of software available is growing like Pinocchio's nose. Since the advent of the computer, the market has been flooded with software, much of it very poor in quality or of a type that should not be used. This makes it necessary for teachers who want to use such materials to consult with the librarian, read current reviews in professional magazines, and check sources published by the American Library Association. And by all means keep in mind that since the quality of these materials varies greatly, they should all be previewed before you use or recommend them for the library or media center.

The Room Library

In this age of television, too many children come to school having had only limited experience with books or with seeing others read. It is the job of the school not only to teach children to read, but to teach them to *enjoy* reading and to turn readily to books for information. The television set can furnish both information and entertainment, but books give depth to understanding and become lifelong companions during leisure hours.

The Newbery Medal is awarded annually for the most distinguished contribution to children's literature published in the United States during the preceding year.

The Caldecott Medal, also awarded annually, is given for the most distinguished picture book for children published in the United States during the preceding year.

The library corner, then, should be the most inviting spot in the classroom and should contain as many books as possible. The teacher must know about books suitable for children and make many of these known to them. There are numerous aids available for this purpose: books on children's literature, such as those by Huck, Sutherland, Glazer and Williams, Stewig, and Cullinan; lists published by professional organizations and publishers; reviews of children's books that appear regularly in magazines such as *Language Arts, School Library Journal, The Horn Book*, and *The Reading Teacher*; and special lists, such as those of the Newbery and Caldecott award winners. The school librarian, if there is one, or the children's librarian at the city or county library should have many of these and should also be able to make recommendations. In addition, you should be familiar with many children's books, particularly those you select for the room library.

Books in the room library should be changed often so that no child will be unable to find one that interests him or her, although special favorites may be retained or brought back, since young children particularly love to "reread." Books should vary in level of difficulty and should be of many types. The following list may serve as a guide.

Picture or "Easy" Books

Carle, Eric. *The Mixed-up Chameleon*. Harper & Row, 1984.
Degen, Bruce. *Jamberry*. Harper & Row, 1983.
Dubanevich, Arlene. *Pigs in Hiding*. Scholastic, 1983.
Jonas, Ann. *Round Trip*. Greenwillow, 1983.
Keats, Ezra Jack. *Pet Show*. Macmillan, 1970.
Rylant, Cynthia. *The Relatives Came*. Macmillian, 1985.
Scarry, Richard. *Best Mother Goose Ever*. Western, 1970.
Seuss, Dr. *Horton Hears a Who!* Random, 1954.
Siebert, Diane. *Truck Song*. Harper & Row, 1984.
Wildsmith, Brian. *Brian Wildsmith's Birds*. Franklin Watts, 1957.
Wood, Audrey. *King Bidgood's in the Bathtub*. Harcourt, 1985.

Idea or Theme Books

Alexander, Martha. *Nobody Asked Me If I Wanted a Baby Sister*. Dial, 1971.
de Paola, Tomie. *Watch Out for the Chicken Feet in Your Soup*. Prentice-Hall, 1974.
Gramatky, Hardie. *Little Toot Through the Golden Gate*. Putnam's, 1975.
Hutchins, Pat. *Happy Birthday, Sam*. Greenwillow, 1978.
Keller, Holly. *Cromwell's Glasses*. Greenwillow, 1982.
Lexau, Joan. *Emily and the Klunky Baby and the Next-Door Dog*. Dial, 1972.
Paris, Lena. *Mom Is Single*. Children's Press, 1980.
Steptoe, John. *Stevie*. Harper & Row, 1969.
Viorst, Judith. *Alexander and the Terrible, Horrible, No Good, Very Bad Day*. Atheneum, 1972.
Wolf, Bernard. *Anna's Silent World*. Lippincott, 1977.

Animal Stories

Bate, Lucy. *Little Rabbit's Loose Tooth*. Crown, 1975.
Brown, Marc. *Arthur Goes to Camp*. Little, Brown, 1982.
Duvoisin, Roger. *Petunia*. Knopf, 1950.
Freeman, Don. *Dandelion*. Viking, 1964.
Hogrogian, Nonny. *Carrot Cake*. Greenwillow, 1977.
Holabird, Katharine. *Angelina Ballerina*. Crown, 1983.
Keats, Ezra Jack. *Hi, Cat!* Macmillan, 1967.
Kent, Jack. *Joey*. Prentice-Hall, 1984.
Lobel, Arnold. *Frog and Toad All Year*. Harper & Row, 1979.
Noble, Trinka. *The Day Jimmy's Boa Ate the Wash*. Dial, 1980.
Tresselt, Alvin. *The Beaver Pond*. Lothrop, Lee and Shepard, 1970.

Many other types should also be included: ABC books, counting books, picture and beginning dictionaries, books that help develop concepts children should learn, stories of other lands, fables, poetry, and so on. Choose

Children's Books about Libraries

Check It Out by Gail Gibbons (Harcourt Brace Jovanovich, 1985)
I Like the Library by Anne Rockwell (Dutton, 1977)
A Visit to the Sesame Street Library by Deborah Hautzig (Random House, 1986)

carefully, keeping in mind the interests, backgrounds, and needs of the particular children in your class. And choose books that you like so that you will be enthusiastic about sharing them. If you love books and if there are books suitable for every child in the class, motivation will be created for acquiring the beginning library skills.

Even in as small a place as the room library, books should be arranged on the shelves in some sort of logical way. This will enable children to learn that there is a pattern to the way libraries are set up and that the purpose of this pattern is to help them find books. The arrangement may be by type, by level of difficulty, or perhaps alphabetically (this would give meaningful practice with alphabetical order). Whatever the arrangement, explain it to the children, show them how to look for particular books, and teach them to return books to their proper places so that others will be able to find them.

When children first begin to handle books, they should also learn how to take care of them, and, as in other matters, they should help to formulate the standards themselves. Perhaps they will come up with something like this:

Taking Care of Books

1. Always have clean hands.
2. Don't write in a book that isn't yours.
3. Protect books from rain or snow.
4. Keep books away from younger brothers or sisters who don't know how to handle them.
5. Be careful not to tear pages.
6. Return books as soon as you are through with them.

As children learn to handle and care for books, they can also learn the terms used in talking about them. The most important terms (and the concepts they represent) that primary children can learn to use when talking about books are *title, author, illustrator*, and *table of contents*.

The concept of *title* is not a difficult one for children to grasp. They are already aware of their own names and those of their pets, the school, and so on. It is a simple matter, then, to explain that the name of a book is called a title and that this often helps to tell what the book is about—for example, *Curious George, My First Pictionary*, or *Millions of Cats*.

Author and *illustrator* can also be related to the children's own names. Just as children put their names on their papers, the person who writes a book puts his or her name on it. Most children know Dr. Seuss, for example, and can understand that if they like *Horton Hatches the Egg* they might also like other books by the same author. Several authors the children are familiar with might be used to illustrate this point, thereby laying the foundation for using the card catalog and the alphabetical arrangement of books by author to find books they will enjoy.

The illustrator is of great importance to a book for young children, who usually select books on the basis of the pictures alone. Again, just as children put their names on their own drawings, a person who draws in a book has his or her name on the cover. And just as authors may write more than one book, they may sometimes illustrate their own books. Show children books by such author-illustrators as Maurice Sendak, Arnold Lobel, Ezra Jack Keats, Nonny Hogrogian, and Leo Lionni and discuss ways in which the illustrations add to the books. Having copies of the same story—a fairy tale, for example—with pictures by different illustrators can add much to this discussion. Children will also enjoy drawing pictures about stories that are read or told; these can be posted, with captions showing the name of the story, the author, and the phrase "Illustrated by _____ ."

At the primary level there is little need for children to be concerned with publication information, but they should know that they can find the title of a book and the names of the author and illustrator on the title page. If they are curious about the other items found on this page, these can be explained simply, but they should not be emphasized, nor should children be required to know them.

Children ought to know that some books contain things other than stories or poems. The selection of books in the room library will demonstrate this, as will the regular use of resource materials. When discussing weather, for example, obtain from the library books that contain factual material at the children's level, including at least one that has a table of contents. Point out again that the title gives a general idea of what the book is about; then turn to the table of contents and show how it gives much more specific information. Competence in using this aid can be furthered by writing the name of the daily story on the chalkboard and having the children look up the page number in the table of contents.

The important concern at this level—or any other—is not the terminology of books, but the concepts related to the terminology and the understanding that books may provide not only pleasure but also knowledge of many kinds.

As soon as possible, arrange to take your class to the school and community libraries. Be sure to go first yourself, so that you will be familiar with the physical set-up and the locations of various types of materials. Involving parents in the class trip to the community library may encourage them to help their children obtain library cards or to get cards themselves and check out books for their children. Many parents may be unaware of the vast array of beautiful children's books that are published. Library visits should be prearranged, so the librarians will be available to talk to the children. It is important for children to know the librarians' names and to look on them as friends and helpers.

Before making these trips, teach library behavior and explain the reasons for library rules. If, as suggested earlier, children have learned how to handle and care for books, they will not be unwelcome guests in the library. If they have learned consideration for others, they will understand the need for quiet. The librarian can explain rules about checking out books, how long they may be kept, and so forth.

In some schools, library rules forbid young children to check out books. If this is true, it is still possible to schedule regular trips to the library to let the children help select books for the classroom. The librarian can explain the fun of browsing, help in selecting books, and show them where the

---

When children write their own books, they can include a page giving information about the author, illustrator, and "publisher"—something like "Miss Elton's Third Grade, Midland School."

Informational Books for Young Children

ABC's of the Ocean by Isaac Asimov (Walker, 1970)

Building a House by Byron Barton (Greenwillow, 1981)

Cars and How They Go by Joanna Cole (Crowell, 1983)

How Much Is a Million? by David Schwartz (Lothrop, Lee and Shepard, 1985)

Less Than Nothing Is Really Something by Robert Freeman (Crowell, 1973)

Once There Was a Tree by Natalia Romanova (Dial, 1985)

Squirrels by Brian Wildsmith (Franklin Watts, 1974)

Up Goes the Skyscraper by Dale Gibbons (Four Winds, 1986)

various kinds of books may be found and how they are arranged. And children should be allowed to explore for themselves as well.

As soon as children are old enough to check out books, they should be taught borrowing procedures. Here again it is a good idea to enlist the aid of the librarian. Actually checking out books is the best way to learn the procedures, but reinforcement and clarification of library terms may be provided by a bulletin board designed around a favorite book, showing the book card and the date due slip in the format used in your particular library. Examples of these two items are shown on the following page.

At this level, call number and copy number, like the publication information on the title page of the book, need not be stressed. If the children ask questions about these items, explain simply that they help to identify the book and show the librarian where it belongs on the shelves.

If your school does not allow primary children to check out books, you might prepare them for later use of the library by making sample cards for the books in the room library. (You may want to do this anyway if children need practice). Let the children select a different librarian daily and practice checking out and returning the books. Be sure to use the same procedure as that in the school library, and show children the importance of placing their full names—in their best printing—in the correct space on the card so that there is no confusion about who has checked out a book.

Many larger libraries use a photocopying or computerized system for book circulation rather than the type discussed here. If this is the case in the library you visit with the children, ask the librarian to show them how the procedure operates—they will not only be fascinated but will also be better prepared for using large libraries.

SKILLS AND ACTIVITIES FOR THE MIDDLE GRADES

Intermediate-grade children's knowledge about books and libraries will vary widely. Most children entering the fourth grade will have visited libraries, will know where to find picture and storybooks, and will have had some experience in checking out books. By this time, too, most children will have had experience with filmstrips, cassettes, picture files, and various types of displays in the classroom and will know that libraries have these items (especially if your school library is the media center) and that they can be checked out or used in the library just as books can.

During the intermediate grades, children will be embarking on more and more independent study and preparing both oral and written reports. Therefore, no later than about the fourth grade you should have a series of lessons and activities specifically designed to help children learn about the many kinds of materials to be found in libraries and how to locate them. It goes without saying, of course, that these lessons should be planned in conjunction with actual needs for finding and using information. Most language arts textbooks for the intermediate grades contain one or more units on using the library. If these are suited to the children, their needs, and the card that is in the pocket inside the cover

call number	j C	2
author title	Cleary, Beverly Ramona Quimby Age 8	

Date Due	Borrower's Name
Feb. 19	David George

call number · copy number · author · title · date due · your name

date due is found inside the book on a slip like this

j
C
Cleary

Ramona Quimby Age 8

Date Due			
Jan. 14 Apr. 29			

Library Name
City, State

particular library or libraries they will be using, by all means use them. Be very sure, however, that the materials you select are both adequate and suitable, for this is one of the most valuable lessons you will teach. There is little point in teaching children to read and enjoy books and the knowledge to be found in them if they are unable to find the books and other materials they want and need.

Basic Library Skills

As suggested previously, children should be exposed to books from the very beginning of the school year. Make sure that the classroom library is stocked with a variety of books—stories, poems, factual books, humor, fantasy, stories about problems children face, and so forth. Read some of these to the children; then talk about the library, mentioning shelf arrangements (left to right), shelf labels, and different classifications (easy books, juvenile, etc.).

Ask the librarian to give the class a tour of the school library, explaining where different books, magazines, and newspapers are located and why they are located in these places. Comparing a library with a supermarket may help children to understand that, just as all the fruits and vegetables are located near each other, all the books on similar subjects are located together: stories are together; biographies are together; and nonfiction books on topics such as conservation, hobbies, sports, and archaeology are grouped.

Intermediate children should have in mind the concepts related to book vocabulary, such as *title, author, illustrator, cover,* and *spine.* These may need review. To aid children in studying efficiently and in gathering and reporting information, they also need to develop an understanding of the purposes and uses of the various parts of a book. This knowledge can be developed over a period of time, as children have need to use various kinds of books and refer to various sections of them. They should become familiar with the following terms:

Factual Books for Older Children

Bats by Sylvia A. Johnson (Lerner, 1985)
Being Blind by Rebecca B. Marcus (Hastings House, 1981)
The Hospital Book by James Howe (Crown, 1981)
Sea Guide to Whales of the World: A Complete Guide to the World's Living Whales, Dolphins, and Porpoises by Lyall Watson (Dutton, 1981)
Seeing What Plants Do by Joan Elma Rahn (Atheneum, 1972)
A Snake Lover's Diary by Barbara A. Brenner (Young Scott, 1970)
To Space and Back by Sally Ride (Lothrop, Lee and Shepard, 1986)
Where the Bald Eagles Gather by Dorothy Patent (Ticknor and Fields, 1984)

Publisher	The company that printed the book and put it together
City	Place where the book was published
Copyright date	When the book was published
Title page	A page giving the title, author, and publisher
Dedication	A special page in the book where the author thanks people, often special friends or members of his or her family
Introduction, Preface, or Foreword	Any one of these names can be used for the section in the front of the book that tells briefly what the book is about or why it was written
List of illustrations	A list usually found in a book with many pictures, maps, or charts
Table of contents	A list of stories or chapters (Refer to this throughout the school year in all subject areas so that children become familiar with it. If you are using a basal reader,

	have children use the table of contents to find their current story.)
Glossary	A small dictionary that defines words used in this particular book (In elementary grades this is often found in the back of basal reading, social studies, or science books. Basal series frequently provide experiences in using the glossary. Capitalize on these.)
Index	A list of subjects, found in the back of most books, that is the principal means for locating information (Several lessons will be needed for children to develop an understanding of the arrangement of indexes, their location, the format used, any subtopic arrangements, and the relationship to the table of contents in amount of detail.)

Ideally, before children are asked to use the library to prepare an oral or written report, they should have visited it many times and checked out books; they should have had opportunities to browse among the different kinds of materials to be found there and to know the librarian as a friend and helper. Try to see that the children in your class have as much preparation of this kind as possible. Improvise where necessary (some suggestions are included throughout this chapter), but try to avoid simply having available in the classroom everything that they will need to prepare a report. Children need to learn how to locate information for themselves; they cannot forever be dependent on the teacher.

However, children should not be expected to learn all at one time both the skills of organizing material from several sources and those of using the library to locate information. Using the room library, give them practice in taking notes and correlating information from two or three sources; then let them advance to using the school library for further information. Using the library to locate information involves using the card catalog, knowing the difference between fiction and nonfiction, understanding what call numbers signify, and perhaps even knowing the basic elements of classification systems. These skills are interdependent. There are many things to be learned at the same time; thus, some practice exercises may need to be provided. If the need for the skills is real, however—that is, if children are preparing reports to be used in connection with a particular unit of study—practice exercises will be more meaningful.

Chapter 13 has suggestions for teaching how to locate specific information and take notes.

The skills discussed in the following sections are interrelated and must be presented at the same time. They are separated here for purposes of organization; for the same reason, practice exercises may also need to be presented separately. But library skills should never be taught in isolation from any real need for their use.

Using the Card Catalog

On children's initial visit to the library, the librarian will undoubtedly show them the card catalog and explain its use. Later, when the opportunity arises, this learning can be reinforced. A child may say "This was a good book. I would like to read another one like it.'' This is the time to suggest that he or she look in the card catalog to see if there is another book by the same author or on the same subject. Another child might report ''Someone told me the name of a good book, but I don't know how to find it in the library.'' Then, the use of title cards can be introduced. Thus, when children are ready to prepare reports, the catalog will not be entirely unfamiliar to them. Before they can be truly independent in using it, however, they will need a lesson or series of lessons demonstrating the various kinds of cards and how they can be of help.

Begin with the physical set-up of the card catalog or catalogs. In most libraries, author, title, and subject cards are all filed together, in alphabetical order. In some, however, each of these categories is filed separately; children should be aware of both possibilities. Similarly, cards for audiovisual materials may be filed in a separate catalog, or they may be with those for books. Libraries that middle-grade children use, however, are likely to file all—or most—cards together. In this case they will probably use a color-coding system, which is especially useful, since it helps both you and the children to discover quickly and easily whether the library has a filmstrip or cassette, for instance, that might be useful in presenting a report or teaching a particular unit. In this system, each type of material is assigned a particular color. That is, cards for filmstrips might have a strip of green tape across the top, cassettes a red one, films a blue one, and so on. These items will be filed alphabetically according to both subject and title.

A helpful technique is to go to the school or community library and sketch the outside of the card catalog, including guide letters. Display this sketch on a chart or bulletin board and use short oral drills to provide practice. Stress the alphabetical arrangement, point out that even the books listed under an author's name are in alphabetical order, and call attention to the fact that articles (*a, an,* and *the*) are not considered in alphabetizing titles.

Chart or Bulletin Board

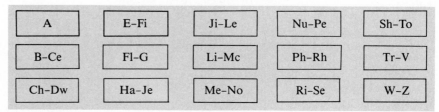

A	E–Fi	Ji–Le	Nu–Pe	Sh–To
B–Ce	Fl–G	Li–Mc	Ph–Rh	Tr–V
Ch–Dw	Ha–Je	Me–No	Ri–Se	W–Z

Ask questions such as these:

> In which drawer would you find:
> *How to Be a Perfect Person in Three Days?*
> information about space travel?
> basketball stories?
> a cassette recording of *And Now Miguel?*
> a Halloween poem?
> a biography of Jim McMahon?

Continue this type of activity only as long as seems necessary, making sure to include a variety of topic headings, as well as many that might be found under more than one heading. And help children learn to explore all possible headings—for example, a Halloween poem might be located under "Halloween," "holidays," or even "poetry" or "poems"; and the cassette could be listed in the general file or in a special one.

Children who are ready to use the card catalog will have already had a great deal of experience in using other materials that are alphabetically arranged, such as dictionaries, indexes, and telephone directories. Therefore, they should have little difficulty in understanding the alphabetical nature of the catalog. The important part of this learning is understanding the different kinds of cards in the catalog and how to use them to find books and information. In conjunction with teaching about the physical set-up of the catalog, then, explain the cards themselves. A bulletin board display showing enlarged drawings of actual cards from the catalog of the school or community library is almost a must. (See pages 405–410 for types of cards that should be included.) These can be placed below the chart showing the outsides of the drawers. Both color and meaning can be added by putting explanatory notes on colored cards and attaching each to the item it refers to with a piece of colored yarn. Be sure to include all types of cards and to keep the display up until after the children have had actual experience in using the catalog to find information for a report.

Children should learn to use a card catalog by using one.

Children will have many questions about the cards and the items on them: "Is a book listed only once in the catalog? What does the call number mean?" Answer these questions as thoroughly as possible to help children feel competent and at ease in using library aids. Some questions may not have particularly logical answers; when this is true, simply say so. For example, why are an author's first *and* last names capitalized when only the first word of a book title is? Why does one card contain more complete information than another card on the same book?

If children have had a limited amount of library experience, they may need to do practice exercises to ensure that they know exactly how to use the card catalog. For example, they might report on how many books the library has by Lois Lenski, Beverly Cleary, or some other author they like; they could begin with a list of book titles (both fiction and nonfiction) and find the names of the authors and where the books are located in the library; or each child could select a subject and find three books containing information about it, what subject headings they are listed under, and where they are located on the shelves. Again use this kind of practice only as much as seems necessary; if some children are already fairly adept at using the catalog, let them work on special reports or serve as "assistant teachers" for those who need practice.

As soon as possible, each child should select a topic and go to the library to find information for a brief oral report; purposeful activities will provide greater reinforcement than any number of practice drills. Frequent opportunities to use the library in connection with units of study in all areas of the curriculum will both enrich the curriculum and help learnings to become well established. A special caution should be observed here, however: *know* your library or libraries and make sure the children choose topics about which information is available. No amount of teaching about library procedures will be successful if a child's first efforts to find material are unsuccessful.

Activities related to using the card catalog should be designed to ensure that the children learn the following:

- Author, title, and subject cards are all arranged alphabetically.
- Cards for media items may be filed in the general catalog or in a separate one. These cards are also in alphabetical order, under both subject and title.
- Titles beginning with *A*, *An*, or *The* are alphabetized according to their second word. (Note that *And* is not included here.)
- A number in the title may or may not be spelled out but the title card is filed as though it were.
- Names beginning with *Mac* or *Mc* are filed together. (Children will be interested in knowing that this is a recent development, brought about by the use of computerized cataloging. Computers apparently don't recognize a difference!)
- Abbreviated words are listed as if they were spelled out. For example, for "U.S. Government," the alphabetical arrangement places this entry as if it were spelled out—"United States Government." The same applies to such abbreviations as *Dr., Mrs., Mr., St.,* and so on.

- Author cards for books by the same writer are filed according to the alphabetical order of the titles of the books: "Politi, Leo, *Butterflies Come, The*" comes before "Politi, Leo, *Song of the Swallows.*"

If your school library does not have a card catalog or if your school does not have a library, make a card catalog for the books in the room library so that children will have an opportunity to learn how to use this valuable aid. Use shoe boxes or metal file boxes for the drawers, making author, title, and subject cards for each book. Set up the library corner as much like a real library as possible, and allow children to take turns being the class librarian, checking out books and seeing that they are returned to their correct places on the shelves. Even though this catalog will be small, children will have fun "playing library" while they learn that the catalog can help them:

> find a book quickly when they know the title but not the author;
> find out whether the library has another book by an author whose work they have enjoyed (it could be checked out and therefore not visible on the shelf); and
> find out whether the library has a book on a particular subject.

Another possibility is to enlist the cooperation of one or two other teachers in making a cooperative catalog. The call number for each book could indicate which room the book is in and where it can be found in that room, and children would be allowed to check books out from any of the several rooms. Thus, many more books would be available to each child. This would entail a great deal of work initially, but it would be well worth the time spent, particularly in a small school or with children who, for one reason or another, do not have the opportunity to use a large library regularly.

Using Call Numbers

Children should learn about call numbers while they are learning to use the card catalog. They should also learn the difference between fiction and nonfiction and the meaning of biography. Middle-grade children can understand that fiction is a story that someone made up, even though some characters may be real people and some incidents true; that nonfiction contains true information that the author has tried to verify and may or may not be in story form; and that biography is the true story of the life of a real person.

The following understandings should be developed:

1. Books of fiction are shelved together and arranged in alphabetical order according to the author's last name. Just as children's books and adult books are in different sections, sometimes picture books and books for older children can be found in separate sections—in fact, many libraries have added a third group that includes books for children in the upper grades. A fiction book for young readers will have the letter j on its spine, possibly followed by a capital letter indicating the first letter of the author's last name. These

letters constitute the call number of the book. If the library has a special section for older children, books found there will be marked with y or ya (young adult) rather than j (juvenile). Cards for both these types, as well as those for picture books, will be found in the children's catalog.

2. Biographies may be shelved in either of two ways. In most libraries children will use, biographies are likely to be together and have either the letter B or the call number 92 on their spines. Some libraries, however, are beginning to shelve biographies along with books about the subject's vocation or area of expertise; that is, a biography of Willie McGee will be found in the sports section, one about Beverly Sills in the music section, and so on. In either case, though, biographies are alphabetized according to the name of the person the book is about rather than the name of the author. Therefore, a biography will have the first letter of the subject's name beneath the call letter or number so that all books about the same person will be together. Thus, a child looking for a biography of a particular person will have only one place to look instead of several.

3. Other nonfiction books (biography is nonfiction) are arranged in numerical order according to numbers that indicate what each book is about. Thus, as with biographies, all the books about the same subject can be shelved together. Call numbers are assigned according to a classification system that has been worked out to include all subject areas. There are two of these systems; one or the other is used in almost every library of any size. General reference books such as encyclopedias and dictionaries, which contain information about many subjects, are another special category of nonfiction. These usually have the letter R on their spines, are kept in a special area, and can seldom be checked out of the library.

4. Media items have call numbers similar to those for books and are often grouped together for ease of care, use, and storage—that is, records are together, cassettes together, pictures in a special file, and so forth. In the juvenile sections of some libraries, however, a record might be found on the shelf next to the book that is recorded, a cassette could be packaged in a plastic bag with its book and kept in a special place, and so on. The librarian should be asked to help if these materials cannot be located.

Children who understand how to use the card catalog and what the call numbers mean are well on their way to being able to find what they are looking for, even in the large libraries they will encounter later. It is important to help them understand that this is not simply a complicated system set up by adults to try to confuse them. Rather, the card catalog is like a telephone directory; just as a child can look in the telephone directory to find out where a friend lives, so he or she can look in the card catalog to find out where a particular book—or information about a particular subject—can be located. The call number is the book's "address"; it shows where the book is shelved in the library, and it helps the librarian to put the book away quickly so that another person will be able to find it.

Children should *never* be required to memorize either the Dewey Decimal or Library of Congress system of classification; there is no more point in this than in memorizing the call numbers of individual books. The important concept to learn is that the numbers will guide them in locating the books they want. If they are curious about what the numbers mean, a simple explanation can help them to understand why books about the same subject have the same or similar numbers and to recognize that there is order in the arrangement.

Although most university and other large libraries now use the Library of Congress system, many small libraries—including those in schools—find the Dewey Decimal system better suited to their needs. Begin with whichever is used in libraries available to the children, although it would be a good idea to point out that this is not the only system. If neither system is used, teaching should be postponed until it can be meaningful.

Children might be interested in learning something about Melvil Dewey, a most interesting man.

Dewey Decimal System. In the Dewey Decimal System, books are arranged numerically on the shelves; therefore, anyone who can count and knows the call number of the book he or she wants can find it easily—the call number, of course, is found by looking in the card catalog. The numbers represent ten general subject areas, as follows:

000–099	Reference books, such as encyclopedias and bibliographies (books about books) (Many of these have the letter R on the spine and can seldom be checked out of a library; those that have call numbers, such as computer science books, usually can be checked out.)
100–199	Philosophy, psychology, ethics (conduct)
200–299	Religion, including mythology and religions of all peoples
300–399	Social sciences: law, government, education, vocations, civics, economics
400–499	Language: dictionaries and books about the study of all languages
500–599	Science: mathematics, physics, chemistry, biology, zoology, botany
600–699	Useful arts: medicine, engineering, agriculture, aviation, manufacturing, etc.
700–799	Fine arts: painting, music, photography, recreation
800–899	Literature: poetry, plays, novels, and criticisms of these
900–999	History, geography, travel, biography

Each of these general areas is divided into many subtopics, each of which has its own number. For example, the 630s are devoted to agriculture, and a book on forestry will be numbered 634, probably followed by a decimal point and another number to indicate a further subdivision of that subtopic.

Library of Congress Classification. The Library of Congress classification may be explained if it is used in your library. By the time children reach the upper grades, they should at least be aware that there is more than one system of classification, since they may be using more than one library.

A	General works—polygraphy
B	Philosophy—religion
C	History—auxiliary science
D	History and topography (except America)
E & F	America
G	Geography—anthropology *(continues on page 411)*

CATALOG CARDS
DEWEY DECIMAL SYSTEM

author card

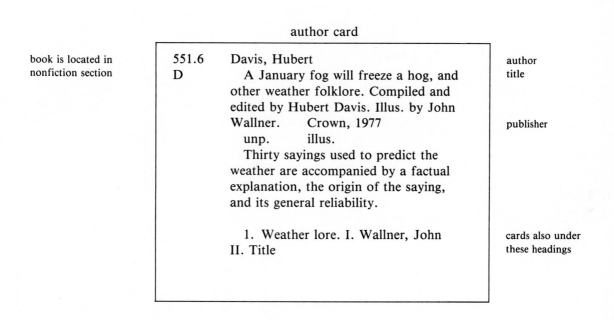

book is located in
nonfiction section

551.6
D   Davis, Hubert
    A January fog will freeze a hog, and
other weather folklore. Compiled and
edited by Hubert Davis. Illus. by John
Wallner.   Crown, 1977
    unp.   illus.
    Thirty sayings used to predict the
weather are accompanied by a factual
explanation, the origin of the saying,
and its general reliability.

    1. Weather lore. I. Wallner, John
II. Title

author
title

publisher

cards also under
these headings

title card

pages are not
numbered; book
is illustrated

A January fog will freeze a hog, and
other weather folklore

551.6
D   Davis, Hubert
    A January fog will freeze a hog, and
other weather folklore. Compiled and
edited by Hubert Davis. Illus. by John
Wallner.   Crown, 1977
    unp.   illus.

    1. Weather lore. I. Wallner, John
II. Davis, Hubert

remember that this
card will be found
under J, not A

subject card

WEATHER LORE

551.6   Davis, Hubert
         A January fog will freeze a hog, and
      other weather folklore. Compiled and
      edited by Hubert Davis. Illus. by John
      Wallner.   Crown, 1977
         unp.   illus.
         Thirty sayings used to predict the
      weather are accompanied by a factual
      explanation, the origin of the saying,
      and its general reliability.

         1. Weather lore. I. Wallner, John
      II. Title

note that cards are
alphabetized by first
letter at top of card,
regardless of
indentation

there will also be a
card for this book under
the illustrator's
name

title card

The great Gilly Hopkins

j   Paterson, Katherine
Fiction   The great Gilly Hopkins. New York:
           Crowell, 1978.

              1. Foster care homes--fiction
           I. Title

book may be found
in juvenile fiction

cards for fiction are
virtually the same in
Dewey Decimal and
Library of Congress
systems

author card

```
j          Paterson, Katherine
Fiction        The great Gilly Hopkins. New York:
           Crowell, 1978.

               1. Foster care homes--fiction
               I. Title
```

when illustrator
is important,
there may be a
third card

see and see also cards

there is nothing
catalogued under
this heading; look
under woodcarving
for information
about whittling

```
WHITTLING      see

WOODCARVING
```

some information
can be found under
this heading; you
may find additional
information under
the second heading

```
AIRPLANES      see also

AERONAUTICS
```

CATALOG CARDS
LIBRARY OF CONGRESS SYSTEM

author card

call number—book
is in juvenile
nonfiction

jPN   Bishop, Ann
6371.5   Noah riddle? Pictures by
B52   Jerry Warshaw. Chicago,
J. Whitman, 1970.

40 p.   col. illus.   22 cm.

A collection of riddles about
Noah and the animals in his
ark.

1. Riddles
I. Warshaw, Jerry
II. Title

book has 40 pages
and color
illustrations

title card

jPN   Noah riddle?
6371.5
B52

Bishop, Ann
Noah riddle? Pictures by
Jerry Warshaw. Chicago,
J. Whitman, 1970.

40 p.   col. illus.   22 cm.

A collection of riddles about
Noah and the animals in his
ark.

1. Riddles
I. Bishop, Ann
II. Warshaw, Jerry

subject card

```
        RIDDLES

jPN     Bishop, Ann
6371.5     Noah riddle? Pictures by
B52     Jerry Warshaw. Chicago,
        J. Whitman, 1970.

        40 p.   col. illus.   22 cm.

          A collection of riddles about
        Noah and the animals in his
        ark.

              1. Bishop, Ann   I. Warshaw, Jerry
              II. Title
```

illustrator card

```
        Warshaw, Jerry

jPN     Bishop, Ann
6371.5     Noah riddle? Pictures by
B52     Jerry Warshaw. Chicago,
        J. Whitman, 1970.

        40 p.   col. illus.   22 cm.

          A collection of riddles about
        Noah and the animals in his
        ark.

              1. Riddles
              I. Bishop, Ann
              II. Title
```

cassette cards

Oversize probably means that the cassette is packaged with the book by the same name and kept in a special place in the library; ask the librarian about location

CASSETTE
j
Oversize
PZ
8.1
.M159
Ar

McDermott, Gerald
    Arrow to the sun.
[Sound recording.] --
Weston Woods, 1975

publisher

1 cassette [LTR 184C]

order number of cassette

1. Pueblo Indians--Legends
I. Title

CASSETTE
j
Oversize
PZ
8.1
.M159
Ar

Arrow to the sun

McDermott, Gerald
    Arrow to the sun.
[Sound recording.]--
Weston Woods, 1975

remember these cards may be color-coded if filed in the general file

1 cassette [LTR 184C]

1. Pueblo Indians--Legends
I. McDermott, Gerald

cards for other media will be similar to these

PUEBLO INDIANS--Legends

CASSETTE
j
Oversize
PZ
8.1
.M159
Ar

McDermott, Gerald
    Arrow to the sun.
[Sound recording.]--
Weston Woods, 1975

1 cassette [LTR 184C]

1. McDermott, Gerald
I. Title

H	Social science
J	Political sciences
K	Law
L	Education
M	Music
N	Fine arts
P	Language and literature
Q	Science
R	Medicine
S	Agriculture—plant and animal industry
T	Technology
U	Military service
V	Naval service
Z	Bibliography and library science

Using Media

As has been stated several times in this chapter, the elementary-school library usually contains many materials other than books. A well-stocked library may have pictures, graphics of many kinds, films and filmstrips, slides, records and cassettes, programmed materials, kits and games, models, videotapes, and computers and software. In some schools some of these materials may be housed separately, for example, in a materials center or computer lab, but learning to find and use them should be considered a part of library instruction.

Most children will have had experience with various kinds of media both at home and in school, but many will need further—or more specialized—instruction. For example, more and more libraries are using computerized cataloging; if there is such a library in your area, arrange for the children to visit it and receive instruction—and, ideally, experience in using it. Computers, like video cassettes, are becoming an inescapable part of our lives, so children should learn how to use them.

Children need practice both in locating the various audiovisual aids and in using them to supplement and/or add interest to reports, just as you use such materials to improve your lessons for the class. Children have some experience with this as early as kindergarten, during "Show and Tell" sessions, and may have used pictures or charts to illustrate simple reports in the primary grades. So, as soon as they have become sufficiently familiar with the card catalog and the library itself to prepare simple reports using more than one source, plan for them to give reports in several subject areas, for which they may use various audiovisual aids. Make sure, however, that children understand that the aids chosen must fit the organizational plan for the report. Point out that if a particular filmstrip, for example, cannot be included in the outline for the report, it should not be a part of that report, however interesting it may be.

Such reports, when well prepared, not only will enrich classroom activities but will help to prepare children for the kinds of presentations that many will be expected to make during later school years and in adult life.

SPECIAL REFERENCES

The use of an encyclopedia, atlas, almanac, biographical dictionary, fact book, or similar reference involves many of the same skills as those needed for effective use of a dictionary or a library card catalog. In addition, skillful use of most reference books requires the ability to locate the particular section, paragraph, or sentence within a topic or a book that gives the specific information sought, and some familiarity with each of the reference sources—familiarity gained through practice in using them.

Encyclopedias

An encyclopedia such as *Childcraft* can provide primary-grade children with good experiences in seeking and locating information in an encyclopedia. Introduce encyclopedia use by demonstrating that you use the index to find where to look for information and that you can then turn to the correct

Children will benefit from familiarity with many kinds of reference books.

page and read the information you were looking for. Do this frequently as more information is needed on subjects being discussed. Tell and show the children what you are doing, and read what you find. Primary-grade children should be permitted to browse in the encyclopedias available to them, and as soon as they have learned to read with sufficient skill, they may be assigned simple facts to look up.

Intermediate-grade children should receive more direct instruction, which should include the following skills and understandings:

- The form in which material in an encyclopedia is arranged, and differences in arrangement in the encyclopedias available for their use
- Knowledge of the location of the index and the meanings of guide letters on the covers of volumes; particular attention should be given to boldface type, parentheses, italics, and so on
- The use of pronunciation keys, cross-reference listings, and bibliographies at the close of articles

Children should discover that there are also many specialized encyclopedias—for example, about science, sports, animals, and so on.

Many good encyclopedias for children are available—*The New Book of Knowledge, Compton's, The World Book, Britannica Junior, Americana*, and *Merit Student's Encyclopedia*, to name a few—and most school libraries have several of these. Children should have experience with all that are available to them. In connection with learning to take notes, each child can select a topic and look for information about it in all of the encyclopedias available. Comparing the information found will help children to discover the importance of looking in several sources for information. This should be done a number of times with a number of subjects; repeated lessons under guidance are essential for effective use of these materials.

Children can work both individually and in groups to gather information for oral reports. A group report can be valuable in several ways: the children can learn organization through planning what information each will look up and report; they can help each other in both finding and organizing material; and together they can present a more complete coverage of material than if each child were working individually.

Opportunities should also arise in an activity of this sort for children to discover that different sources sometimes present conflicting or different facts. Discuss how this might happen and emphasize the importance of using several sources to try to verify facts as far as is possible. It is also helpful to point out that the copyright date of a book may have a bearing on the accuracy of certain facts—population figures and scientific data, for example. In other words, information might not have been wrong—or known to be wrong—at the time it was printed.

Children enjoy working with encyclopedias and other reference tools, and this type of experience provides opportunities for learning to locate information; to read critically; to take notes on, summarize, and outline what they have read; to prepare an oral or written report; to use handwriting, spelling, and punctuation skills; to compose with specific information and an audience in mind; and to do proofreading and editing. Thus, learning to use the encyclopedia not only is valuable in itself but also involves practice in a wealth of related language skills.

Atlases

Use of the atlas is frequently taught in connection with social studies, but, as with most teaching in social studies and other subject matter areas, the tools and skills are those of the language arts.

Like use of the encyclopedia, use of the atlas should be taught first through demonstration. If the atlas includes a section that tells how to get the most out of it, this should be used as an aid. *The World Book Atlas*, for example, has at the beginning a section called "How to Get the Most out of *The World Book Atlas*," which explains how to find places, directions, and distances; how to understand symbols and population figures; how to pronounce names of cities; and how to understand abbreviations and foreign geographical terms. This atlas is also color-keyed to help the user find quickly sections such as the United States, Asia, Africa, the index, and so on. Children using this atlas to learn about the United States can find both physical and political maps of the entire country, as well as maps of regions and individual states. There are historical maps showing colonial America, the colonies at the time of the Revolution, territories opened up by 1800, and westward expansion from 1800 to 1850; maps showing positions and routes of the forces during the Vicksburg, Chattanooga, and Atlanta campaigns of the Civil War; plus two maps of the eastern theater of battle in 1862–1863 and 1864–1865. Other maps show principal air routes, railroads, and highways; charts give populations and areas of states and major cities and distances between these cities. In addition, one can learn that Mexico City is the largest city in North America, that the highest elevation is Alaska's Mt. McKinley at 20,320 feet, and that the lowest spot is California's Death Valley, 282 feet below sea level. And this is only part of what the atlas can reveal; there are maps and charts showing weather, population density, average income, available medical care, and so on. Children will be truly amazed at the variety of information that can be gleaned from a single book.

To give children experience with the atlas, have each child choose a city in the United States that he or she would like to visit. Help to direct selections so that each city chosen is large enough to be shown on maps and listed in at least some tables. Then have each child see how much information can be found about his or her city and write this information on a small card. Perhaps the class could discuss the kinds of facts they want to know and formulate a list of questions such as the following:

> How far is the city from where we live?
> What route would I take to get there by plane? train? car?
> What kind of weather does the city have?
> What is its population?
> How many feet above sea level is the city?
> Is it located in an agricultural or industrial area?

The information gained through such an activity can be used to make a very attractive bulletin board—a map of the United States surrounded by the cards the children have made, each connected with a piece of colored yarn to a pin showing the location of the city. A map can be made very easily by taping a piece of white shelf paper or tagboard to the chalkboard,

There are specialized atlases, too—for example, *The Historical Atlas, Atlas of Exploration,* and *Atlas of Archeology.*

using the opaque projector to focus an image of the map on the paper, and then drawing the outline with a felt pen. The children can color the states and locate their cities and other points of interest.

Once the children have learned to find places through the use of the index and map searching, teach them about directions and aids to pinpointing places. Parallels of latitude and meridians of longitude should be explained and discussed. Ask the children questions: "Which is farther from our city—Houston, Texas or Tallahassee, Florida? If you were traveling from Louisville, Kentucky to Memphis, Tennessee, which direction would you travel?"

Other atlas activities include these:

1. The reading of map symbols is necessary for understanding a map. The children can make a bulletin board display showing the common map symbols and their meanings. Allow the children to copy these symbols from actual maps in an atlas. Perhaps the class could make up a game that involves identifying map symbols.

2. Determining distances on maps can and should be taught as part of an arithmetic lesson. This is another example of the way language arts can be integrated with other subject areas.

3. Abbreviations and foreign geographic terms become understandable to children once they are able to read and understand the tables where these are listed. Once children are aware of such tables, they will enjoy looking for the new-found words or abbreviations on the maps.

4. An atlas also gives a great deal of information about a country—the area in square miles, the population and population density, the form of government, the capital and the largest cities, official and major languages—all on one easy-to-read table. It also gives information about the world as a whole— the largest countries of the world in population and in area, climates, rainfall, and so forth. Give the children questions that require them to find such information: "What is the coldest it ever got in North America and where was this? Where was it the warmest in North America, and what was the temperature? In what countries—or on which continents—do most of the people in the world live?"

5. Teaching about relief maps found in an atlas can be related to the making of salt-and-flour maps. Salt-and-flour maps can be made of a state, of a country, or of areas to help develop concepts such as peninsula, gulf, bay, or plateau. A child who uses an atlas as a guide in making a salt-and-flour map of a plateau will have solid knowledge of that term. Activities of this type are particularly beneficial for children who have difficulty with reading. (Make the salt-and-flour mixture with one cup each of salt, flour, and water, plus one tablespoon of powdered alum. The mixture can be stored in old coffee cans until you are ready to use it. If it dries out, add more water.)

Other References

A library contains a wealth of other reference materials with which children should become familiar; the following may be of particular interest. In addition, permitting children to browse in libraries and encouraging them to report on interesting things they discover may suggest other areas of study.

Children will be fascinated with the many kinds of one-volume references to be found in the library. A few are listed below; let them see how many others they can find.
Book of Lists
Dictionary of Art and Artists
Dictionary of Costume
The Ethnic Almanac
Geographical Dictionary
Guiness Book of World Records
Webster's Sports Dictionary

The Kid's World Almanac of Records and Facts, by Margo McLoone-Basta and Alice Siegel (World Almanac Publications, 1985), contains a special chapter of questions children ask, such as "How much does the earth weigh?" and "What makes popcorn pop?"

Children will also enjoy *First of Everything: A Compendium of Important, Eventful, and Just-Plain-Fun Facts about All Kinds of Firsts,* by Dennis Sanders (Delacorte, 1981).

Almanacs. Children should learn that an almanac is a source of all kinds of fascinating information. The best way to teach them what an almanac contains and how to use it is to provide them with copies and allow them time to explore. Once they have done some browsing, a few specific lessons should be sufficient to familiarize them with this interesting reference. The following are a few suggestions:

1. Ask each child to write the name of a magazine or newspaper that is available locally. Then let each one use the almanac to find out what the circulation of that periodical is.
2. Have each child select a city and use the almanac to find out its population, the height of its tallest building, and so on.
3. Let each child look for a famous person who shares his or her last name. The class might even like to make a *Who's Who* of these famous "relatives."
4. Have children make up questions for which answers can be found in the almanac—for example, "Who won the National League batting championship in 1971?" These can be placed on cards and exchanged, perhaps with children divided into teams and competing to see which team can find all the answers first.

Famous First Facts. Intermediate-grade children have been known to get into the "he did"–"he didn't" type of argument. Many times such an argument can be settled by referring to *Famous First Facts.* The index in this book is different from others children may be familiar with; it is divided into five separate sections with information listed by topic, person involved, geographic location, year, and day of the year. This index can be used in many ways. For example, the children could make a map of their state, showing the locations of many famous "firsts." Or each child could make a list of the important events that occurred on his or her birthday or on a particular holiday. These lists might be incorporated into a bulletin board display entitled "Famous Days," which would include a picture of each child, the date of his or her birthday, and the list of events compiled by the child. A similar display could focus on famous events of a particular year—perhaps the year most of the children were born or the year they started attending school. This type of activity can stimulate conversation and lead to other language activities.

Books of Quotations. Books of quotations may be introduced in a manner similar to that used to introduce almanacs and *Famous First Facts.* The primary objective is for children to become aware that there are books like this and to understand how they are organized and in what ways they are helpful. Again, a bulletin board can be useful. It might be entitled, "I Wish I'd Said That," with each child selecting an author—perhaps just because the name appeals—and then finding a quotation from the author selected. These may be written on cards, along with credit to the author and the source, and placed on the board. To extend this activity, children might check for facts about the person in an encyclopedia, take notes, and give orally or write a brief report.

The reference works mentioned above are intended as suggestions only—so many excellent books are available that it would be impossible to teach about all of them. The important thing is for children to become aware of the many resources to be found in libraries and to become familiar with ways to use them. Plan lessons around those that are of special interest to your class or that may be used in conjunction with class activities or units of study.

ACTIVITIES FOR THE UPPER GRADES

Children in the upper grades are apt to vary widely with respect to library skills, perhaps at least partly because of the mobility of today's population. Some may still be learning to use the card catalog and the special references discussed in the preceding sections. Many will still be taking notes that are either too copious or inadequate. And nearly all will need help in combining information from several sources into an organized report. These are learnings essential to a child's success in school and to his or her personal growth. Make sure, then, that upper-grade children have practice in these skills as need is indicated.

Begin with simple, short reports, possibly even requiring only one source of information. Or perhaps you might assign group reports, with each child responsible for only one aspect. Go with the class to the library and observe children as they work, to discover individual and group needs. Then, if necessary, design individual or group exercises (similar to those suggested for the middle grades) to meet these needs. Continue this sort of practice, along with short reports, as long as necessary.

As children advance to preparing longer reports using several sources of information, stress the need for beginning with an outline so they will know what they are looking for and thus not take unnecessary notes. And, of course, emphasize the importance of outlining as a means of organizing material after it is obtained. These outlines need not be formal, though children should know outline form by the time they reach the upper grades.

At *no* point should elementary-school children be required to write long "term papers." Instead, emphasize the skills of locating information, organizing it, using audiovisual aids to supplement oral reports, and choosing the best way to convey ideas, either orally or in writing.

Children in the seventh or eighth grade who have become adept at locating and using materials may be ready for an introduction to *The Reader's Guide.* It should be stressed, however, that the child who has not learned to use an encyclopedia easily, who does not readily use the table of contents or index of a book to locate information, or who has not learned to organize materials from two or more sources is *not* ready for this more complicated source. If, however, you do have a few children who seem ready, select a time when these few are working on group or individual reports to introduce them to this valuable research tool. Bring in a volume of *The Reader's Guide*—or if this is not possible, photocopy a few pages from a

Alert the public library when students are going to be preparing reports. Perhaps additional materials can be borrowed from other libraries, shorter borrowing periods arranged, special displays set up, and so forth.

volume. Show the children how to find out what periodicals are included and how to interpret the entries; then let them practice looking up sources of specific information. (Very little instruction or practice should be needed if they are truly familiar with other references.) Then arrange a trip to the library, either specifically for these children or with the entire class, to provide actual experience in using the *Guide* and finding magazine articles listed there.

Again, learning to use a public library is crucial, since it is the public library that will be used or not used by adults.

Upper-grade children should be aware that a city, county, or university library is a veritable treasure house of records, tapes and cassettes, picture files, films, micro-recorded materials, and equipment to use them. In addition, there are pamphlet files, newspaper files, bound volumes of innumerable periodicals, art objects, dioramas, and exhibits of many kinds. There are soundproof rooms where one may go to listen to recordings, and machines for copying pages from books. If there is such a library in your area, upper-grade children should visit it. Possibly you could arrange a guided tour by the children's librarian or someone else who knows and understands children. This may help them to be less awed when they are ready to take advantage of the library's resources.

A FINAL WORD

Teaching children to know about and use the library and all its resources should be a vital part of your program in all areas. There is little doubt that the child who knows how to use library aids will, in all probability, be a better student. But the greatest reward will come when the child reaches maturity, for then he or she will be able to find information and to locate books and other materials that enrich life and aid personal fulfillment.

References

Bell, Irene W., and Brown, Robert B. *Gaming in the Media Center Made Easy*. Libraries Unlimited, 1982.

Bell, Irene W., and Weikert, Jeanne. *Basic Media Skills Through Games*, 2nd ed. Libraries Unlimited, 1985.

Hart, Thomas L. *Instruction in School Library Media Center Use*, 2nd ed. American Library Association, 1985.

Jay, M. Ellen, and Jay, Hilda L. *Building Reference Skills in the Elementary School*. Shoe String Press, 1986.

Lewis, Marguerite. *Hooked on Research*. Center for Applied Research in Education, 1984.

Margrabe, Mary. *Media Magic: Games and Activities for Total Curriculum Involvement*. Acropolis, 1979.

———. *New Library Media Center: A Stations Approach with Media Kit*. Acropolis, 1975.

Montgomery, Paula K., and Walker, H. Thomas. *Teaching Library Media Skills: An Instructional Program for Elementary and Middle School Students*. Libraries Unlimited, 1983.

Richardson, Selma K. *Magazines for Children: A Guide for Parents, Teachers, and Librarians*. American Library Association, 1983.

———. *Periodicals for School Media Programs*. American Library Association, 1972.

———, ed. *Children's Services of Public Libraries*. University of Illinois, Graduate School of Library and Information Science, 1978.

School Library Media Activities Monthly, published by LMS Associates.

Teaching Resources

The following are examples of resources that may aid in teaching library skills.

Adventures in Library Land. Random House (six sound filmstrips and teacher's guides; K–grade 6).

Brigance, Albert H. *Study Skills: Strategies and Practice.* Curriculum Associates (reproducible study sheets on reference skills, reading graphs, and maps; grades 3–8).

Doing Research and Writing Reports. Scholastic (workbooks and teacher's editions; grades 4–6).

The Elementary School Library. Society for Visual Education (four filmstrips, four cassettes, worksheets, and teacher's guide; grades 3–6).

Lathrop, Ann. *How Can I Find It If I Don't Know What I'm Looking For: Library Skills.* Sunburst Communications, 1985 (computer program).

Library Skills. Scholastic (workbooks and teacher's editions; grades 2–6).

Library Skills Series. Random House (six filmstrips with cassettes and teacher's guide; grades 4–6).

Mallett, Jerry J. *Library Skills Activities.* Center for Applied Research in Education (workbook—pages can be duplicated).

Meet the Card Catalog. Library Filmstrip Center (filmstrip, cassette, and teacher's guide; grades 4–7).

My Library. Spoken Arts (four filmstrips, four cassettes, and teacher's guide; upper grades).

Reference Skills. Random House (audio cassettes and worksheet masters; grades 4–9).

Ripley's Library Research Skills. Society for Visual Education, 1986 (four filmstrips, four cassettes, twenty-four skillsheets, two computer disks, and teacher's guide; intermediate grades).

Using the Library. Society for Visual Education (four filmstrips, four cassettes, worksheets, and teacher's guide; upper grades).

Where in the World Is Carmen Sandiego? Broderband Software (computer program; grades 6–12).

Activities for Preservice Teachers

1. Investigate the possibility of involving parents as librarians or library helpers. Be prepared to report to the class.

2. Gather materials on book fairs. What has to be done to get a traveling exhibit to come to a school?

3. Survey several classrooms to determine how many pupils have public library cards. Inquire how often those with cards use them.

4. Plan a lesson for a particular primary grade that will necessitate looking up information in a beginning encyclopedia. Be sure to find out whether this information can be found in an encyclopedia that might be available to a class at this grade level.

5. Visit the library to obtain lists of Newbery and Caldecott award winners. Familiarize yourself with as many of these books as possible, and begin a card file of annotations for primary, middle, or upper grades.

6. Select a fifth-grade text for a specific subject area. Using the text as a base, make a unit lesson plan that would require children to go to the library for added information. Be sure to provide for differences in library experience and language skills.

7. Familiarize yourself with at least one set of encyclopedias, one atlas, and one of the other references listed in this chapter. Note particularly organization, teaching aids provided, types of information included, and grade levels for which each might be suitable.

8. Plan an activity designed to familiarize children with the use of a reference tool other than the encyclopedia. Demonstrate to the class exactly how you would present it.

9. Plan a unit for a particular subject area and grade level. Include at least three different types of audiovisual aids and tell how you would use them.

10. Examine a number of teaching aids such as those listed above and begin a file of ones you would like to use in teaching library skills at a particular grade level. Give reasons for your choices.

Activities for Inservice Teachers

1. Visit libraries in your area. Discuss with librarians the ages, interests, and reading abilities of your class. Find out what each library has to offer of a special nature for children. Find out what the librarian would like children of the ages of those in your class to know about the library.

2. Prepare a bulletin board display designed to teach the use of the card catalog. Make large sample cards, similar to those in this chapter, with explanations (including pictures) of the various entries on the cards.

3. Plan a library skills unit for your class. Include visits to libraries in your plans.

4. Prepare activities that require children to use particular library skills—for example, finding several references about a topic, using an atlas, finding fiction books by a particular author, or locating a specific issue of a magazine.

5. Make a survey of the amount of library-use teaching done in your school. Report the results of your survey.

6. Plan a unit in some subject area for which children will prepare individual or group reports, using audiovisual aids. Report to the class on the number and types of aids used—and how successful they were.

7. List the media aids or other resources you have used in teaching library skills to your class. Which would you use again and why?

Independent Activities for Children

1. Individual children can go to the library and report back to the class about one or more kinds of reference books or sets. For example, one child might go to find out about the different kinds of atlases the library has. Each report should be complete enough for the children to appreciate the differences among the references in a category. Permission might be obtained to bring one or more of the reference works to the classroom at the time of the report for purposes of illustration.

2. Ability to read symbols—verbal and pictorial—related to air and auto travel is a true part of literacy. A child or group of children could prepare a chart or bulletin board display showing the different types of signs that would be seen in an airport or on the highway, for example.

3. Ask a child to find the title and call letters for a book by each of these authors:

Tomie de Paola	Lila Perl
Marguerite Henry	Joan Lexau
Robert Lawson	Maurice Sendak

Then reverse the process and give a few titles of books for which the child is to find the names of the authors.

4. Prepare sheets containing various informational statements, some true and some false. Individual children who need additional practice in library and study skills can find out whether or not the information is true. Sample statements might be as follows:

Julie of the Wolves was written by Roald Dahl.
Hailstones and Halibut Bones is a book of poems about holidays.
Chicago is approximately 850 miles from Boston by air.
The piranha is a flesh-eating fish that lives in the Amazon River.

5. During the football season (or that of baseball, hockey, etc.), a sports-minded pupil might prepare a bulletin board display using pictures cut from magazines and newspapers, along with interesting information about the sport gathered from almanacs and other sources.

6. Have a child prepare a report on the library to present to another class. This should include the use of visual aids—for example, reproductions of various types of cards from the card catalog, a floor plan of the library, books with different types of call numbers, and so forth.

7. A child can use an atlas to plan an imaginary trip, plotting the route to be taken, places of interest to visit, time necessary for traveling, method of travel, kinds of clothing needed, and so on.

8. An individual child can prepare a report for the class about the Caldecott or Newbery Medal. This might include such items as when the award was first given, what factors enter into the selection, and which books and authors that the class is familiar with have

won it. Several books that have received the award might be used to illustrate the report.

9. When the class is working on a project for which supplementary material is needed (this will occur often in a program that is vital and broad), a child— or several children—can go to the library to locate and examine materials that might be useful. The child can either check out these materials for class use (arrangements will need to be made with the librarian for this) or prepare a list to be placed on the bulletin board, giving title, author, a few words about content, and the call number or location for each item.

Chapter 15

Literature for Children

*T*eaching a child the basic reading skills is necessary if the child is to succeed in school, since such a large portion of the learning that takes place in school involves reading. However, if teaching also results in the child's learning to *enjoy* reading, that learning will aid the child in becoming a more complete person throughout life. The reading program, then, should be two-pronged. First, it must give each child the skills he or she needs to read well, for if these skills are not learned there will be little or no seeking of the knowledge, pleasure, and insights that reading can provide. Second, if a child is to discover these things, there must also be specific provision for the kinds of literary experiences that will encourage and develop appreciation of the written word and the desire to read.

VALUES OF LITERATURE

The principal value of literature is surely the pleasure and enrichment it brings to the individual. A child who loves to read will never be at a loss for something to do and will spend many pleasant hours with books as companions. This reading will enlarge and extend the reader's world and should result in his or her gaining greater appreciation of the beauty and power of language—the way words can stir the imagination, arouse the emotions, and develop new insights.

Books can also help children to understand both themselves and their relationships with other people, and this understanding can often help an individual child to improve his or her self-concept. This is a central theme of an increasing number of books written for primary-grade children. For example, there is Pat Hutchins's *Titch*, which exemplifies the frustrations of innumerable small children, for Titch is the youngest and smallest member of his family. *Emily and the Klunky Baby and the Next-Door Dog*, by Joan Lexau, will strike a response not only from children of divorced parents but also from those whose parents are very busy and those who must help care for younger brothers and sisters. The illustrations in this book will bring gleeful giggles as the huge, shaggy next-door dog steals rides on Emily's sled, making it heavier and heavier for her to pull until she finally decides not to run away from home after all. A fifth-grade girl whose family has recently moved might find solace in *The Cat Across the Way*; one who lives in a foster home will surely respond to *The Great Gilly Hopkins*, whose heroine yearns to find her "real" mother; and Lila Perl's *Fat Glenda* should appeal to any girl in the upper grades who is overweight and longs to be attractive to boys. A boy who is beginning to feel independent will surely empathize with Dave, in Emily Neville's *It's Like This, Cat*, who wants a cat simply because his father thinks he should have a dog. There are books about old age, death, the problems of adolescence, the insecurity of illegitimate children, the tragedy of teen-age suicide, and so on. In short, there are innumerable opportunities for children to discover that they are not alone in their troubles, to find inspiration for setting and seeking goals, and to learn how they can adjust to situations and personal problems.

Children need not only to understand their own problems, but also to recognize that other people have problems not unlike their own. This may lead to the realization that people are not so different after all. For example, the white child who reads Ezra Jack Keats's *Whistle for Willie* will not be able to help identifying with this black boy who cannot whistle for his dog; similarly, the child of divorce—or of poverty—must surely feel kinship with Rafer in Joan Lexau's *Me Day*. Such books as *Stevie* by John Steptoe, *Watch Out for the Chicken Feet in Your Soup* by Tomie de Paola, *How My Parents Learned to Eat* by Ina R. Friedman, *In the Year of the Boar and Jackie Robinson* by Betty Bao Lord, *The Turning Point* by Naomi Karp, and *Water Sky* by Jean Craighead George can lead children to a better understanding of other cultures and other races. When selecting books for your room library, look especially for some about cultures represented by children in your class, as well as some that are not. And perhaps a unit centered around several of these might prove fruitful.

Equally important in these days of mainstreaming and the struggle for equality for the handicapped are books that help to develop an awareness of those who are physically or mentally different. There are many of these, even at the primary level, for example: Joe Lasker's *He's My Brother* (slow learner), Bernard Wolf's *Anna's Silent World* and Jean Peterson's *I Have a Sister—My Sister is Deaf* (deafness), Ezra Jack Keats's *Apt. 3* (blindness), Tricia Brown's *Someone Special, Just Like You* (various handicaps), and even Mary Ellen Powers's *Our Teacher's in a Wheelchair*.

Reading these kinds of books can help children gain a greater understanding of people and the world in which they live. This understanding can be further increased by reading literature of and about the past. It has long been recognized that literature is a major avenue for transmitting to the present the values, ideas, and experiences of past generations. Knowing about the past can provide a new perspective on problems of the present and increase children's appreciation of both their own heritage and that of others.

There can be little doubt that wide experience with books increases a child's vocabulary. Children whose parents have bought them books and have read to them frequently are better prepared for the language of school. In Chapter 4 teachers of primary grades were advised to use many books and to read and tell many stories, activities that help children learn new words and acquire new meanings of words they already know. As children advance in school, reading can continue to enrich vocabulary in these ways.

Reading is also an important way to build and extend concepts. For example, a common word like *home* may have different connotations for different children. One may think of home as a two-story frame house in a typical suburban neighborhood; another may think of it as a crowded

See also suggested books for special children listed at the end of Chapter 16.

apartment in a city tenement; and possibly neither has ever heard of a home called an *igloo* or *hogan*. Books may introduce these and many other words that hold the concept of *home,* along with the emotional factors with which this word may be associated. And as they advance in reading skills and experience, children can acquire and broaden many concepts and ideas.

In addition to providing vocabulary and ideas, books can help children learn to express their own thoughts and to become familiar with the language patterns they meet in reading and in listening to others. The child who comes to school with a limited language background is especially helped by hearing many stories both read and told, but all children need to become acquainted with many types of sentence structure, the use of figurative language, the language of poetry, the formal language of research, and so forth, if they are to learn to use language effectively. And perhaps one of the most valuable corollaries of reading is that it stimulates the child's imagination and helps to stir creative talents. There is no child who cannot write something creative given the proper encouragement and a wealth of models.

Reading is total involvement.

Finally, any program that is tied to a single textbook is almost bound to be both narrow and uninteresting. Resource materials are invaluable, but why not add a third dimension through the use of imaginative literature? Benjamin Franklin becomes a real person, not just a character in history, when viewed through the delightful *Ben and Me*; Patricia Clapp's *Witches' Children* helps readers experience vicariously the events that culminated in the infamous Salem witch trials; stories such as *Susanna of the Alamo* and the *Little House* series have surely made the hardships of the westward expansion more real to many; while Mike Fink, Paul Bunyan, and Pecos Bill lend color and humor to that same study. Pupils with a scientific bent may enjoy reading science fiction and trying to decide whether the events depicted could really happen; a letter-writing unit can be enriched by the addition of letters written by famous people; and, of course, biography can be useful in any area. Finding just the right materials to ensure the best use of literature in the total program may take a little time, but the rewards are immeasurable.

CREATING THE CLIMATE

Ideas

Children's Book Week in early November is a good time to promote children's books. Write to The Children's Book Council, 67 Irving Place, New York, NY 10003.

If you want to have a book fair, write to The Children's Book Council and to *Scholastic Teacher*, 50 W. 44th Street, New York, NY 10036.

Also remember National Library Week, observed in April of each year; write to the American Library Association, 50 E. Huron Street, Chicago, IL 60611.

Just as you are the model for children's speaking, so are you a model for their attitude toward books and reading. Thus a cardinal requisite for guiding children toward a love of reading is to enjoy books yourself. Even an avid reader of adult books may find it difficult to communicate this enjoyment to children; it is therefore vital that you become widely acquainted with books written expressly for children. A good first step is to take a course in children's literature, if this is possible. In addition, books written about children's literature, book reviews, and bibliographies of various types can serve as guides to specific titles. (See the list of guides to book selection at the end of this chapter.) But these are only guides. Simply knowing *about* books or knowing specific titles and authors is only the beginning; to really *know* children's books, it is necessary to read them. Spend time regularly in the children's section of the library making notes of books that would be good for reading aloud, those that would be good additions to the room library, those that would interest a particular child in your class, those that would be useful as supplementary reading for a particular unit of study, and so on. This will not be an onerous task; the world of children's books is a delightful and colorful one.

Demonstrating Interest in Books

The daily activities of the classroom provide many opportunities to demonstrate to the children your own interest in and dependence on books. First, make it a point to show your reliance on books. Let the children see you reading, use stories and poems to illustrate situations and to show how ideas have been expressed by others, and use quotations when they are appropriate—perhaps putting a daily or weekly quotation on the bulletin board. The latter can be overdone, however; quotes should be used naturally and only when they are suitable to the occasion, or children will become bored with them.

Second, make time in the schedule to read aloud to the children at least once every day. This practice should be continued even after children have acquired the skills to read on their own. In fact, it is perhaps more important in the upper grades, since young children are ordinarily eager to read and to be read to, whereas the interest of older children, whose horizons are expanding, may tend to diminish unless it is carefully nurtured. The reading may be only a short poem, or it may be a story, a chapter in a book, or something interesting and informative that you wish to share with them. Learn to read well, and let the children see that you enjoy reading.

Third, discuss books with the children. Ask them questions about books they are reading or have read, let them recommend selections to be read aloud to the class, help individual children to find books that are suited to their interests and needs, and seek their opinions about books that you have especially liked—or perhaps even ask them to evaluate a book you did not like and see if they can decide why you didn't. Your attitude should show that you value their opinions and that not everyone has to like the same book, even if it is one that is supposed to be "good."

And, finally, although reference materials are not, strictly speaking, "literature," you can foster the idea that books are friendly helpers by turning to books regularly for information and assistance. Children need to learn that not even the teacher knows everything—that it is the most natural thing in the world to turn to the dictionary to check a spelling, to seek out additional information on a subject you are studying, or to look up something you do not know.

For aids to teaching literature, write to The Children's Book Council, 67 Irving Place, New York, NY 10003.

The Room Library

The appeal of the corner of the classroom devoted to the room library is an important factor in creating an atmosphere that encourages reading. If the reading corner is nothing more than simply an area with some bookshelves and perhaps a table and a chair or two, it will do little to reinforce the attitude that reading is a pleasant and satisfying experience. The reading corner should be warm and bright—one of the most attractive spots in the room—and should have enough light so the children can read comfortably and can see to find books on the shelves. Chairs arranged invitingly in groups around a low table on which books are attractively displayed will provide motivation.

Some teachers like to obtain children's lounge or rocking chairs to make the reading corner inviting. Another possibility is to seek contributions from parents—an outmoded sofa, chairs, lamps, even a plant or two. A more informal atmosphere can be created by strewing large cushions on the floor, bringing in bean bag chairs, or even filling an old bathtub or rowboat with pillows. Let space, availability of furnishings, your own imagination, and the ages and backgrounds of the children be your guides.

A bulletin board devoted exclusively to books is also an important part of the reading corner. The children themselves can help to make displays and see that they are changed regularly. Here are a few ideas:

Developing Learning Skills through Children's Literature: An Idea Book for K–5 Classrooms and Libraries, by Mildred Knight Laughlin and Letty S. Watt (Oryx Press, 1988), is an excellent source of ideas.

1. Place at the top a caption reading "Can You Match These?" On one side put pictures of well-known authors of children's books, and on the other put either actual book jackets or some that have been drawn by the children for books that were written by these authors. Provide lengths of colored yarn that the children can use to connect each writer with his or her book as they discover which ones belong together.

2. Use the type of set-up described above to match characters and the books they are in or quotations and the characters who said them (Chicken Little and "The sky is falling"; The Little Engine and "I think I can, I think I can"; etc.).

3. Create interest in a particular book by cutting pictures representing characters and scenes in the book from publishers' advertisements, book jackets, or magazines, mounting them attractively, and arranging them around a replica of the book.

4. Let children write captions for pictures or draw their own illustrations for stories they particularly like. These can be used to make a bulletin board about a particular book or about several books with a common theme, the same author, or the same setting.

5. Let the children write "advertisements" for books they particularly like and post them on the bulletin board. This would be excellent in connection with a study of advertising techniques.

6. Regularly center a display around a particular ethnic or national group. This might include authors, illustrators, or even favorite characters in books.

7. Cut a large tree from construction paper and place it in the center of the bulletin board. At the lower corners tack envelopes containing apples, oranges, or whatever, also cut from construction paper (it could even be a magic tree, bearing many different kinds of fruit). When a child finishes a book, the child writes his or her name and the name of the book on one of the pieces of fruit and fastens it to the tree.

8. Have the children write letters to their favorite authors, and make a display of the answers received so that all the children can enjoy them.

9. Many of the activities suggested in the later section on book reports can provide attractive and interesting bulletin boards.

Of course, there is no point in making an attractive library corner unless the children are allowed to use it. The library area can certainly be used for the Sustained Silent Reading discussed in earlier chapters. However, the schedule should provide for additional time for children to read, listen to stories, discuss the books they've read, and work on book reports and other projects related to their reading and writing. Writing about their reading can be done by the children in the library area or nearby. And, of course, children should be allowed and encouraged to browse when they arrive at school early or when they have finished assigned work and the other children are still busy. There is no need for absolute quiet in the room library—if the children enjoy books, they will want to share their pleasure. The classroom atmosphere—not just during the library period, but at all times—should be one in which children feel free to ask questions, share information, and help each other. However, they should at the same time recognize that consideration for others demands that they do this without disturbing others or disrupting the activities of the class.

Every classroom should have an extensive library.

Naturally, the most important furnishings for the room library are the books themselves. Beginning with the very first day of school, the library should be well stocked with both fiction and nonfiction books of many types. Filmstrips, records, and cassettes may be in the room library or in a media center nearby, and many of these materials should be related to books that are in the library so a child may, for example, listen to the audio cassette while reading the story. Of course, the books should have eye appeal—attractive illustrations and easy-to-read type—and there should be a few books for advanced readers that are above grade level, as well as a good number having high interest and simple vocabulary for the reluctant and poor readers, who are especially difficult to entice. Books should be changed regularly so that no child will be unable to find something of interest that he or she has not already read.

Knowing the children, their interests, and their abilities is the best aid in selecting books and other materials that will be particularly suitable for them. Another aid is the children themselves. Allowing several (not the same ones each time) to go along on trips to the library will help them to become familiar with the library and library procedures. They can help not only in selecting books, but also in "taking orders" for particular kinds of books from the other children, freeing you to browse among new additions and find those suitable for children with special interests or needs. In the middle grades (if this is permitted in the school or library) two or three children might occasionally go by themselves to select books, again filling requests from the others. To avoid confusion and the "bandwagon" effect that might result from taking requests orally, these could be written on slips of paper and placed in a box kept on the table in the library corner or in a colorfully decorated envelope thumbtacked to the bulletin board. Pupil selection, however, should be an addition to, not a substitute for, teacher selection, since pupils cannot have a total picture of class needs.

Reading Aloud

As suggested earlier, providing time during each school day for reading aloud to the children will do much to stimulate interest in books. Sometimes this reading will be spontaneous (a particular situation simply demands the reading of a certain selection), but most of the time reading should be planned. There are two reasons for this: first, it is not possible to have at hand every selection that you might want to read; second, reading aloud requires preparation.

Many selections are available on records or cassettes; both the quality and quantity of these are increasing almost daily. However, allowing individual children to select and listen to records or cassettes—or playing them for the entire class—should supplement, not supplant, reading aloud. This is a time for sharing an enjoyable experience with the children, for building rapport, for discovering their interests and tastes, and for broadening interest and improving tastes. Sometimes, of course, you may wish to use a recording in order to free your hands for manipulating visual aids or in order to join the children in enjoying an especially well-read story or poem. But this should be the exception rather than the rule; the avenue of this kind of pleasure for children should most often be your own voice rather than that of an unseen actor.

Becoming a good oral reader requires practice; even if you are experienced in reading to a class, you should not read a selection without going over it first. It may be a good idea to record yourself while reading and then listen to the tape to determine such things as whether the pitch is pleasant and loud enough to be heard, whether the speed and enunciation make effective listening possible, how much time the reading takes, and, finally, whether the selection is likely to give the desired impression. This technique can also be helpful if a selection you have read to the class has not seemed to "go over" well. Was it not read well? Did the reading take too long? Was the content too difficult or of little interest to these particular children? Answering these and other questions can make future reading experiences more successful.

In general, select for reading aloud only those stories or poems that you personally enjoy. Just as you would probably do a poor job of teaching something you don't really think the children need to learn, you will not read well a story you do not particularly like. The pleasure the children get from listening is in direct proportion to the pleasure you have in reading.

Be constantly on the alert for selections that are appropriate for reading aloud. Making a card file is one way to be sure you will find the right story for the right time. Cards might be organized according to the particular units or areas the class will be studying, or they might simply be under rather general headings, possibly including special categories such as "Holidays," "Personal Problems," and "Stories for a Dreary Day." Each card should contain enough information to aid you in choosing the best story to use and in finding it quickly. Thus a card might include the following items:

1. Title and author
2. Where it may be found—Is it in a collection? In what library? Call number?
3. Audiovisual possibilities—Are the illustrations suitable for showing? Are filmstrips or slides particularly good? Is there a record or cassette that might be used with visual aids?
4. Time required for reading
5. Brief summary—only as much as is needed for a reminder

With the exception of poetry, which in most cases is meant to be read aloud, there is no point in reading something the children could just as easily read for themselves. Reading time is precious; it should be reserved for those things which children might have difficulty reading for themselves or which they might not appreciate as thoroughly. For example, humor—particularly subtle humor—is sometimes not evident to children when they read silently, although they respond delightedly when it is read well to them.

Unless you are one of the few who read dialect well, use a recording of a story that makes extensive use of dialect—but be *sure* it's a good one!

Dialect, too, often poses a problem, as do stories containing foreign words and names, because the words do not *look* familiar. For example, *The People Could Fly*, by Virginia Hamilton, might be confusing to some children because the *g*'s are dropped from words ending in *-ing* and *gone* is used for *going* or *went*, but middle-grade children will be delighted to hear such stories as "He Lion, Bruh Bear, and Bruh Rabbit." The dialect in these stories does not present the usual problem of being difficult to read aloud. Try reading one to your children; then they can easily handle others themselves.

In addition, many children's classics contain a number of words that children can understand in context but have difficulty reading for themselves. Marguerite Henry's *King of the Wind*, for instance, is neglected by many middle-graders until the teacher selects it for reading aloud. Thus, reading aloud is an excellent way to improve children's tastes and increase their perception. Reasons for reading aloud, then—or for using records and cassettes—might include one or more of the following:

- The selection is high in interest level, but vocabulary or sentence structure is difficult for the children. (This might apply to anything read to kindergarten or first-grade children, but should be particularly considered at higher levels.)
- The selection is of particular interest, but not enough copies are available for individual reading.
- The selection is of high interest, but print in available copies is difficult to read and illustrations are poor.
- The selection is particularly suitable for reading aloud. Sounds of the words and phraseology add markedly to enjoyment, and/or appreciation is particularly heightened by oral interpretation.

Not everything that is of value is suitable for reading aloud. Check by asking yourself these questions:

1. Is the action (of a story) fast moving and easy to follow?
2. Is the length suitable for reading at one sitting (the length of a sitting should depend on the age and maturity level of the children)? If it is long, could it be satisfactorily divided (for example, chapters of a novel)?
3. Is the vocabulary such that children will understand what is happening even if there are a few words they do not know?
4. Will it be of interest and value to all the children?
5. Is the content pertinent to something the children are studying or something they are interested in?

The atmosphere for reading or storytelling should be pleasant and informal. If at all possible, gather the children around you in such a way that they can all see illustrations without delaying the reading unduly. Illustrations are often important to enjoyment (it would be a shame to read *Where the Wild Things Are* without letting the children see those marvelous "wild things"), so they should be large enough to be seen by all the children. If not, consider other possibilities: larger pictures placed on a flannel board, transparencies made for the overhead projector, or perhaps a filmstrip. In such cases it might be helpful to tape the story or to use a commercially produced tape, thereby freeing your hands to manipulate the aids. This is useful also when realia (objects related to daily life) are being used, as, for instance, when reading is being used to develop vocabulary for primary children. It is not necessary, however, to use visual aids every time a story is read. In fact, with some children (such as educationally disadvantaged children, whose attention spans may be short), visual aids may prove to be a distraction. A child may become more interested in what makes the figures stick on the flannel board or how the projector works than in the story and may interrupt the reading to investigate. Thus discretion is needed in deciding when and how to use visual aids. Certainly, good illustrations should always be shared, and visual aids can add variety. They can also be incorporated into the discussions that precede or follow the reading of a selection when this seems appropriate.

Successful reading or storytelling is an act of sharing. Hold the book away from your face so the children can see your expression as you read, and maintain eye contact by looking up at them occasionally. The reading should move along smoothly or interest will lag, but children should be allowed to see illustrations, to laugh at a humorous line or situation, or even to ask a question that can be answered in one or two words. Other questions can be answered with a friendly smile and "Let's find out" or some similar remark. Too many interruptions may mean that you are not reading well or loudly enough or that the children find the story uninteresting. In the latter case, it may be best simply to put the book away until another time. The possible cause of the inattention should then be considered. Possibly the story was too difficult in concepts or language, there was too little action, or the characters did not seem believable. If so, look for another story that will serve the same purpose but have more appeal for the children. However, if you consider the story suitable and wish to try it again at a later time, perhaps the visual aids could be changed or omitted entirely, the story told instead of read, or some other variation applied.

In some schools teacher's aides, senior citizens, cafeteria workers, and others who have the time and interest are enlisted to read to children. This makes possible reading to small groups or even to individual children (with the child perhaps sitting on the reader's lap), as well as providing a more informal atmosphere and allowing for greater attention to the needs, interests, and abilities of each child. When taking advantage of the availability of such helpers, try to include both men and women since children, especially boys, need male reading models as well as female ones. But remember to use these people to enrich the program, not to substitute for reading done by you or to free you for grading papers or going to the teachers' room. Always work closely with them: aid them in finding suitable stories, familiarize them with the children's needs and interests, and make them an integral part of your total program.

Volunteer readers not only enrich a language arts program but can do much to foster good school/community relations.

Storytelling

A good storyteller is always in demand. None of us ever grows too old to enjoy a well-told story, but storytelling is a particularly useful tool with young children, since their attention span is short. Telling a story instead of reading it also frees your hands for illustrating it with flannel-board figures or some other aid. More importantly, it permits you to maintain eye contact and makes you seem closer to the children—there is not even a book between you. Furthermore, storytelling permits the insertion of synonyms or appositive phrases to explain an unfamiliar word or a definition of a foreign term (*"hombre*—that means *man* in Spanish"*) without interruption of the story.

The criteria for selecting a story to be told are much the same as those for choosing one to read, with one important addition: it is important that the story not lose by being translated into your own words. For example, *The Elephant's Child* without Kipling's "great, gray-green, greasy Limpopo River" or *The Wonderful O* in any language but Thurber's own would surely be less effective. Of course, it is possible to memorize a story, but that is not advisable except in very special cases. Memorization takes a great deal of time, and a story can be ruined if you forget something at a crucial point. Therefore, if the author's words are vital to full enjoyment, reserve the story for reading aloud.

For stories told by real storytellers, not read by actors, send for Catalog of Storytelling Resources from NAPPS, P.O. Box 112, Jonesboro, TN 37659.

A good storyteller commands a great fund of words and can find exactly the right way to describe a character or an event. A good storyteller loves words, loves telling stories, and communicates this enthusiasm to the listener. There are few "born storytellers"; thorough preparation is the key to success.

Like reading aloud, storytelling is an act of sharing, but it is even more intimate. Therefore, the experience should be truly enjoyable for both the teller and the listeners. Choose a physical setting that is comfortable and

Books with Many Helpful Ideas about Storytelling

Children's Literature through Storytelling by Joseph A. Wagner (William C. Brown, 1970)

Handbook for Storytellers by Caroline Feller Bauer (American Library Association, 1977)

Just Enough to Make a Story by Nancy Schimmel (Sisters' Choice Press, 1982)

The Story Vine: A Source of Unusual and Easy-to-Tell Stories from Around the World by Anne Pellowski (Macmillan, 1984)

Storyteller by Ramon R. Ross (Charles E. Merrill, 1972)

Storytelling by Eileen Colwell (The Bodley Head, 1981)

Storytelling, Art and Technique by Augusta Baker and Ellin Green (R. R. Bowker, 1987)

Twenty Tellable Tales by Margaret Read MacDonald (H. W. Wilson, 1986)

The Way of the Storyteller by Ruth Sawyer (Viking Press, 1970)

relaxing—possibly the library corner, where children may sit beside you, on the floor, or on cushions, each one close enough to hear well and to see gestures, facial expressions, or other aids used. Select for telling only stories that you particularly enjoy, with plots that are easily followed and with characters and situations suited to the age and experiential backgrounds of the children. Study the characters thoroughly and decide what kinds of voices and mannerisms they would have. Visualize the setting and think of words that will convey this image concisely. Determine the mood of the story and what vocabulary, phrasing, and tone of voice will best express it. Examine the wording of the story to see whether retaining some of the author's words or phrases will heighten enjoyment, either because they are particularly colorful or because they form a repetitive pattern. Decide where gestures might be effective and whether visual aids are needed, such as pictures, flannel-board figures, puppets, or realia. In selecting and using these aids, however, keep in mind that children should sometimes hear language *without* pictures and that a well-told story often needs no embellishment. Finally, make sure that you know the exact sequence of events, especially any details that are important to appreciation or to events that come later. We have all had the experience of having a joke spoiled when the teller had to insert "Oh, I forgot to tell you that . . . " Don't let this happen to you!

Practice and rigid self-evaluation are essential to good storytelling. Using a tape recorder, experiment with pitch, intonation, phrasing, and use of pauses; practice telling the story before a mirror to judge the effect of gestures and facial expressions; time several tellings so you will know how much time is needed to tell the story effectively. All this will seem very time-consuming at first, but it will prove to be time well spent. And a story once learned can be told again and again—possibly even to the same children. It should be noted, though, that even a story that has been told many times before should be mentally reviewed to make sure of details and sequence. A set of cards containing names of characters, important details, the sequence of events, and useful visual aids can help you to review. These cards can be filed with those containing information about stories for reading aloud.

Using Media

There is little doubt that the media have become an important part of our lives. The school cannot—and does not—ignore this fact. The school library, or more often the media center, is likely to be well stocked with files of book jackets, pictures, flannel-board figures, overhead transparencies, films, filmstrips, tapes, records, cassettes, and computer software, as well as the equipment for utilizing all of these. Familiarize yourself with these materials early in the year and keep up with new additions, since they can be valuable assets to your literature program. Make sure, however, that they are used to enhance that program, *not* replace it.

Plan carefully, and use media items to add variety and interest to your program. When reading or telling stories, use flannel-board figures on one day, puppets on another, a filmstrip on another, and so on—choosing the medium best suited to the material being presented, of course. Occasionally you may even wish to use an audio cassette to replace your own voice or a cassette-with-filmstrip combination; this might be especially appropriate for presenting a story containing dialect, since, as suggested earlier, dialects are difficult to read well. It might also be worthwhile to use a recording of an expert reading of certain poetry, or an author reading his or her own work. Use these sparingly, however, since reading or storytelling time should be one for building rapport between you and the children. In addition, remember that *any* addition to reading or telling a story creates some interference or distraction, so plan for frequent times when no audiovisual or other aids are used.

Various types of audiovisual aids can, of course, be effective in providing motivation for reading. A filmstrip can motivate children to read the book or story on which the film is based, especially younger children, who love familiar things. Only a portion of a filmstrip or cassette can be used as a ''teaser,'' as can a recently developed form called the MovieStrip, which presents scenes from educational or commercial films (such as *Roots*) in filmstrip-with-cassette format.

An audio cassette can be helpful as a ''read-along'' aid when a story contains some difficult words, or it can help a poor reader to enjoy a book that his or her peers have liked. The computer is also becoming a valuable aid for slow readers. For some reason, reluctant readers seem to like computers, and it has been discovered that sometimes a child who seems unable to read suddenly can when the text appears on a computer monitor. Furthermore, there are even computer games that require reading—that is, the game cannot be won unless a particular book is read either before or during play. Several noted science fiction writers, such as Isaac Asimov and Ray Bradbury, are designing books specifically for such games; these should surely entice many reluctant readers in the upper grades.

Media can also be used in follow-up activities. For example, the film or television version of a book the class has read might initiate discussion of whether the production was true to the book, why certain characters or events were omitted or changed, and even the difficulties of translating ideas from one medium to another. Or perhaps children might obtain a comic book edition of a popular novel and compare it to the original. Such activities are valuable for developing appreciation as well as critical reading and thinking.

An almost endless number and variety of commercial materials are available. Many children's stories have been made into films or videotapes that are available to schools at low cost. Well-known actors have recorded stories and poems; some authors have recorded their own works. Nearly all of the Newbery Medal books are available in several types of media, as are interviews with well-known authors and illustrators. In addition, multimedia kits are available that include multiple copies of a book, and a filmstrip, a cassette or record, a teacher's guide, and sometimes duplicating masters for children's responses. Computer software also comes in various types of ''packages.''

The range of these materials being marketed increases daily, so it is difficult to know how much or what to use. Two suggestions may prove helpful. First, keep information about media items you have used successfully in your book file. For convenience the cards can be color-coded in a manner similar to that used by some libraries (see Chapter 14); they may be marked with colored tape, crayon, or felt-tipped pen. Second, evaluate media items carefully and use only those that will truly enrich your literature program and help lead the children toward more and better reading. Your librarian or media specialist can help you, and there are reviews of new media items in such periodicals as *Booklist*, *The Horn Book*, *Library Journal*, *Learning*, and *Media and Methods*. Some specialists say that the mere inclusion of an item in *The Horn Book*'s listing means that it is worth purchasing. However, this does not mean that it will be best for your program or the particular children in your class, so don't rely entirely on the opinions of others, helpful though they may be. Do preview all materials, and make your selections carefully.

HELPING CHILDREN SELECT BOOKS

Developing an understanding of each child's interests, expanding those interests, and helping the child to develop new interests is the responsibility of each teacher. In order to help a child select books, it is vital to know the child and his or her interests. This is one reason for staying with the class when they go to the library. The librarian can offer suggestions and help children find books, and there is also computer software that purports to identify books for children of particular ages and interests. (This software can even be programmed to suggest only the books that are available to the children.) However, it is difficult to believe that either a librarian or a computer can respond to individual interests and abilities as well as a teacher can.

Begin by reading the cumulative records for your class before school starts. These records will furnish background information on age, sex, health problems, family structure, abilities, and perhaps interests. Knowing that Lily Jones hates her name or that the biggest child in your fifth grade has first-grade reading ability, for example, will be helpful when you select books for the class and for individuals.

A list of children's choices for reading is published annually by The International Reading Association and The Children's Book Council. For a free copy, write to Children's Choices, c/o International Reading Association.

Children are no different from adults with respect to having likes and dislikes in reading. Age, gender, environment, interests, and ability all influence what a person selects to read. A wise teacher knows each child in the class and guides each one in the selection of books.

Again, a useful aid is a set of file cards. In this case, the cards can be used to record the children's interests so that you can help them to discover books they will enjoy and profit from. Let the children start the cards themselves; at the beginning of the year, have each child fill out a card, giving his or her name and age and the answers to a few simple questions, such as:

Of all the books you have read (or stories you have heard), which did you like the best?
What was one you didn't like very well?

Many children enjoy reading several books by the same author.

What is your favorite TV show?
What do you like most to do after school or at recess?
If you could go anywhere you wanted, where would you go? Why?

Other questions may be more suitable for a particular class or grade; the important thing is to keep to a few that can be answered briefly. Use the cards as a beginning and add to them as you talk to the children, jotting down names of books they seem to enjoy, hobbies, problems, and so on. Thumb through the cards before going to the library, making notes of particular types of books or authors the children have enjoyed, special problems, and so forth, to guide you in the selection of books for the room library or for reading to the class. In addition, a "request box" might be kept in the library corner, where individual pupils can place requests for particular books or books about specific subjects. And, whenever possible, several children should go with you to the library to help make selections.

Interests by Age and Sex

For a free copy of *Choosing a Child's Book*, write to The Children's Book Council. This pamphlet gives suggestions for choosing books for various age levels and lists other sources of information about children's reading.

Naturally, children differ in reading interests just as they do in every other respect. Children in general, however, appear to show certain preferences at certain age levels, and these are discussed below. They should not be thought of as absolutes, but only as guidelines to be used in conjunction with a knowledge of the interests of the specific children in a class.

Primary Grades. Primary-grade children select books principally by their pictures; therefore, the illustrations are of primary importance. Bright colors are preferred over pastels, and pictures should occupy a major por-

Magazines for Children

Artsporation, College of Fine Arts, The University of Texas, Austin, TX 78712 (grades 4–6)

Children's Digest, Children's Health Publications, Box 567B, Indianapolis, IN 46206 (grades 3–6)

Cobblestone, Cobblestone Publishing Company, 20 Grove Street, Peterborough, NH 03458 (grades 1–4)

Cricket, Box 2670, Boulder, CO 80302 (grades 1–4)

Highlights for Children, P.O. Box 269, Columbus, OH 43216 (grades 3–6)

National Geographic World, National Geographic Society, 17th and M Streets, N.W., Washington, DC 20036 (grades 3–6)

Odyssey, Astromedia Corp., P.O. Box 92788, 625 E. St. Paul Avenue, Milwaukee, WI 53202 (grades 4–8)

Ranger Rick's Nature Magazine, National Wildlife Federation, 1412 18th Street, N.W., Washington, DC 20036 (grades 2–5)

3-2-1 Contact, Children's Television Workshop, P.O. Box 2934, Boulder, CO 80321 (grades 4–8)

tion of the space, with only a few words on each page. Illustrations may be fanciful, but objects should be readily recognizable. Young children love animal stories, such as *The Surprise Party* and *It's Not My Fault*, as well as those about prehistoric monsters, such as *My Visit to the Dinosaurs*. They also enjoy stories about mechanical objects, such as *Little Toot Through the Golden Gate*, and both fiction and nonfiction about objects, events, and places in the world around them, for example, *Up Goes the Skyscraper* and *The Dallas Titans Get Ready for Bed*. Equally popular are stories about children who have problems young readers can identify with, such as Jim in *Will I Have a Friend?*, who wonders apprehensively if he will find a friend on his first day at school, or the boy in Marchette Chute's poem, who says,

> I told them I didn't WANT mittens
> And they've given me mittens again!*

Folk and fairy tales are perennial favorites, and children love fantasy as long as the characters have human feelings and reactions. For example, Horton may sit on the egg without breaking it, but he must shiver when the winter winds blow and grow lonely sitting there on the nest alone.

Middle Grades. Middle-grade children continue to like fantasy and folk tales, but as their knowledge and experiences broaden so do their reading interests. They are interested in the world around them, both near and far, today and yesterday. Many books appeal to the middle-grader: histories, biographies, stories of other lands; adventure tales about pirates, cowboys, and the frontier; and books such as *Bats* that explain the wonders of the world around them. Mysteries begin to be popular, especially those with young detectives, such as Donald Sobol's Encyclopedia Brown. In the upper middle grades, boys particularly begin to be interested in sports and science, and both sexes continue to enjoy animal stories, particularly those about horses. As a rule, middle-grade children are interested in a wide variety of subjects and types of books; their principal criterion as far as fiction is concerned is that the plot move fast and include plenty of action.

Upper Grades. Most of the interests pupils have in the middle grades continue into the upper gardes. At this level, however, the sexes begin to differ. The boys often prefer sports, action, adventure, and mystery, while many girls begin to enjoy a bit of love interest. It might be said that the girls' interests are broader, since they often enjoy the books the boys do, whereas the boys scoff at love and tend to avoid books in which the principal character is female.

At all ages, children enjoy and should be exposed to humor as well as to stories about those who have problems to which they can relate. Humor is a safety valve for emotions, and it is important that children learn to

---

*"Presents" by Marchette Chute. Copyright 1932, 1960 by Marchette Chute. From the book *Around and About* by Marchette Chute. Copyright © 1957 by E. P. Dutton & Co., Inc., publishers, and used with their permission.

More Magazines for Children

Ebony Jr., Johnson Publishing Company, 820 S. Michigan Avenue, Chicago, IL 60605 (grades 4–8)

The Electric Company Magazine, P.O. Box 2924, Boulder, CO 80321 (grades 1–4)

Jack and Jill, Children's Better Health Institute, P.O. Box 567B, Indianapolis, IN 46206 (grades 1–3)

Penny Power, Consumer's Union of the United States, P.O. Box 1906, Marion, OH 43302 (grades 4–8)

Stone Soup, Children's Art Foundation, P.O. Box 83, Santa Cruz, CA 95063 (grades 4–8; articles and illustrations by children)

Your Big Back Yard, National Wildlife Federation, 1412 18th Street, N.W., Washington, DC 20036 (preprimary)

The American Library Association Review and *Booklist* regularly review books for poor readers.

laugh, at themselves as well as others. By all means encourage the enjoyment of humor—problems at which we can laugh grow small enough to attack. Similarly, children need to be exposed to stories about both personal and social problems. The important factor is to make sure that the problem is not too great for the children's experience and is one to which they can relate.

Another factor to be considered at all levels is the size of print and general attractiveness of the books. As mentioned earlier, young children select books primarily by their illustrations. Appearance continues to be important even in the upper grades; children will seldom select a book that has very small print and no illustrations. Naturally, the size of print can decrease as children mature, as can the amount of space devoted to illustrations, but it is important that books be attractive and not too difficult to read. This is especially true for children who do not read well.

Reading Ability

It is relatively easy to find books for good readers, but a major problem for most teachers is helping those children who have limited reading ability select books that will interest them and that they can read. This is not an easy task; it is one that will require a great deal of patience and ingenuity. A few guidelines may prove helpful:

- Determine the child's independent reading level. If you don't know how this is done, consult a diagnostic reading book or the reading consultant in your school or district. (A frequently used "rule of thumb" is to estimate a child's independent reading level to be one grade level below his or her instructional level.)
- Determine the child's interests by observing and listening.
- Use the knowledge you have gained about the child's interests and particular characteristics to guide you in selecting material for that child.
- Branch out in the use of resources. Perhaps magazines rather than books can furnish the necessary stimulus.
- Help the child maintain self-respect by finding easy-to-read materials that are not beneath his or her age level. Help the child gain standing in the other children's eyes. Make the most of other abilities the child has.

Children have been known to extend themselves in reading ability if they are sufficiently motivated. For example, a thirteen-year-old with third-grade reading ability and an interest in fast cars might be successfully tempted by Lerner Publications' series about racing. This series includes books about the Indianapolis 500, race-car drivers, drag racing, motorcycle racing, and even snowmobile racing. Franklin Watts has a similar series, written by E. and R. S. Radlauer, which has great appeal to children in the middle and upper grades. Both series have middle-grade reading levels and are amply illustrated with real-life photographs filled with action and excitement. Mysteries may also entice slow readers; William Butterworth has written a pair—*Stop, Thief* and *The Air Freight Mystery*—that have blue-collar, teen-aged heroes. Girls with low reading levels might enjoy *A Love for Violet,* and the popularity of the *Jaws* movies and horror movies in general is sure to draw both sexes to *The Great White Shark* or *Monsters You Never Heard Of.* The former contains stories of real-life shark encounters, whereas the latter is about mythical or reported monsters (who could resist reading about the Chicago Phantom Kangaroo?). Materials such as these, along with those mentioned in the section on using media, may be utilized to improve reading skills so that reluctant readers can advance to higher levels of ability and appreciation.

Book Lists

Ask the librarian to help you compile lists of suggested books for:
1. Reading aloud
2. Helping children to find in the library
3. Suggesting to relatives as gifts
Give the lists to parents at parent-teacher conferences, possibly making specific recommendations for individual children.

Although you and the children will make the final selection of books for the room library, the librarian can be extremely helpful in making suggestions. Most librarians will go to great pains to help find exactly what is wanted, if they are asked. In addition, a librarian usually has a number of book lists to guide him or her in book selection. Such lists are generally annotated and arranged by subject areas, with age or grade levels indicated. The librarian will also have lists of Newbery and Caldecott Medal winners; these are excellent both for the children and for reading aloud.

Naturally, you will want to read or skim all the books you select for the room library, but book lists and the librarian can save you a considerable amount of time by leading you to specific titles and authors.

THE INSTRUCTIONAL PROGRAM

If children are exposed to a wide variety of good books, have a teacher who enjoys reading, and are given the time to become acquainted with literature, they will be more likely to develop a taste for reading and some discrimination in selecting what they read. If literature is integrated with other areas of the curriculum, there is little doubt that both the curriculum and individual children will be enriched. And if the kinds of activities discussed in later sections result from reading, children's language skills will surely improve. But if careful planning of literary experiences coordinates all of these, the benefits will be even greater.

Planning, however, does not mean that children's reading should be circumscribed, nor that they should be limited to a specific reading list. Experience with this type of approach in the secondary school has shown that it does little to inspire enthusiasm for reading. Instead, the program should include both planned experiences and free choice, and it must be built around the interests, needs, and abilities of the particular children for whom it is planned. There should *not* be a specified reading list for each grade that all children are expected to follow, but there should be specific planning for the *kinds* of literary experiences that will be included in the program, not just at one grade level but at all levels. With planning, one experience builds on and relates to another. Without it, children may have many valuable and enjoyable experiences, but they may also wind up being "introduced" to haiku (for example) in the fifth grade, again in the sixth grade, once more in the seventh grade—and even again in the secondary school.

Instructional Considerations

A number of factors must be considered in planning, both for a single grade level and for the entire program. These are discussed in the following sections.

Variety. Selections chosen for the entire group—to be read either by or to the children—should include a variety of kinds and styles. This variety should embrace genre (stories, poems, plays, etc.), theme, tone, humorous selections as well as serious ones, and type (fantasy, folklore, adventure, history, biography, etc.). In addition, there should be some older classics and some newer ones. Not all of these are suitable at every grade level, of course, but every effort should be made to see that children at all levels become acquainted with many kinds of writing and many styles.

Experience Level. Like any other area of the curriculum, the literature program must begin where the children are. If the language and sentence structure are too difficult for them, they will probably find a selection boring. Furthermore, the concepts must be ones to which they can relate. For example, a first-grader who has never seen snow is less likely to respond to *A Snowy Day* than is one accustomed to wintry weather. This is not to say that children can relate only to that which is within their immediate experience—part of the value of literature lies in the vicarious experience it provides—but there must be a basis for relating. Primary-grade children, for instance, can enter readily into a story in which animals speak, since they themselves frequently carry on lengthy conversations with pets, dolls, and even imaginary playmates. This is "pretend," and they understand that, as long as there is some other basis for relating. Thus, they delight as Roald Dahl's "Fantastic" Mr. Fox outwits Farmers Boggis, Bunce, and Bean, because they recognize the parent's role as provider for the family and also because the three obnoxious farmers represent the adult world that so often circumvents their own desires.

Integration. If literature is to be an integral part of the curriculum, consideration must be given to how this integration is to be accomplished. Just as overall planning requires decisions about experiments, field trips, and audiovisual aids, it also requires decisions about literary experiences that may enrich and be supplemented by other curriculum areas and that are suited to the particular children involved. Should a social studies unit include the tall tales of the expanding frontier? If so, should this be balanced by a realistic story of life in the early days? Does a group of reluctant readers need a story to "spice up" their interest in the American Revolution, such as *A Spy in Williamsburg* by Isabelle Lawrence? How can poetry be used? What kinds of literary experiences have these children had, and what kinds do they need?

Books for Special Events

Candles, Cakes, and Donkey Tails by Lila Perl (Clarion Books, 1984). Describes birthday customs in various countries.

Children's Books for the Holidays (National Council of Teachers of English). An annotated list of books for Christmas and Hanukkah (K–7).

The Crowell Holiday Books (Thomas Y. Crowell). Include books about St. Valentine's Day, Halloween, Thanksgiving Day, Passover, and others.

First Book of Holidays by Bernice Burnett (Franklin Watts, 1974).

Jewish Holidays by Betty Morrow and Louis Hartman (Garrard Publishing, 1967).

Clarion Books publishes a series of books about various holidays, all written by Edna Booth; Holt, Rinehart and Winston produces a series by Gail Gibbons; and Messner offers a series by Judith Hoffman Corwin.

Several books by Judith Conway suggest things to make and do for holidays (Troll Associates).

Flexibility. If the literature program is truly to be adapted to the needs of the children and if it is to supplement and enrich their experiences as well as the curriculum, it must be flexible. No plan is so good that it cannot be changed. Suppose, for example, you had planned to have the children read a particular book as a group, but, as the year progresses, you discover that it is too difficult for a number of them. Possibly you might read it aloud if it is suitable for oral reading; perhaps the substitution of another book that is easier to read but has a similar theme or setting would be desirable; or the class might be divided into several groups, each reading a different book and preparing some sort of report on it for the rest of the class. The important fact to remember is that the interests, needs, and abilities of the children are at the heart of any successful program.

Growth. In order to provide for the needs of *all* the children, the program must include both group and individual experiences. Such selections can be read to or by the entire class, so that they develop understandings and broaden concepts through guided discussions and shared reactions. Sometimes small groups may read different selections to accommodate differing interests and abilities. Above all, the program must provide opportunity and encouragement for each child to explore in the area of his or her own interests, to discover new ones, and to grow in understanding and appreciation through individual reading. Be sure to make recreational reading a part of your daily plan. Do not allow time and subject matter constraints to interfere with the establishment of lifetime habits.

Objectives of the Literature Program

Underlying all of the considerations discussed above is the most important element in planning—consideration of the objectives of the literature program. First, of course, are the underlying objectives, embodied in the earlier section on the values of literature as well as in the preceding paragraphs. These must be the overriding considerations in planning for both group and individual reading. Second are the immediate objectives—what are the specific outcomes desired from reading? These will be discussed in the following sections.

An earlier chapter grouped the language arts into two categories: receptive and expressive. The specific objectives of the literature program may be characterized in the same way. Those having to do with reception involve understanding and appreciating what is read; those having to do with expression involve both oral and written responses to what is read, including creative responses.

Receptive Abilities. In considering the objectives of the literature program, it is vital to remember that elementary-school children should *not* engage in critical analysis—this should be reserved for university students and possibly some secondary students. However, some understanding of genre, theme, plot, setting, characterization, and point of view can be developed gradually during the elementary and secondary years, and these will lay the foundation for greater perception and appreciation. Children need not know the meanings of words such as *genre*, but they will understand the concepts all these terms embody if they have been exposed throughout the elementary years to a program that has provided many experiences with them. For example, the primary-grade child can certainly understand that Nonny Hogrogian's *One Fine Day* is a story but the book that tells about the weather or how to feed the fish in the class aquarium is not. Perhaps factual material might even be kept on a different shelf in the room library to further this concept. The young child also begins to realize that some stories are about people who could be real (*A Snowy Day*, for example), but ones like *Where the Wild Things Are* are pure make-believe. Thus, the child is laying the foundation for understanding the difference between fiction and nonfiction and between fantasy and realism, although none of these words are known.

The child can also begin to recognize that poetry is different from prose, particularly if rhyme and rhythm are pointed out. Both rhythm and rhyme play a prominent role in readiness activities, and many children's stories are written in rhyme. Primary-grade children will enjoy clapping their hands softly to the rhythm of a poem or song, and they may even attempt to write simple poems if poetry has been made a part of their reading experiences.

Talking about things is an important part of language development, especially at the primary level. Suppose you interrupt the reading of a story to ask "What do you think will happen next?" You are giving the children an opportunity not only to express themselves and to think critically, but also to understand a basic element of plot construction—the way a story turns out is built on the events that have gone before and the kinds of characters involved. Having children recap the sequence of events in a story builds organizational skills and also helps to develop the concept of plot. Questions such as "Why did Horton keep sitting on the egg when he was so cold and miserable?" "What kind of boy is Archie?" and "What did you learn from this story?" are concerned with theme and characterization and will help children learn to think about and evaluate what they read.

In the middle and upper grades these concepts can be further developed. Children who are going to use the library independently need to know the difference between fiction and nonfiction and to understand what biography is. To write reports and stories they must understand sequence and organization. Some direct instruction will be needed, but the best teacher is example. Certainly no child should be asked to write a story without having heard or read many stories. In addition, discussions can point out sequence in plot development and the need for *cause* to be established before *effect* is reasonable.

Children in the middle and upper grades should also be aware of figurative language. They can talk about phrases like "the *heart* of the problem" and "matters came to a *head*." They can compose similes and metaphors (note that they should compose these, not just identify them in someone else's writing); they may even experiment with personification, describing an event from the viewpoint of an old house, a pet, or a piece of furniture. Dealing with figurative language, however, requires many examples and great familiarity with both written and spoken language.

As children discover the thought and work that go into writing well, their appreciation for good writing will grow. This appreciation and the understandings that effect it develop slowly, and only as a result of wide acquaintance with books over a long period of time. Children cannot be told to understand a concept or to appreciate a poem—the foundation for understanding and appreciation must be carefully laid through experience.

Expressional Abilities. If literature is truly made an integral part of the activities and program of the classroom, it will be inextricably interwoven with the use of language in all its aspects. Children may develop both oral and organization skills as they plan the dramatization of a scene from a favorite story (see Chapter 5 for suggestions). Shy children who have difficulty in making oral presentations may tell a story through the use of puppets, thus taking a first step toward developing oral abilities (Chapter 5 gives directions for making several kinds of puppets). Children may read aloud stories or poems they particularly like, or they may participate in choral reading activities.

A good literature program should also stimulate creative writing of many kinds; children may write stories, poems, accounts of incidents that might have occurred before or after the action of a particular story, letters from one character to another, and so on. Book reports, too, can take both conventional and creative forms (this will be discussed in the next section).

In doing any kind of writing or talking about a book (other than merely recounting the plot), the child must do some evaluation. If he or she is going to write a different ending for a story, it must fit the events that have gone before and the characters who are involved. If a poem is written, it should capture the mood of the story. If an illustration is drawn, the setting must be accurate. Discussions of selections the whole class has read are a good way to help children see the considerations that must enter into this kind of expression. Such evaluation, in turn, should help them to make their own writing and speaking more effective.

In planning the literature program, then, you should take into account the kinds of expressional activities the children need to engage in. Naturally, not all oral and written expression must result from literature, nor is it necessary that expressional activities result from everything that is read—this would be proselytizing in the worst way. However, reading *may* stimulate expression, and it certainly can and should provide models, particularly for creative writing.

Book Reports

Make book reports—like science reports or those in any other curriculum area—an integral part of your oral language program.

The book report has been used and abused for years. Too often it is dull to read or hear and consists of little more than a recounting of the plot. This type of report does have some value; it gives practice in using the skills of writing or speaking as well as in selecting important details and arranging events in sequence. But a good book report can do this and much more.

To begin with, not every book read needs to be reported on. If you wish to keep a record of the childrens' reading—and this is a good idea for many reasons—each child might keep a card on which he or she records the names

Children should go to a school or public library frequently.

and authors of the books read, along with the date on which each was finished. As an added incentive, the children might use a numerical system to evaluate books:

> 1—Excellent. I recommend it highly.
> 2—Very good, but not everybody would like it.
> 3—Not bad, but I wouldn't particularly recommend it.
> 4—I didn't like it much.

These cards might be kept in a room file; children could glance through them for recommendations, and they could serve as an extra checkpoint before the regular trips to the library.

However, most books read should be reported on, because a pleasant experience should be shared and because books make excellent springboards to both oral and written expression. Some suggestions follow, and both you and the children can probably think of more.

Oral Activities. Oral activities for reporting on books may take a variety of forms. A few suggestions are these:

1. A child might read a particular incident from the book to the class. This requires preparation so that it will be read well; also, the incident selected should be complete in itself or listeners will lose interest.

2. Several children who have read the same book could dramatize a scene.

3. Children who have read books about the same period of history could have a panel discussion comparing the information learned—or developing different aspects of life during the period.

4. An individual child could demonstrate skills learned from a book—card tricks or a sports skill, for instance.

5. A child could pretend to be one of the characters in a book giving an interview to a newspaper or TV reporter. Another pupil would act as interviewer and would be given a list of questions to ask.

6. A child could prepare a speech explaining why a particular character would or would not make a good friend.

Written Activities. These should vary according to the age and abilities of the children; some of the following might be appropriate:

1. An imaginary letter written by one character to another at a particular point in the story.

2. An estimate of what kind of person might enjoy the book and why.

3. A review or advertisement for the class or school paper.

4. A first-person description of a particular event in the story, told as though the writer had been an onlooker (this observer could even be a dog or some inanimate object rather than a human being).

5. A character sketch of one of the people in the book, which should include both a physical description and a discussion of the kind of person this character was (using specific actions to prove points).

6. A description of the setting of the book, telling why it was or was not important to the story.

7. A TV script based on the book (if equipment is available, it might actually be dramatized and videotaped as a group or class activity, thus calling for both oral and written expression as well as planning and organizational skills)

8. Book reviews (as children reach the upper grades, they should learn how to write a good book review; prepare for this by bringing in sample reviews from magazines and papers).

Other Activities. Nonlanguage activities related to books read can be useful in two ways; they create an opportunity for children who are not highly verbal to make something the other children will admire, and the products can add interest and color to the library corner. Such activities might include the following:

1. Making models, dioramas, or maps (for example, one child might use sand, twigs, and other items to show the setting for the battle at Little Big Horn, another might make a scale model of the Kon Tiki, another might draw a map showing Huck Finn's trip down the Mississippi, etc.).

2. Drawing illustrations for a particular story (these can make excellent bulletin board displays).

3. Drawing a cartoon strip showing the action in a certain event (also good bulletin board material).

4. Dressing a doll in a costume that might have been worn by a character in a story.

5. Making a mobile depicting characters or objects in a book (it can be hung in the library corner).

Activities such as these can be used to encourage a shy child to speak before the group. For instance, a child who drew a map might be asked to explain briefly where various incidents took place, or one who made a model could explain what it represents. These explanations can be done very informally, with the children grouped around and looking at the object being shown rather than at the child who is speaking.

POETRY IN THE CLASSROOM

Many adults think they do not like poetry, but children love rhythm, rhyme, and the sounds of words. Mother Goose has remained in good standing for years, and Dr. Seuss is an undisputed favorite with young readers. Unfortunately, teachers and textbooks must take a large share of the blame for this shift in values. Selections inappropriate to the age, experience, and interests of children have made poetry dull; teachers have read beautiful poems badly; forced memorization has placed poetry in the same category as multiplication tables; and an overemphasis on analysis has made poems seem like scientific data to be studied rather than an experience to be enjoyed.

Poetry offers a way to express ideas and feelings; it stimulates the imagination and provides an outlet for the emotions; it motivates children to express their own creativity; and it furnishes a way of showing children the beauty and expressiveness of language. What better reasons can be offered for using poetry with children?

Guidelines

Poetry has its birth in song, and, as with song, its aural qualities are among its chief assets. Thus, with a few rather obvious exceptions, poems are meant to be heard, not seen. This does not mean that the children may not have copies to follow as a poem is read—in fact, this may sometimes increase their enjoyment—but the poem should be read aloud, not silently, and it should be read in such a way that the greatest appreciation is obtained. This means preparation; attention must be given to the speed at which individual lines should be read, what the cadence is, which words should be emphasized, and what tone and pitch will best express the poem's meaning. Reading poetry well requires even more practice than reading stories well; again, recording yourself reading can be very useful to your preparation. Cassettes and records can be used to present poetry; some poems almost require a professional reading, and many fine ones are available. The difficulty, of course, is that you often will not want to use a record or cassette in its entirety, and it isn't always easy to find quickly the exact portion desired. Also, it must be stressed once more that your enjoyment and appreciation are best expressed through your own voice.

Poetry should become a natural part of the ongoing classroom activities. Opportunities are endless; what better way to spice up a social studies lesson than with songs of the river boatmen, Indian chants, or folk ballads? Many of these are available on records or in filmstrip-with-cassette packages, and this is an excellent use of such aids. Or possibly arrangements could be made to have someone come in to play and sing some folk songs to the class; older children will particularly enjoy this.

The use of poetry may be instigated by a holiday, a change in the weather, a circus in town, or animals or insects brought in by the children. There have been poems written about every imaginable subject or situation, for poetry is truly a natural form of expression. For example, sixth-graders struggling with fractions might find a moment of relaxation with Carl Sandburg's "Arithmetic"; or on a dreary day when the schoolyard is a sea of mud, you might say to the children "Do you know what? I know a poem about mud."

Celebrations by Myra Cohn Livingston (Holiday House, 1985) is a collection of poems about holidays. This book, illustrated by Leonard Everett Fisher, is worthwhile for its lovely illustrations alone, but is also remarkable for its inclusion of poems about holidays other than the usual ones—for example, Martin Luther King Day.

MUD

Mud is very nice to feel
All squishy-squash between the toes!
I'd rather wade in wiggly mud
Than smell a yellow rose.
Nobody else but the rosebush knows
How nice mud feels
Between the toes.*

Be selective—gather quality, not quantity. And by all means choose only poems you like yourself.

Select poems carefully and choose only those you and the children will enjoy. Too few children have regular exposure to enjoyable experiences with poetry after they have passed the nursery-rhyme stage. Therefore, at any grade level it is important to start with poems that the children will understand and like. Children will not learn to love poetry or any other type of literature by being forced to read particular poems simply because they are reputed classics or because they are in a particular textbook. There are plenty of good poems; it requires only a little time and effort to find those that appeal to the children in a particular class.

A Few Suggestions

Blackberry Ink by Eve Merriam (Morrow, 1985)
Doodle Soup by John Ciardi (Houghton Mifflin, 1985)
Earth Songs by Myra Cohn Livingston (Holiday House, 1986)
The New Kid on the Block by Jack Prelutsky (Greenwillow, 1984)
Read-Aloud Rhymes for the Very Young, edited by Jack Prelutsky (Alfred A. Knopf, 1985)

Studies have shown that children prefer humorous poems to serious, meditative ones and that they like narrative poems and poems about animals or about experiences that are familiar and enjoyable to them. They respond to rhythm, rhyme, and sound in poems, but they reject poems that rely heavily on imagery and figurative language, finding these difficult to understand. Select poems that contain concrete, well-defined images. Ask questions that bring forth individual responses and encourage appreciation for the "special" language of poetry. Help children to *discover* images; do not test for "correct" responses. For example, if you read the poem quoted above, you might ask "What are a rosebush's toes? Do you suppose it can really feel the mud?" Or possibly say "I like the words squishy-squash, don't you? Can you think of other words about mud?" Sandburg's fog that comes "on little cat feet" might initiate a discussion of which animals might represent other weather phenomena: could a distant thunderstorm be

*By Polly Chase Boyden. From *Child Life,* copyright © 1930. Used by permission.

a growling dog threatening to attack, fleecy clouds be swans floating grace-fully across the sky? Through such questions and discussion, children can develop a true understanding of such techniques as metaphor or onomato-poeia without ever hearing the words. And, with encouragement, they will experiment with their own word pictures and colorful language when they write. As they grow in experience and understanding, they will be ready for figurative language and more subtle types of imagery.

Older children will enjoy learning the names of poetic techniques, but keep in mind that a poem should *never* be analyzed like a specimen under a microscope lens. Call attention to rhythm, a particular rhyme pattern, alliteration, metaphor, onomatopoeia, and other techniques as they aid in creating the total effect of a poem, not as items to be memorized and tested for at a later date. If children can see that the "Beat, beat, beat of the tom-tom" not only imitates the sound of the drums by its rhythm but empha-sizes it through the use of hard vowels, they can begin to appreciate that the ordering and the sounds of words do much more than merely state facts. As you point out these techniques, follow with writing activities in which they are used—as a class, in groups, or individually.

Poetry may be reacted to in many ways other than writing or discussion, of course. Children may simply clap to the rhythm of a poem, dramatize all or a part of it, make a drawing or painting, or create a dance reflecting its rhythm or feeling. A poem with a repeated refrain might inspire choral reading, either spontaneous or planned. Encourage many kinds of re-sponses; but, above all, make every effort to ensure that poetry is an avenue for the enjoyment, enrichment, and appreciation of the beauty and power of words.

Poetry File

The file in which you keep records of stories to be told or read should also contain poems. A file is probably even more important for poetry than for stories, since poems are short and it is virtually impossible to remember exactly where to find any particular one. Very short poems may simply be clipped or copied and placed in the file; other entries might show only where the particular poem is to be found. It is also a good idea to keep at least one good anthology (preferably several) in the classroom so that poems are quickly available. These should not be the only sources of poems, but they should be selected with great care.

Another possibility is to clip cards with titles and sources of poems to pictures in your picture file. These can provide a quickly assembled—and effective—bulletin board display for some special occasion.

Suggested Activities

Primary children should participate in rhythmic activities to help them de-velop coordination and aural discrimination. Select poems with a strong, regular beat, preferably ones the children know and like, and let them clap out the rhythm as you read. They will also enjoy acting out nursery rhymes as you read them; try simple ones first, such as "Humpty, Dumpty," "One, Two, Buckle My Shoe," "Jack and Jill," and "Three Little Kittens."

Children love familiar poems just as they love to have the same story read again and again. When they ask for particular poems, you can begin to develop appreciation by asking questions such as the following: "Why do you like this poem so much? Which words do you like the best? Does this line make you see a picture? When the three little kittens say 'Mew, mew, mew,' does it sound as though they're crying? How do you feel when they say 'Purr, purr, purr?'" Such questioning should not be overdone, however. The important goal is to have the children enjoy the poem. Let the questions come as a spontaneous expression of your own appreciation; use them to increase pleasure, just as you point out illustrations in a book to make the story more enjoyable.

Young children love rhythm and rhyme. Seek out opportunities to capitalize on and develop this interest whenever you can. For example, when you talk about rhyming words in developing reading skills, let the children make couplets using the words that rhyme. You be the scribe, furnishing spelling, punctuation, and capital letters. They will enjoy this and learn to put a thought into a few words:

> The sky is black
> Because night came back.
>
> See what I found!
> A ball that's round.

Primary-grade children can also participate in simplified choral reading—that is, you read the verse, and they recite the refrain. Intermediate-grade children can progress to more complex types of choral reading; in fact, students of all ages will enjoy this activity if poems are carefully selected.

Intermediate- and upper-grade children also enjoy reading aloud poems they particularly like. This is an excellent way to introduce a poetry unit. It is important to accept any poem a child selects, even if it is not a very good one. The selections children make can serve as a guide for discovering other poems that they can understand and enjoy.

As middle-grade children expand concepts and vocabulary and begin to feel more at ease with writing and spelling, they should also be increasing their appreciation of the ways words are used. Choosing exactly the right word to use is important to all writing, but it is especially vital to poetry. Emphasize the fact that the sound of a word, as well as its meaning, contributes to the effect of a poem. An excellent vehicle for demonstrating this is a sampling from Mary O'Neill's *What Is That Sound!*, for instance:

> **GROWL?**
>
> When a surly dog
> Complete with scowl
> Goes rumbly-grumbly
> That's a growl.
> Growl's sound is surly

> Snarly-gray,
> And when you hear it
> Back away. . . . *

Talk about the sound of words such as *rumbly-grumbly*, *surly,* and *snarly,*: "Do they sound unpleasant? Why do you suppose she called a snarl *gray* instead of some other color? Certainly it rhymes with *away*, but is that the only reason?"

The introductory poem from the same volume is excellent for building vocabulary as well as for talking about the images words create:

SOUND OF WATER

The sound of water is:
Rain,
Lap,
Fold,
Slap,
Gurgle,
Splash,
Churn,
Crash,
Murmur,
Pour,
Ripple,
Roar,
Plunge,
Drip,
Spout,
Slip,
Sprinkle
Flow,
Ice,
Snow.*

Experiment with reading this poem in such a way that each word sounds like its meaning, and be sure to point out the rhyme if children have missed it. Then let them try to create a similar poem about the sound of paper, the classroom, the school bus, or whatever. Be sure to give at least several choices.

Almost every child can be inspired to be creative in some ways. Perhaps this creativity will consist merely of finding and cutting out pictures from magazines that will illustrate a particular poem for a bulletin board display, but even this is a beginning and should be praised. Many children can write surprisingly good poems if they are motivated. Free verse may be a good vehicle for some children because they can concentrate on choosing the best

*Reprinted with permission of Atheneum Publishers, an imprint of Macmillan Publishing Company, from *What Is That Sound?* by Mary O'Neill. Copyright © 1966 by Mary O'Neill.

words instead of on form. However, free verse is not as easy as it seems, and many children prefer poems that rhyme. Middle- and upper-grade children like limericks and consider it fun to try writing them. They will also achieve success in writing a form such as cinquain (see Chapter 10).

Children should begin by writing short poems and forms they can execute successfully. Praise for efforts made and helpful—but limited—suggestions will encourage further efforts with other types of poetry. If there is sufficient interest, the children can create a class poetry book; some children may do the major portion of the writing, while others may draw illustrations, develop a format, plan organization, design a cover, and so on. It is vital to remember, however, that, before being asked to write, children should see and hear many models and should thoroughly understand the particular characteristics of the kind of poem they are going to write; *this* is the time for talking about poetic techniques.

EVALUATION OF THE PROGRAM

Since the principal value of literature is the pleasure and enrichment it brings to an individual, some people oppose evaluating the literature program. The viewpoint expressed throughout this book, however, is that evaluation is an integral part of teaching. Without evaluation, how does a teacher know what he or she has done well or needs to do? Also, there is a special need for a teacher to evaluate the literature program since literature so frequently receives only peripheral attention in the crowded school curriculum.

What one gains from literature is a very personal matter; thus, tests should probably not be given on literature selections. Such tests usually measure reading comprehension and reflect an adult's point of view as to what should have been gained from the reading. However, you should ask yourself a number of questions:

1. Do the children show interest in reading beyond that which is assigned?
2. Do I read to the children and in reading introduce them to various genres and types of content?
3. Do the children share their reading with me and the other children?
4. Is the reading corner or center a busy place when children have "spare" time?
5. Do the children use the library or media center?
6. Is there evidence that children with personal problems have been affected by their reading?

These are not the only questions that could be asked, and the answers to them may be more reminders to you than measures of the program in any objective sense. But consider them carefully in deciding whether your program is meeting its objectives and in making future plans. Strive for a hearty "yes" in answer to each question.

A FINAL WORD

We are fortunate to live in a time when hundreds of trade books intended for children are published each year. Although only a few families can afford to purchase many of these, public and school libraries make them readily available. You can make a worthy contribution to society by informing yourself about children's books and introducing your students to the best of them. Everyone agrees that the time and effort required to do this will pay rich dividends, but someone—you, very likely—has to accept the responsibility for performing this crucially important service.

References

Bauer, Caroline Feller. *This Way to Books*. H. W. Wilson, 1983.

Carlson, Ruth K. *Literature for Children: Enrichment Ideas*. William C. Brown, 1970.

Chambers, Aiden. *Introducing Books to Children*, 2nd ed. The Horn Book, 1983.

Cullinan, Bernice. *Literature and the Child*. Harcourt Brace Jovanovich, 1981.

Glazer, Joan I. *Literature for Young Children*, 2nd ed. Charles E. Merrill, 1986.

Huck, Charlotte S.; Hepler, Susan; and Hickman, Janet. *Children's Literature in the Elementary School*, 4th ed. Holt, Rinehart and Winston, 1987.

Lamme, Linda Leonard. *Raising Readers: A Guide to Sharing Literature with Young Children*. Walker, 1980.

Lonsdale, Bernard I., and Mackintosh, Helen K. *Children Experience Literature*. Random House, 1973.

Lukens, Rebecca. *A Critical Handbook of Children's Literature*. Scott, Foresman, 1986.

Paulin, Mary Ann. *Creative Uses of Children's Literature*. Shoe String Press, 1982.

Purves, Alan C., and Monson, Dianne L. *Experiencing Children's Literature*. Scott, Foresman, 1984.

Shapiro, Jon E., ed. *Using Literature and Poetry Affectively*. International Reading Association, 1979.

Stewig, John Warren. *Children and Literature*, 2nd. ed. Houghton Mifflin, 1988.

Sutherland, Zena, et al. *Children and Books*, 7th ed. Scott, Foresman, 1986.

Trelease, Jim. *The Read-Aloud Handbook*, rev. ed. International Reading Association, 1985.

Teaching Resources

GUIDES FOR SELECTING BOOKS FOR CHILDREN

Arbuthnot, May Hill, et al. *Children's Books Too Good to Miss*, 7th ed. University Press Books, 1979.

Carroll, Frances Laverne, and Meacham, Mary. *Exciting, Funny, Scary, Short, Different, and Sad Books Kids Like about Animals, Science, Sports, Families, Songs, and Other Things*. American Library Association, 1984.

Freeman, Judy. *Books Kids Will Sit Still For*. Alleyside Press, 1984.

Frizzell, Dorothy B., and Andrews, Eva L., eds. *Subject Index to Poetry for Children and Young People*. American Library Association, 1977.

Gillespie, John T., ed. *Elementary School Paperback Collection*. American Library Association, 1985.

Gillespie, John T., and Gilbert, Christin B., eds. *Best Books for Children: Preschool Through the Middle Grades*. R. R. Bowker, 1985.

Griffin, Barbara. *Special Needs Bibliography*. The Griffin (P.O. Box 195, DeWitt, NY 13214), updated annually.

Haviland, Virginia, ed. *Children's Books of International Interest*. American Library Association, 1978.

Hopkins, Lee Bennett. *The Best of Book Bonanza*. Holt, Rinehart and Winston, 1980.

Kimmel, Margaret Mary, and Segel, Elizabeth. *For Reading Out Loud: A Guide to Sharing Books with Children*. R. R. Bowker, 1983.

LiBretto, Ellen V., ed. *High/Low Handbook*, 2nd ed. (covers books, materials, and services for the problem reader). R. R. Bowker, 1985.

Lima, Carolyn W. *A to Zoo: Subject Access to Children's Books*. R. R. Bowker, 1986.

Paperback Books in Print. R. R. Bowker, published annually.

Sinclair, Patricia Kennelly. *Children's Magazine Guide: Subject Index to Children's Magazines*. Pleasant T. Rowland, 1985.

Sunderlin, Sylvia, ed. *Bibliography of Books for Children*. Association for Childhood Education International, 1983.

Tway, Eileen, ed. *Reading Ladders for Human Relations*. National Council of Teachers of English, 1981.

CHILDREN'S BOOKS REFERRED TO IN THIS CHAPTER

Aliki. *My Visit to the Dinosaurs*. Crowell, 1969.

Brandenberg, Franz. *It's Not My Fault*. Morrow, 1980.

Brown, Tricia. *Someone Special Just Like You*. Holt, Rinehart and Winston, 1984.

Bunting, Eve. *The Great White Shark*. Messner, 1982.

Butterworth, William. *The Air Freight Mystery*. Scholastic, 1979.

——. *Stop, Thief*. Scholastic, 1975.

Clapp, Patricia, *Witches' Children*. Morrow, 1982.

Claypool, Jane. *A Love for Violet*. Westminister, 1982.

Cohen, Daniel. *Monsters You Never Heard Of*. Dodd, Mead, 1980.

Cohen, Miriam. *Will I Have a Friend?* Macmillan, 1967.

Dahl, Roald. *The Fantastic Mr. Fox*. Alfred A. Knopf, 1970.

de Paola, Tomie. *Watch Out for the Chicken Feet in Your Soup*. Prentice-Hall, 1974.

Friedman, Ida R. *How My Parents Learned to Eat*. Houghton Mifflin, 1984.

George, Jean Craighead. *Water Sky*. Harper & Row, 1987.

Gibbons, Gale. *Up Goes the Skyscraper*. Four Winds Press, n.d.

Gramatky, Hardie. *Little Toot Through the Golden Gate*. Putnam's, 1975.

Hamilton, Virginia. *The People Could Fly*. Alfred A. Knopf, 1985.

Henry, Marguerite. *King of the Wind*. Macmillan, 1945.

Hogrogian, Nonny. *One Fine Day*. Macmillan, 1971.

Huston, Anne. *The Cat Across the Way*. Seabury Press, 1968.

Hutchins, Pat. *The Surprise Party*. Macmillan, 1986.

——. *Titch*. Macmillan, 1971.

Jakes, John. *Susanna of the Alamo*. Harcourt Brace Jovanovich, 1986.

Johnson, Sylvia A. *Bats*. Lerner Publications, 1985.

Karp, Naomi. *The Turning Point*. Harcourt Brace Jovanovich, 1976.

Keats, Ezra Jack. *Apt. 3*. Macmillan, 1986.

——. *The Snowy Day*. Viking, 1962.

——. *Whistle for Willie*. Penguin, 1977.

Kipling, Rudyard. *The Elephant's Child*. Follett, 1969.

Kuskin, Karla. *The Dallas Titans Get Ready for Bed*. Harper & Row, 1986.

Lasker, Joe. *He's My Brother*. Albert Whitman, 1974.

Lawrence, Isabelle. *A Spy in Williamsburg*. Rand McNally, 1955.

Lawson, Robert. *Ben and Me*. Dell, 1973.

Lexau, Joan. *Emily and the Klunky Baby and the Next-Door Dog*. Dial, 1972.

——. *Me Day*. Dial, 1971.

Lord, Betty Bao. *In the Year of the Boar and Jackie Robinson*. Harper & Row, 1984.

Neville, Emily. *It's Like This, Cat*. Harper & Row, 1964.

Perl, Lila. *Hey, Remember Fat Glenda?* Clarion Books, 1981.

Peterson, Jean Whitehouse. *I Have a Sister—My Sister Is Deaf*. Harper & Row, 1977.

Powers, Mary Ellen. *Our Teacher's In a Wheelchair*. Albert Whitman, 1986.

Sendak, Maurice. *Where the Wild Things Are*. Harper & Row, 1963.

Steptoe, John. *Stevie*. Harper & Row, 1969.

Thurber, James. *The Wonderful O*. Simon & Schuster, 1957.

Wolf, Bernard. *Anna's Silent World*. Lippincott, 1977.

BOOKS ABOUT AUTHORS AND ILLUSTRATORS OF CHILDREN'S LITERATURE

de Montreville, Doris, and Crawford, Elizabeth D. *Fourth Book of Junior Authors and Illustrators*. H. W. Wilson, 1978.

Holtze, Sally Holmes, ed. *Fifth Book of Junior Authors*. H. W. Wilson, 1983.

Kirkpatrick, D. L. *Twentieth Century Children's Writers*, 2nd ed. St. Martin's, 1983.

Something about the Author (a regularly updated series containing facts and pictures about contemporary authors and illustrators of books for young people). Gale Research, 1971– .

ADDITIONAL RESOURCES

The American Storytelling Series. H. W. Wilson (series of video cassettes featuring stories of many types, countries, and ethnic traditions, with a viewer's guide with each tape; all ages).

Bookbrain. Oryx Press, 1987 (fiction-finding software, grades 4–6).

Caedmon Records offers recordings of both prose and poetry suitable for every grade level and read by both authors and actors; for example, Carl Sandburg tells the Rootabaga Stories and Ed Begley tells tall tales.

Dailey, Sheila. *Storytelling: A Creative Teaching Strategy*. Paradigm Video (curriculum guide, video cassette, and teacher's guide, K–grade 8).

Davidson, Tom. *Share It If You Read It! 100 Ways to Get Kids to Want to Read on Their Own*. Freline, Inc., 1986. (ideas for book sharing, book reports, etc.; grades 1–8).

Electronic Bookshelf. Electronic Bookshelf, Inc. (computer software offering multiple-choice quizzes on books read; teacher can add additional ones; grades 3–up).

England, Claire, and Fusick, Adele M. *Children: Evaluating and Reviewing Materials for Children*. Libraries Unlimited, 1987.

Enna, Peter, and Forsberg, Glen. *Stories That Live*. STL International, 1985 (six volumes and cassettes).

Fritz, Jean. *And Then What Happened, Paul Revere?* Weston Woods (book with cassette; one of a series about Revolutionary War figures, including Benjamin Franklin, John Hancock and others).

Greeson, Janet, and Taha, Karen. *Name That Book! Questions and Answers on Outstanding Children's Books*. Scarecrow Press, 1986.

Hunt, Mary Alice, ed. *A Multimedia Approach to Children's Literature*. American Library Association, 1983.

Knowledge Unlimited produces video cassettes of such classics as *Charlotte's Web*, *The Yearling*, and others.

Live Oak Media offers a number of "Read-alongs" (cloth or paperbound book plus cassette) specially designed so that children may follow without frustration.

Livo, Nora J., and Rietz, Sandra A. *Storytelling Activities*. Libraries Unlimited, 1987 (all grades).

Martin, Bill, Jr. *Treasure Chest of Poetry*. DLM Teaching Resources (box of poems, divided by seasons, plus videotapes of stories, poetry, and songs).

Moss, Joy F. *Focus Units in Literature*. National Council of Teachers of English, 1984.

Prizzi, Elaine, and Hoffman, Jeanne. *Beginning Book Reporting*. Fearon (worksheets and teacher's notes; grades 2–5).

Random House produces listening cassettes or filmstrip-and-cassette packages of Newbery Medal books as well as many about Newbery-winning authors (middle and upper grades). Random House also produces sound filmstrips and read-along cassettes (with books) of Caldecott Medal winners (primary) and video cassettes of many favorites for all grade levels.

R. Caldecott: The Man Behind the Medal. Weston Woods (sound filmstrip and utilization guide; primary grades).

Veitch, Carol J., and Boklage, Cecelia M. *Literature Puzzles for Elementary and Middle Schools*. Libraries Unlimited, 1983.

Veitch, Carol J., and Crawford, Jane. *More Literature Puzzles for Elementary and Middle Schools*. Libraries Unlimited, 1986.

Weston Woods offers sound filmstrips, films, and video cassettes of many Caldecott Medal winners as well as other children's favorites.

What Is Poetry? Caedmon Records (sound filmstrips, teacher's guides, and duplicating masters).

Activities for Preservice Teachers

1. Read several research studies about children's interests in literature and compare the results. Report your findings to the class.

2. Look in a media or instructional materials center for video and audio cassettes, films, and filmstrips based on children's literature. Preview a variety of these and decide which ones you would—or would not—use in a classroom. Give reasons for your decisions.

3. Learn a story to tell to children. Review the section

on storytelling and read some of the suggested references before you begin.

4. Begin a collection of pictures of authors of children's books.

5. Visit the children's section of a public library. Inquire about the most popular books, the frequency of children's visits, and the method used to select books for the collection.

6. Visit a library or bookstore and investigate collections of poetry for children. Select at least one that you would like to have as a part of your personal collection of children's literature.

7. Begin a collection of poems about holidays that occur during the normal school year. Confine your selec-

tions to those suitable for a particular age group (primary, middle, or upper grades), and try to include as many poems and as many holidays as possible.

8. Begin a file of stories for reading or telling to children. Concentrate on primary, middle, or upper grades.

9. Plan an activity designed to aid sixth-grade children in understanding and using figurative language. Use a story or poem as a motivating device. Outline carefully each step you would use in teaching the concept.

10. Visit a public library during the storytelling hour. Observe and report to the class on storytelling techniques used, choice of stories, and the children's reactions.

Activities for Inservice Teachers

1. Instead of, or in addition to, providing comfortable spots for readers in the library corner, some teachers like to set up "quiet areas" where children can sit on chairs or recline on mats while they enjoy books. Experiment with this, and, with the children, set up standards for behavior in these areas.

2. Read one of the books on storytelling listed on page 435. Then preview a video or audio cassette of a particular story and compare the techniques used with those suggested in the book.

3. Investigate the availability of paperback books for children. Where can they be obtained? How durable are they? What do they cost?

4. Add to the independent activities for children suggested in this chapter.

5. Compile a file of poetry appropriate for particular days, such as the first day of spring, the first snow, a foggy day, Valentine's Day, and so on.

6. With your class, make a bulletin board display about a favorite author.

7. With the children, organize a book fair and book

swap. The children can bring favorite books, books they want to trade, and books obtained from neighbors (watch these for appropriateness). Assemble the books in an attractive and organized manner in an area of the room where children can easily go to browse and to make selections. Bulletin boards, book displays, mobiles, posters, and the children's own book-sharing devices (a card file of reactions to books that have been read, dioramas, art work, objects that have been constructed or collected, etc.) may be used to enhance the appeal of the area.

8. List the stories, poems, and books you have read to your class this year. Are you reading a variety of literature, presenting new authors, and introducing new literary forms?

9. List five media items you have used with your class this year. Describe your purposes and methods for using these and evaluate their effectiveness.

10. A walk to the local library with your class can be an enjoyable learning experience. Check with your library to make arrangements for a visit. A librarian may plan to read a special story to your class.

Independent Activities for Children

1. Encourage children to make their own poetry anthologies and illustrate the poems with their own drawings or pictures cut from magazines. These should not be collected or graded (although they may

be shared if the children wish). Poems might be written by the children themselves, might be ones they especially like, or both.

2. Have individual children select favorite poems and record them on tape. They can then use the tapes to judge their own reading for speed, expression, enunciation, and so forth. After a child feels that an effective reading level has been achieved, he or she may read the poem to the class.

3. Allow a child to go to the library and select books about a topic being studied by the class. This child may then be responsible for helping other children choose among them either for personal enjoyment or for reporting to the class.

4. Have a child interview classmates and other children in the school about their favorite books. Urge the child to find out *why* each book is a favorite. He or she may report the results of the interviewing to the class and show copies of some of the books.

5. One or several children might stage a puppet show based on an incident in a story or book.

6. Have a child look through magazines for pictures to illustrate a favorite story for telling to the class.

7. A child can prepare a bulletin board display advertising a favorite book. A colorful jacket, sketches of characters, and a biography of the author might be included. Lists of "good" words, appealing passages, and chapter titles may also be part of the display.

8. Have the child select a character from a story that he or she knows well and finds especially appealing. The child then lists words, phrases, or sentences (either those used in the story or ones selected from his or her own impressions) that describe the character.

9. In the upper grades many children are beginning to play the guitar. Such a child may prepare for the class a program of ballads or folk songs from a particular era or locality in conjunction with a social studies or literature unit.

10. Mobiles illustrating a story or several stories may be made. These might show principal characters, location of action, or anything else the child wishes to express.

11. Many opportunities for independent activities are presented by audiovisual aids. Individual children or groups can listen to taped or recorded stories and poems, view videotapes or filmstrips, prepare flannelboard stories to tell, etc. Sometimes this individual activity can be followed up by class viewing or listening.

12. An upper-grade student might write a comparison of two versions of the same story, presented through different forms of media, telling which he or she liked best and why.

13. A child may write a letter to an author or illustrator of a book that he or she has particularly enjoyed. Make sure that the letter includes particular reasons for liking the book (or the illustrations) or points out parts that were especially enjoyed. As an alternative, some piece of creative writing or art work that resulted from the reading might be sent to the author or illustrator.

Chapter *16*

Children with Special Needs

*I*n several earlier chapters it was suggested that you refer to this chapter as you consider the children in your classroom or, if you're not teaching, those in a classroom you might have. The point of the suggestions was to further remind you of the differences among children, particularly in intellectual abilities and levels of achievement. Too often teaching suggestions tend to regard children of the same age as a homogeneous group— yet we all know that this is not true. This book has frequently pointed out that modifications of the suggested program and procedures must be made to meet individual needs. Chapter 2, for example, described a specific instructional approach for determining differences among children in ability and achievement and discussed how the differences might be incorporated in planning your program. Other chapters emphasized children's individuality and suggested what you could do to teach each as effectively as possible. This chapter extends the examination of differences, particularly those of children identified here as "special," and makes further teaching suggestions.

Every child is special and has special needs, but for the past 150 years it has been the practice in the United States to identify some children as "special" or "exceptional." This practice began with concern for educating children with visual impairments, referred to until relatively recent times as "blind children." Later, special attention was given to children with hearing losses, speech impairments, physical handicaps, and mental retardation. Next, children of high intelligence were identified as "special," and then those with special talents, but attention to these has been somewhat sporadic. More recently, the category of special children has been extended to include those with learning disabilities and emotional problems. Parents and teachers prompted much of the attention given to these children over the years, were largely responsible for the establishment of special schools and classes, and are the forces behind recent changes in policies specifying which children are "special" and how they should be educated.

In addition to those children defined as special, there are thousands of children entering classrooms each year who are unable to speak English and are unprepared by their cultural backgrounds for the environment of the school. Still other children enter school speaking a dialect different from that used by the teacher and found in textbooks. Both of these groups of children are also special and add to the range of differences among children. It is important, though, that the extent of differences among children not be overemphasized. In most classrooms there is a rather wide range in the intellectual abilities of children, and even if the range is rather narrow, they will still differ in learning rates and styles.

Since this book is intended for teachers in "regular" classrooms, suggestions in this chapter relate to the special children identified above who are increasingly found there. There is no attempt to discuss the needs and teaching of children who are so severely handicapped mentally, physically, emotionally, or in some combination of these that they will seldom if ever be assigned to a regular classroom. Also, the proliferation of subcategories within the category "learning disabled" will receive less attention than some readers might desire.

SPECIAL CHILDREN: AN OVERVIEW

For information, write to:

Council for Exceptional
  Children
1920 Association Drive
Reston, VA 22091

National Easter Seal Society
2023 W. Ogden Avenue
Chicago, IL 60612

Office of Handicapped Individuals Clearing House
Rm. 3517 Switzer Building
330 C Street, S.W.
Washington, DC 20201

Although historically the attention given to the educational needs of special children resulted in some improvements, authorities conceded in 1975 that many children with impairments, handicaps, and learning problems were not being adequately served by the existing programs. One reason was that the education offered these children differed from state to state, with some of the children denied schooling altogether, others placed in institutions that emphasized care rather than education, and still others labeled mentally retarded on faulty evidence. Demands for reform by leaders of minority groups, teachers, and, particularly, parents led to the passage of the Education for All Handicapped Children Act (P.L. 94–142). Since the passage of this law, there has been a huge jump in the number of school-age handicapped children receiving special education, including education in regular classrooms; but few would maintain that the educational needs of the special children have been met.

How Many Children?

Estimates as to the number of children directly affected by P.L. 94–142 vary. One textbook (Hewitt, see References) indicates the following percentages of children with various handicaps:

Visually handicapped	0.07%
Hearing impaired	0.19%
Orthopedic and health impaired	0.34%
Multihandicapped	0.18%
Seriously emotionally disturbed	0.85%
Speech impaired	2.83%
Learning disabled	4.04%
Mentally retarded	1.96%

In addition, there are estimates that 3 to 5 percent of school-age children are gifted and/or talented. Although the estimates regarding the numbers of children whose handicaps can be specifically identified do not vary greatly, such is not the case for all categories of "special" children. Learning disabled and emotionally disturbed are two such categories. And, of course, the estimates of the numbers of gifted and talented children vary greatly. As one publication (see Lewis and Doorlag in the References) put it, "If those with different viewpoints as to what constitutes giftedness could fill a small auditorium, scholars with irreconcilable views as to what constitutes learning disabilities (LD) could fill Yankee stadium."

As to the numbers or percentages of children whose cultural backgrounds make them "special," there are no satisfactory estimates. One reason is that increasing numbers of children whose native language is not English are being enrolled in the schools. At the same time, the number of children who speak English dialects that are enough different from school and textbook English to cause learning difficulties for the speakers seems to be decreasing.

Mainstreaming

The term *mainstreaming* does not appear in Public Law 94–142, but the philosophy embodied in it does, since the law requires that states provide, to the maximum extent appropriate, that handicapped children be educated along with children who are not handicapped. The law implies, too, that some alternatives for educating special children are more appropriate than others. This has led to the term *least restrictive environment* and the assumption that *all* children fall along a continuum of special needs. Thus, mainstreaming should include:

- Providing each child with the most appropriate education in the least restrictive environment
- Looking at the educational needs of children rather than at their clinical or diagnostic labels
- Seeking and creating alternatives in the educational programs of regular classrooms to serve minimally handicapped children
- Uniting special education programs with general education programs for the educational benefit of these children

The law prescribes that a written educational plan must be developed and maintained for each handicapped child placed full- or part-time in a regular classroom; that this plan should be developed by a team consisting of the classroom teacher, principal, school psychologist, and support specialists; and that parents must be permitted to examine the school records, methods of instruction used, and support services available for their child. Note that the law does not eliminate self-contained special education classrooms for the education of children whose handicaps are so severe that participation in a regular classroom is impossible. Interpretations of what constitutes the "least restrictive environment" vary, but there is general agreement that the regular teacher should have primary responsibility for the child's schooling and that more than one-half of the school day should be spent in the regular classroom.

The philosophy of mainstreaming is applicable to all school settings and all children. All children are entitled to an environment that maximizes their growth, and their needs should be the bases of instruction.

Labeling Children

Traditionally, various labels have been attached to special children—often misleading ones. For example, individuals who have relatively minor hearing losses have been labeled "deaf." And labeling of children as "slow learners" has sometimes limited their development—the so-called self-fulfilling prophecy. Too often such labeling has been a diversion used by the educational system to avoid facing up to the teaching problem some children present. And although there has been a decline in such labeling, some relatively new labels—such as "learning disabled" and "emotionally and behaviorally maladjusted"—are being increasingly applied. Whether this labeling has resulted or will result in more effective instruction of the children so labeled, rather than extending the stigmatizing of children or providing an excuse for poor teaching or parental neglect, remains to be seen. Children should be put into a category or given a label only if doing so helps in the selection of an educational program or other treatment, provides evidence of what can be expected from such a program, and achieves desirable results.

Use of labeling has diminished in some communities, partially because of a trend toward what has come to be called "noncategorical special education." This term is interpreted in different ways. A few educators believe that, except for the gifted, children considered "special" or "exceptional" have so much in common that in terms of educational needs they can be considered as a single group. Other educators are unwilling to go that far but do believe that the learning disabled, the mildly disturbed, and the mildly retarded are more alike than different (with respect to intelligence, personality and adjustment, and achievement) and therefore may be placed in classrooms where similar teaching methods are used.

Labeling has not disappeared, and it will not, since proper planning of educational programs requires its use to some degree. However, combining categories for instructional purposes and reducing the harshness of some labels by using such terms as "visual impairments," "hearing disorders," and "orthopedic impairments" helps reduce the differences in the minds of both special children and so-called normal children and will lead to better understanding and a better education for all.

Instructional Considerations

Help parents to accept their children's limitations and to recognize their potential.

Mainstreaming is intended to help special children gain more positive self-concepts and greater peer acceptance and to foster more positive expectancies in teachers and parents. Special children need to learn the concepts, skills, abilities, and attitudes that other children need to learn. Thus many of the teaching procedures normally used are suitable for use with these children. In some situations, though, modification of instructional methods is needed. Specifically, the individualized educational plan for each child being mainstreamed should have: (1) a description of the child's present level of functioning, (2) short- and long-term educational goals in specific terms, (3) specific services which will be provided and the amount of time required, (4) the starting times and duration of special teaching, and (5) evaluative criteria to be used for determining whether the objectives are

Working relationships between teachers and parents are important in teaching all children, but such relationships are especially important in teaching special children.

being achieved. The intent of such a plan is to be specific as to the child's strengths and weaknesses. For example, a child may be in a regular classroom for social studies instruction because social studies is not an area of weakness, but at certain times he or she will be in a special setting to receive remedial instruction in reading because this is a weakness.

CHILDREN WITH SPEECH DISORDERS

Write to American Speech-Language-Hearing Association, 9030 Old Georgetown Road, Washington, DC 20014.

Although problems of speech are the handicapping condition most frequently encountered by classroom teachers, the number of children in a given classroom with problems that may be called speech disorders—disorders requiring extended attention from specialists—is likely to be rather small. However, it is important that teachers identify these children and provide for their instruction, as well as help others whose speech problems are less severe or are transitory.

Normal Speech Problems

When a child first enters school, his or her speech may retain vestiges of "baby talk." Estimates indicate that over 40 percent of kindergarten children and 25 percent of those in the first grade show such retention. The speech of many of these children is characterized by one or more of the following: reversals (for example, *aminal* for *animal*), inability to articulate some blends (*st, th, str*, etc.) and individual speech sounds, mispronunciations, and divergencies in pitch and loudness. A child with any of these speech characteristics may be referred to a speech therapist, who will probably simply wish to observe the child's maturation but may suggest activities similar to those in this chapter.

The child of eight or nine (at the latest) certainly should be able to produce all of the speech sounds unless he or she has a genuine speech handicap. The child may, of course, have certain speech habits (saying *deese* for *these*, for example) that need attention and may continue to have problems of voice quality and control.

Speech handicaps that go beyond the speech characteristics of many young children, with the exception of those associated with a psychological disturbance, are discussed below. Most of these problems call for the services of a speech specialist, either working directly with the child or giving the classroom teacher suggestions or assistance. However, since speech specialists are not always available, the teaching considerations and activities suggested may be useful.

For material on speech problems, write to Alexander Graham Bell Association for the Deaf, 3417 Volta Place, N.W., Washington, DC 20007.

Types of Abnormal Speech

Speech problems may be manifested in a variety of forms. These can be grouped, though, in four major categories: (1) articulatory, or pronunciation, disorders; (2) voice disorders—malfunctioning of the sound-producing mechanism; (3) linguistic, or language, disorders; and (4) disorders of speech rhythm.

Articulation Disorders. Probably as many as 70 percent of all speech problems found in the typical elementary-school classroom are those in which the speaker cannot make certain speech sounds either in isolation or in blends with other speech sounds. Most frequently, these articulation problems consist of sound substitution, omissions, reversals, and additions in the speech of children older than eight years. This persistence of common speech characteristics of young children is called "infantile perseveration" and may be caused by poor muscular coordination, illness, retarded physical maturation, low intelligence, short auditory memory span, poor auditory discrimination, or various environmental factors (overprotection by a parent, desire for attention, jealousy of a younger sibling, etc.). There are other articulatory disorders identified by speech specialists—the most common of which is probably lisping—but they are also manifested through problems with specific individual speech sounds.

Voice Disorders. Voice disorders are those in which speech sounds are articulated acceptably but the voice has a quality that is unpleasant to the hearer. Few children have this problem beyond the primary years. The most common voice disorder is nasality, usually caused by a physical problem, the most serious of which is a cleft palate. Other voice disorders include hoarseness, an unnaturally high or low pitch, and excessive loudness or softness.

Language Disorders. Language disorders are the result of physical, environmental, or psychological problems that have interfered with language learning. The language disorders most often found in the elementary school are delayed speech and childhood aphasia. Delayed speech may mean that a child does not know some sounds or has a very limited vocabulary. Victims of delayed speech range from the child who suffers a mild delay in the appearance of a few sounds to the one who reaches the primary grades with the ability to say only three or four words. When seriously delayed language development is shown, the cause is usually brain damage; the condition is known as aphasia.

Rhythm Disorders. The principal speech disorder of a rhythmic nature is stuttering. Some stutterers block on producing sounds; some repeat sounds, syllables, or words; some speak very slowly or very rapidly; some prolongate sounds; and others have spasms of the speech mechanism. There may be combinations of the above in the speech of a stutterer, and there are usually times when there is no evidence of stuttering. Speech specialists generally state that there is no definite cause of stuttering, and no certain cure. However, many stutterers can learn procedures that enable them to control the problem.

Instructional Considerations

Children who have been identified, by a screening procedure, as possibly having a speech disorder should be referred to a specialist for diagnosis and remediation. After seeing the child, the speech specialist will contact the parents and will involve a physician, a psychologist, and others if there is a serious speech disorder. Unless the child is totally removed from his or her regular classroom, the teacher will be brought into the planning for remediation. The reduction of anxieties is important in treating any speech problem. Cutting off a child's attempts to say what he or she wants to say is devastating. Classmates should not be permitted to cut the child off or to make fun of his or her speech. A program that makes it possible for children to talk together in small groups will benefit a child with a speech problem. The activities suggested in Chapters 4 and 5 that avoid singling the child out will help. In addition, a teacher should give special attention to the way he or she speaks to such a child. Looking directly at the child when speaking helps, as does speaking in a well-modulated voice and in an unhurried and pleasant manner.

Never display impatience with a child who has faulty speech. The child must feel accepted and secure.

Activities

Activities that may modify or remedy speech defects should be used to meet specific needs; they should not be used indiscriminately. It is much more important for children—including those who have speech handicaps—to engage in genuine communication situations than to practice speech exercises. Activities such as those suggested here are certainly important and necessary when speech correction is needed, but they are only part of a total speech improvement program.

Relaxing exercises such as falling completely relaxed into a chair, dropping the head and letting the arms dangle, shaking the hands and arms, and rotating the head on the chest and shoulders may help a child whose speech problem is related to tenseness. Breathing exercises, such as taking short quick breaths, inhaling deeply, taking in a quick breath and exhaling slowly (by counting), and doing specific acts (smelling a flower, saying "ah" for the doctor, showing surprise), may also be helpful. To correct excessive nasality, try such activities as yawning, panting, and "blowing out" vowel sounds (or blowing out a candle, blowing a pinwheel, etc.).

Hearing exercises are also important, since good speech depends on aural acuity and the ability to discriminate between correct and incorrect production of a sound. These exercises include discriminating among sounds (the ringing of a small bell and the sound of a triangle, for example), telling when two words begin with the same sound (or end with the same sound, or have the same middle sound), and selecting objects whose names contain a particular sound.

In helping the child who retains vestiges of baby talk, the first task is to identify the particular sounds the child does not produce correctly. Then attempt to have the child distinguish between words correctly and incorrectly spoken: *fadder-father, wittle-little, thithter-sister*. It may be necessary for the child to use a mirror so that he or she can watch lip and tongue movements. Tape recording these efforts may also help. Another useful technique is to have the child recite poems and sing songs containing the sounds that are troublesome.

Tongue exercises are helpful in remedying simple articulation problems. These should be done individually with the aid of a mirror. They include stretching the tongue out and down, up toward the nose, inside the lips, and so on. There are also activities suitable for groups, such as saying the following rhymes

> Little kitty laps her milk,
>   Lap, lap, lap!
> Her tongue goes out,
> Her tongue goes in,
>   Lap, lap, lap!
>
> Little kitty likes her milk,
>   Lap, lap, lap!
> Oh, see her tongue
> Go out and in,
>   Lap, lap, lap!
> ("Make your tongue go like kitty's.")
>
> Tick! Tock! Tick! Tock!
> The clock goes ticking all the day.
> Tick! Tock! Tick! Tock!
> It has no other words to say.
> Tick! Tock! Tick! Tock!
> It ticks all night; it ticks all day.
> And when I sleep, or when I play,
> The clock goes on the same old way.
> Tick! Tock! Tick! Tock!

Exercises for correcting the production of specific sounds may be used when particular faults have been identified. For example, for the sound represented by /s/ the following might be done:

- Say lists of words.

see	pencil	nice
sit	answer	dress
sun	dressing	house
soup	insect	base
salt	groceries	tennis

- Repeat /s/ sentences.

    My sister is sick.
    We ate soup, salad, roast, and carrots.

- Say contrasting words.

some–thumb	sick–thick	so–though
seem–theme	thin–sin	

These are only examples of exercises that may be appropriate. A speech therapist can provide many more that will be helpful for specific problems.

THE HEARING IMPAIRED

The total incidence of hearing losses among the children in schools is not known, since these losses range from very slight ones to total deafness. Hearing losses and learning difficulties are not necessarily related, but the fact that so much instruction is on an aural-oral basis means that there may be problems. Most children with hearing losses that are less than total deafness can be successful in the regular classroom if sensitivity is shown for their handicaps and instructional adjustments are made.

Screening for Hearing Losses

The best procedure for a school to use to determine whether a child has a hearing loss is to test the child with an audiometer. This test requires a competent operator for the equipment, so often children are screened on a systemwide, regional, or statewide basis. If such a testing service is not available, a child with a suspected hearing loss should be referred to a physician.

It is possible to test children informally to determine the need for audiometric testing or referral by having them listen to a ticking watch or to whispering. The watch should have a fairly loud tick, one that would be heard at about four feet from the ear by a child with normal hearing. Each ear should be tested separately; the actual testing is done by holding the watch near the ear and moving it away until the child signals that he or she can no longer hear it. The whispering testing is done by whispering directions ("raise your left hand," "close your fist," etc.) at increasing distances from the ear being tested.

A child with a speech or hearing impairment may also be a "quiet one."

A teacher must also be alert to children's behavior or habits that indicate a hearing impairment or an impending difficulty with hearing properly. These conditions include recurring earaches, the tendency to favor one ear in listening, rubbing an ear, headaches, head noises, and dizziness. Excessive inattention, reflected in poor achievement and the failure to follow directions, may also signal a hearing problem. Sometimes, too, faulty pronunciation, heavy breathing through the mouth, and an unnatural pitch of voice are signs of hearing impairment.

Children with hearing losses often need professional treatment. The teacher is usually informed about the diagnosis and treatment, particularly if there is a responsibility the physician thinks the school should assume. For example, if a child is given a hearing aid, he or she has to be helped in getting accustomed to using it. If a child is receiving instruction in lip reading, the teacher should know this. If there is medication prescribed, this should be known. Do not hesitate to inquire of parents or the school physician about these matters.

Helping the Child

Children don't like to be too different. The child with a hearing loss should be given the consideration needed to aid learning without excessive attention being called to the problem. For example, when directions are given or other talking is done with this child, he or she should be faced as directly as possible. The child will learn to watch faces (some children even learn by themselves to read lips). Do not shout or exaggerate lip and facial movements. (Try looking in the mirror sometime while reciting "Mary Had a Little Lamb" with exaggerated facial expression and a shouting voice. Who would want to look at such efforts all day?) Remember to hold hands and books away from the face when speaking to a child with a hearing loss. And if the child does not understand, rephrasing or restating is better than repeating what was said.

Seating arrangements should be such that a child with a hearing loss has his or her back to the light (actually a good idea for seating all children). With the light off the child's face, he or she will be better able to watch the speaker.

It is also important to keep in mind that lip reading requires constant attention and concentration (try it for half an hour; ask a friend to whisper while you watch his or her lips). Thus, the child who depends heavily on lip reading will get tired and need time to rest.

Because hearing loss often affects speech and confidence in oral language situations, particular attention should be given to structuring activities that the child can engage in successfully. Others in the school—special teachers, clerks, and so on—should be aware of the child's hearing loss so that they can cooperate with you in your efforts. A child with a hearing loss often needs to develop skill in auditory discrimination. Although not every child with a hearing loss has undeveloped auditory discrimination skill, and not every child who needs teaching attention to his or her auditory discrimination ability is suffering from a hearing loss, being able to discriminate among speech sounds is important to success in using language. Listening and readiness activities suggested in earlier chapters will help children develop this ability.

CHILDREN WITH VISUAL IMPAIRMENTS

For information, write to:

American Foundation for the Blind
15 W. 15th Street
New York, NY 10011

Division for the Blind and Physically Handicapped
Library of Congress
Washington, DC 20542

National Society for the Prevention of Blindness
78 Madison Avenue
New York, NY 10016

Children who are visually impaired may, depending on the severity of the handicap, present particular teaching problems in most areas of the language arts. Children who are blind or nearly so generally will not be in a regular classroom, although with mainstreaming they may be for a portion of the school day. Regular classrooms do contain, however, a good many children who have visual problems of a less severely handicapping nature. These children often have difficulty seeing the board, charts, and/or the print in books. They may also reflect such handicaps in their writing.

Identifying the Children

Symptoms of possible visual problems include losing one's place while reading, avoiding close work, poor posture while reading, holding the reading material closer or farther away than normal, holding one's body rigid while looking at distant objects, rubbing the eyes, tilting the head to one side, frowning, blinking, scowling while reading or writing, excessive head movement while reading, inflamed eyelids, and frequent headaches. Children in the primary grades who have difficulty learning their colors may be suspected of having color "blindness."

Most schools make some provision for screening children's vision. Usually the screening is done using the Snellen Chart, a procedure that checks vision at 20 feet but does not check near-point vision or measure fusion ability, muscular imbalance, or other visual abnormalities. A lesser number of schools also screen with a chart held at a distance of 14 inches from the eye, which does adequately screen near-point vision.

Other testing instruments are sometimes used in schools (such as the Keystone Telebinocular or the Titmus Vision Tester), usually administered by a school nurse or some other specialist rather than the classroom teacher. The classroom teacher can check on symptoms by asking children to read aloud material on the chalkboard and by close questioning about letters and words in near-point reading. All children suspected of having problems seeing properly should be referred to specialists.

Instructional Considerations

When referred to a specialist, a child who has a vision problem usually receives attention: glasses, contact lenses, supervised muscle training, and so on. However, the attention needed may take most of the school year to materialize. And even if a child does receive the kind of special assistance he or she needs, there are still some ways a teacher can help. These include the following:

- Seat the child so that he or she can see the board as well as possible.
- Arrange the child's desk to avoid glare.
- Prevent the child from facing sharp contrasts in the amount of direct or reflected light.
- Use reading materials that are not "slick" or glossy.
- Remove the glossy finish from the top of the child's desk.
- Use a typewriter with large type to make materials for the child.

Assignments can be given orally, the child can be read to by other children, and the answers to questions can be given orally rather than in writing. Information, directions, and even literary selections can be recorded on tape for the child to listen to, particularly if other pupils are enlisted in helping to prepare the tapes. Extra attention should be given to teaching listening skills, since the child with a vision problem must depend more heavily on listening than does the child with normal vision. Recognition will need to be given to the fact that partially sighted children usually take longer to complete assignments than those with normal vision. Teachers may need to shorten written assignments for these children or allow them more time for completion.

CHILDREN WITH OTHER PHYSICAL HANDICAPS

Many children with physical handicaps or limitations can participate in a regular classroom. However, adjustments may need to be made in order that learning problems do not develop or are not aggravated. These special children may also need help in acquiring a commonsense attitude regarding their personal strengths and limitations, one that will be sustained as they get older.

Types of Handicaps

There are many types of physical handicaps other than hearing and vision losses, and some speech problems have a physical base. Many of these physical handicaps are manifested in slight impairments of movement. Children with severe handicaps, such as serious cardiac conditions, will usually not be placed in regular classrooms. But many children with serious physical problems, such as epilepsy or the loss of a limb, have learned to function in group settings like the classroom. In general, doctors recommend that physically handicapped children associate with their peers in normal settings. There are also many borderline "special" children, those having a rather minor physical defect, a physical problem such as being grossly overweight, or a temporary restrictive condition. These children are generally included in the regular classroom, and they may be especially sensitive to their physical problems, even though the problems may not be of a serious nature. Certainly any child who regards himself or herself as handicapped must be treated as a "special" child.

Instructional Considerations

Many children with serious physical defects have gaps in their experiential lives, although, considering the effects of television, the gaps are not as great at present as they once were. However, there are differences between watching an activity on TV and participating in a trip to a supermarket, a dairy, or a museum, for example. Such activities can be the bases for much language learning, and physically handicapped children in a regular classroom can engage in most activities if they are properly planned.

Attention often needs to be given to the child's special social needs—relationships with parents, peers, and the personnel of the school. The child may need social contacts that have not been experienced, physical activity that has been avoided, and the general opportunity to extend himself or herself as a person. Certainly physical limitations and any special problems related to them must be thoroughly understood before efforts are made in these areas. This means that the teacher must have some contact with the child's physician, parents, and other specialists who are also working with him or her.

A physical handicap often brings about an emotional condition that is reflected in behavior and learning problems. Helping the child to overcome such problems and to adjust to conditions that cannot be overcome is often the teacher's most important task, and there is no easy way to do this. Certainly a teacher must extend himself or herself as a sensitive human being—this is a broad concept, one that includes the very best of teaching practices and true attention to needs, interests, and abilities. The basis for the teaching that needs to be done is often in providing a means for the child to recognize his or her own problem and to work on it.

CHILDREN WITH LEARNING PROBLEMS

For information, write to:

Association for Children
with Learning Disabilities
4156 Library Road
Pittsburgh, PA 15234

League for Emotionally
Disturbed Children
171 Madison Avenue
New York, NY 10017

National Association for
Retarded Citizens
2709 Avenue E East
P.O. Box 6109
Arlington, TX 76011

This section discusses children in typical classrooms who have more difficulty learning than most of their classmates but whose problems are not so severe that they need to be excluded from at least some participation in such a classroom. These children may be mildly mentally retarded or mildly emotionally disturbed or have a learning disability. Although the disabilities of these children differ to some extent, they do have similar characteristics. Thus, some common instructional efforts can be made.

Definitions and Characteristics

The issue of labeling is particularly critical with respect to the category of "mentally retarded." Estimates have been made that 80 to 90 percent of the students identified as mentally retarded have no organic brain damage. They are retarded educationally, and this retardation is attributed to lack of early educational stimulation, malnutrition, poor health, parental deprivation, and other factors.

Children who have been labeled (whether openly or not) as mentally retarded have many of the same needs all other children do. They want and need to explore and extend their environment, perhaps even more than children not so identified. They need first-hand experiences—concrete ones more than abstract. The abilities of these children vary, although a common characteristic is that their development has been and is slower than average. Yet they can learn much that is taught to other children if the teaching takes into account their limitations and the causes of them.

**Possible Symptoms of
Learning Disabilities**

inattentiveness
aggressiveness
impulsiveness
shyness
lack of organization
overexcitability
speech irregularities
perceptual difficulties
lethargy

A learning disability may be defined as a condition that prevents an intellectually and physically normal child from absorbing knowledge, organizing experience, and expressing the synthesis of these in ideas and actions at the level of his or her true potential. This is a broad definition—and deliberately so, since there tend to be many definitions and interpretations of definitions. The common element in the definitions—and in terminology related to them—is that learning achievement is highly unsatisfactory when compared to the apparent learning potential. As with children who are mildly retarded, attention and memory are the two characteristics showing consistent deficiencies. Most identifications of children as learning disabled occur because of the difficulties these children have with reading comprehension.

Some educators use the term *learning disorder* rather than learning disability, since they believe that something is out of order and can be remedied. Others state that learning disabilities may be due to brain injuries, perceptual handicaps, or minimal brain dysfunctions. Although some children who have been identified as learning disabled may have an organic base for their disabilities, often the cause is poor teaching and/or parental neglect.

As with the learning disabled, how the emotionally or behaviorally disturbed child is characterized or identified depends largely on who is doing the defining. Many teachers, at one time or another, have considered a child who misbehaves more than the other children in a class to be emotionally disturbed. The same feelings have surely also been experienced by some parents.

In considering emotional and behavior problems, one must recognize the fact that every child is growing, changing, and developing in a nonstatic world and that so-called normal behavior in that world is difficult to describe. What is acceptable behavior at one time and place may not be in another. Definitions which indicate that an emotionally disturbed child is one who cannot function emotionally, socially, and intellectually in a manner acceptable to all the individuals he or she encounters at home, at school, or in the community are less than helpful, since they bring to mind the question "Who can?"

It is true that there are children with psychoses, neuroses, and personality disorders—just as there are such people in the adult population. A physical or intellectual handicap may bring about emotional maladjustments. Similar maladjustments may arise from the child's size, appearance, or degree of social maturity. The child who is careless, lazy, spoiled, or immature has a learning maladjustment. So does the one who displays an antisocial attitude, emotional instability, or hyperactive behavior.

On the other hand, many children manifest transient and situational behaviors that do not warrant their being identified as emotionally disturbed. The increase in the number of children labeled emotionally disturbed and the trend toward treatment by drugs should cause all teachers to think seriously about whether the roots of many of the problems of these children may not lie in the teaching practices and the school program. Simply identifying children's particular problems is not providing the teaching they need. Of course, the determination of a child's specific problems and needs should lead to more effective instruction; the question is whether or not this is happening.

Instructional Considerations

Many teaching techniques and procedures have been suggested and tried with children who have learning problems, but there is little conclusive evidence to support particular procedures or techniques. However, the techniques and procedures *proven by research and practice* to be effective with so-called normal children appear to be, with some modifications, generally effective with these children. The modifications made are usually in terms of the rate of learning and the reinforcement of perception and retention, but the teacher of a child with a learning problem—whatever the subcate-

Children from other cultures and those who are economically or socially handicapped may have emotional and/or motivational problems in some school settings. This does not mean that these children are disabled learners. Of course, some may be.

For guidance concerning the hyperactive child, consult *Hyperactive Child, Adolescent, and Adult: Attention Deficit Disorder Through the Lifespan* (available from the National Institute of Child Health and Human Development, P.O. Box 2911, Washington, DC 20040).

A teacher should know if a child is receiving medical or psychological treatment. If you do not know but suspect that this may be the case, ask the parents.

gorization within this larger one—needs to try various procedures. What works for some children will not necessarily work for others. In short, attention must be given to individual differences in attitudes, interests, needs, and abilities—which of course is the essence of all good teaching.

Usually, children with learning problems need to develop patterns of behavior that they can follow without conscious thought. They need to be taken to foundational levels of visual, auditory, and motor skills that were not acquired in earlier learning opportunities. Attention must be focused on specific needs and problems, and what is to be learned should be presented in a graduated sequence of small steps. Teachers should stress the social value of what is to be learned and respect each child as an individual.

These children do not respond positively to prodding or coercing. Such procedures will usually reactivate or reinforce behaviors that may well be major aspects of their learning problems: withdrawal, rebelliousness, negativism, or escapism. To gain any rapport at all with many of these children requires a great deal of patience. This patience should be manifested in understanding, sympathy, and friendliness, but it also needs to be shown in firm controls and fair limitations. The children need to feel that they are accepted, but that they are expected to learn.

In sum, the instructional planning described in Chapter 2 and the many activities suggested throughout this book are appropriate for children who have learning problems—particularly if the following suggestions are kept in mind:

1. Establish short-range goals, and be sure the child understands them.
2. Break up the content of the material into smaller than usual units.
3. Keep directions simple; ask that they be repeated.
4. Provide materials the child is capable of using.
5. Make instruction systematic and orderly.
6. Provide adequate time for the child to accomplish selected or assigned tasks.
7. Talk to the child directly and calmly.
8. Minimize the complexity of language used, the number of items or concepts presented at a given time, and the memory load required.
9. Minimize distractions.
10. Make sure the child attains a measure of success.
11. Make sure the child is aware of his or her accomplishments.
12. Be patient and understanding and sensitive to interests and needs.

TEACHING GIFTED AND TALENTED CHILDREN

A point of view held by many people is that extremely bright children will learn under almost any conditions. Children with special talents are often considered to be maturing lopsidedly, not making equal effort in areas other than that in which they show talent, or simply being rebellious. Although

For information, write to:

American Association for
Gifted Children
15 Grammercy Park
New York, NY 10003

Association for Gifted
Children
2179 Gregory Drive
Hot Springs, AR 71901

little concern is likely to be shown in schools for talented children as being "special," particularly if the talents are not in academic areas, there have been efforts in recent years to establish special programs for the intellectually gifted.

Identifying the Children

Various definitions have been advanced to characterize the gifted and talented. Possibly the most practical one is that these are children who show outstanding ability in any or several of a variety of areas: general intelligence, specific aptitudes, creativity, leadership, or artistic skill. The identification of children as gifted or talented should be done by professionals, that is, by teachers, psychologists, and other trained specialists. The identification should not be based solely on intelligence tests, since high intelligence as measured by these tests may not correlate highly with some of the talents, aptitudes, and other characteristics of children who are gifted, particularly for children from minority groups.

Giftedness generally means above-average general ability, a high level of task commitment, and a high level of creativity. Individuals possessing some talents may not have all of these characteristics; however, most people would agree that the creative and/or talented individual in our society is generally quite intelligent and is committed to his or her specialty, whether that is ice skating, writing fiction, designing buildings, or whatever. Thus, evidence of task commitment is a criterion that should not be overlooked when gifted and talented individuals are being identified. It is also important to remember that handicapped children may be gifted and/or talented.

Keep in mind that an individual may be gifted and also handicapped. The best-known example is Helen Keller.

Instructional Considerations

Children who are gifted or talented are still children, not adults. Their interests and needs are often little different from those of other children. They may have broader interests, however, if they are academically gifted, or they may have special interests if they possess particular talents or aptitudes. A major question regarding the academically gifted is whether their movement through the normal school curriculum should be accelerated or whether the curriculum should be enriched at each level to better accommodate their needs and interests. This question is most frequently answered in favor of the latter alternative; that is, these children often leave the regular classroom for part of the school day in order to engage in enrichment activities. This exiting from the classroom is not necessary, though, if *all* children in a classroom are treated as unique individuals, are permitted to pursue their interests, and have appropriate challenges presented to them.

Gifted Child Quarterly is published by the National Association for Gifted Children (5100 North Edgewood Drive, St. Paul, MN 55112).

If the classroom experiences of gifted children are to meet their needs, the extension of the curriculum should not be "more of the same." Gifted children don't need longer lists of spelling words, more questions to answer, more book reports, and the like. They do need more stimulating ideas, more opportunities to extend their interests, and most of all a teacher who is neither threatened by their intellects and talents nor prone to be too demanding of them. The teacher should share interests with these children,

Bringing Out the Best: A Resource Guide for Parents of Young Gifted Children is published by Free Spirit Publishing (123 N. Third Street, Suite 716, Minneapolis, MN 55401).

Older children, particularly gifted ones, can help younger students.

discuss things with them—particularly abstract ideas—introduce areas of potential interest, encourage wide exploring of topics, and pose questions that require critical thinking and problem solving.

Children who are especially creative or talented in some area may need curriculum enrichment of a different type from that needed by the academically gifted. However, enrichment is often necessary to meet their needs. Perhaps they can be given leadership roles in small group discussions, on the class or school newspapers, in planning a dramatization, or in organizing class sporting events. Extra time might be given to them to pursue their special interests, or assignments might be tailored to capitalize on their talents. Possibly they are (or could become) interested in and capable of taking photos; making films, filmstrips, slides, or audio and video cassettes; or preparing other materials for classroom use. If computers are available, that opens another avenue for the extension of the curriculum. Many of the activities suggested throughout this book can be made challenging to the gifted and talented; these should be reviewed and considered in planning curriculum enrichment.

OTHER SPECIAL CHILDREN

Education has always been a major road to social advancement and economic success in society, but there have been blocks in this road, and many of them remain. In the past, the schools dealt reasonably well with some

Who are the children?

Black children who live in the ghettos of cities or in poor rural areas

Children without English language backgrounds, especially Puerto Ricans, Cubans, and immigrants from Southeast Asia and Mexico

Children of poor whites in the South, the Appalachian mountain regions, and the city locations to which these people have moved

Native American children

Children of migrant workers

For information, write to:

Council on Interracial Books for Children, 1841 Broadway, New York, NY 10023.

immigrant children and less well with others. However, the failures of those times received little general attention. Today, with the influx of immigrants from Spanish-speaking areas of the Americas and from some sections of Asia, failure to properly educate the children of these immigrants is receiving widespread attention. Possibly one reason for this failure is a decline in public acceptance of the "melting pot" concept—a decline evidenced in the desire of many groups to preserve aspects of their cultural heritages. Recently, though, concern has been voiced by some authorities that this desire results in children's not learning English well, or even not learning it at all. In the view of most people, this handicaps these individuals in achieving their potential in our society.

Children of racial minorities—blacks and native Americans—have also encountered road blocks in their educational progress, though to some extent these are fewer in recent years. And, as suggested earlier, there are children of all races and national backgrounds who have been deprived of intellectual stimulation early in their lives because of living in remote areas (and some areas of large cities fit this category) or having been neglected by parents and schools. All of these children—the undereducated, those whose native language is not English or whose dialect is too different from the school's "standard" one, and those of racial minorities—should be considered "special," and the school should make provision for their proper education.

Understanding the Children

Since the use of language is fundamental to the task of educating, children who do not speak English are faced with a problem that may affect them psychologically as well as limit their learning. Children whose native language is English but whose dialect is substantially different from what they hear at school have a similar problem. Such directions as "Hang up your wraps" or "Wash after you go to the lavatory" may be confusing for them and may result in what is interpreted by the teacher as defiance or inattention. The non–English speakers will be even more confused. In either case, the cause of this lack of understanding must be overcome if the development of feelings of insecurity and inferiority is to be avoided; either the teacher must change what he or she says so that it will be understood, or the child must learn the language the teacher uses.

If communication is limited because of either language or dialect difference, the children will withdraw from situations and activities in which their participation would otherwise be natural. Other possible causes of withdrawal and seeming inattention may be hunger and fatigue, for these children often come from poor homes and these are conditions often associated with poverty.

These children need a great deal of understanding and assistance in overcoming inferiority feelings and in becoming contributing members of their group. At the same time, they need to get this help in a manner that does not single them out as being particularly different from or inferior to the other children. They and the other children need to be shown that all children are much more alike than different, but that each child is different in minor ways from any of the others.

Building a Child's Identity

Build each child's self-concept:

1. By taking pictures of him and things he has done.
2. By listening to her tell about herself and sometimes writing accounts of her experiences for her.
3. By having objects or pictures related to his race or culture in the classroom.
4. By making her the leader in games and other activities she does well.
5. By respecting him as a person at all times.

In teaching a child the English used in the school, it is crucial to truly believe that neither a child's thinking abilities nor any other of his or her qualities as a human being are being "improved." Yet in order to function as adults in our society non-English speakers do need to learn to speak and write English with some effectiveness. And native English speakers should probably not use a dialect that will handicap them in school or when they seek employment as adults. Of course, many who learn English as a second language need not become so proficient that they could qualify as TV commentators. Likewise, it is impossible to define, for all possible conditions, what might be considered a "handicapping" dialect.

A teacher must remember that family and cultural ties are important to every person and must be given prime consideration in instruction. A child's earliest thoughts are of home and family, and his or her native language or dialect is a very important part of this background. Personal dignity is inseparable from early background—a fact that every teacher should remember. To abuse or dishonor a child's heritage by condemning his or her language in any way degrades the child and shows a lack of sensitivity. Beyond that, there is the very practical fact that the desire a child has to learn a new language depends heavily on an attitude about his or her own worth as an individual.

A first step in helping non-English speaking children retain their identity while they learn the language of the school is to understand their heritage. Learn as much as possible about the children's native country, its customs and history, its values and traditions, and its language. Although it will probably not be possible to learn the language, some expressions—greetings, school and home words, and other words that are used often—can be learned and used with the whole class.

Perhaps the children themselves can be encouraged to teach the other children words and customs that have been and still are important to them. Someone from the children's native land—possibly an English-speaking parent—can be invited to the classroom for a special program or as a resource person when the children's homeland is being studied. Since all children are interested in the dress, art, music, customs, and food of a country, this is a good opportunity not only to enhance the non-English-speaking children's self-images but also to make all the children knowledgeable about and appreciative of other cultures.

In a similar manner, children who speak nonstandard English can be made to feel that their identities are important. This will not be as difficult as some might imagine, since we are a mobile people and many of us retain at least some elements of our varied heritages. Exchanging information about words and expressions, customs, favorite foods, and so on, can enrich all the children.

In addition to having a positive feeling about himself or herself, the child has to have a similar attitude toward school and the language used in school. Thus the child needs affirmation not only of his or her identity as a person but also of the ability to achieve success in this new realm. Whether in the kindergarten or a higher grade, the child needs to participate in classroom activities—games, duties, projects—that he or she is capable of handling and that are enjoyable. The child needs to gain new confidence about this strange place before undertaking difficult tasks.

Self-images are not built in a few months or even a few years; the feelings children have about themselves are the result of all their experiences, including their environment, their family, and their observations of others. But working for even a short time (that is, the year a child is in your class) on helping a child build a more positive feeling about himself or herself is worthwhile and is fundamental to teaching the skills and knowledge the child needs.

Dialects and Teaching

It is important for a teacher to be fully aware of the implications of the fact that all people speak in different ways as they engage in different activities. Not only do well-educated, partly educated, and uneducated people speak the dialects of their geographical regions and societal settings, but they all speak different varieties of those dialects. In addition, almost everyone shows differences in levels of style or formality in speaking and writing.

Educators have increasingly come to accept the point of view that it is educationally unsound to attempt to obliterate a child's native dialect and to replace it with standard English. This has led to an emphasis on functional bidialectalism, in which the speaker uses the dialect appropriate to the situation in which he or she happens to be. Yet even this viewpoint has come under attack by those who insist that in a pluralistic society, the child's language should not be tampered with at all. However, dialect switching is essentially little different from the switching of speech styles that most of us do in moving from a formal to a casual situation.

As noted earlier, it seems apparent that children who speak dialects that differ quite noticeably from standard English should at least learn to use language that is not stigmatizing. There is often a problem motivating this learning, though, since a speaker of a nonstandard dialect has little or no trouble understanding most speakers of standard English—or at least grasping their fundamental meaning (though the opposite is less likely to be true). But the level of understanding may suffer considerably when standard English is encountered in print.

Points of interference or difference between standard and nonstandard English have been identified by linguists. These features or points of interference can serve as the bases for teaching standard English using procedures developed for teaching foreign languages. The question, however, is how much of this teaching to provide in the elementary-school classroom. Teachers themselves can determine in a nontechnical way the features of two dialects that are different. Both phonological and grammatical differences should be noted if they appear consistently and are such that their use would sound out of place in conversation among educated Americans.

In essence, the strategy for teaching a second dialect is to identify a limited number of items—genuinely significant ones—and make every effort possible to have the children use them consistently in the classroom.

Successful implementation of this strategy requires a long-term teaching effort, perhaps a schoolwide one. This effort must be directed toward helping children to recognize that the dialects are different, to understand the reasons for language differences among people, and to know the social situations in which it is appropriate to use the second dialect rather than the first. Even though children may be taught to hear phonological differences and to recognize grammatical ones and may be drilled so that they repeat phrases and sentences in the new dialect, that dialect will not be used effectively if the children do not have a favorable attitude toward it and the occasions to use it.

English as a Second Language

A catalog listing materials, objects, and symbols related to learning English as a second language can be obtained from Bilingual Education Services, P.O. Box 669, 1603 Hope Street, South Pasadena, CA 91030.

Various approaches and programs have been used with children whose native language is not English in attempts to bring these children into the mainstream of education. The research literature shows that no one way of teaching English to these children allows for all aptitudes, attitudes toward learning, outside influences, ages, and amounts of time available for the teaching. This fact has produced considerable controversy among proponents of various approaches.

One approach is that of immersion; that is, the non–English-speaking child is placed in a classroom in which English is the only language used. The child is therefore forced to learn English. This approach may be traumatizing to the child, however, and in fact immersion may not really occur, since the child will spend more time in his or her home than in school and English is not likely to be the language spoken in that home. On the other hand, if there are only a few children in a school who do not speak English, it may be the most practical approach to use.

The teacher does not need to assume total responsibility for teaching the non–English-speaking child; the children in the class who speak English can help. Although children are naturally accepting, they can at times be cruel, so they must be shown how to give this help. First, like the teacher, they must learn to respect the child's native language and culture. Imitation of the teacher's attitudes and general classroom atmosphere are factors here, but it is also a good idea to plan a study of the country, language, and customs of each non-native child early in the year.

Even before that, though, a child who speaks English can be asked to serve as a "special friend" to a non–English-speaking one. This special friend will be particularly helpful, since the two children will soon learn to communicate with each other. Children assigned as special friends can be given some quick coaching, but they will usually take their assignments seriously and may do more for the non–English-speaking child than you can.

In many sections of the country there will be more than a few non–English-speaking children in each classroom. In fact, in areas where there are many families or entire communities speaking the same native language (most often some dialect of Spanish), there will be entire classes of children who speak little or no English. In such cases, direct instruction is called for. Approaches to this instruction vary, but the following are useful guidelines:

1. The focus should be on oral activity. Specific English expressions should be listened to and spoken.

2. The language forms or patterns taught should be taken from the natural English speech of children. Attention should be given to the conversational speed, intonation patterns and stress, and idiomatic uses of the child who is a native speaker of English.

3. A tape recorder provides a good means for gaining samples of speech, for listening to the forms being taught, and for allowing the child to listen to himself or herself. Other audiovisual aids are particularly helpful in teaching meanings of words and expressions through pictures and actual objects.

4. The teacher sets a model for quality of speech, so he or she must actually act as the model or provide the model by means of tapes and records.

5. The child should not be pushed into reading. Not only does the child have a language handicap, but he or she has had a different experiential background from that of native speakers of English. Attempting to teach a child to read before he or she has the language and experiential readiness for it is an inexcusable waste of both your time and the child's.

6. The basic procedure should be one of drill on language patterns selected on the basis of a contrastive analysis of English and the child's native language. The emphasis in the drill should be on the language patterns known to be the most difficult to learn.

7. Language drills should be related as closely as possible to actual classroom experiences. The emphasis in the drill is on imitation of the model, including the pronunciation the model gives to words. Some separate drill on making particular sounds will probably be needed.

8. Making the sounds of English is difficult, so a sympathetic noncritical climate in the classroom is important. Overcorrecting a child's pronunciation, accent, or speech patterns should be avoided.

9. The child's native language should not be used during the teaching or drill sessions, since translation interferes with the automatic responses that are necessary.

Suggested Items for an Object Box

knife	mirror
fork	comb
spoon	hairbrush
plate	watch
glass	button
chalk	eyeglasses
notebook	purse
scissors	string
key	hammer
soap	nail
money	shoelaces

Whenever possible, an object, a specific action, or an idea should be associated with the word or expression that names, describes, or explains it. A very useful tool to have is an "object box." Objects can be selected from the box and identified by a simple sentence, for example, "This is a spoon." At first, the teacher should select the object, but later a child can select objects, or two children can use the box for a game (one should be a native speaker of English). The child should always repeat the entire sentence, preferably while handling the object. For direct teaching of action words and expressions, objects will not be helpful (except in the teaching of words such as *cut*, in which case scissors or a knife could be used). Many actions can be demonstrated by the teacher, an aide, or other children.

Ideas can be directly shown by placing something *in* a box, holding an object *above* a desk, taking a book *from* a shelf, and so on. Of course, more complicated ideas are difficult to show directly because they involve several concepts. Some of these—for example, "helping one another"—can be demonstrated in the classroom if a little time and thought are devoted to the effort.

Pictures can be helpful in teaching about ideas and actions. For example, they can become the basis for stories and games in which the idea or action is pointed to and appropriate sentences are constructed for the child to repeat. Pictures can also be used as the basis for questions that require the beginning speaker of English to formulate responses. A picture file (added to regularly) is of course helpful to every teacher, whether or not he or she has non–English speakers in class. The file should be organized by major topics—communications, sports, animals, ways people live, bodies of water, foods, and so forth—with subdivisions for each and perhaps some cross-referencing so that pictures can readily be found and related to the vocabulary and structures that need to be taught. In a similar way, other materials can be used for children to talk about and as a basis for the construction of drill sentences. These include advertisements, news items, comic strips, games, and books.

Stories and poetry can also be used to present new vocabulary and structures. The selection should be read and reread—possibly only one section at a time—until the children show understanding by their ability to answer specific questions. Using several readings will also help lead children into understanding new concepts by relating them to known ones and will aid them in memorizing many structures. If this memorization does not occur from repetition of the reading, memorization drills may be used for teaching the most important structures.

For direct instruction to be effective a teacher must have at least a basic knowledge of the child's native language. Because many teachers are likely not to have such a knowledge of even one language other than English,

Motivating language learning with games.

many schools place non–English-speaking children in a classroom taught by a teacher who is competent in the children's native language, sometimes for only part of the school day. A variation of this, and the type of program probably most widely used, calls for the non–English-speaking children to be taught subject matter in their native language for half of a school day, with the other half devoted to learning English—particularly learning to read it. Still another type of program seeks first to teach the children to use their native language more effectively, since many, particularly some Hispanic children, do not speak the standard dialect of their native language. Proponents of this program stress the need for children to be proficient in their first language in order to develop their cognitive abilities. In this type of program, children are mainstreamed only after several years of schooling in their native language.

Bilingual programs have been controversial for a number of years, and the controversy shows no signs of abating. Primarily, concern is expressed that not enough stress is given to teaching English and too much attention is given to the cultures of the children's native countries. Also, the growing use of Spanish in many areas of the country has given rise to a fear that if a sizable number of people cannot use English, the character of the country will change. Probably a more realistic concern is that inadequate effort to teach English will condemn non–English-speaking individuals to second-class citizenship.

A FINAL WORD

Careful planning of language arts programs and sensitive and informed teaching are necessary for learning to occur in a classroom containing special children, and most classrooms include children with some of the impairments, disabilities, handicaps, or problems identified in this chapter. The increased mainstreaming of children formerly segregated into special education classrooms and the increasing elimination of racial and social/economic segregation of children mean that a good many schools need to look at their curriculum and teaching practices. But, as has been stressed throughout this book, there is no substitute for good teaching. Good teaching means acceptance of all children, diagnosis of their needs and interests, and direct and individualized attention to those needs and interests.

References

Ambert, Alba, and Melendez, Sarah E. *Bilingual Education: A Source Book*. Garland Publishing, 1985.

Anderson, Betty, and Joels, Rosie Webb. *Teaching Reading to Students with Limited English Proficiencies*. Charles C. Thomas, 1985.

Baskin, Barbara H., and Harris, Karen H. *Notes from a Different Drummer: A Guide to Juvenile Fiction Portraying the Handicapped*. R. R. Bowker, 1977.

———. *Books for the Gifted Child*. R. R. Bowker, 1980.

Baum, Dale D. *The Human Side of Exceptionality*. PRO-ED, 1982.

Berdine, William H., and Blackhurst, A. Edward, eds. *An Introduction to Special Education*, 2nd ed. Little, Brown, 1985.

Blatt, Barton. *The Conquest of Mental Retardation.* PRO-ED, 1987.

Cohen, Sandra, and Plaskon, Stephen. *Language Arts for the Mildly Handicapped.* Charles E. Merrill, 1980.

Friedberg, Joan B.; Mullins, June B.; and Sukiennik, Adelaide W. *Accept Me As I Am.* R. R. Bowker, 1985.

Hewitt, Frank M. (with Steven R. Forness). *Education of Exceptional Learners*, 3rd ed. Allyn and Bacon, 1984.

Jeffree, Dorothy, and Skeffington, Margaret. *Reading Is for Everyone.* Prentice-Hall, 1984.

Lewis, Rena B., and Doorlag, Donald H. *Teaching Special Students in the Mainstream.* Charles E. Merrill, 1983.

Litchfield, Ada B. *Making Room for Uncle Joe.* Albert Whitman, 1984.

Lucas, Linda, and Karrenbreck, Marilyn H. *The Disabled Child in the Library.* Libraries Unlimited, 1983.

Makohon, Linda, and Fredericks, H. D. Bud. *Teaching Expressive and Receptive Language to Students with Moderate and Severe Handicaps.* PRO-ED, 1985.

Norton, Donna. *Through the Eyes of a Child.* Charles E. Merrill, 1984.

Phelps-Terasaki, Diana; Phelps-Gunn, Trisha; and Stetson, Elton G. *Remediation and Instruction in Language.* Aspen Systems, 1983.

Pollette, Nancy, and Hamlin, Marjorie. *Exploring Books with Gifted Children.* Libraries Unlimited, 1980.

Schon, Isabel. *A Hispanic Heritage, Series II: A Guide to Juvenile Books about Hispanic People and Cultures.* Scarecrow Press, 1985.

Schulz, Jane B., and Turnbull, Ann P. *Mainstreaming Handicapped Students*, 2nd ed. Allyn and Bacon, 1984.

Shore, Kenneth. *The Special Education Handbook.* Teachers College Press, 1986.

Spodek, Bernard; Saracho, Olivia N.; and Lee, Richard C. *Mainstreaming Young Children.* Wadsworth, 1984.

Teaching Resources

There are many books and other materials related to this chapter that are for children or for teachers to use with children—and more are coming out each year. The items listed here are merely suggestions of some that you may want to examine.

BOOKS ABOUT CHILDREN WITH SPEECH, HEARING, AND VISUAL PROBLEMS

Brown, Marc. *Arthur's Eyes.* Little, Brown, 1979.

Cunningham, Julia. *The Silent Voice.* Dutton, 1981.

Garfield, James. *Follow My Leader.* Scholastic, 1987.

Keats, Ezra Jack. *Apt. 3.* Macmillan, 1986.

Little, Jean. *From Anna.* Harper & Row, 1972.

Whitehouse, Jean Peterson. *I Have a Sister—My Sister is Deaf.* Harper & Row, 1977.

Wolf, Bernard. *Anna's Silent World.* Lippincott, 1977.

BOOKS ABOUT CHILDREN WITH OTHER PHYSICAL DISABILITIES

Burnett, Frances H. *The Secret Garden.* Penguin, 1987.

de Angeli, Marguerite. *The Door in the Wall.* Scholastic, 1984.

Greenfield, Eloise. *Darlene.* Methuen, 1980.

Greenfield, Eloise, and Revis, Alesia. *Alesia.* Philomet, 1981.

Howard, Ellen. *Circle of Giving.* Atheneum, 1984.

Little, Jean. *Mine for Keeps.* Little, Brown, 1962.

MacLachlen, Patricia. *Through Grandpa's Eyes.* Harper & Row, 1980.

Miner, Jane C. *New Beginning: An Athlete Is Paralyzed.* Crestwood House, 1982.

Phipson, Joan. *A Flowing.* Atheneum, 1981.

Powers, Mary Ellen. *Our Teacher's in a Wheelchair.* Albert Whitman, 1986.

Seuling, Barbara. *I'm Not So Different: A Book about Handicaps.* Western Publishing, 1986.

Southall, Ivan. *Let the Balloon Go.* Bradbury Press, 1985.

Weik, Mary Hays. *The Jazz Man.* Atheneum, 1986.

BOOKS ABOUT CHILDREN WITH LEARNING PROBLEMS

Booth, Zilpha. *Finding a Friend.* Windswept House, 1987.

Byars, Betsy. *Summer of the Swan*. Viking, 1970.

Cassedy, Sylvia. *M. E. and Morton*. Crowell, 1987.

Clifton, Lucille. *My Friend Jacob*. Dutton, 1980.

Jansen, Larry. *My Sister Is Special*. Standard Publishing, 1984.

Lasker, Joe. *He's My Brother*. Albert Whitman, 1974.

Little, Jean. *Take Wing*. Little, Brown, 1968.

Smith, Lucia B. *A Special Kind of Sister*. Holt, Rinehart and Winston, 1979.

Wartsi, Maureen Crane. *My Brother Is Special*. Westminster, 1979.

Wrighton, Patricia. *A Racecourse for Andy*. Harcourt, 1968.

BOOKS ABOUT GIFTED CHILDREN

Fitzhugh, Louise. *Harriet the Spy*. Dell, 1986.

Lowry, Lois. *Anastasia Krupnik*. Houghton Mifflin, 1979.

Sadler, Marilyn. *Alistar's Time Machine*. Prentice-Hall, 1986.

Warren, Sandra, ed. *Being Gifted: Because You're Special from the Rest*. Trillium Press, 1987.

BOOKS ABOUT CHILDREN WITH APPEARANCE PROBLEMS

Blume, Judy. *Blubber* (overweight). Dell, 1986.

Branson, Mary K. *It's Not Easy Being Small* (size). Broadman, 1981.

Christopher, Matti. *The Twenty-One Mile Swim* (size; middle grades). Little, Brown, 1979.

Kaye, M. M. *The Ordinary Princess* (ordinary looking). Doubleday, 1984.

BOOKS ABOUT CHILDREN WITH PERSONALITY AND BEHAVIOR PROBLEMS

Barrett, John M. *No Time for Me: Learning to Live with Busy Parents*. Human Science Press, 1985.

Brooks, Bruce. *The Moves Make the Man*. Harper & Row, 1984.

Estes, Eleanor. *The Hundred Dresses*. Harcourt Brace Jovanovich, 1974.

Fassler, Joan. *The Boy With a Problem: Johnny Learns to Share His Troubles*. Human Science Press, 1971.

L'Engle, Madeline. *Meet the Austins*. Vanguard Press, 1960.

Paterson, Katherine. *Bridge to Terabithia*. Harper & Row, 1987.

Peck, Richard. *Remembering the Good Times*. Delacorte, 1985.

Schlein, Miriam. *The Way Mothers Are*. Albert Whitman, 1963.

Stolz, Mary. *The Bully of Barkham Street*. Harper & Row, 1985.

BOOKS ABOUT ASIAN-AMERICAN CHILDREN

Ashabranner, Brent, and Ashabranner, Melissa. *Into a Strange Land*. Dodd, Mead, 1987.

Friedman, Ina. R. *How My Parents Learned to Eat*. Houghton Mifflin, 1984.

Lord, Betty Boa. *In the Year of the Boar and Jackie Robinson*. Harper & Row, 1984.

Rau, Margaret. *Holding Up the Sky*. Lodestar Books, 1983.

Surat, Michele Maria. *Angel Child, Dragon Child*. Raintree, 1983.

Yashima, Taro. *The Umbrella*. Viking, 1958.

Yep, Laurance. *Child of the Owl*. Harper & Row, 1977.

BOOKS ABOUT PUERTO RICAN CHILDREN

Bouchard, Lois. *The Boy Who Wouldn't Talk*. Doubleday, 1967.

Fife, Dale H. *Rosa's Special Garden*. Albert Whitman, 1985.

Lexau, Joan. *The Christmas Secret*. Dial, 1963.

Mann, Peggy. *How Juan Got Home*. Coward-McCann, 1972.

Mohr, Nicholasa. *Felita*. Dial, 1979.

———. *Nilda*. Harper & Row, 1973.

Sonneborn, Ruth A. *Friday Night Is Papa Night*. Penguin, 1987.

BOOKS ABOUT MEXICAN-AMERICAN CHILDREN

Brown, Tricia. *Hello, Amigos!* Holt, Rinehart and Winston, 1986.

Ets, Marie Hall. *Gilberto and the Wind*. Penguin, 1978.

Krumgold, Joseph. *And Now Miguel*. Harper & Row, 1984.

Schweitzer, Byrd Baylor. *Amigo*. Macmillan, 1973.

Taha, Karen T. *A Gift for Tia Rosa*. Dillon Press, 1986.

BOOKS ABOUT NATIVE AMERICAN CHILDREN

Baker, Betty. *Little Runners of the Longhouse*. Harper & Row, 1962.

Carlson, Vada, and Witherspoon, Gary. *Black Mountain Boy*. Navajo Curriculum Center Press, 1982.

Dalgliesh, Alice. *The Courage of Sarah Noble*. Macmillan, 1987.

de Paola, Tomie. *The Legend of the Bluebonnet*. Putnam's, 1983.

Roop, Peter. *Little Blaze and the Buffalo Jump*. Council for Indian Education, 1984.

Wolfson, Evelyn. *Growing Up Indian*. Walker, 1986.

BOOKS ABOUT BLACK CHILDREN

Blume, Judy. *Iggie's House*. Bradbury, 1970.

Caines, Jeannette. *Daddy*. Harper & Row, 1977.

Green, Betty. *Philip Hall Like Me. I Reckon Maybe*. Dial, 1974.

Greenfield, Eloise. *She Come Bringing Me That Little Baby Girl*. Lippincott, 1974.

Hamilton, Virginia. *The House of Dies Drear*. Macmillan, 1968.

Irwin, Hadley. *I Be Somebody*. Macmillan, 1984.

Keats, Ezra Jack. *Hi Cat*. Macmillan, 1970.

Mathis, Sharon Bell. *The Hundred Penny Box*. Viking, 1975.

Steptoe, John. *Stevie*. Harper & Row, 1969.

Taylor, Mildred D. *Song of the Trees*. Dial, 1973.

Washington, Vivian E. *I Am Somebody, I Am Me: A Black Child's Credo*. C. H. Fairfax, 1986.

BOOKS ABOUT CHILDREN OF OTHER NATIONALITIES

Coerr, Eleanor. *Sadako and the Thousand Paper Cranes* (Japanese). Putnam's, 1977.

Cohen, Barbara. *Gooseberries to Oranges* (Russian). Lothrop, Lee and Shepard, 1982.

de Paola, Tomie. *Strega Nona* (Italian). Prentice-Hall, 1975.

Estes, Eleanor. *The Hundred Dresses* (Polish). Harcourt, 1974.

Greene, Constance. *The Unmaking of Rabbit* (Polish). Viking, 1972.

BIBLIOGRAPHIES AND SOURCES OF BOOKS AND IDEAS

Carroll, Frances Laverne, and Meacham, Mary. *Exciting, Funny, Scary, Short, Different, and Sad Books Kids Like about Animals, Science, Sports, Families, Songs, and Other Things*. American Library Association, 1984 (lists books about children with various handicaps).

Griffin, Barbara. *Special Needs Bibliography*. The Griffin, 1984, P.O. Box 295, DeWitt, NY 13214 (lists new books for and about children and young adults regarding social concerns, emotional concerns, and the exceptional child).

Griffin, Louise. *Multi-Ethnic Books for Young Children* (3 vols.). National Association for Education of Young Children, 1981.

High/Low Handbook: Books, Materials, and Services for the Problem Reader. R. R. Bowker, 1985.

Leonard, Phyllis. *Choose, Use, Enjoy, Share: Library Skills for the Gifted Child*. Libraries Unlimited, 1985.

Rogovin, Anne, and Cataldo, Christine Z. *What's the Hurry? Developmental Activities for Able and Handicapped Children*. University Park Press, 1983.

Souweine, Judith, and Crimmins, Sheila. *Mainstreaming: Ideas for Teaching Young Children*. National Association for the Education of Young Children, 1981.

OTHER RESOURCES

Big Book ESL Library. Scholastic (big books, cassettes, and guides).

Carlson, Nancy. *Loudmouth George and the Cornet*. Society for Visual Education, 1986 (books, cassette, and guide; K–grade 3).

Children of Courage. Spoken Arts (four color filmstrips and audio cassettes or records of ethnic tales).

Himmel, Roger J. *Taking Turns*. Society for Visual Education, 1978 (ten books and one audio cassette).

McGraw-Hill offers a number of films related to this chapter, including *First Steps, Nicky: One of My Best Friends*, and *It's Cool to Be Smart*.

Society for Visual Education produces the videotapes *Stage One: The Natural Approach to English* and *Stories From the Attic*.

Special Education for the Handicapped: Like You, Like Me. Encyclopaedia Britannica (videotape).

Activities for Preservice Teachers

1. Familiarize yourself with materials used in schools for testing children's vision. Visit a school when vision screening is being done. Report your observations to the class. If possible, repeat the activity for hearing screening.

2. At an elementary school that is mainstreaming children, ask for permission to examine a written educational plan for a child. Consider its completeness and be prepared to report to the class about your experience. (In reporting, do not identify the child or even the school, if possible.)

3. Inquire at one or more nearby elementary schools about the special teaching considerations in effect to meet the needs of gifted and talented children. Report to the class about what you found out—and possibly observed.

4. Examine the educational literature published during the past five years for definitions of "learning disabled." What are your conclusions?

5. With others in the class, plan a panel discussion on the issues involved in identifying and working with those who have "special learning disabilities." Make certain you deal with the apparent increased incidence of learning disabilities and the influx of commercial materials presumed to attack learning disorders.

6. Visit special classrooms for mentally retarded children. Note the basic language arts emphasized in these classrooms.

7. Find out if schools in your local community are teaching English as a second language. If they are, what procedures are being used?

8. If you have not observed classes in schools in ghetto or slum areas, do so in connection with reading this chapter. What differences do you note among the children? How do the classroom conditions and activities compare with those you have observed in more prosperous areas?

9. Visit an Indian reservation and/or a migrant labor camp to observe the environment of the children living there.

10. Develop a plan for learning songs, stories, customs, and history of a particular country whose emigrants you might sometime have in class. Begin the execution of your plan.

Activities for Inservice Teachers

1. How do the percentages of children with various types of handicaps as given in this chapter compare with those in your school and the other institutions and agencies in your community? Does your school district compile such statistics? If not, is there a city, county, or state agency that does?

2. What problems with mainstreaming are present in your school? What do the teachers think about mainstreaming? Do you and they believe that the concept is working in practice?

3. Current research and theory suggest that children who are mildly mentally retarded, learning disabled, or mildly mentally disturbed be considered as a single group for instructional purposes. What is your opinion? Is it the policy of your school system to take this point of view? If not, do you know why not?

4. Prepare activities "special" children can do individually to learn language skills. Those suggested in the following section will give you a start.

5. What evidence do you see in your classroom or in other classrooms in your school that such things as impoverished background, different sociocultural mores, or different native language have resulted in categorizing children as mentally retarded or slow learners?

6. What sort of evaluation of the mainstreaming program is done in your school? Report to the class your opinion of this evaluation.

7. Many professionals believe mainstreaming adds to the instructional tasks teachers have. What is done in your school to alleviate this—for example, teacher aides or reduced pupil/teacher ratios? How effective are the measures taken?

8. As you look at your class, identify in your mind children who may be "special" as described in this chapter. Search through all records (test results, etc.) that you can find. Confer with parents. Then plan changes in your program to better meet the needs of these children.

Independent Activities for Children

Each previous chapter has activities that can be used or adapted for the children discussed in this chapter.

CHILDREN WITH SPEECH HANDICAPS

1. Emotions play a major role affecting the expression of children with speech problems; therefore, plan for activities that reduce anxieties. Letting the children use puppets as ''speakers'' in conversational and discussion situations will help, as will providing for these children to talk principally in small-group situations.

2. Provide short selections that a child can read aloud and record. The child can then listen to the recording, practice needed corrections, record again, and compare the readings.

3. Prepare tapes that focus on the specific words and sounds a child has difficulty with so that he or she can listen to them and practice saying them.

4. Consult a speech therapist for specific activities and exercises that may help a child who has a speech problem.

CHILDREN WITH HEARING IMPAIRMENTS

1. Provide the child with reading material containing the information provided in oral reports given by other children—children speaking before a group are often difficult to hear.

2. Let each child keep a word file or dictionary of interesting new words she or he encounters. Have the child look up the correct pronunciation and meaning of each word, and fix it in her or his memory by using it as many times as possible, both in speech and in writing.

3. Children with hearing impairments frequently have smaller vocabularies than do children with normal hearing. Having these children find synonyms, antonyms, and homonyms of words they use is one kind of activity that will build vocabularies.

VISUALLY HANDICAPPED CHILDREN

1. Provide recorded and taped stories and poems for the visually handicapped child to listen to as a substitute for at least a part of the independent reading other children do. The child can report on these as others report on their reading.

2. Make tapes of simple directions for activities that

the children will enjoy—activities involving body movements, drawing, collections of materials, games, and so forth.

3. Provide short exercises to help visually handicapped children practice their listening skills. For example, give the children short lists of words to remember; explain that they are to write the words you will say, but only after you have finished saying them. Adaptations can be made of this type of listening activity.

SLOW LEARNERS

1. Slow learners will profit from many kinds of readiness games, such as matching objects of the same shape, size, or color or putting pictures in sequence for a story.

2. Provide many recorded or taped stories for the children to listen to; these will help build vocabulary and concepts for reading and writing.

3. Obtain an old book of wallpaper samples from a store. Let individual children use the sheets of paper to trace and cut out letters. They can use these letters to become more familiar with letter shapes and to put together spelling words.

4. Let the slow learner make captions for pictures or write titles for stories in the class newspaper, for example, so that he or she will feel included in regular class activities.

GIFTED CHILDREN

1. Gifted children can make spelling and vocabulary charts, design bulletin boards, design and make games, and do many similar tasks that interest and challenge them.

2. Provide time and a place for them to write stories, scripts, reports, and so forth. Encourage them to write to favorite authors, TV producers, politicians, and so on.

CHILDREN WITH PHYSICAL HANDICAPS OR PERSONALITY MALADJUSTMENTS

1. Make it a special point to provide stories for independent reading that may help these children. Learning that others, too, have problems may help them to adjust to theirs.

2. Seek out the special talents these children have and

provide opportunities to use them. For example, the child who likes to draw might illustrate a story the class has written or design the cover for a creative writing booklet; a very shy child could tape a story for individual listening activities; a hyperactive one might be put in charge of keeping library books shelved.

CHILDREN SPEAKING A DIVERGENT DIALECT OR OTHER LANGUAGE

1. Children can make alphabet books with words for each letter in their own language as well as in English.

2. Have a child make a bulletin board display around the country of his or her origin. This might include a picture of the flag of that country, pictures of its people and their homes, a map, a list of principal occupations and products, and so forth.

3. Let a child prepare for the class a program of folk songs, stories, and/or poems from her or his native land or culture.

4. A child may invite a speaker to talk to the class about his or her native country. The child will be responsible for introducing the speaker and providing any audiovisual aids or other articles that might be needed (a table for displaying handiwork, a projector and screen, etc.).

5. Children working in pairs with a simple camera can take pictures of one another. Each child can then use the pictures, examples of classwork (stories, pictures drawn, etc.), and pictures from magazines of things of interest to make a booklet about herself or himself.

6. Materials suggested above might also be used by individual children to make bulletin board displays about themselves. Perhaps a bulletin board could be divided into quarters and entitled "Our Class." A child can gather the particular objects he or she would like to display and arrange them in one of the sections to make a picture story.

7. Provide materials for children to read and record individually so they can listen to their own speech; have short stories and poems that they can listen to for cadence and word order, record questions to answer, and so on.

8. A child who speaks a nonstandard dialect might prepare a story for the class using particular idioms or expressions that are peculiar to that dialect. This may be used in connection with a study of dialects to help children understand the many variations that are present in speech, even within the same country.

Addresses of Publishers, Distributors, and Organizations

Ablex Publishing Corporation
355 Chestnut Street
Norwood, NJ 07648

Acropolis Books
2400 17th Street, NW
Washington, D.C. 20009

Addison-Wesley Publishing Company
1 Jacob Way
Reading, MA 01867

Allyn and Bacon, Inc.
160 Gould Street
Needham Heights, MA 02194-2320

Amereon, Ltd.
P.O. Box 1200
Mattituck, NY 11952

American Library Association
50 E. Huron Street
Chicago, IL 60611

Aquarius People Materials, Inc.
Box 128
Indian Rocks Beach, FL 33535

Aspen Publishers, Inc.
1600 Research Boulevard
Rockville, MD 20850

The Association for Childhood Education
    International
11141 Georgia Avenue, Suite 200
Wheaton, MD 20902

Atheneum Publishers
866 Third Avenue
New York, NY 10022

Barr Films
P.O. Box 5667
3490 E. Foothill Boulevard
Pasadena, CA 91107

Basil Blackwell, Inc.
432 Park Avenue South, Suite 1530
New York, NY 10016

R. R. Bowker Company
245 W. 17th Street
New York, NY 10011

Boynton/Cook Publishers, Inc.
P.O. Box 860
52 Upper Montclair Plaza
Upper Montclair, NJ 07043

Bradbury Press
866 Third Avenue
New York, NY 10022

Broadman Press
127 Ninth Avenue North
Nashville, TN 37234

Broderbund Software
17 Paul Drive
San Rafael, CA 94903

William C. Brown Group
2460 Kerper Boulevard
Dubuque, IA 52001

C and C Software
5713 Kentford Circle
Wichita, KS 67220

Caedmon Records, Inc.
1995 Broadway
New York, NY 10023

Cambridge University Press
32 E. 57th Street
New York, NY 10022

Carolrhoda Books, Inc.
241 First Avenue North
Minneapolis, MN 55401

The Center for Applied Research in Education
P.O. Box 430
West Nyack, NJ 10995

Children's Art Foundation
Box 83
Santa Cruz, CA 95063

Children's Press
1224 W. Van Buren Street
Chicago, IL 60607

Clarion Books
52 Vanderbilt Avenue
New York, NY 10017

Computer Advanced Ideas, Inc.
1442A Walnut Street
Berkeley, CA 94709

Coronado Press
P.O. Box 3232
Lawrence, KS 66044

Coronet, The Multimedia Co.
108 Wilmot Road
Deerfield, IL 60015

Council For Indian Education
517 Rimrock Road
Billings, MT 59102

Coward-McCann (*See* Putnam's)

Creative Education, Inc.
P.O. Box 227
Mankato, MN 56001

Crestwood House, Inc.
P.O. Box 3427
Mankato, MN 56002

Crowell-Collier (*See* Macmillan)

Curriculum Associates, Inc.
5 Esquire Road
North Billerica, MA 01862-2589

Davidson and Associates
3135 Kishawa Street
Torrance, CA 90505

Delacorte Press
1 Dag Hammarskjold Plaza
New York, NY 10017

Dell Publishing Company
245 E. 47th Street
New York, NY 10017

Delmar Publishers, Inc.
2 Computer Drive
Albany, NY 12212

Developmental Learning Materials
P.O. Box 4000
One DLM Park
Allen, TX 75002

Dial Press (*See* Doubleday)

Dillon Press, Inc.
242 Portland Avenue South
Minneapolis, MN 55415

DLM Teaching Resources
One DLM Park
Allen, TX 75002

Dodd, Mead and Company
71 Fifth Avenue
New York, NY 10003

Doubleday and Company, Inc.
501 Franklin Avenue
Garden City, NY 11530

E. P. Dutton, Inc.
2 Park Avenue
New York, NY 10016

EBSCO Curriculum Materials
Box 11542
Birmingham, AL 35202

Educational Activities
Box 392
Freeport, NY 11520

Educational Leadership
125 N. West Street
Alexandria, VA 22314-2798

Electronic Bookshelf, Inc.
Rt. 9, Box 64
Frankfort, IN 46041

Encyclopaedia Britannica, Inc.
310 S. Michigan Avenue
Chicago, IL 60604

Evans Publishing House
431 Post Road East, Suite 708
Westport, CT 06880

C. H. Fairfax Company, Inc.
P.O. Box 502
Columbia, MD 21045

Family Communications
4802 Fifth Avenue
Pittsburgh, PA 15213

Farrar, Straus and Giroux, Inc.
19 Union Square West
New York, NY 10003

Fearon Teaching Aids
19 Davis Drive
Belmont, CA 94002

First Byte
2845 Temple Avenue
Long Beach, CA 90806

Follett Publishing Company
1010 W. Washington Boulevard
Chicago, IL 60607

Four Winds Press
P.O. Box 824
Soquel, CA 95079

Freline, Inc.
P.O. Box 889
32 East Avenue
Hagerstown, MD 21740

Gale Research Company
Book Tower
Detroit, MI 48226

Garland Publishing Inc.
136 Madison Avenue
New York, NY 10016

Greenleaf Software
2101 Hickory Drive
Carrollton, TX 75006

Greenleaf Video, Inc.
3230 Nebraska Avenue
Santa Monica, CA 90404

Greenwillow Books (*See* Morrow)

Grosset and Dunlap
51 Madison Avenue
New York, NY 10010

Harcourt Brace Jovanovich, Inc.
1250 Sixth Avenue
San Diego, CA 92101

Harper and Row Publishers, Inc.
10 E. 53rd Street
New York, NY 10022

Hart Publications, Inc.
P.O. Box 1917
1900 Grant Street, Suite 400
Denver, CO 80201

Hartley's Courseware, Inc.
Dimondale, MI 48821

Harvest House Publishers
1075 Arrowsmith
Eugene, OR 97402

D. C. Heath and Company
125 Spring Street
Lexington, MA 02173

Heinemann Educational Books
70 Court Street
Portsmouth, NH 03801

Holt, Rinehart and Winston
383 Madison Avenue
New York, NY 10017

Holt, Rinehart and Winston of Canada
55 Horner Avenue
Toronto, Ontario M8Z 4X6
Canada

The Horn Book
31 St. James Avenue
Park Square Building
Boston, MA 02116

Houghton Mifflin Company
One Beacon Street
Boston, MA 02108

Houghton Mifflin Educational Software
Box 683, Dept. 217
Hanover, NH 03755

Human Resources Development Press
22 Amherst Road
Amherst, MA 01002

Human Science Press, Inc.
72 Fifth Avenue
New York, NY 10011

Humanities Ltd.
P.O. Box 7447
Atlanta, GA 30309

Humanities Software
P.O. Box 590727
San Francisco, CA 94159

IBM
1133 Westchester Avenue
White Plains, NY 10604

InterLearn, Inc.
Box 342
Cardiff-by-the-Sea, CA 92007

International Reading Association
P.O. Box 8139
800 Barksdale Road
Newark, DE 19714-8139

Jamestown Publishers
P.O. Box 9168
Providence, RI 02940

JMH Software of Minnesota
7200 Hemlock Lane, Suite 103
Maple Grove, MN 55369

Kendall/Hunt Publishing Company
P.O. Box 539
2460 Kerper Boulevard
Dubuque, IA 52001

Thomas S. Klise Co.
P.O. Box 3418
Peoria, IL 61614

Alfred A. Knopf, Inc.
201 E. 50th Street
New York, NY 10022

Knowledge Unlimited
P.O. Box 52
Madison, WI 53701-0052

The Learning Company
545 Middlefield Road, Suite 170
Menlo Park, CA 94025

Learning Well
200 South Service Road
Roslyn Heights, NY 11577

Lerner Publications
241 First Avenue North
Minneapolis, MN 55401

Libraries Unlimited, Inc.
P.O. Box 263
Littleton, CO 80160-0263

J. B. Lippincott Company
E. Washington Square
Philadelphia, PA 19105

Listening Library, Inc.
P.O. Box L
Old Greenwich, CT 06870

Little, Brown and Company
34 Beacon Street
Boston, MA 02106

Live Oak Media
P.O. Box 34
Ancramdale, NY 12503

Lodestar Books
2 Park Avenue
New York, NY 10016

Longman, Inc.
95 Church Street
White Plains, NY 10601

Lothrop, Lee and Shepard Books
105 Madison Avenue
New York, NY 10036

Macmillan Publishing Company
866 Third Avenue
New York, NY 10022

McDougal, Littell and Company
P.O. Box 1667
Evanston, IL 60204

McGraw-Hill Book Company
1221 Avenue of the Americas
New York, NY 10020

Media Basics
Larchmont Plaza
Larchmont, NY 10538

Charles E. Merrill Publishing Company
1300 Alum Drive
Columbus, OH 43216

Julian Messner
1230 Avenue of the Americas
New York, NY 10020

Methuen, Inc.
29 W. 35th Street
New York, NY 10001

Milliken Publishing Company
P.O. Box 21579
1100 Research Boulevard
St. Louis, MO 63132

Milton Bradley, Inc.
443 Shaker Road
East Longmeadow, MA 01028

Mindscape, Inc.
Dept. S
3444 Dundee Road
Northbrook, IL 60062

Modern Curriculum Press
13900 Prospect Road
Cleveland, OH 44136

William Morrow and Company, Inc.
105 Madison Avenue
New York, NY 10016

NAESP Educational Products Center
P.O. Box 1461
Alexandria, VA 22313

National Association for the Education of
Young Children
1834 Connecticut Avenue, NW
Washington, D.C. 20009

National Council of Teachers of English
1111 Kenyon Road
Urbana, IL 61801

National Textbook Company
4255 W. Touhy Avenue
Lincolnwood, IL 60646

Navajo Curriculum Center Press
Rough Rock Demonstration School
Star Route 1
Rough Rock, AZ 86503

Thomas Nelson Australia
480 La Trobe Street
Melbourne 3000, Australia

New Plays Books
Box 273
Rowayton, CT 06853

Open University Press
242 Cherry Street
Philadelphia, PA 19106-1906

Oryx Press
2214 N. Central Avenue
Phoenix, AZ 85004-1483

Richard C. Owens Publishers, Inc.
Rockefeller Center, Box 819
New York, NY 10185

Oxford University Press
200 Madison Avenue
New York, NY 10016

Pantheon Books
201 E. 50th Street
New York, NY 10022

Paradigm Video
127 Greenbrae Boardwalk
Greenbrae, CA 94904

A. W. Peller and Associates
P.O. Box 106
249 Goffle Road
Hawthorne, NJ 07507

PEM Press
Box 3000
Communications Park
Mount Kisco, NY 10549

Penguin Books
40 W. 23rd Street
New York, NY 10010

Penguin Software
830 Fourth Avenue
Geneva, IL 60134

Philomel (*See* Putnam's)

Phoenix/BFA Films and Video
470 Park Avenue South
New York, NY 10016

Plays, Inc.
8 Arlington Street
Boston, MA 02116

Potomac MicroResources, Inc.
P.O. Box 277
Riverdale, MD 20737

Prentice-Hall, Inc.
Route 9W
Englewood Cliffs, NJ 07632

PRO-ED
5341 Industrial Oak Boulevard
Austin, TX 78735

G. P. Putnam's Sons
200 Madison Avenue
New York, NY 10016

Raintree Publications, Inc.
310 W. Wisconsin Avenue, Mezzanine Level
Milwaukee, WI 53203

Rand McNally and Company
P.O. Box 7600
Chicago, IL 60680

Random House, Inc.
201 E. 50th Street
New York, NY 10022

Reading Is Fundamental, Inc.
Smithsonian Institution
600 Maryland Avenue, SW
Washington, D.C. 20560

Renfro Studios
1117 W. Ninth Street
Austin, TX 78703

St. Martin's Press, Inc.
175 Fifth Avenue
New York, NY 10010

Scarecrow Press, Inc.
Box 656
52 Liberty Street
Metuchen, NJ 08840

Scholastic, Inc.
P.O. Box 7501
2931 E. McCarty Street
Jefferson City, MO 63102

Scholastic Software
730 Broadway
New York, NY 10003

Schoolhouse Press (*See* Simon and Schuster)

Science Research Associates
155 N. Wacker Drive
Chicago, IL 60606

Scott, Foresman and Company
1900 East Lake Avenue
Glenview, IL 60025

Scribner-Laidlaw Educational Publishers
866 Third Avenue
New York, NY 10022

Seabury Press
Icehouse 1-401
151 Union Street
San Francisco, CA 94111

Sensible Software, Inc.
24011 Seneca
Oak Park, MI 48237

Dale Seymour Publications
P.O. Box 10888
Palo Alto, CA 94303

Shoe String Press, Inc.
P.O. Box 4327
Hamden, CT 06514

Simon and Schuster, Inc.
1230 Avenue of the Americas
New York, NY 10020

Society for Visual Education, Inc.
1345 Diversey Parkway
Chicago, IL 60614

Spinnaker Software
One Kendall Square
Cambridge, MA 02139

Spoken Arts
P.O. Box 289
New Rochelle, NY 10802

Springboard Software
7808 Creekridge Circle
Minneapolis, MN 53435

Standard Publishing Co.
8121 Hamilton Avenue
Cincinnati, OH 45231

Sterling Publishing Company
2 Park Avenue
New York, NY 10016

STL International, Inc.
P.O. Box 35918
Tulsa, OK 74153-0918

Stuart Finley
3428 Mansfield Road
Falls Church, VA 22041

Sunburst Communications
39 Washington Avenue
Pleasantville, NY 10570

Teachers College Press
Columbia University
1234 Amsterdam Avenue
New York, NY 10027

Charles C. Thomas, Publisher
2600 S. First Street
Springfield, IL 62794-9265

Thompson Book and Supply Company
P.O. Box 11600
Oklahoma City, OK 73136

Times Books
201 E. 50th Street
New York, NY 10022

Trillium Press
Box 209
Monroe, NY 10950

Unicorn Software Co.
1775 E. Tropicana Avenue, No. 8
Las Vegas, NV 89109

University of California Press
2120 Berkeley Way
Berkeley, CA 94720

University of Chicago Press
5801 Ellis Avenue
Chicago, IL 60628

University of Illinois
Graduate School of Library Service
249 Armory Building
505 E. Armory Street
Champaign, IL 61820

University of Wisconsin Press
114 N. Murray Street
Madison, WI 53715

University Park Press
P.O. Box 434
Grand Central Station
New York, NY 10163

University Press Books
Box 460
Middletown, NY 10940

Vanguard Press
424 Madison Ave.
New York, NY 10017

Viking Penguin Inc.
40 W. 23rd Street
New York, NY 10010

Wadsworth Publishing Co.
10 Davis Drive
Belmont, CA 94002

Walker and Company
720 Fifth Avenue
New York, NY 10019

Warner Books, Inc.
Juvenile Division
666 Fifth Avenue
New York, NY 10103

Western Publishing Company, Inc.
850 Third Avenue
New York, NY 10022

Westminster Press
925 Chestnut Street
Philadelphia, PA 19107

Weston Woods
389 Newtown Pike
Weston, CT 06883

Albert Whitman and Company
5747 W. Howard Street
Niles, IL 60648

The H. W. Wilson Company
950 University Avenue
Bronx, NY 10452

Windswept House, Publisher
P.O. Box 159
Mt. Desert, ME 04660

The Wright Group
10949 Technology Place
San Diego, CA 92127

Yale University Press
302 Temple Street
New Haven, CT 06520

Zaner-Bloser, Inc.
P.O. Box 16764
2300 W. Fifth Avenue
Columbus, OH 43216

Index

DEMCO